THE NEW NATURALIST LIBRARY

A SURVEY OF BRITISH NATURAL HISTORY

PLANT PESTS

*

The aim of this series is to interest the general reader in the wildlife of Britain by recapturing the enquiring spirit of the old naturalists. The editors believe that the natural pride of the British public in the native flora and fauna, to which must be added concern for their conservation, is best fostered by maintaining a high standard of accuracy combined with clarity of exposition in presenting the results of modern scientific research.

THE NEW NATURALIST LIBRARY

PLANT PESTS

A Natural History of Pests of Farms and Gardens

DAVID V. ALFORD

Collins

This edition published in 2011 by Collins,
An imprint of HarperCollins Publishers

HarperCollins Publishers
77–85 Fulham Palace Road
London W6 8JB
www.collins.co.uk

First published 2011

A CIP catalogue record for this book is available from the British Library.

Set in FF Nexus, designed and produced by
Tom Cabot/ketchup

Printed in Hong Kong by Printing Express

Hardback
ISBN 978-0-00-733849-8

Paperback
ISBN 978-0-00-733848-1

Contents

Larvae of silver Y moth (*Autographa gamma*) are important pests of both outdoor and greenhouse-grown plants.

Editors' Preface

PESTS OF FARMS AND GARDENS have not received the recognition they deserve from naturalists, many of whom view the purest natural history as that of plants and animals in habitats hardly touched by man. Nowadays, such habitats are few and far between, as much of the UK is under farm or garden crops, habitats in which plant feeders are generally regarded as pests. A simpler assemblage than that in a natural stand of vegetation, the fauna of a uniform crop offers an accessible introduction to the complex web of interactions of herbivorous insects with their plant hosts and with other creatures, including the predators and parasites that act as their natural enemies. The entomologists' abiding problem of identification is less formidable here, because a limited and somewhat predictable range of insect species is associated with each type of crop, and although this book is not a monograph on pest identification, its illustrations and descriptions will help to narrow the range of possibilities. Whether in crop monocultures or in the more diverse vegetation of gardens, an understanding of the natural history of these very accessible communities is welcome, both for its intrinsic interest and as a basis for management. Further, as more people come to focus on the insects associated with cultivated plants, we may expect an improvement in our ability to monitor the changing spectrum of pests over the years, as some decrease in importance and new species invade our crops from abroad.

Drawing on a lifetime's experience, David Alford introduces the natural history of the insects and mites that inhabit our plants, by day and by night, and shows how and why the different operations of cultivation affect their world. Until now books on plant pests have generally been more concerned with controlling pests than with exploring their lives. We hope this book will help more people to appreciate the fascinating communities of insects and mites that inhabit our farms and gardens, and feed on our cultivated plants.

Author's Foreword and Acknowledgements

PLANT PESTS, INCLUDING THOSE attacking our crops, have claimed the attention of man for millennia. However, it is only in the last two centuries or so that we have come to study them in any detail. The nineteenth century saw many advances in our knowledge, succinctly captured in John Curtis's classic 1860 book on *Farm Insects*. Since then, our understanding of pests has escalated beyond all recognition, and notable contributions on their habits and on ways to protect cultivated plants from attack or damage have been made by a vast number of people, both at home and abroad.

Man's over-reliance on pesticides, which followed the discovery and introduction of DDT and other 'weapons of mass destruction' from the mid-1900s onwards, has been replaced by a far more enlightened approach to plant protection. Admittedly, chemical pesticides still have a role to play. However, today, more and more emphasis is placed on environmental issues and non-chemical means of pest control. This requires a greater appreciation of ecosystems, coupled with a greater understanding of individual pests, including their habits and their role in the environment. To this extent, plant pests should not be viewed as different from other wildlife. Of course there will be times when measures must be taken to limit numbers of pests or even to eliminate them. However, killing everything that moves is not the right approach, and ill-considered protective measures can prove counterproductive.

The purpose of the present work is to provide naturalists and other readers with an account of the fascinating world of pests of cultivated plants. To this end, the text concentrates on the natural history of such creatures and includes frequent mention of their natural enemies. The book is not intended as an identification guide to pests; nor does it aim to be encyclopaedic or attempt to address the vexed question of how to control them.

Writing the book has been very much a personal journey, albeit tempered by reference to the publications of many other scientists and practitioners, and I make no apology for any apparent bias. Nevertheless, apologies are offered to those whose work might have been misinterpreted or has not been adequately acknowledged or covered.

To avoid unnecessary elaboration, citation of synonyms for names of species (pests and otherwise) has been kept to a minimum, and largely restricted to changes adopted during the past two decades. Earlier name changes for insects and other invertebrates associated with cultivated plants are mostly well known, and conveniently catalogued in Seymour's 1989 *Invertebrates of Economic Importance in Britain. Common and Scientific Names.*

It is a pleasure to thank my wife Inge and daughter Ingaret for their help in obtaining specimens during various field trips, and also for maintaining insect cultures during my absence. My wife's editorial skills and eye for detail are similarly acknowledged. In addition to various landowners who have allowed access to their property over the years, thanks are also due to A. T. Bilton, C. I. Carter, S. C. Gordon, A. C. Howells, Dr J. Moeser, Dr M. Saynor, P. R. Seymour, Dr B. Ulber and R. A. Umpelby, several of whom provided live material for me to photograph. Finally, I am particularly grateful to Dr Sally Corbet of the New Naturalist Editorial Board for her editorial guidance and encouragement, and for making many helpful suggestions on the draft manuscript.

CHAPTER 1

Plant Pests and Their Natural Enemies

In one of the earliest and most successful New Naturalist books, *Insect Natural History* by A. D. Imms,[1] a pest was defined as 'an animal or plant that has become too abundant for man's comfort or convenience, or has even become a danger to his interests.' Most if not all organisms causing damage to cultivated plants, or in some other way having a deleterious impact on man's attempts to grow, harvest, store or market them, could be covered by this definition. However, this is true only if pathogens (e.g. disease-inducing plant-pathogenic fungi, phytoplasmas and viruses) in addition to weeds are categorised albeit very loosely under the general heading of plants. Although the term 'pest' can be applied very widely, unrestricted by the kind of organism, it is usually used in a far more restrictive sense to embrace insects, mites and other animals but not weeds or plant pathogens. This more targeted approach has been adopted here. Nevertheless, a somewhat liberal view has been taken as to what creatures qualify as pests. At one extreme there are species that cause significant damage to cultivated plants. These include both primary and secondary invaders (the latter requiring prior attack by some other organism – whether a pest or a pathogen). At the other, there are those whose depredations are at worst no more than cosmetic or whose presence (perhaps as contaminants at harvest time) is merely an inconvenience. Considered in isolation, some invaders are of little or no significance as pests. However, collectively, infestations of several individually innocuous species can become a problem. Further, some pests introduce and spread the organisms responsible for causing plant diseases. Such species are termed vectors. Virus vectors, in particular, are of considerable economic importance in both agriculture and horticulture.

The present work deals mainly with pests of outdoor plants cultivated for food, seed, ornament and so forth. For completeness, as there is considerable overlap, pests of plants grown in permanently protected environments (e.g. greenhouse-grown vegetables and ornamentals) are also discussed. However, other than passing mention in relation to nursery beds and those of significance during the production of Christmas trees, forestry pests are excluded – our timber-generating woodlands being considered non-agricultural enterprises. Pests of stored products such as grain and flour (i.e. pests that give rise to post-harvest problems) inhabit a very different world from those of growing crops; they are also excluded.

Most plant pests are insects or mites and, in the following chapters, emphasis is unashamedly placed upon them. In passing, however, other invertebrates (including plant-parasitic nematodes, slugs and snails) are also mentioned, as are a few birds and mammals. Consideration of natural enemies of pests, especially parasitoids (parasites that kill their hosts) and predators, also focuses on insects and mites, although various other beneficial species (ranging from micro-organisms to vertebrates) receive some attention. For readers requiring such information, the main features of invertebrate plant pests, parasitoids and predators are outlined in Appendix I.

WHAT MAKES A PLANT PEST A PEST?

Ever since man first cultivated plants and grew crops, herbivorous insects, mites and other creatures have risen to prominence as pests. Today, herbivorous animals are usually regarded as pests when their depredations exceed or have the potential to exceed perceived economic thresholds. Direct or indirect contamination of plants and plant products (e.g. fruits) can also elevate organisms to pest status, even if they are not active herbivores. As already mentioned, some creatures qualify as pests because they carry and spread plant diseases.

Some of our most important plant pests have relatively short lifecycles, and within limits and under suitable conditions, as often on offer in field crops and in greenhouses, they are capable of completing many generations annually. Aphids, thrips*, whiteflies and spider mites are examples. Such rapidly reproducing pests are particularly liable to develop resistance to pesticides, further enhancing their likely pest status: peach/potato aphid[2] (*Myzus persicae*), western flower thrips

* Note: there is no such word as 'thrip'.

(*Frankliniella occidentalis*), glasshouse whitefly (*Trialeurodes vaporariorum*) and two-spotted spider mite (*Tetranychus urticae*) are common examples. Some pests have become regular antagonists of crops and cause economic damage in most if not all years, whereas others are damaging only sporadically or under special circumstances. Many examples are cited in the following chapters. In a changing world, cultivated plants are also under constant threat of attack by new pests from both home and abroad.

FEEDING HABITS

Phytophagous (plant-feeding) pests gain nourishment by sucking or biting their hosts. Leafhoppers, mirid (capsid) bugs and mites, for example, typically pierce cell walls with their stylet-like mouthparts (Fig. 1) before injecting digestive juices and sucking out the cell contents. As a consequence, leaves in particular often become russeted or bronzed, or may develop a distinctive pallid mottling or speckling, and sometimes appear extensively blanched (Fig. 2). Thrips cause similar damage, and affected tissue often also becomes contaminated by tiny grains of black frass (solid excrement). Some sucking pests, such as aphids, scale

FIGS 1 & 2. True bugs, as exemplified by the hawthorn shield bug (*Acanthosoma haemorrhoidale*), have complex, needle-like mouthparts (above left). These are used to pierce host plants, to inject saliva and then to ingest food in a semi-liquid state. Foliage damaged by leafhoppers (above right) is often blanched following removal of sap from the underlying cells.

FIG 3. Globules of honeydew, upon which sooty moulds may develop, frequently contaminate leaves infested by glasshouse whiteflies (*Trialeurodes vaporariorum*).

FIG 4. The head of a biting phytophagous larva, as exemplified by that of a death's head hawk moth (*Acherontia atropos*) caterpillar, bears a pair of powerful mandibles (jaws), as well as sensory palps.

insects and whiteflies, typically penetrate the plant's sap-conducting vessels (the phloem). In many cases, as a result of the copious intake of sugary fluid, such insects excrete masses of sticky honeydew upon which sooty moulds may develop (Fig. 3). Biting pests include adult and larval beetles, as well as larvae (caterpillars) of various butterflies, moths (Fig. 4) and sawflies (Fig. 5). Such insects are armed with a pair of mandibles, used to bite off and chew plant material. Millepedes, symphylids and woodlice are also biting pests. Larvae of many flies (here tenuously also regarded as biting pests) have a pair of rasping mouth-hooks that tear at the food plant prior to the ingestion of tissue.

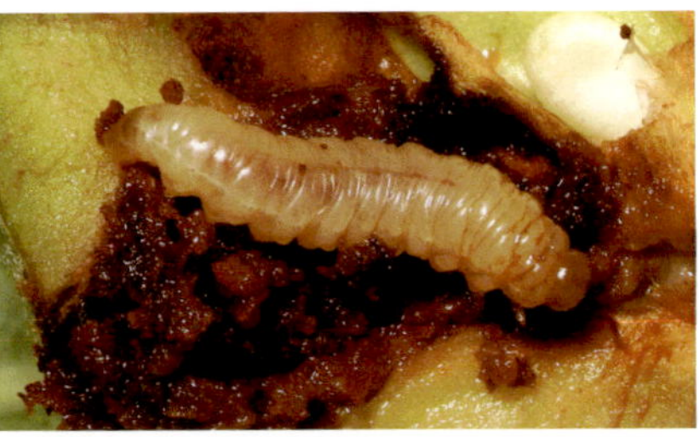

FIG 5. Sawfly larvae are destructive pests of trees, shrubs and some herbaceous plants. Leaf-browsing species, such as (above left) Solomon's seal sawfly (*Phymatocera aterrima*), are significant pests in commercial nurseries and private gardens. Some species, including apple sawfly (*Hoplocampa testudinea*) (above right), are important fruit-boring pests.

Biting pests include defoliators, shoot miners, stem borers and leaf miners; buds, fruits and roots are also attacked. Some pests feed indiscriminately on a wide range of plants and are described as polyphagous (i.e. generalist feeders). Most, however, are oligophagous and exhibit some degree of host selectivity, restricting their attacks to members of one botanical family; a few are monophagous (i.e. specialist feeders), and attack just one species of plant.

Parasitoids of pests are also specialist feeders, and many have evolved as enemies of just one (or a very narrow range of) target species. Characteristically, parasitoid lifecycles are intimately linked to that of the host, and they feed and develop internally (as endoparasitoids) or externally (as ectoparasitoids) (Fig. 6). By contrast, predators tend to be generalist feeders. Of these, ground beetles, rove beetles and spiders are amongst the most important natural enemies of

FIG 6. Larvae of various wasps are ectoparasitic on crop pests. Here, an almost fully fed ichneumonid wasp larva (on left) lies alongside its paralysed tortricid larval host

pests in annual field crops, whereas predatory bugs and predatory mites commonly hold sway in perennial field crops such as orchards (see Chapter 7). Although predators are frequently opportunist feeders, some specialise in attacking particular groups of prey. Various ladybirds, lacewings and the larvae of certain hover flies and midges, for example, are aphidophagous, feeding mainly if not entirely on aphids.

Host location by herbivorous insects

Herbivorous insects commonly use chemical odours emitted by plants to locate their hosts. Such volatiles often operate at a distance, but short-distance chemical responses may also be involved. Some host-seeking insects, as in the case of certain aphids, need to make contact with the plant, or even to initiate feeding, before confirming a plant's suitability. Colour is often used as a visual host-seeking cue, and can also determine the frequency with which some host-seeking winged (alate) aphids alight on the leaves of possible food plants prior to exploratory probing with the mouthparts.[3] Many insects find yellow objects highly attractive.

HOST PLANT RESISTANCE TO PESTS

Crop cultivars (cultivated plant varieties: cvs) often vary in their susceptibility to pests, some being to a greater or lesser extent resistant or, if attacked, showing some degree of tolerance. As long ago as the early nineteenth century, the apple cvs Siberian Bitter-Sweet and Winter Majetin were known to be resistant to woolly aphid (*Eriosoma lanigerum*)[4] and, probably as the first reported example worldwide, in the previous century the old wheat cv. Underhill was shown to be resistant to hessian fly (*Mayetiola destructor*).[5] More spectacularly, in the late 1800s, resistance in American grapevine rootstocks to grape phylloxera (*Viteus vitifoliae*) saved the European wine industry (see Chapter 12). For a range of reasons, pests might also 'prefer' to feed or breed on particular cultivars of host plants. Preference or non-preference is related either to the presence or absence of toxic plant chemicals or to the structural characteristics of plants, such as the toughness or hairiness of leaves.

Over evolutionary time, plants have developed biochemical defences that reduce the likelihood of their being attacked by phytophagous insects and other herbivores, and many plants contain high levels of alkaloids, glucosinolates (previously known as mustard oil glucosides) or other toxins.

Solanaceous plants, including potato and tomato, contain the toxic steroidal

FIG 7. Colorado beetle (*Leptinotarsa decemlineata*) larvae feed voraciously on the foliage of potato crops and are not deterred by the plant's chemical defences.

glycoalkaloids (SGAs) chaconine and solanine. Levels are particularly high in the sprouting shoots of potato plants.[6] Colorado beetle (*Leptinotarsa decemlineata*) (Fig. 7), the most notorious herbivorous pest of potato crops worldwide, feeds exclusively on SGA-containing plants, and unlike many other insect herbivores it is not deterred by such chemicals. However, SGAs are neither sequestered nor metabolised by the pest. Instead, they are excreted.[7] There are many other examples of defensive chemical toxicity in the plant kingdom.

Pyrrolizidine alkaloids (PAs) are widespread in the botanical family Asteraceae (particularly *Senecio* spp.). They also occur in other families, notably in the Boraginaceae, although at low levels in borage. Like other chemicals, they often impart a bitter taste to plant tissue, perceptible by man and other vertebrates in which they act as cumulative poisons (for example, causing problems when cattle and horses eat ragwort). Many herbivorous insects avoid PA-containing plants, but larvae of tiger moths (family Arctiidae) for example have become specialist feeders upon them. Having fed on PA-laced tissue, larvae store the alkaloids in their bodies, a process known as sequestration. As feeding deterrents and toxins, the sequestered PAs afford protection against parasitoids and predators, in both adult and larval stages of the insect.

Cabbage white butterflies *Pieris* spp. interact with the glucosinolates in brassicas in a similar way. Breakdown products of glucosinolates, emitted by

FIG **8.** Cabbage white butterfly (*Pieris* spp.) larvae are specialist feeders on brassicaceous plants. Those (above left) of large white butterfly (*P. brassicae*) and (above right) small white butterfly (*P. rapae*) rate as important pests.

brassicaceous plants, elicit egg-laying by the butterflies, and the caterpillars (Fig. 8) benefit from the sequestration of glucosinolates derived from their hosts.[9] However, it is not all one sided. Just as cabbage whites have become able to respond positively to compounds thought to have evolved originally as biochemical defences, so some of their natural enemies have become able to respond positively to toxins sequestered in the host caterpillars. Chemical volatiles arising from larva-damaged brassicaceous plants are particularly attractive to the parasitoid wasp (*Cotesia glomerata*),[10] an important enemy of cabbage white butterflies (Chapter 6). Insects capable of feeding on plants containing such toxins are mainly specialists. On brassicas, various ceutorhynchid weevils (*Ceutorhynchus* spp.), mustard beetles (*Phaedon* spp.), as well as the larvae of cabbage white butterflies, diamond-back moth (*Plutella xylostella*), garden pebble moth (*Evergestis forficalis*) and turnip sawfly (*Athalia rosae*), are examples. The highly polyphagous cabbage moth (*Mamestra brassicae*) is a notable exception; its larvae feed on Brassicaceae and many other kinds of plant.

Oil derived from oilseed rape seeds can be high in both acrid-tasting glucosinolates and erucic acid, a potentially toxic fatty acid. This has direct implications for the use of rapeseed oil in margarine manufacture, and also for the use of rapeseed meal as animal fodder. As a consequence, modern (so-called 'double-low' or 'double-zero') cultivars have been bred which are low in glucosinolates and erucic acid. The impact on invertebrate pests of the change to double-low oilseed rape cultivars is uncertain. One might expect loss of glucosinolates to result in decreased attack by specialist pests, but increased attack by generalist insects not adapted to deal with the toxins – but is this what happens? This question is discussed in Chapter 4.

FIG 9. Tomato moth (*Lacanobia oleracea*) larvae are important pests of many outdoor and greenhouse crops.

Toxic lectins occur as defences in many plants.[11] These chemicals are naturally occurring sugar-binding proteins, and some have antifeedant properties. Although some are highly toxic to man and other vertebrates, there is potential to use such chemicals to protect crops. Concanavalin A (conA) and snowdrop lectin (galanthus nivalis agglutinin: GNA), for example, have been shown in transgenic plant breeding programmes to confer a degree of resistance to tomato moth (*Lacanobia oleracea*) (Fig. 9) and other insect pests.[12] Similarly, on genetically modified (GM) oilseed rape, lectins are known to reduce the survival of pollen beetle (*Meligethes aeneus*) larvae.[13]

Physical features of plants also influence the likelihood of their being damaged by herbivores. The defensive potential of hairs (trichomes) in plants such as stinging nettles is well known. In addition, the mere presence of hairs on plants may offer a defence against pest attack; various phytophagous insects and mites show a preference for smooth leaves. Conversely, the smooth leaves of brassicaceous plants are made slippery by their waxy bloom, and hairy-leaved plants are favoured by some pests, such as watercress beetle (*Phaedon cochleariae*).[14]

Plant breeding programmes can address such issues to the benefit of man. However, until GM crops become legitimised tools in farming strategies the potential on offer to protect crops from pests and other agents cannot be fully realised.

THE IMPACT OF PESTS ON PLANTS

Most pests are directly damaging to their host plants, and cause sufficient injury to affect quality, growth or yield, even if they do not actually destroy them. Fortunately, however, few pests boast the destructive power of locusts. As indicated above, the mere presence of pests on plants or in plant tissue can also be an issue. Many pests (including various insects, mites and plant-parasitic nematodes) inject toxic saliva into their hosts, and this may cause malformation if not death of tissue. Such pests sometimes initiate the development of distinctive galls, and these vary from minor distortions and discolorations – sometimes classified as pseudogalls (Fig. 10) – to more complex structures that are usually of characteristic appearance for the causal organism[15] (Fig. 11). Many examples are cited in the following chapters. Herbivorous pests can also be of

FIG 10. As exemplified by rosy leaf-curling aphid (*Dysaphis devecta*) on apple, many phytophagous insects initiate and inhabit pseudogalls on host plants.

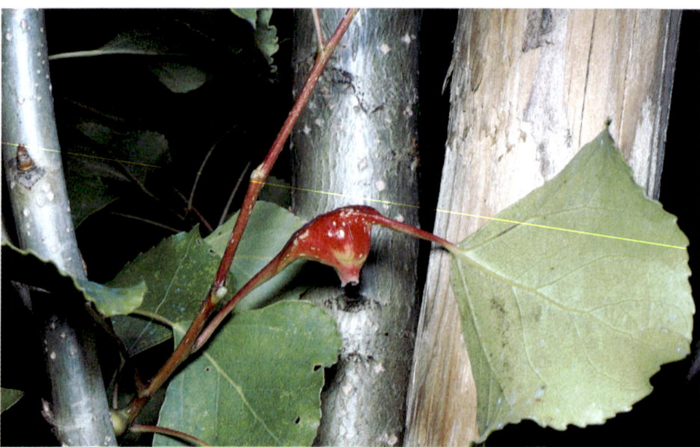

FIG 11. In springtime, lettuce root aphid (*Pemphigus bursarius*) initiates and breeds within flask-like galls on the leaf stalks of poplar trees.

FIG 12. Many phytophagous pests cause 'windowing' of leaves by removing part of the leaf tissue but leaving either the upper or lower epidermis intact. Such damage is often caused by young larvae of cabbage moth (*Mamestra brassicae*).

indirect significance, the damage they cause predisposing plants to infection by bacteria, fungi and other pathogens. This is in addition to their activity as vectors of plant diseases. Plant viruses, spread by aphids, leaf beetles, leaf bugs, leafhoppers, thrips, weevils, whiteflies and nematodes (Appendix II), are sometimes more important antagonists than the pests themselves.

Damage caused by biting pests is wide ranging, and varies from indiscriminate browsing or grazing on the aerial or underground parts of plants to more targeted attacks on buds, leaves, flowers, fruits, stems or roots. Leaf-infesting insects sometimes remove tissue from just one side of an expanded leaf blade, leaving behind a more or less transparent outermost layer of tissue on the other; such damage is termed 'windowing', and is typically caused by the young larvae of some lepidopterous pests (Fig. 12) and larvae of certain leaf beetles, weevils and sawflies. Some leaf-feeding pests – adults of pea & bean weevil (*Sitona lineatus*) and vine weevil (*Otiorhynchus sulcatus*) are examples – attack the margins of expanded leaves, creating characteristic notches. Others, such as larvae of many sawflies, destroy much of the leaf blade, perhaps at best leaving behind a mere skeletal tracery of major veins.

Leaf-mining insect larvae (of which there are many) are often highly modified structurally as either sap feeders or tissue feeders. Sap feeders, as in the moth family Phyllocnistidae, penetrate cells and then imbibe sap, whereas tissue feeders

FIG 13. Protective webs are formed and inhabited by larvae of several pests, including gregarious species such as apple small ermine moth (*Yponomeuta malinellus*).

(e.g. leaf-mining larvae of various beetles, moths and sawflies) chew the cells with their mandibles or, as in the case of dipterous leaf miners (e.g. family Agromyzidae), scythe their way through the cells with their mouth-hooks and then imbibe the severed tissue. Some leaf miners are sap feeders in their early larval stages but then moult into tissue feeders; during the course of their development larvae of the moth genus *Phyllonorycter* (family Gracillariidae), for example, pass through three sap-feeding and then two tissue-feeding instars (growth stages).[16]

Leaves attacked by insect larvae are often rolled or folded to form distinctive habitations, frequently held in position by strands of silk.[17] Larvae of many tortrix moths (family Tortricidae), collectively described as 'leaf tiers' or 'leaf rollers', are common examples. Silk is also widely used by insect larvae to build protective webs (Fig. 13) or to construct cocoons within which the larvae then pupate. As described in later chapters, silk has other uses too.

CLIMATE CHANGE AND WEATHER

Current and future trends towards hotter drier summers and wetter warmer winters, and an increase in the frequency of extreme weather events, are bound to impact directly or indirectly on crop pests. Increases in temperature are of particular significance, perhaps advancing the timing of a pest's seasonal activity and increasing the rate of development, thereby allowing certain species to complete more generations per year than normal. For better or worse, such changes can also affect pest complexes on crops, and alter the abundance and distribution of particular species. Hot, dry conditions certainly favour pests such as cereal ground beetle (*Zabrus tenebrioides*), leopard moth (*Zeuzera pyrina*) and turnip moth (*Agrotis segetum*) but they can disadvantage others, including some root-infesting species that deposit eggs in or on the soil; eggs of carrot flies (*Psila rosae*) and crane flies (e.g. *Tipula* spp.), for example, are particularly prone to desiccation. Pest development and survival may also be affected if the food plants become drought stricken or are otherwise forced into early senescence. Milder winters encourage survival of certain pests, especially aphids such as potato aphid (*Macrosiphum euphorbiae*) whose lifecycle does not involve a winter egg stage. Similarly, mild conditions enable clones of peach/potato aphids to overwinter as nymphs and adults rather than as eggs, resulting in the earlier production of winged spring migrants. Wetter, frost-free winters also favour activity by slugs. Pests programmed to undergo an obligatory period of winter diapause (as eggs or other stages), however, are disadvantaged by such changes; mild winters certainly present a greater risk of infection by fungal pathogens.

Strong winds and heavy rain can affect crop pests, dislodging them from their food plants or knocking them to the ground where they become vulnerable to attack by ground-dwelling predators. Inclement weather may also prevent pests such as newly emerged midges and adult carrot flies from taking flight. Conversely, wind and rain aid the dispersal of tiny creatures such as gall mites, and dispersing wind-borne aphids are a particularly important component of the aerial plankton.[18] Soil-inhabiting pests are inevitably influenced not only by soil type but also by soil condition, which is in part affected by rainfall. Adequate soil moisture levels are an important precursor for the emergence of wheat blossom midges from subterranean cocoons in which they have overwintered and pupated. Thus, the summer emergence of the midges can be delayed if soil conditions are unfavourable, and this may allow wheat crops to pass through their most susceptible growth stages before they are attacked.

In the longer term, owing to expected ongoing changes in our climate, some crops (such as black currants, which require hard winter frosts to ensure proper bud break and subsequent fruiting) could well decline in importance, whereas others (such as maize or sweet corn, which are favoured by hot, dry summers) might be grown more widely and intensively. This would inevitably affect the status and distribution of certain pests. Induced modifications in cropping patterns and sowing dates, and longer growing seasons, could also have an impact, advantageous or otherwise. More and more vineyards are being established in Britain. Also, in the southwest of England fruit-bearing olive trees have already been raised, albeit on a very limited scale. This is not to say, however, that southern European pests such as olive fruit fly (*Bactrocera oleae*) are now poised to descend upon us!

THE IMPACT OF FARMING PRACTICES

Agroecosystems are essentially unstable environments, and this is especially so in the case of annual as opposed to perennial crops. Populations of pests, parasitoids and predators within perennial crops are subject to relatively little disturbance unless pesticides are applied. Admittedly, pruning and fruit picking can be disruptive. However, these operations are as nothing compared with the dramatic changes and disruptions associated with growing rotational arable and vegetable crops. These disruptions are caused by physical disturbance of soil and vegetation (for example, by annual ploughing), by application of pesticides, and by changes in microclimate associated with the annual harvest and preparation for the next crop.

Field crops tend to be grown as monocultures (one and the same kind of crop), with plants at an identical stage of development (Fig. 14). Such uniformity facilitates harvesting and other farming activities. However, it also offers pests potentially rich pickings – on occasions resulting in epidemics – and contrasts markedly with uncultivated habitats, which are typically more varied and also inherently more stable. Natural habitats usually support a wide range of plants and animals, including herbivores (which occupy the bottom of the animal food chain), detritus feeders and an assorted entourage of parasitoids and predators. Pests are particularly likely to flourish in the absence of their natural enemies, which may be less numerous in annual crops because of the instability of such environments. However, the establishment and survival of parasitoids and predators within crops can be encouraged by the adoption of appropriate management strategies. Although more appropriate to tropical than temperate

FIG 14. Crops are typically grown as monocultures, with plants all at an identical stage of development.

agriculture,[19] intercropping (the growing of two or more crops in the same piece of land at one and the same time) can increase biodiversity and subsequently prove detrimental to pests, especially specialist feeders.[20]

Physical disturbance

Cultivation techniques on arable farms range from traditional deep ploughing (Fig. 15) to non-inversion methods, and these (along with seedbed preparation) can have important consequences for crop pests and their natural enemies. In particular, ploughing may expose pests to predatory birds, or leave them on or near the surface to die from desiccation. However, such techniques can also have adverse effects on important ground-dwelling predators such as ground beetles, thereby potentially enhancing pest survival rates. Ploughing is also known to deplete populations of hymenopterous parasitoids which pupate in the soil.[21]

The time of sowing of field crops has a considerable bearing on pests. In oilseed rape, for example, the pest spectra of autumn- as opposed to spring-sown crops are rather different (see Chapter 4). Also, whether crops are sown early or late can enhance or reduce the likelihood and impact of pest attacks, as clearly demonstrated in the case of cabbage stem flea beetle (*Psylliodes chrysocephala*) which is potentially more damaging the earlier the autumn-sown host crop germinates and develops.[22] Similarly, there might be differences in pest complexes on younger as opposed to older crops. Strawberry mite (*Phytonemus pallidus fragariae*), for example, is more likely to be found in mature strawberry plantations than in maiden beds. The stage of growth of a crop can also be of significance.

Crop rotation also influences pest populations, both directly and indirectly. In particular, cyst nematodes on potato crops thrive and escalate if host plants

FIG 15. Deep ploughing of fields, whether post-harvest or otherwise, unearths soil-inhabiting pests and is also disruptive to various natural enemies.

are grown in the same fields year after year. Accordingly, in the presence of the pest, strict crop rotation (perhaps growing no more than one potato crop in six years) is often advised and implemented, with the nematode populations subsequently declining. Management of cyst nematodes in sugar beet crops demands a similar approach, backed by statutory pest control orders (see Chapter 5). Other examples, although not calling for mandatory controls, are to be found in the insect world. Perennial crops, where short-term or perhaps medium-term if not long-term rotation is inappropriate, present a different scenario. Following successful invasion and establishment within a crop, pest numbers might be expected to increase year on year unless control measures are implemented. However, the same is true of populations of natural enemies and, as can be demonstrated in unsprayed or rarely sprayed orchards, where parasitoids and predators are allowed to thrive, pest populations often stay below economically damaging levels.

Crop microclimates

Plant architecture, spacing and stage of growth play a major role in governing microclimates within crops. Microclimatic differences (especially in temperature and humidity) are particularly well displayed in annual arable crops. In early spring, for example, the soil surface in root crops such as beet and potato is largely bare – exposed to the warmth of the sun in the daytime but likely to become cold at night as heat is lost by radiation to a largely clear sky. Only later in the season does a significant leaf canopy develop, reducing fluctuations in temperature and humidity in the sheltered air within the crop by shifting the exposed zone of extreme temperature to the top of the canopy. Springtime microclimates are more stable in winter-sown field crops, including cereals.

FIG **16.** In spring, an autumn-sown oilseed rape crop develops very rapidly and the canopy soon becomes very dense. The microclimate below the canopy is typically cool and dank.

At the extreme, winter oilseed rape crops (which grow very rapidly in spring and soon develop a dense leaf canopy; Fig. 16) present a rather cool and humid micro-environment beneath the canopy. Such microclimatic differences can influence communities of polyphagous predators such as ground beetles, of which there are cold-tolerant, warmth-loving, drought-tolerant and moisture-loving species. However, other factors that govern predator activity and breeding in fields and their immediate surroundings can be overriding.[23]

The microclimate is consistent in perennial crops, especially if they are evergreen, but it suffers periodic disruption in sites where annual crops are grown, especially if the soil is ploughed or in some other way laid bare. Some species of pests and predators can weather such changes by overwintering below the soil surface. However, many cannot, and must recolonise the field every year from surrounding vegetated habitats which offer more stable conditions. Often, herbivores multiply faster than natural enemies, so that in field crops parasitoids and predators may not exercise a sufficient degree of control over their prey until pest populations have reached or exceeded damaging proportions. This delay is particularly evident in the case of multi-brooded pests such as aphids, whose populations on the crop often escalate before any colonising or recolonising natural enemies have had a chance develop their populations and exercise an adequate degree of natural control.

Pest management

Farming practices vary considerably, ranging from low-input (extensive) agriculture, including organic farming, where artificial inputs are strictly limited and perhaps avoided altogether, to high-input (intensive) agriculture, in which artificial fertilisers, insecticides, fungicides and herbicides may be applied

FIG 17. Pheromone traps are used to monitor pests in various crops. They allow farmers or growers to assess pest numbers and flight times, and to judge if and when insecticides should be applied. Frequently monitored pests include codling moth (*Cydia pomonella*) and fruit tree tortrix moth (*Archips podana*) in apple orchards, plum fruit moth (*C. funebrana*) in plum orchards and pea moth (*C. nigricana*) in pea crops.

routinely. These two extremes flank a range of other systems. Pest management systems include so-called 'supervised control', where pesticides are applied but only if monitoring, perhaps using pheromone traps (Fig. 17), indicates that numbers of specified pests are likely to prove economically damaging. More sophisticated strategies include Integrated Pest Management (IPM) and Integrated Crop Management (ICM). These can involve the use of artificially introduced or naturally occurring biocontrol agents (BCAs) – parasitoids, predators and pathogenic micro-organisms – and chemical pesticides (ideally selective ones which have a strictly limited spectrum of activity and will not harm BCAs or counteract their impact), which are used only when absolutely necessary. Biological control, i.e. control of a pest by one or more natural enemies, is a key component and overall aim of IPM. Classical biological control, however, is a specific entity within crop protection, and involves the introduction of a non-indigenous BCA to kill an alien pest. IPM techniques may also include push–pull strategies whereby the behaviour of pests and/or BCAs is manipulated by using deterrent and repellent stimuli (push) along with attractant and stimulant stimuli (pull).[24] The latter might include a trap crop to which pests are attracted and in which they are killed before they can move elsewhere.[25]

Insecticides and other pesticides are frequently used to control pests in intensive agricultural systems, often with little or no regard for the presence of naturally occurring BCAs. Unintended slaughter of the parasitoid wasp (*Trichomalus perfectus*) in English oilseed rape crops in the 1990s is a classic example of collateral damage that can follow sometimes misguided or overenthusiastic use of insecticides.[26] Pesticides often affect beneficial predatory insects, mites and spiders. Pesticides can also harm non-target organisms other than BCAs, including pollinating insects such as bees. In general, modern farming practices are tuned to avoid harmful side effects. However, in spite of man's best efforts, unexpected problems can still arise, as in the case of bee deaths in Germany in 2008 that followed the drilling of insecticide-treated maize seed under exceptional drought conditions; here, harmful dust arose from the abraded seed coating and then drifted onto nearby flowering weeds.[27]

Where chemical pesticides are applied, pest populations tend to recover more quickly than those of parasitoids and predators. However, the impact on natural enemies is lessened if a suitably selective pesticide is used. In controlled environments, such as greenhouses, commercially available BCAs are widely used in IPM systems. These can be introduced at the optimum time to maintain adequate control of the target pest(s) throughout the growing season, and growers adopting such techniques often do not need to apply chemical pesticides (Chapter 10).

FIG 18. Naturally occurring entomopathogenic fungi infect a wide range of insects, including sawfly larvae, but their impact is lessened following the application of fungicides.

Most fungicides and herbicides do not have a direct impact on insects or other invertebrates, whether pests or otherwise. However, some field-applied fungicides are known to affect springtails active on the soil surface.[28] Fungicides can also have a deleterious effect on entomopathogenic fungi (EPFs) (Fig. 18). More specifically, the fungicide benomyl is toxic to earthworms.[29] As for herbicides, trifluralin (a widely used weedkiller in both agriculture and horticulture) inhibits the development and growth of certain EPFs.[30] Also, following the use of herbicides, loss of weeds can have indirect effects on invertebrates, resulting in a less abundant food supply for herbivores (including seed feeders) and reduced cover (shelter) for ground-dwelling species.

The farm landscape

Flocks of seagulls following the plough epitomise part of the traditional arable farming scene, as do vociferous skylarks and various other farmland birds. Similarly, bees and other insects foraging on flowering weeds within fields or on the flowers of rotational broadleaved crops such as field beans and oilseed rape are a familiar sight on farmland. Particularly in spring and summer, field surroundings – hedgerows, grassy banks and the like – can also visibly teem with life. Apart from such examples, arable land might at times seem relatively 'lifeless', at least to the casual observer, even when fields are carpeted by developing crops. However, closer examination (with permission from the landowner) can unearth a fascinating and often unimaginable hive of activity within the crops themselves, both above and below ground level. This is in part generated by a wide range of phytophagous insects and other creatures deemed to be pests, whose presence can support an intricate web of predators and other natural enemies. The soil is also, of course, a hidden world of macro- and micro-organisms in its own right.

Farmland landscapes range from large, prairie-like fields, more or less devoid of hedges and other such habitats, to sites that offer a compact, often undulating, patchwork of cropped and uncultivated land. Grasslands aside, cultivated areas include mainly annual crops (in Britain, primarily cereals) but also perennial crops such as those in fruit plantations, orchards and vineyards, all of which are major landscape elements. These are complemented by a few highly specialised habitats such as hop gardens (Fig. 19) and watercress beds (Fig. 20).

Uncropped areas (e.g. hedgerows, grassy banks, copses, woodlands, ditches and dykes) are also significant landscape elements, and for many insects and other invertebrates they not only provide ideal overwintering sites but also function as alternative feeding or breeding grounds. Provision of flowering strips within farmland landscapes can provide essential nectar and pollen for both parasitoids and predators; these BCAs may subsequently disperse and attack pests in adjacent crops.[31] However, flowering strips do not affect all natural

FIG 19. Traditional hop gardens, with bines supported by tall poles and wirework, are far less common than in former years.

FIG 20. Watercress beds are minor but highly specialised habitats, confined mainly to the southern-most counties of England.

enemies in the same way. For example, they are of no benefit to single-brooded parasitoids that do not undergo a period of maturation feeding prior to egg-laying – the ichneumonid wasps (*Phradis interstitialis, P. morionellus* and *Tersilochus heterocerus*), parasitoids of pollen beetle on oilseed rape, are examples.[32]

It is often thought that pest abundance, or at least the potential for pest populations to develop and flourish, is related to the extent to which suitable crops are available in the landscape. However, the crop itself can become a hostile environment if insecticides are applied. Unless there is subsequent reinvasion from elsewhere, survival of the pest within the landscape might then depend upon the availability of untreated host plants. In this regard, specialist feeders are at greater risk of localised extinction than generalists. Mobility of pests also has a role to play, and pests with high dispersal potential are less likely to be lost than relatively immobile ones.

Pest damage is typically reduced in landscapes offering a wide diversity of plant life.[33] In part this is due to the activities of predators, which find such environments more conducive for survival. However, a pest does not necessarily pass its whole lifecycle on the crop, and most are subject to predation in fields for just part of the year. Black bean aphid (*Aphis fabae*), which feeds and breeds on annual crops (such as field bean, potato and sugar beet) during spring and summer but overwinters in the egg stage on wild spindle bushes, is a prime example. In the absence of pests, survival of predators depends upon their being able to local alternative food sources in fields, in adjacent areas or elsewhere.[34] Management of field margins can be key.

Arable field margins typically comprise three zones:[35]

- **the field boundary** – for example a hedge, a wall, a grassy bank, a windbreak and/or a ditch, which separates one field from another or from an alternative land-use feature;
- **the boundary strip** – the area between the field boundary and the edge of the crop, often including a cultivated, mown or sprayed strip and, perhaps, a farm track;
- **the crop margin** – the area within the crop between the edge and the first tractor wheeling (usually equivalent to one boom width of the farmer's sprayer).

In the interests of biodiversity, crop margins (then termed 'conservation headlands') are sometimes less-intensively managed than the rest of the crop. They may, for example, be left more or less unfertilised and unsprayed.[36] This allows flowering weeds and a range of wildlife to flourish, and by safeguarding beneficial insects (particularly polyphagous predators) can aid pest management

FIG 21. Grassy banks within or around arable fields are ideal overwintering sites for predators such as ground beetles, rove beetles and spiders.

on the farm. In addition, season-to-season survival of ground beetles, rove beetles and spiders within large arable fields can be enhanced following the establishment of ridges of dense, tussocky grass and other kinds of perennial vegetation (Fig. 21); these artificial refuges are popularly known as 'beetle banks'.[37]

In spite of ever-increasing demands for new housing, roads and so forth, a large proportion of the British countryside is still devoted to crops. Arable crops in England and Wales alone, for example, currently occupy around 4.5 million hectares. The arable farmer's main objectives are to meet the demands of agricultural production and to run a profitable business. However, this does not mean that arable farms must be treated as barren industrial sites. Today, the need to consider the environment, to conserve wildlife and to enhance on-farm biodiversity is becoming more and more widely recognised. Encouraged by schemes such as Countryside Stewardship and Environmental Stewardship, farmers are increasingly aware that they are major custodians of our precious countryside. Working with rather than against nature is a laudable and viable aim, and this is of particular significance when considering crop pests and their natural enemies.

CHAPTER 2

An Overview of Cereal Pests

ARABLE FARMING IN THE British Isles is dominated by cereal production, primarily based on wheat and barley crops which occupy over 2.2 million ha and *c.* 1.3 million ha, respectively. Oats also feature, although at about 0.1 million ha far less prominently than in the past. Other cereal crops, forage maize, rye and triticale, are relatively unimportant. Cereals are attacked by a wide range of pests. Some are of particular significance at the establishment phase (from sowing to seedling emergence) and many others invade at a more advanced stage of crop development. However, once crops have flowered and the plants have begun to senesce and harden off prior to harvest field pests become of little or no importance, although birds and mammals sometimes plunder the ripening grain. Cereal crops share many pests that are commonplace on cultivated and wild grasses. They are also subject to attack by some that are very catholic in their choice of food plant – leatherjackets (the larvae of crane flies) and wireworms (the larvae of click beetles) are common examples. In detail, however, pest complexes and the relative importance of individual species vary from one kind of cereal to another. They also depend on whether crops are sown in the autumn (as in the case of winter wheat and winter barley, which constitute the vast majority of British cereal crops) or in the spring. Other influencing factors (direct or otherwise) include the method of pre-sowing cultivation (whether traditional ploughing, minimal cultivation or direct-drilling techniques are employed) and the nature of the previous crop in the rotation (whether grass, a cereal or some other crop). As highlighted later in this chapter, cereals may be sown into recently ploughed-up grassland or pastures, and this is of particular importance because it can result in their being attacked by various pests capable of transferring from the 'old' grass.

GRAIN HOLLOWING BY PESTS

Recently drilled (sown) cereal seeds are attacked by pests both before and immediately following germination. In particular, slugs often remove the germ, so that the seeds fail to develop. Such damage, commonly termed grain hollowing, is particularly significant on winter wheat and is caused by several species, of which the field slug (*Deroceras reticulatum*) is usually most important. Slugs also attack cereal seedlings, severing the shoots close to the seeds and shredding the developing leaves above soil level. Slugs are mainly nocturnal and most active in warm, damp conditions. They are also most likely to inflict damage to crops grown on heavy soils and in cloddy seedbeds, and where crops follow cereals, oilseed rape or peas. Cereal seeds are similarly hollowed-out by various other pests, including certain insects and wood mice.

In the 1990s grain hollowing by adults of the aptly named Wessex flea beetle (*Psylliodes luteola*) was observed for the first time, in winter cereals in various parts of Dorset, Hampshire and Wiltshire. Little is known of the bionomics of this insect, which has since rapidly expanded its pest range within England well beyond the Wessex epicentre of attacks; reports of damage have extended northwards to Oxfordshire, eastwards to Kent and westwards to Devon. Observations on cereal crops suggest that mid-September sowings are particularly susceptible. Damage has also been reported on recently drilled herbage seed crops and winter oilseed rape. Until recently Wessex flea beetle was considered a rare British insect[1] and the current upsurge in populations is unexplained. The change does, however, mirror a similar but more dramatic escalation and spread of the closely related cabbage stem flea beetle (*P. chrysocephala*), which followed the rise in importance of winter oilseed rape in eastern England (and subsequently elsewhere) from the late 1970s onwards.[2] Wireworms (e.g. *Agriotes* spp. and in upland districts *Ctenicera* spp.) surviving from ploughed-up grassland are also frequently responsible for grain hollowing in recently sown cereal crops.

PESTS OF ESTABLISHED CROPS

Soil-inhabiting insect pests

Young cereal plants are attacked by a range of phytophagous (plant-eating) soil-inhabiting insects, including many so-called 'ley pests' (see Chapter 3) that are primarily associated with grasses and readily transfer from ploughed-up grassland

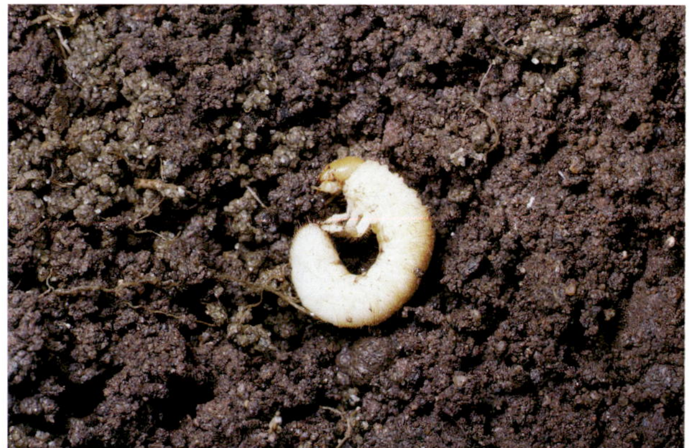

FIG 22. Brown chafer (*Serica brunnea*) larvae feed on the roots of cereals and many other plants.

or grassy stubbles to following crops such as cereals. Soil-inhabiting examples include chafer grubs, wireworms and leatherjackets. Sometimes, cereal plants are also damaged by bibionid larvae: e.g. *Bibio hortulanus* and *B. johannis*[3] and fever fly (*Dilophus febrilis*).[4] Bibionids are discussed further in the following chapter.

As for chafer grubs, those of three grassland species – the brown chafer (*Serica brunnea*) (Fig. 22), the cockchafer (*Melolontha melolontha*) and the summer chafer (*Amphimallon solstitiale*) – are sometimes harmful to cereals, individuals grazing indiscriminately on the roots of host plants. They will also sever the stems of seedlings. In all three species the lifecycle (governed by temperature and humidity) extends over two or more years; cockchafer larvae, for example, typically require three or four years to complete their development.[5] Wireworms also have extended life histories (see Chapter 3). On established plants they typically damage stems below soil level, either fraying the shoot close to the seed or biting a ragged hole into the base. Attacked plants often turn yellow and die, but sometimes just the central shoot is affected. Damage on cereals is seen mainly during the spring and early summer. Wireworms are primarily denizens of old, established grassland and they became particularly significant agricultural pests during and immediately after the Second World War, when a considerable number of old pastures were broken up and planted with cereals and other crops. It was then not unusual for wireworm numbers in grassland and following crops to exceed several million per hectare. However, populations in grass fields declined considerably in the 1950s,[6] coinciding with the introduction and widespread use of persistent organochlorine insecticides. On environmental grounds, such materials have long since been withdrawn from use, and there is a perception that this is now leading to a recovery in wireworm populations.

FIG 23. Common crane fly (*Tipula paludosa*) larvae, known as leatherjackets, feed on the roots of various plants.

Cereal crops that follow grass are frequently attacked by leatherjackets (Fig. 23). These familiar pests tear through the plant stems at or just below the soil surface, leaving behind characteristically ragged wounds. Leatherjackets also feed on expanded leaves whose tips or blades are touching the ground. Damage occurs mainly in the spring and is most prevalent in damp situations. The leatherjackets themselves are often found resting in the soil close to the damaged plants. The main culprit tends to be the common crane fly (*Tipula paludosa*), the adults of which often appear in plague proportions in the early autumn, frequently generating considerable but usually unjustified media attention. However, damaging populations of *T. oleracea* have also been reported on cereals, usually when cereals follow winter oilseed rape crops. Typically, the largely impenetrable rape canopy will have confined the egg-laying females and prevented their wider dispersal, thereby concentrating the forthcoming leatherjacket attack.[7]

Agriphila straminella,[8] a species of grass moth (see Chapter 3), is also, occasionally, found on cereals, typically having spread from previously infested ploughed-up grassland or grassy stubbles. Such attacks have occurred on both autumn-sown and spring-sown wheat and barley in various parts of central, eastern and southern England.[9] However, problems on cereals are sporadic and uncommon. Damage caused to cereal plants is most evident in the spring, when stems and tillers are completely severed. But for the clean-edged (rather than ragged) incisions, such damage could easily be mistaken for that inflicted by leatherjackets and wireworms. *A. straminella* larvae also burrow into the stems, causing similar injury to that ascribed to pests such as common rustic moth (*Mesapamea secalis*) (p. 34). Pupation occurs in the soil, close to the surface, in small oval cocoons. In North America, the larvae of such insects are known as sodworms or webworms and are important pests of a wide range of crops.

FIG 24. Soil-inhabiting garden swift moth (*Hepialus lupulinus*) larvae often attack the roots of cereals.

Attacks on cereals by larvae of swift moths are by no means uncommon, again often following grass or where patches of grass weeds, especially common couch, have been killed off. The larvae emerge at night from subterranean, silk-lined burrows to attack cereal plants, individuals typically working along a row of plants which they sever at or about soil level. Although ghost swift moth (*Hepialus humuli*) can be responsible, attacks on cereals are more usually attributable to garden swift moth (*H. lupulinus*) (Fig. 24). Swift moth larvae are readily disturbed and immediately retreat backwards down their burrows if they sense the approach of an intruder. Since their burrows often extend downwards below spade depth, it is not unusual for the larvae to remain undetected.

Cereal ground beetle (*Zabrus tenebrioides*), previously a local and scarce British species, is another soil-inhabiting pest of cereals and one that has risen to prominence over the past 30 years or so. Infestations in Britain were first recorded in 1977, on winter wheat near Swaffham Prior in Cambridgeshire.[10] Since then, damage to cereals has occurred in several other parts of southern England, including Dorset, Oxfordshire, Sussex and Wiltshire. Attacks on wheat and barley crops continue to be reported to this day, especially on chalkland sites. Cereal ground beetle is better known as a pest in eastern Europe, where infestations can be of considerable significance.[11] Grasses such as annual meadow-grass and common couch are also attacked. The upsurge of this species in England could well be a result of the increased frequency of hot, dry summers which apparently favour its development. Cereal ground beetle larvae (Fig. 25) inhabit subterranean tunnels which they excavate in the soil, and these habitations are readily found adjacent to attacked plants. The larvae emerge at night to attack their food plants, the leaves of which become extensively

FIG 25. Cereal ground beetle (*Zabrus tenebrioides*) larvae are found mainly in chalkland sites in southern England.

FIG 26. Leaf shredding by cereal ground beetle larvae is often very noticeable.

shredded (Fig. 26). Severed leaf fragments are also dragged into the burrows and later devoured during the daytime. Severe attacks by cereal ground beetle larvae can lead to the complete destruction of plants, with just tangled mats of dead or dying tissue left on the soil surface. The larvae feed from autumn onwards, and complete their development in the following May or June. The rather stout-bodied, sombre-looking adults occur in July.

Finally, the shoots of young wheat plants are sometimes attacked by larvae of the wheat shoot beetle (*Helophorus nubilus*). This local pest is found mainly in eastern England, and usually occurs on cereals following short-term grass leys.[12] The larvae feed from November onwards, causing damage that typically becomes evident over the following few months. They bite into the base of the shoots, leaving a small but distinct and often ragged hole; attacked shoots may also be completely severed. As in the case of wireworm attack, the central shoots of plants often turn yellow and die. Wireworm damage, however, is not usually seen in the field until March at the earliest. Owing to its small size (adults 3–4 mm long; larvae up to 7 mm long) and cryptic, mud-like coloration, this soil-inhabiting pest is often overlooked.

FIG 27. The deadheart symptom (i.e. death of the central shoot) is typical of attack by larvae of many pests, including wheat bulb fly (*Delia coarctata*).

Shoot-borers

Cereal plants are frequently invaded by stem-boring insect larvae, many of which cause the central shoots of developing plants to turn yellow and die, especially in the spring. Such damage (Fig. 27) is universally described as the deadheart symptom and is attributable to several well-known agricultural pests, in particular frit fly (*Oscinella frit*), wheat bulb fly (*Delia coarctata*) and yellow cereal fly (*Opomyza florum*). Various non-dipterous pests (wireworms, for example, have already been mentioned) are also responsible for central-shoot damage.

True flies

Frit fly, which has three or more generations annually, is a notorious pest of cultivated ryegrasses and spring-sown cereals, especially oats and maize (including sweet corn). First-generation adults are active in May and early June, and eggs are then deposited on the basal part of young host plants. Following egg hatch, each larva bores into a central shoot, typically destroying the growing point. The larvae (Fig. 28) are fully grown in about three weeks and, characteristically, complete their development within a single shoot. Their skins then harden and darken to become reddish-brown puparia within which pupation takes place. New adults appear shortly

FIG 28. Frit fly (*Oscinella frit*) larvae are important pests of cereals, particularly oats.

afterwards. On spring-sown oats, these flies deposit eggs close to the developing ears. However, such plants are susceptible to attack for only a short time – from ear emergence to the end of flowering. Where attacks are established, the larvae damage the developing grain and cause a blackening of the inner tissue, a condition known as fritted grain. Frit fly puparia are often gathered with the grain, and swarms of the tiny black adults subsequently emerge from buildings in which the harvested crop is stored. Third-generation flies occur in late summer to early autumn. They often deposit eggs on recently germinated, early-sown cereal plants, including wheat and barley. However, Italian ryegrass is a more preferred host. If grass leys infested by frit fly are ploughed up and then planted with cereals, the larvae are capable of transferring from the buried turf to the young cereal plants. Accordingly, frit fly is designated a ley pest, in common with several other grass- and cereal-feeding insects, including larvae of certain moths, beetles and flies, including grass & cereal flies in the genera *Cetema*, *Geomyza* and *Meromyza*.[13]

Unlike frit fly, wheat bulb fly (a locally important pest of wheat, barley, rye and triticale, especially in eastern England and Scotland) has just one generation annually. In this case, the grey-bodied, housefly-like adults (Fig. 29) are long-lived and occur in the field from June to early September. Unlike most other phytophagous pests, they lay eggs speculatively in bare soil (for example, in fallows or between the rows of root crops such as potato and sugar beet), in the

FIG 29. Wheat bulb fly (*Delia coarctata*) is a major pest of winter wheat.

FIG 30. Wheat bulb fly (*Delia coarctata*) larvae feed in the central shoots of wheat plants, and plant losses are often considerable.

absence of suitable host plants. Wheat bulb fly population densities vary considerably from season to season and from place to place, but can be of considerable significance. In some years, egg numbers in particularly susceptible fields (designated as hot spots) exceed several million per hectare. Eggs are particularly numerous in fields following fallows or potatoes.[14] Mortality of eggs during the winter is often considerable and is due to a range of factors, including desiccation, pathogens and the activity of predators.[15] Wheat bulb fly eggs usually hatch from mid-January to mid-March, depending on temperature. Larvae (Fig. 30) then work their way vertically upwards through the soil, and (at least in sandy soil) can successfully invade host plants even if eggs have been buried to some depth by ploughing.[16] If suitable host plants are present, larvae then invade the central shoots. Unlike those of frit fly, wheat bulb fly larvae each attack and kill more than one shoot during the course of their development, tearing at the basal tissue with their hook-like mouthparts. Also, fully fed (third-instar) larvae bite their way out of plants through a ragged hole to form puparia in the soil rather than within the host plant. Careful examination of a vacated plant will often reveal the black skeletal remains of the first- or second-instar larval mouthparts, including the so-called 'mouth-hooks' that form part of the cephalopharyngeal skeleton (see Fig. A.4, p. 416) which is discarded when the individual moults from one growth stage to the next. This is further confirmation, if required, of the former presence of the pest. Although wheat bulb fly larvae tend to escape the attentions of parasitoids and predators, the pupae are often parasitised by larvae of rove beetles (*Aleochara bilineata* and *A. bipustulata*); pupal losses following predation by ground beetles are also of some significance.[17] In addition, adult wheat bulb flies are attacked by dance flies (namely, *Empis livida*) and yellow dung flies (*Scathophaga stercoraria*).[18, 19]

At about the time that wheat bulb fly larvae are approaching maturity and beginning to vacate infested plants, crops can also be attacked by late-wheat shoot fly (*Phorbia securis*), another shoot-infesting cereal pest. In this case, the adult flies (active in March and April, especially in warm, sunny conditions) deposit their eggs directly onto host plants, each egg being inserted singly beneath the leaf sheath of a secondary shoot (tiller). Infestations of over 600,000 larvae per hectare have been reported, which sounds a lot.[20] However, the detrimental impact on a crop is greatly reduced since damage by this pest is restricted to the secondary shoots.

Adult yellow cereal flies occur from mid-June onwards and are long-lived, surviving well into the autumn. They are, however, most numerous in July. Numbers in fields then decline rapidly,[21] as adults seek sheltered situations (such as coppices and woodlands) in which to spend the summer. In late September the flies migrate to early-sown winter wheat crops, where eggs are deposited on soil close to the developing seedlings. Egg-laying is largely completed by the end of October, so that crops sown from October onwards usually escape attention.[22] The eggs hatch in February. Each larva then burrows into a central shoot, and familiar deadheart symptoms soon become visible within infested crops. However, unlike larvae of wheat bulb fly, those of yellow cereal fly do not tear holes through the shoot tissue. Instead, they make a circular, brownish incision or a characteristic spiralling around the shoot base or immediately above the first node. This becomes visible if the surrounding leaf sheath of an infested plant is removed (Fig. 31). Like those of frit fly, yellow cereal fly larvae complete their development within a single shoot, where pupation also takes place. Adults of the related dusky-winged cereal fly (*Opomyza germinationis*) are also often abundant in cereal crops. Their larvae then occur in wheat and oat plants but are more often associated with grasses.[23]

FIG 31. Shoot spiralling, visible when the outer-most leaf sheath is removed, is typical of attack by yellow cereal fly (*Opomyza florum*).

One further shoot-infesting dipteran deserves attention: gout fly (*Chlorops pumilionis*). This pest is a

FIG 32. Gout fly (*Chlorops pumilionis*) larvae feed within the shoots of host plants.

FIG 33. When fully fed, gout fly (*Chlorops pumilionis*) larvae pupate *in situ*.

distinctive, black and yellow fly that occasionally causes damage to wheat, barley, rye and triticale. Common couch, particularly when growing in arable fields, is also attacked,[24] but oats and maize are immune. First-generation adults are active in May and June, and eggs are deposited singly on the upper leaves of host plants. Following egg hatch the larva bores into the central shoot to begin feeding. Working downwards the larva (Fig. 32) eventually reaches the developing ear, which either fails to emerge or does appear but is stunted and distorted. Larvae are fully fed in about a month. They then pupate *in situ*, each in a brown and characteristically elongated puparium (Fig. 33). A second generation of flies appears from August onwards, and in mild conditions individuals often survive into late October. Eggs from these flies are laid on the leaves of early-sown cereals. Volunteer cereals and grasses (especially common couch) are also attacked. The second-brood larvae feed singly within the central shoots, and complete their development in the following spring. The main shoot of an infested plant eventually becomes noticeably swollen (gouty) (Fig. 34) – a characteristic feature of gout fly attack. The secondary tillers produced by an infested plant are also killed. Deadheart, however, is not a symptom of attack. Nowadays, in cereal crops, gout fly is found mainly on September-sown

FIG 34. A swollen stem is typical of attack by gout fly (*Chlorops pumilionis*).

winter wheat and winter barley. Larvae are frequently parasitised, especially by the double-brooded endoparasitoid *Stenomalus micans*,[25] a pteromalid wasp.[26]

Beetles

Wheat flea beetle (*Neocrepidodera ferruginea*)[27] is a common ley pest, the larvae readily transferring to cereals sown in recently ploughed infested grassland. The adult beetles are active from June to mid-September, eggs being laid in late summer at the base of various plants but especially grasses. The eggs hatch in the autumn and larvae bore into the shoots to begin feeding. The larvae complete their development in May. They then vacate their hosts and enter the soil to pupate, new adults appearing about a month later. In late winter or early spring, the central shoots of invaded winter cereal plants turn yellow and die, and are often thought to have been attacked by frit fly or wheat bulb fly. Wheat flea beetle larvae (up to 5 mm long), however, are readily distinguished from dipterous pests by the presence of three pairs of thoracic legs, a distinct head and an anal plate. Careful examination of a damaged plant will also reveal a tiny rounded hole in the side of the stem base, through which the larva initially gained access.

Moths

Larvae of several noctuid moths feed within the stems of cereals and grasses, those of the common rustic moth being amongst the most frequently encountered. Common rustic moth (Fig. 35) occurs throughout Britain and Ireland, and is on the wing from June or July to August or September. Eggs are then deposited in rows on the leaf sheaths of various grasses and hatch about a fortnight later. In the following spring, larvae feed in the stems of grasses and cereal plants, especially wheat, an invaded shoot having a distinct ragged hole in the side, close to the base. Damage also results in the death of the central shoot – again, the familiar deadheart symptom. If an infested shoot is split

FIG 35. Common rustic moth (*Mesapamea secalis*) is a minor pest of cereals.

FIG 36. Common rustic moth larvae feed in the stems of cereals and grasses.

open, a green (in the final instar, also purplish-striped) larva may be found feeding within (Fig. 36).[28] Each larva attacks several tillers during the course of its development, the hollowed-out shoots typically containing tell-tale particles of dark-green frass. Pupation occurs in silken cocoons formed within the soil, there being just one generation annually. Insufficient information is available to assess the pest status (if any) of the lesser common rustic moth

(*Mesapamea didyma*) and Remm's rustic moth (*M. remmi*); until the mid-1980s both were considered merely forms of *M. secalis* but they are now regarded as distinct species.[29]

FIG 37. Rosy rustic moth (*Hydraecia micacea*) larvae sometimes burrow within the shoots of cereal plants. They are also associated with various other crops, including hop, potato, rhubarb and strawberry.

In parts of mainland Europe the moth *Oria musculosa* (in Britain known as the Brighton wainscot moth) is also a pest of cereals.[30] This species overwinters in the egg stage, the eggs hatching in the spring. Young larvae then feed singly within the shoots of host plants. Older larvae later attack the developing ears, which are often devoured completely. This rare and very local British insect became established in parts of central England during the 1900s in association with wheat and oat crops, especially in and around the county of Wiltshire. Barley, rye and wild grasses are also hosts. Although it became locally very numerous in the mid- to late 1940s,[31] the insect has never reached pest status in Britain. Indeed, it may now be extinct or at best on the edge of extinction in Britain,[32] and is currently named in the UK Biodiversity Action Plan as a species that warrants conservation. Various reasons for its demise in Britain have been proposed, including crop rotation, stubble burning (a practice that ceased in 1993), spraying crops with insecticides and the use of combine harvesters.

Several other shoot-infesting noctuids occur on cereal crops in Britain and Ireland. However, their association with cereals is primarily that of incidental ley pests, the larvae usually spreading to crops sown in ploughed-up infested grassland. Examples include: flounced rustic moth (*Luperina testacea*), marbled minor moth (*Oligia strigilis*), rosy minor moth (*Mesoligia literosa*) and rustic shoulder-knot moth (*Apamea sordens*). Occasionally, larvae of the rosy rustic moth (*Hydraecia micacea*) (Fig. 37) also feed in the stems of cereals, but (as described in later chapters) these are more often associated with crops such as hop, potato, rhubarb and strawberry.

FIG 38. Wheat stem sawfly (*Cephus pygmeus*) is often mistaken for a wasp.

FIG 39. Wheat stem sawfly (*Cephus pygmeus*) larvae bore within the stems of wheat plants.

Sawflies

Wheat stem sawfly (*Cephus pygmeus*) is a minor pest of winter wheat and, more rarely, barley, oats, rye and spring wheat. The mainly black, yellow-striped and narrow-bodied adults (Fig. 38) are active in sunny weather from late May to early July, and are most often seen around the edges of cereal crops, where they often settle on the flowerheads of wild Apiaceae. They are also attracted to various other plants, including late-flowering oilseed rape, and are then sometimes mistaken for ichneumonid wasps. Eggs are laid singly in wheat stems, each inserted in a small slit close to the uppermost node. Following egg hatch the larva (Fig. 39) bores downwards within the pith, taking about a month to reach the base. After biting around the wall to form a point of weakness the larva spins a silken cocoon in which it overwinters and eventually pupates. Attacked plants are dwarfed and weakened, and strong winds and heavy rain often cause them to break off a few centimetres above ground level.

Stubble burning is known to kill fully fed wheat stem sawfly larvae sheltering in wheat stems, and in the past post-harvest burning of cereal stubbles might well have helped keep the pest in check. To the relief of many country dwellers this widely polluting and sunshine-quenching activity was banned in the early 1990s. However, its cessation has not resulted in a resurgence of the pest in these islands. Perhaps this is because parasitoids (the most important being the braconid wasp *Bracon terebella* and the ichneumonid wasp *Collyria coxator*),[33] were also placed at risk by stubble burning and are now better placed to exert a controlling influence on the pest. In North America, where a different species of wheat stem sawfly, *Cephus cinctus*, is a particularly important pest, sheep grazing of fallows is a major cause of mortality of the overwintering larvae.[34]

Sucking pests

Aphids

Aphids are notorious pests of cereals, infestations affecting grain quality and overall crop yields. Damage results not only from direct feeding but also following the contamination of plants by honeydew upon which sooty moulds develop. Cereal aphids are also important virus vectors (see below).

Grain aphid (*Sitobion avenae*) (Fig. 40) is a particularly important pest[35] and one of the most frequently encountered cereal-infesting species, especially on wheat. The whole lifecycle is spent on cereals and grasses, the pest overwintering in the egg stage. Grain aphid also survives the winter as wingless females, although it rarely does so in cereal fields.[36] Colonies develop from spring onwards, populations on cereals being enhanced in late May or early June by the arrival of winged migrants raised on wild grasses. During the summer (particularly in hot, dry conditions) aphid numbers on cereal crops can increase rapidly, colonies eventually spreading to the emerging ear. A temperature of 20°C is considered the optimum for reproduction and development.[37] Although currently at a low ebb, the pest has in the past sometimes reached epidemic

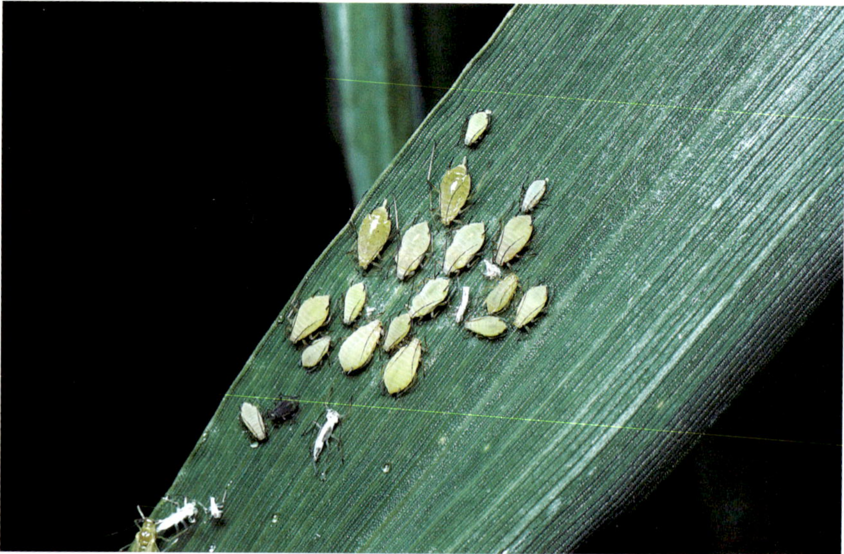

FIG 40. Grain aphid (*Sitobion avenae*) is an important cereal pest, and of particular significance when infestations arise on the developing ears.

proportions (as in the still memorable 1976 summer), notably in the southern counties of England.[38] Populations usually reach their peak in July or August. They then decline as plants mature and become unsuitable hosts. There can then be a small autumn migration to early-sown winter cereals and grasses. Colonies of grain aphid are very obvious, particularly when on the developing ears, and usually include individuals of different colour morphs (green, reddish brown or yellowish green), all with long, uniformly black siphunculi.[39]

In common with grain aphid, cereal leaf aphid (*Rhopalosiphum maidis*)[40] and fescue aphid (*Metopolophium festucae*)[41] – both relatively minor cereal pests – are similarly restricted to cereals and grasses throughout their entire lifecycle. Some species of cereal aphid, however, show an alternation between secondary (summer, herbaceous) hosts, where breeding is entirely parthenogenetic, and primary (winter, woody) hosts upon which, following a sexual phase, winter eggs are laid. Bird-cherry/oat aphid (*R. padi*), blackberry/cereal aphid (*Sitobion fragariae*) and rose/grain aphid (*M. dirhodum*) are examples.

In the northern half of Britain bird-cherry/oat aphids usually overwinter in the egg stage on bird-cherry trees, fulfilling the requirement for a sexual phase in the lifecycle. However, in more southerly regions (and also further north in favourable years) populations survive the winter as live aphids on early-sown winter cereals and grasses, thereby omitting a sexual phase. Colonies are then to be found just below the soil surface on the shoots of cereal plants. Geographically, the latter lifestyle has increased greatly in recent years, probably as a consequence of milder winters and the predominance on farms of autumn-sown as opposed to spring-sown cereals. In summer, bird-cherry/oat aphids infest the lower leaves of cereal plants, particularly barley and oats. They can also be abundant between the husk leaves surrounding the cobs of maize and sweet corn (Fig. 41). Blackberry/cereal aphid is merely a minor pest of cereals and, during the summer, small colonies sometimes develop on the ears; it overwinters in the egg stage on wild bramble bushes. Rose/grain aphid, however, occurs mainly on the lower leaves and does not spread onto the ears. Even so, when numerous, the aphids are still capable of causing appreciable yield losses, as occurred on winter wheat crops in the outbreak year of 1979.[42]

Aphids also occur on the roots of cereal plants. Apple/grass aphid (*R. insertum*), dogwood/grass aphid (*Anoecia corni*) and elm/grass-root aphid (*Tetraneura ulmi*) are examples, all of which adopt cereals and grasses as their summer (secondary) hosts.

Cereal aphids are often of significance as vectors of barley yellow dwarf virus (BYDV), the most important virus disease of cereals worldwide. There are several viral strains (isolates),[43] three of which are of significance in Britain:

FIG 41. Bird-cherry/oat aphid (*Rhopalosiphum padi*) is an important cereal pest, both as a direct feeder and as a vector of barley yellow dwarf virus. In summer, dense colonies sometimes develop on the leaves of maize and sweet corn plants.

- **RPV** – transmitted by bird-cherry/oat aphids;
- **MAV** – transmitted by grain aphids;
- **PAV** – transmitted most efficiently by bird-cherry/oat aphids but also by grain aphids, apple/grass aphid and various other species.

Of these, BYDV-RPV is most virulent and of greatest economic importance.[44] Aphids introduce and spread BYDV in various ways. Typically, in autumn, winged aphids (having first acquired the virus from grasses or volunteer cereals on which they were reared) invade and pass the infection to early-sown winter cereal crops. Their wingless offspring are then responsible for limited in-field spread of the virus. In the southern half of Britain, bird-cherry/oat aphid is the main agent of autumn transmission. However, in the north (where bird-cherry/oat aphid overwinters in the egg stage on bird-cherry trees) grain aphid becomes the primary vector. There are also other geographical differences. In west Wales, for example, BYDV is spread mainly by bird-cherry/oat aphids and apple/grass aphids.[45] As a second autumn pathway, if cereals are sown immediately after grass that has not been totally destroyed (by herbicides or during cultivation) aphids can readily transfer BYDV to the emerging new crop. This is often described as a green-bridge infection. Either way, cereal crops are at particular risk following wet summers that encourage growth of grasses, and warm autumns and winters that favour survival of live aphid vectors. Finally, as a third pathway, in late spring winged aphids arriving on summer hosts can transfer BYDV to spring-sown cereal crops.

Cereal aphids are often attacked by hymenopterous parasitoids. The aphelinid wasps *Aphidius rhopalosiphi* and *A. uzbekistanicus* are common examples. Both species are solitary endoparasitoids, depositing eggs singly in their hosts.

Following egg hatch, the wasp larva begins to feed on its host, the body of which becomes bloated, mummified (parchment-like) and typically beige in colour. Parasitised individuals are then readily visible amongst their unaffected brethren. The fully fed parasitoid larva finally pupates inside the remains of its host, and the young wasp eventually emerges through a small rounded exit hole. *A. rhopalosiphi* can lay a large number of eggs,[46] but its long-term impact is somewhat blunted as it is often itself attacked by hyperparasitoids.[47] Both parasitoid species are active throughout the spring, summer and autumn months. Overwintering cereal aphids (whether on cereal crops or grasses), however, are parasitised mainly by *A. uzbekistanicus*.[48]

Various predators are of significance as natural enemies of cereal aphids. These include aphidophagous specialists (e.g. hover fly larvae, lacewing larvae and ladybird adults and larvae) as well as generalists such as earwigs, ground beetles, rove beetles, soldier beetles and spiders.[49] Cereal aphids also fall victim to entomopathogenic fungi. Within integrated farming systems, flowering strips of lace phacelia are sometimes established on field margins in order to attract hover flies and other aphid-specific predators. Phacelia flowers are also visited by many other nectar- or pollen-seeking insects, including *Aphidius* spp. and many other hymenopterous parasitoids. However, such strips (although usefully providing sustenance) do not necessarily enhance predator or parasitoid activity on adjacent cereal crops.[50]

Of the many non-specialist predators that attack crop pests, ground beetles are particularly championed.[51] Commonplace examples in British agroecosystems include *Anchomenus dorsalis*,[52] *Bembidion lampros*, *Demetrias atricapillus*, *Harpalus affinis*, *H. rufipes*, *Poecilus cupreus*, *Pterostichus melanarius* and *Trechus quadristriatus*, of which *A. dorsalis* and *D. atricapillus* are generally considered the most important predators of cereal aphids (Fig. 42). To maximise

FIG 42. The ground beetle *Demetrias atricapillus* is one of the most important predators of cereal aphids.

the impact on aphid infestations, winter survival of ground beetles (allowing them to re-establish in spring) is critical. Some species successfully overwinter within crops: *T. quadristriatus*, for example, does so in the larval stage. Others, however, move to suitable shelter nearby, many then hibernating in field boundaries (as in the case of *A. dorsalis* and *D. atricapillus*)[53] or (if available) in artificially created 'beetle banks'.[54] Nearby wild flower areas, especially older ones, are also useful hibernation sites, not only for ground beetles but also for rove beetles.[55] Ground beetles usually crawl rather than fly, and some species (e.g. *Trechus quadristriatus*) have both fully winged and partially winged forms. *Amara plebeja*, which breeds in summer in open arable fields, develops temporary functional flight muscles in autumn and again in spring, allowing migration by flight to and from overwintering sites in distant woodlands and forests.[56]

Thrips

Many householders, especially those living in the vicinity of cereal crops, regularly experience summer plagues of dark brown or black-bodied cereal thrips (commonly known as thunderflies). These tiny creatures are notorious for causing considerable irritation when present on human skin. Their attacks are especially severe in hot, sultry weather, when clouds of the creatures emerge from ripening cereal fields, often in advance of thunderstorms. Walkers and picnickers in the countryside are especially vulnerable and often victimised. However, people in towns and cities are far from immune. Once airborne, the winged thrips (carried aloft in air currents) can travel considerable distances. The insects have an innate ability to squeeze into seemingly impenetrable gaps, and their corpses often accumulate *en masse* in glass-fronted framed pictures, and around fridge and freezer seals and many other household objects. Thrips can also force their way into and set off burglar alarms and fire alarms. The generally abundant grain thrips (*Limothrips cerealium*) is most frequently responsible but other species, including barley thrips (*L. denticornis*), are also involved. On cereal crops, grain thrips is probably the most studied species.[57] The mated females overwinter in wooded areas and emerge in the spring. They then invade cereal fields to lay eggs in the young plants. Following egg hatch, the pale yellowish-orange nymphs live and feed between the leaf sheaths, causing usually inconspicuous silvering of the tissue. There are from one to two generations annually. Later in the season, nymphs move into the ears. Although capable of damaging the developing grain,[58] attacks are usually of little significance unless the pests are present in large numbers. Unlike females, the adult males are wingless and cannot fly. They die shortly after mating.

Blossom midges

Midges are frequent inhabitants of cereal fields. Some species are cereal pests and a few (such as *Aphidius rhopalosiphi* and *Aphidoletes aphidimyza*, already cited as predators of aphids) are beneficial. Yet others may be associated with non-cereal host plants, including grasses and other weeds. Arable land is also inhabited by large numbers of mycetophagous (fungivorous) midges.[59]

Orange wheat blossom midge (*Sitodiplosis mosellana*) is an important cereal pest in many wheat-growing areas, and damage was particularly widespread in England in 1993. Since then, the pest has maintained a high profile (possibly as a result of climate change which appears to be encouraging the pest) and populations have frequently exceeded treatment thresholds. The adoption of minimal tillage post-harvest (nowadays often preferred in arable cropping systems to more traditional deep ploughing) may also be a contributory factor, as this practice is thought to be less damaging to midge survival. The adult midges are active at dusk in early summer, particularly in warm, calm conditions, and then often occur in noticeable swarms. Infestations in wheat crops tend to be most severe on headlands, the adults typically having migrated downwind from their emergence sites.[60] Eggs are laid in the freshly emerging ears of wheat plants and hatch about a week later. The orange-coloured larvae feed in the flowers (florets), either singly or in small groups (Fig. 43), and have a detrimental effect on grain quality.[61] Fully fed individuals drop to the ground and enter the soil where they form small silken cocoons in which to overwinter. In the following year, but sometimes up to ten or more years later, the larvae emerge from their cocoons and move closer to the soil surface. They then pupate and adult midges emerge shortly afterwards. Warm, damp weather during May encourages larval emergence and pupation, and such conditions are

FIG 43. Orange wheat blossom midge (*Sitodiplosis mosellana*) larvae feed in the flowers (florets), either singly or in small groups.

indicative of potential outbreaks of the pest.[62] Predation of adult midges by dance flies (especially *Platypalpus* spp.) is commonplace, and predators such as soldier beetles (e.g. *Cantharis* spp.) attack the larvae. In addition, the pteromalid wasp *Macroglenes penetrans*[63] is a widely known and important endoparasitoid, both in Europe and Canada.[64] The parasitoid deposits eggs singly in those of the midge, but the parasitoid eggs do not hatch until the host larva is fully grown and has overwintered. Wheat blossom midge larvae are also parasitised by the platygastrid wasp *Leptacis tipulae*.[65]

The lemon-yellow larvae of the yellow wheat blossom midge (*Contarinia tritici*) occur gregariously in the ears of wheat plants, where they attack the developing florets, inhibiting fertilisation and thereby preventing grain formation. Attacks are most likely to occur where wheat is grown continuously. However, significant outbreaks such as those experienced in Ireland in 1951[66] and in Yorkshire in the late 1970s[67] are rare.

British wheat fields are occasionally inhabited by hessian fly (*Mayetiola destructor*) – actually a midge – a potentially devastating and virtually worldwide pest of particular importance in North America. First-generation adults occur in early spring and deposit eggs on the leaves of host plants (usually wheat but sometimes also barley, rye and wild grasses such as common couch). Following egg hatch the larvae move downwards, squeezing between the leaf and leaf sheath. They then attack the stem and feed on the exuding sap. When larvae are fully fed, their skins harden and darken into brown, seed-like structures (puparia) within which pupation eventually takes place (Fig. 44) – owing to its appearance, the puparium is widely known as the flax-seed stage. Groups of these puparia occur at the base of infested plants or just above a node, between the base of a leaf and the stem. Damaged plants, with their stems weakened by the pest larvae, often lodge. Oat stem midge (*M. avenae*) causes similar damage on oats.

FIG 44. Hessian fly (*Mayetiola destructor*) puparia represent the so-called flax-seed stage in the lifecycle.

Hessian fly, which has two or more generations annually, was believed to have been introduced into America in straw carried by Hessian troops who landed in Long Island in August 1776 during the American Revolution. It was George Morgan, a gentleman farmer and former army colonel, who (with a friend) subsequently coined the name 'hessian fly'. As later penned by Morgan in 1788:

> *It is now become the most opprobrious Term our Language affords & the greatest affront our Chimney Sweepers & even our Slaves can give or receive, is to call or be called Hessian.*[68]

This clearly shows the contempt in which the pest was then held. Hessian fly was not found in England until 1886. Fortunately, damage to our cereal crops has never reached the devastating proportions reported from America.

Minor outbreaks of saddle gall midge (*Haplodiplosis marginata*) are sometimes reported on cereal crops growing in the heavy-land districts in England. This insect has also long been known to occur in Wales, from whence the first British records came.[69] The red-bodied adults emerge in May. Eggs are then laid on the uppermost leaves of host plants in reddish, raft-like groups. Following egg hatch the larvae invade the stems to begin feeding. Saddle-like galls soon develop in a line along the stem, each containing a single larva. When fully grown the larvae vacate their galls and enter the soil where they eventually overwinter. Pupation occurs shortly before the appearance of the adults. Spring crops are more vulnerable than autumn-sown ones, and earlier-sown crops are at greatest risk; also, wheat is preferred to barley for egg-laying.[70]

Leaf grazers

Beetles

Cereal leaf beetle (*Oulema melanopa*) is a colourful, metallic insect – black head, reddish-brown thorax and dark bluish-green elytra – and is often a common component of the cereal insect fauna. The adults emerge from hibernation in April. They then feed on the leaves of wild grasses before moving onto cereal plants. The beetles graze away longitudinal strips of leaf tissue from the upper surface, the damaged areas appearing pale brown or as dirty-white stripes between the veins. Adults of the similarly coloured – but stouter and more rounded – polygonum leaf beetle (*Gastrophysa polygoni*) are also often found on cereal plants, especially on or close to weedy headlands and field margins. However, they do not cause damage as they are merely casual visitors, being associated with knotgrass and other Polygonaceae. Eggs of cereal leaf beetle are laid on the uppermost leaves of host plants and hatch about 12 days later.[71] The period of egg-laying, however, is

FIG 45. Cereal leaf beetle (*Oulema melanopa*) infestations are particularly harmful when flag leaves are attacked. Note the excrement-coated larva settled at the base of the leaf.

very protracted and, during the summer months, all stages of the pest often occur together. Cereal leaf beetle larvae, which feed on the upper surface of the expanded leaves and cause damage similar to that caused by the adults, cover themselves in blackish, slimy excrement (Fig. 45) and are often mistaken for tiny slugs. After about a month the larvae drop to the ground and pupate in the soil, a few centimetres below the surface. New adults appear a couple of weeks later. These beetles feed on the leaves of wild grasses before entering hibernation, usually in October or November. Infestations of cereal leaf beetle are favoured by hot, dry conditions but damage, although often spectacular, is not of significance unless loss of photosynthetic tissue (especially on the flag leaves during grain filling) is very extensive. *O. obscura*[72] – a metallic-blue species – also occurs in the UK but is far less often reported. In mainland Europe, however, it is often an abundant and significant cereal pest, especially on wheat[73] (Fig. 46). Both species are vectors of cocksfoot mild mosaic virus (CMMV)[74] and cocksfoot mottle virus (CoMV).[75]

Leaf-striping on cereals is also indicative of attacks by adult flea beetles, especially barley flea beetle (*Phyllotreta vittula*) – a black insect with a broad, yellow, longitudinal stripe down each elytron – and the mainly reddish-brown adults of wheat flea beetle. Both are to be seen on the foliage during daytime. Compared with damage caused by cereal leaf beetles, however, grazing by flea beetles is far less extensive.

FIG 46. *Oulema obscura* is less common than *O. melanopa*, but also a known virus vector.

Moths

Wheat and maize plants are sometimes attacked by larvae of the tortricoid moth *Cnephasia longana*. This relatively polyphagous pest is of particular significance in southern England, especially in chalkland and coastal districts. Adults occur in July (Fig. 47). Eggs are then laid singly on tree trunks and inanimate objects such as wooden posts and telegraph poles, often several metres above ground level. The eggs hatch within two to three weeks. The young larvae

FIG 47. The tortricoid moth *Cnephasia longana* is a minor pest of cereals.

then spin silken hibernacula in which to overwinter. In spring, the minute larvae become active and seek suitable host plants, producing strands of silk to aid their dispersal in wind currents. Wild Asteraceae and various other herbaceous plants are frequently attacked. On cereals, the larvae (called omnivorous leaf tiers) feed within folded-over leaves. They eventually invade the flag leaves and developing ears (Fig. 48), to feed amongst silken webbing within which pellets of frass soon accumulate.[76] Larvae are fully grown in June. They then pupate on host plants, each in a silken cocoon, and adults emerge shortly afterwards. In mainland Europe, especially in northern France and Germany, the

FIG 48. Larvae of *Cnephasia longana* sometimes graze on the developing ears of cereal plants.

FIG 49. Foliage-feeding sawfly larvae, such as *Dolerus* spp., are often found on cereal plants. They are a welcome food source for partridges and other game birds.

related cereal tortrix moth (*C. pumicana*), whose larvae are widely known as cereal leaf rollers, causes significant damage to the ears of wheat and barley plants. This pest appears to be extending its range in Europe but has not yet been confirmed as present in Britain.

Sawflies

Leaf-grazing sawfly larvae (Fig. 49) often feed fully exposed on the leaves of cereal plants and grasses, especially in early summer. Several species are involved, including *Dolerus haematodes* and *Pachynematus clitellatus*.[77] The larvae graze away irregular patches of tissue, commencing at the tip or at the leaf margins, but damage is usually of little or no significance. Within cereal and grassland ecosystems, leaf-feeding sawfly larvae are of greater importance as a food source for game birds, especially grey partridge chicks.[78] To the detriment of game birds, however, sawfly larvae are frequently killed by pesticides applied against other more important cereal pests.[79] If unscathed, the fully fed larvae pupate in the soil. They then overwinter, there being just one generation annually.

Vertebrates

Various birds and mammals qualify as pests of cereal crops, either grazing upon or trampling crops and sometimes (as in the case of jackdaws, rooks and starlings) stealing recently sown seeds or uprooting young plants in their search for soil-inhabiting insects such as leatherjackets and wireworms.[80] In particular, in coastal areas, geese sometimes graze on overwintering crops.[81] Damage is also caused by moorhens and swans. Rabbit grazing around the edges of fields has become legendary,[82] and in many areas deer, including red deer, have become a perennial problem not only on cereals but also on other arable crops.

Leaf miners

The activities of leaf-mining insects are sometimes in evidence on cereal crops. This is especially so during the summer months when pale, broadly linear or blotch-like mines are formed on the leaves (Fig. 50). Most cereal leaf miners are larvae of agromyzid flies, with *Agromyza nigrella*, *A. nigrociliata*, *A. rondensis*, *Phytomyza nigra* and *Pseudonapomyza atra* the most frequently encountered species.[83] Considering that the fully grown larvae are no more than a few millimetres long, the mines are often surprisingly large, some up to 9 cm or more in length. Leaf-mining species are either solitary feeders (e.g. *A. nigrella* and *A. rondensis*) or gregarious (e.g. *A. nigrociliata*) (Fig. 51). If an affected leaf is held up to the light, a tiny larva or larvae may be seen feeding within the mine. An empty mine usually indicates that larval development has been completed and that the former inhabitant or inhabitants have dropped to the ground to pupate. Careful examination of the surface of the mine may then disclose a minute slit through which the larva or larvae escaped. Although agromyzid larvae usually pupate in the soil, those of *Cerodontha incisa* (a widely distributed and gregarious species) do so *in situ*,

FIG 50. Blotch mines formed by *Agromyza nigrociliata* and certain other leaf miners are often common on winter wheat plants.

FIG 51. Unlike many cereal leaf miners, *Agromyza nigrociliata* larvae feed gregariously.

the metallic-black, barrel-shaped puparia being stuck to the inner surface of the mine by fine threads of silk. This species often attacks maize or sweet corn, but breeds mainly on wild grasses and reeds. Damage caused to cereal crops by cereal leaf miners is usually slight. However, heavy infestations have been reported, as in the mid-1960s in southeast England.[84] Mines formed on flag leaves are of particular significance.

Leaf-mining larvae of shore flies, notably *Hydrellia griseola*, also occur on cereals. *H. griseola* has two generations annually, larvae of the first developing during the summer months and those of the second feeding throughout the autumn and winter. Infested leaves turn yellow. Unlike agromyzids, the larvae of shore flies lack anterior spiracles; they are also larger, attaining a length of about 6 mm.

Mites

Cereal crops growing in Britain and Ireland are rarely attacked by mites, although several species, e.g. the cheese mite (*Tyrolichus casei*),[85] the cosmopolitan flour mite (*Lepidoglyphus destructor*)[86] and the flour mite (*Acarus siro*) infest stored grain.[87]

Cereal crops are sometimes inhabited by the grass & cereal mite (*Siteroptes avenae*), a minor pest with a most unusual lifestyle. The microscopic adult females (individuals less than 0.2 mm long) occur on both cereals and grasses, populations developing in the shelter of the leaf sheaths. The mites not only feed on the leaf tissue but also on hyphae of the fungus *Fusarium poae*, with which they are said to form a symbiotic relationship.[88] *S. avenae* is considered part of a complex of species (called the *S. cerealium* complex). This includes

S. graminum (now considered a synonym of *S. cerealium*), the name under which grass & cereal mite has been most frequently cited in the literature. However, owing to confusion between *S. avenae* and *S. cerealium*, published accounts of the biology of the mites vary. Laboratory studies indicate that there are distinct differences between the two species. In the case of *S. avenae* there are no free-living juvenile stages in the lifecycle; eggs develop directly into adults. Also, the eggs are retained throughout their development within the body (hysterosoma) of the maternal mite, which gradually swells to become a glistening balloon-like structure up to 3 mm or more in diameter. This phenomenon (which is also a feature of *S. cerealium*) is known as physogastry. It is at this stage that the pregnant mites are most likely to be seen in the field, typically in association with whitening of the inflorescences of infested host plants (a condition often described as 'silver top'). Eventually, the bloated hysterosoma bursts and releases its quota of new adult males and females. There are no nymphal stages. Occasionally, eggs are laid by *S. avenae* but these contain fully formed encapsulated adults which emerge within minutes of oviposition. The mite *S. cerealium* differs in having three pre-adult stages: egg, 'larva' and pupa. On bursting, eggs having hatched within, the swollen hysterosoma releases a hundred or more motile 'larvae'. These eventually become sedentary pupae, from which new adults soon emerge. In the case of grass & cereal mites, there are several generations annually, populations reaching their peak in the late summer or autumn.[89] In hot, dry autumns, grass & cereal mites are sometimes also found on greenhouse-grown carnations (presumably having drifted in through open doors or ventilators). Here, along with *Fusarium poae*, they attack the flower buds, leading to a condition described as bud rot or central bud rot.[90] Adult females of *S. avenae* have an eversible, sac-like structure (the sporotheca) which may be used to transport spores of *F. poae*. However, no such structure has been found in *S. cerealium*, supporting suggestions that *S. avenae* is the mite associated with carnation bud rot.

Few other mites are likely to be seen on cereal crops, although symptoms of the damage they cause can become evident in some years. In the presence of the oat spiral mite (*Steneotarsonemus spirifex*), for example, the flowerheads of late-maturing oat plants sometimes fail to emerge properly. Instead, they become distorted and spirally twisted (Fig. 52). Affected plants also appear noticeably reddened and stunted, and the leaf margins tightly rolled. This microscopic pest also breeds on grasses and, occasionally, on wheat. Finally, in hot summers, maize plants are sometimes infested by two-spotted spider mites (*Tetranychus urticae*). The mites feed on the underside of the leaves and if populations are particularly large invaded tissue becomes coated in silk webbing.

FIG 52. Oat spiral mite (*Steneotarsonemus spirifex*) damage occurs mainly on oats, although the pest also attacks wheat and various grasses.

Nematodes

Cereals are attacked by various plant-parasitic nematodes, especially if grown in light-textured soils. Infestations often result in the appearance of patches of yellowish, stunted plants, symptoms similar to those caused by acidity, virus infection and waterlogging. Cereal cyst nematode (CCN) (*Heterodera avenae*), for example, was a formerly important and widespread cereal pest, especially on oats. CCN became especially significant from the early 1940s to the mid-1950s.[91] Nowadays, however, populations have dwindled following a decline in the importance of oat crops and the introduction of resistant crop cultivars; reductions in CCN populations are also a feature of continuous cereal growing,[92] due at least in part to the activities of soil-inhabiting fungal parasites that kill female nematodes and eggs.[93] The widespread replacement of oats by spring barley in the second half of the twentieth century has further helped to reduce the overall impact of CCN. Where this pest is established, plant roots are invaded in autumn or spring by minute, second-stage juveniles. Males swell slightly whilst developing as juveniles. However, when moulting to adulthood they emerge as narrow, eel-like worms and eventually escape back into the soil. Individuals destined to develop into adult females swell considerably throughout their development. They finally burst through the root surface to become visible as white, lemon-shaped cysts, each about a millimetre long. Mating eventually takes place. Following the death of the fertilised female, the body wall darkens and becomes a tough, protective capsule containing hundreds of eggs. These cysts eventually drop into the soil, where they remain viable for several years. Agriculturally, cyst nematodes in Britain are of greatest significance on potato and sugar beet crops (see Chapter 5).

Cereal root-knot nematode (*Meloidogyne naasi*), named after the acronym for the Government's former National Agricultural Advisory Service (NAAS),[94] is another cereal-infesting species, attacking both wheat and barley. Patches of poor growth become evident in affected crops from late spring onwards, with distinctive elongate galls developing on the roots. This nematode also invades a range of non-cereal plants, including Italian ryegrass and perennial ryegrass.

Several other nematodes are associated with cereals. The oat race of stem nematode (*Ditylenchus dipsaci*), for example, attacks both oats and rye. Affected plants are stunted and typically have a bulb-like swelling at the base of the shoots. This condition is commonly described as 'tulip root' or in the north of England 'segging'. Various soil-inhabiting migratory nematodes (e.g. *Longidorus* spp., *Pratylenchus* spp. and *Trichodorus* spp.) also damage the roots of cereals.

CHAPTER 3

Grasslands

THE AREA OF AGRICULTURAL land in the UK amounts to some 17.3 million hectares, of which over 11 million hectares is grassland. Grassland over five years old (representing most of the total) is regarded as permanent, and includes meadows, pastures and rough grazing. Meadows are essentially grass swards within which wild flowers and other herbaceous plants flourish (Fig. 53) – the fields being cut periodically for hay.

FIG 53. A traditional hay meadow.

Meadows are home to an eclectic mix of insects and other invertebrates, which often form balanced communities. Many inhabitants are phytophagous but these cannot necessarily be singled out as pests. On the contrary, their presence is likely to be fundamental to the stability and well-being of the environment. Also, many species (attractive butterflies, moths, grasshoppers and other familiar insects, for example) are particularly welcomed by naturalists and other country folk as creatures that greatly enrich our lives. Pastures are similarly long-term grassland habitats but unlike meadows (*sensu stricto*) they are grazed by animals. Pastures range from idyllic, meadow-like fields in peaceful river valleys to upland grasslands that more properly qualify as rough grazing and may finally grade into moorland. These too can support a rich flora and fauna.

Temporary or rotational grasslands (often termed arable grass leys) are of short duration. These grass leys are regularly cut for forage (hay or silage), and eventually ploughed up prior to replanting with a new crop such as potatoes or cereals. By way of example, a six-year arable/grass rotation often includes a two-year grass break. Nowadays, three-quarters of our short-term grass leys are sown along with white clover to improve the nutritional value of the crop. This widens the potential pest spectrum in such fields. However, pest damage within them often goes unnoticed, and recognising where yield losses in such crops have occurred is difficult. Grass leys frequently harbour pests which, after the grass has been ploughed, transfer their attentions to the next crop in the rotation. These ley pests (as already mentioned in Chapter 2) include a wide range of soil inhabitants (e.g. chafer grubs, leatherjackets and wireworms, all of which are indiscriminate feeders) and also various shoot-boring larvae (especially those of grass & cereal flies and certain other dipterans). Following ploughing, larvae of grass & cereal flies can survive burial with the old grass, and are well capable of migrating vertically upwards through the soil to attack a following cereal crop.

Although, as indicated above, it is often difficult if not impossible to quantify damage caused by any particular insect or other antagonist, there are notable exceptions. This is particularly so in the case of grass seed crops and when crops are at the establishment phase. In the latter case, for example, field slugs (*Deroceras reticulatum*) (Fig. 54) are sometimes singled out as responsible for losses.[1] In general, foliage-feeding pests (often of significance on arable and horticultural crops) cause little or no economic damage to established grasses – grass was born to be cut or grazed! Nevertheless, there are occasions when grazing pests can be of significance if the root systems or growing points of plants are targeted.

FIG 54. Field slugs (*Deroceras reticulatum*) are common pests of grasses and many other crops.

FOLIAGE GRAZING AND ROOT-FEEDING PESTS

Beetles

Many beetles are regarded as grassland pests. These include species with root-feeding larvae and also those that, as adults and/or larvae, attack the aerial parts of plants. In hilly or mountainous districts, upland click beetles (*Ctenicera* spp.), especially *C. cupreus* (Fig. 55), frequently cause damage. The robust-bodied adults occur in May and June, depositing eggs mainly in the latter month. The eggs hatch about 34 days later.[2] The tough-skinned, subterranean larvae (known as upland wireworms) (Fig. 56) then feed on the roots and underground parts of the stems of grasses and various other plants. Upland wireworms are capable of

FIG 55. Upland click beetle (*Ctenicera cupreus*).

FIG **56.** Upland wireworms (*Ctenicera* spp.) are generally abundant pests of acid grasslands in many parts of Britain and Ireland.

causing considerable damage, not only to grasses but also to succeeding arable crops such as cereals and potatoes. Development is slow and individuals usually do not pupate until they are in their fifth year. At lower altitudes, the place of upland click beetles is taken by species such as the garden click beetle (*Athous haemorrhoidalis*) and the three common, widely distributed species of *Agriotes*: *A. lineatus*, *A. obscurus* and *A. sputator*. These pests (their larvae known simply as wireworms) also take several years to complete their development. They often occur in abundance in long-term grassland or grassy sites, and are greatly advantaged by undisturbed habitats.[3] Arable or horticultural crops that follow grass are at considerable risk if planted or sown in wireworm-infested sites. Click beetles are so named because of their habit, when disturbed, of flicking themselves into the air with an audible click – the body being armed with a spring-like peg (the prosternal process) located ventrally on the thorax between the first and second pairs of legs.

In a typical lifecycle, as exemplified by *A. lineatus*, eggs are laid in the soil during May or June, either singly or in small batches, and they hatch four to six weeks later. The larvae (i.e. wireworms) then begin to feed on plant roots. Development is slow (larvae often fast after moulting from one instar to the next),[4] and usually extends over four or five years. Individuals pass through several (perhaps as many as eight) instars before pupating,[5] each in a subterranean cell formed 5–30 cm or more below the soil surface. The adult stage is reached about a month later. Adults then hibernate, usually still within the pupal cell, and emerge in the following year.

Grassland is also often infested by chafer grubs. Upland pastures, for example, can be ravaged by a range of species, including the cockchafer

FIG 57. Garden chafer (*Phyllopertha horticola*) larvae are common in light soils, especially in grassland areas.

(*Melolontha melolontha*), the garden chafer (*Phyllopertha horticola*), the summer chafer (*Amphimallon solstitiale*) and the Welsh chafer (*Hoplia philanthus*). Adult chafers are often seen during daylight hours, some species regularly foraging on the inflorescences of wild plants, especially the umbels of Apiaceae; cockchafers, however, remain comatose during daytime but become active at dusk. Chafer grubs (Fig. 57) cause extensive damage by attacking and destroying the grass roots. The quality of swards then deteriorates owing to the ingress of weeds. Populations of garden chafer grubs in excess of 280,000 per hectare have been recorded in fell-side swards in the Lake District.[6] Garden chafer grubs feed throughout the summer and are fully grown by the end of October. Pupation takes place in the following spring, and adults appear shortly afterwards.[7]

Flea beetles are common inhabitants of grasslands, although the damage they cause is of little significance. The most frequently encountered grass-feeding species include barley flea beetle (*Phyllotreta vittula*), *Chaetocnema aridula*, *C. hortensis* and wheat flea beetle (*Neocrepidodera ferruginea*).[8]

Cereal ground beetle (*Zabrus tenebrioides*) has already been mentioned as a pest of both cereals and grasses (Chapter 2). Other ground beetles are also known to cause damage in grassland, including *Amara plebeja*, *Harpalus aeneus* and *H. affinis*. Adults of *A. plebeja* (a rather small species, less than 7 mm long), for example, often ascend the stems of grasses such as annual meadow-grass, false oat, meadow fescue and meadow foxtail to graze on the flowerheads. In the greater scheme of things, however, ground beetles generally play a beneficial role as predators of pests.

Root-feeding weevil larvae frequently occur in grasslands and, if numerous, contribute to the overall decline of plants. Species such as the generally abundant common leaf weevil (*Phyllobius pyri*) attack recently established

FIG 58. Amenity grasslands, as here on the gallops at Newmarket, Suffolk, are not immune from damage by common leaf weevil (*Phyllobius pyri*) larvae.

FIG 59. Common leaf weevil larvae feed on the roots of grasses and various other plants.

pastures and leys, and are also a problem on long-term amenity swards, including horse-racing gallops (Fig. 58). In severe cases, as occurred in the Newmarket area in Suffolk in the 1990s, large areas of turf become loosened, turn brown and die. At two heavily infested grassland sites in East Yorkshire in 1960, common leaf weevil populations exceeded 8 and 12 million larvae per hectare.[9] The larvae (Fig. 59) feed from May to September and then pupate. Adults eventually appear in the following spring.

Attacks by clover weevils and pea weevils (*Sitona* spp.) often develop on clovers growing in grass swards. Three species are of particular significance: clover weevil (*S. lepidus*), common clover weevil (*S. hispidulus*) and pea & bean weevil (*S. lineatus*);[10] *S. humeralis* and *S. puncticollis* also occur. Various species of *Sitona* are important in clover leys and other leguminous fodder or forage crops such as common vetch, lucerne and yellow trefoil.[11] Adult *Sitona* weevils graze on the leaves, sometimes causing extensive notching of the margins; shoots are also damaged. Larvae attack the root system, feeding on the tap roots and the nitrogen-fixing root nodules. Forage legumes (either growing alone or in mixtures with grasses) are also attractive to a range of other weevils, including clover leaf weevils (*Hypera* spp.) and clover seed weevils (*Protapion* spp.[12]); examples of such pests include *H. nigrirostris, H. postica, P. apricans, P. dichroum* and *P. trifolii*. Adults graze on the leaves and cause extensive tattering, shot-holing and blanching of tissue. Larvae of *H. nigrirostris* and *H. postica* damage the young leaves and flowers, and can have a detrimental effect on seed production. They feed externally on the aerial parts of host plants and are essentially yellowish green (*H. nigrirostris*) or green (*H. postica*) in colour.

True flies

Crane flies, also known as daddy long-legs (*Nephrotoma* spp. and *Tipula* spp. – the former often known as tiger crane flies owing to their black and yellow-patterned bodies (Fig. 60)), are common inhabitants of grasslands. Two species (*Tipula oleracea* and *T. paludosa*) in particular are frequently recognised as pests. Both are widely distributed in these islands but *T. paludosa*, which is single brooded, is generally more numerous and of greater significance. Adults of *T. paludosa*

FIG **60.** Crane flies, including tiger crane flies (*Nephrotoma* spp.), are common inhabitants of grasslands.

FIG 61. The distinct head and fleshy outgrowths on the body immediately distinguish bibionid fly larvae from leatherjackets.

appear in considerable numbers during late August and September, often emerging *en masse*. *T. oleracea*, however, is essentially double brooded, with a main flight period in May/June and a second in August/September. In *T. paludosa*, mating occurs soon after the females have emerged. Eggs are then laid in the soil at the base of grass stems, and hatch about two weeks later. The tough-skinned larvae (leatherjackets) feed for several months on roots, and perhaps other tissue, and are usually fully fed by mid-June or so. In summer, prior to pupation, they undergo a period of aestivation which is considered a means of synchronizing the eventual time of adult emergence.[13] Females of *T. oleracea* usually disperse from their emergence sites prior to mating and egg-laying. As a result, subsequent larval infestations are more dispersed than those of *T. paludosa*. Arable and horticultural crops planted in ploughed-up infested grassland are liable to suffer considerable damage, making leatherjackets very important ley pests. Leatherjacket damage in grassland itself, however, is often insidious. Nevertheless, in both established and newly sown crops, infestations can result in the appearance of yellow patches, within which plants subsequently die. Further, in mixed swards, clover plants can be singled out for attack and damaged more severely than the grass.[14]

In common with leatherjackets, the soil-inhabiting, root-feeding larvae of bibionid flies are often found in grassland, especially in the close vicinity of hedges.[15] Although superficially of similar appearance to small leatherjackets, bibionid larvae have a distinct, shiny, dark brown or black head and fleshy outgrowths on the body (Fig. 61). These outgrowths, however, are absent at the pupal stage. Eggs are laid in tight batches, typically within earthen cells,[16] the egg-laying females being strongly attracted to dung heaps and other rotting organic matter. Following egg hatch, the larvae tend to remain aggregated, so

FIG 62. St Mark's fly (*Bibio marci*).

that large numbers are often found close together. Larvae of several species, but especially St Mark's fly (*Bibio marci*) and fever fly (*Dilophus febrilis*), are known to damage crops. St Mark's fly (Fig. 62), with a wingspan of up to 25 mm or so, is the largest British bibionid and single brooded. Eggs are laid mainly in May and hatch just over a month later. The larvae then feed gregariously on the roots of grasses and other plants. Larval development is relatively slow, individuals eventually becoming fully grown during the winter. Fever fly, unlike St Mark's fly, tends towards being double brooded, adults occurring mainly in May, with a smaller second emergence in August and September. St Mark's flies, in particular, are very familiar to country folk, and are so named following their tendency magically to appear in the spring on or about St Mark's Day (25 April). In sunny weather, the hairy, black-bodied adults often congregate over hedges and grassland, forming loose, slowly bobbing swarms, their long legs dangling characteristically downwards. Adult bibionids, including St Mark's flies and fever flies, are often also attracted to the open blossoms of fruit trees, where they play a useful role as supplementary pollinators.

Moths

Larvae of the antler moth (*Cerapteryx graminis*) (Fig. 63) occasionally cause extensive damage to grassland, particularly in upland pastures. The adults occur mainly from July to September, egg-laying females typically broadcasting their eggs at random whilst flying low over the ground. Most eggs hatch in the following spring. Larvae then feed at night on various grasses, favouring harder-textured types such as meadow fescue, mat-grass and purple moor-grass; they also attack rushes, including club-rushes. On occasions,

FIG 63. Antler moth (*Cerapteryx graminis*) larvae sometimes appear in vast numbers, and are then very damaging.

antler moth larval populations in upland areas escalate to plague proportions. Vast numbers of larvae then feed both at night and during the daytime, advancing in legions and devouring all before them. In such situations, farmers have resorted to digging ditches ahead of the larvae in an attempt to halt their advances.

Of the various other leaf-grazing larvae on grasses, those of the drinker moth (*Euthrix potatoria*)[17] sometimes attract attention on account of their attractive, hairy, somewhat velvety appearance and relatively large size (individuals up to 60 mm or so long when fully grown) (Fig. 64). Drinker moth larvae, which feed in the autumn and again (after hibernation) in the spring, have long been known to imbibe droplets of dew: hence the vernacular name which has been used in English entomological literature since the seventeenth century. The broad-winged adults (Fig. 65) are less often encountered.

FIG 64. Drinker moth (*Euthrix potatoria*) larvae often remain fully exposed on the leaves of grasses during the daytime.

FIG 65. Drinker moths (*Euthrix potatoria*) are far less often encountered than their larvae.

FIG 66. Timothy tortrix moth (*Aphelia paleana*) larvae sometimes damage seed heads of timothy grass; they also feed on various other plants.

The unmistakeable black-bodied and white-spotted larvae of timothy tortrix moth (*Aphelia paleana*) (Fig. 66) are sometimes reported as pests of timothy grass; they feed amongst spun leaves and also invade the seed heads.[18] Adults fly in July and August, and there is just one generation annually. The polyphagous larvae, which occur from September to May or June, attack a wide range of plants, including various grasses and clovers within grassland swards. Larvae of the single-brooded allied shade moth (*Cnephasia incertana*) may also be found feeding amongst the spun leaves of clovers and other forage legumes.

Grass moths, including *Agriphila straminella* (already cited in Chapter 2 as an occasional pest of cereals) and the generally abundant garden grass veneer moth (*Chrysoteuchia culmella*),[19] are common inhabitants of grasslands. Characteristically, when disturbed, grass moths fly a short distance before resettling head downwards on a grass stem or other temporary perch (Fig. 67). Adults of *A. straminella* occur

FIG 67. Garden grass veneer moth (*Chrysoteuchia culmella*) is a widespread and generally abundant species.

from June to August, and those of garden grass veneer moth from June to July. Larvae of grass moths attack the roots and basal parts of the stems of host plants. Those of *A. straminella* feed from September onwards, each constructing a silken, more or less U-shaped tube that extends into the soil from the base of the food plant. This serves as a shelter within which the larva hides and where particles of green frass soon accumulate. The larvae feed throughout the winter and eventually pupate in the spring. Garden grass veneer moth is a more important pest and especially abundant in acid grasslands. During an outbreak in the Yorkshire Dales in 1941, for example, the equivalent of over 1,300 larvae per square metre were present, resulting in severe damage to the turf.[20] Larvae of this species, which do not inhabit silken galleries (Fig. 68), are fully grown in October. They then form silken cocoons (Fig. 69), but do not pupate until the following spring. Other root-feeding moth larvae that inhabit grasslands include those of swift moths (*Hepialus* spp.), flounced rustic moth (*Luperina testacea*) and heart & dart moth (*Agrotis exclamationis*).

FIGS 68 & 69. (Above left) Garden grass veneer moth (*Chrysoteuchia culmella*) larvae feed on the roots of various grasses. (Above right) When fully grown the larvae form cocoons within which they eventually pupate.

SHOOT BORERS

Various shoot-infesting fly larvae infest forage grasses and grass seed crops, and they are of particular significance when attacks are launched at the seedling stage. Typically, eggs are laid on or close to host grasses, including seedlings. Volunteer cereal plants are also attacked. Following egg hatch the larvae bore into the base of tillers and seedlings, often resulting in the death of the central shoots (the familiar deadheart symptom already described in Chapter 2). Common examples, all of which overwinter as final-instar larvae and also infest cereal crops (frequently as ley pests), occur in the families Chloropidae and Opomyzidae (Table 1); the species of *Cetema*, *Geomyza* and *Meromyza* are known collectively as grass & cereal flies. Larvae of various moths also feed within the stems of grasses, although infestations usually pass unnoticed and are of little or no significance. Examples include common rustic moth (*Mesapamea secalis*), marbled minor moth (*Oligia strigilis*) and rosy rustic moth (*Hydraecia micacea*), all of which also invade cereal crops.

TABLE 1. Examples of shoot-infesting Diptera associated with grasses.

Species	*Maximum length of fully grown larva*[21]	*Number of generations annually*	*Grass host(s)*
Family Chloropidae			
Cetema elongata	8 mm	1	Various
Cetema neglecta	8 mm	1	Various
Meromyza saltatrix	10 mm	1	Cocksfoot
Meromyza variegata	10 mm	1	Various, but not cocksfoot
Oscinella frit	5 mm	3	Various (highly polyphagous)
Oscinella vastator	5 mm	2 or 3	Ryegrasses etc., but not cocksfoot
Family Opomyzidae			
Geomyza tripunctata	5.5 mm	2	Mainly ryegrasses, especially Italian
Opomyza germinationis	8 mm	1	Various

The life histories of single-brooded flies with shoot-boring larvae are all very similar, although they differ somewhat in detail. Typically, overwintered larvae of *Cetema* spp. pupate in May and adults emerge in late June; those of *Meromyza* spp. usually pupate in early June and adults appear in July. Development of the

FIG 70. Puparia of *Geomyza tripunctata* are formed in the shoots of grasses.

dusky-winged cereal fly (*Opomyza germinationis*), however, is slightly more advanced, pupation taking place in early May and adults emerging in early or mid-June; the adults, however, are long-lived and often survive well into November, depositing eggs in the autumn.[22] In frit fly (*Oscinella frit*), a multi-brooded species, first-generation adults are active in May and early June, followed by two summer flights – in July (second-generation adults) and August (third-generation adults). Developmental times for *Geomyza tripunctata* (which is double brooded) differ markedly, pupation of overwintered larvae occurring in March (Fig. 70) and first-generation adults emerging in April, if not earlier;[23] eggs are then laid in early May and the resulting larvae pupate in June, second-generation adults in their turn appearing in July and ovipositing in August. These timings, of course, are subject to a degree of site to site and year to year variation, not least in response to weather conditions.

FIG 71. The sawfly *Cephus cultratus* breeds on grasses, but is not an important pest.

The midge *Mayetiola dactylis,* a close relative of the cereal-infesting hessian fly (*M. destructor*) (Chapter 2), breeds on cocksfoot. The larvae inhabit the basal parts of the shoots, sheltered by the leaf sheaths, where pupation in characteristic seed-like puparia also takes place. External signs of damage are slight, but infested shoots appear slightly swollen and the inner tissue sometimes discolours and rots. Winter- and spring-collected puparia produce adults from mid-May to late September, and results from breeding experiments suggest that there is just one protracted generation annually.[24] Up to 25 puparia per infested shoot have been recorded. Such puparia are readily seen if the leaf sheath is prised back, as are those of hessian fly on cereals.

Other stem-boring insects include wheat stem sawfly (*Cephus pygmeus*), a pest of forage grasses as well as cereals (see Chapter 2). It occurs widely over much of England and Wales. The more southeasterly distributed species *C. cultratus* (Fig. 71) attacks grasses such as cocksfoot and timothy, but is not of economic significance.

PESTS OF INFLORESCENCES AND SEED HEADS

Gall midges

Many gall midges (Fig. 72) are associated with grasses[25] and some rate as highly significant pests of seed crops, especially cocksfoot and meadow foxtail. In the early part of the twentieth century, for example, gall midges devastated the New Zealand foxtail seed industry, a consequence of their accidental introduction from Europe.[26] Common examples of British grass-infesting midges include *Contarinia dactylidis, Dasineura dactylidis* and *Sitodiplosis dactylidis* on cocksfoot, *C. merceri* and *D. alopecuri* on meadow foxtail, and *C. geniculati* on both. Collectively, and individually, these species are known as either cocksfoot midges or foxtail midges. The pests are essentially single brooded, although some species, including *C. merceri,* sometimes achieve a partial second generation; *C. geniculati* is double brooded, at least in favourable areas.[27] Exemplifying the life history of a typically single-brooded species, adults of *C. dactylidis* occur from late May onwards. Eggs are laid in the developing florets of cocksfoot and hatch shortly afterwards. The tiny, lemon-yellow to golden-yellow larvae then feed gregariously for about a month before overwintering in the soil, each in a silken cocoon. Pupation takes place in the spring, shortly before the emergence of adults. The midges (as in some other species, including *C. merceri*) typically fly in swarms during the evening and again in the early morning.[28]

Clover plants are attacked by various gall midges, of which the clover leaf midge (*D. trifolii*) and the clover seed midge (*D. leguminicola*) are most often reported. The former species is widely distributed but not an important pest. It

FIG 72. Midges, of which there are many grass-infesting species, often swarm around the flowerheads of grasses.

deposits eggs in the unopened leaflets. Later, after expanding, each infested leaflet folds upwards along the midrib to form a pod-like gall within which larvae develop and finally pupate. There are several generations annually. In clover seed midge, which can be of great significance in seed crops, eggs are laid amongst the florets whilst the flowerheads are still green, usually several eggs per head. Larvae feed within the florets and also attack the developing seeds, becoming full grown in four to six weeks. They then pupate in the soil, a second generation of adults emerging one to two weeks later.[29] Some midge larvae lodging within midge-infested clover flowerheads are predators: *Lestodiplosis trifolii*, for example, is known to be associated with clover leaf midge.[30] Others (*Clinodiplosis* spp.) are inquilines and feed on saprophytic fungi.[31]

Timothy flies

Timothy flies (*Nanna* spp.) are common pests of timothy grass. The housefly-like adults occur in mid-May and deposit eggs singly on the upper leaves of host plants, close to the stems. The eggs hatch five to seven days later. Larvae then feed on the developing flowerheads in the shelter of the leaf sheaths. They destroy many of the florets and, once the flowerheads have emerged, the characteristic loss of tissue (with damage often spiralling up the flowerheads) becomes a common sight on both wild and cultivated plants. However, by the time symptoms are seen, the maggot-like larvae will have long since departed. Timothy flies overwinter in the soil, in the pupal stage, there being just one generation annually.[32]

Moths

Cocksfoot moth (*Glyphipterix simpliciella*) is a widely distributed and generally abundant insect, the larvae feeding in the seeds of wild and cultivated cocksfoot. The tiny, metallic adults (Fig. 73) are active in sunny weather from May onwards. They often swarm around the inflorescences of their food plants, where eggs are

FIG 73. Cocksfoot moth (*Glyphipterix simpliciella*).

eventually laid. Larvae feed in the seed heads during the summer months and are sometimes sufficiently numerous to be regarded as pests of cocksfoot seed crops, sometimes causing complete crop loss.[33] When fully grown the larvae bore into the stem, often sharing a small entry hole formed beneath one of the uppermost leaf sheaths. The larvae then spin small, whitish cocoons within which to overwinter. Pupation occurs in the spring shortly before the appearance of the adults.

Seed heads of grass are also a food source for various other lepidopterous pests, including the larvae of noctuids such as dark arches moth (*Apamea monoglypha*), light arches moth (*A. lithoxylaea*) and rustic shoulder-knot moth (*A. sordens*). As youngsters, these clamber up grass stems during the night to feed on the heads. However, the larvae are essentially nocturnal stem-base feeders, and they rest in the soil during the daytime.

LEAF MINERS

Although of little or no economic importance, leaf mining insects are common denizens of grassland swards. Examples include the ephydrid fly *Hydrellia griseola* and various leaf-mining agromyzids, e.g. *Agromyza nigripes, Liriomyza flaveola* and *Phytomyza nigra*, all of which infest grasses.[34] Leaf-mining larvae of certain moths (*Elachista* spp.) also attack grasses, the widely distributed species

FIG 74. Leaf mines formed on clover by *Agromyza nana* larvae are very conspicuous, but not of great significance.

Elachista albifrontella being a particularly common example. However, these do not appear to be of significance as pests.[35] Leaf miners are also found on clovers and other herbaceous components of grassland swards. *Agromyza nana*, for example, forms conspicuous white blotch mines on the upper side of the leaves of clovers (Fig. 74).

SUCKING PESTS

Insects

Various foliage-infesting aphids are associated with grasses. The most frequently encountered species are bird-cherry/oat aphid (*Rhopalosiphum padi*), cocksfoot aphid (*Hyalopteroides humilis*), fescue aphid (*Metopolophium festucae*),[36] grain aphid (*Sitobion avenae*) and rose/grain aphid (*M. dirhodum*). As on cereal crops (Chapter 2), bird-cherry/oat aphids and grain aphids can be of significance as vectors of barley yellow dwarf virus (BYDV), to which many grasses are susceptible.[37] Aphids also occur on the roots of grasses. Dogwood/grass aphid (*Anoecia corni*), for example, overwinters in the egg stage on the stems of dogwood and eventually migrates to grasses where colonies develop parthenogenetically on the roots during the summer months. Winged forms eventually return to dogwood in the autumn. Other root-infesting aphids include apple/grass aphid (*R. insertum*) (a species that overwinters in the egg stage on apple trees), elm/grass-root aphid (*Tetraneura ulmi*) (most widely known for the large, balloon-like galls it forms in springtime on the leaves of elm trees) and *Aploneura lentisci* (which persists on grass roots throughout the year, the colonies being surrounded by flocculent masses of whitish wax). Aphids also infest clover plants and other legumes in grassland swards, or legumes growing as stand-alone forage or fodder crops. Black bean aphid (*Aphis fabae*), cowpea aphid (*A. craccivora*), pea aphid (*Acyrthosiphon pisum*) and vetch aphid (*Megoura viciae*) are examples.

Besides aphids, grasslands host many other phytophagous bugs, and the species complex in non-cropped habitats can be extremely rich. As an example, 45 species of leafhopper were recorded in chalk grassland in Bedfordshire.[38] Phytophagous bugs (leafhoppers and others) are also abundant in meadows and pastures. Grass-feeding species, well capable of attracting attention in farmland swards, include the cereal leafhopper (*Javesella pellucida*) – recognisable as a delphacid by the presence of a large, articulating apical spur on each hind tibia (see Fig. A.3, p. 413) – the slim-looking mirid *Stenodema laevigatum*, and cicadellid leafhoppers such as *Euscelis incisus* and *Macrosteles sexnotatus*. Leafhoppers and other plant bugs are also of some significance on the leguminous component of grass swards. The clover-infesting strawberry leafhopper (*Aphrodes bicinctus*), for example, is particularly renowned as a vector of mycoplasma-like organisms (MLOs), including clover phyllopody. A closely related MLO is readily transferred from clover to strawberry plants by this leafhopper, resulting in a condition on strawberry called green petal.[39] The highly polymorphic and polyphagous common froghopper (*Philaenus spumarius*), widely known abroad as the meadow spittlebug, is also a frequent inhabitant of grasslands, where it infests a wide range of herbaceous plants, again including clovers.

Thrips are common inhabitants of grasslands. Barley thrips (*Limothrips denticornis*), grass flower thrips (*Chirothrips manicatus*), grass thrips (*Aptinothrips rufus* and *A. stylifer*), meadow foxtail thrips (*C. hamatus*) and striate thrips (*Anaphothrips obscurus*),[40] for example, are generally abundant. The nymphs and adults feed by probing the surfaces of host plants and imbibing sap from the underlying cells.

Mites

Cereal rust mite (*Abacarus hystrix*) is a frequent pest of ryegrasses, the microscopic, whitish and narrow-bodied mites breeding on the upper surface of leaves in the longitudinal grooves between the veins. There are several overlapping generations annually, populations reaching their peak in late August or early September. Owing to their small size, cereal rust mites are unlikely to attract attention in the field, although heavy infestations can cause discoloration of leaves. The mites, which are most abundant on uncut or ungrazed perennial ryegrass,[41] are of greatest significance as vectors of ryegrass mosaic virus (RgMV);[42] they also transmit agropyron mosaic virus (AgMV), a disease first found in Britain in 1974.[43] Exceptionally amongst eriophyid mites (which tend to be host specific), cereal rust mites have been recorded from well over 50 different hosts worldwide. Comparative host-related studies,[44] however, suggest that the mites may actually be a complex of highly specialised host-specific races.

Bryobia mites sometimes attract attention on grasses, such creatures being immediately recognisable by their oval, reddish or reddish-brown bodies and greatly elongated front pair of legs. Two species of almost identical appearance are involved: the clover bryobia mite (*Bryobia praetiosa*) and the grass/pear bryobia mite (*B. cristata*). Bryobia mites on grasses are parthenogenetic, and pass through several generations annually.

In winter, red-legged earth mites (*Penthaleus major*) have been associated with patches of poor growth in fields of cultivated cocksfoot. The mites (also known abroad as blue oat mites or winter grain mites) stunt growth and produce silvery feeding areas on the leaves.[45] Such damage, however, largely disappears following regrowth of grass in the spring and is rarely reported. The pest is largely favoured by cool conditions and undergoes extended diapause (in the egg stage) throughout the summer months.[46] Red-legged earth mite – a vernacular name also applied outside Europe to the non-European pest *Halotydeus destructor* – is more important in North America and Australia than in Europe. Other mites associated with grasses include the grass & cereal mite (*Siteroptes avenae*) and the oat spiral mite (*Steneotarsonemus spirifex*), both already mentioned under cereals. Some authors credit the former (in association with the pathogen *Fusarium poae*) with causing a condition on grasses called silver top; not all, however, agree.[47]

CHAPTER 4

The World of Oilseed Rape Pests

OILSEED RAPE IS AN important arable crop. In late spring or early summer the bright yellow expanses of flowering rape fields brighten many a countryside view and, love it or loathe it, the crop is now an integral part of our arable farming landscape (Fig. 75). During the flowering period, fields of oilseed rape visibly teem with life. Not only are they inhabited by pests and a range of natural enemies, including many important

FIG 75. Winter oilseed rape is now a major crop in Britain, and over the past few decades it has transformed the arable farming landscape.

parasitoids and predators,[1] but their floral canopies are also visited by hoards of nectar- and pollen-seeking bees and other insects. Oilseed rape, therefore, is an important rural resource and contributes enormously towards maintaining and enhancing on-farm biodiversity. In 1970, fewer than 4,000 ha of oilseed rape were grown in the UK, and most of this was spring-sown (known as spring rape). Throughout the mid- and late 1970s and early 1980s, however, following Britain's entry into the European Community in 1973, the area of autumn-sown oilseed rape (known as winter rape) increased dramatically, owing to the availability of subsidies for oilseed production. Winter rape was quickly adopted as a break crop in cereal rotations, often at the expense of field beans, and it has now become a major component of British agriculture in its own right. By 1981, the area of oilseed rape in England had topped 100,000 ha, and three or so years later this had almost trebled to around 300,000 ha. From the early 1980s, oilseed rape crops also became a regular feature in the Scottish arable sector. Today, at around 600,000 ha, winter rape continues to be prominent in the UK arable farming scene, in terms of cropped area (ignoring grassland) being third to wheat and barley. Spring rape is still grown. However, at little more than 2 per cent of the total oilseed rape area, it is a comparative rarity on modern arable farms.

The change from spring to winter rape has had a marked impact on pest profiles. For example, since the 1970s, autumn-invading species unable to breed on spring-sown crops at last found a ready stage for their activities. Conversely, some key pests of spring-sown crops are of little significance on the winter crop. Their importance has declined. In part, this is due to the greater robustness of the winter crop and to its ability to compensate for damage caused.

There have been other changes: notably, a move away from oilseed rape cultivars whose seeds contained high levels of erucic acid and glucosinolates.[2] Such cultivars have now been replaced by those whose seeds are low in these chemicals. This does not appear to affect plant susceptibility to insect pests.[3] However, greater yield increases in response to insecticide applications on these so-called 'double-low' or 'double-zero' cultivars have been reported.[4] Also, slugs (which are often important oilseed rape pests at the establishment phase) have been found to graze preferentially on seedlings of double-low cultivars.[5] This does at least indicate the potential vulnerability of such cultivars, which now totally dominate the marketplace.

Non-vegetable brassicaceous crops other than oilseed rape, whether grown for seed or as fodder or forage crops, are susceptible to many of the pests discussed in this chapter. Such crops include brown mustard[6] and to a lesser extent white mustard, as well as kale, swede, turnip and turnip rape.

AUTUMN AND WINTER PESTS OF OILSEED RAPE

Aphids

Green-bodied aphids, almost invariably peach/potato aphids (*Myzus persicae*), commonly occur in the autumn on winter rape seedlings and young established plants. However, unless crops are examined closely, such aphids are often overlooked as they are cryptically coloured and do not form dense colonies. Also, there are usually no obvious signs of attack. This is because the aphids rarely do direct harm, unless plants are growing poorly or are under drought stress. Nevertheless, such aphids are of importance on oilseed rape as potential vectors of beet western yellows virus (BWYV), which they introduce into crops in the early autumn. This virus not only infects oilseed rape but also occurs in common arable weeds such as goosegrass,[7] shepherd's purse and wild radish (see also Chapter 6). Although infected rape plants often show few symptoms of debility, BWYV can affect both growth and yield.[8] The well-known cabbage aphid (*Brevicoryne brassicae*) (Fig. 76) also transmits BWYV, but is of greater significance as a vector of cauliflower mosaic virus (CaMV) and turnip mosaic virus (TuMV) – two other aphid-transmitted virus diseases of winter oilseed rape.[9] Cabbage aphid is also significant in its own right if early-sown crops become infested soon after germinating. The aphids may then cause discoloration, stunting and malformation of plants, and this can affect establishment. Under favourable conditions, cabbage aphids persist on oilseed rape plants throughout the autumn and winter as adults and nymphs. Their numbers then increase once spring arrives and breeding recommences. Alternatively, as is usually the case in more northerly regions, the pest overwinters as eggs on the stems of host plants.

FIG 76. Colonies of cabbage aphid (*Brevicoryne brassicae*) often occur on oilseed rape crops during the summer.

Parasitoids of aphids are of little or no importance as natural enemies in autumn and winter. The tiny wasp *Diaeretiella rapae*, for example, although known to attack peach/potato aphid,[10] is not active at that time of year. The same holds true for specialist predators of aphids, such as ladybirds, which typically reach their peak in summer. Nevertheless, peach/potato aphids are preyed upon in autumn by non-specialist feeders, including ground beetles, rove beetles and spiders. Larvae of soldier beetles are the most important enemies of aphids during the late autumn and winter, and such predators are especially active at temperatures ranging from 0 to 10°C.[11]

Other sap-sucking bugs

European tarnished plant bugs (*Lygus rugulipennis*) occasionally feed on overwintering oilseed rape plants. Potato capsids (*Closterotomus norvegicus*)[12] also occur on oilseed rape, but mainly on spring-sown crops.[13] Similarly, in summer, the tips of plants on field margins sometimes support developing cuckoo-spit-coated nymphs of the common froghopper (*Philaenus spumarius*). Such insects, however, are merely incidental pests of oilseed rape, and their occurrence is of no significance.

Flea beetles

Two species of flea beetle attack winter oilseed rape: Wessex flea beetle (*Psylliodes luteola*) and cabbage stem flea beetle (*P. chrysocephala*) (Fig. 77). The former has recently become locally significant in the early autumn on winter oilseed rape, the adults causing extensive shot-holing of the cotyledons and youngest leaves. Attacks are ephemeral, and have been centred in southern England where this insect has also damaged herbage seed crops or recently drilled winter cereals (see Chapter 2).

FIG 77. (Above left) Cabbage stem flea beetle (*Psylliodes chrysocephala*) is an important pest of winter oilseed rape. (Above right) The larvae feed singly or gregariously within host plants, attacking the stems, leaf stalks and growing points.

Cabbage stem flea beetle is nowadays a well-established pest of winter rape crops in Britain. Owing to the extended periods of adult activity, egg-laying and larval development, the pest is sometimes thought to have two generations annually. The true lifecycle, however, shows young (newly reared) adults first appearing in summer, their emergence in fields more or less coinciding with the rape harvest. Back in the 1970s, when the pest was particularly abundant locally on oilseed rape (see below), loaded seed trailers could sometimes be seen with the surface of their cargoes literally seething with 'harvested' beetles. After a brief dispersal phase, the young adult beetles seek shelter and enter a short period of summer diapause or rest (known as aestivation). These beetles reappear, from late August or early September onwards, and move to newly germinated, autumn-sown rape where they feed on the young foliage. At that time, the adults are often seen as drowned casualties in puddles on farm tracks in the vicinity of infested fields. Following mating, eggs are laid in the soil, close to host plants. Egg-laying continues over many weeks, but most eggs are deposited in the autumn. They hatch from mid-October onwards. There is a direct relationship between the rate of egg development and temperature.[14] Thus, eggs laid in advanced crops (when temperatures are generally higher) tend to hatch well in advance of those deposited in association with more retarded ones. As autumn turns to winter, such differences are inevitably exacerbated by seasonally declining ambient temperatures. Following egg hatch, the larvae invade their hosts, where they feed either singly or gregariously. At first they bore into the leaf stalks, their mines characteristically breaking through the surface tissue at intervals to form distinctive open wounds. The larval feeding galleries are later extended into the stems, and may also reach the growing points. Damage can be extensive (Fig. 78). Larvae are fully fed in the spring, but sometimes not until early June. They then pupate in the soil.

FIG **78.** Stunted and weakened, multi-stemmed plants are symptomatic of a heavy infestation of cabbage stem flea beetle (*Psylliodes chrysocephala*).

Before winter oilseed rape became a significant UK crop, cabbage stem flea beetle was a relatively insignificant pest in Britain. Spring-sown crops are not attacked, and so the pest was absent from spring rape and mustard. It was, however, a minor problem on overwintering brassicaceous vegetables, with its apparent headquarters in East Anglia.[15] Initially, back in the 1970s, cabbage stem flea beetle infestations on winter rape were largely restricted to Bedfordshire, Huntingdonshire (today, part of the administrative county of Cambridgeshire) and Northamptonshire. However, from these humble beginnings, infestations soon followed the expansion of winter rape as a crop in England, spreading inexorably to neighbouring counties and beyond. The pest was clearly boosted by the seemingly infinite food source and the welcoming new breeding grounds. By the late 1980s, infestations had reached most rape-growing areas in England and Wales, and it was only a matter of time before winter rape crops in Scotland also fell foul of the pest.

Weevils

Weevils do not usually occur in oilseed rape crops during the autumn/winter period, either as adults or as larvae. Nevertheless, infestations of one species – the rape winter stem weevil (*Ceutorhynchus picitarsis*) – are sometimes found on winter oilseed rape crops, especially in eastern and northeast England (essentially East Anglia, Lincolnshire and South Humberside). Rape winter stem weevil was of particular significance in England in the 1980s. Although it has since extended its range into southern Scotland, it remains merely a local and minor pest. The mainly shiny-black adults, with a distinctive yellowish mark on the shoulder of each wing case, are active in the autumn, from late September onwards. Eggs are then deposited in the leaf stalks of host plants, either singly or in small groups.

FIG 79. Rape winter stem weevil (*Ceutorhynchus picitarsis*) larvae cause stunting, and infested plants often split open.

FIG 80. Rape winter stem weevil (*Ceutorhynchus picitarsis*) larvae feed in the stems of young oilseed rape plants.

Following egg hatch, the larvae feed gregariously within the leaf stalks. Later, they move into the crowns, where they are capable of causing considerable damage (Fig. 79). Heavily attacked plants are stunted and distorted, and growing points may be destroyed. Larvae (Fig. 80) feed throughout the winter and become fully grown in March or April. They then pupate in the soil, a few centimetres below the surface. New adults emerge in late May and early June, and these feed briefly before dispersing. The weevils aestivate during the summer in hedgerows and other sheltered sites, reawakening and moving into new host crops in the autumn.

Defoliators

Few leaf-browsing insects are likely to attract attention on oilseed rape plants, except at the early stages of crop development. Larvae of cabbage moth (*Mamestra brassicae*), small white butterfly (*Pieris rapae*) and diamond-back moth (*Plutella xylostella*), along with a few others, occur on occasions. However, compared with damage caused to seedlings and young plants by slugs, such attacks are usually patchy and inconsequential. Slug damage is most prevalent in autumn, and is recognised unerringly by the presence on holed cotyledons and leaves of silvery mucous trails. Piles of black excrement may also be in evidence. Particularly on shallow, chalky soils, losses to establishing crops can be such that re-drilling becomes necessary. In wet weather, slugs (which are essentially nocturnal animals) often rest during the daytime on the underside of the invaded leaves. However, in dry conditions, on completing their night-time activities they typically retreat back into the soil.

Turnip sawfly (*Athalia rosae*) (Fig. 81) was once an important defoliating pest of brassicaceous plants. Reports of severe damage to turnips in the late eighteenth century and early- to mid-nineteenth century are well documented.[16] From the

FIG 81. After an absence of many years, turnip sawfly (*Athalia rosae*) has again appeared in Britain, having successfully invaded from mainland Europe.

late 1800s, however, the pest declined and is believed to have become extinct as a breeding species in Britain. Wet summers are unsuitable for survival,[17] and this may well explain the rise and fall in the pest's fortunes in Britain. Turnip sawfly re-established itself as a pest in the eastern, midland and southern counties of England from the early 1940s onwards.[18] However, little or nothing was heard of this pest in the second half of the twentieth century, and it was certainly never encountered when winter oilseed rape began its major advance as an agricultural crop in England from the 1970s onwards. In recent years, turnip sawfly has emerged from obscurity and has once again become a noticeable pest. The larvae are most often reported in the autumn on the leaves of winter oilseed rape crops and other host plants. In addition, the adults may be found in water traps used to monitor more established pests such as cabbage stem flea beetle. Turnip sawfly infestations in the first decade of the twenty-first century have occurred widely on winter oilseed rape in southern England, from Hampshire and Wiltshire to Kent, and northwards through Essex to Suffolk. Attacks have also been reported in the Midlands and as far afield as Shropshire and Yorkshire. There is little or no doubt that the resurgence of turnip sawfly in England is the direct result of immigration from mainland Europe, where the pest is well established. The wretched summer of 2008, however, will have done nothing to support its continued survival in Britain. The ebb and flow, and migratory nature of this insect have been known for many years. In 1783, for example, Marshall[19] reported as follows:

> *From their more frequently appearing on the sea-coast, and from the vast quantities which have, I believe, at different times, been observed on the beach washed up by the tide, it has been a received opinion among the farmers, that they*

> [turnip sawflies] *are not natives of this country, but come across the ocean, and observations this year* [1782] *greatly corroborate the idea. Fishermen upon the eastern coast declare, that they actually saw them arrive in cloud-like flights; and from the testimony of many, it seems to be an indisputable fact, that they first made their appearance on the eastern coast; and, moreover, that on their first being observed, they lay upon and near the cliffs so thick and so languid, that they might have been collected into heaps, lying it is said, in some places two inches thick. From thence they proceeded into the country, and even at the distance of three or four miles from the coast they were seen in multitudes resembling swarms of bees.*

Yarrell,[20] in discussing the periodicity of turnip sawfly attacks, reported that:

> *The crops of turnips in the counties of Kent, Essex, Sussex, part of Buckinghamshire, Hampshire, and Wiltshire were considered a failure* [in 1835]; *and so long did the various broods continue their attacks, that the produce of a second and even a third sowing did not escape destruction, nor was it till the occurrence of the rains in September, after an unusually dry summer in many districts, that the mischief ceased.*
>
> ... *happily* [turnip sawfly] *does not make its appearance in great numbers except at wide intervals, and during those seasons that are remarkable for the almost total absence of rain.*

Turnip sawfly has up to three generations annually. Adults first appear in late April or early May. Those of the second and third generations occur in the summer and early autumn, respectively. Eggs are laid on the underside of leaves, each inserted within tissue close to the leaf margin. They hatch about five days later. However, egg development is greatly protracted in cool conditions. The mainly black-bodied larvae (Fig. 82) graze on the leaves of host plants during the daytime and at night, and often bask in sunshine. They are quite unlike any other pest associated with the crop – their wrinkled and hairless body, shiny black head, three prominent pairs of thoracic legs and eight pairs of abdominal prolegs making them unmistakeable. If disturbed, the larvae often curl up and

FIG **82.** In former times, turnip sawfly (*Athalia rosae*) larvae were major pests of brassicaceous crops.

FIG 83. Various species of tachinid fly are known to parasitise turnip sawfly larvae.

drop to the ground. They may also exude small drops of haemolymph through the body wall – a process known as reflex bleeding. The haemolymph contains chemicals, such as sinalbin, which accumulate in the body following the sequestration of glucosinolates from the larval food plant and are capable of deterring predators.[21] This does not, however, prevent larvae being attacked by tachinid flies[22] (Fig. 83) and parasitoid wasps. The larva of turnip sawfly was known to nineteenth-century farmers under several derisive common names, including 'black canker', 'black palmer' and 'black slug'.[23] References to canker and slug are self-evident; the term palmer, however, is less obvious, being an old name for a destructive, hairy (the latter term not really appropriate for a turnip sawfly larva) caterpillar. Historically, years when turnip sawfly reached epidemic proportions were described as 'canker years'.[24] Today, of course, the term canker is applied exclusively to diseases such as stem canker which is caused on oilseed rape and other Brassicaceae by the fungal pathogen *Leptosphaeria maculans* – anamorph *Phoma lingam* (the anamorph being the imperfect, asexual reproductive state of the fungus). Turnip sawfly larvae feed for three to four weeks, and cause extensive defoliation. They then pupate in the soil, each in a relatively large, oval cocoon. Individuals of the final generation generally complete their development by mid-October.

Insects and slugs are by no means the only defoliators to have an impact on oilseed rape. Crops that are slow to establish, for example, are often ravaged by rabbits. They are also grazed indiscriminately by birds such as grey partridges, pheasants and woodpigeons. In addition, during the autumn and winter months, flocks of woodpigeons frequently descend upon established oilseed rape crops. Unchecked, they cause considerable damage to the foliage, especially in February and early March.[25] Winter grazing by mute swans (Fig. 84) has also become a nuisance on oilseed rape and other winter crops, especially in the fenlands of East Anglia.

FIG 84. Mute swans soon learn that overwintering oilseed rape crops are a highly palatable food source.

Leaf miners

Seedlings and young oilseed rape plants frequently play host to dipterous leaf miners. The generally common species *Phytomyza rufipes* and *Scaptomyza flava* are most frequently involved, and both are said to be oligophagous – being restricted to a narrow range of host plants. Larvae of *P. rufipes* (known as cabbage leaf miners) form long, inconspicuous galleries in the midribs and leaf stalks. The larvae also enter the stems of young plants. Damaged leaves often turn bright yellow, and are a common sight on infested crops during the winter months. There are three generations annually. Mined leaves on older plants, whether in winter, spring or summer, are often dismissed as due to natural senescence. However, if the leaf stalks are split open, evidence of mining (if not the larvae themselves) may be found. Unlike larvae of many related species, cabbage leaf

FIG 85. Larvae of *Scaptomyza flava* pupate within their mines, each in a relatively long puparium.

miners usually pupate externally, so the puparia usually escape attention. Leaf mines formed by *S. flava* larvae appear as irregular, whitish blotches, each extending upwards and outwards from near the base of the infested leaf blade. Although often extensive, and then very noticeable, the mines are of little or no significance on oilseed rape. Larvae of *S. flava* pupate within their mines, each in a relatively long puparium (Fig. 85).

SPRING AND SUMMER PESTS OF OILSEED RAPE

Aphids

Especially following mild winters, cabbage aphid colonies often escalate on winter rape during the spring and summer, and may persist right up to harvest time. Although rarely of significance, infestations are often very noticeable on individual plants at the edges of fields. Affected plants become plastered with aphids, the grey, mealy-coated colonies extending over the upper branches and racemes. The shoots of heavily affected plants are distorted, and developing leaves and pods (more correctly called siliquae) often become tinged with red or purple. Cabbage aphid is also a frequent inhabitant of spring-sown crops.

In summer, cabbage aphid colonies on oilseed rape are targeted by predators, including larvae of the hover fly *Episyrphus balteatus*. However, these natural enemies arrive too late in the season to have a marked impact on populations. The same is true of parasitoids such as *Diaeretiella rapae*. This solitary endoparasitoid characteristically pupates in the bloated, pale beige remains (skin) of its host, and these mummified aphids are a common sight within colonies. Overall, however, *D. rapae* appears to have little impact on aphid numbers.[26] Seven-spot ladybirds (*Coccinella septempunctata*) and their larvae sometimes feed on the aphids during the summer, although cabbage aphids are not particularly suitable as a food source.[27] Interestingly, the harlequin ladybird (*Harmonia axyridis*) avoids cabbage aphids.[28] Thus, this newcomer to Britain (see Chapter 12), although generally regarded as a voracious predator of aphids, cannot be viewed as a possible future controlling agent for this particular pest.

Unlike cabbage aphids, peach/potato aphids rarely attract attention on rape plants. As spring arrives, winged forms soon leave the crop and migrate to non-brassicaceous hosts such as potatoes and sugar beet (Chapter 5). Overwintering populations on oilseed rape then die out. Summer infestations – small colonies on developing pods, for example – sometimes occur (Fig. 86) but are of no significance. In the late 1980s, concern was expressed that winter

FIG **86.** Tiny colonies of peach/potato aphid (*Myzus persicae*) sometimes occur in summer on the developing pods of oilseed rape plants. Note that one of the aphids is parasitised and has become mummified.

oilseed rape might serve as a reservoir of insecticide-resistant peach/potato aphids, thereby posing a risk to arable crops. Surveys conducted during two mild winters showed that there was certainly a build-up of highly resistant forms on winter rape in the autumn. However, from January onwards these were virtually absent in populations, suggesting that such variants were less fitted to survive the winter than non-resistant ones.[29]

Flea beetles

Various small, black and shiny flea beetles (*Phyllotreta* spp.) – some with a metallic-blue or metallic-green sheen and others with a yellow longitudinal stripe on each wing case – attack spring-sown brassica seed crops. Turnip flea beetles (*P. atra, P. consobrina* and *P. cruciferae*), the small striped flea beetle (*P. undulata*) and the large striped flea beetle (*P. nemorum*) are amongst the most common crop invaders in Britain.[30] The adult beetles are active from April onwards. They then attack germinating or recently germinated brassica crops, to feed on the cotyledons, young leaves and stems. Tiny pits are made in the tissue, and these often develop into distinct holes as the plants grow. Attacks on spring oilseed rape can have a detrimental effect on establishment, especially under warm and dry conditions when growth is retarded. Flea beetle eggs are laid in the soil and, depending on the species, the larvae either feed on the roots or mine within the leaves, leaf stalks and stems. Although infestations can be significant on vegetable brassicas, they are of little or no importance on seed crops such as oilseed rape. Development is completed in the early summer. New adults appear from late June onwards and then hibernate. There is just one generation annually.

Pollen beetles

Pollen beetle (*Meligethes aeneus*) has also generated concern as a result of the development of resistance to insecticides (see below). Adults overwinter amongst leaf litter in hedgerows or woodlands, and in other similar situations. They then invade winter oilseed rape crops from late April or early May, the first arrivals appearing at about the green-bud growth stage.[31] Pollen beetles usually remain active in crops until June. The beetles feed on pollen, and they must bite into the unopened buds in order to locate it. In so doing, they often cause damage to the floral parts, resulting in the eventual abortion of buds. Pollen is more readily available in open flowers and these become particularly attractive to the beetles. In winter rape fields essentially still at the green-bud stage, for example, the adults often congregate on bolted plants with open or opening flowerheads. Aggregations of pollen beetles on such plants, which come into flower ahead of (and stand proud of) the rest of the crop, can be alarming. However, acting in effect as magnets, they give a false indication of the overall size of the pest invasion. The same is true of early-flowering arable weeds such as charlock, whose flowerheads often become plastered with the beetles. After mating has occurred, eggs are laid in the flower buds of host plants, either singly or in small groups. The eggs hatch a week or so later. Larvae (Fig. 87) then feed on pollen for up to a month, moulting to their second (and final) instar at about the time that the flower buds open.[32] The second-instar larvae regularly ascend the inflorescences at intervals of a few days, to gain access to younger flowers, before eventually becoming fully fed and dropping to the ground to pupate in the soil.[33] It is at this time (often called the dropping period) that the larvae become vulnerable to attack from ground beetles, wolf spiders and other

FIG **87.** A nearly fully grown pollen beetle (*Meligethes aeneus*) larva.

ground-dwelling predators that may be lurking within the dank confines beneath the crop canopy (see below). Young adult pollen beetles emerge from the soil three to four weeks later, usually in July. They then fly to various flowering plants, where they again feed on pollen. Such infestations are not limited to Brassicaceae, the beetles' pollen requirements being drawn from flowers of a wide range of plants. Having fed on pollen, the young adults enter hibernation. There is just one generation annually.

Pollen beetles in oilseed rape are frequently cited as *Meligethes* spp., since more than one species can occur. However, the generally abundant *M. aeneus* greatly predominates. As for others, the bronzed pollen beetle (*M. viridescens*) is sometimes found on rape crops but in just small numbers. The life histories of both species are similar. However, bronzed pollen beetles prefer higher temperatures for both egg-laying and development,[34] and appear slightly later in the spring than *M. aeneus.*

Pollen beetle damage to the buds of oilseed rape results in the appearance of blind stalks (the remains of aborted buds) on the racemes. However, damage attributed to the pest is often overestimated since physiological factors can produce similar symptoms. Further, winter rape is capable of compensating for early loss of buds by setting more pods, thereby reducing the overall impact of the pest on this crop.[35] Winter rape crops are also often beyond the susceptible green- to yellow-bud stages[36] before the majority of overwintered beetles arrive on them. Spring-sown rape, on the other hand, is more vulnerable as it often has to face the full force of any invasion whilst still to reach the flowering stage. The invaders on spring rape include mated adult females migrating from winter rape in search of buds in which to lay their eggs. Spring rape plants are also less vigorous, and therefore less able to compensate for bud losses. This having been said, in spite of the dominance of winter rape in these islands, pollen beetle is becoming a more significant pest of oilseed rape generally, a situation exacerbated in part by changes in crop cultivars. The recent development of resistance to pyrethroid insecticides in pollen beetle populations also has to be considered – pyrethroids are now the standard chemical control measure for use against pollen beetle, and are widely used on oilseed rape crops in the spring (albeit often unnecessarily). Such resistance was initially confirmed in 1999, in pollen beetle populations from northeast France. It has also now become widespread and highly significant in other parts of mainland Europe (for example, in Denmark, Germany and Poland). In 2007, resistance to pyrethroids was finally demonstrated in pollen beetles from the UK, although in just a small sample of beetles from a frequently sprayed area.[37]

Away from agriculture, pollen beetle infestations can be a problem on crops such as calabrese and cauliflower (Chapter 6). Calls to control pollen beetles on oilseed rape as a means of overcoming such attacks, however, are unrealistic. Pollen beetles also have a nuisance value. The adults often alight in numbers on yellow clothing, to which they are strongly attracted. They may also be brought indoors on cut flowers, to the annoyance of florists and householders alike.

Pollen beetle larvae are attacked by various hymenopterous parasitoids. On winter rape, for example, the single-brooded ichneumonid wasps *Phradis interstitialis* and *Tersilochus heterocerus* hold sway. The life histories of these two generally common endoparasitoids are similar, but they differ in detail. Adults of *P. interstitialis* tend to appear on winter rape crops in the spring, well before flowering has begun. After mating, the adult females investigate the developing buds, searching for pollen beetle eggs or first-instar larvae. When a female locates a suitable host, a single egg is inserted through the bud wall, using the needle-like ovipositor.[38] Adults of *T. heterocerus* become active somewhat later, arriving in rape crops during the flowering period. Males arrive slightly ahead of females, often appearing above the crop canopies at the field borders in noticeable swarms. It is not unknown for such parasitoids to be mistaken for brassica pod midges (see below), and erroneously then perceived as a portent of impending doom! After mating, the females of *T. heterocerus* visit open flowers in their search for suitable hosts, preferring to oviposit in large, second-instar larvae.[39] The eggs of both parasitoid species hatch just before the pollen beetle larvae are fully fed. However, the parasitoid larvae do not complete their development until after their hosts have dropped to the ground and formed subterranean pupal chambers. The parasitoid larvae eventually pupate and individuals reach adulthood about a month later. They then overwinter *in situ*, eventually emerging in the spring. Parasitoids such as *P. intersitialis* and *T. heterocerus* can cause significant mortality within pollen beetle populations. Therefore, to minimise pesticide use it is important these natural enemies are conserved. Indeed, with the evolution of resistance to insecticides within pollen beetle populations, the role of such parasitoids in sustainable pest management strategies seems set to adopt an even higher profile.[40]

The natural enemies of pollen beetles include a range of predators. For example, adult pollen beetles are occasionally trapped in the webs of spiders, especially those of *Theridion* spp. (Fig. 88) and orb-web-forming species such as *Araneus cucurbitinus* and *Tetragnatha montana* (Fig. 89). They may also be ambushed by blossom-inhabiting hunters such as the crab spider *Misumena vatia*. Further, pollen beetle larvae feeding in oilseed rape flowers are vulnerable to predators such as ladybirds.[41] However, most losses amongst pollen beetle populations

FIG 88. Webs formed by spiders such as *Theridion* spp. frequently ensnare adult pollen beetles and other pests.

FIG 89. The orb-web spider *Tetragnatha montana* is often found in summer at the tips of oilseed rape plants, where it feeds on various invertebrates, including aphids, midges and other pests.

result from attacks on fully fed larvae, prepupae and pupae by polyphagous ground-dwelling predators. The common British ground beetle *Poecilus cupreus*,[42] whose peak numbers in oilseed rape fields (along with those of *Amara similata*) more or less coincide with the dropping of pollen beetle larvae,[43] is considered of particular importance. Species such as *Clivina fossor* and *Trechus quadristriatus*, which prey on the pre-adult stages in the soil, are also of significance.[44]

Susceptibility of pollen beetle to micro-organisms has been exploited in attempts to control larval populations.[45] For example, spraying crops with entomopathogenic nematodes (EPNs) can reduce pollen beetle numbers. Further, in cage experiments, the entomopathogenic fungus *Metarhizium flavoviride*[46] has been deployed on infested oilseed rape with the aid of honey bees (*Apis mellifera*) as vectors; 61 per cent control of pollen beetle larvae on winter rape and complete control of those on spring rape was obtained.[47] Open-field results, however, might prove less encouraging, since honey bees tend to avoid rape flowers infested by pollen beetles.[48]

Cabbage seed weevil

Cabbage seed weevil (*Ceutorhynchus assimilis*)[49] is a generally common pest of winter and spring oilseed rape. The weevils also breed on other brassica seed crops, but they do not attack white mustard. Overwintered adults (Fig. 90) first arrive on winter rape crops from about the yellow-bud stage onwards, becoming active at temperatures of 15°C and above. Numbers reach their peak in May, during the flowering period. In fine, still weather, mating pairs are often a common sight as they sit or wander over the racemes of host plants. Eggs are laid singly in the developing pods, the female inserting her ovipositor through a tiny hole bitten into the pod wall. Having deposited an egg, she marks the surface of the pod with a pheromone to deter other egg-laying females. The deterrent effect, however, lasts for no more than an hour or two.[50] Following egg hatch the larva feeds on the developing seeds, damaging several during the course of its development. When fully fed, the larva bores its way through the pod wall (leaving behind a characteristic pinhead-sized exit hole) (Fig. 91) and

FIG 90. In spring, cabbage seed weevils (*Ceutorhynchus assimilis*) often assemble on the flowers of oilseed rape plants.

FIG 91. Exit hole in the pod wall through which a fully fed cabbage seed weevil (*Ceutorhynchus assimilis*) larva has escaped, to pupate in the soil.

drops to the ground. If it evades the attentions of surface-dwelling predators, the larva then weaves its way into the soil, where it pupates in an earthen cell a few centimetres below the surface. New adults appear in July. These weevils feed briefly on various brassicaceous plants, including field vegetables, before hibernating. As in the case of pollen beetle, there is just one generation annually.

The pteromalid wasp *Trichomalus perfectus* ranks as the most influential natural enemy of cabbage seed weevil, and high rates of parasitism, often well in excess of 70 per cent, are frequently reported.[51] The importance of this vanguard species is such that it has been promoted as a key component of an integrated pest management (IPM) strategy for use on winter oilseed rape in England.[52] The metallic-green adult females appear in the spring, usually arriving on flowering winter rape crops two to four weeks after adult cabbage seed weevil numbers have reached their peak. The build-up of parasitoids then continues throughout June and into July.[53] Females arriving on the crop have immature ovaries and, in order to develop their eggs, the wasps must feed on cabbage seed weevil larvae – a phenomenon known as host feeding. Firstly, the parasitoid has to locate a larva inside a pod. Then, using the ovipositor, a crystalline feeding tube is formed that extends through the pod wall down to the prospective host. Once the tube is in place, and the body wall of the host breached, body fluids are drawn outwards by capillary action and the waiting female is able to imbibe them.

T. perfectus is a solitary ectoparasitoid which usually deposits eggs on third-instar host larvae. Females examining rape pods for the presence of suitable hosts perform a series of ritual antennal movements, described as 'radaring', 'touching', 'drumming' and 'stroking'; in the presence of a larva this

FIG 92. A larva of the encyrtid wasp *Trichomalus perfectus* feeding on that of its host – cabbage seed weevil.

activity is followed by tapping with the tip of the abdomen, insertion of the ovipositor and, finally, deposition of an egg.[54] The host larva is also stung, and immediately paralysed. The parasitoid egg hatches a few days later. The tiny larva then begins to devour its host (Fig. 92), and is fully fed a week to ten days later. Pupation occurs *in situ*, a young adult wasp emerging after about three weeks and escaping by biting its way out of the pod. Mating occurs soon afterwards, the mated females eventually overwintering.

Several other hymenopterous parasitoids are known to attack eggs, larvae or adults of cabbage seed weevil.[55] However, although they contribute to the overall natural mortality of the pest, none is as important as *T. perfectus*.

Other weevils

Cabbage stem weevil (*Ceutorhynchus pallidactylus*)[56] (Fig. 93) often breeds on oilseed rape, but is more important on spring-sown than on autumn-sown crops. Nevertheless, the adults are by no means uncommon on winter rape at the flowering stage, although they form but a fraction of ceutorhynchid weevil populations likely to be encountered at that time. Eggs are laid in the leaf stalks during the spring, inserted from below, either singly or in small groups. Following egg hatch, the larvae (Fig. 94) feed within the leaf stalks, and later invade the stems. Individuals are fully grown within a few weeks. They then enter the soil and pupate. Young adults emerge in the summer. They often then migrate in numbers to vegetable brassicas, where they graze briefly on the foliage before seeking overwintering sites. Infestations on winter rape are of little or no importance, but attacks on spring-sown crops can be harmful[57] and frequently justify the implementation of chemical control measures. The pest is also of

FIGS 93 & 94. (Above left) Cabbage stem weevil (*Ceutorhynchus pallidactylus*) occurs on oilseed rape crops from spring onwards. (Above right) Cabbage stem weevil larvae are more important on spring-sown rape than on the winter crop.

some significance on mustard crops.[58] It is possible that larval damage on crops can exacerbate problems of stem canker, allowing the pathogen more readily to gain entry to plants.[59] Abroad, as in northern France and northern Germany, winter rape crops are attacked by another species of stem weevil – the rape stem weevil (*C. napi*). This insect (Fig. 95) can be very damaging and is also a precursor of stem canker infections.[60] In addition, infested plants are particularly attractive to egg-laying cabbage stem weevils.[61] It has been speculated that rape stem weevil might sometimes spread from the near Continent to winter rape crops in southeast England. However, this has not been confirmed.

The small, black-bodied weevil *Ceutorhynchus typhae*[62] often inhabits oilseed rape fields. It is not in itself harmful, being associated mainly with brassicaceous

FIG 95. Larvae of rape stem weevil (*Ceutorhynchus napi*) cause extensive damage to winter rape crops in mainland Europe, but this pest has yet to be confirmed as occurring in Britain.

weeds such as shepherd's purse. Nevertheless, when present on flowering rape plants, the weevils are sometimes thought to be pests. Also, cases of mistaken identity are possible, especially after the weevils have blundered into water traps used to monitor cabbage seed weevils (their bloated corpses tending to be more difficult to distinguish from the target species than live weevils). The resulting erroneous elevation of recorded cabbage seed weevil numbers could result (and, in the past, might well have resulted) in the unnecessary application of insecticides.

Midges

Brassica pod midge (*Dasineura brassicae*) is a potentially important pest of oilseed rape and other brassica seed crops. However, like cabbage seed weevil (see above), it does not attack white mustard. The adults emerge from mid-May onwards. Mating takes place at emergence sites – primarily fields in which rape was grown during the previous year or so. The short-lived mated females then disperse to new crops. They are, however, weak fliers, and usually travel no more than few hundred metres. On arriving on winter rape or other suitable hosts, the midges begin to lay eggs in the developing pods, typically in batches of up to 30. The midges are unable to attack undamaged pods, and most frequently utilise feeding wounds or egg-laying punctures made in the pod walls by cabbage seed weevils. The midge eggs hatch a few days later. The whitish midge larvae (Fig. 96) then feed on the pod walls, or on the seeds, for up to four weeks. Infested pods (Fig. 97) split prematurely, and this allows the fully fed larvae to escape. The larvae then fall to the ground and eventually pupate in the soil, a few centimetres

FIGS 96 & 97. (Above left) Brassica pod midge (*Dasineura brassicae*) larvae feed gregariously on the walls of the pods. They do not attack the seeds, but ripening seeds are lost when the infested pods split open prematurely. (Above right) Pods damaged by the larvae show signs of premature splitting and senescence. On some hosts they are also noticeably swollen – hence the old epithet 'bladder pod midge'.

below the surface, each in a tiny silken cocoon. Second-generation adults emerge about two weeks later, and the females often utilise seed weevil larval exit holes in pod walls when seeking to oviposit. Some first-generation larvae in the soil do not pupate. Instead, they enter diapause, and the proportion doing so increases with each successive generation.[63] Diapause is eventually broken, some larvae remaining quiescent for up to three or more years before pupating. Third-generation midges appear too late in the season to be able to breed on winter rape. However, they may be able to attack spring rape or other such hosts if these are available nearby.[64]

As harvest time approaches, it is not uncommon for ripening oilseed pods to be damaged by birds, especially house sparrows. In such cases, V-shaped beak marks may be visible on the pod walls and the pods often break open, tulip fashion, from the tip. Also, the septum between the two splayed valves is usually broken. This premature pod shattering often occurs in patches on the field margins, and is sometimes blamed on brassica pod midges.[65] However, the midge larvae leave the septum intact. Also, when midge-infested pods split prematurely they do so along their length and open up from the base not the tip. Midge larvae (albeit usually pinkish in colour) are sometimes found inside bird-damaged pods, heightening confusion, but these are mycetophagous – merely feeding on fungi.

Many hymenopterous parasitoids attack brassica pod midge larvae.[66] However, by no means all published records can be substantiated. Not only are specimens sometimes misidentified, but host records themselves are by no means always reliable.[67] Published reports of several species of *Platygaster*, for example, might well in reality refer to *P. subuliformis*, a species first described as British in 1999.[68] In England, recent studies have centred on the platygastrid *P. subuliformis* and the eulophid *Omphale clypealis*. These are currently considered amongst the most important parasitoids of brassica pod midge, both here and elsewhere in Europe. *Platygaster* spp. are endoparasitoids, the parasitoid eggs being laid singly in those of their hosts. However, further development is deferred until host larvae reach maturity. Pupation eventually takes place in the pupal cocoons of the host, either immediately after completion of parasitoid larval development or after a period of diapause. *O. clypealis* is a solitary endoparasitoid, depositing eggs in older midge larvae shortly before they vacate the infested pods and enter the soil. Adults of both species are strongly attracted to isothiocyanates[69] (chemicals that emanate from damaged rape plants and thereby aid host location), as are female brassica pod midges and other specialist brassica-feeding insects.[70] As explained by Bernays and Chapman: 'glucosinolates are the *in vivo* precursors of the mustard oils, or isothiocyanates, and yield these acrid volatiles after enzymic hydrolysis. Whenever insects chew on such plants, myrosinase [an enzyme] acts on the glucosinolates to release isothiocyanates.'[71]

Naturally occurring predators also play a part in reducing brassica pod midge populations. The midges, for example, frequently fall victim to dance flies, long-legged flies, crab spiders, jumping spiders and orb-web spiders. Of these, dance flies have the greatest potential as natural biocontrol agents, owing to their general abundance in oilseed rape fields (up to 59 flies emerging/m^2)[72] and their rate of feeding (individuals devouring three midges/day).[73] The spider *Theridion impressum*, whose webs often abound in oilseed rape canopies, is also of some significance. Finally, on dropping to the soil, fully fed brassica pod midge larvae are inevitably vulnerable to attack from ground-dwelling predators; ground beetles, for example, prey avidly upon them.

CHAPTER 5

Pests of Beet, Mangold and Potato Crops

AROUND 150,000 HECTARES OF SUGAR beet and 140,000 hectares of potatoes are grown annually in the UK, usually as break crops in arable rotations. In addition, fodder beet and mangolds[1] are grown as food for cattle and sheep. Beets can be fed to animals as fresh roots. However, owing to the mild toxicity of the freshly lifted roots, mangolds must be stored in clamps for a couple of months (or more) before they can be used. In store, the roots are subject to attack by various pests, notably aphids and rats. They may also be invaded by fungi and other pathogens. There are similar problems with lifted potato tubers, especially in chitting houses (buildings in which potatoes are induced to sprout, i.e. induced to produce small shoots, prior to planting). Sugar beet, fodder beet and mangolds are all derived from our wild sea beet. Potatoes, however, are not indigenous to Europe, and it was not until the late sixteenth century that they first appeared here, probably having been introduced from South America by the Spanish. As a member of the family Solanaceae, the potato plant has few native British relatives.[2] Nevertheless, several highly polyphagous pests have found potato a suitable host, as have some more specialised herbivores. Indeed, the regularity with which several members of our fauna have adopted the crop and become regular pests is emphasised by their vernacular names: 'peach/potato aphid', 'potato capsid', 'potato flea beetle' and 'potato stem borer' – the last-mentioned referring to larvae of the rosy rustic moth (*Hydraecia micacea*) (Fig. 98) – are examples. Non-indigenous potato pests that have spread from South America and become established here are few and far between, although mention should be made of potato cyst nematodes (*Globodera* spp.) (see p. 117). In mainland Europe, the infamous Colorado beetle (*Leptinotarsa decemlineata*) can also be cited.

Production of sugar beet is dependent upon the availability and accessibility

FIG 98. Rosy rustic moth (*Hydraecia micacea*) is particularly common in weedy sites, and sometimes of significance as a pest of potato and other crops. When infesting potato plants, the larvae are commonly known as potato stem borers.

of sugar-processing factories. These are fewer in number than previously. Consequently, sugar beet crops are nowadays centred mainly in the West Midlands (Herefordshire and Shropshire) and eastern England (from Yorkshire in the north to Essex in the south). Potatoes are grown far more widely, in England, Scotland, Wales and Ireland.

SUCKING INSECT PESTS

Aphids

Beet and potato crops are frequently invaded by aphids. Not only do such pests cause direct damage to host plants but, more significantly, they introduce and spread virus diseases. Several species are involved (Table 2), varying from major to minor pests. On beet, two species – black bean aphid (*Aphis fabae*), a typical blackfly, and peach/potato aphid (*Myzus persicae*), a typical greenfly – are of particular concern, the latter primarily as a virus vector. On potato, glasshouse & potato aphid (*Aulacorthum solani*) (Fig. 99), peach/potato aphid and potato aphid (*Macrosiphum euphorbiae*) are usually of greatest significance.

Black bean aphid overwinters in the egg stage on wild spindle bushes. The eggs hatch in early spring, and wingless females then feed on the bursting buds and unfurling leaves. When mature, these first-generation aphids give rise to a second generation of wingless females which in turn usually produce winged females. In late May or early June, these spring migrants depart for summer (secondary) hosts, including sugar beet and (rarely) potato. Other targeted plants include field bean, fodder beet, lettuce, mangold, red beet, runner bean and spinach, and weeds such

TABLE 2. Examples of aphid pests of beet and potato crops.

Species	*Beet*	*Potato*	*Lifecycle (see text)*
Black bean aphid (*Aphis fabae*)	+	+	Holocyclic
Buckthorn/potato aphid (*Aphis nasturtii*)	–	+	Holocyclic
Bulb & potato aphid (*Rhopalosiphoninus latysiphon*)	+	+	Anholocyclic
Glasshouse & potato aphid (*Aulacorthum solani*)	+	+	Anholocyclic and holocyclic
Mangold aphid (*Rhopalosiphoninus staphyleae*)	+	–	Anholocyclic
Peach/potato aphid (*Myzus persicae*)	+	+	Anholocyclic, rarely holocyclic
Potato aphid (*Macrosiphum euphorbiae*)	+	+	Mainly anholocyclic
Shallot aphid (*Myzus ascalonicus*)	+	+	Anholocyclic
Violet aphid (*Myzus ornatus*)	–	+	Anholocyclic

+ Present.
– Absent.

FIG 99. Glasshouse & potato aphid (*Aulacorthum solani*) often occurs on potato plants but, unlike some aphid species, it is not an important virus vector.

as fat-hen. Reproduction on these hosts is entirely parthenogenetic and viviparous, there being a succession of wingless, asexual generations throughout the summer months. Colonies reach their peak in July or August and, eventually, perhaps in response to a deteriorating food supply or colony overcrowding,[3] winged female morphs are produced, followed by winged males. The winged female migrants fly to their primary hosts (spindle bushes), where they give rise to a generation of wingless, egg-laying females. These mate with immigrating winged males and finally deposit the winter eggs. As outlined in Chapter 2, aphids adopting this kind of lifecycle, in which both sexual and asexual reproduction occurs, and where the winter is passed in the egg stage, are described as holocyclic; anholocyclic aphids, on the other hand, breed asexually throughout the year and do not undertake a sexual phase. In Britain, peach/potato aphid (a typically holocyclic species, with nectarine and peach trees acting as the primary hosts) overwinters largely as adults and nymphs, having developed clones that are anholocyclic. Winter hosts for such aphids include outdoor vegetable brassica crops and various other herbaceous plants.[4] Oilseed rape is also now an important winter host for peach/potato aphid (Chapter 4), and an early source of spring immigrants to beet, mangold and potato crops. Aphids (including glasshouse & potato aphid, peach/potato aphid and potato aphid) can similarly overwinter in greenhouses and subsequently give rise to spring migrants that may invade outdoor crops.[5]

The aphid menace continues on stored crops. Mangold aphid (*Rhopalosiphoninus staphyleae*) and peach/potato aphid, for example, frequently overwinter in mangold clamps. Winged migrants are then produced in the spring. These pose a particularly significant risk to nearby beet and mangold crops since most if not all clamps are likely to harbour aphids that carry transmissible virus diseases.[6] Bulb & potato aphid (*R. latysiphon*), glasshouse & potato aphid, peach/potato aphid and potato aphid commonly infest the sprouting shoots of stored potato tubers. Shoots can be killed, most frequently following infestations of bulb & potato aphid and glasshouse & potato aphid on seed potatoes.

Aphid-borne viruses are classified as non-persistent, semi-persistent or persistent. A non-persistent virus is acquired by an adult aphid or nymph within a few minutes if not seconds of feeding, the virus particles adhering to the mouthpart stylets. The stylet-borne virus is then immediately capable of being transmitted, but the aphid vector remains infective for only a short time. A semi-persistent virus is acquired after the potential vector has fed for about ten minutes, and the aphid remains infective for several days; the virus is lost, however, if (as might be the case in an aphid nymph) the insect moults. Persistent viruses are acquired after several hours to a day or more, usually following extended feeding from the phloem of the host plant. This is followed by a protracted latent period, during which the virus particles pass from the aphid's digestive tract, via the haemolymph, into the salivary glands. Transmission then becomes possible, and infectivity is long-term and not halted by moulting.

Various aphids act as virus vectors on beet and potato crops. However, peach/potato aphid is by far the most effective and efficient. Viruses transmitted by this species include:

- **beet mosaic virus (BMV)** and **potato virus Y (PVY)**, both of which are non-persistent;

- **beet yellows virus (BYV)**, which is semi-persistent;
- **beet chlorosis virus (BChV)**, **beet mild yellowing virus (BMYV)** and **potato leaf roll virus (PLRV)**, all of which are persistent.

Either individually or in combination, viruses on beet crops produce a condition widely known as virus yellows disease. Unlike peach/potato aphid, black bean aphid is an ineffective vector of beet viruses and unimportant as a vector of PVY. Bulb & potato aphid, buckthorn/potato aphid (*Aphis nasturtii*), glasshouse & potato aphid, potato aphid, shallot aphid (*Myzus ascalonicus*) and violet aphid (*M. ornatus*) are also of minor significance as virus vectors.

There is also some field transmission of non-persistent viruses by winged aphids that neither feed upon nor colonise beet or potato crops. This is accomplished when such aphid visitors probe the foliage with their mouthparts whilst seeking out their legitimate summer hosts. They thereby acquire and spread non-persistent viruses. In this regard, leaf-curling plum aphid (*Brachycaudus helichrysi*) is a well-known casual vector of PYV in the UK,[7] and particularly important in years when vast numbers of spring migrants arise from their primary *Prunus* hosts. Such aphids then spread widely as part of the aerial plankton. Other casual virus vectors on potato include bird-cherry/oat aphid (*Rhopalosiphum padi*), damson/hop aphid (*Phorodon humuli*) and rose/grain aphid (*Metopolophium dirhodum*). Non-persistent viruses of beet crops are spread similarly. During the growing season, numbers of aphids on beet and potato crops are likely to be depleted by natural enemies, especially polyphagous and specialist aphidophagous predators. However, these cannot be expected to exert adequate levels of control, and they are of little or no direct value in preventing the spread of non-persistent viruses.

Miscellaneous plant bugs

Apart from aphids, plant bugs are relatively unimportant on beet, mangold and potato. Nevertheless, several species inhabit such crops and some breed on the foliage during the spring and summer. Leafhoppers, for example, frequently occur on potato crops, infested leaves developing whitish speckles or patches and often appearing mottled. Two kinds of lifecycle are demonstrated by these insects. *Empoasca decipiens*, for example, overwinters in the adult stage, individuals finding shelter amongst evergreen trees and shrubs (including ivy). With the arrival of spring the adults invade herbaceous plants, where eggs are eventually laid. Nymphs develop during June and July, and new adults appear from August onwards. Many leafhoppers exhibit a quite different lifecycle, overwintering in the egg stage. This is so in the case of *Eupteryx aurata* (Fig. 100), a species associated with stinging nettles but commonly found feeding on potato

FIG 100. Potato leafhopper (*Eupteryx aurata*) is often found on potato plants, but is far more abundant on nettles.

foliage during the late summer. Other leafhoppers known to occur on potato include *Empoasca vitis* and *Eupteryx atropunctata*. These are joined by mainly tree-infesting species (such as *Edwardsiana flavescens* and *Eupterycyba jucunda*) which spread into crops during the summer from nearby hedgerows. Although adult leafhoppers often feed on the foliage of sugar beet, the damage they cause is insignificant. Abroad, leafhoppers are known to transmit beet curly top virus (BCTV).[8] However, this virus does not occur in Britain; nor do the known vectors, such as the North American beet leafhopper (*Circulifer tenellus*).

Again abroad, another sugar beet virus – beet leaf curl virus (BLCV) – is transmitted by the beet leaf bug (*Piesma quadratum*). In East Anglia, this insect inhabits grass-leaved orache, sea beet, sea purslane and other coastal or salt marsh plants. However, although in the past recorded on sugar beet, the bugs do not appear to migrate from their wild hosts into neighbouring sugar beet crops, and they are not regarded as pests.[9] The related spinach leaf bug (*P. maculatum*), although recorded in sugar beet fields in England, including the Brecklands of Norfolk, also has no pest status. It is most often found on fat-hen.

Mirids (capsids) are sometimes numerous in sugar beet and potato fields, especially on headland plants growing close to hedgerows. Common green capsid (*Lygocoris pabulinus*) and potato capsid (*Closterotomus norvegicus*),[10] for example, spend the winter as eggs laid in the rind of woody or succulent plants. Later, following egg hatch, the highly active nymphs feed on a wide range of hosts, including potato and sugar beet. When common green capsid nymphs attack beet seedlings they retard growth; damaged cotyledons typically become brittle, thickened and noticeably elongated.[11] Potato capsid is particularly well-known for causing shot-holing and tattering of foliage on both sugar beet and potato plants. A third species, the European tarnished plant bug (*Lygus*

FIG 101. European tarnished plant bug (*Lygus rugulipennis*) is a pest of many crops, including potato and sugar beet.

rugulipennis) (Fig. 101), also occurs during the growing season, especially on sugar beet. This species overwinters in the adult stage, hibernating amongst leaf litter in ditches, dykes and hedgerows. The bugs become active in the spring and are then numerous on various weeds, notably Chenopodiaceae. They often attack sugar beet seedlings, injecting toxic saliva into the plants as they feed; this can result in the death of growing points.[12] Damage later in the season can lead to the development of backward, multi-headed plants. In Scotland, although European tarnished plant bugs are recorded on various crops, including potatoes, they are not considered of significance. This relates to the slow development of nymphs, and their tendency to inhabit and feed selectively on

FIG 102. Common nettle capsid (*Liocoris tripustulatus*) feeds on various plants, including potato, but is most abundant on nettles.

weeds during the early part of the season (the time when crop plants would be most susceptible to damage).[13] Other species on potato include common nettle capsid (*Liocoris tripustulatus*) (Fig 102) and slender grey capsid (*Dicyphus errans*). Common nettle capsid is entirely phytophagous and most abundant on stinging nettles. However, it also invades other plants. In recent years it has even become a pest of vegetable crops being raised in commercial greenhouses (Chapter 9). Slender grey capsid is essentially predacious, attacking aphids and other arthropods. Nevertheless, it also probes potato leaves and imbibes the sap, plant food being an essential component of its overall diet.[14] This bug has long, slender legs and is well adapted for walking over plants (such as potato) that have hairy leaves, the leaf hairs proving no barrier to its progress.[15]

MITES

Mites are rarely of significance as pests of arable crops. However, in summer or early autumn, two-spotted spider mite (*Tetranychus urticae*) sometimes becomes evident in potato and sugar beet crops. The mites form colonies on the underside of the leaves, amongst strands of silken webbing, where they feed and breed. Infested leaves are discoloured and may develop a yellow mottling. On sugar beet, such symptoms are easily mistaken for those of virus yellows disease. Mite attacks are favoured by long, hot summers and generally appear to be on the increase, especially on sugar beet.[16]

LEAF GRAZERS

Leaf-grazing moth larvae (caterpillars) frequently occur on sugar beet and potato plants. Examples include the larvae of angle-shades moth (*Phlogophora meticulosa*), silver Y moth (*Autographa gamma*) (Fig. 103) and tomato moth (*Lacanobia oleracea*) – the last-mentioned species is also known amongst lepidopterists as the bright-line brown-eye. All three pests are associated with a wide range of crops, both agricultural and horticultural. On beet, there is also the likelihood in late spring and early summer of finding larvae of the flax tortrix moth (*Cnephasia asseclana*) (Fig. 104) spun up on the leaves. Less often, as famously happened in 1958 (when conditions particularly favoured development of indigenous populations and these were further swollen by mass immigration from mainland Europe),[17] diamond-back moth (*Plutella xylostella*) also invades sugar beet crops. This worldwide pest, however, is associated mainly with Brassicaceae. Rarely,

FIGS 103 & 104. (Above left) Silver Y moth (*Autographa gamma*) larvae are sometimes numerous in potato and sugar beet fields. Note the reduced number of abdominal prolegs compared with most members of the family Noctuidae; this is typical of the subfamily Plusiinae. (Above right) Flax tortrix moth (*Cnephasia asseclana*) larvae are sometimes found amongst spun leaves on sugar beet plants.

larvae of the death's head hawk moth (*Acherontia atropos*) (Fig. 105) – unlike diamond-back moth an infrequent migrant to these shores – are encountered in potato fields, especially during the autumn. The large pupae (Fig. 106) might also be unearthed when potatoes are lifted. In spite of their appetites and size –

FIG 105. Death's head hawk moth (*Acherontia atropos*) larvae are a rare sight on potato plants in Britain. They are never numerous and, in spite of their large size (individuals up to 125 mm long when fully grown), do little damage.

FIG 106. Death's head hawk moth (*Acherontia atropos*) pupae are sometimes unearthed when potatoes are lifted.

individual larvae exceed 125 mm in length when fully grown – larvae should not be considered worthy of destruction as they are never numerous. Also, the damage they cause to potato crops is restricted to localised loss of foliage and is not of economic importance. With a wingspan that sometimes exceeds 135 mm, the death's head hawk moth (Fig. 107) is one of our largest insects. It is a spectacular prize sought by many a lepidopterist, usually without success!

FIG 107. With a wingspan of up to 135 mm, death's head hawk moth (*Acherontia atropos*) is the largest of all British moths.

FIG 108. Sand weevil (*Philopedon plagiatum*) inhabits light soils, and adult sometimes graze on the leaves of sugar beet plants. Attacks on seedlings are of particular significance.

Although not leaf-grazing pests, the reddish-brown to pinkish larvae of rosy rustic moth attack the aerial parts of potato plants. They bore into the stems at about ground level and then tunnel upwards within the pith, eventually causing plants to wilt and collapse. Such larvae are known as potato stem borers. This polyphagous pest is associated with many herbaceous plants, including docks, horsetails, plantains and sedges, and the presence of such weeds increases the likelihood of attacks developing on field crops.

Various herbivorous beetles graze on the leaves of beet or potato plants, some as adults and others as both adults and larvae. Excluding the alien Colorado beetle on potato, these include beet carrion beetle (*Aclypea opaca*), sand weevils (*Philopedon plagiatum*)[18] (Fig. 108) and tortoise beetles (*Cassida* spp.), all of which occur on sugar beet. Beet carrion beetle adults hibernate in grass tussocks and leaf litter, and in other sheltered situations, especially at the margins of copses or other wooded sites. The beetles become active from mid-April onwards, and then invade beet crops to feed on the cotyledons and developing leaves. Eggs are eventually laid in the soil and hatch a few days later. The flattened, shiny black and distinctly segmented, woodlouse-like larvae then feed openly on the foliage. Characteristically, large, irregular sections of leaf tissue are grazed away and slimy black excrement is deposited on the plants. The larvae are fully fed in about three weeks. They then pupate in the soil and new adults emerge about a fortnight later. Although there is just one generation annually, a protracted period of egg-laying means that all stages of the pest occur together during the summer months. Beet carrion beetle was formerly of some significance in beet and mangold crops.[19] However, nowadays infestations are rarely found. Sand weevils are usually minor pests of sugar beet crops growing on sandy soils, as in the Brecklands of East Anglia. The adult weevils notch the margins of cotyledons and leaves, and heavy infestations on seedlings have been known to cause complete crop failure. Feeding follows the emergence of overwintered weevils in April, and can persist into June. However, the rather bulbous-bodied weevils usually escape attention as they are generally active at night and hide in the soil during daytime. The soil-inhabiting larvae feed on the roots of grasses and various other plants, and take about 18 months to complete their development.

Tortoise beetles, of which three species are recorded on sugar beet, are interesting but inconsequential crop pests in Britain. The yellowish-brown or greenish, tortoise-shaped adults overwinter in leaf litter and other shelter, emerging in spring from April onwards. They then feed on the foliage of weeds such as fat-hen and sea beet; at this time they also damage sugar beet seedlings. In the case of beet tortoise beetle (*Cassida nobilis*), a single-brooded species, eggs are laid on the foliage, either singly or in small groups. They hatch about two weeks later. The flattened, distinctly spinose larvae, each armed with a bifid fork-like caudal spine, then feed on the foliage from mid-May onwards. Presumably as protection against predators, larvae of tortoise beetles often adorn themselves with frass and cast skins of earlier instars, such debris readily adhering to their spiny bodies (Fig. 109). Beet tortoise beetle larvae are fully grown in about a month. Pupation then takes place on the underside of the expanded leaves, and new adults emerge about two weeks later. *Cassida vittata*, a greenish and somewhat metallic-looking species, also occurs on sugar beet and can complete two generations annually. However, the cloudy tortoise beetle

FIG 109. Beet tortoise beetle (*Cassida vittata*) larvae partly coat themselves with excrement.

(*C. nebulosa*), another double-brooded species, is rarely found on sugar beet. It breeds mainly on common orache and fat-hen.

Flea beetles also inhabit beet and potato fields, and adults immediately leap into the air when disturbed. Some, as in the case of many *Phyllotreta* spp., are associated with charlock and other brassicaceous weeds, and have no interest in the planted crops (other than, perhaps, as possible landing stages). However, mangold flea beetle (*Chaetocnema concinna*) and potato flea beetle (*Psylliodes affinis*) are regarded as potentially harmful (the former to beet and mangold, the latter to potato), causing shot-holing of cotyledons and leaves. Beet seedlings are particularly vulnerable, but damage is rarely of significance unless plants are invaded at an early stage of development. Both pests are single brooded. Their larvae feed during the summer on the roots of host plants.

Warm, damp weather in late spring and early summer encourages foliage-feeding springtails such as the lucerne-flea (*Sminthurus viridis*) (see Fig. A.2, p. 410) to attack sugar beet plants. But for their mobility and habit of jumping, these tiny, yellowish or greenish, globular insects could easily be mistaken for small wingless aphids.

LEAF MINERS

Mangold fly (*Pegomya hyoscyami*) is a generally common leaf-mining pest of sugar beet. Attacks also occur on related plants, including fodder beet, mangold, red beet and spinach. The housefly-like adults are active in the early spring from April to early June. Eggs are then deposited in small batches on the underside of the leaves of host plants and hatch about five days later. The robust, maggot-like larvae (Fig. 110), known as beet leaf miners, feed gregariously in large, blister-like

FIG 110. Mangold fly (*Pegomya hyoscyami*) larvae feed gregariously in blotch mines on the leaves of mangold and sugar beet.

FIG 111. Blotch mines formed by mangold fly (*Pegomya hyoscyami*) larvae are a common sight in sugar beet fields.

blotch mines (Fig. 111) and are fully fed in about two weeks. They then pupate in the soil and adults of the next generation appear in July. Larvae of a second brood complete their development in late summer or early autumn. At least in favourable situations there can be another full or partial generation. Affected leaves appear scorched, such damage being most obvious in August and September. Although attacks can result in the death of young plants (mines often occupying complete leaves and totally destroying cotyledons), the impact of the pest is usually minor. However, this might not be so where beet crops are drilled to a stand – i.e. where the seed rate is set to provide the required number of plants per unit area, with little or no allowance for post-germination losses.

SOIL-INHABITING INSECT PESTS

Polyphagous soil-dwelling insect pests such as bibionid fly larvae, chafer grubs, leatherjackets and wireworms sometimes damage sugar beet and potato crops. Infestations most often develop when long-term grassland is brought into arable production. Wireworms in particular have long been considered important on potatoes. The pests often bore into the tubers, forming narrow, more or less straight channels that extend well into the flesh. Wireworms are long-term but periodic feeders, and tend to cause most damage from March to May and from September to October. Several species are involved, especially the generally common lowland species *Agriotes lineatus*, *A. obscurus* and *A. sputator*. Of these, *A. lineatus* (Fig. 112) is the dominant species in eastern and southern England, whereas *A. obscurus* occurs mainly in the north. Other species known to damage potatoes include *Athous haemorrhoidalis* (Fig. 113) and upland wireworms (*Ctenicera* spp.). Wireworm problems on potato crops have increased in recent years, but the reasons for this are unclear.[20]

FIGS 112 & 113. (Above left) *Agriotes lineatus* is the dominant species of click beetle in eastern and southern England, and the larvae frequently bore into potato tubers. (Above right) Garden click beetle (*Athous haemorrhoidalis*) larvae attack potatoes and roots of many other plants.

FIG 114. Ghost swift moth (*Hepialus humuli*) larvae are often a problem in weedy sites.

Weedy sites similarly encourage attacks by polyphagous soil-inhabiting pests. Garden swift moth (*Hepialus lupulinus*) and ghost swift moth (*H. humuli*) (Fig. 114), for example, are particularly troublesome in fields where perennial weeds such as dandelions, docks and nettles are rampant.[21] The dusk-flying adults occur mainly in May and June (garden swift moth) or June and July (ghost swift moth). At dusk, the mainly white-winged males of the latter species (which are very different from the yellowish-ochreous, reddish-tinged females) (Fig. 115) are sometimes to be seen hovering ghost-like in the air: hence the insect's vernacular name.

As on carrots, lettuces and other vegetables (Chapter 6) cutworms also cause damage to beet and potato crops, especially on lighter soils and in hot, dry conditions. Turnip moth (*Agrotis segetum*) (Fig. 116) is the most important species, and the larvae (most of which arise from eggs laid in June) attack the subterranean parts of plants from July through to lifting. On potato, large but typically shallow wounds are often formed in the flesh of the tubers (Fig. 117);

FIG 115. Ghost swift moth (*Hepialus humuli*) is a pest of many crops. Males (above left) and females (above right) differ markedly in appearance.

FIG 116. Turnip moth (*Agrotis segetum*) is generally the most abundant and important species of cutworm.

FIG 117. Cutworms frequently bore into potato tubers, forming distinctive cavities.

similar but deeper cavities are usually the work of chafer grubs, swift moth larvae or slugs.[22] Larvae of garden dart moth (*Euxoa nigricans*) (another cutworm species) are also pests of potato and sugar beet, particularly on fenland soils in eastern England.[23] Unlike turnip moth larvae, they cause damage from March to June, rather than in the summer and autumn (see Chapter 6).

Other soil-inhabiting insect pests include pygmy mangold beetle (*Atomaria linearis*), a minute reddish-brown to blackish insect about 1.5 mm long, which is a common pest of beet and mangold crops. Indeed, before the introduction of strict crop rotations in the mid-1930s – essentially to avoid cyst nematode infestations (see below) – it was one of our most important pests of seedling sugar beet. Pygmy mangold beetles overwinter in the fields where they were reared. From March or April onwards they then move into new beet or mangold crops. The beetles undertake mass migration flights from their former breeding grounds, the first usually occurring in fine weather in the early spring at ambient temperatures around 20°C. Cool, inclement conditions, however, mean that such flights are delayed, perhaps until the end of May if not later. The beetles attack germinating seedlings at or below ground level, damaging the hypocotyl and developing rootlets. Affected tissue develops characteristic oval pits which turn black, and heavily infested seedlings may die. The adult beetles also feed amongst the developing heart leaves of emerged seedlings. Egg-laying takes place in the soil over an extended period, from April onwards. Subsequently, tiny whitish larvae feed on the roots of host plants but the damage they cause is not of significance. New adults appear throughout the summer and autumn months. Early-emerging individuals are themselves able to breed and produce a second generation. Pygmy mangold beetle is periodically abundant and populations in

FIG 118. Spotted snake millepede (*Blaniulus guttulatus*) is a minor pest of potatoes. Attacks also occur on other crops; for example, particularly in dry conditions, ripening strawberries in contact with the soil may be damaged.

heavily infested fields can reach several million per hectare. However, owing to their small size and secretive nature, the beetles and their larvae are often overlooked even when they are present in large numbers.

Root damage similar to that caused by pygmy mangold beetle is also inflicted on sugar beet by white blind springtails (*Onychiurus* spp.), and by non-insect pests such as glasshouse symphylids (*Scutigerella immaculata*) and spotted snake millepedes (*Blaniulus guttulatus*) (Fig. 118). Symphylids and millepedes also cause injury to potato tubers.

NEMATODES

Free-living, ectoparasitic nematodes

Various free-living (migratory) plant-parasitic nematodes inhabit arable soils, especially (although by no means exclusively) in well-drained sites. Such pests include needle nematodes (*Longidorus* spp.) and stubby-root nematodes (*Paratrichodorus* spp. and *Trichodorus* spp.), some of which attack sugar beet and potato crops. Direct or indirect damage (the latter following transmission of plant-pathogenic viruses or subsequent invasion of nematode-damaged tissue by other pathogens) is of considerable significance, and can have a profound effect on plant growth and crop yields. Such nematodes feed externally on the roots, probing the tips with their piercing stylets. Although infestations most often occur in light, open-textured soils, *L. leptocephalus* is a denizen of heavy land and renowned for reducing potato yields by feeding on roots below cultivation depth.

Needle nematodes are long-lived and develop slowly. The well-known crop pest *L. elongatus*, for example, develops from egg to adult in about a year, egg-laying typically coinciding with active root growth of host plants. Stubby root nematodes develop far more quickly than needle nematodes. Under favourable, moisture-rich conditions they complete several generations annually, and this allows a rapid escalation of field populations.

Sugar beet crops attacked by needle nematodes and stubby-root nematodes are stunted, and often develop distorted, fangy roots. Such symptoms were originally mistaken for those caused by acidity, soil compaction, waterlogging and other abiotic factors, and it was not until 1948 that soil-inhabiting nematodes were eventually implicated as primary antagonists. Nematodes typically give rise to a condition described as Docking disorder – so named after the parish of Docking in Norfolk where such damage was first found. In some beet-growing regions, needle nematodes are the main culprits, but in others stubby-root nematodes are more important. Field symptoms of Docking disorder become apparent from the two-rough-leaf stage onwards, appearing as patches of irregular growth within crops. Characteristically, a so-called 'hen and chicks' symptom develops, with large plants (the 'hens') occurring adjacent to several small, stunted ones (the 'chicks'). Owing to the vigorous growth exhibited by the former, size differences between such plants can be as much as twentyfold.[24]

Stubby-root nematodes are also of note as vectors of tobacco rattle virus (TRV), a disease of potato and certain other crops. These nematodes occur mainly in light, open-textured soils, as in the sandy parts of Norfolk and the Vale of York;[25] stubby-root nematodes are also common in light, well-drained arable soils in Scotland.[26] TRV induces a condition called spraign. This disorder affects the quality of tubers, but there are no field symptoms. Typically, the flesh (parenchymatous tissue) develops chestnut-brown streaks or other such markings, which become visible when tubers are sliced through. Potato mop top virus (PMTV) causes identical symptoms, but is transmitted by *Spongospora subterranea* – the fungal pathogen which causes powdery scab disease. Potato cultivars vary in their susceptibility to spraign; cvs Maris Bard and Pentland Dell, for example, are highly susceptible.[27] Needle nematodes are also well-known vectors of plant viruses. *L. attenuatus* and *L. elongatus*, for instance, transmit tomato black ring virus (TBRV) to potato, sugar beet and various other crops.

Nematode virus vectors must first acquire a viral pathogen by feeding at the root tip of an infected host plant. The ability to do so is shared by both adults and juveniles, and infection is acquired after a relatively short period of feeding (up to an hour). The virus particles adhere to the mouthparts (for example, the stylet sheath or the cuticular lining of the oesophagus or pharynx), and are transferred to new hosts when the nematode again feeds. Infectivity persists in adults, but is lost when a juvenile nematode moults and thereby sheds its old stylet and cuticle.[28]

Cyst-forming nematodes

Cyst nematodes are serious pests of sugar beet and potato, and they rank very highly in terms of their economic importance. The threat posed by cyst nematodes is emphasised by the presence of Plant Health orders that relate specifically to them. Such controls were initially drawn up as domestic statutory instruments. These included the Beet Eelworm Order (which applied to England and Wales, and was first introduced in 1943) and the first Potato Root Eelworm Order (Northern Ireland) which dated back to 1945. In addition, a Potato Cyst Eelworm (Great Britain) Order was imposed in 1973, to meet the requirements of a

European Commission directive. In essence, these are restriction orders to limit the frequency at which host crops can be grown in any particular field. Regulatory control of crop pests in Britain began with the Destructive Insects Act of 1877. This followed the discovery, in 1877, of a live Colorado beetle (even then feared as a major potato pest) at Liverpool docks on a ship carrying a consignment of wheat from America. Colorado beetle is discussed further in Chapter 12.

Beet cyst nematode (*Heterodera schachtii*) causes stunting of sugar beet and mangold crops, leading to a condition known as beet sickness or mangold sickness. This pest is well established in peaty fenland soils in East Anglia, particularly where the water table is high. Other hot spots include northeast Norfolk and the Isle of Axholme in north Lincolnshire. In addition to sugar beet and related crops, the nematode often infests vegetable brassicas, as in the West Midlands. It also breeds on oilseed rape and various weeds, including charlock, shepherd's purse and many other Brassicaceae.[29] Beet cyst nematodes survive the winter in the soil as first-stage juveniles, curled within minute eggs which are themselves packed inside brown, lemon-shaped cysts. Each cyst is formed from the dead body wall of a swollen female nematode, and typically contains hundreds of eggs. The eggs often remain viable for several years. However, usually about half hatch in their first year, each egg giving rise to an infective second-stage juvenile. Hatching is enhanced by the presence of root exudates from suitable host plants.[30] The highly mobile second-stage nematodes invade the roots, where they eventually develop through two further juvenile stages before reaching adulthood. As previously described for cereal cyst nematode (*Heterodera avenae*) (Chapter 2), greatly enlarged adult females break through the root surface. Here they remain temporarily attached until, after mating, they eventually die and become detached from the root. There are normally two generations annually, and frequency of cropping is particularly important in governing the build-up of field populations in beet-growing areas.[31] Under the current British Sugar contract with growers, sugar beet must not be sown where any *Beta* crop (i.e. beet or related) has been grown during either of the previous two years (i.e. closer than one year in three). Appropriate rotation of sugar beet crops in England has been encouraged or enforced since the mid-1930s,[32] and restricting the frequency with which beet or mangolds are grown on any particular site has also, fortuitously, led to a reduction in the importance of pygmy mangold beetle (p. 114).

Potato cyst nematode (PCN) is a major pest of potatoes worldwide, and can have a dramatic impact on crop yields.[33] PCN was probably first introduced to these islands from its Andean homeland in the mid-1800s. At that time much seed material was being imported from South America in attempts to find blight-resistant cultivars that might halt the Irish potato famine. Although the pest had been known for many years, it was not until the 1970s that it was recognised as comprising two distinct species: white potato cyst nematode (*G. pallida*) and yellow potato cyst nematode (*G. rostochiensis*).[34] Specific differences are best appreciated as the females on host roots mature, their swollen bodies temporarily appearing white or cream in the former and golden yellow in the latter before eventually turning brown and becoming soil-borne cysts. Unlike cysts of beet cyst nematode and other species of *Heterodera*, those of *Globodera* spp. are rounded, not lemon-shaped. The life history of PCN is similar to that of beet cyst nematode, but there is usually just one generation annually. There is also noticeable spontaneous hatching of eggs in the spring, in addition to that stimulated by host root exudates. Nevertheless, cysts surviving in the soil often contain viable eggs for more than a decade. Of the two potato-infesting species, white PCN has become dominant in areas where potatoes are grown for consumption (i.e. as ware crops) rather than for seed. This is due, in part, to the slower decline of soil populations of this particular species in the absence of host plants and to the lack of potato cultivars resistant to attack.

Non-cyst-forming endoparasitic nematodes on beet crops

Cereal root-knot nematode (*Meloidogyne naasi*) and northern root-knot nematode (*M. hapla*), which inhabit knot-like galls on the roots of various hosts (Fig. 119), sometimes occur on sugar beet plants. However, although important pests in other parts of the world, they are not considered of significance on beet crops in Britain.[35]

FIG **119.** Galls inhabited by northern root-knot nematode (*Meloidogyne hapla*) are sometimes found on the roots of sugar beet plants.

Non-cyst-forming endoparasitic nematodes on potato crops

Potato tuber nematode (*Ditylenchus destructor*), once thought to be merely a biological race of the ubiquitous and notorious stem nematode (*D. dipsaci*), invades potato tubers via the 'eyes' and lenticels. The endoparasitic nematodes then feed and breed within the flesh (parenchyma), especially around the periphery. Adults, eggs and juveniles occur together, and breeding is continuous so long as conditions remain favourable. Infested tissue eventually becomes desiccated and spongy, and gradually darkens as secondary pathogens (e.g. bacteria and fungi) gain a foothold. The overlying skin also dries out and cracks, becoming noticeably wrinkled and papery. Unless heavily infested tubers are planted out as seed, the pest has no impact on the growth of host plants and there are no obvious above-ground symptoms. However, damage to the tubers may be seen when crops are lifted and is exacerbated if infested potatoes are stored under damp conditions. Over the years, infestations on potato crops have been particularly significant on fenland farms in East Anglia. The underground parts of various other plants, including dahlia tubers, bulbous iris and tulip bulbs, also serve as hosts, as do the creeping rhizomes of corn mint and, less frequently, corn sow-thistle. The presence or absence of wild hosts such as corn mint probably determines whether or not the pest survives on land supporting typical potato-growing crop rotations.

Stem nematode, although a common endoparasite of many crops (e.g. Chapter 6), is rarely found on potato crops in Britain. However, when present, the nematodes cause stunting, swelling and distortion of leaves and stems. Infestations may also occur in the tubers, damage typically extending deeper into the flesh than that caused by potato tuber nematode.[36]

Although of minor importance, root-lesion nematodes (*Pratylenchus* spp.) are sometimes associated with potato crops. These nematodes (of which *P. penetrans* is the most abundant British species)[37] are known as migratory endoparasites, the adults and juveniles feeding both on and in the roots. Lesions made in the roots subsequently become invaded by pathogenic bacteria and fungi.

SLUGS

In appropriate conditions, slugs often find potato fields ideal feeding and breeding grounds. They not only graze on the foliage but, as subterranean feeders, also benefit from a readily available and seemingly inexhaustible food supply in the developing tubers. In common with several other potato pests,

TABLE 3. Examples of slugs attacking potato crops.[38]

Species	*Remarks*
Family Agriolimacidae	
Field slug (*Deroceras reticulatum*)	Generally abundant, feeding mainly above soil level
Family Arionidae	
A white-soled slug, *Arion circumscriptus*	A mainly subterranean feeder
A white-soled slug, *Arion fasciatus*	A mainly subterranean feeder
A white-soled slug, *Arion silvaticus*	A mainly subterranean feeder
Garden slug (*Arion hortensis*)	An important pest, especially on non-acidic soils, feeding both above and below soil level
Family Milacidae	
A keeled slug, *Milax gagates*	Most numerous in southwest England and Wales
Budapest slug (*Tandonia budapestensis*)	A mainly subterranean feeder
Sowerby's slug (*Tandonia sowerbyi*)	A mainly subterranean feeder

including chafer grubs, cutworms and swift moth larvae, slugs form cavernous holes in the flesh. Slug damage to potato tubers, however, is typified by the relatively small entry holes and, often, by the presence of slime if not the slugs themselves. Slugs are essentially crepuscular or nocturnal creatures. However, when conditions are particularly dull and damp, they can also remain active during the daytime. This is especially so in the case of the surface-feeding or leaf-grazing species, of which the field slug (*Deroceras reticulatum*) is a common example. Several species are associated with potato crops (Table 3), all of which occur in both mainland Britain and Ireland.[39] Of these, the Budapest slug (*Tandonia budapestensis*), the field slug and the garden slug (*Arion hortensis*) are often most numerous. Many slugs have annual lifecycles, eggs being laid mainly in mid- to late summer or in the autumn. Field slug, however, is double brooded, breeding in the spring and again in the autumn. As crop pests, slugs are usually of greatest importance in heavy, moisture-retentive soils. Nevertheless, in high-rainfall areas, as in the beet-growing regions of western Ireland, damage can also be of significance on light, medium-textured soils.[40] Field slugs are renowned crop pests and frequently kill sugar beet seedlings; they cause particularly significant damage in steckling beds. Stecklings are young sugar beet plants, stored over the winter and then planted out for the production of seed. Root-feeding by the white-soled slug (*Arion fasciatus*) can also result in the death of young sugar beet plants.[41]

CHAPTER 6

Pests of Field Vegetables

FIELD VEGETABLES ARE AN important component of the British horticultural industry, ranging from large-scale production of field crops (as in the black fens of East Anglia) to small-scale production of salad crops on traditional smallholdings. In England and Wales, vegetable crops occupy around 100,000 ha, about a quarter of which is devoted to the production of brassicas. Overall, beans (*Vicia* and others) and peas also continue to be major players, with carrots, outdoor lettuces, onions and parsnips similarly maintaining a strong foothold. The area committed to field vegetables or salad crops varies considerably from year to year, governed largely by market forces. Cheaper, year-round imports from mainland Europe and many other parts of the world have certainly had a major impact on the British horticultural industry, and in the wake of such competition land formerly devoted to vegetable production has often been diverted to arable cropping (nowadays, mainly cereals and oilseed rape). Demands for high-quality vegetables also place considerable pressure on producers, who are required to keep pests and pest damage to a minimum. However, the situation is far from static, with processors and other customers perhaps showing zero tolerance to pest damage in times of plenty but relaxing their rules when the crops they require are in short supply.

On a field scale, habitats presented by vegetable crops vary from relatively stable ones (where perennial crops such as asparagus and rhubarb are being grown) to typically unstable ones with more or less annual or (as in the case of certain salad crops) far shorter rotations. Cropping patterns inevitably govern the availability of food plants for pests (whether specialists or polyphagous herbivores) and can also have a direct or indirect impact on natural enemies, particularly ground-dwelling predators. The vast majority of pests associated with field vegetable crops are insects, and these are reviewed below. To avoid unnecessary repetition elsewhere, it is also convenient here to consider pests associated with non-vegetable legumes – essentially, field beans.[1]

SUCKING PESTS

Aphids

Aphids rank amongst our most important plant pests, and few arable or field vegetable crops are totally immune from attack. Aphids associated with such crops range from highly polyphagous species such as peach/potato aphid (*Myzus persicae*), which feeds and breeds on hundreds of different kinds of plant, to those with a far more restricted host range (e.g. Table 4).

Cabbage aphid (*Brevicoryne brassicae*) is one of the most widespread and significant pests of vegetable brassicas. The aphids, their bodies liberally coated in mealy wax, form dense colonies on host plants, and they are a common sight on crops such as broccoli, Brussels sprout, cabbage, cauliflower, radish and swede. Turnip, however, appears to be largely immune. The pest is directly damaging and is also an important vector of viruses, especially cauliflower mosaic virus (CaMV) and turnip mosaic virus (TuMV). In cooler, more northerly parts of it range, cabbage aphid overwinters as eggs laid in the autumn on the stems and leaves of winter brassicas. The eggs hatch from February onwards, and colonies then develop on the shoots and leaves. Winged aphids are produced from May to July, and these spread infestations to newly emerged or newly planted hosts. Colonies in overwintering sites then decline rapidly and are often said to crash. Populations build up on new hosts during the summer, autumn and early winter. There is also a second period of winged migration and population spread in mid-October, followed

FIG 120. Hawthorn/carrot aphid (*Dysaphis crataegi*) is a minor pest of carrot and parsnip.

TABLE 4. Examples of aphids associated with field vegetables.

Species	*Lifecycle**	*Main crop host(s)*
Black bean aphid (*Aphis fabae*)	Holocyclic	Beans, red beet
Cabbage aphid (*Brevicoryne brassicae*)	Anholocyclic and holocyclic	Brassicas
Carrot root aphid (*Pemphigus phenax*)	Holocyclic	Carrot
Currant/lettuce aphid (*Nasonovia ribisnigri*)	Holocyclic	Lettuce
Hawthorn/carrot aphid (*Dysaphis crataegi*)	Holocyclic	Carrot, parsnip
Hawthorn/parsley aphid (*Dysaphis apiifolia petroselini*)	Holocyclic	Celery, parsley
Lettuce root aphid (*Pemphigus bursarius*)	Holocyclic	Lettuce
Parsnip aphid (*Cavariella pastinacae*)	Holocyclic	Parsnip
Pea aphid (*Acyrthosiphon pisum*)	Mainly holocyclic	Broad bean, pea
Peach/potato aphid (*Myzus persicae*)	Mainly anholocyclic**	Brassicas, lettuce, red beet etc.
Potato aphid (*Macrosiphum euphorbiae*)	Mainly anholocyclic	Lettuce
Shallot aphid (*Myzus ascalonicus*)	Anholocyclic	Lettuce, onion, shallot
Vetch aphid (*Megoura viciae*)	Holocyclic	Broad bean, pea
Willow/carrot aphid (*Cavariella aegopodii*)	Holocyclic	Carrot, celery, parsley, parsnip
Willow/parsnip aphid (*Cavariella theobaldi*)	Holocyclic	Parsnip

* See Chapter 5, p. 100.

** See Chapter 1, p. 13; Chapter 5, p. 101.

eventually by egg-laying. In many areas (and increasingly so nowadays) cabbage aphid overwinters as adults and nymphs rather than eggs. Where this is so, particularly in warm springs, populations increase more rapidly than would otherwise be the case. The lifecycle and overwintering strategies of peach/potato aphid, yet another virus vector, have already been discussed (Chapter 5).

Various aphids are pests of carrot and parsnip crops. These include three species of *Cavariella* (all of which overwinter in the egg stage on willow trees), hawthorn/carrot aphid (*Dysaphis crataegi*) (Fig. 120) (which overwinters as eggs on hawthorn) and carrot root aphid (*Pemphigus phenax*) (Fig. 121) (whose primary host is poplar) (Table 4). Willow/carrot aphid (*C. aegopodii*) (Fig. 122) is the most important pest, albeit as a vector of carrot motley dwarf virus (CMDV – a complex of carrot red leaf and carrot mottle viruses) and parsnip yellow fleck virus (PYFV).

Foliage-feeding aphids are major pests of lettuce. Examples include currant/lettuce aphid (*Nasonovia ribisnigri*), peach/potato aphid, potato aphid (*Macrosiphum euphorbiae*) and shallot aphid (*Myzus ascalonicus*) (Fig. 123), all of which cause malformation and stunting. Aphid-infested leaves are often contaminated by honeydew amongst which the cast nymphal skins accumulate.

FIG 121. Carrot root aphid (*Pemphigus phenax*) breeds on the roots of carrots during the summer months.

FIG 122. Willow/carrot aphid (*Cavariella aegopodii*) damages the foliage of carrot crops, but is of greater significance as vector of carrot motley dwarf virus.

FIG 123. Shallot aphid (*Myzus ascalonicus*) infests onion and many other plants. It is a major vector of plant viruses.

Peach/potato aphid is of particular significance as a vector of beet western yellows virus (BWYV), today an important pathogen of summer-maturing butterhead lettuces. Lettuce root aphid (*Pemphigus bursarius*) colonises the roots of lettuce plants, stunting growth and causing leaves to turn yellow; particularly in dry conditions infested plants may even be killed. Lettuce root aphid overwinters as eggs on poplar trees. In spring, following egg hatch, the aphids invade the stalks of the young leaves where they initiate characteristic pouch-like galls. Breeding continues within these galls until the early summer, when winged forms are produced. These aphids then disperse to lettuces and other summer hosts, including sow-thistles. Breeding on the roots of summer hosts continues until late summer when, following the production of new winged forms, a return migration to poplar takes place. Egg-laying females (oviparae) are then produced, and these eventually mate with incoming winged males before depositing the winter eggs. These oviparae are very small and they each lay just one egg, placed deeply within a bark crevice.[2] This lifecycle, however, is not always followed. On occasions, wingless aphids persist in the soil, even after plants are lifted, and these can subsequently infest the roots of newly planted lettuces, either in the autumn or in the following spring.[3] The progeny of these overwintered asexual aphids eventually produce winged female morphs which, in common with those arising in summer from populations on poplar, then spread infestations to summer herbaceous hosts.[4]

FIG 124. Black bean aphid (*Aphis fabae*) is a major pest of field bean and several other crops.

Black bean aphid (*Aphis fabae*) is a notorious farmland pest, especially on sugar beet (Chapter 5) and spring-sown field beans (Fig. 124). It also causes considerable concern on horticultural crops such as broad bean, dwarf French bean, red beet, runner bean and spinach. Although regarded as one of our most well-known garden aphids,[5] it can be confused with similar-looking black-bodied species that colonise various weeds and ornamental plants: dock aphid (*A. rumicis*), ivy aphid (*A. hederae*) and viburnum aphid (*A. viburni*) are common examples.

FIG 125. Pea aphid (*Acyrthosiphon pisum*) occurs on various leguminous plants, but is of particular importance as a pest of pea crops.

In common with forage maize, sweet corn plants are attacked by bird-cherry/oat aphid (*Rhopalosiphum padi*) and grain aphid (*Sitobion avenae*). The former species is of greater importance, colonies typically developing in the shelter of the overlapping modified leaves that form the husk and sheathe the cobs. Infested tissue becomes contaminated by sticky honeydew and subsequently blackened following the development of sooty moulds.

Pea aphid (*Acyrthosiphon pisum*), which has green and red colour forms, occurs on broad beans and field beans but is most important as a pest of peas. The winter is passed as eggs on the leaves and stems of perennial leguminous hosts, including clovers, lucerne, trefoils and vetches.[6] The eggs hatch early in the year, and colonies of wingless viviparous female aphids soon develop on host plants. Winged aphids are produced from the second or third generation onwards and these disperse to summer leguminous hosts, including pea crops, usually from early May onwards. The green-bodied aphids invade the growing points, and their presence is often overlooked until infestations have spread onto the foliage or developing pods (Fig. 125). Aphid numbers on pea crops generally reach their peak in June and July. However, numbers vary considerably from year to year. Later-sown crops (which tend to be at a more susceptible growth stage at the time of aphid arrival) become more heavily infested than earlier-sown ones. Winter temperatures are considered an important factor governing the likely significance of the pest in any particular year as they influence both early-spring colony development and the time of sowing of pea crops.[7] Pea aphids are rather spindly and long-legged, and are readily dislodged from host plants by heavy rain;[8] they also drop to the ground when otherwise disturbed. Yet another species, the vetch aphid (*Megoura viciae*), is sometimes noticed on broad bean, field bean and pea crops but is usually unimportant as a pest.

Naturally occurring predators, parasitoids and pathogens of aphids are justifiably heralded as of great benefit to farmers and growers. In many instances, however, their impact comes too late to protect untreated crops from damage or to prevent the introduction and spread of aphid-borne viruses. The guild of predators attacking aphids on crops such as field beans and field vegetables includes a range of non-specialist feeders (ground beetles, rove beetles, spiders and harvestmen, for example), along with aphidophagous lacewings, ladybirds, hover fly larvae and so on. Predators not only contribute to the decline of colonies by devouring aphid adults and nymphs but (as has been shown in the case of pea aphid) may also trigger the production of winged dispersal morphs by stimulating the aphids to emit an alarm pheromone,[9] thereby heralding a premature end to aphid colony development. Induction of winged aphids by predators, however, is not universal, and does not occur in the case of black bean aphid or vetch aphid.[10] The endoparasitoid wasp *Diaeretiella rapae* has already been mentioned as a natural enemy of cabbage aphid and peach/potato aphid (Chapter 4), and populations are frequently established on aphid-infested vegetable brassicas during the spring and summer months. Unharvested brassica plants bearing parasitised aphid mummies are useful overwintering sites for this parasitoid, and they serve as useful reservoirs from which attacks are launched in the coming season.[11] Other naturally occurring parasitoids of cabbage aphids include *Aphidius ervi*, yet another solitary endoparasitoid that pupates within its mummified host. This species also attacks pea aphid, targeting green rather than red forms. Conversely, given a choice, predators of pea aphids tend to target the red morphs.[12] Known fungal pathogens of foliar-feeding aphids include *Beauveria bassiana*, *Lecanicillium muscarium*,[13] *Paecilomyces fumosoroseus* and *Pandora neoaphidis*.[14] An isolate of *Metarhizium flavoviride*[15] is known to kill lettuce root aphid.[16]

Miscellaneous pests

Thrips often cause noticeable harm to agricultural and horticultural crops, and infested leaves and petals frequently develop a silvery or whitish appearance where the cell contents have been withdrawn. Thrips also cause stunting and distortion of plants, especially when the growing points have been attacked. Crops such as *Vicia* beans, brassicas, peas and red beet are often invaded. Several species are involved, including field thrips (*Thrips angusticeps*), a widespread, locally common and polyphagous species that has two distinct generations annually. The brown-bodied adults of the overwintering generation – individuals little more than a millimetre long – have reduced wings and are described as brachypterous. These emerge from the soil in the early spring to breed on a range of hosts, producing nymphs (after an egg stage) that eventually develop (through a propupal and a pupal stage) into fully winged (macropterous) adults. In particular, the spring-feeding nymphs often cause significant damage to pea seedlings, such plants being stunted and their foliage distorted and discoloured.[17] The nymphs are also damaging to various other plants, including beet seedlings. In late May or early June the young macropterous adults feed on a range of summer hosts, upon which their nymphs develop into the next round of brachypterous, overwintering adults. Pea and *Vicia* bean crops are also hosts of pea thrips (*Kakothrips pisivorus*), a more specialist invader of leguminous plants.[18] The adults of this southerly distributed, single-brooded and fully winged species occur in spring and early summer, infesting the flowers, young leaves and developing pods. Eggs are deposited in the flowers, often in a row along the sheath of a stamen, and they hatch about ten days later. The nymphs are most numerous in June and July. They feed for about three weeks and then burrow into the soil where they overwinter. Individuals eventually pass through a brief propupal and then a pupal stage before emerging as adults. Damage to crops is especially severe in drought conditions during June and July. Infested flowers fail to develop, and pods and whole plants often become stunted and distorted.

Relatively large (*c.* 2 mm long) dark-brown thrips with distinctly banded, black and white forewings and noticeably rounded wing-tips sometimes attract attention on field crops such as field beans and vegetable brassicas. The adults (commonly known as banded thrips or banded-wing thrips) occur from May to August; the pale-bodied nymphs are present from July onwards. Two species are involved: *Aeolothrips intermedius*[19] and *A. tenuicornis*. The true status of these insects needs clarification, but they appear to be of greatest significance as predators of thrips and other small invertebrates rather than as pests.

Onion thrips (*T. tabaci*) is yet another commonly encountered species, but is associated mainly with leek, onion and various greenhouse-grown crops (Chapter 10). Its presence on leeks and onions is often indicated by the development of noticeably deformed, silvered or whitish-speckled leaves. Damage to salad onions and leeks can be considerable, particularly in dry conditions. Outdoors there are typically two generations per year, adult females reared in the autumn overwintering in the soil.

Other sap-feeding insects associated with field crops include polyphagous bugs such as common green capsid (*Lygocoris pabulinus*), European tarnished plant bug (*Lygus rugulipennis*) and potato capsid (*Closterotomus norvegicus*).[20] Brassicas, carrots, legumes and many other crops are regularly infested. Mirids (capsids) are usually most numerous on weedy sites or around field margins. Owing to fundamental differences in their biology, European tarnished plant

FIG 126. Cabbage whitefly (*Aleyrodes proletella*) is often abundant on brassicaceous crops, especially in allotments and gardens.

bugs (which overwinter as adults) invade such crops as adults, whereas the others (which overwinter as eggs) do so as nymphs.

As a specialist feeder, cabbage whitefly (*Aleyrodes proletella*) (Fig. 126) is commonly associated with brassica crops such as broccoli, Brussels sprout, cabbage and cauliflower, particularly in allotments and gardens. Disturbance of infested plants often invites clouds of the tiny, superficially moth-like adults (their bodies and wings coated in white, waxen powder) to rise into the air, immediately betraying the presence of the pest. In spring, the females deposit characteristically semicircular batches of eggs on the underside of leaves. The eggs hatch a week or two later. Flattened, scale-like, first-instar nymphs then wander briefly over the leaves before settling down to sink their mouthparts into host plants and begin feeding. These sedentary nymphs moult twice before entering a short-lived pseudo-pupal stage within which the transformation to adulthood takes place. Cabbage whiteflies breed continuously throughout the summer, and are capable of completing four or more overlapping generations. The winter is passed in the adult stage or occasionally as pseudo-pupae. Whitefly nymphs excrete copious amounts of honeydew. This contaminates host plants and also serves as a substrate upon which sooty moulds soon develop.

DEFOLIATING PESTS

Moths and butterflies

Foliage-feeding larvae (caterpillars) of various lepidopterous pests regularly occur on arable and vegetable crops. Common examples include those of silver Y moth (*Autographa gamma*) and flax tortrix moth (*Cnephasia asseclana*). Silver Y moth (Fig. 127) is a well-known migrant which arrives in Britain annually from North Africa, often in considerable numbers. As members of the subfamily Plusiinae the larvae possess just three pairs of prolegs (lacking those on the third and fourth abdominal segments), and they progress with a somewhat looping gait. As a consequence, they are often called semi-loopers. The pest is highly polyphagous and larvae occur during the summer on a wide range of crops, including *Vicia* beans, carrot, celery, lettuce, pea, red beet and runner bean. Under favourable conditions, silver Y moth completes two generations here. However, populations then die out as the pest is unable to survive British winters. Flax tortrix moth is also polyphagous, and is often a common pest of field bean crops. The larvae also attack field vegetables, including peas and beans. Arguably, however, flax tortrix moth is of greatest significance on lettuce, the larvae

FIG 127. Silver Y moth (*Autographa gamma*) is a well-known migrant to Britain and Ireland.

FIG 128. Straw-coloured tortrix moth (*Clepsis spectrana*) larvae feed on various crops, including onion and rhubarb.

damaging the leaves, soiling plants with frass and also occurring on lifted plants as post-harvest contaminants. The essentially grey, sombre-looking adults are active from June to August. Eggs are then laid on various herbaceous plants, either singly or in groups of two or three. Following egg hatch the larvae initially mine the leaves, forming tiny linear or blotch-like mines.[21] The larvae overwinter whilst still quite small, each sheltering in a silken hibernaculum. Activity is resumed in the spring, usually in April. No longer leaf miners, the larvae draw leaves or other tissue together with silk to form suitable habitations. When disturbed, unlike many tortricids they do not wriggle violently backwards but instead curl up and drop to the ground. Pupation takes place in a folded leaf edge or amongst dead leaves or other debris. Allied shade moth (*C. incertana*) has a similar life history and host range. Amongst field crops, it is probably most often reported on field beans, peas, clovers and vetches. *C. longana*, whose larvae are known as omnivorous leaf tiers and whose life history is slightly different from that of its aforementioned relatives (see Chapter 2), frequently occurs on field bean crops. A few other tortricid moths also attack field vegetables. Examples include straw-coloured tortrix moth (*Clepsis spectrana*) (Fig. 128) on onion and rhubarb, and *Ditula angustiorana* on French bean and runner bean.

In years of mass immigration and abundance (as in 2003, 2004 and 2009 when many adults reached these shores) painted lady butterflies (*Cynthia cardui*) extend their range of food plants beyond thistles and other wild hosts, and deposit eggs on the leaves of French bean and runner bean crops. The larvae subsequently cause some defoliation before finally pupating on the food plant (Fig. 129). However, it is questionable whether the epithet 'crop pest' in any serious sense really applies to them. Nevertheless, it must be accepted that some of our most beautiful and revered insects can on occasions prove damaging to crops. Polyphagous lepidopterans more

FIG 129. Painted lady butterfly (*Cynthia cardui*) pupae (and other life stages) are sometimes found on French bean and runner bean crops.

frequently associated with weeds also feed occasionally on field crops. Again, however, such species hardly deserve pest status.

Some Lepidoptera are of considerable significance as pests of vegetable brassicas. Several species are involved (Table 5) and larvae sometimes reach plague proportions. Home gardeners will be all too familiar with cabbage white butterflies and the havoc their larvae can wreak on broccoli, Brussels sprout, cabbage and other such plants in vegetable gardens and allotments. Two species are involved – large white butterfly (*Pieris brassicae*) and small white butterfly (*P. rapae*) – both familiar sights from spring to autumn throughout these islands. Large white butterflies lay their eggs in batches, mainly on the underside of leaves. Following egg hatch, the larvae feed gregariously and rapidly defoliate host plants, riddling leaves with holes or reducing them to mere skeletons of major veins. Infested plants are also indelibly fouled by larval excrement. Large white butterfly larvae become less gregarious in

TABLE 5. Some lepidopterous pests attacking vegetable brassicas.

Species	*Family (subfamily)*
Angle-shades moth (*Phlogophora meticulosa*)*	Noctuidae (Noctuinae)
Cabbage moth (*Mamestra brassicae*)	Noctuidae (Noctuinae)
Diamond-back moth (*Plutella xylostella*)	Yponomeutidae (Plutellinae)
Dot moth (*Melanchra persicariae*)*	Noctuidae (Noctuinae)
Flax tortrix moth (*Cnephasia asseclana*)*	Tortricidae (Tortricinae)
Garden pebble moth (*Evergestis forficalis*)	Pyralidae (Evergestiinae)
Large white butterfly (*Pieris brassicae*)	Pieridae (Pierinae)
Silver Y moth (*Autographa gamma*)*	Noctuidae (Plusiinae)
Small white butterfly (*Pieris rapae*)	Pieridae (Pierinae)
Tomato moth (*Lacanobia oleracea*)*	Noctuidae (Noctuinae)

* Usually of minor significance.

FIG 130. Cabbage moth (*Mamestra brassicae*) larvae are very polyphagous, but favour brassicaceous hosts.

their later stages of development and usually pupate alone – occasionally on the food plant (as often occurs in the first brood) but usually some distance away in sheltered situations on fences, posts, tree trunks and other structures. Although they often cause great distress to home gardeners, large white butterfly infestations are patchy and rarely of significance on a field scale. By contrast, small white butterfly is potentially important on both field and garden crops. The eggs of this species are laid singly on the underside of leaves, although several may be found on one and the same leaf. Unlike those of large white butterfly, the larvae are essentially solitary feeders and being cryptically coloured they frequently pass unnoticed until a considerable amount of damage has been caused. Both species are double brooded in Britain, although they are sometimes able to complete a third generation, and immigrants arriving from abroad regularly boost indigenous populations.

Vegetable brassicas are also frequently attacked by cabbage moth (*Mamestra brassicae*), another generally common leaf-grazing pest (Fig. 130). This species, unlike cabbage white butterflies, is extremely polyphagous. However, as aptly described by Bretherton *et al.*,[22] it is 'particularly addicted to *Brassica* crops'. The moths (Fig. 131) are active throughout much of the year, but are most numerous in early summer and autumn. The hemispherical, distinctly ribbed eggs are laid in batches, mainly in June or July. They hatch just over a week later. Larvae then feed voraciously for up to four or five weeks, causing extensive damage and also contaminating plants with their faeces. They then pupate in the soil and either overwinter or produce a new wave of adults. As in the case of other lepidopterous pests, parasitoids not infrequently emerge from the pupae instead of moths (Fig. 132). Cabbage moth is often described as single brooded. However, the number of generations per year in Britain is uncertain as there is considerable

FIGS 131 & 132. (Above left) Cabbage moth (*Mamestra brassicae*). The ichneumonid wasp *Amblysteles armoratus* (above right) is an endoparasitoid of various lepidopterous pests.

FIG 133. Diamond-back moth (*Plutella xylostella*) is an important crop pest, and a frequent migrant to Britain and Ireland.

FIG 134. Garden pebble moth (*Evergestis forficalis*).

overlapping of the developmental stages and larvae may be found at any time from early summer to November. Although described here as a field pest, cabbage moth infestations frequently develop on protected crops (Chapter 10).

Diamond-back moth (*Plutella xylostella*) (Fig. 133) and garden pebble moth (*Evergestis forficalis*) (Fig. 134) are also potentially important pests of brassicaceous crops. In some years, as happened in 1891[23] and 1958,[24] diamond-back moths occur in considerable numbers. Their larvae, which are particularly serious pests in tropical and subtropical parts of the world, are then liable to cause extensive defoliation. Garden pebble moth is a locally common and sporadically important pest of brassicas, particularly in allotments, home gardens and market gardens. In addition to being defoliators, the larvae (Fig. 135) are renowned for spoiling the spears of broccoli and calabrese, for boring into the hearts of

FIG 135. Garden pebble moth (*Evergestis forficalis*) larvae damage brassicaceous plants and also contaminate them with silken webbing and frass.

cabbages and for launching attacks on the developing buttons of Brussels sprout plants. Infested plants are also contaminated by silken webbing, amongst which grains of frass accumulate. Garden pebble moth is double brooded but if conditions are favourable a partial third generation can be completed.

Larvae of cabbage white butterflies often fall victim to the braconid wasp *Cotesia glomerata*,[25] and the pupal cocoons of this gregarious externally pupating endoparasitoid are often seen alongside the remains of host larvae. Volatile chemicals released by larva-damaged leaves and similar volatiles arising from regurgitated gut contents of larvae assist the parasitoids in locating prospective hosts.[26] Pre-pupae and pupae of large white butterflies are also attacked by adults of the wasp *Pteromalus puparum*, a gregarious endoparasitoid of pupae. In this case, the parasitoids pupate internally and new metallic-green wasps eventually emerge via tiny holes bored through the skin of their host.

FIG 136. Large white butterfly (*Pieris brassicae*) larvae often succumb to virus disease. Infected specimens appear greyer than healthy ones.

Eggs of cabbage white butterflies are also taken by garden warblers and house sparrows.[27] Large white butterflies are far less numerous in Britain than they were 50 or so years ago, following the natural introduction of a virus from mainland Europe. Virus-infected caterpillars are often seen in the field and readily distinguished from healthy specimens by their dull, greyish appearance (Fig. 136).

Beetles

Asparagus beetle (*Crioceris asparagi*) (Fig. 137) is a colourful and well-known pest of edible and ornamental asparagus plants. Adults emerge from hibernation in the late spring, and then invade asparagus beds where they graze on the fronds and other aerial parts. Their relatively large, upright eggs are laid from June onwards and hatch a week or so later. The rather sedentary larvae (Fig. 138) then feed for about three weeks before eventually entering the soil to pupate in parchment-like cocoons a few centimetres below the surface. Second-generation adults emerge two to three weeks later. Adults and larvae cause extensive defoliation. They also strip rind from the stems and branches, thereby weakening host plants. *Tetrastichus asparagi*, a tiny, metallic-green eulophid wasp, parasitises the eggs of asparagus beetle, and the adults are sometimes seen buzzing around or settled upon beetle-infested plants.[28]

FIG 137. Asparagus beetle (*Crioceris asparagi*).

FIG 138. Asparagus beetle (*Crioceris asparagi*) larvae feed gregariously and cause extensive defoliation.

Arable and vegetable crops have few other such enemies, although dock beetles (*Gastrophysa viridula*) sometimes spread from polygonaceous weed hosts to cultivated rhubarb and garden sorrel. The adults and larvae feed on the expanded leaves, forming holes between the major veins. The leaf

FIG 139. Flea beetles (*Phyllotreta* spp.) commonly attack radish and other brassicaceous seedlings.

beetle *Galerucella grisescens* also occurs on cultivated rhubarb but is more usually associated with wetland plants such as frog-bit and yellow loosestrife. Adult and larval damage is restricted to windowing or holing of the foliage and is of no economic importance. Celery leaf beetle (*Phaedon tumidulus*) has been regarded as a minor pest of celery plants, but nowadays is found mainly on wild umbelliferous hosts such as hogweed.

Around the time of their emergence above ground level, untreated brassica seedlings are manna from heaven for flea beetles (*Phyllotreta* spp.). The adult beetles attack the cotyledons, hypocotyls and young leaves, forming distinctive pin-prick-like holes that gradually enlarge as the plants grow (Fig. 139). Later, the larvae attack or burrow within the roots, often causing extensive damage. Such infestations are especially damaging on young radish and turnip plants. Several species are involved, including the large striped flea beetle (*P. nemorum*), the small striped flea beetle (*P. undulata*) and various turnip flea beetles (*P. atra*, *P. consobrina* and *P. cruciferae*).

Pea & bean weevil (*Sitona lineatus*) is a generally abundant and well-known pest of legume crops. The weevils become active in the spring, and invade crops such as broad beans, field beans and peas. Here, the weevils graze on the foliage, forming characteristic marginal U-shaped notches which are often the first indication of the presence of the pest (Fig. 140). Growing points and cotyledons of recently germinated plants are also attacked. Eggs are laid in the soil from April onwards and hatch about three weeks later. The grub-like larvae then feed on the root nodules for several weeks before pupating. Adults of the new generation appear two to three weeks later, usually from late July or early August onwards. These weevils feed on the leaves of legumes and various other plants, including non-hosts such as firethorn and strawberry, before eventually overwintering in

FIG **140.** Leaves attacked by pea & bean weevils (*Sitona lineatus*) are characteristically notched.

hedge bottoms, amongst long grass, in stacks of straw and in other sheltered situations. In clover stubbles, they are also recorded hibernating 'more or less exposed on the earth between the plants'.[29] There is just one generation annually.

Autumn- and spring-sown field bean crops also play host to the bean flower weevil (*Eutrichapion vorax*).[30] This tiny, metallic-blue insect produces small feeding punctures on the flower petals and leaves, but such damage is of little or no significance. The adults, however, are vectors of viruses, including broad bean true mosaic virus (BBTMV) and broad bean stain virus (BBSV).[31] Crops are invaded by adult weevils from May onwards. Eggs are then laid in the developing flowers, where larval development and pupation eventually take place. Young adults appear in the summer and then disperse to woodlands and other sheltered habitats in which to overwinter. Pea & bean weevils also transmit viruses but are far less efficient vectors.

Nowadays, vegetable leaf brassicas are increasingly invaded by young cabbage stem weevils (*Ceutorhynchus pallidactylus*)[32] that have been reared on nearby oilseed rape crops. The stems and underside of the midrib and other major veins are grazed, resulting in the development of unsightly callused wounds. Attacks are ephemeral and occur prior to the pests seeking their overwintering quarters.

Vertebrates

Particularly in winter, birds such as pheasants and mammals such as rabbits and muntjac frequently attack overwintering brassicas and other vegetable crops. Badgers too can be a minor problem, and seem to have an uncanny ability to raid carrot beds just ahead of the planned harvest date! Damage caused by birds and mammals, however, is usually of greatest significance in rural allotments and gardens rather than in field crops.

MINING PESTS

The leaves of celery, parsnip and various other cultivated or wild umbelliferous plants (Apiaceae) are often destroyed by blister-like mines, which come to occupy much if not all of the available tissue. Such damage is caused by celery leaf miners, the larvae of celery fly (*Euleia heraclei*) (Fig. 141). The distinctive, mottled-winged, green-eyed adults first appear in late spring. Eggs are then deposited on the underside of leaves of host plants and hatch about a week later. The larvae are often visible through the walls of their mines, feeding singly or gregariously for two to three weeks. Infested foliage becomes distorted and eventually turns through yellow to brown (Fig. 142). Heavily infested plants appear scorched, as if damaged by herbicides. If the condition of infested leaves deteriorates before larvae are fully grown, as might occur following infection by celery leaf spot (*Septoria apiicola*) (a common fungal pathogen), the pests vacate their original mines and initiate others on foliage elsewhere.[33] Fully fed larvae pupate

FIG 141. Celery fly (*Euleia heraclei*) larvae inhabit blotch mines and are known as celery leaf miners.

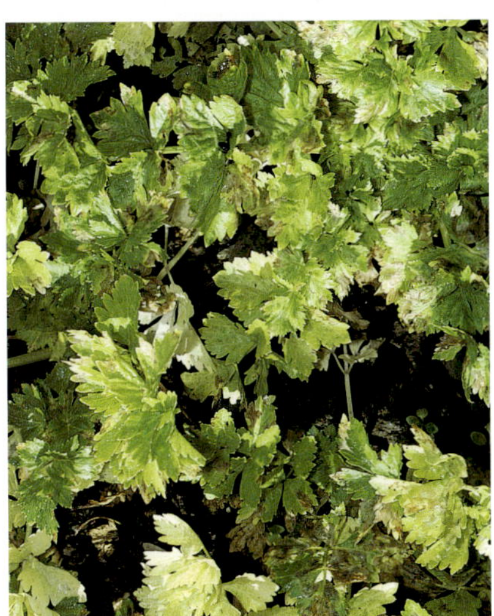

FIG 142. Blotch mines on celery plants are indicative of attack by celery fly (*Euleia heraclei*).

FIG 143. Celery fly (*Euleia heraclei*) puparium.

in situ (Fig. 143) or in the soil, and adults of the next generation emerge about a month later. Larvae of a second brood occur during the summer. When conditions are favourable those of a third generation may be found feeding during the autumn. Similar-looking damage on parsnip but with associated external silken webbing is indicative of an infestation by the common lancewing moth (*Epermenia chaerophyllella*). This minor pest is most often found in gardens and allotments, the larvae mining leaves during their early life but later feeding externally (Fig. 144). The strands of webbing associated with an attack are often adorned with tiny beads of moisture. Larvae of another species, the carrot lancewing moth (*Epermenia aequidentellus*), similarly target the foliage of carrot plants.

FIG 144. Common lancewing moth (*Epermenia chaerophyllella*) larvae sometimes occur on cultivated parsnip. They mine leaves during their early life but later feed externally, partly sheltered by strands of silken webbing.

FIG 145. Parsnip moth (*Depressaria pastinacella*) larvae sometimes occur on cultivated parsnip but are more often associated with wild umbelliferous plants.

Occasionally, cultivated parsnip plants are attacked by fleshy, bluish-grey, black-spotted larvae of parsnip moth (*Depressaria pastinacella*), a minor pest more frequently associated with wild umbelliferous hosts such as hogweed and wild parsnip. Such larvae (Fig. 145), known as parsnip webworms, feed amongst the flowerheads during the summer months, each larval habitation drawn into a tight bunch of tissue by tough strands of silk amongst which grains of frass accumulate. The larvae also mine within the stems of host plants, where pupation eventually takes place. Adult parsnip moths make their appearance in the autumn and then overwinter. The moths reappear in the spring and eventually deposit eggs on the leaves of host plants.

Larger stem-boring lepidopterans include rosy rustic moth (*Hydraecia micacea*) larvae, which are sometimes found tunnelling in the crowns of rhubarb plants during the spring and early to mid-summer. Very occasionally, outdoor tomato plants are also attacked. Similarly, the distinctly fleshy larvae of a near relative, the frosted orange moth (*Gortyna flavago*), occasionally bore within globe artichoke and Jerusalem artichoke plants. They cause shoots to wilt, but are more usually associated with wild herbaceous plants such as burdocks, foxgloves and thistles.

Asparagus fly (*Pliorecepta poeciloptera*)[34] is a pest of asparagus, the larvae tunnelling within the stems and causing plants to collapse. This insect is important in mainland Europe but no infestations have been found in Britain since the 1930s.[35] Unconfirmed records of asparagus fly attacks continue to this day. However, these probably refer to *Hexomyza simplex*,[36] an agromyzid fly whose larvae (known as asparagus miners) also mine the stems of cultivated asparagus plants. Unlike those formed by larvae of asparagus fly, such mines are restricted to the surface layers of plants and the damage is usually unimportant.[37] Nevertheless, affected tissue can become infected by fungal pathogens (*Fusarium* spp.),[38] increasing the overall significance of the pest.

Whitish, linear mines formed by larvae of other agromyzid flies are a common sight on the leaves of field bean and pea plants. Although the mines themselves are relatively small, and attacks usually innocuous, infestations are at least potentially harmful.[39] On pea crops, the mines often occur in the stipules and are also known to enter the tendrils. The species most frequently involved are *Liriomyza congesta* and *Phytomyza horticola* (Fig. 146). In applied entomology, larvae of *L. congesta* (along with those of *L. pisivora* – yet another pea-infesting species) are known as pea leaf miners.

Parsnip plants are often attacked by the leaf miner *Phytomyza spondylii*. The larvae feed within extensive, whitish mines; fully fed larvae eventually vacate their feeding galleries through the underside of the leaf and pupate externally. Adult feeding punctures are often visible if infested leaflets are held up to the light. The pest is of little or no importance, and most often observed in gardens and allotments rather than field crops. The same holds true for *Cerodontha incisa* which forms expansive mines in the leaves of sweet corn and other Poaceae. The larvae of *C. incisa* feed gregariously and eventually pupate within the communal mine, each in a metallic-black puparium.

Mention has already been made of *Phytomyza rufipes* and *Scaptomyza flava* as minor pests of oilseed rape (Chapter 4). These species also occur regularly on

FIG 146. Mines formed on pea leaves by larvae of *Phytomyza horticola* often attract attention.

FIG 147. Larvae of *Scaptomyza flava* mine the leaves of various brassicaceous plants, including radish.

vegetable brassicas. The former is particularly well-known on crops such as broccoli, cabbage, calabrese and swede, albeit usually as a minor pest. The larvae (cabbage leaf miners) feed within the leaf stalks and stems, and damage is of greatest significance on young plants. There are records of situations where eggs have been laid on all available plants. However, there is considerable natural mortality of both eggs and young larvae, and this lessens the impact of the pest.[40] Hosts of *S. flava* (the larvae of which develop in blotch-like rather than linear mines) include broccoli, Brussels sprout, cauliflower and radish (Fig. 147). Both pests are multi-brooded, and evidence of their activities can be seen throughout the year.

In addition to its impact as a pest of mangold and sugar beet (Chapter 5), mangold fly (*Pegomya hyoscyami*) also damages red beet and spinach. Attacks on seedlings are most debilitating, and heavily infested leaves or even entire plants can be killed. On older plants the expansive leaf mines formed by the usually gregarious larvae are of particular significance on spinach, since the foliage is the saleable part of the crop. Spinach plants are also attacked by spinach stem fly (*Delia echinata*). The solitary, maggot-like larvae feed within the midribs and hollowed-out leaf stalks. Damaged tissue often splits open and the tips of affected shoots turn black. Occupied mines may be found at any time from May through to October, there being up to three if not four generations annually.

Leek moth (*Acrolepiopsis assectella*) is occasionally found on leek crops in Britain, most frequently in the coastal regions of southeast England. Attacks on onions, as in Devon in 1973,[41] are also reported. Where established, adults emerge from hibernation in the spring and deposit their eggs singly at the base of host plants. Larvae initially mine within the outer leaves. Later, they bore through the leaf sheaths to feed at the heart of their hosts, thereby forming a series of small

FIG 148. When fully fed, leek moth (*Acrolepiopsis assectella*) larvae pupate in net-like cocoons.

holes. On onions, the larvae frequently occur within the hollow leaves and later move downwards to enter the bulbs. Leek moth larvae often feed gregariously, soiling plants with their frass. Each larva eventually pupates in a flimsy, net-like cocoon, spun on the food plant (Fig. 148) or amongst debris on the ground. Adults of the next generation emerge about three weeks later. In southern Europe, where leek moth is a serious pest, there are many generations annually. In Britain, however, the pest is usually double brooded. Leek moth (a near relative of diamond-back moth) is an habitual migrant, but was not reported in Britain until the 1940s.[42] Today, it is uncertain to what extent infestations on crops are initiated by locally established moths or by recently arrived immigrants.

Root vegetable crops such as carrot, celeriac, celery and parsnip (and parsley, another umbellifer) are frequently attacked by carrot fly (*Psila rosae*), a well-known and serious pest of garden and commercial crops. There are typically two generations annually,[43] although in some years, as in the fenland districts of East Anglia, a partial third generation is possible. First-generation adults usually become active in May, and are most numerous from mid-May to early June. These first-generation flies feed on the flowerheads of cow parsley and hemlock,[44] favouring sheltered sites.[45] During windy weather the adults assemble on the leeward side of hedges, where they often hide on the underside of leaves of rough chervil, hogweed and other Apiaceae.[46] Eggs are laid singly, or in small groups, in soil-surface cracks close to host plants, especially at the edges of fields in the vicinity of hedgerows.[47] The eggs hatch about a week later. The narrow-bodied larvae (Fig. 149) initially burrow through the soil to feed on the surface tissue of the rootlets or developing tap roots. Later, when in their third instar, but sometimes also as second instars, they mine within the roots, causing extensive damage. Fully grown larvae eventually pupate in the soil, each

FIG 149. Carrot fly (*Psila rosae*) larvae are major pests of carrot and parsnip crops.

in an elongated, yellowish-brown puparium. Second-generation adults are active and often numerous in late July, August and early September, the flight period sometimes overlapping imperceptibly with that of any third-generation individuals that might arise. In northern England and Scotland timings are somewhat different, with flies of the first generation occurring mainly in June and July, followed in August and September by those of a smaller second generation. Carrot fly typically overwinters as either larvae or pupae. Field symptoms of attack vary according to the kind of host plant and the stage of host-plant development. Early-season attacks on carrots, for example, are usually restricted to the side (lateral) roots rather than the tap root. Further, when plants are under drought stress, the foliage of affected plants turns reddish, and may wilt and die, mirroring symptoms resulting from infestations of willow/carrot aphid or even virus infection. Root damage caused by larvae can also result in the death of seedlings. Later in the season, in response to second-generation attacks, the tap roots of older plants become riddled with open rusty-looking galleries, the extent of damage increasing steadily throughout the autumn. Celery plants often turn yellow, following larval infestations of the crowns, leaf stalks and roots. Such damage, attributable to first-generation carrot fly larvae, is often particularly severe in Lancashire and can result in crop failures, both there and in eastern England.[48] On parsnip, larval damage mirrors that found on carrot, although feeding tends to be restricted to the uppermost parts of the tap root. First-generation larvae also kill young plants by severing tap roots; they also bore into leaf stalks. Several natural enemies attack carrot fly,[49] and predation of eggs by small rove beetles (subfamily Aleocharinae) and ground beetles such as *Trechus quadristriatus* can be of some significance, especially in spring and autumn.[50]

Larvae of another root-mining fly, *Napomyza carotae*, also feed on carrot. However, they are uncommon and rarely reported. *N. carotae* was unknown as a pest in Britain until 1974 when infestations were found in Cambridgeshire. Adults produce characteristic feeding punctures in the leaves, and larvae mine the tap roots. Compared with carrot fly, however, larval damage is less extensive and more superficial. Nevertheless, particularly in wet conditions, mined tap roots are liable to be invaded by secondary pathogens. As in the case of asparagus miners (see above) this serves to enhance the potential status of the pest. Eggs of *N. carotae* are deposited mainly in the leaves and leaf stalks. Following egg hatch, the larvae bore downwards and enter the tap root where they form elongated galleries just below the surface. Fully fed larvae eventually pupate within their mines, and adults emerge shortly afterwards. There are two if not three generations annually. The ichneumonid wasp *Phygadeuon punctiventris* is known to attack the pupae of *N. carotae*, with parasitism recorded at around 20 per cent.[51]

Few leaf-mining or stem-boring beetle pests are associated with field vegetable crops. However, vegetable brassicas are sometimes damaged by larvae of the large striped flea beetle, individuals forming small blister-like leaf mines. Also, from late summer onwards, cabbage stem flea beetle (*Psylliodes chrysocephala*) sometimes invades such crops. The larvae of this well-known oilseed rape pest (see Chapter 4) feed within the leaf stalks and stems, and the damage they cause to winter brassicas can be extensive. Larvae of cabbage stem weevil (as previously mentioned, yet another oilseed rape pest) may also be found on vegetable brassicas. These mine within the leaf stalks and stems from late spring to early summer, and are particularly harmful in spring-sown brassica seedbeds.

SEED-INVADING INSECTS

Pea moth (*Cydia nigricana*) (Fig. 150) is a major pest of pea crops, especially in southern and eastern England. Wild hosts capable of maintaining populations in the absence of pea crops include meadow pea and tufted vetch. Pea moths are active in sunny afternoons and warm evenings (typically from 16.00 to 18.00 hrs British Summer Time (BST) and at temperatures in excess of 18°C), from late May or early June to mid-August, populations usually reaching their peak in mid-July.[52] Eggs are laid on the underside of leaves and stipules of host plants, either singly or in small groups, and hatch about a week later. The young larvae then invade the pods to attack the developing seeds (peas) (Fig. 151). Larvae are

FIG 150. Pea moth (*Cydia nigricana*).

FIG 151. Pea moth (*Cydia nigricana*) larvae feed inside pods, causing direct damage to the developing peas (seeds).

fully grown in about three weeks. They then bite their way out of the pods and drop to the ground. Here, they burrow into the soil and spin tough, silken cocoons in which to overwinter. Pupation occurs in the spring and adults emerge about two weeks later.[53] There is typically just one generation annually. Crops differ in their susceptibility to pea moth attacks, early-maturing vining (fresh-picked) pea cultivars, for example, suffering less than later-maturing ones.[54] Also, dry-harvesting peas (harvested when the peas are dry rather than fresh), are exposed to attack for far longer than vining peas, irrespective of cultivar. Pea moth can be a particularly serious problem if such crops are intended for human consumption or seed.

The braconid wasp *Ascogaster quadridentata* (a solitary egg/larval endoparasitoid) and the ichneumonid wasp *Pristomerus vulnerator* (a solitary larval/prepupal endoparasitoid) both attack pea moth. These polyphagous parasitoids are also associated with other tortricid pests, including codling moth (*Cydia pomonella*), the well-known apple pest (Chapter 7). Two further ichneumonid parasitoids of pea moth are known: *Glypta haesitator* and *Hemiteles ridibundus*.[55] Both occur in Britain, and the latter is known to attack pea moth in Essex.[56]

The bean beetle (*Bruchus rufimanus*) frequently occurs on broad bean and field bean crops. Another bruchid, the pea beetle (*B. pisorum*) is also recorded in Britain, but only in imported produce. Bruchids are somewhat unusual-looking, hunch-backed beetles that lay their eggs singly in the fresh pods of host plants. Subsequently, larvae feed inside the developing seeds, within which pupation takes place. New adults eventually emerge from the seeds through small, pinhead-sized flight holes, either before or after crops have been harvested. Bean beetle larvae typically attack the cotyledonous tissue of seeds, without damaging the germ. Thus, infested beans remain viable and, if subsequently planted out (as is often the case in farm-saved seed) are quite capable of germinating. Adult bean beetles are commonly encountered in barns or other buildings in which recently harvested beans are kept. However, the beetles are not storage pests, as they are unable to infest the dried seed; those emerging in or accidentally carried into stores cause no damage and merely seek to escape back into the field at the earliest opportunity. Wild oat seeds often lodge in the beetle emergence (flight) holes, each stuck fast and standing aloft like a feather in a Red Indian's head-dress. Batches of harvested beans contaminated in this way can be a problem to processors.

On sweet corn, the tight spaces between the husk and developing ear are favourable roosting sites for common earwigs (*Forficula auricularia*). Although of no significance on a field scale, this can become a slight problem in private vegetable gardens when the insects bite into the developing grains, ruining the apical portion of the cobs (Fig. 152).

FIG 152. Sweet corn cobs are sometimes damaged by earwigs.

ROOT FLIES

Root flies are common denizens of market gardens, private gardens and field crops, and they constitute an important group of vegetable pests. These range from polyphagous feeders such as bean seed flies, of which two species (*Delia florilega* and *D. platura*) occur in Britain, to more specialised ones such as onion fly (*D. antiqua*), spinach stem fly and turnip root fly (*D. floralis*) (Table 6). As the most formidable of such pests, however, cabbage root fly (*D. radicum*) tends to grab the headlines.

Bean seed flies first appear in the spring, having overwintered in the pupal stage. The flies are especially attracted to soils rich in organic matter, and as general scavengers their larvae are often associated with trashy conditions created when crops such as cereals have been harvested. Eggs are laid in May or early June, usually into freshly disturbed soil. They hatch a few days later. The maggot-like larvae then seek out germinating seeds or young seedlings (of peas and beans, for example), where they burrow within the cotyledons, hypocotyl and other tissue. Damage is often extensive. Larvae are fully grown in about three weeks. They then pupate in the soil, each in a barrel-shaped puparium. Adults of the next generation appear two to three weeks later and these initiate a similar cycle, there being up to three or four overlapping generations annually. Onion fly has a similar life history, but the adults tend to appear in spring about a month later than spring-emerging bean seed flies.[57] Also, onion flies do not lay eggs speculatively. Instead, the eggs are either deposited in soil close to host plants or placed directly onto the leaves and stems. Following egg

TABLE **6.** Anthomyiid pests of vegetable crops.

Species	***Host(s)***
A bean seed fly, *Delia florilega*	Dwarf French bean, onion, runner bean
A bean seed fly, *Delia platura*	Brassicas, dwarf French bean, lettuce, onion, pea, runner bean etc.
Cabbage root fly (*Delia radicum*)	Brassicas (ornamentals, including stock and wallflower, are also attacked)
Mangold fly (*Pegomya hyoscyami*)	Red beet and spinach (see Chapter 5, p. 110)
Onion fly (*Delia antiqua*)	Leek, onion and shallot
Spinach stem fly (*Delia echinata*)	Spinach
Turnip root fly (*Delia floralis*)	Brassicas, especially swede and turnip

FIG 153. Onion fly (*Delia antiqua*) larvae feed singly or gregariously inside onion bulbs, eventually causing considerable damage.

hatch the larvae (Fig. 153) bore into the plants in order to feed, either singly or gregariously. Attacks are most frequent in central and eastern England, and often result in the collapse and eventual death of seedlings. Immature larvae then move through the soil to attack adjacent plants. Bean seed fly larvae also attack onion seedlings, and this can result in misidentification of the species involved.[58] In the case of germinating pea and bean seeds and seedlings, it is not uncommon to find spotted snake millepedes (*Blaniulus guttulatus*) and other soil-inhabiting creatures enlarging the original wounds caused by dipterous larvae.

Brassica plants are at particular risk of attack from cabbage root fly. The housefly-like adults are active from spring onwards, the actual timing of emergence varying according to temperature. Time of emergence is also genetically determined, there being distinct early-emerging and late-emerging biotypes.[59] Members of the former biotype tend to appear in late April and early May, and those of the latter in June and early July; mixed populations occur in many areas. Cabbage root fly eggs are laid on the ground or in cracks in the soil close to the stems of host plants. Sometimes they are also laid on the foliage of host plants, including the crinkled leaflets around the developing buttons of Brussels sprout plants. In warmer parts of the country, egg-laying commences in late April or early May, often coinciding with the flowering of cow parsley. However, eggs are laid two to three weeks or so later in more northerly regions, including Scotland. The eggs hatch within a week. Creamy-white larvae (Fig. 154) then attack their hosts, rasping at the surface tissue of the tap root and destroying the fibrous side roots. Larvae also feed within the stems, crowns and growing points or bore into Brussels sprout buttons. The larvae are fully fed in three to four weeks. They then pupate in the soil, and adults of the next

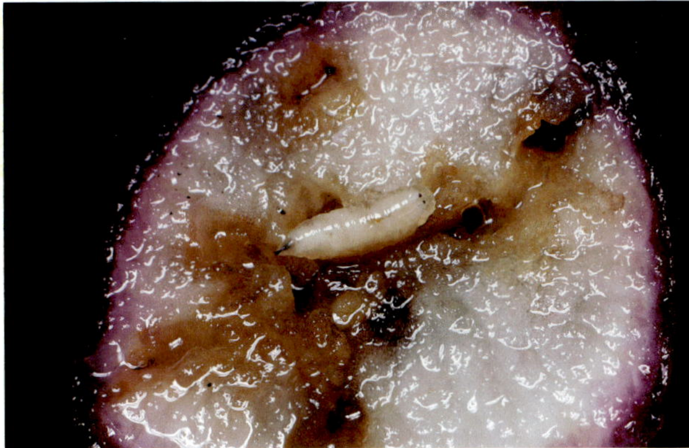

FIG 154. Cabbage root fly (*Delia radicum*) larvae are major pests of brassicaceous crops, including radish.

generation eventually make their appearance. Egg-laying by second- and third-generation adults generally occurs in July and September, respectively. However, a full third generation is not always completed, and larvae caught out by the onset of winter die without completing their development. The extent of damage on host plants varies from superficial, almost imperceptible grazing, as on the tap roots of swedes and turnips, to the collapse and death of young plants. Brassica seedlings and recent transplants, for example, are often killed by the larvae. Infestations are particularly significant in the case of summer cabbages and both summer and autumn cauliflowers. Internal damage to Brussels sprout buttons is often undetected at harvest, and infested buttons (even when the incidence of attack is low) can prove a significant problem in crops sent for freezing. Brassica root crops intended for human consumption (where quality is often a key issue) have a lower acceptable damage threshold than those grown as stock feed where yield alone tends to be paramount.

Compared with all the aforementioned species, turnip root fly has a noticeably northerly distribution, and is found mainly in northern Britain. It is also essentially single brooded, adults occurring during the summer months and the larvae feeding on the roots of brassica plants from early autumn onwards. Infestations most often occur on swedes and turnips, the larvae typically burrowing deeply into the tissue. Larvae of the turnip gall weevil (*Ceutorhynchus pleurostigma*)[60] also feed in the roots of swedes and turnips, but each is housed within a distinctive, single-chambered, marble-like gall (Fig. 155). Cabbage and cauliflower plants are also attacked. Such galls are sometimes mistaken for symptoms of clubroot, a disease caused by the protozoan *Plasmodiophora brassicae*.[61] Root swellings induced by clubroot, however, are solid not hollow.

FIG 155. Turnip gall weevil (*Ceutorhynchus pleurostigma*) larvae inhabit marble-like galls on the roots of host plants.

A considerable number of root fly eggs and larvae are lost to predators. In the case of cabbage root fly, for example, the ground beetles *Bembidion lampros* and *Harpalus affinis*[62] have been recognised as particularly useful in spring (April and May), followed later in the season by *H. rufipes*, *Pterostichus melanarius* (Fig. 156) and *Trechus quadristriatus*.[63] Rove beetles also play an important predatory role. Adults of *Aleochara bilineata*, for example, will feed on cabbage root fly eggs and larvae.[64] *A. bilineata* acts as both a predator and a parasitoid. Eggs are laid in the soil close to infested plants. Following egg hatch each tiny beetle larva searches for a host puparium and having located one bores into it. The parasitoid then attacks and kills the developing pupa. The parasitoid larva eventually pupates and finally emerges from the host puparium as a fully fledged adult. The related *A. bipustulata* also parasitises cabbage root fly pupae.

FIG 156. Ground beetles such as *Pterostichus* spp. are important predators of cabbage root fly eggs.

The cynipid wasp *Trybliographa rapae*[65] is a common endoparasitoid of cabbage root fly. It deposits eggs in first- and second-instar larvae but hosts are not killed until they have pupated.[66] Various braconid and ichneumonid wasps are also recorded as parasitoids, but are of lesser significance.[67] Adult cabbage root flies are often infected by naturally occurring fungal pathogens. These include *Entomophthora muscae*,[68] a generally common pathogen with a wide range of dipterous hosts (including house flies, onion fly and other *Delia* spp.). In central England, the pathogen 'becomes particularly common during mid-summer conditions, when dead, diseased [cabbage root fly] adults can readily be seen clinging in a characteristic manner to the foliage of many hedgerow plants'.[69]

CUTWORMS

Cutworms (the larvae of certain noctuid moths) are important polyphagous pests and often cause extensive crop damage. They are of particular significance in the major vegetable-growing areas of England, as in the black fens of East Anglia. Turnip moth (*Agrotis segetum*) is usually the most important and most destructive species, although others also occur (see below). Adult turnip moths are on the wing in May and June. Eggs are then laid in small, irregular groups on various plants, and hatch about two weeks later. The larvae spend most of their time in the soil, feeding at night. In their youngest stages they ascend host plants to graze on the leaves. However, as older individuals they typically attack the stems of plants which they often partially or completely sever at or about soil level – hence the term 'cutworm'. They also attack tap roots, tubers and other subterranean parts of plants. In drilled crops, cutworms often work along the rows of young plants, leaving trails of destruction behind them as a direct result of their night-time activities. During the day, the comatose larvae may be found sheltering in the uppermost layers of the soil or under nearby stones or other debris. Turnip moth larvae are usually fully grown by the autumn, but most do not pupate until the following spring. Sometimes, however, a few pupate early and give rise to a partial second generation of adults. Cutworms such as turnip moth are usually most important in hot, dry summers. Damage to cabbages, carrots, celery, leeks, lettuces, onions, potatoes, swedes, turnips and other root vegetables can then be particularly severe. Attacks are also most frequent in light or medium soils. Early-instar larvae are very susceptible to rainfall, and inclement weather during the initial stages of larval development results in considerable mortality.[70] Moist soil is also unfavourable to them, hampering survival.[71]

FIG 157. Heart & dart moth (*Agrotis exclamationis*) larvae are often common pests of vegetable crops.

Other species whose larvae behave as cutworms and cause damage to vegetable crops include garden dart moth (*Euxoa nigricans*), heart & dart moth (*Agrotis exclamationis*) (Fig. 157) and white-line dart moth (*E. tritici*). The life history of heart & dart moth is similar to that of turnip moth, although adults tend to appear slightly later in the season. Those of garden dart moth and white-line dart moth, however, are fundamentally different. In these two species eggs form the overwintering stage, larvae feed from March to June and adults occur mainly in July and August. Larvae of dark sword-grass moth (*A. ipsilon*), a regular and sometimes common migrant to Britain, also behave as cutworms. This species, however, cannot survive British winters. In addition, larvae of the often abundant large yellow underwing moth (*Noctua pronuba*) similarly inhabit the soil and adopt a cutworm-like habit, although they are essentially leaf grazers; they are generally known as climbing cutworms.

MIDGES

Pea midge (*Contarinia pisi*) is a potentially important pest of vining peas, particularly in Humberside, Lincolnshire, north Cambridgeshire and Norfolk. First-generation adults emerge from the soil in June or early July, often following heavy showers of rain. They are most likely to emerge in fields where peas were grown during the previous year. Mating takes place at these emergence sites, the mated females then dispersing in order to locate suitable host plants. Dispersal flights most often occur in calm weather conditions in the early morning and towards dusk. Once suitable hosts are located eggs are laid in association with the buds or flowers, typically in groups of about 20–30. The eggs hatch a few days later. Larvae then feed gregariously for about ten days before dropping to the soil and forming subterranean silken cocoons in which to pupate. Pea midge larvae (in common with those of other members of the genus *Contarinia*) possess the ability to jump by flexing their bodies, and this aids their dispersal over the ground prior to entering the soil and spinning their subterranean cocoons. Two kinds of cocoon are produced:[72] rounded ones in which larvae pupate immediately and give rise to a second generation of adults (in England, in late July and early August), and oval ones in which pupation occurs after an extended period of diapause. Larvae that have overwintered usually pupate in late May or early June. However, some remain in their cocoons for several years before eventually doing so. Following attack by pea midge larvae, developing flowers become swollen, crinkled and noticeably distorted. Terminal shoots also develop into stunted, tight clusters of tissue, a symptom often described as 'nettle-head'. Later in the season, larvae may also feed inside developing pods – reminiscent of brassica pod midge (*Dasineura brassicae*) larvae in the siliquae of brassicaceous plants. Overall, pea midge is capable of causing extensive damage. However, infestations vary considerably in size from one year to another and from place to place, with years of great abundance or relative scarcity. Outbreak years in which heavy infestations occurred in England include 1905, 1906, 1926, 1955 and 1956.[73] Midge-infested flowerheads or growing points are often co-inhabited by pea thrips and by the pteromalid wasp *Macroglenes gramineus*,[74] a tiny endoparasitoid that lays its eggs singly in the larvae of pea midge. A parasitised midge larva continues to develop, and is not killed until it has entered the soil and spun a cocoon. It is here that the parasitoid larva eventually pupates. In common with its host, *M. gramineus* has two generations annually.[75] *Leptacis tipulae*, the platygastrid parasitoid of wheat blossom midge (Chapter 2), also attacks pea midge.[76]

Particularly in dry weather during June the heads of brassicas (primarily swede and to a lesser extent turnip) become infested by tiny, yellowish-white larvae of swede midge (*Contarinia nasturtii*). Such larvae cause distortion of leaves (the 'crumpled leaf' symptom), swelling of flowers and death of growing points. Loss of growing points subsequently results in the development of numerous secondary shoots (the 'many neck' symptom). Damaged plants are also subject to rotting that follows infection by bacterial pathogens. Swede midge is multi-brooded and can be very damaging,[77] especially on late-sown swede seed crops, but only in years when growing conditions are poor.[78]

Occasionally the stems of field beans are attacked by larvae of bean stem midge (*Resseliella* sp.). Infestations of this as yet undescribed species were first found in eastern England (in Cambridgeshire) in the early 1980s.[79] The midges appear in late May and June. Eggs are then laid in lesions on the stems of autumn-sown beans – at that time of year there are relatively few suitable lesions on spring-sown beans. Following egg hatch, the larvae feed in groups, lined up immediately beneath the epidermis. The covering epidermal tissue eventually turns black, and this is often the first sign of an infestation. Fully fed larvae pupate in the soil and adults of a second generation emerge in mid-summer. Direct damage is of no immediate importance. However, following secondary invasion of the larval feeding sites by fungal pathogens (*Fusarium* spp.), midge-damaged plants frequently lodge.

SLUGS

Particularly in moist conditions, slugs cause noticeable damage to vegetable crops. They not only damage the tap roots of crops such as red beet (Fig. 158) but may also graze on the aerial parts of plants, including celery (Fig. 159).

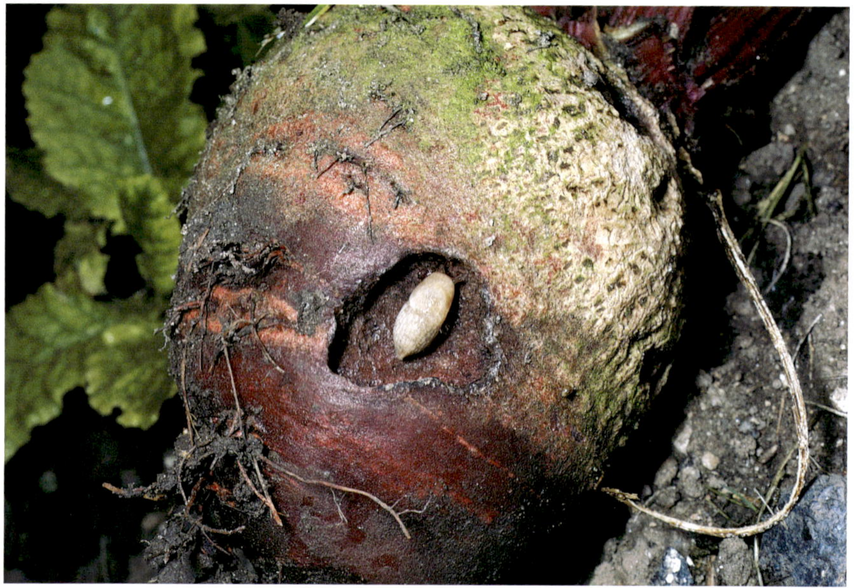

FIG 158. Slugs often bore into tap roots of crops such as red beet.

FIG 159. Slugs sometimes graze on the stems of celery, rendering plants unmarketable.

NEMATODES

Various plant-parasitic nematodes are associated with vegetable crops (Table 7). These range from soil-inhabiting ectoparasitic needle nematodes and stubby-root nematodes to endoparasitic species that feed and breed internally. Plant symptoms resulting from nematode attacks (patches of poorly growing, discoloured, distorted and stunted plants, for example) may well attract attention, but they are often difficult to distinguish in the field from those caused by other debilitating factors. Nevertheless, it may be possible in summer to find the lemon-shaped cysts of *Heterodera* spp. on the roots of carefully lifted infested host plants. This is especially so in the case of pea cyst nematode (*H. goettingiana*). This pest is well established in central and eastern England, and often present in private gardens and allotments.

TABLE 7. Examples of plant-parasitic nematodes associated with vegetable crops.

Species	***Host crop(s)***
Beet cyst nematode (*Heterodera schachtii*)	Brassicas, red beet, spinach etc.
Brassica cyst nematode (*Heterodera cruciferae*)	Brassicas
Carrot cyst nematode (*Heterodera carotae*)	Carrot
Needle nematodes (*Longidorus* spp.)	Carrot, parsnip
Northern root-knot nematode (*Meloidogyne hapla*)	Bean, carrot, parsnip, pea etc.[80]
Pea cyst nematode (*Heterodera goettingiana*)	Broad bean, pea
Stem nematode (*Ditylenchus dipsaci*)	Carrot, onion, pea, rhubarb etc.[81]
Stubby-root nematodes (*Paratrichodorus* spp.)*	Pea
Stubby-root nematodes (*Trichodorus* spp.)*	Carrot, parsnip, pea

* Some species are vectors of pea early browning virus (PEBV).

Stem nematode (*Ditylenchus dipsaci*) is probably the most important nematode pest of field vegetables. As one biological race or another, it is also associated with many other crops. Crinkled leaves, dead or discoloured foliage, distorted crowns and the presence of stem lesions and swollen leaf stalks or stems are all symptomatic of attack. The transparent, thread-like adults (each little more than a millimetre long) feed and breed continuously within the tissue of their hosts. Individuals pass through an egg and four juvenile (pre-adult) stages, the first of which occurs whilst still within the egg. Development is rapid, and the lifecycle is completed in about three weeks at 15°C.[82] Onion is usually acknowledged as the most frequently and severely affected vegetable host.[83] Here, the infested stems become noticeably swollen (a condition often described as 'bloat'). Also, leaves become thread-like and distorted, and plants eventually rot and die. Other frequently attacked crops include beans, carrots, parsnips, peas and rhubarb – on rhubarb, stem nematode and the pathogenic bacterium *Erwinia rhapontici* are associated with a wasting condition called crown rot. Broad bean and field bean plants are susceptible to the oat race of stem nematode. A so-called 'giant race', the adult females of which often exceed 2 mm in length,[84] also occurs on beans. This giant race is particularly damaging and especially liable to invade the flowers and developing seeds. Unlike most plant-parasitic nematodes, stem nematode is capable of surviving prolonged periods of desiccation. The nematodes often do so within dried-out infested plant tissue by clumping together as fourth-stage juveniles to form so-called 'nematode wool'. They then remain in suspended animation until moisture eventually brings about their revival.

CHAPTER 7

Life in Orchards

OVER THE PAST HALF CENTURY or so the land area occupied by orchards in the UK has more than halved. The area of dessert apple orchards, for example, which extended to over 25,000 ha of farmland in England and Wales during the 1960s, had shrunk to less than 8,000 ha by the year 2000, a staggering drop of over 75 per cent. Regrettably, this general decline has continued into the new millennium (Table 8), although new plantings are to be found.

UK commercial orchards are dominated by dessert and to a lesser extent culinary apple production, concentrated in East Anglia, Kent and the West Midlands. Cider apples, however, whether in modern bush or traditional orchards, are grown mainly in Devon, Herefordshire and Somerset. There is also a small, but thriving, apple industry in Co. Armagh, Northern Ireland.[1] Plums

TABLE 8. Land area (ha) devoted to orchards in England and Wales, 2000 to 2004.*

	2000	2001	2002	2003	2004
All orchards	20,823	21,104	18,739	17,671	16,909
Dessert apples	7,662	6,630	5,628	5,349	6,018
Culinary apples	3,795	3,340	2,745	2,446	2,405
Cider apples	5,043	7,010	6,738	6,551	5,190
Pears	2,355	2,330	2,041	1,742	1,673
Perry pears	165	22	61	58	23
Plums	1,213	1,072	947	1,003	978
Cherries	459	473	428	381	389

* Source: Orchard Fruit Survey – July 2004 (Defra).

(including damsons and greengages) are widely grown in Britain. However, commercial production is centred in southeast England and the West Midlands, the latter including the Vale of Evesham. Nowadays, most cherry and pear orchards are to be found in Herefordshire and Kent, with perry pears located mainly in Gloucestershire, Herefordshire and Worcestershire. Hop and nut crops, often discussed in tandem with orchard fruits, are excluded from this chapter and will be addressed later (Chapter 11).

Orchards are home to a rich diversity of wildlife, associated not only with fruit trees and the overall ground flora but also with windbreaks and surrounding hedges. The guild of temporary or more permanent inhabitants includes a wide range of invertebrates. Admittedly, some of these might be pests (Tables 9 and 10). However, at the other extreme there are likely to be beneficial species acting as pollinators or as natural enemies of pests. As potentially attractive habitats, orchards are frequented by many ephemeral, casual or purposeful visitors, including nectar- and pollen-seeking insects. Insect pollination in orchards, whether by honey bees (perhaps temporarily imported by man) or by naturally occurring pollinators such as bumblebees, is a key component of the fruit production cycle. As long-term habitats, old orchards

TABLE 9. Examples of insect pests (genera) associated with rosaceous fruit trees in Europe.[2]

Order	*Family*	*Genus (number of species)*
Saltatoria	Tettigoniidae	*Leptophyes* (1), *Phaneroptera* (1)
	Acrididae	*Locusta* (1)
Dermaptera	Forficulidae	*Forficula* (1)
Hemiptera	Acanthosomatidae	*Acanthosoma* (1)
	Pentatomidae	*Dolycoris* (1), *Palomena* (1), *Pentatoma* (1)
	Tingidae	*Stephanitis* (1)
	Miridae	*Atractotomus* (1), *Camplylomma* (1), *Closterotomus* (1), *Lygocoris* (2), *Lygus* (1), *Orthotylus* (1), *Plagiognathus* (2), *Psallus* (1)
	Cercopidae	*Cercopis* (1), *Philaenus* (1)
	Flatidae	*Metcalfa* (1)
	Membracidae	*Stictocephala* (1)
	Cicadellidae	*Aguriahana* (1), *Alnetoidia* (1), *Cicadella* (1), *Edwardsiana* (3), *Empoasca* (2), *Fieberiella* (1), *Ribautiana* (2), *Typhlocyba* (1), *Zygina* (1)
	Psyllidae	*Cacopsylla* (6)

	Aphididae	*Anuraphis* (2), *Aphis* (4), *Brachycaudus* (3), *Dysaphis* (5), *Eriosoma* (2), *Hyalopterus* (2), *Melanaphis* (1), *Myzus* (3), *Phorodon* (1), *Pterochloroides* (1), *Rhopalosiphum* (2)
	Phylloxeridae	*Aphanostigma* (1)
	Diaspididae	*Chionaspis* (1), *Diaspidiotus* (1), *Epidiaspis* (1), *Lepidosaphes* (1), *Pseudaulacaspis* (1), *Quadraspidiotus* (3)
	Coccidae	*Ceroplastes* (1), *Eulecanium* (1), *Parthenolecanium* (1), *Sphaerolecanium* (1)
Thysanoptera	Thripidae	*Frankliniella* (1), *Taeniothrips* (1), *Thrips* (2)
Coleoptera	Scarabaeidae	*Melolontha* (2)
	Buprestidae	*Agrilus* (1)
	Cantharidae	*Cantharis* (1)
	Bostrychidae	*Sinoxylon* (1)
	Cerambycidae	*Tetrops* (1)
	Chrysomelidae	*Agelastica* (1), *Aphthona* (1), *Longitarsus* (1)
	Rhynchitidae	*Involvulus* (1), *Neocoenorrhinus* (2)
	Attelabidae	*Byctiscus* (1), *Deporaus* (1)
	Apionidae	*Protapion* (3)
	Curculionidae	*Anthonomus* (2), *Furcipes* (1), *Magdalis* (3), *Mecinus* (1), *Otiorhynchus* (2), *Peritelus* (1), *Phyllobius* (4), *Polydrusus* (5), *Rhyncaenus* (1), *Scolytus* (2), *Xyleborinus* (1), *Xyleborus* (1)
Diptera	Cecidomyiidae	*Contarinia* (2), *Dasineura* (3), *Putoniella* (1), *Resseliella* (1)
	Tephritidae	*Ceratitis* (1), *Rhagoletis* (2)
	Agromyzidae	*Phytomyza* (1)
	Muscidae	*Mesembrina* (1)
Lepidoptera	Nepticulidae	*Stigmella* (4)
	Cossidae	*Cossus* (1), *Zeuzera* (1)
	Zygaenidae	*Agalopa* (1)
	Lyonetiidae	*Bucculatrix* (1), *Leucoptera* (1), *Lyonetia* (2)
	Gracillariidae	*Callisto* (1), *Parornix* (1), *Phyllonorycter* (7)
	Sesiidae	*Synanthedon* (1)
	Choreutidae	*Choreutis* (1)
	Yponomeutidae	*Argyresthia* (5), *Scythropia* (1), *Swammerdamia* (1), *Yponomeuta* (3), *Ypsolopha* (1)
	Coleophoridae	*Coleophora* (5)
	Oecophoridae	*Batia* (1), *Carcina* (1), *Diurnea* (2)

	Gelechiidae	*Anarsia* (1), *Gelechia* (1), *Recurvaria* (2)
	Blastobasidae	*Blastobasis* (1)
	Momphidae	*Spuleria* (1)
	Tortricidae	*Acleris* (4), *Adoxophyes* (1), *Ancylis* (3), *Archips* (4), *Argyrotaenia* (1), *Cacoecimorpha* (1), *Choristoneura* (2), *Cnephasia* (2), *Croesia* (1), *Cydia* (6), *Ditula* (1), *Enarmonia* (1), *Exapate* (1), *Hedya* (3), *Neosphaleroptera* (1), *Pammene* (2), *Pandemis* (4), *Ptycholoma* (1), *Rhopobota* (1), *Spilonota* (1), *Syndemis* (1)
	Pyralidae	*Cryptoblabes* (1), *Ostrinia* (1), *Udea* (2)
	Papilionidae	*Iphiclides* (1)
	Pieridae	*Aporia* (1)
	Lycaenidae	*Satyrium* (1), *Thecla* (1)
	Lasiocampidae	*Eriogaster* (1), *Gastropacha* (1), *Malacosoma* (1), *Odonestis* (1), *Poecilocampa* (1)
	Geometridae	*Abraxas* (1), *Agriopis* (3), *Alcis* (1), *Alsophila* (1), *Apocheima* (1), *Biston* (2), *Campaea* (1), *Chloroclysta* (1), *Colotois* (1), *Crocalis* (1), *Ectropis* (1), *Epirrita* (1), *Erannis* (1), *Eupithecia* (1), *Lycia* (1), *Opisthograptis* (1), *Operophtera* (2), *Ourapteryx* (1), *Pasiphila* (1), *Peribatodes* (1), *Phigalia* (1), *Selenia* (1), *Theria* (1)
	Sphingidae	*Mimas* (1), *Smerinthus* (1)
	Notodontidae	*Phalera* (1)
	Dilobidae	*Diloba* (1)
	Lymantriidae	*Calliteara* (1), *Euproctis* (2), *Lymantria* (2), *Orgyia* (1)
	Arctiidae	*Hyphantria* (1), *Spilosoma* (1)
	Nolidae	*Nola* (1)
	Noctuidae	*Acronicta* (4), *Allophyes* (1), *Amphipyra* (1), *Conistra* (1), *Cosmia* (2), *Eupsilia* (1), *Mamestra* (1), *Melanchra* (1), *Naenia* (1), *Orthosia* (6), *Phlogophora* (1)
Hymenoptera	Pamphiliidae	*Neurotoma* (2)
	Cephidae	*Janus* (1)
	Tenthredinidae	*Ametastegia* (1), *Caliroa* (1), *Endelomyia* (1), *Hoplocampa* (4), *Micronematus* (1), *Nematus* (1), *Priophorus* (1), *Pristiphora* (1)
	Torymidae	*Torymus* (1)
	Formicidae	*Lasius* (1)
	Vespidae	*Vespa* (1), *Vespula* (2)

TABLE 10. Examples of mite pests (genera) associated with rosaceous fruit trees in Europe.[3]

Order	*Family*	*Genus (number of species)*
Prostigmata	Eriophyidae	*Acalitus* (1), *Aculus* (2), *Diptacus* (1), *Epitrimerus* (1), *Eriophyes* (3), *Phyllocoptes* (1)
	Tetranychidae	*Amphitetranychus* (1), *Bryobia* (2), *Eotetranychus* (2), *Panonychus* (1), *Tetranychus* (2)
	Tenuipalpidae	*Cenopalpus* (1)
Cryptostigmata	Mycobatidae	*Humerobates* (1)

provide suitable conditions for the establishment and survival of a large number of plants and animals.[4] This includes great rarities such as the noble chafer (*Gnorimus nobilis*), and restoration of traditional orchards has been advocated under the Countryside Stewardship Scheme to halt the decline of such species and encourage their survival.

Less-intensively managed orchards offer particularly rich pickings for insects and mites, whether phytophagous or otherwise. However, pests are not necessarily rampant in such places, since a balance may well have become established between them and their natural enemies. Intensively managed commercial orchards are inevitably more clinical than others, and even where pesticide use is commonplace trees are unlikely to remain totally pest-free throughout the whole season. Nor will parasitoids, predators or pathogens be entirely absent.

DEFOLIATING PESTS

Over the course of a growing season, apart from any impact that might follow the application of pesticides, fruit trees provide highly suitable conditions for the development of leaf-browsing insects. Some of these are regular orchard inhabitants, including economically important pests such as fruit tree tortrix moth (*Archips podana*) (Fig. 160) and winter moth (*Operophtera brumata*) (Fig. 161). Many others are casual, infrequent visitors which, in themselves, are unlikely to be of concern to fruit growers. However, even the least harmful phytophagous species contribute to the overall assault upon host trees. Collectively, they can become of some significance and are worthy of attention. Just how many juvenile

FIG 160. Fruit tree tortrix moth (*Archips podana*) is a major orchard pest. Males (above left) are smaller and darker than females (above right). Larvae (left) attack buds, leaves and developing fruits.

FIG 161. Winter moth (*Operophtera brumata*) is an important pest of fruit trees. Males (above left) are fully winged but the inconspicuous females (above right) are virtually wingless and cannot fly.

pests (nymphs or larvae) successfully complete their development through to adulthood is questionable since all must run the gauntlet of natural enemies, including various parasitoids, predators and pathogens. There are of course other mortality factors to be overcome, and these include pesticides applied by man.

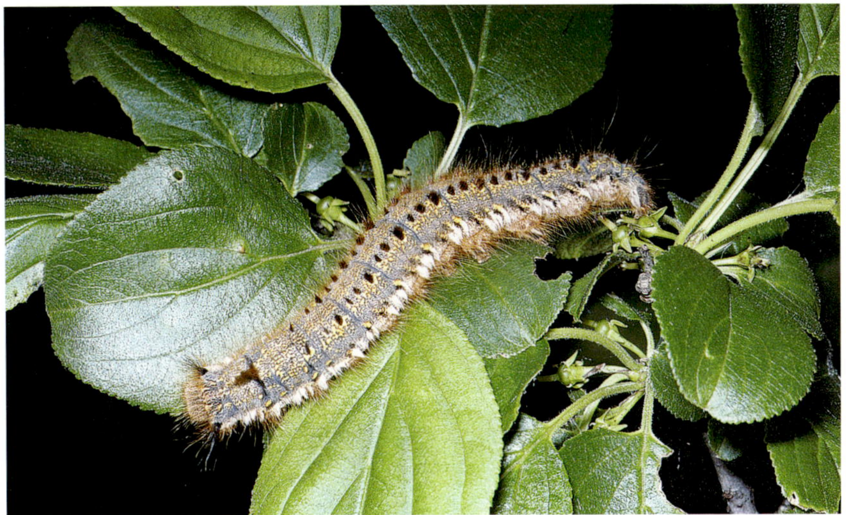

FIG 162. Lappet moth (*Gastropacha quercifolia*) larvae occasionally occur on fruit trees, but are usually restricted to old, unsprayed orchards.

Moth larvae on fruit trees range from small, often overlooked, species (fully grown individuals perhaps no more than a centimetre or so in length) to a few extremely large ones. At up to 100 mm in length, fully grown larvae of the lappet moth (*Gastropacha quercifolia*) (Fig. 162) are probably the largest. Although nowadays a local and declining British species, this unmistakable insect does occasionally deposit eggs on apple and plum trees. Eyed hawk moth (*Smerinthus ocellata*), another large species and by no means an uncommon orchard visitor, has gained a reputation for causing extensive damage to the foliage of young apple trees. During their later instars the larvae, which often occur in pairs, rapidly strip the foliage from the new shoots. It is then that they most often attract attention.

Leaf-rollers or leaf-tiers (family Tortricidae) are particularly important orchard pests, and many species are associated with fruit trees. The larvae typically web leaves together with silken threads or form a shelter from a folded leaf, their habitations often being characteristic for the species.[5] Fruit tree tortrix moth is the most widely known orchard-inhabiting species, but many others also occur, including the locally important summer fruit tortrix moth (*Adoxophyes orana*) (Fig. 163) and generally common species such as barred fruit tree tortrix moth (*Pandemis cerasana*), bud moth (*Spilonota ocellana*) and plum tortrix moth (*Hedya pruniana*). Damage is not necessarily restricted to foliage. At some time in

FIG 163. Summer fruit tortrix moth (*Adoxophyes orana*) larvae are locally important pests in orchards, especially in southeast England.

their development, the larvae may also browse on buds, blossoms, fruitlets and fruits, and collateral damage such as this is often particularly serious. Most tortrix larvae wriggle violently backwards when disturbed. This behaviour, however, is not unique and is shared by larvae of various other groups, including gelechiids (family Gelechiidae) and pyralids (family Pyralidae).

Apple leaf skeletonizer moth (*Choreutis pariana*) is a frequent inhabitant of unsprayed apple orchards, the larvae (each protected by a small web, within which black grains of frass soon accumulate) grazing away tissue from the upper surface of leaves. Typically, the lower surface of the leaf remains intact and eventually turns brown, as if burnt.[6] There are two generations annually, larvae occurring in May and June, and again in August. Pupation takes place in opaque, white, cigar-shaped to boat-shaped cocoons, which are often formed on the underside of leaves. Adults of the second generation spend the winter amongst dead leaves and in other sheltered situations. Although this insect is usually of only minor significance in orchards, larvae of the second brood sometimes attack the surface of maturing fruits, and this subsequently leads to surface russeting.

Various looper caterpillars (family Geometridae – larvae typically with functional prolegs present on just the sixth and tenth abdominal segments) also occur on fruit trees. Of these, winter moth larvae (Fig. 164) are the most damaging and best known. Other orchard-inhabiting geometrids include March moth

FIG 164. In spring, winter moth (*Operophtera brumata*) larvae often cause extensive damage to foliage. Developing fruitlets are also attacked.

FIG 165. Pale brindled beauty moth (*Phigalia pilosaria*) females are flightless ('wingless').

(*Alsophila aescularia*), mottled umber moth (*Erannis defoliaria*) and pale brindled beauty moth (*Phigalia pilosaria*)[7] (Fig. 165). In common with winter moth, all three species have 'wingless' females – in reality, however, pale brindled beauty moth and winter moth females are not strictly wingless, as they possess wing stubs. Reinvasion by such species in regularly sprayed orchards is achieved mainly by first-instar larvae that drift in the wind (from nearby infested hedgerows or woodlands) on fine threads of silk. Wingless females are also a feature of some non-geometrids, including the vapourer moth (*Orgyia antiqua*) (family Lymantriidae), an often abundant, polyphagous species in both urban and rural areas. Here, dispersal following egg hatch is achieved by the highly mobile, nomadic larvae.

Larvae of the light emerald moth (*Campaea margaritata*), another polyphagous arboreal geometrid, are unusual in that they continue to feed on fruit trees in mid-winter, individuals removing the rind from the young shoots and thereby

FIG 166. Light emerald moth (*Campaea margaritata*) larvae feed throughout the winter and, in the absence of leaves, they browse on the rind of the young shoots.

exposing the pale underlying tissue. They are mainly grey, somewhat flattened creatures, with a characteristic fringe-like skirt of short protuberances along either side of the body (Fig. 166). Also, unlike most other geometrids, they have an additional pair of functional prolegs. Other orchard-inhabiting geometrid larvae sporting additional prolegs include March moth (with a pair of small, stump-like, non-functional prolegs on the fifth abdominal segment) and brimstone moth (*Opisthograptis luteolata*) (with two additional pairs of functional prolegs – on the fourth and fifth abdominal segments).

Although the vast majority of leaf-browsing larvae on fruit trees lead independent, solitary lives, some species are gregarious. Young larvae of the yellow-tail moth (*Euproctis similis*) feed in large communal groups before dispersing and becoming independent. The downy, yellow, black and orange-yellow larvae of the buff-tip moth (*Phalera bucephala*), however, continue to feed gregariously for much of their lives. When fully grown, buff-tip larvae can exceed 50 mm in length and, collectively, are capable of causing extensive defoliation. Although sometimes present on fruit trees, they are far more often found on wild hosts such as alder, birch, elm and hazel. Gregarious web-inhabiting species are discussed later.

Larvae of several noctuid species are frequent inhabitants of fruit trees. Of these, species of *Orthosia*, including the clouded drab moth (*O. incerta*) (Fig. 167), are most often reported as causing damage, although colourful larvae of species such as the dark dagger moth (*Acronicta tridens*) and the grey dagger moth (*A. psi*) are more likely to attract attention. Larvae of the dunbar moth (*Cosmia trapezina*), sometimes mistaken for those of clouded drab moth, are partly cannibalistic and renowned as habitual predators of winter moth larvae.

FIG 167. (Above left) Clouded drab moth (*Orthosia incerta*) is a generally common pest, whose larvae (above right) sometimes bite into developing apple fruitlets.

Butterflies do not rate as pests of fruit trees in the British Isles. Abroad, however, larvae of some species can cause damage, including those of the brown hairstreak butterfly (*Thecla betulae*) on plum[8] and the black-veined white butterfly (*Aporia crataegi*) (long-since extinct in Britain) on apple and pear. A hundred years or so ago, the large tortoiseshell butterfly (*Nymphalis polychloros*) was to be found breeding on fruit trees in southern England, especially in cherry orchards,[9] but this is no longer so.

Various leaf-browsing sawfly larvae are also associated with fruit trees. Of these, the most important are undoubtedly those of the pear slug sawfly (*Caliroa cerasi*) (Fig. 168), an often abundant inhabitant of cherry and pear trees. Other hosts for this species include rowan and whitebeam. The larvae (known as pear & cherry slugworms) are slug-like in general appearance and their bodies are coated in olive-black slime. Although they possess thoracic legs, and also seven

FIG 168. Pear slug sawfly (*Caliroa cerasi*) larvae feed on the upper surface of leaves, and are often mistaken for small black slugs. Note cast skin of an earlier instar (top right).

pairs of abdominal prolegs, these are all very short and inconspicuous. Pear & cherry slugworms remove tissue from the upper surface of the leaves, and often cause extensive damage. There are usually two broods per year, the slugworms occurring throughout the summer and early autumn.

In continental Europe, pear leaf sawfly (*Micronematus abbreviatus*) is an important pest of pear trees, the larvae being capable of causing extensive defoliation and consequent yield losses. Individual larvae feed around the leaf margins throughout May into early June, completing just one generation annually. Although this species is present on pear trees in Britain, its potential as a pest seems largely to have been ignored. Larvae of the sawfly *Nematus lucidus* similarly feed along leaf margins, in this case on damson and plum trees. When at rest the larvae grasp the leaves with their thoracic legs and hold the abdomen aloft. Damage is of little or no economic importance, but is probably much under-reported. Foliage on plum trees is also damaged by larvae of the plum leaf sawfly (*Priophorus pallipes*), a smaller yet more well-known pest.

In springtime, the foliage of fruit trees can be ravaged by adult leaf weevils (e.g. *Phyllobius* spp. and *Polydrusus* spp.). These insects are particularly abundant in grassland areas, and they often invade rosaceous trees and shrubs where they bite characteristic notches into the leaf margins. If trees are in flower, the pests also damage the blossoms. Although sometimes extensive, such damage is short term and the weevils disappear from the orchards almost as quickly as they arrived.

FIG 169. In spring, first-generation green pug moth (*Pasiphila rectangulata*) larvae attack fruit blossom, destroying the floral parts.

Some leaf-browsing moth larvae preferentially feed on fruit blossoms, and damage not only the petals but also the stamens and ovaries. First-generation larvae of the green pug moth (*Pasiphila rectangulata*)[10] (Fig. 169) are frequent culprits, especially on apple trees.

A few pests are dependent upon the presence of flower (fruit) buds in order to complete their lifecycle. Apple blossom weevil (*Anthonomus pomorum*) (Fig. 170) is a well-known example. Prior to the introduction of DDT in 1946, this pest was of great importance in commercial orchards, and resultant yield losses were often considerable.

FIG 170. Apple blossom weevil (*Anthonomus pomorum*) is a notorious pest.

Following the widespread use of organochlorine insecticides, however, the importance of this pest rapidly declined. Adults overwinter in woodlands, dense hedgerows, wood piles and other shelter, and become active in the early spring from February onwards. They then invade apple trees, and lay eggs singly through the side of flower (fruit) buds. Following egg hatch, each larva feeds on the developing anthers and style; they also bite into the petals and these, instead of expanding and opening, remain closed as a protective cover – the characteristic and, to the seasoned fruit grower, familiar capped blossom – that eventually turns brown (Fig. 171). Fully grown larvae eventually pupate (Fig. 172), and new adults

FIG 171. Capped blossom is characteristic of apple blossom weevil (*Anthonomus pomorum*) infestations.

FIG 172. Apple blossom weevil (*Anthonomus pomorum*) larvae pupate within the shelter of capped blossom.

emerge from the capped blossoms about three weeks later. Today, in the wake of more liberal pest management regimes, apple blossom weevil appears to have become more numerous than in, say, the 1960s or 1970s, but it does not rank as a major twenty-first-century antagonist. Indeed, in years when there is a particularly heavy set of fruit, loss of blossoms as a direct result of an attack can be considered beneficial, the weevil acting as a natural thinning agent.

Cherry fruit moth (*Argyresthia pruniella*) occurs mainly in unsprayed cherry orchards, the adults frequently being seen resting on the trunks of host trees during June and July. Eggs are deposited on the shoots and spurs, typically no more than a couple of metres or so above ground level. The eggs usually hatch in the following spring. However, they sometimes do so in advance of this, in which case the larvae hibernate within small silken cocoons spun beneath the empty eggs shells. Flower (fruit) buds are invaded at or just before bud burst, the larvae boring into the developing tissue. Larvae also invade the blossoms, destroying the ovary. Later, they may also tunnel within young fruitlets. Crop losses on heavily infested trees can be considerable. Cherry fruit moth also causes damage on plum.[11] The related *A. curvella*[12] is similarly associated with fruit trees, and can be very numerous in neglected apple orchards. The adults occur during June and July, and eggs deposited on the shoots and spurs of host trees hatch in the following spring. The larvae then bore into flower (fruit) buds, eventually destroying the ovaries and other floral parts. Fully grown larvae drop to the ground and pupate in the soil. Adults emerge shortly afterwards.

SHOOT AND STEM BORERS OR BROWSERS

Several orchard pests damage the young shoots of fruit trees, browsing upon their surface, biting or boring into them. Apple twig cutter (*Involvulus caeruleus*),[13] for example (a small, metallic-blue weevil), is a generally common pest of young apple trees. From May onwards, the egg-laying females climb to the tips of the new vegetative shoots which they then sever or partially sever a few centimetres below the unfurling apical cluster of leaves. A single egg is then deposited in each shoot. The damaged shoot (which subsequently becomes the larval habitation) wilts and usually falls to the ground. The larva feeds in the pith of the severed shoot and eventually pupates in the soil. Pear leaf-roller weevil (*Byctiscus betulae*) causes similar damage to pear trees; attacked shoot tips dry out, shrivel and soon turn black.

Clay-coloured weevil (*Otiorhynchus singularis*) sometimes damages young fruit trees, the nocturnal adults ascending under cover of darkness to browse on the rind of the small branches and new shoots. Recent grafts in orchards and nurseries are also subject to attack. The cause of such damage is often unsolved, since the culprits shelter throughout the day on the ground beneath the trees and thereby escape attention. The comatose weevils are particularly difficult to find, not only because of their dull, greyish-brown, soil-like coloration, but also because their bodies are frequently caked in mud. Where young trees are surrounded by straw mulch, the weevils often shelter between this and the underlying soil.

Two potentially important wood-boring insects occur in orchards: goat moth (*Cossus cossus*) and leopard moth (*Zeuzera pyrina*). The former is likely to be found only on older trees, the larvae (often in numbers) boring within the heart wood and sometimes leading to the eventual death of the host. Larvae of the latter (Fig. 173), however, attack branches, stems and trunks no more than 10 cm in diameter.[14] Leopard moth damage to fruit trees is sporadic, and in Britain

FIG 173. Leopard moth (*Zeuzera pyrina*) larvae tunnel within the shoots and smaller branches of host trees.

most frequently initiated in hot summers. Apart, perhaps, from death of buds attacked at the earliest stages of larval development, the first sign of an infestation is often the accumulation of sawdust on the ground beneath an infested tree, usually in the year following that in which eggs were laid. The fleshy, yellow, black-spotted larvae (which take up to two or three years to complete their development) feed within the pith of shoots and branches, weakening and sometimes killing them. Fully grown individuals attain a length of 50–60 mm, so it is not surprising that their impact on young trees can be dramatic. Open wounds in the bark of infested trees, which may be caused or further extended by woodpeckers seeking out the larvae, are also potential entry points for pathogenic fungi.

Cherry bark tortrix moth (*Enarmonia formosana*) is a persistent pest of old cherry trees. The larvae feed within the bark and underlying cambial layers of the trunks, forming extensive galleries which are extended by successive generations year after year. Distinctive rusty-looking frass tubes protrude from infested bark and (along with silken webbing and quantities of exuded gum) are an immediate sign of the presence of the pest. Plum trees are similarly affected. Attacks on apple are most often established on the underside of the larger branches, the bark becoming noticeably galled.[15] The trunks and branches of older apple trees are also subject to attack by apple clearwing moth (*Synanthedon myopaeformis*)[16] (Fig. 174). The larvae tunnel within or just below the bark, and take almost two years to complete their development. During the summer, the day-flying adults are active in sunny weather. Eggs are then deposited in cracks or crevices in the bark of host trees. Infestations are often established in cankerous wood already attacked by cherry bark tortrix moth.

Although primarily feeding as leaf rollers or invaders of blossoms or flowerheads, tortrix moth larvae of a few species sometimes bore into the new shoots of fruit trees. Shoots of young apple trees, for example, may be invaded by larvae of *Cnephasia longana*, especially in weedy, thistle-strewn sites. Abroad, larvae of the oriental fruit moth (*Cydia molesta*) do likewise on peach trees. Larvae of several other small moths also feed within the shoots of fruit trees. These range from incidental invaders, such as *Argyresthia albistra* and *A. spinosella* on damson and plum (two species more often associated with wild blackthorn bushes), to pith moth (*Spuleria atra*) which was once a persistent pest in commercial apple orchards.[17] Nowadays, pith moth is most often encountered on unsprayed trees. Eggs of this species are laid on the bark in the summer and hatch about a fortnight later. Larvae then bore into host trees, close to an unopened bud, to commence feeding singly within a shoot or spur. Larvae continue to feed throughout the autumn and winter months, and complete their

FIG 174. (Left) Apple clearwing moth (*Synanthedon myopaeformis*) occurs mainly on older apple trees. Larvae (below left) tunnel within or just below the bark, and take almost two years to complete their development.

development in the spring. Leaves and blossom on infested shoots wilt and die, immediately betraying the presence of a larva. There may also be external signs by way of accumulated frass, forced out of the larval gallery through cracks in the bark. Pith moth larvae are pinkish in colour, with the head and prothoracic plate dark brown; there are also, characteristically, three caudal plates. The golden-brown pupae, each with a pair of ventral projections directed obliquely forwards from the tip of the body, are equally unmistakable.

Death of young shoots in spring also follows in the wake of attacks by adult bark beetles. Large fruit bark beetles (*Scolytus mali*) and fruit bark beetles (*S. rugulosus*), for instance, often bore into shoots and the base of buds prior to forming breeding galleries in the trunks and branches. Bark beetles, however, usually attack ailing trees and are of secondary importance. The same is true of ambrosia beetles, including the fruit-tree wood ambrosia beetle (*Xyleborinus saxeseni*).[18]

GREGARIOUS WEB INHABITANTS

Gregarious larvae of several web-forming insects occur on fruit trees, and these sometimes cause noticeable but usually localised defoliation. Webs formed by apple small ermine moth (*Yponomeuta malinellus*)[19] on apple (Fig. 175) and the closely related common small ermine moth (*Y. padella*)[20] on damson or plum are probably most frequently encountered. However, compared with the often extensive and catastrophic outbreaks of small ermine moth larvae in the wild – e.g. *Y. cagnagella* on spindle bushes, *Y. evonymella* on bird-cherry trees,[21] and common small ermine moth on blackthorn and hawthorn hedges – damage to fruit trees is generally slight. Although associated mainly with hawthorn and (notably in parks and gardens) cotoneaster, larvae of the hawthorn webber moth (*Scythropia crataegella*) sometimes also occur in orchards, usually on damson trees

FIG 175. (Above left) Apple small ermine moth (*Yponomeuta malinellus*) is often common on unsprayed apple trees. Larvae (left) feed gregariously in silken webs.

or on adjacent hawthorn bushes. However, the pest usually escapes attention until the later stages of development when the reddish-brown, late-instar larvae and the darker, reddish-brown to blackish pupae become evident within the confines of an often expansive, although relatively flimsy, communal web. The attractive, silvery-white adults make their appearance in late June and July.

Lackey moth (*Malacosoma neustria*) is by no means an uncommon insect in fruit-growing areas, and communal webs (tents) formed by the larvae sometimes occur in orchards. The inhabitants, in their striking red, black, blue and white livery, often bask in sunshine on the outside of the tents or on nearby branches, and are then very conspicuous. Lackey moth eggs are laid in compact batches that girdle the shoots of host plants, where they overwinter. The larvae feed from April or early May onwards and complete their development in about July, individuals attaining a length of 40–50 mm. Web-forming larvae of the notorious brown-tail moth (*Euproctis chrysorrhoea*) also bask in sunshine on the outside of communal webs, typically as recently overwintered youngsters before launching springtime attacks on the foliage of host plants. Their dense, polythene-like winter tents are particularly noticeable during the winter months when host plants are devoid of foliage. At the start of the twentieth century this pest could be found in English apple, pear and plum orchards,[22] at least in Kent. Today, however, brown-tail moth occurs mainly (but not exclusively) on blackthorn and hawthorn hedges, and on other wild hosts such as bramble. This contrasts with continental Europe, where the pest still often damages apple and other rosaceous fruit trees. Following its accidental introduction from France in the late 1880s, brown-tail moth became, and still is, an important orchard pest in the USA. Brown-tail moth is discussed further in Chapter 9.

Certain non-lepidopterous pests also form webs on fruit trees. The gregarious larvae of the social pear sawfly (*Neurotoma saltuum*), for example, occur on pear trees during the early summer, their webs sometimes extending along complete branches to encompass the leaves and developing fruits. With their orange-yellow, naked bodies, their shiny black heads and the total absence of abdominal prolegs, the larvae (Fig. 176) are unmistakable. Nevertheless, their unusual and somewhat primitive appearance, and habit of wriggling violently (sometimes as a seething mass) when disturbed, often causes considerable puzzlement and alarm. Social pear sawfly larvae are fully fed by the end of July. They then drop to the ground to overwinter deep within the soil.

Mites also form webs on the leaves of fruit trees, but these structures are likely to be noticed by only the most fastidious of observers. Perhaps the most frequently encountered are the webs formed along the midrib on the underside of the leaves of apple trees by the hornbeam spider mite (*Eotetranychus carpini*). The mite

FIG 176. When fully fed, social pear sawfly (*Neurotoma saltuum*) larvae drop to the ground to pupate in the soil.

colonies are rarely populous, and damage resulting from feeding by the inhabitants is usually restricted to local discoloration of the foliage, albeit visible from above and below. Although capable of producing silk, the ubiquitous fruit tree red spider mite (*Panonychus ulmi*) does not construct webs. Two-spotted spider mite (*Tetranychus urticae*) does so, but usually only when populations are particularly dense. However, when present in orchards, this species is far more likely to be found on inter-row strawberry plants or other herbaceous hosts than on fruit trees.

LEAF MINERS

Several leaf mining pests are associated with orchard trees, most commonly the larvae of small moths. Although the majority are likely to occur in unsprayed orchards, it is by no means unusual to find leaf miners active in regularly sprayed sites. Perhaps the most frequently encountered orchard-inhabiting species is *Lyonetia clerkella*, whose larvae feed on apple and various other hosts, including cherry. The larvae (known as apple leaf miners) are pale green and have distinctive, bead-like bodies. They form very long, linear galleries, and eventually cause the death of leaf tissue as this becomes isolated by the mines. Fully fed larvae vacate their mines and each pupates in a characteristic, hammock-like cocoon (Fig. 177) on a cupped leaf or on the bark of the host tree. In Britain, there are usually two generations annually (and occasionally a partial third), with adults overwintering. Other species forming linear mines on the leaves of fruit trees include apple pygmy moth (*Stigmella malella*). This pest is of some significance as a pest of apple trees in mainland Europe. However, infestations in the UK are rarely of economic importance.

FIG 177. Pupal cocoons of *Lyonetia clerkella* are often common on unsprayed fruit trees, especially apple and cherry.

Larvae of several orchard pests form blotch mines in the leaves. Again, the vast majority are small lepidopterans. However, the assemblage of leaf-mining insects associated with fruit trees also includes an agromyzid fly, *Phytomyza heringiana*, albeit a relatively uncommon and usually overlooked species in Britain. Each of the grub-like fly larvae forms a brownish mine at the tip of an apple leaf and eventually pupates in a small, barrel-shaped puparium, with a pair of horn-like respiratory processes protruding through the leaf surface. Such mines are, therefore, instantly recognisable. Lepidopteran leaf miners include several members of the genus *Phyllonorycter*, of which the most commonly encountered species in orchards are undoubtedly the apple leaf blister moth (*P. blancardella*) (Fig. 178) and its close relative *P. corylifoliella*. Their blotch mines are often abundant on apple trees, the former on the underside of a leaf and the latter on the upper side. In the case of apple leaf blister moth, a characteristic mosaic pattern is visible on the upper surface of the mine. Mines of both species sometimes occur on one and the same leaf. Species of *Phyllonorycter* pupate within their mines, and the empty pupal case typically remains protruding from the surface following emergence of the adult (Fig. 179).

FIG 178. Apple leaf blister moth (*Phyllonorycter blancardella*) mines are clearly visible from above but formed on the underside of leaves.

FIG 179. Apple leaf blister moth (*Phyllonorycter blancardella*) is a generally common pest in apple orchards. Note the empty pupal case protruding from the mine, and the newly emerged moth resting nearby.

In recent years, another species of *Phyllonorycter* – namely, the firethorn leaf miner moth (*P. leucographella*) – has appeared in English orchards, although usually in non-commercial situations. This Mediterranean species, having spread northwards through Europe, first reached these islands in the late 1980s.[23] Although associated mainly with firethorn (critically, an evergreen plant), and now widely distributed in England, it also breeds on certain deciduous rosaceous plants, including apple and cherry. The unmistakable silvery-white blotch mines are formed along the top of the midrib of leaves (Fig. 180). On firethorn, they cause infested leaves to fold upwards and become elongated, pod-like shelters within which larvae of the second or partial third generation (still within the mines) overwinter. Larvae cannot survive the winter in the fallen leaves of apple and cherry, and the insect is likely to remain no more than a curiosity on fruit trees.

FIG 180. Firethorn leaf miner moth (*Phyllonorycter leucographella*) mines often occur on apple trees.

Circular blotch mines formed on the leaves of apple and pear trees by larvae of the pear leaf blister moth (*Leucoptera malifoliella*) are an uncommon sight in commercial orchards. They are more frequently found on wild hosts such as crab-apple and hawthorn. Populations of this pest in orchards and elsewhere are subject to periods of scarcity or abundance, possibly reflecting the impact of disease or parasitism. The more or less circular blotch mines formed by coleophoran case-bearing larvae (*Coleophora* spp.) on the leaves of apple, cherry, plum and other fruit trees are regularly encountered in orchards, especially in unsprayed or rarely sprayed sites. Examples include the apple & plum casebearer moth (*C. spinella*), the cherry pistol casebearer moth (*C. anatipennella*) (Fig. 181) and the fruit tree casebearer moth (*C. hemerobiella*). Following emergence from the egg, a coleophoran larva first mines within the leaf tissue to form a minute blotch. On moulting to the second instar, however, the larva becomes free-living and uses some of the original leaf tissue to build itself a small protective case. Subsequent feeding results in the production of a series of blotch mines, with small portions of leaf tissue and silk being added to the case as the larva grows. During the course of development, the larva may abandon its old case and construct an entirely new one. However, details of case formation vary considerably from species to species.[24] Even in the absence of the causal organism, a coleophoran leaf mine is at once recognisable by the presence of a small round hole, about the size of a pinhead, through which the mining larva gained access to the inner leaf tissue; the hole also marks the point of attachment of the case during feeding. Further, examination of the host plant in the vicinity of an unoccupied coleophoran mine may result in the discovery of a case on a nearby leaf, shoot or twig. The cases are usually brown or blackish and are often

FIG 181. Cherry pistol casebearer moth (*Coleophora anatipennella*) larvae feed and pupate in distinctive pistol-shaped cases formed from leaf fragments, frass and silk.

cigar-shaped or pistol-shaped, depending on the species. They are a common sight on infested fruit trees throughout the summer months. However, the small, narrow-winged and mainly dingy-coloured adults usually escape attention.

Larvae of *Callisto denticulella*, a generally common gracillariid on wild crab-apple trees throughout the British Isles, mine leaves during their earliest growth stages, each larva forming an irregular blotch. Later, however, individuals inhabit a tightly folded-down leaf edge. These highly characteristic habitations are often abundant on unsprayed apple trees in orchards and gardens during July and August. Similar larval habitations are formed on hazel leaves by *Parornix devoniella* and on blackthorn (and, rarely, cultivated plum) by *P. torquillella*.

SUCKING PESTS

A large number of phytophagous pests with probing and suctorial mouthparts feed on fruit trees, piercing the surface tissue and imbibing sap. Examples include aphids, mirids (capsids), leafhoppers, psyllids, scale insects, midges, gall mites, rust mites and spider mites. Many species are important orchard pests, causing direct damage to the foliage, and some also act as vectors of harmful phytoplasmas and plant viruses. Similarly, when sap-feeding pests attack blossoms, they can inflict injury that leads to the development of distorted or otherwise imperfect fruitlets; damaged blossoms or fruitlets may also abort.

Aphids

Aphids are frequent inhabitants of orchards. Green apple aphid (*Aphis pomi*), for example, is a generally common pest on apple trees. Throughout the spring and summer months ant-attended colonies develop at the tips of young shoots, the aphids often causing significant leaf curl. Compared with many other species, green apple aphid has a relatively simple lifecycle as there is no summer migration to secondary host plants. It is also more frequently a pest of young rather than established trees. Apple/grass aphid (*Rhopalosiphum insertum*) is another generally common species in apple orchards. Here, the pest overwinters as eggs on the bark of host trees. These eggs hatch in the spring from the green-cluster stage[25] onwards, and colonies then develop on the young foliage; later, blossom trusses also become infested. Winged forms are produced during the blossom period, and these migrate to the roots of cereals and grasses (especially annual meadow-grass). A return migration to apple occurs in the autumn. Populations of apple/grass aphid on apple trees vary considerably from year to year, and are usually greatest following wet summers which favour the growth of grasses.[26] Pear/grass aphid

FIG 182. Woolly aphid (*Eriosoma lanigerum*), originally from North America, is a notorious pest of apple trees.

(*Melanaphis pyraria*) similarly overwinters in the egg stage on fruit trees (in this instance, pear and quince) and spends the summer on grasses.

Woolly aphid (*Eriosoma lanigerum*) is a worldwide pest of apple, often responsible for the development of large cankerous galls on the shoots, branches and trunks of infested trees (Fig. 182). Infestations are usually most intense on older trees, and watershoots emanating from the trunks and larger branches are especially liable to be attacked. The aphids feed and breed within cottonwool-like masses of sticky, flocculent wax (wool). Along with the soft bodies of the wax-coated nymphs and adults, the wool can be a considerable nuisance to pickers at harvest time. Casual contact is often sufficient for skin or clothes to become sticky and stained red by the squashed bodies of the occupants; in Germany, the pest has rightly earned the name Blutlaus (blood louse).[27] Most of the aphids are wingless, although a few winged individuals are produced in July. Most natural spread of this species, therefore, is by active crawling from tree to tree or accidental transfer by wind or innocent animal carriers. Perhaps unexpectedly, the pest overwinters beneath flakes of bark or in bark crevices as naked individuals devoid of the familiar waxen wool.

Several aphid pests on apple trees feed and breed amongst curled leaves, infested foliage becoming noticeably galled and characteristically embellished

FIG 183. Rosy apple aphid (*Dysaphis plantaginea*) infestations often result in significant fruit damage.

with red or yellow. Common examples include apple/anthriscus aphid (*Dysaphis anthrisci*), rosy apple aphid (*D. plantaginea*) and rosy leaf-curling aphid (*D. devecta*). There is also the pear/bedstraw aphid (*D. pyri*) on pear. All of these pests overwinter in the egg stage. Rosy leaf-curling aphid is a rather sedentary and local pest. The colonies usually occur on just a small number of trees in an orchard, and such trees continue to be infested from one year to the next. The other species all migrate in the summer to secondary, herbaceous hosts. There, breeding continues before a return autumn migration to the primary (winter) hosts, where eggs are eventually laid. As an orchard pest, rosy apple aphid (commonly known by fruit growers as blue bug) is particularly serious, the pinkish to bluish-grey, wax-coated nymphs and adults causing severe damage to leaves and young shoots, and also leading to the development of dwarf, much-distorted fruits (Fig. 183). Unchecked, spring infestations in apple orchards can be devastating and culminate in considerable yield losses. Leaves galled by rosy apple aphid are usually tinged with red, as are those affected by apple/anthriscus aphid and rosy leaf-curling aphid. Pear leaves affected by pear/bedstraw aphid become severely twisted and, often, tinged with yellow.[28]

Two other gall-forming aphid pests of pear deserve comment: pear/coltsfoot aphid (*Anuraphis farfarae*) and pear/parsnip aphid (*A. subterranea*). As their common names imply, both species alternate between fruit trees (their winter hosts) and herbaceous summer hosts. In spring, following egg hatch, individual aphids develop on the underside of young pear leaves, each causing the affected leaf to bend downwards along the midrib; both sides of the leaf then meet to form a purse-like gall. Foliage galled by the latter species turns distinctly reddish, whereas leaves invaded by the former usually remain green (at least while the tissue is still alive!). *Anuraphis* galls on pear are usually abandoned by the end of May, departing winged aphids being produced after just one generation of wingless forms. The abandoned galled leaves then turn brown and die, leaving only the white, cast nymphal skins as indicators of the former inhabitants.

Plum trees are subject to attack by three generally common aphids, damson/hop aphid (*Phorodon humuli*), leaf-curling plum aphid (*Brachycaudus helichrysi*) and mealy plum aphid (*Hyalopterus pruni*), all of which overwinter in the egg stage. Damson/hop aphid, although a potential vector of plum pox virus (PPV – the cause of plum pox or Sharka disease), is of little significance on plum. Nevertheless, small colonies do develop on the leaves during the spring. Winged forms then depart for wild and cultivated hop plants from mid-May onwards. Leaf-curling plum aphid is an important pest in orchards. The winter eggs are unusual in that they hatch soon after being laid and most have done so well before the turn of the year.[29] The young nymphs then invade the flower (fruit) buds, feeding around the base even before they open. Dense colonies develop on the shoots in the spring, causing extensive, often very severe, leaf curl (Fig. 184). In May, winged forms appear and these migrate to summer hosts such as ox-eye daisy and tansy. Colonies on plum then die out, although breeding on the primary host can continue so long as suitable young growth remains available. Leaf-curling plum aphid also transmits PPV. Mealy plum aphid is a persistent

FIG 184. Leaf-curling plum aphid (*Brachycaudus helichrysi*) damage appears early in the season, and is often severe.

FIG 185. Mealy plum aphid (*Hyalopterus pruni*) colonies are coated in mealy wax. Note the presence of predatory midge larvae amongst the aphids.

pest on plum trees; dense wax-coated colonies (Fig. 185) occur on the underside of leaves from April onwards. Heavily infested young shoots appear greyish white as they become coated by the secreted wax. Foliage is also contaminated by copious amounts of honeydew, upon which sooty moulds later develop. Reeds and waterside grasses are the summer hosts, but colonies of wingless aphids may persist on plum well into August.

Finally, cherry trees are often invaded by shiny, black-bodied aphids: namely, the cherry blackfly (*Myzus cerasi*). It now appears that aphids on sweet cherry are different from those on sour cherry, but whether at a specific or a lesser level is open to debate. Aphids on sweet cherry (cited as the sweet cherry aphid, *M. pruniavium*, as opposed to the sour cherry aphid, *M. cerasi*) are more damaging. Unlike sour cherry aphid they cause foliage at the tips of infested shoots to become extensively gnarled and fist-like. These pseudogalls eventually desiccate and turn brown or black. Summer hosts of cherry aphids, to which winged individuals depart from May onwards, include bedstraws, eyebright and speedwells.

Leafhoppers

Leafhoppers are often abundant on fruit trees. Collectively, if numerous, they cause considerable damage to the foliage (especially on apple, damson, greengage and plum trees), attacks resulting in noticeable mottling or overall silvering of

FIG 186. Examples of leafhoppers that infest fruit trees: (clockwise from top left) cherry leafhopper (*Aguriahana stellulata*), *Typhlocyba quercus* and *Zygina flammigera*.

tissue. Leafhopper nymphs typically feed on the underside of leaves, where the cast nymphal skins often remain after the bugs have reached adulthood and have long since dispersed. In the absence of the pests on damaged leaves, these exuviae clearly identify the causal agents as leafhoppers. Many fruit tree leafhoppers are creamy or greenish in colour, and individual species such as *Alnetoidia alneti*, *Edwardsiana crataegi* and *E. prunicola* are difficult to identify with certainty in the field. Some species, however, are very characteristic in appearance. These include the striking and unmistakable cherry leafhopper (*Aguriahana stellulata*), with its brilliant white, dark-marked elytra, *Typhlocyba quercus*, with brownish-red, greenish or orange-red spots on the creamy-white elytra, and *Zygina flammigera*, which has distinctive red or reddish-brown zigzag markings on the elytra and thorax (Fig. 186). Particularly on unsprayed fruit trees, adult leafhoppers often arise in clouds when the branches are jarred.

Mirids (capsids)

A hundred years or so ago, apple capsid (*Lygocoris rugicollis*)[30] was considered one of the most important pests in British orchards.[31] The insect caused severe distortion of young shoots and developing fruits, and had a profound effect on tree growth and fruit yields. As a consequence, the pest was greatly feared by apple growers. Apple capsid continued to be of significance throughout the 1920s, 1930s and early 1940s. However, the post-war introduction of DDT into orchard spray programmes virtually eliminated this pest from apple orchards and populations never fully recovered. Today, apple capsid's place as a potentially important pest in orchards has been taken largely (albeit to a far lesser degree) by the common green capsid (*L. pabulinus*). This insect was long considered an associate of mainly herbaceous plants,[32] although its presence on apple had been noted in Ireland towards the end of the First World War.[33] In England, common green capsid was first found on apple in 1926.[34] Nowadays, it is a frequent pest of orchard trees, causing damage to buds, leaves and developing fruits. As a fruit pest, however, it is of greater significance in bush-fruit plantations (Chapter 8). Both apple capsid and common green capsid overwinter in the egg stage, their flask-shaped or banana-shaped eggs being inserted in the bark of their hosts.[35] The life histories of the two species, however, differ markedly. Apple capsid is single brooded and completes is lifecycle on its woody host, adults being active mainly in late June and July. Common green capsid, however, is double brooded, nymphs of the first generation departing from the trees to complete their development on herbaceous hosts. Here, a second generation develops. Young adult females arising from this generation then seek woody hosts (including apple trees) in which to deposit their winter eggs. Most other orchard-inhabiting mirids (capsids) are beneficial, being important predators of pests. A few predacious species, however, including the black apple capsid (*Atractotomus mali*), the dark green apple capsid (*Orthotylus marginalis*) and the red apple capsid (*Psallus ambiguus*), are partly phytophagous. In addition to playing a beneficial role by helping to control pests, such species also puncture the foliage and developing fruits; this causes a range of symptoms. On pear, in particular, considerable amounts of sap weep from the wounds, and fruits become noticeably malformed. Attacked fruits also develop so-called 'stony pits' in the flesh.[36]

Psyllids

Apple sucker (*Cacopsylla mali*)[37] (Fig. 187) is frequently abundant in unsprayed apple orchards, adults (in common with leafhoppers) leaping into the air in some numbers if a heavily infested branch is disturbed. Eggs overwinter on the bark, and nymphs develop on the young leaves and blossom trusses during the spring. Infested blossoms often turn brown, as if killed by frost. Nymphs secrete copious quantities of whitish wax and also excrete honeydew, so that infested foliage quickly becomes contaminated; the overall whitish appearance of infested unfurling leaves is often reminiscent of mildew infection. Adult apple suckers are bright green, and they occur throughout the summer and autumn months, there being just one generation per year. Psyllids also invade pear trees, pear sucker

FIG 187. (Top) Apple sucker (*Cacopsylla mali*) nymphs and (above) adults are often abundant on unsprayed apple trees.

(*C. pyricola*)[38] being a potentially important pest both in commercial orchards and private gardens. This species overwinters as adults, either on pear trees or amongst nearby non-host trees and shrubs. Although they mainly remain on the bark in such situations, they sometimes fly about in mid-winter sunshine. Eggs are laid on pear shoots in the early spring. Nymphs then invade the expanding buds, young foliage and blossom trusses. New adults appear several weeks later and these deposit eggs along the midrib, on the upper surface of leaves. There are usually three generations annually. Unchecked, populations in pear orchards become progressively larger as the season develops. In hot summers, pear sucker can be a very significant pest. Particularly in the absence of rain, the foliage and fruits of infested trees become extensively contaminated by honeydew excreted by the nymphs, and then blackened by sooty moulds which disrupt photosynthetic activity. Such contamination is the main cause of damage to host trees. Winfield *et al.*[39] discussed the history of pear sucker in Britain, from its apparent rarity in the late 1880s, to years of increased abundance during the mid- to late twentieth century, and concluded that the insect becomes a serious pest only when summers are hotter than average. Commercial control strategies for pear sucker require careful selection of pesticides, not only to avoid unnecessary damage to natural enemies, especially anthocorid bugs, but also because the pest has developed resistance to many materials. Timing of any chemical treatment is also critical.

Scale insects

Orchard trees are often infested with scale insects, of which the ubiquitous and generally abundant mussel scale (*Lepidosaphes ulmi*) is perhaps the best-known example. The scales usually occur on the bark of host trees, but on occasions can

FIG 188. Yellow pear scale (*Quadraspidiotus pyri*) is one of several species of scale insect to infest fruit trees.

also be found on the developing fruits. Mussel scale has one generation per year, eggs overwintering and hatching in the late spring. First-instar nymphs then wander over host trees before finally settling down to feed and develop. The sedentary second- and third-instar nymphs (and finally adults) are covered by wax and the cast remains of the nymphal skins which together come to form the familiar mussel-shaped 'scales'. Winter eggs are laid beneath the scales in late summer or early autumn. Although the maternal females then die, the scales remain *in situ* and protect the eggs throughout the winter. Generations of dead scales often cover the bark of heavily infested trees, often as a virtual additional outer skin. The same is true of various other armoured scale insects (family Diaspididae) associated with orchard trees, including yellow plum scale (*Quadraspidiotus ostreaeformis*), yellow pear scale (*Q. pyri*) (Fig. 188) and several others. These species are close relatives of the San José scale (*Diaspidiotus perniciosus*),[40] a notorious fruit pest of Far Eastern origin. San José scale is of particular significance in the USA but does not occur in Britain.

Interestingly, although certain populations of mussel scale produce males, those on fruit trees do not appear to do so; thus, in orchards, reproduction is entirely parthenogenetic. Males do, however, feature as part of the lifecycle of *Quadraspidiotus* spp. These are minute (< 0.5 mm long), yellow to orange-yellow insects, each with a single pair of wings, a long caudal spine and a prominent black thoracic crossband. Morphological characters of the males are often useful for distinguishing between the various species.[41] Soft scales (family Coccidae) are less numerous on fruit trees than are armoured scales. However, brown scale (*Parthenolecanium corni*) is sometimes present on plum trees, and nut scale (*Eulecanium tiliae*) is known to occur on apple, pear and plum. Both of these species are parthenogenetic on fruit crops and overwinter as young nymphs, not as eggs.

Miscellaneous plant bugs

Fruit trees are also infested by a range of other phytophagous bugs. Of these, the red & black froghopper (*Cercopis vulnerata*) deserves brief mention. Adults of this unmistakable insect sometimes invade apple trees, where they attack the foliage and cause angular, greenish-yellow markings that eventually turn brown. Such damage (commonly known as angular leaf spot) was once thought to be due to a fungal pathogen. Attacks also occur on cherry and pear, where fruitlets rather than leaves tend to be injured, their surfaces bearing corky scars or noticeable splits. Red & black leafhoppers breed on the roots of dock plants, where their nymphs feed within protective masses of cuckoo-spit. In common with some other pests, they are most likely to occur in weedy orchards. Weeds, however, are not necessarily detrimental, and their presence in orchards can enhance the activities of aphidophagous predators.[42]

Gall mites and rust mites

Gall mites do not cause major problems in orchards, although trees (especially pear and plum) are often infested. The mites, all of which overwinter in the adult stage, become active in the early spring and immediately invade the buds or unfurling leaves. Pear leaf blister mite (*Eriophyes pyri*) inhabits hollow, blister-like galls on the upper surface of leaves, each a few millimetres across. The galls, which change in colour as they mature from yellow through red to black, frequently develop in distinct patches on infested trees. A biological race of this pest also occurs on apple. Unsprayed apple trees are sometimes invaded by another eriophyid, the apple leaf erineum mite (*Phyllocoptes malinus*). This pest inhabits dense mats (termed erinea) of white or rusty-brown hairs on the underside of the leaves. The erinea are very obvious, but attacks are localised and not of significance. It is not clear whether this mite is a separate species or merely a subspecies of the generally abundant, hawthorn-inhabiting mite *P. goniothorax*, the leaf-edge-rolling form of which is a common sight in hedgerows.

The plum leaf gall mite (*Eriophyes padi*) breeds within small, finger-shaped galls that project upwards in clusters from the upper surface of leaves. By contrast, galls formed by the closely related and usually in the UK far more numerous plum pouch-gall mite (*E. similis*) are irregularly pouch-like and pale-coloured, sometimes reddish-tinged, swellings on the leaves (Fig. 189). Such galls are often clustered towards or along the leaf margins. On some plum cultivars (e.g. cv. Yellow Egg), galling by the latter species sometimes occurs on the developing fruitlets, the surface subsequently becoming distinctly irregular and the fruits unmarketable. Such symptoms are sometimes confused with those of plum pox (Sharka) disease.[43] Galls of both species regularly occur on

FIG 189. Plum pouch-gall mite (*Eriophyes similis*) is a generally common pest on damson and plum trees.

blackthorn. Plum spur mite (*Acalitus phloeocoptes*) also infests blackthorn and, sometimes, cultivated plum trees. In spring, adult females invade unopened buds. Here, they feed beneath the bud scales, initiating localised swellings (galls) within which eggs are then laid. Breeding continues throughout the summer, the galls gradually hardening as they age. Mites become trapped within these galls and it is not until the following spring that (following the death and cracking of the galls) the overwintered adult females can finally escape.

Rust mites often cause damage on fruit trees. In plum orchards, for example, infestations of plum rust mite (*Aculus fockeui*) can result in extensive and intense bronzing of the foliage; populations commonly reach many hundreds if not thousands of mites per leaf. Similar damage to apple and pear by apple rust mite (*A. schlechtendali*) (Fig. 190) and pear rust mite (*Epitrimerus piri*) also occurs. All three species have similar lifecycles, involving the presence of two quite distinct winter and summer female forms, known respectively as deutogynes and protogynes. Such species are termed deuterogenous. Here, the deutogynes overwinter beneath bud scales on the youngest wood. The mites then emerge in the spring and invade the new foliage where they begin to feed and breed. Several generations of females (as protogynes) and males occur during the summer, with new deutogynes appearing in increasing numbers as the breeding season advances. Protogynes and males eventually die out, leaving the

FIG 190. Leaves infested with apple rust mite (*Aculus schlechtendali*) are distorted and discoloured. The mites also damage the fruits.

deutogynes to ensure the future survival of the species. In Kent, overwintered deutogynes of apple rust mite die out in May and production of new ones commences in late June.[44] New deutogynes of pear rust mite, however, do not appear until July.[45] Deutogynes and protogynes are structurally different, the former being somewhat larger and often, for example, having noticeably fewer and broader so-called 'tergites' and 'sternites' – these are annulations on the hysterosoma (see Fig. A.6, p. 424). Indeed, differences in some deuterogenous mites are so great that deutogynes and protogynes have been regarded and described as quite different species! When rust mites, such as apple rust mite and pear rust mite, invade blossoms their feeding on the receptacles and developing fruits often results in subsequent surface russeting of the fruitlets.[46] At harvest, russeted fruits are often rejected by supermarkets, even though they are completely edible and disease-free: presumably, 'they don't look right'. In this respect it is ironic that a russeted surface is a natural feature of apple cultivars such as Ashmead's Kernel and Egremont Russet.

Spider mites

Fruit tree red spider mite is one of the most important pests to occur in apple orchards (Fig. 191), and modern pest management strategies are usually structured to ensure that populations of the mite are kept in check. This is often achieved by

FIG 191. Fruit tree red spider mite (*Panonychus ulmi*) is one of the most important orchard pests. Infested foliage becomes bronzed and photosynthetic activity is greatly impaired.

the adoption of an integrated approach to mite management.[47] The pest also occurs on cherry, pear and plum, although less frequently. Fruit tree red spider mite overwinters as eggs on the bark of host trees, mainly on the spurs and smaller branches. The eggs hatch from about late April to mid-June, the timing varying considerably as there are both early- and late-hatching strains.[48] There is also an inbuilt strategy whereby premature hatching during unseasonally warm weather in early spring is avoided, as is delayed hatch of overwinterd eggs in the event of prolonged cold weather.[49] The mites feed and breed on the underside of expanded leaves, where summer eggs are also laid. Individuals pass through a 'larval' and several nymphal stages, and development from egg to adult takes about a month. This allows the completion of several overlapping generations annually. Dispersal of mites from tree to tree, and from site to site, is accomplished by adult females which parachute in the wind on fine threads of silk. Fruit tree red spider mite was formerly of little significance in orchards. However, in the second half of the twentieth century it became a major pest. This followed the introduction of broad-spectrum pesticides which dramatically depleted populations of natural enemies, especially anthocorid bugs and predatory mirids (capsids). Viable present-day pest control programmes in orchards are constructed to take account of predators. The mite's ability to develop resistance to pesticides also needs to be addressed.[50]

LEAF-CURLING GALL MIDGES

Two species of gall midge are common denizens of fruit orchards: apple leaf midge (*Dasineura mali*) and pear leaf midge (*D. pyri*). In both cases, larvae develop gregariously within the tightly rolled leaf margins of host plants (Fig. 192).

FIG **192.** Apple leaf midge (*Dasineura mali*) larvae develop in distinctive, often colourful, rolled leaf margins.

Damaged (galled) tissue is often tinged with red or purple and, on pear, eventually turns black. Infestations, although by no means uncommon in established orchards, are of greatest importance in nursery beds and on young trees. There are usually three generations annually.

FRUITLET- AND FRUIT-INVADING INSECTS

Some insect pests in orchards are obligate fruit feeders, their larvae developing within apples, pears, plums or other fruits. Amongst these, codling moth (*Cydia pomonella*) (Fig. 193) must rate as one of the most important worldwide. Although it is primarily associated with apple, it also attacks other hosts, including pear, quince and walnut. The pest usually overwinters as fully grown larvae in cocoons spun on the bark of host trees or in other similarly sheltered situations. Pupation occurs in the spring and adults appear from June onwards. Pheromone-baited sticky traps, set for codling moth, are routinely deployed in commercial orchards. These enable growers to assess the risk to their crops and if necessary to apply treatments before larvae enter the fruits. Codling moth larvae (Fig. 194) – often known as apple maggots – can cause considerable yield losses in both commercial

FIG 193. Codling moth (*Cydia pomonella*) is a notorious apple pest throughout the world.

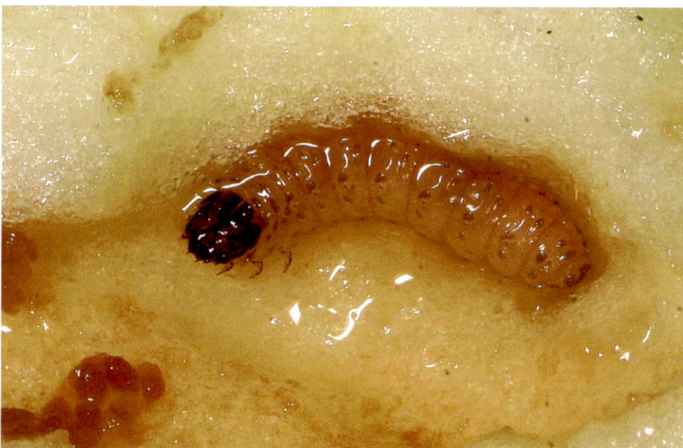

FIG 194. Codling moth larvae feed inside apple fruits, and often burrow down to the core.

and non-commercial apple orchards. They can also be troublesome on apple trees in private gardens. Infested fruits tend to drop to the ground prior to harvest, but this is not always so. Although in Britain the pest usually has just one generation a year, if the summer is hot and larval development can be completed by the end of July, a significant (and potentially more devastating) second generation can occur. Plum fruit moth (*Cydia funebrana*) has a similar lifecycle to that of codling moth (although, as its vernacular name implies, it attacks plum). Again, there is usually just one generation annually in England, although under favourable conditions there may be a partial second. Interestingly, second-generation plum fruit moth adults tend to be smaller than those of the first: mean forewing lengths of 5.5 and 6.5 mm, respectively.[51] Plum cultivars vary in their susceptibility. The cultivar Coe's Golden Drop, for example, is considered highly susceptible,[52] and cv. Burbank was most affected during studies on the pest in the Wisbech area of

FIG 195. Plum fruit moth (*Cydia funebrana*) larvae are known as red plum maggots.

Cambridgeshire.[53] Fruits infested by plum fruit moth larvae (Fig. 195) – commonly known as red plum maggot – do not necessarily drop to the ground prior to harvest.[54] It is not unusual, therefore, to find larvae in harvested fruits. This also applies to cherries infested by larvae of the European cherry fruit fly (*Rhagoletis cerasi*), a common pest in mainland Europe but one that does not occur in Britain.

Larvae of the fruitlet-mining tortrix moth (*Pammene rhediella*), a pest of apple, cherry and plum, are sometimes mistaken for those of codling moth and plum fruit moth. The larvae, however, occur earlier in the season and are noticeably smaller. Also, unlike codling moth and plum fruit moth larvae, they do not attain a pinkish coloration. Fruitlet-mining tortrix moth larvae characteristically web several fruitlets together with silk, and expel frass into the webbing as they develop. The pest also completes just one generation annually, irrespective of weather conditions. Larvae of *P. argyrana* have also been found inside developing apples, usually in old orchards. Such attacks were first reported in the 1950s in the Netherlands[55] and in Switzerland.[56] *P. argyrana* is more usually associated with oak trees, where the larvae feed as inquilines inside the spongy galls (called oak-apples) initiated by the oak-apple gall wasp (*Biorhiza pallida*). However, the moth occasionally frequents British apple orchards,[57] which suggests that a direct association with apple might be more common than the paucity of reports suggests. It has certainly bred on an old apple tree (cv. Keswick Codlin) in my Cambridgeshire garden.

Apple and plum fruits are also subject to attack by apple sawfly (*Hoplocampa testudinea*) and plum sawfly (*H. flava*), respectively, the former being the more common pest. Apple sawflies are active during the blossom period, when mating occurs. Eggs are then deposited singly, each inserted in a blossom receptacle just below the calyx. The eggs hatch a few weeks later and the young larvae then bore

FIG 196. Apple sawfly (*Hoplocampa testudinea*) larvae cause significant damage to young fruitlets.

FIG 197. A ribbon-shaped scar on a maturing apple indicates an earlier failed attack by a young apple sawfly (*Hoplocampa testudinea*) larva.

into the by now developing fruitlets and commence feeding. An infested fruitlet shows clear signs of attack, often bearing external scars and a small hole through which wet frass is expelled by the larva (Fig. 196). The larvae eventually vacate the original fruitlets and invade adjacent ones, individuals usually attacking several during the course of their development. Invaded fruitlets often drop prematurely and yield losses can be considerable. At harvest, mature apples are sometimes found with a curved, scimitar-like scar on their surface (Fig. 197). This characteristic blemish was once thought to be the remains of an oviposition slit made by an apple sawfly female. However, it is actually due to the breakdown of tissue following an aborted attempt by a young larva to penetrate a fruitlet, the originally damaged area of skin expanding as the surviving fruitlet grows to maturity.[58] Plum

FIG 198. Plum sawfly (*Hoplocampa flava*) larvae develop inside plum fruitlets, and crop losses are sometimes considerable.

FIG 199. Apple fruit moth (*Argyresthia conjugella*) is associated mainly with rowan but also invades apple trees. The larvae feed gregariously within the flesh, and infested fruits are distinguished by the presence of several small holes in the skin.

sawfly follows a similar lifecycle, the larvae feeding singly in damson and plum fruitlets (Fig. 198). Also, as in the case of apple sawfly, larvae attack more than one fruitlet before completing their development.

Occasionally, mature apples are discovered with narrow tunnels and rotting tissue in the flesh, and sunken, blotch-like markings and small pinhead-sized pits on the surface (Fig. 199). Such damage is caused by larvae of the apple fruit

FIG 200. Apple fruit rhynchites (*Neocoenorrhinus aequatus*) is most often found on young apple trees.

moth (*Argyresthia conjugella*), a species normally breeding in the fruits (berries) of rowan trees. Attacks in orchards are sporadic, and most often discovered in orchards close to woodlands and in years when rowan berries are in short supply. There is just one generation annually.[59]

Two other fruitlet-invading pests are worthy of mention, although both are more important on garden trees than in commercial orchards. The first, apple fruit rhynchites (*Neocoenorrhinus aequatus*),[60] is a small, reddish-brown weevil (Fig. 200) that lays its eggs in apple fruitlets, each at the base of a small hole bored a few millimetres into the flesh. The larvae develop over a period of about three weeks before vacating the fruit and dropping to the ground to pupate. At maturity, an attacked fruit may bear several small, corky pits on the skin and would then be unmarketable. The second, pear midge (*Contarinia pyrivora*), is a potentially devastating pest. The adults are active during the spring, depositing eggs in open pear blossoms or in those still at the white-bud stage. Following egg hatch, the larvae feed gregariously within the developing fruitlets. Compared with healthy fruitlets these initially become noticeably enlarged as they compete more successfully for assimilates. However, attacked fruitlets soon become distorted, shrunken and blackened, and eventually drop to the ground. Although capable of causing complete loss of crop on isolated trees, pear midge is not of such significance in commercial orchards.

Many phytophagous insects and mites damage developing fruits, but are not dependent upon them for completion of their lifecycle. Damage caused in orchards by these facultative fruit feeders, however, can be extensive and, collectively, highly significant.

FIG 201. Common quaker moth (*Orthosia stabilis*) larvae are often common on apple and other trees.

In spring, several pests have gained a reputation for biting chunks out of young fruitlets. These include adult cockchafers (*Melolontha melolontha*) (ephemeral, casual pests in orchards during their flight period in May) and larvae of various moths, notably clouded drab moth and winter moth. Damaged fruitlets often continue to grow and, at maturity, sometimes have a navel-like pit in the side which can extend right down to the core. Less severe injuries on fruitlets quickly heal over, but are expressed in the mature fruits as corky patches or other minor skin blemishes. Clouded drab moth larvae often damage several fruitlets in a cluster,[61] the final two (fifth and sixth) larval instars being responsible.[62] Larvae of various other related species, including the common quaker moth (*Orthosia stabilis*) (Fig. 201), occur on apple, but to what extent they too attack fruitlets is unclear. In North America, larvae of *O. hibisci* are certainly known to do so, as are those of the North American species *Amphipyra pyramidoides* and *Lithophane laticinerea*, all three (amongst many others) known collectively as green fruitworms.[63]

In the summer and autumn young tortrix moth larvae (although primarily leaf feeders) often web leaves to the surface of maturing fruits. They then pare away the skin and outermost parts of the underlying tissue. Damage to apples is especially severe in the wake of attacks by summer fruit tortrix moth; fruit tree tortrix moth can also be of significance. In Britain, summer fruit tortrix moth was first noted in Kent in 1950.[64] Since then, it has become a notorious pest in apple and cherry orchards in various parts of southeast England; its current range extends deep into East Anglia. Unlike many related species, it has two substantive generations annually. It is the young larvae of the second generation that overwinter.

FIG 202. Autumn apple tortrix moth (*Syndemis musculana*) larvae browse on leaves, and also damage the surface of ripening apples.

Direct damage to maturing apples in late summer and early autumn is often inflicted by larvae of *Syndemis musculana* (Fig. 202). This polyphagous tortricid species was not recognised as an orchard pest until the early 1980s when infestations on apple were reported in southwest England.[65] At that time of year, larvae of this species are usually older (and, hence, larger) than those of related species. They are, therefore, able to cause significant damage. In the UK, this pest is now known as the autumn apple tortrix moth. It has also become recognised as a pest of apples in the Netherlands.[66]

Another new pest, the moth *Blastobasis decolorella* (Fig. 203), was found in Essex apple orchards in the late 1970s. In this case, the larvae were causing major damage to the maturing fruits of cv. Egremont Russet.[67] Damage to fruits and the bark of tree branches also occurred at about the same time in apple orchards in Kent.[68] Larvae of this species (Fig. 204), a native of Madeira, are usually described as detritus feeders and tend to inhabit confined spaces. On apple trees, for example, they

FIG 203. Straw-coloured apple moth (*Blastobasis decolorella*) is a relatively new orchard pest, having first been discovered attacking orchard fruits in the late 1970s.

FIG 204. Straw-coloured apple moth larvae cause extensive damage around the base of maturing fruits. On apple, they prefer short-stalked cultivars such as Egremont Russet.

usually occur on short-stalked cultivars, and feed where the base of the fruit is in contact with the shoot. Fear amongst some English growers was such that in the 1980s control measures against the pest were included in routine spray programmes, even in parts of the country where the pest had never been found! This potentially devastating pest (now known as the straw-coloured apple moth) has not become a major problem in commercial orchards, although attacks continue to be reported. Infestations have also been noted on non-commercial fruits, including almonds and peaches, as well as on hawthorn berries, rose hips and stored apples.

Earwigs (*Forficula auricularia*) are sometimes harmful to orchard fruits. They are, for example, notorious for contaminating fruits with their frass and for enlarging flesh wounds made by other agents such as birds. However, earwigs are also useful predators, as they frequently attack codling moth eggs, aphids and many other invertebrate pests.

Particularly in weedy sites, fully fed larvae of the dock sawfly (*Ametastegia glabrata*) often bore into apple fruits in their search for overwintering sites. However, they then vacate the fruits as these are found to be unsuitable. Dock sawfly larvae also bore into plastic irrigation pipes, which they soon find equally uninhabitable.

Orchard fruits are also considered fair game by vertebrates, including various birds and mammals. In particular, cherries are greatly prized by blackbirds and marauding mobs of starlings. Indeed, some cherry crops require protection with netting if fruits are to survive to harvest. Recently, ring-necked parakeets have been reported attacking orchard fruits in Kent. Mammals are usually a lesser problem. However, wood mice and grey squirrels sometimes clamber over trees to feed on ripening fruits. Fruits on branches close to the ground are also destroyed by rabbits. In winter-time, rabbits also strip the bark from the trunks and lowermost branches of unprotected apple trees, a habit increasingly shared by muntjacs.

NATURAL ENEMIES OF ORCHARD PESTS

Predatory bugs form an important component of orchard ecosystems and in common with other natural enemies they can help to reduce populations of aphids, psyllids, moth larvae, phytophagous mites and various other pests. Their overall abundance is such that they play a useful role in both sprayed and unsprayed sites.

Black-kneed capsid (*Blepharidopterus angulatus*) (Fig. 205) (a mainly green species with a black, knee-like mark at the base of each tibia) is a particularly useful and well-known enemy of fruit tree red spider mite,[69] and it is generally common in apple orchards. When spider mites are in short supply, the bugs often feed on eriophyid mites, including apple rust mite. These alternative food sources are helpful in maintaining predator populations throughout the season. Predacious phytoseiid mites adopt the same survival strategy.[70] Many other mirids (capsids) also prey on fruit tree red spider mite.[71] These include black apple capsid (with its noticeably swollen first and second antennal segments), dark green apple capsid, red apple capsid, delicate apple capsid (*Malacocoris chlorizans*), *Heterotoma planicornis* (with its greatly enlarged and laterally flattened second antennal segment), *Phytocoris reuteri*, *P. tiliae* and the ant-like *Pilophorus perplexus* (Fig. 206).

Predatory mirids (capsids) also attack aphids and other prey, including eggs of pests such as codling moth.[72] Further, *P. tiliae* frequently attacks winter moth larvae,[73] and *P. perplexus* is an extremely effective predator of pear leaf midge larvae.[74] There are many other examples.[75] Most mirid (capsid) species have just one generation per year and typically overwinter in the egg stage, the eggs usually being inserted into the young wood of trees. Species that overwinter as adults include *Deraeocoris lutescens* and *D. flavilinea*, the latter (Fig. 207) a rather large species that has spread rapidly in southeast England since its first arrival in

FIG 205. Black-kneed capsid (*Blepharidopterus angulatus*), here a nymph, is an important predator of small invertebrates in orchards.

FIG 206. The ant-like mirid (capsid) *Pilophorus perplexus* is a common predator of small invertebrates in orchards.

FIG 207. The predatory mirid (capsid) *Deraeocoris flavilinea* is a recent arrival in England, where it was first noticed in 1996. It has spread rapidly and may often be found on unsprayed fruit trees.

Britain in 1996.[76] Both species attack aphids on apple, plum and other fruit trees.

Various other predatory bugs are also frequent inhabitants of orchards. These include shield bugs, damsel bugs and, especially, anthocorids. Anthocorid bugs often abound on fruit trees. *Anthocoris nemoralis* (Fig. 208), for example, is a particularly important predator in pear orchards, whereas its close relative *A. nemorum* tends to breed on apple trees.[77] During the first part of the season (April to June), *A. nemoralis* occurs only in small numbers on pear trees, the bugs instead feeding on aphids infesting nearby non-fruit trees and shrubs. In July and August, however, *A. nemoralis* populations on pear trees can be very large, particularly if pear sucker eggs and nymphs (of which *A. nemoralis* is a major predator) are abundant.[78] Certain insecticides are effective against pear sucker nymphs and are non-damaging to anthocorids. Accordingly, if required, such products 'may be used against the pest in summer without disrupting the biocontrol potential of the predators'.[79]

FIG 208. *Anthocoris nemoralis* is an important predator, particularly in pear orchards.

Many orchard pests spend part of their lifecycle in the soil beneath host trees, usually as fully grown larvae and pupae. They are then subject to attack by a range of ground-inhabiting predators, including ground beetles such as *Pterostichus melanarius* and rove beetles such as the devil's coach-horse beetle (*Staphylinus olens*)[80] (Fig. 209).

A few ground beetles and some rove beetles have adopted an arboreal habit, and actively seek prey within the tree canopy. Common examples include *Demetrias atricapillus*, a mainly yellow, black-headed species, and *Dromius quadrimaculatus*, a brownish-black to reddish-black species with two pairs of pale yellowish patches on the elytra. In addition, adults and larvae of *Oligota flavicornis*, a minute black-bodied rove beetle no more than 1 mm long, regularly feed on the active stages of fruit tree red spider mite; mite eggs are also acceptable food. The adult of *O. flavicornis* hibernate beneath bark or amongst leaf litter and invade apple trees in

FIG 209. Devil's coach-horse beetle (*Staphylinus olens*) is a ground-dwelling predator, and often found in orchards.

FIG 210. Fourteen-spot ladybird (*Propylea quattuordecimpunctata*) is a predator of aphids and other small invertebrates in orchards.

May and June, to lay eggs amongst spider mite colonies. The beetle larvae feed on their prey for a couple of weeks or so before dropping to the ground and pupating in the soil. New adults appear shortly afterwards. In favourable conditions there may be a partial second generation. A few other rove beetles occur on fruit trees, including the shiny-black to orange-yellow ('Duracell' battery-like) species of *Tachyporus*, which are frequent predators of aphids and other small invertebrates. Cantharid beetles also seek prey on fruit trees. The well-known orange-red soldier beetle *Rhagonycha fulva*, for example, devours aphids, including rosy apple aphids.

Coccinellid beetles (ladybirds) are often found on fruit trees. Both adults and larvae of predacious species (i.e. members of the subfamily Coccinellinae) attack aphids and various other small invertebrates. Frequent orchard inhabitants include the fourteen-spot ladybird (*Propylea quattuordecimpunctata*) (Fig. 210), the seven-spot ladybird (*Coccinella septempunctata*) and the two-spot ladybird (*Adalia*

FIG 211. Harlequin ladybird (*Harmonia axyridis*) larvae often develop amongst aphid colonies on fruit trees.

FIG 212. Kidney-spot ladybird (*Chilocorus renipustulatus*) larvae (above left) are abundant on unsprayed fruit trees. They and the adults (above right) feed on scale insects and other small invertebrates.

bipunctata). The harlequin ladybird (*Harmonia axyridis*) (see Chapter 12) (Fig. 211) also attacks aphids on fruit trees, including cherry blackfly. The conifer ladybird (*Exochomus quadripustulatus*) is a predator of scale insects, as are the kidney-spot ladybird (*Chilocorus renipustulatus*) (Fig. 212) and certain other species. Also, the minute black ladybird (*Stethorus punctillum*) (adults no more than 1.5 mm long) is often present on fruit trees, where it preys mainly on rust mites and fruit tree red spider mites; predatory typhlodromid mites are also attacked.[81] In English apple

FIG 213. Brown lacewings, such as *Hemerobius humulinus*, are generally common in orchards.

FIG 214. (Top) Green lacewings, such as *Chrysoperla cunea*, are abundant and widely distributed, and often common on fruit trees. Their larvae (above) are voracious predators of aphids and other small invertebrates.

orchards during the 1950s, this ladybird was renowned as having developed a degree of resistance to the then widely used insecticide parathion.

Lacewings are important predators of aphids, psyllids, scale insects, spider mites and other invertebrates, and representatives of all three of the main neuropteran families commonly occur in orchards. These include the brown lacewings *Hemerobius humulinus* (Fig. 213) and *H. lutescens*, the green lacewings *Chrysopa perla*, *Chrysoperla curnea* (Fig. 214), *Cunctochrysa albolineata* and *Nineta flava*, and the tiny whitefly-like powdery lacewings *Conwentzia pineticola*, *Coniopteryx tineiformis* and *Semidalis aleyrodiformis*.

Adult green lacewings usually feed on honeydew and pollen grains. However, their somewhat crocodile-shaped larvae are voracious predators, especially of aphids and other plant bugs. Brown lacewings and powdery lacewings are entirely predacious, as adults and as larvae.[82] Larvae of some lacewings, including *Cunctochrysa albolineata* (Fig. 215), carry debris on their bodies, as camouflage, and when moulting from one instar to another, as described by Killington,[83] 'debris-carrying forms of Chrysopid larvae throw off the packets of debris with the old skin and then proceed to build up a new coat with fresh material'.

Various dipterans are either parasitoids or predators of orchard pests. Amongst the former, tachinid flies are probably the most frequently encountered, and many species are well-known endoparasitoids of fruit pests.[84] Adult tachinids are rather bristly, housefly-like flies that attack caterpillars, including those of many important orchard pests. Common examples include *Compsilura cocinnata* (on various Noctuidae), *Cyzenis albicans* (on winter moth), *Elodia morio* and *Nemorilla floralis* (on codling moth and other microlepidoptera), *Pales pavida* (on Noctuidae and other macrolepidoptera; occasionally also on Tortricidae), and *Phryxe nemea* and *P. vulgaris* (on, for example, Geometridae and Noctuidae). Tachinid flies adopt a wide range of strategies for parasitising their

FIG 215. Larvae of the lacewing *Cunctochrysa albolineata* often camouflage themselves with debris.

hosts. In some instances, the adult female incubates her eggs internally and subsequently places tiny larvae on the skins of suitable hosts; such larvae then bore their way into the host, using their rasping mouth-hooks. Other tachinids deposit eggs on the skin of the host. Yet others lay their eggs on leaves. Such eggs are either accidentally ingested by a passing herbivorous host or, following egg hatch (if still on a leaf), the young tachinid larva must itself locate a suitable host.

Predacious Diptera are also important natural enemies of orchard pests. Larvae of several species of hover fly, for example, are considered of significance, especially (but not exclusively) as predators of aphids. Attacks on apple aphids in Europe are exemplified as follows:[85]

- **apple/grass aphid:** from April to May, attacked by *Episyrphus* and *Scaeva*;
- **green apple aphid:** from June to September, attacked by *Episyrphus* (Fig. 216), *Melangyna triangulifera* and *Syrphus*;
- **rosy apple aphid:** from April to July, attacked by all the above-mentioned;
- **woolly aphid:** from May to September, attacked by *Episyrphus*, *Pipiza* and *Syrphus*.

Predation is not, of course, confined to apple orchards. Larvae of one species or another also feed avidly amongst aphid colonies on cherry, pear, plum and other fruit trees.

The predatory midge *Aphidoletes aphidimyza* is also a frequent inhabitant of orchards. The tiny larvae (up to 3 mm long) develop within aphid colonies, attacking the adults and nymphs by seizing them at a leg joint and then sucking out the body contents. Even wax-coated aphids such as mealy plum aphid cannot escape their attention. The delicate adult midges feed on honeydew.

FIG 216. Hover flies such as *Episyrphus balteatus* (left) frequently invade orchards. Their larvae (below left) are well-known predators of aphids.

The orchard environment offers many opportunities for parasitoid wasps to find hosts, not only within the pest community but also more widely. For example, predators of pests as well as other parasitoids may also be victimised. Hymenopterous parasitoids attracted into orchards are drawn from many different families, ranging from relatively large species (adults of some members of the family Ichneumonidae, for instance, are 20 mm or more long) to minute ones whose adults may be no more than a fraction of a millimetre in length. Some parasitoids are highly specialised and host specific, attacking just one species: examples include the aphelinid *Aphelinus mali* (on woolly aphid) and the polyembryonic chalcid *Copidosoma flavomaculatum* (on pith moth). Others have more catholic tastes, targeting a group of related hosts or perhaps an even wider range.

The platygastrid *Platygaster demades* (a parasitoid of apple leaf midge) and the ichneumonid *Lathrolestes ensator* (a parasitoid of apple sawfly) are heralded as particularly useful natural antagonists in modern orchard IPM programmes.[86]

FIG 217. The ichneumonid wasp *Scambus pomorum* (above left) is a common parasitoid of apple blossom weevil. The larvae (above right) feed as ectoparasitoids within capped apple blossom.

P. demades is a tiny, black-bodied wasp that lays its eggs singly in those of apple leaf midge and various other midges, including pear leaf midge. Development of this parasitoid is rapid, and there are several generations annually. As an enemy of apple sawfly, *L. ensator* launches its attacks primarily on second-instar larvae. These are likely to be available for no more than a week on any particular apple cultivar within an orchard, potentially lessening the parasitoid's impact on the pest population; further, the egg-laying parasitoid females apparently have no mechanism for avoiding hosts that are already parasitised.[87] Populations of apple sawfly are also reduced by the activities of *Aptesis nigrocincta*, another orchard-inhabiting ichneumonid wasp. Females of *A. nigrocincta* have vestigial wings and are flightless. They lay eggs in the cocoons of full-grown sawfly larvae which they must locate in the soil beneath the trees. Interestingly, unlike its host, this parasitoid has two generations annually.[88]

Apple blossom weevil larvae and pupae are liable to be parasitised by the ichneumonid wasp *Scambus pomorum* (Fig. 217). This was formerly a very common ectoparasitoid in British apple orchards, and one to which over a quarter of apple blossom weevil larvae and pupae have been known to fall victim.[89] Eggs are laid singly in the spring, each placed in a capped blossom occupied by an apple blossom weevil larva or pupa. Following egg hatch, the parasitoid larva gradually devours its host before eventually pupating, still within the confines of the capped blossom. Young adult wasps typically emerge in mid-June. Interestingly, as recently discovered in the Netherlands,[90] these then become predatory and feed on the larvae of non-host insects. The leaf-mining larvae of apple leaf blister moth are most frequently victimised. Such larvae are attacked using the ovipositor and mouthparts, the wasps exposing their prey by scraping away the outer leaf tissue. Haemolymph weeping from the body of the injured larva is then imbibed. In spring, following emergence from hibernation, the female wasps again attack non-host (lepidopterous leaf miner) larvae. Host feeding (see Chapter 4, p. 92) on apple blossom weevil larvae also occurs.

Within orchard communities, moth larvae are attacked by many other hymenopterous parasitoids. Small leaf miners (apple pygmy moth, for example) are victimised by eulophids, including *Chrysocharis prodice* and *Cirrospilus vittatus*. The first-named is a solitary endoparasitoid, which completes its development only after the leaf-mining host has vacated its mine and spun a pupal cocoon in the soil; the latter, however, is an ectoparasitoid and feeds on the host larva within the mine. Species of *Phyllonorycter* are similarly afflicted; d'Aguilar *et al.*,[91] for example, cite nine eulophid species as parasitoids of apple leaf blister moth. They also record four, eight and ten species as parasitoids of *Lyonetia clerkella*, apple pygmy moth and pear leaf blister moth, respectively. Tortricid pests are parasitised mainly by braconid and ichneumonid wasps (e.g. the braconids *Ascogaster quadridentata* and *Macrocentrus linearis*, and the ichneumonids *Glypta pedata*, *Itoplectis alternans* and *Pristomerus vulnerator*). Named hosts of one or more of these parasitoids include bud moth, codling moth, fruit tree tortrix moth and many others.

Larger lepidopterans are far from immune. Indeed, they often fall victim to many hymenopterous parasitoids. For example, at least three braconids and five ichneumonids are known to attack larvae of the clouded drab moth.[92] Further, eggs of noctuids and other lepidopterans (large and small) are often parasitised by chalcid wasps, especially the well-known biological control agent *Trichogramma evanescens* and its near relatives.[93] *Trichogramma* can be mass-reared for use in field crops as well as in forestry, and in European orchards (but not in the UK) tortricid pests such as codling moth have been targeted.

Man's exploitation of the relationship between woolly aphid and its parasitoid *Aphelinus mali* is one of many examples of classical biological control, where a non-native parasitoid was deliberately introduced into Europe during the first half of the twentieth century in an attempt to combat an invasive alien North American pest. The parasitoid still survives in some UK orchards, where (along with native predators such as earwigs, ladybirds and various insectivorous birds) it continues to contribute towards the natural control of woolly aphid. Massee[94] usefully summarised the techniques originally adopted by apple growers in Kent to ensure survival of the parasitoid in their orchards from one year to the next.

Leaf-feeding aphids in orchards are attacked by many parasitoids. Such wasps are solitary, and often highly polyphagous, occurring not only in orchards but also in many different locations, including field crops. Common examples include *Diaeretiella rapae* (which pupates within the mummified remains of its aphid host) and *Praon volucre* (which pupates in a silken cocoon spun beneath the empty shell of its former host).

Scale insects too are often victimised by parasitoids. *Aphytis mytilaspidis*, for example (a near relative of *Aphelinus mali*), is a common natural enemy of mussel scales.

Phytoseiid mites are well-known predators of mites in orchards and play an important role in the regulation of pests such as fruit tree red spider mite.[95] They also destroy eggs of pests such as codling moth.[96] The key species is *Typhlodromus pyri*, but *Amblyseius umbraticus*, *Euseius finlandicus*[97] and *Phytoseius macropilus*, amongst others, are also of significance. The mites (often affectionately known as 'typhs') are active within spider mite colonies, where they breed throughout the spring and summer months. They occur in greater or lesser numbers in both sprayed and unsprayed sites.

Various other predatory mites are also of significance in orchards, and a few examples are mentioned below.

The whirligig mite (*Anystis baccarum*), so called because if its rapid and erratic movements over leaves and other surfaces, is a common predator of small invertebrates. It occurs in various habitats, and is often a useful predator of apple rust mite and fruit tree red spider mite in apple orchards. In Bramley orchards in Northern Ireland, whirligig mites have also been confirmed to be major spring-time predators of apple/grass aphid.[98] Although an entirely beneficial species, whirligig mites can be confused with fruit tree red spider mites, and growers have sometimes then mistakenly applied pesticides in attempts to 'control' them.[99]

By contrast, the yellow predatory mite (*Zetzellia mali*) is a rather sedentary species. It feeds and breeds mainly within the colonies of pests such as apple rust mite, flat scarlet mite (*Cenopalpus pulcher*) and fruit tree red spider mite. Although contributing to natural control of such pests, they also feed on eggs of predatory mites such as *Typhlodromus pyri*.[100]

In the spring, fruit growers often notice very large (2.5 mm long), red-bodied mites crawling purposefully over the foliage, shoots and branches of fruit trees, and fear they have encountered a giant form of spider mite! These mites, *Allothrombium fuliginosum* (Fig. 218), however, are general predators of small invertebrates such as aphids (including woolly aphid) and young lepidopteran larvae. *Allothrombium* has a striking velvety appearance, hence the common name red velvet mite. Compared with the other cited orchard-inhabiting predatory mites, the life history of red velvet mite is unusual in that there is just one generation annually and their eggs are laid in the soil. Also, the very earliest developmental stages are temporarily ectoparasitic, attaching themselves to soil-inhabiting hosts for a week or so before becoming free-living and adopting a predatory existence.[101] The adults of red velvet mite (the stage in the lifecycle

FIG 218. The velvet red mite (*Allothrombium fuliginosum*) is a common predator of aphids and other small invertebrates.

most likely to be encountered) overwinter in the soil or amongst dead leaves; they become active in the spring, and then ascend fruit trees and other plants in search of prey.

Spiders and to a lesser extent harvestmen prey upon orchard pests, and they are often found on fruit trees and amongst the ground flora. Common arboreal spiders include orb-web spinners such as the greenish-bodied *Araneus cucurbitinus*, crab spiders, money spiders and many others. The spectrum of natural enemies of orchard pests also includes a range of naturally occurring micro-organisms (e.g. bacteria, entomopathogenic fungi and insecticidal baculoviruses) and vertebrates. Insectivorous birds, for example, feed avidly on larvae and other foliage-feeding pests. They similarly destroy scale insects and fully grown larvae or pupae in cocoons spun on the bark of fruit trees. Hibernating codling moth larvae, amongst others, are frequently taken by birds (especially blue tits and great tits), and such depredations can lead to a marked reduction in pest populations.[102] Not all bird activity in orchards in winter, however, is beneficial – bullfinches, in particular, regularly destroy dormant flower (fruit) buds and the damage they cause can be extensive.[103]

CHAPTER 8

Life in Soft-Fruit Plantations

OVER THE PAST TWENTY-FIVE years or so soft-fruit production in these islands has changed out of all recognition. Escalating labour costs, competition from foreign imports and (often albeit unrealistic) demands from modern-day consumers for year-round supplies of fresh produce have all played their part in remoulding the industry. Strawberry production in the fenlands of East Anglia, for example, as in the areas around King's Lynn (Norfolk) and Wisbech (Cambridgeshire), has all but disappeared. Similar declines have occurred elsewhere. Also, nationally, strawberries are often now grown as annual or semi-perennial rather than perennial crops (and then, as is also the case of raspberries in parts of Scotland, frequently in permanent or temporary walk-in structures rather than in the open). Such changes inevitably impact on pests, as do changes in cultivars and other agronomic practices. These sometimes reduce the likelihood of pest attacks. Conversely, they might offer greater opportunities for pest development or establishment. Although hardy soft fruits can be raised under protection (strawberries, for example, under cloches or in walk-in plastic tunnels known as Spanish tunnels, and sometimes even in greenhouses), they are regarded here as essentially non-protected field crops. Land in the UK devoted to soft-fruit production currently exceeds 9,000 ha. This is dominated by strawberries, followed by black currants and raspberries (at *c.* 4,400 ha, 2,500 ha and 1,500 ha, respectively). In spite of declines in some sectors, wine production has increased, and there are now almost 400 commercial vineyards in England and Wales, covering a total area of around 800 ha.

SUCKING PESTS

Aphids

Aphids are common pests of soft-fruit crops (Table 11) and significant infestations are often encountered, especially in unsprayed sites. Various species occur on protected strawberry plants. These include melon & cotton aphid (*Aphis gossypii*), glasshouse & potato aphid (*Aulacorthum solani*) (Fig. 219) and violet aphid (*Myzus ornatus*). However, field crops are most often invaded by shallot aphid (*Myzus ascalonicus*) and strawberry aphid (*Chaetosiphon fragaefolii*). Damage caused by shallot aphid arises in the spring, usually from April onwards, the foliage of infested plants becoming noticeably stunted and deformed. Developing blossoms

TABLE 11. Examples of aphids associated with soft-fruit crops.

Species	***Host soft-fruit crop(s) – remarks***
Black currant aphid (*Cryptomyzus galeopsidis*)	Currant
Blackberry/cereal aphid (*Sitobion fragariae*)	Blackberry
Currant stem aphid (*Rhopalosiphoninus ribesinus*)	Currant
Currant/lettuce aphid (*Nasonovia ribisnigri*)	Gooseberry, occasionally red currant
Currant/sow-thistle aphid (*Hyperomyzus lactucae*)	Black currant, occasionally other currants
Currant/yellow-rattle aphid (*Hyperomyzus rhinanthi*)	Red currant
Glasshouse & potato aphid (*Aulacorthum solani*)	Strawberry
Gooseberry aphid (*Aphis grossulariae*)	Gooseberry, occasionally currant
Gooseberry/sow-thistle aphid (*Hyperomyzus pallidus*)	Gooseberry
Large blackberry aphid (*Amphorophora rubi*)	Blackberry – virus vector
Large raspberry aphid (*Amphorophora idaei*)	Raspberry – virus vector
Melon & cotton aphid (*Aphis gossypii*)	Strawberry – usually protected crops
Pelargonium aphid (*Acyrthosiphon malvae*)	Strawberry – virus vector
Permanent blackberry aphid (*Aphis ruborum*)	Blackberry, loganberry, rarely strawberry
Permanent currant aphid (*Aphis schneideri*)	Currant, especially black currant
Potato aphid (*Macrosiphum euphorbiae*)	Strawberry, occasionally loganberry and raspberry
Red currant blister aphid (*Cryptomyzus ribis*)	Currant, mainly red currant – inhabiting leaf galls
Red currant/arrow-grass aphid (*Aphis triglochinis*)	Red currant, rarely black currant
Scarce blackberry aphid (*Macrosiphum funestrum*)	Blackberry
Shallot aphid (*Myzus ascalonicus*)	Strawberry
Small raspberry aphid (*Aphis idaei*)	Raspberry, loganberry – virus vector
Strawberry aphid (*Chaetosiphon fragaefolii*)	Strawberry – virus vector
Violet aphid (*Myzus ornatus*)	Strawberry – usually protected crops

FIG 219. Glasshouse & potato aphid (*Aulacorthum solani*) occurs on strawberry plants throughout the year, but colonies are typically small.

are also affected. Winged aphids are produced from May onwards, and these soon migrate to agricultural crops such as potato and sugar beet. Populations on strawberry then die out. Cast nymphal skins on abandoned host plants may then be the only immediate sign that aphids have been at work. Damage typically occurs in patches within the beds, and is reminiscent of that caused in late summer and autumn by tarsonemid mites (see below). Infestations of shallot aphid in strawberry plantations are most severe when the weather is mild in late winter/early spring (particularly in February and, to a lesser extent, March).[1] Strawberry aphid, unlike shallot aphid, spends its whole life on strawberry, breeding parthenogenetically throughout the year. Infested plants are not stunted but do become contaminated with sticky honeydew. Strawberry aphid is also an important vector of viruses, including strawberry crinkle virus (SCV) and strawberry mottle virus (SMoV).[2] The aphids feed and breed mainly on the young leaflets rather than the older leaves. On established plants, populations peak in late May or June, after which numbers decline rapidly. On maidens (first-year plants), however, peak numbers are not reached until late summer or early autumn. Winged aphids, which are responsible for spreading viruses to new areas,[3] occur mainly from early May to late June or July, with smaller numbers present in colonies from October through to January or February.[4]

Cane fruit crops are similarly vulnerable to aphid-vectored virus diseases such as black raspberry necrosis virus (BRNV), raspberry leaf mottle virus (RLMV), raspberry leaf spot virus (RLSV) and rubus yellow net virus (RYNV). All of these are transmitted by the large raspberry aphid (*Amphorophora idaei*). In addition, raspberry vein chlorosis virus (RVCV) is spread by the small raspberry aphid (*Aphis idaei*).[5] Aphids on cane fruits also cause direct damage, and well-established colonies often develop on the young shoots. Blackberry/cereal aphid (*Sitobion fragariae*) on blackberry, and small raspberry aphid on loganberry and raspberry are most often encountered. Both of these species overwinter in the egg stage. However, whereas small raspberry aphid occurs on cane fruits throughout the year, blackberry/cereal aphid migrates in summer to cereal crops and other Poaceae (such as annual meadow-grass); it then returns to primary (winter) hosts in the autumn. The vast majority of aphids infesting currant and gooseberry bushes show a similar seasonal alternation between woody and herbaceous plants (Table 12), using currant or gooseberry bushes as their primary hosts. The locally distributed permanent currant aphid (*Aphis schneideri*) is an exception, lacking alternate hosts and breeding on currant throughout the summer. Colonies of gooseberry aphid (*A. grossulariae*) also persist on *Ribes* throughout the summer, even after winged migrants have been produced and have departed for summer hosts (in this case, willowherbs). As on other soft fruits, aphids on bush fruits also act as virus vectors. Currant/lettuce aphid (*Nasonovia ribisnigri*), currant/sow-thistle aphid (*Hyperomyzus lactucae*) and gooseberry aphid, for example, all transmit gooseberry vein-banding virus (GVBV). This virus affects gooseberry, black currant and red currant.

TABLE 12. Summer hosts of various currant- and gooseberry-infesting aphids.

Species	*Summer host(s)*
Black currant aphid (*Cryptomyzus galeopsidis*)	Hemp-nettles, red dead-nettle and other Labiatae
Currant/lettuce aphid (*Nasonovia ribisnigri*)	Hawksbeards, hawkweeds, lettuces, speedwells etc.
Currant/sow-thistle aphid (*Hyperomyzus lactucae*)	Sow-thistles
Currant/yellow-rattle aphid (*Hyperomyzus rhinanthi*)	Yellow-rattle
Gooseberry aphid (*Aphis grossulariae*)	Willowherbs
Gooseberry/sow-thistle aphid (*Hyperomyzus pallidus*)	Corn sow-thistle
Red currant blister aphid (*Cryptomyzus ribis*)	Hedge woundwort
Red currant/arrow-grass aphid (*Aphis triglochinis*)	Marsh arrow-grass, watercress etc.

Scale insects

Woolly vine scale (*Pulvinaria vitis*) (Fig. 220) and brown scale (*Parthenolecanium corni*) are often found in currant and gooseberry plantations. They also occur on a range of other woody hosts, including grapevine. The life histories of these closely related species are very different – woolly vine scale usually reproduces sexually, whereas brown scale populations (at least on fruit crops) are typically asexual and breed parthenogenetically.

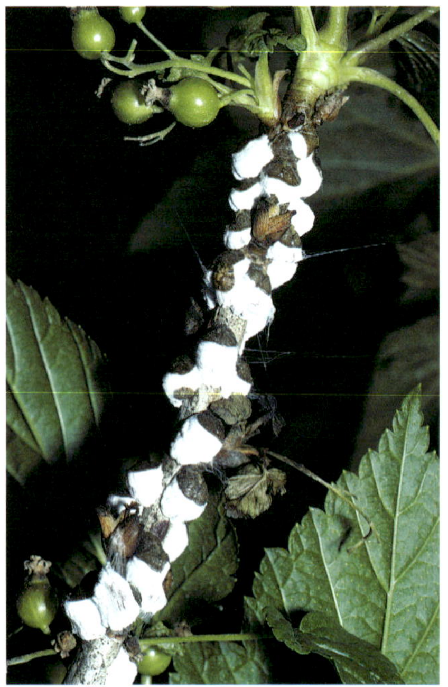

FIG 220. Woolly vine scale (*Pulvinaria vitis*) is sometimes present on bush fruits, such as black currant. Heavily infested plants are contaminated by honeydew and accumulations of white waxen 'wool'.

For many years, woolly scales on currant and gooseberry were considered a distinct species, and described as the woolly currant scale (*Pulvinaria ribesiae*). However, as long suspected by Newstead[6] (who treated *ribesiae* merely as a variety of *vitis*), the scales on currant, gooseberry and grapevine are now confirmed as representing one and the same species, with the name *P. vitis* holding sway. Adult woolly vine scales, including the delicate, pinkish-red and short-lived males, occur in September and October. After mating, the females hibernate and do not develop fully or mature until May. Each then produces a prominent white, cushion-like ovisac, within which up to a thousand or so eggs are laid. The eggs hatch in June or July. First-instar nymphs then move throughout the bushes before settling down on the shoots to continue their development. At the time of female maturation, heavily infested bushes can be an extraordinary sight as strands of white waxen 'wool' secreted by the mature females are wafted about in the wind and soon festoon the foliage, shoots and developing fruits. Infested plantations also become alive with the sound of foraging flies, wasps and other insects attracted to honeydew excreted by the pests. Unlike woolly vine scale, brown scale overwinters on outdoor hosts as second-instar nymphs, and the adult females (which do not secrete flocculent masses of wax) first appear in May. Development of this species is greatly affected by temperature, often being noticeably delayed in cool conditions,[7] and greatly advanced by high temperatures. The pest is usually single brooded in the field in Britain but it can complete two or more generations annually under glass. Brown scale is by no means an uncommon pest of currant and gooseberry bushes, although it tends to occur mainly in unsprayed sites.

Miscellaneous plant bugs

Harmful mirid (capsid) bugs – especially the common green capsid (*Lygocoris pabulinus*) (Fig. 221) and the European tarnished plant bug (*Lygus rugulipennis*) – are frequent inhabitants of soft-fruit plantations. They not only attack bush and cane fruit crops but also cause damage in strawberry beds and vineyards. Common green capsid is an important and highly active pest, overwintering as eggs on woody hosts such as currant and gooseberry. The flask-shaped eggs are inserted into the new wood, usually with their caps level with the surface of the rind. At least on currant, two-year-old shoots are also favoured oviposition sites.[8] The eggs hatch in the spring and the young nymphs feed from April onwards. The nymphs can mature and produce a summer generation on their winter hosts.[9] However, more usually, whilst still young they migrate to herbaceous summer hosts such as strawberry, potato and various weeds. Here, the next generation will eventually develop. Second-generation (summer) nymphs reach the adult stage in September. These adults then migrate back to woody hosts, upon which winter eggs are eventually laid. Common green capsid nymphs and adults often cause extensive distortion of the new shoots and foliage of host plants. Invaded leaves also become puckered, shot-holed and tattered. Such injury, resulting from puncturing of leaves by the bugs and injection of toxic saliva, is often severe on cane fruit crops such as raspberry. Attacks can also result in death of the main shoots, followed by the development of unwelcome lateral branches.

Unlike common green capsid, European tarnished plant bug overwinters in the adult stage. This insect has been of concern mainly on non-fruit crops such as beet, flax, linseed and potato. In recent years, however, it has also become a significant problem where late-season strawberries are being grown. Here, infestations result in the development of unmarketable, malformed fruits.[10]

FIG 221. Common green capsid (*Lygocoris pabulinus*) is a common pest of bush fruits.

FIG 222. Loganberry leafhoppers (*Ribautiana tenerrima*), here a male and female *in copula*, are abundant on unsprayed loganberry and raspberry canes.

Adults reared during the spring and early summer invade strawberry fields in July, and give rise to nymphs that complete their development from late August onwards. These bugs then overwinter on the strawberry plants before finally dispersing to other hosts.[11] Malformed strawberry fruits also arise following poor pollination, sometimes masking the impact of insect pests.

Various other sap-feeding plant bugs inhabit soft-fruit plantations. The foliage of cane fruit crops, for example, can become severely mottled and discoloured following the attention of pests such as the loganberry leafhopper (*Ribautiana tenerrima*) (Fig. 222), *R. debilis* and the rose leafhopper (*Edwardsiana rosae*). The common froghopper (*Philaenus spumarius*) also often occurs, the nymphs developing on host plants (including many herbaceous weeds but also red currant and strawberry plants) amongst a protective coating of cuckoo-spit. Some plant bugs are vectors of plant diseases. The strawberry leafhopper (*Aphrodes bicinctus*), for example, is a vector of green petal disease of strawberry. The causal organism, as previously mentioned in Chapter 3, is a mycoplasma-like organism (MLO), and this is acquired by the leafhoppers when they feed on infected clover plants. Green petal disease is usually most in evidence following dry summer conditions, which encourage migration of the vectors from clover to strawberry crops.

Thrips

Over the past couple of decades or so, thrips have become troublesome on everbearer strawberry crops. Attacks launched on the flowers and developing fruitlets result in surface bronzing, although fruits do not become malformed. Carnation thrips (*Thrips atratus*), rubus thrips (*T. major*) and, to a lesser extent, onion thrips (*T. tabaci*) are most often the culprits.[12] Following its establishment in Britain, western flower thrips (*Frankliniella occidentalis*) has also become a pest on strawberry crops raised under protection.

Mites

In addition to gall mites (considered elsewhere in this chapter), members of two other groups also occur as pests of soft-fruit crops: tarsonemid mites and spider mites.

Strawberry mite (*Phytonemus pallidus fragariae*),[13] a typical tarsonemid mite, is an important fruit pest. Adult females occur on strawberry throughout the year, hibernating within the crowns of host plants during the winter months. Adult males also overwinter but in very small numbers. The tiny, typically barrel-shaped mites emerge in the spring, to commence feeding on the still furled or unfurling leaves. The mites are light-shy, and tend to hide amongst the leaf hairs where humidity is high. Infested foliage becomes crinkled, stunted and discoloured (Fig. 223), although symptoms vary somewhat between host cultivars. As a general rule, fully expanded leaves are not occupied. During the springtime, breeding is mainly if not entirely parthenogenetic. However, males become numerous during the summer, and sexual reproduction is then commonplace. The relatively large eggs are laid singly, from March onwards. These soon give way to active, six-legged 'larvae' which feed briefly and then become noticeably bloated, entering a quiescent (non-feeding) nymphal stage within the skin of which development to adulthood takes place. These so-called resting nymphs are sometimes carried around by young adult males, each holding his potential bride aloft with the aid of a dorsal sucker. Overall effects on plant growth, plant vigour and crop production can be considerable, especially in the case of highly susceptible strawberry cultivars such as Cambridge Favourite;[14] fruit size

FIG 223. Strawberry mite (*Tarsonemus pallidus fragariae*) infestations stunt growth. Severely affected plants may be killed.

and quality are also affected,[15] as is the number of flowers produced per inflorescence.[16] The pest tends to be more important on longer-term crops, especially those grown in a matted-row system, where plants and their progeny (runners) are allowed to crop for several seasons. Uncontrolled, patches of stunted plants become more extensive year by year and the life of infested beds might have to be terminated prematurely. At least in western Europe (including Britain), most damage is caused in summer and early autumn, when mite populations are at their peak and, critically, when flower bud initiation for the following season is taking place. Leaf damage caused on strawberry by chrysanthemum nematode (*Aphelenchoides ritzemabosi*) (essentially, a basal silvering or greying of tissue on the upper surface of the young leaves) is sometimes mistaken for that inflicted by strawberry mite but is most evident in the spring.

Two-spotted spider mite (*Tetranychus urticae*) is an important pest of strawberry and other soft-fruit crops, especially black currant. It is also a notorious pest of hop and protected crops such as cucumber, tomato and a wide range of ornamentals, and often causes flecking or bronzing of infested leaves. Particularly in hot, dry summers, populations can escalate rapidly, sometimes reaching plague proportions. The mites may then spread to less-frequently invaded crops such as potato, sugar beet and sweet corn. Two-spotted spider mites overwinter as diapausing adult females, clustered beneath dead leaves, amongst straw mulch or in other sheltered situations. Activity is resumed in the spring. Unlike strawberry mite, the mites typically establish colonies on the underside of fully expanded leaves, more or less sheltered by strands of fine silk. Individuals develop from egg to adult through a 'larva' and, usually, two nymphal stages (protonymph and deutonymph), the rate of development varying considerably according to temperature. There are several overlapping generations annually, usually six or seven on outdoor crops. Although summer adults are greenish in appearance, characteristically marked by a large dark patch on either side of the body (hence the common name), the winter females are brick-red. Fruit tree red spider mite (*Panonychus ulmi*) also occurs in soft-fruit plantations, attacking various bush fruit crops, cane fruit crops and grapevines, but is far more important in orchards (see Chapter 7).

In the past, gooseberry bryobia mite (*Bryobia ribis*) was a frequent pest of gooseberry bushes. Today, however, it is rarely found in commercial plantations. Heavy infestations cause extensive discoloration of foliage and premature leaf fall, and the impact on fruit yields and quality is then considerable. Gooseberry bryobia mite, which is readily distinguished from two-spotted spider mite by its flattened, oval body-shape and noticeably elongated front pair of legs, does not produce silk webbing and is single brooded, overwintering in the unusually prolonged egg stage after just one generation. The pest is also entirely parthenogenetic, males being unknown. Published accounts of the life history and habits of gooseberry bryobia mite vary since this species has often been confused with the clover bryobia mite and then erroneously described under *B. praetiosa*. So have several others, namely, the apple & pear bryobia mite (*B. rubrioculus*), the grass/pear bryobia mite (*B. cristata*) and the ivy bryobia mite (*B. kissophila*). Although such species are structurally rather similar, their life histories are quite distinct.[17]

DEFOLIATING PESTS

Moths

Leaf-browsing moth larvae (caterpillars) are often abundant in soft-fruit plantations, those of tortrix moths usually being of greatest significance. The tortricid complex is especially extensive on strawberry, with at least ten species recorded attacking commercial crops in England. Of these, the strawberry tortrix moth (*Acleris comariana*) (Fig. 224) is most frequently cited as a pest and, over the years, has often been the dominant species. This is especially so in lowland sites such as Cambridgeshire and Cheshire, but not in all strawberry-growing areas.[18]

FIG 224. Strawberry tortrix moth (*Acleris comariana*) is most often found in lowland sites.

FIG 225. Dark strawberry tortrix moth (*Celypha lacunana*) frequently attacks plants grown under cloches.

Strawberry tortrix moth, a highly polymorphic species,[19] overwinters in the egg stage, most eggs being laid on the underside of the fully expanded leaves.[20] In the distant past,[21] probably with reference to the old cultivar Royal Sovereign, stipules have also been recorded as egg-laying sites. However, this does not hold true for more modern cultivars (such as Cambridge Favourite) whose stipules, unlike those of Royal Sovereign, are rather small and not at all leaf-like. Most other tortrix pests associated with strawberry crops overwinter as young larvae. These include species such as allied shade moth (*Cnephasia incertana*), flax tortrix moth (*C. asseclana*), *C. longana* (all three of which are single brooded), and essentially double-brooded species such as dark strawberry tortrix moth (*Celypha lacunana*)[22] (Fig. 225) and straw-coloured tortrix moth (*Clepsis spectrana*) (Fig. 226); the more locally distributed *Ancylis comptana*, however, usually passes the winter as fully grown larvae.

FIG 226. Straw-coloured tortrix moth (*Clepsis spectrana*), here a female, is a polyphagous pest which sometimes attacks strawberry crops.

Overwintered eggs of strawberry tortrix moth hatch in the spring and the larvae then feed amongst spun leaves, eventually pupating in early to mid-June. Adults appear about two weeks later. These also then lay eggs

FIG 227. Dark strawberry tortrix moth (*Celypha lacunana*) larvae wriggle backwards very rapidly when disturbed.

singly on the leaves of host plants. Second-brood larvae occur from late July to September. Second-generation adults are active from August onwards, individuals often surviving well into November.

Larvae of strawberry tortrix moth feed mainly on the leaves of strawberry plants, which reduces their immediate impact on the crop.[23] However, those of *Cnephasia* spp., dark strawberry tortrix moth (Fig. 227) and straw-coloured tortrix moth, and also those of the day-flying carnation tortrix moth (*Cacoecimorpha pronubana*) (a potentially multi-brooded, highly polyphagous species), although not averse to feeding on leaves, show a particular liking for the blossoms. As individuals, they frequently tie the petals down with silk to form a cover whilst they destroy the underlying stamens and other floral parts. These capped or partially capped blossoms are readily seen in infested sites. On occasions, early-instar larvae of the powdered quaker moth (*Orthosia gracilis*) – a noctuid (family Noctuidae) – cause similar damage.

Other moths also occur in strawberry beds, especially in weedy sites. These include large yellow underwing moths (*Noctua pronuba*) which, although not strictly diurnal, are often observed during the daytime. When disturbed by pickers or other visitors the moths career wildly through the air (their wings seeming to pulse with yellow) before crashing to the ground and resettling, usually several metres away. Larvae of this polyphagous species attack the roots and crowns of strawberry plants, feeding mainly at night.[24] Known as climbing cutworms, they also graze on the foliage.

Several strawberry-feeding tortricids are also associated with other soft-fruit crops. Examples include: allied shade moth and *Cnephasia longana* on currant and raspberry; dark strawberry tortrix moth on blackberry and raspberry; also, straw-coloured tortrix moth on blackberry and black currant. On black currant,

FIG 228. Bramble shoot moth (*Epiblema uddmanniana*) is a common pest of cane fruits.

egg-laying by straw-coloured tortrix moth is restricted largely if not entirely to the new growth. As a consequence, infestations tend to be greatest on bushes where fruit has been harvested mechanically (i.e. where breakage of shoots and branches stimulates the development of fresh vegetative growth).[25] Species associated with trees and shrubs are also frequent inhabitants of bush fruit and/or cane fruit plantations. These include fruit tree tortrix moth (*Archips podana*) and several other common and widely distributed leaf-rolling species such as *Acleris variegana, Archips rosana, Ditula angustiorana, Pandemis cerasana* and *P. heparana*. Larvae of the bud moth (*Spilonota ocellana*) may also be encountered. None of these species qualifies individually as an important pest in soft-fruit plantations. However, the bramble shoot moth (*Epiblema uddmanniana*) (Fig. 228), yet another tortrix, can be of some significance on blackberry, raspberry and other cane fruit crops, causing death of buds, checking cane growth and having an adverse effect on cropping potential for the following year. Adults occur mainly in July, depositing their eggs singly on the foliage close to the tips of the young canes. The eggs hatch about two weeks later. Young larvae, typically one per infested cane, may then be found amongst the youngest leaves which they web together with strands of silk. In mid-August, whilst still quite small, the larvae vacate the leaves and each spins a tough cocoon in the axil of a leaf, towards the base of a cane.[26] The larvae remain in these cocoons throughout the autumn and winter months, and reappear in the spring. They then invade the apical leaves, webbing the foliage tightly together to form tough tent-like habitations. The larval tent contains masses of dark frass (accumulating amongst a mat of silken webbing) as well as the occupant: a rather plump, brown-bodied larva. The larvae (Fig. 229), commonly known as bramble shoot webbers, feed within their tents but, at night, they also emerge to attack nearby leaves, buds and flowers. After the blossom period, larvae infesting fruiting

FIG 229. Bramble shoot moth (*Epiblema uddmanniana*) larvae develop within tough habitations of webbed and distorted leaves.

canes usually migrate to the new vegetative growth, where further tents are formed. Pupation takes place in the larval habitation from late May onwards, there being just one generation annually.

In addition to tortricids, various polyphagous leaf-browsing geometrids and noctuids (amongst others) also regularly grace soft-fruit plantations with their presence. Examples include: currant pug moth (*Eupithecia assimilata*) on currant; dot moth (*Melanchra persicariae*) (Fig. 230) and magpie moth (*Abraxas grossulariata*) (Fig. 231) on currant and gooseberry; mottled umber moth (*Erannis defoliaria*) and

FIG 230. Dot moth (*Melanchra persicariae*) larvae feed on various plants. They are minor pests of soft-fruit crops, including currant and gooseberry.

FIG 231. Magpie moth (*Abraxas grossulariata*) is a minor pest of currant and gooseberry, and more often found in private gardens than in commercial plantations.

winter moth (*Operophtera brumata*) on blueberry and other bush fruits (at least in woody districts); gothic moth (*Naenia typica*) and *Orthosia* spp. on raspberry; angle-shades moth (*Phlogophora meticulosa*) and cabbage moth (*Mamestra brassicae*) on strawberry. In addition, the double dart moth (*Graphiphora augur*) has become recognised as a pest in Scottish raspberry plantations.[27] Larvae of this pest not only damage the foliage but also attack the buds. If bud burst in the spring is delayed, even small numbers of individuals can be of significance. In one instance,[28] for example, over a third of buds were destroyed in an infested block of raspberry canes.

Sawflies

Foliage-feeding sawfly larvae are often active in soft-fruit plantations. Generally, gooseberry sawfly (*Nematus ribesii*) (a pest all too frequently encountered by amateur gardeners) is the most devastating species, the larvae attacking various kinds of *Ribes*, including gooseberry, red currant and white currant but never black currant. The pale-spotted gooseberry sawfly (*N. leucotrochus*) and the small gooseberry sawfly (*Pristiphora pallipes*) are also common, although less important, pests. Their larvae infest currant (other than black currant) and gooseberry bushes. Sawfly larvae, intermediate in appearance between those of gooseberry sawfly and pale-spotted gooseberry sawfly, do occur on black currant bushes but these belong to a quite separate species, first recognised as distinct in the early 1950s.[29] This pest, known as the black currant sawfly (*N. olfaciens*), also attacks red currant and gooseberry.

FIG 232. Gooseberry sawfly (*Nematus ribesii*) larvae are gregarious and voracious feeders. Infested shoots and branches, if not entire bushes, are rapidly defoliated.

FIG 233. Gooseberry sawfly prepupae are active but do not feed. They lack the prominent black pinacula of larvae, and are often thought to be a different species.

Gooseberry sawfly adults occur in April and May. Characteristically, eggs are laid in rows along the major veins on the leaves of host plants. Following egg hatch, the mainly green, black-speckled and black-headed larvae (Fig. 232) feed gregariously for about three weeks. They can cause extensive defoliation, and often reduce bushes or parts of bushes to a sorry skeleton of leafless shoots and branches. Males pass through four larval instars and females through five. They then moult to an active, but non-feeding, prepupal stage which is of a very different appearance, being paler in colour and lacking the prominent black spots (pinacula) so typical of the larvae. These prepupae (Fig. 233) are sometimes erroneously thought to be larvae of a quite different species of sawfly or merely recently moulted larvae yet to develop their full livery. The prepupae soon vacate host bushes. They then burrow into the soil where they spin parchment-like cocoons within which pupation takes place. Adults of the next generation emerge a few weeks later. Gooseberry sawfly is a particularly prolific, double-brooded (if not triple-brooded) and damaging pest, females depositing up to 50 (usually 15–30) eggs per leaf. Pale-spotted gooseberry sawfly, however, rarely lays more than five and often just one per leaf,[30] and has just one generation annually. Its larvae (Fig. 234) are rarely if ever numerous.

Sawfly larvae also attack cane fruit crops. These include those of the raspberry sawfly (*Empria tridens*) (Fig. 235) and the small raspberry sawfly (*Priophorus morio*) (Fig. 236). Similarly, larvae of antler sawflies (*Cladius* spp.), so named because of the antler-like antennae of the adults, are often common but minor pests of

FIG 234. Pale gooseberry sawfly (*Nematus leucotrochus*) larvae occur in small numbers on gooseberry and currant bushes, but not black currant.

strawberry. The noticeably hairy larvae form large holes in the expanded leaves and most often occur at the ends of rows. Quite different leaf damage on strawberry is caused by larvae of the day-flying banded rose sawfly (*Allantus cinctus*). The adult of this slender-bodied species is mainly black, with a long, cylindrical abdomen and (in females) a distinctive white cross-band towards the hind end of the body. The adults are very strong fliers and especially active in sunny weather.[31] Eggs are deposited in the leaves of host plants, forming a series of wart-like swellings. Following egg hatch, the larvae feed on the leaf margins (Fig. 237), eating away considerable areas of leaf tissue. This pest, which has two generations per year, is mainly associated with rose bushes and is more numerous in private gardens than in commercial strawberry fields. It also occurs on raspberry.

FIG 235. Raspberry sawfly (*Empria tridens*) larvae are usually of minor importance.

FIG 236. Small raspberry sawfly (*Priophorus morio*) larvae are generally common, but cause only minor damage.

FIG 237. Banded rose sawfly (*Allantus cinctus*) larvae are sometimes found on strawberry plants, but the pest is more often associated with rose bushes.

Beetles

Browsing adult beetles often cause damage to the foliage of soft-fruit crops. Otiorhynchid weevils (genus *Otiorhynchus*) and several of their close relatives, for example, often form large notches in leaf margins. Such damage can be very extensive, especially in strawberry fields. Most crop damage, however, is caused by the root-feeding weevil larvae. These are discussed later, under soil pests. Similar, but much smaller, U-shaped notches around the leaf margins of strawberry plants are caused by adult pea & bean weevils (*Sitona lineatus*). Such symptoms are most often noticed in districts where legume crops (typically, peas and field beans) are grown, and occur in summer when newly reared weevils feed avidly on non-leguminous plants prior to taking up their winter quarters and hibernating.

Flea beetles often occur on cane fruit and strawberry crops, where they browse on the leaves. Large flax flea beetle (*Aphthona euphorbiae*) and the raspberry flea beetles *Batophila aerata* and *B. rubi* are the most frequent visitors. However, the injury they cause, although sometimes attracting attention, is of little or no significance.

Finally, a species of soldier beetle (*Cantharis obscura*) has been highlighted as a pest of raspberry plants in eastern Scotland.[32] The adults feed in May on the expanding fruiting laterals, causing direct damage to the nodes and internodes which sometimes results in the loss of shoots.

LEAF MINERS

Damage caused by leaf-mining insects, albeit usually of an insignificant nature, can attract attention in soft-fruit plantations, especially on cane fruit crops. Causal agents include the larvae of two raspberry leaf-mining sawflies (*Metallus albipes* and *M. pumilus*) (Fig. 238) and, less frequently, larvae of the tiny moth

FIG 238. Raspberry leaf-mining sawfly (*Metallus pumilus*) larvae feed in large blotch mines.

FIG 239. The tiny moth *Tischeria marginea* (above left) is a minor, often overlooked pest of loganberry and raspberry. The larvae (above right) feed within blotch mines on the leaves.

Tischeria marginea (Fig. 239). All three species form whitish to pale-brown blotch mines in the expanded leaves. First-brood larvae of *T. marginea* feed from June to July and those of a second brood from September onwards. The latter do not complete their development until the early spring and can survive the winter only on evergreen *Rubus*. In the case of raspberry leaf-mining sawflies, which are also double brooded, second-generation larvae are fully grown in the autumn; therefore, the annual cycle can be completed on either a deciduous or an evergreen host. The sawfly larvae pupate in the soil. In *T. marginea*, however, pupation takes place in the mine.

Serpentine leaf mines of the blackberry pygmy moth (*Stigmella aurella*) are sometimes in evidence on cultivated blackberry but must be considered of little or no significance to the fruit grower. Their general abundance in the countryside on wild bramble bushes in England, Wales and Ireland, if not Scotland, however, makes them worthy of a passing mention. Similar mines formed by the less well-known species *S. fragariella* occur on loganberry and raspberry, especially in southeast and south-central England. Both insects are double brooded but details of their biology are quite distinct, especially regarding their overwintering strategies – blackberry pygmy moth, owing to the later and more protracted development of the second-brood larvae, is unable to survive the winter except on evergreen forms of *Rubus*, as highlighted previously for *T. marginea*.[33]

Amongst the guild of leaf-mining flies just one species is of interest in soft-fruit plantations: *Agromyza potentillae*, the larvae of which are known as strawberry leaf miners. The characteristic mines sometimes occur on cultivated raspberry and strawberry plants, each commencing as a linear gallery but then widening into an expansive blotch. There can be several mines on an infested leaf, and these have a deleterious effect on the growth of very small strawberry plants. They are, however, of little or no consequence on raspberry.

FIG 240. Strawberry casebearer moth (*Coleophora potentillae*) sometimes occurs on cultivated strawberry plants. The shell-like larval cases are easily mistaken for those of tiny snails.

Another leaf-mining insect to be found on strawberry, but of no more than minor pest status, is the strawberry casebearer moth (*Coleophora potentillae*). The larval cases (Fig. 240), which are formed from silk and plant debris, could easily be mistaken for conical snail shells but are likely to attract the attention of only the most diligent of observers. This species feeds on various wild plants, and also on cultivated cinquefoil, rose, raspberry and other cane fruits.

Blossom weevils

Two small weevils, strawberry blossom weevil (*Anthonomus rubi*) and strawberry rhynchites (*Neocoenorrhinus germanicus*),[34] are responsible for the loss of buds or blossoms in strawberry beds. These insects also occur on blackberry, loganberry and raspberry. The adult weevils have a long, curved trunk-like snout (rostrum) and, in profile, are not dissimilar in appearance to minute elephants. Accordingly, both species have been blessed by growers with the name elephant bug, but never with affection! Indeed, the activities of these pests have often caused considerable concern, especially on strawberry crops. Other colloquial names bestowed upon these weevils (at least on the strawberry blossom weevil) include elephant beetle, elephant fly and needle bug. The two weevils have often been confused, although, with even superficial examination, they are readily separated; for example, the strawberry blossom weevil is essentially greyish black and the strawberry rhynchites black with a metallic blue-green sheen; also, the antennae of the former (in common with other members of the family Curculionidae) are elbowed, with a long basal section, whereas those of the latter (a member of the family Rhynchitidae) are straight and the individual 'segments' (called flagellomeres) are all of a similar length.

Strawberry blossom weevil adults appear in strawberry crops in April and May. At first they inhabit the field margins, close to hedges and other sheltered sites where they hibernated, but they soon migrate into the crop. They fly readily in sunny weather.[35] The weevils feed on the young foliage in the crowns of plants and also congregate on the open blossoms. After mating, females deposit eggs singly in the unopened flower buds, each weevil boring a hole through the side with the aid of her rostrum. Having laid an egg, the weevil crawls down the flower stalk, which she then partially girdles a few centimetres from the base of the calyx. This causes the stalk to fold over. Affected buds fail to open and remain temporarily suspended from the partially severed stalk and eventually drop to the ground. The weevil egg hatches within a few days and the larva then feeds on the floral parts, protected by the calyx and the wilting remains of the undeveloped petals. Larvae eventually pupate *in situ*, and new adults emerge shortly afterwards, usually from mid- to late July. The young weevils feed briefly on young foliage and then disperse to seek their winter quarters.

For many years dusting with DDT was a standard treatment against strawberry blossom weevils in strawberry plantations, and afterwards the beds would appear white as if dusted with snow. In Cambridgeshire if not elsewhere this practice continued as a routine well into the 1960s, even though the status of the pest had by then largely diminished. At least in part, the decline in the importance of the pest may have been linked to the replacement in commercial fields of susceptible older cultivars (such as Royal Sovereign) by more even-ripening and heavier-cropping cultivars such as Cambridge Favourite and Red Gauntlet. Where chemical treatments are warranted, dusting with DDT has long since been replaced by more targeted spraying with a less persistent and more selective insecticide. Even so, due regard needs to be given to the possible impact that any pesticide could have on overall pest management within the crop. The mere presence of the weevil is no excuse for treatment; minor infestations can have a beneficial bud-thinning effect and increase overall fruit size.

The life history of the strawberry rhynchites is similar to that of strawberry blossom weevil but the egg-laying period extends over a far longer period, lasting from mid-April to late August.[36] Also, the eggs are laid in the stalks of leaves or blossom trusses, often several per stalk. Having deposited the required complement of eggs the female bites a ring of tiny holes around the stalk, just below the lowermost egg, and the complete leaf or blossom truss (within which larval development will take place) eventually wilts and dies. In addition to strawberry, attacks are often noticed on blackberry, loganberry, raspberry and other cane fruit crops, the partially severed blossom clusters sometimes dangling by a thin piece of rind, reminiscent of injury caused on young fruit trees by the related apple twig cutter (*Involvulus caeruleus*)[37] (Chapter 7).

FRUIT INVADERS

Raspberry beetle (*Byturus tomentosus*) (Fig. 241) must rate as one of the most well-known pests of soft-fruit crops. The adults and larvae attack cane fruit crops such as blackberry, loganberry and raspberry. Unchecked, the pest is capable of causing considerable damage, and it is of significance both to the fresh fruit market and to fruit processors. Raspberry beetle is also a notorious pest in private gardens and allotments. Adults overwinter in the soil and emerge in the spring, the timing of their emergence varying according to temperature. In the main raspberry-growing areas of eastern Scotland, for example, emergence typically begins in mid-May.[38] However, the beetles appear earlier (often from April onwards) in southern England. Following emergence, the adults are attracted in sunny weather to a range of rosaceous plants, including non-hosts such as apple, pear and hawthorn, where they feed on pollen within the open blossoms. On loganberry and raspberry, adults cause damage to the developing buds, unopened and opened flowers. The harm they do is especially serious in years when large numbers of beetles invade plants before the flowers have opened.[39] Eggs are usually laid singly in the flowers of raspberry and other hosts, and they hatch ten or so days later. Larvae (Fig. 242) then feed on the surface of

FIG 241. Raspberry beetle (*Byturus tomentosus*) is a major pest of cane fruits.

FIG 242. Raspberry beetle larvae attack cane fruits, and are common in commercial plantations and private gardens.

the developing fruits, remaining exposed for an extended period before eventually entering the berries.[40] Damage is caused to the developing drupelets, especially at the base (at the calyx end) of the fruit. Later, the larvae also burrow into the fruit plugs. Fully grown larvae drop to the ground and eventually pupate in the soil. Although the adult stage is reached in the autumn the beetles do not appear above ground until the following spring.

The lifecycles of relatively few other soft-fruit pests are dependent for their completion upon the presence of actual fruits, although developing or ripe ones are fair game for a wide range of opportunist invertebrate and vertebrate invaders. In particular, adult ground beetles (including common species such as *Nebria brevicollis*, *Pterostichus madidus* and *P. melanarius*, which are otherwise welcome as predators of pests) target ripe strawberries, excavating deep cavities into the flesh. Such damage is often particularly evident in damp conditions following periods of dry weather.[41] Similar damage is caused by slugs. However, the holes they cause tend to be more irregular and often house an accumulation of slimy, macerated tissue; slime trails are also present.[42] Other pests known to cause direct damage to fruits include broad-nosed weevils (*Barypeithes araneiformis* and *B. pellucidus*), the adults of which bore into developing strawberry fruits, and larvae of the carnation tortrix moth, which often feed directly on ripe or ripening strawberries.[43]

In dry conditions, strawberries in contact with the ground can be a welcome source of moisture for invertebrates such as spotted snake millepedes (*Blaniulus guttulatus*). Similarly, ripe or over-ripe raspberries, and other such fruits, often attract the attention of moisture-seeking insects which might not otherwise be classifed as pests. Also, the forest bug (*Pentatoma rufipes*) and the green shield bug (*Palomena prasina*) (Fig. 243) sometimes mark raspberries and other fruits with an evil-smelling secretion. Affected fruits are then rendered unpalatable. On the

FIG 243. Green shield bugs (*Palomena prasina*) produce an evil-smelling secretion which sometimes taints raspberries and other fruits.

plus side, however, forest bugs are also predators of caterpillars and other invertebrate pests.

One ground beetle, the strawberry seed beetle (*Harpalus rufipes*) (Fig. 244), is a more discerning feeder. This beetle, which is active at night,[44] regularly removes seeds (achenes) from ripening strawberries (Fig. 245). In doing so, it typically damages the surrounding flesh and renders the fruits unmarketable. Achenes on the side of fruits close to and facing the ground are most often selected. Linnets also remove achenes from strawberries, but from the exposed surfaces of the fruits and without causing physical damage to the fruit surface.[45] Nevertheless, such symptoms are often mistakenly attributed to seed beetles by strawberry growers.[46] Various other birds, including blackbirds and woodpigeons, launch indiscriminate attacks on soft-fruit crops. Although an unmitigated nuisance in private gardens, where they often strip fruits from red currant, white currant and gooseberry bushes (even before the fruits have ripened), their depredations on a field scale are usually of minor significance. Ring-necked parakeets, however, have recently become a problem in some soft-fruit plantations and vineyards. As harvest time approaches flocks of

FIG 244. Although strawberry seed beetle (*Harpalus rufipes*) is a common and well-known predator, the adults also attack ripening strawberries.

FIG 245. Strawberries attacked by strawberry seed beetle (*Harpalus rufipes*) are unmarketable. Seeds (achenes) are ripped from the fruits, damaging the flesh. Damage is often confused with that caused by linnets.

starlings can be a serious problem in commercial vineyards, much to the frustration of growers. In some parts of Europe (as in Burgenland, Austria, close to the Austro-Hungarian border) pilots of light aircraft are sometimes hired to chase the flocks away in mock dog-fights! Helicopters have also been used. Another tactic is to employ the services of falconers.

Developing blackberries are sometimes invaded by blackberry mite (*Acalitus essigi*). As the fruits ripen and become black, the basal drupelets of mite-infested ones remain hard and greenish to red – a condition known as red-berry disease. Late-maturing fruits are especially affected. Uneven ripening of drupelets can also be caused by other factors, and the presence of mites needs to be confirmed before concluding that the pest is responsible.

SHOOT BORERS

Three kinds of day-flying moths with shoot-boring larvae inhabit soft-fruit plantations. Currant clearwing moth (*Synanthedon tipuliformis*), for example, is a widely distributed pest of currant and gooseberry bushes. The wasp-like, transparent-winged adults occur in May and June, and are active in sunny weather. They may then be seen foraging on the open blossoms of brambles and other plants growing in the vicinity of infested plantations. Their larvae feed singly within the shoots and branches of host bushes throughout the summer and autumn, tunnelling in the pith towards the younger wood. Fully grown individuals pupate in the spring, each in a tough, silken cocoon formed in a small chamber at the end of the feeding gallery. Prior to the emergence of the adult, the pupa breaks out of the cocoon and through the rind of the infested shoot, leaving behind a characteristic emergence hole. These are often noticed during winter pruning, and are a useful indication of the presence of the pest. Currant clearwing moth is said to have little economic impact on crop yields in commercial black currant plantations, with no indication of a long-term deterioration of bushes, even in the face of heavy infestations.[47] However, this may not be the case in plantations where regular frost protection (overhead spraying with water) at flowering time is practised. This is because drenched bushes can become weighed down with ice and clearwing-infested branches are then liable to snap off. Infestations can certainly be of significance in gooseberry plantations,[48] resulting directly in the death of bushes. They also hasten the decline of host plants by predisposing them to infection by grey mould (*Botryotinia fuckeliniana* – anamorph, *Botrytis cinerea*), to which black currant bushes are also far from immune. Currant shoot borer moth (*Lampronia capitella*) is another diurnal pest of currant and gooseberry. This species is widely distributed in England but more local in Scotland, where it was not found until the mid-1950s.[49] In parts of northern Europe (e.g. in Scandinavia) currant shoot borer is an important pest in commercial holdings. In Britain, however, it is found mainly in private gardens. Adults occur from the end of flowering onwards. Eggs are then deposited within the developing green fruits, usually in batches of four to seven.[50] Following egg hatch, larvae feed briefly on the developing seeds before vacating the fruits and spinning overwintering cocoons in sheltered situations on host plants. The overwintered larvae reappear in the following spring. They then attack the buds and also burrow into the new shoots. Pupation occurs in April or May, typically within a mined shoot. Attacks result in the death of buds and shoots, and also the loss of developing fruits. The third species, raspberry moth (*Lampronia rubiella*), is generally the most abundant and most widely known. Adults are active in spring and early summer, not only in daytime but also at night. Eggs are deposited singly in the flowers of host plants. Following egg hatch, the young larvae feed within the developing fruitlets, each burrowing into the plug. Whilst still tiny they vacate the fruit to overwinter in the soil.[51] Larvae reappear in the following spring, at bud burst. They then ascend the canes to bore into the buds and young shoots. Damage caused by such larvae can

FIG 246. Canes attacked by loganberry cane fly (*Pegomya rubivora*) wilt and die.

be considerable. In Ireland, for example, 75 per cent of raspberry shoots were destroyed in the wake of a particularly heavy infestation.[52] Raspberry moth tends to be more damaging to raspberry than to loganberry, probably because larvae in the plugs are eliminated when loganberries are harvested (the plugs usually remaining within the fruits).[53] On raspberry, the plugs usually remain attached to the bushes when fruits are picked, allowing young larvae to continue their development.

Occasionally, young blackberry, raspberry and loganberry canes are attacked by loganberry cane fly (*Pegomya rubivora*). The larvae (maggots), which feed during June and July, tunnel downwards within the pith and also girdle the canes. This causes the tips to keel over and die (Fig. 246). Pupation occurs at the base of the hollowed-out canes, and adults eventually emerge in the following spring. At least in Scotland,[54] raspberry crops are also attacked by rosy rustic moth (*Hydraecia micacea*). The larvae bore within the canes, causing them to wilt. Rosy rustic moth is more widely known as a strawberry pest, the larvae burrowing within the crowns. Swift moth and otiorhynchid weevil larvae may also be found lodged in the crowns of wilting, dead or dying strawberry plants. The former, however, are usually temporary inhabitants, feeding at night and usually hiding in the soil during daytime.

GALL INHABITANTS

Several gall midges are associated with soft-fruit plantations. These include the black currant leaf midge (*Dasineura tetensi*) and the raspberry cane midge (*Resseliella theobaldi*).

First-generation black currant leaf midges occur from April to early June, the actual timing of their appearance depending very much upon ambient temperatures. Eggs are laid in the furled leaves at the tips of new shoots and hatch shortly afterwards. Several larvae then feed on the leaves, which soon become distorted and discoloured. Shoot growth is checked, and affected tissue can be killed, resulting in the development of secondary, lateral shoots. Fully fed larvae drop to the ground and then pupate in their subterranean cocoons. There are two, and occasionally three, further generations during the year. The blackberry leaf midge (*D. plicatrix*), another multi-brooded species, causes similar damage on wild and cultivated blackberry but is of little or no commercial significance.

Raspberry cane midge is a locally important pest, capable of causing extensive damage within raspberry plantations. Although this pest has been known in England since the 1920s,[55] it was another half century before attacks were eventually reported from the important raspberry-growing regions of Scotland.[56] In southern England, midges first appear in early May, but emergence is about a month later in Scotland. Within an area, the midges also tend to emerge earlier in warmer sites such as south-facing as opposed to north-facing slopes.[57] Eggs are deposited in cracks in the rind of young canes, including sites of mechanical injury and natural growth splits. The pinkish larvae feed beneath the rind for two to three weeks before eventually pupating in the soil, each in a tiny silken cocoon. Attacked parts of canes become susceptible to invasion by *Leptosphaeria coniothyrium* (a pathogenic fungus), resulting in a condition known as cane blight or midge blight.[58] Raspberry cane midge typically has three overlapping generations annually, the number of larvae present in later broods often being considerable. The pest causes most damage on raspberry cultivars whose canes are liable to split in the spring. It is of far less significance on loganberry, tayberry and non-splitting raspberry cultivars.

Black currant gall mite (*Cecidophyopsis ribis*) is another notorious eriophyid fruit pest, acting as a vector of black currant reversion virus (BRV) and also causing direct damage to black currant bushes.[59] From early spring onwards, effectively from the onset of flowering to the initial stages of fruit swelling, the mites are free-living on the leaves of host plants. At this time they may be seen to jump into the air, behaviour that aids their dispersal in wind currents.[60] Following this dispersal phase, new buds are invaded and eggs laid. A succession of rapidly developing generations follows, the infested buds swelling considerably into the familiar big-buds (Fig. 247). If prised open, a galled bud may be seen to be teeming with thousands, if not tens of thousands, of mites. Breeding peaks in September and, apart from a brief halt in early winter, continues throughout the dormant season. It reaches a second peak in the early

FIG 247. Buds invaded by black currant gall mite (*Cecidophyopsis ribis*) become greatly swollen (big-buds). Growth of infested bushes is disrupted, but the pest is of greater significance as a vector of blackcurrant reversion virus.

spring, shortly before the free-living dispersal stage. Infested buds, which eventually shrivel and die, sometimes exceed 15 mm in diameter, and are especially obvious after leaf fall. The impact of BRV, however, is more significant than direct mite damage. The presence of this disease (indicated by bushes that develop characteristic leaf symptoms and are then said to be reverted)[61] often signals the premature end to the productive life of a plantation.

Gall mites also invade the buds of gooseberry and red currant bushes. However, as the buds do not then swell infestations usually escape attention. The mites responsible – gooseberry gall mite (*C. grossulariae*) and red currant gall mite (*C. selachodon*), respectively – are close relatives of black currant gall mite, and all three have often been considered one and the same species. However, the validity of regarding them as distinct[62] has been confirmed by molecular studies.[63]

Another eriophyid, the raspberry leaf & bud mite (*Phyllocoptes gracilis*), causes a yellow blotching of the upper surface of leaves of raspberry and other cane fruits. The mites inhabit the buds, developing fruits and underside of expanded leaves, and heavy infestations can cause extensive damage.[64] The pest occurs mainly in warm, sheltered situations, populations reaching their peak in mid-summer. In the autumn, the adult females seek hibernation sites, typically

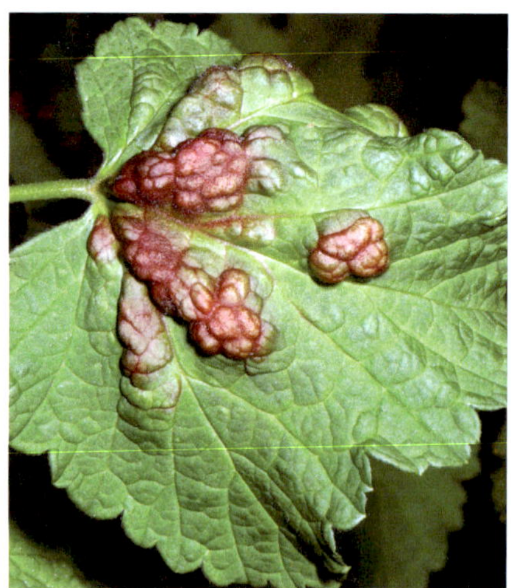

FIG 248. Blister-like galls inhabited by red currant blister aphid (*Cryptomyzus ribis*) are a common sight on red currant bushes.

hiding away beneath bud scales. Here, however, they face an uncertain future, and many fail to survive. Mean autumn mortality rates of 71 per cent/bud and 61 per cent/cane have been recorded, the mites probably being squashed when the buds swell prior to becoming dormant.[65]

Blackberry stem gall midge (*Lasioptera rubi*), a minor pest of blackberry, raspberry and other cane fruits, initiates walnut-like galls that often completely encircle the infested stems (canes). Each gall encloses a single cavity within which several (up to 15 or more) orange-red midge larvae may be found throughout the summer, autumn and winter. Similar but more irregular galls are formed on canes by the rubus gall wasp (*Diastrophus rubi*). In this case, however, the galls are multi-chambered, each chamber enclosing a single, whitish wasp larva. Rubus gall wasp is not uncommon in the wild but it is rarely reported on cultivated plants.

Various other gall-forming pests occur in soft-fruit plantations, including the red currant blister aphid (*Cryptomyzus ribis*). This pest overwinters in the egg stage. In spring, small colonies of pale-bodied, wingless aphids develop on the underside of red currant leaves, resulting in the formation of distinctive galls. These are clearly visible from above as large, red or purplish-red blisters (Fig. 248). The aphids also occur on black currant, but here the galls are yellowish green and far less obvious. Following the production of winged forms (which migrate in summer to hosts such as hedge woundwort), colonies on currant bushes eventually die out. A return migration to currant (the primary host, upon which winter eggs are laid) occurs in the autumn.

Blister-like galls (erinea), indicative of attack by vine leaf blister mite (*Colomerus vitis*), are often found on the leaves of grapevines (Fig. 249). Characteristically, the lower surface of each gall is lined with a dense, velvet-like mass of distorted hairs, forming a whitish or brownish erineum within which the microscopic mites feed and breed. Vine leaf blister mite is a generally common pest in vineyards throughout the world. Several physiological strains

FIG 249. Vine leaf blister mite (*Colomerus vitis*) occurs widely in vineyards. The mites inhabit felt-like galls (erinea) on the leaves.

are known, each causing a specific host plant symptom. However, the erineum-forming strain is the only one recorded from Britain.[66] The galls should not be mistaken for the more prominent, wart-like structures initiated on grapevine leaves by the infamous grape phylloxera (*Viteus vitifoliae*) (Chapter 12). They are also quite different from those formed by the vine leaf gall midge (*Janetiella oenophila*), a common but minor pest in vineyards in mainland Europe.

SOIL PESTS

New plantings, especially in weedy sites or in recently destroyed pasture, are at particular risk from a range of soil pests. These include several of those already discussed as pests of cereals and other field crops, especially chafer grubs, wireworms, leatherjackets and cutworms. Migratory nematodes such as *Longidorus attenuatus, L. elongatus, L. macrosoma* and the dagger nematode (*Xiphinema diversicaudatum*) can also be a problem, not only as direct feeders but also as important carriers of arabis mosaic virus (ArMV) and strawberry latent ringspot virus (SLRV). Species of *Longidorus* are also vectors of raspberry ringspot virus (RpRSV) and tomato black ring virus (TBRV), notably in Scotland. Other non-insect soil pests that can be troublesome to soft-fruit crops, especially in strawberry plantations, include slugs and symphylids.[67]

Among soil insects, root-feeding weevil larvae probably pose the greatest economic threat in both new and established plantations. Many species are involved. These range from minor and uncommon pests such as the hop root weevil (*Mitoplinthus caliginosus*)[68] and the sand weevil (*Philopedon plagiatum*) to various, often common, strawberry weevils. Strawberry weevils include many

FIG 250. The root weevil *Otiorhynchus rugosostriatus* is a generally common pest of strawberry and many other plants.

species of *Otiorhynchus*, collectively known as wingless weevils because their wing cases are fused and they cannot fly. Vine weevil (*O. sulcatus*) is an example. This notorious pest is not only a major problem in commercial fruit plantations but also a common adversary of many an amateur gardener or professional nurseryman. Damage caused to host plants is particularly severe on light, sandy soils and in drought conditions.

At least four species of *Otiorhynchus* have been labelled pests of strawberry crops – *O. ovatus, O. rugifrons, O. rugosostriatus* (Fig. 250) and *O. sulcatus*.[69] These weevils all breed parthenogenetically, and males are largely if not entirely unknown. In essence, new adults emerge from the soil in the spring (usually in late April or in May). These then feed on leaves of host plants, and egg laying begins a week or so later. The eggs may be laid in the soil or deposited on the leaf stalks or crowns of plants. The eggs hatch about three weeks later and larvae then attack the roots. First-instar larvae are also known to mine the leaves of host plants prior to entering the soil.[70] Otiorhynchid larvae feed throughout the summer and autumn, and eventually overwinter. In spring they pupate, each in an earthen cell. The adult stage is reached about three weeks later. However, individuals remain in their earthen cells for several days whilst their body shell (cuticle) hardens before eventually sallying forth. Larval attacks on the root system of host plants can be devastating, especially to strawberry plants. Larvae of the nettle leaf weevil (*Phyllobius pomaceus*) also cause major harm in strawberry plantations (Fig. 251). Damage is essentially similar to that inflicted by otiorhynchid weevils, the larvae stripping the outermost tissue from the roots and also boring into the crowns.

During the 1950s, red-legged weevil (*O. clavipes*) was the most important otiorhynchid species on strawberry crops in the Cheddar district of Somerset,

FIG 251. Nettle leaf weevil (*Phyllobius pomaceus*) larvae sometimes attack the roots of strawberry plants, causing extensive damage.

where other root weevils (*O. ovatus, O. rugifrons, O. rugosostriatus* and *O. sulcatus*) were either infrequent or absent.[71] As a soft-fruit pest, however, red-legged weevil is mainly of importance in raspberry plantations. By contrast, in Cambridgeshire in the 1960s and 1970s, and probably earlier, *O. rugosostriatus* was the dominant root weevil in strawberry beds. Throughout the 1980s and 1990s, however, in East Anglia, southwest England and elsewhere, vine weevil (unknown as a fruit pest 100 or so years ago)[72] became the most frequently encountered species. This was so not only in commercial strawberry beds but also in black currant and gooseberry plantations. Today, vine weevil continues to cause growers most concern, and over the past few decades it has received considerable attention as a pest of soft fruits and other horticultural crops,[73] far outweighing that given to its many relatives.[74]

In soft-fruit plantations, adult vine weevils often congregate in large numbers under plastic sheeting and elsewhere, and such behaviour may well be governed by an aggregation pheromone.[75] Plastic sheets, when used as mulches in crops such as strawberry and black currant, can have a deleterious impact on vine weevil management.[76] They not only provide a protective environment for the pest, including hibernation sites for overwintering adults,[77] but also raise soil temperatures and thereby favour the pest's development. Plastic mulches are also a major barrier to the penetration of insecticides into the soil. In summer, adults often roost during the daytime on black currant bushes. They are then not infrequently included as contaminants amongst mechanically harvested fruits. Roosting snails – frequently the larger banded snail (*Cepaea nemoralis*) and the smaller banded snail (*C. hortensis*) – are also unwelcome guests in harvested black currants, and their mere presence (even in small numbers) has resulted in whole consignments of fruits being rejected by processors.

NATURAL ENEMIES OF PESTS

In common with habitats formed by other perennial crops, especially orchards, soft-fruit plantations are home to a wide range of beneficial insects, mites and other creatures. Many of these (collectively if not always individually) are important natural enemies of pests. Some species are merely casual, opportunist visitors to plantations. Others, however, may be long-term residents.

Predators

Pest populations in soft-fruit crops are often reduced by the action of predators. Two-spotted spider mites, for example, often fall victim to predatory thrips and other insects, including the larvae of predatory midges. More significantly, however, they are often preyed upon by mites such as *Euseius finlandicus*[78] and *Typhlodromus pyri*. On strawberry, even where crops are not grown perennially, predatory mites such as *Amblyseius californicus*[79] and *A. cucumeris*[80] can still gain a foothold, albeit temporarily. Both of these species also attack strawberry mite. *A. californicus* is not native to Britain. However, with the aid of man it has become established here following inundative field releases during biological or integrated pest control programmes. The well-known predatory mite *Phytoseiulus persimilis* is similarly used on outdoor strawberry crops to combat two-spotted spider mite, and may also be encountered. However, this exotic species is unable to survive British winters, except under glass and in similarly protected environments. Although it is used mainly against spider mites, when introduced early in the season it has also proved effective against strawberry mite.[81]

Highly active predatory bugs form a significant component of soft-fruit ecosystems, and many native species are likely to be encountered on bush and cane fruit crops. This is especially so in unsprayed sites. As non-specialist feeders such predators attack a wide range of invertebrate prey, including aphids, mites and many other pests. Common examples include the ant damsel bug (*Aptus mirmicoides*), the common flower bug (*Anthocoris nemorum*), the oak flower bug (*Anthocoris confusus*), *Anthocoris nemoralis*, *Orius majusculus* and the raspberry bug (*Orius vicinus*). Predatory mirids (capsids) such

FIG 252. Delicate apple capsid (*Malacocoris chlorizans*) is a common predator on unsprayed currant bushes.

FIG 253. Dark green apple capsid (*Orthotylus marginalis*) is a voracious predator of aphids, mites and other invertebrates. It is often present on unsprayed fruit bushes.

as the delicate apple capsid (*Malacocoris chlorizans*) (Fig. 252), the black-kneed capsid (*Blepharidopterus angulatus*), the dark green apple capsid (*Orthotylus marginalis*) (Fig. 253), *Deraeocoris lutescens*, *D. ruber* and *Heterotoma planicornis* may also be abundant. Anthocorids regularly bite (more correctly, pierce) the skin of man, causing considerable irritation, as many a raspberry picker has cause to remember. Other predatory bugs, including black-kneed capsids,[82] behave similarly.

Aphid colonies, notably but by no means exclusively those on bush and cane fruit crops, frequently harbour predatory midge larvae (essentially those of the ubiquitous species *Aphidoletes aphidimyza*). Aphid colonies also serve as highly lucrative breeding grounds for hover flies, lacewings and ladybirds, including many of those known to inhabit orchards. A range of other opportunist feeders also take their toll of aphids in soft-fruit plantations, including rove beetles such as *Tachyporus hypnorum* and *T. obtusus* (whose larvae feed on strawberry aphids),[83] ground beetles (including arboreal species such as *Demetrias atricapillus*) and spiders.

Insectivorous birds, such as tits, frequently feed on aphids, scale insects and other small invertebrates. Similarly, rooks are known to forage around the base of fruit bushes in search of vine weevil larvae and other soil-inhabiting creatures. Vine weevils are also an acceptable food source for small mammals such as wood mice.

Parasitoids

Some pests within soft-fruit plantations, including raspberry beetle,[84] raspberry cane midge and other gall midges,[85] rarely host naturally occurring parasitoids. However, many pests commonly do so. Parasitoid wasps (mainly ichneumonids), for example, frequently victimise gooseberry sawfly larvae.[86] Other sawfly pests are similarly targeted. Larvae of lepidopterous pests are universally exploited by parasitoids, many of which have a wide or moderately wide host range. There are, however, some true specialists: the encyrtid wasp *Litomastix aretas*, for example, depends exclusively on strawberry tortrix moth.

In England, 17 species of parasitoid or hyperparasitoid have been found in association with strawberry tortrix moth[87] (probably the most studied host species). These include three tachinid flies, several braconid and ichneumonid wasps, and the encyrtid wasp *Litomastix aretas*. The tachinids include *Elodia morio* and *Nemorilla floralis*, both of which have a wide host range, and often occur in soft-fruit plantations and elsewhere. They have already been mentioned in Chapter 7 as attacking codling moth in apple orchards. Amongst the range of braconid and ichneumonid parasitoids associated with strawberry tortrix moth three species deserve special mention: *Microgaster laeviscuta*, a solitary ectoparasitoid that pupates in a small, white cocoon spun alongside the remains of its larval host; *Glypta monoceros*, a solitary endoparasitoid which, having devoured the host larva, pupates in a transparent, thin-walled cocoon; and *Phytodietus polyzonias*, a solitary endoparasitoid which, having feasted on the host pupa, pupates externally in a large, brown cigar-like cocoon.[88] The ichneumonid *Itoplectis alternans*, a solitary pupal endoparasitoid of many tortrix pests, including those which invade strawberry crops, should also be highlighted.

Litomastix aretas is a potentially important natural control agent of strawberry tortrix moth. This tiny wasp lays its eggs singly in those of its host. Subsequently, following hatching of the host egg, the embryo of the parasitoid egg subdivides into numerous discrete parts during a process known as polyembryony. When the host larva is fully fed, these subdivided embryos themselves become larvae, all of the same sex (all males or all females). They then feed avidly on the inner tissue of the host. When fully grown they come to fill the by now bloated and desiccated skin of their long-since dead host (Fig. 254). They then pupate, all tightly bunched together, and adult wasps eventually emerge. Up to 69 wasps have been reared from a single host larva, and the number of female offspring emerging per host tends to exceed that of males.[89] Reported levels of parasitism vary considerably: normally up to 7 per cent but exceptionally about 90 per cent;[90] up to 5 per cent (in the first host generation) and up to 33 per cent (in the second host generation);[91] from 6 to 76 per cent, and frequently well in excess of

FIG 254. The encyrtid wasp *Litomastix aretas* is an important parasitoid of strawberry tortrix moth. Fully fed larvae pupate *en masse* in the bloated skin of the host larva.

FIG 255. The braconid wasp *Macrocentrus linearis* attacks various tortricid larvae. The parasitoid larvae develop gregariously within the body of the paralysed host.

50 per cent in both host generations.[92] Add to this the impact of other parasitoids, and natural control of strawberry tortrix moth can become of real significance. As a benchmark, levels of parasitism in excess of 36 per cent are considered necessary for achieving 'substantial' control of a pest.[93]

Polyembryony as a reproductive strategy is also found in hymenopteran families other than the Encyrtidae. The braconid wasp *Macrocentrus linearis*, for example, attacks the larvae of various tortrix moths, including the straw-coloured tortrix moth (Fig. 255). In this case about 40 individuals subsequently develop within one and the same host.

Relatively few detailed records exist of parasitoids or parasites of other soft-fruit pests in Britain, although species of *Campoplex* (family Ichneumonidae) are known to target some. For example, *C. mutabilis* attacks the larvae of the bramble shoot moth (i.e. bramble shoot webbers),[94] as do a species of *Cotesia* (family Braconidae),[95] the tachinid fly *Nemorilla notabilis* and, at least in Poland, the microsporidian parasite *Nosema carpocapsae*.[96] Further, *Campoplex ensator* victimises currant clearwing moth larvae,[97] as do tachinid flies (e.g. *Pelatachina tibialis*) and the braconid wasp *Macrocentrus marginator*. Little information on the impact of such biocontrol agents is available, although relatively high (36 to 48 per cent) mortality rates of bramble shoot webbers as a result of the activities of *C. mutabilis* have been reported.[98]

As parasites, rather than parasitoids, certain nematodes also deserve a mention. These include the mermithid *Mermis nigrescens*, a large, thread-like endoparasite (often up to 200 mm or so in length). This entwines itself within the bodies of a range of soil-inhabiting hosts, including chafer grubs, cutworms and larvae of root weevils. More significantly, microscopic nematode species such as *Heterorhabditis bacteriophora* and *Steinernema carpocapsae*[99] infect a range of insects. Both parasites occur naturally in soils, and are now cultured as biocontrol agents for use against vine weevil. In Australia, drench treatments using *S. carpocapsae* have been applied successfully to control currant clearwing moth larvae in black currant cuttings and bushes.[100]

Several naturally occurring entomopathogenic fungi are known to infect pests in soft-fruit plantations. These include *Empusa planchoniana,*[101] *Hirsutella noduosa, Paecilomyces eriophytis* and *Metarhizium flavoviride.*[102] Recorded hosts include aphids, strawberry mite, black currant gall mite and vine weevil, respectively.

CHAPTER 9

Hardy Ornamentals

HARDY ORNAMENTALS INCLUDE A wide range of native or non-native trees and shrubs, produced as either open-bedded (field-grown) or containerised plants, the latter often raised as regimented pot plants (known as liners) set on matting or plastic sheeting. Such plants, along with other outdoor ornamentals (alpines, bedding plants and herbaceous plants), must run the gauntlet of an eclectic armada of phytophagous insects, mites and other creatures,[1] some of which rate as highly significant pests. These can affect the vigour, structure and overall quality of host plants, and may even kill them. Other antagonists are far less important, and their depredations are often at worst merely cosmetic. Pest attacks also range from the persistent to the ephemeral. Inevitably, however, as in other cropping situations, the vulnerability of hosts varies according to the time of year, and might also depend on the age and growth stage of plants. The risk and impact of pests can also differ from area to area and from one year to the next. The following, necessarily highly selective account of pests associated with hardy ornamental plants is but a snapshot, and based on the more common, interesting or unusual species likely to be encountered in outdoor nurseries. Pests of ornamental bulb crops are discussed in Chapter 11.

SUCKING PESTS

Aphids

Colonies of aphids on the shoots of ornamental plants often attract attention in nurseries. This is especially so if the colonies are attended by ants or when infested leaves are strongly curled and young shoots deformed. The presence of

FIG 256. Broom aphid (*Aphis cytisorum*) colonies occur on laburnum and Spanish broom. Infested shoots and pods soon become coated in sticky honeydew and blackened by sooty moulds.

aphids (or, perhaps, other sap-imbibing plant bugs such as scale insects and whiteflies) may also be disclosed when plants become contaminated by honeydew and sooty moulds. Black or blackish-brown aphids (blackflies) associated with ornamental plants include broom aphid (*Aphis cytisorum*) on laburnum and Spanish broom (Fig. 256), *A. cytisorum sarothamni* on broom, cowpea aphid (*A. craccivora*) on Fabaceae, and black bean aphid (*A. fabae*) on various shrubs and herbaceous plants; other examples include elder aphid (*A. sambuci*), ivy aphid (*A. hederae*), holly aphid (*A. ilicis*) and viburnum aphid (*A. viburni*) on their respective hosts. Commonly occurring green aphids (greenflies) include *Acyrthosiphon pisum spartii* on broom, rose aphid (*Macrosiphum rosae*) (Fig. 257) and rose/grain aphid (*Metopolophium dirhodum*) on rose, and green apple aphid (*Aphis pomi*) on cotoneaster and other Rosaceae. Spectacularly damaging infestations of species such as honeysuckle aphid (*Hyadaphis passerinii*),[2] Essig's lupin aphid (*Macrosiphum albifrons*) and iris aphid (*Aphis newtoni*) may also be encountered. Small willow aphid (*Aphis farinosa*), a greenish, yellow-mottled species associated with broadleaved and narrow-leaved willows, is often common on nursery stock, but of little significance; the reddish-orange male nymphs appear from June or July onwards and whilst developing within colonies these are often mistaken for the similarly coloured larvae of the predatory midge *Aphidoletes aphidimyza*. The bodies of some aphids on nursery stock are profusely coated in white, mealy wax.

FIG 257. Rose aphid (*Macrosiphum rosae*) is a very important pest of rose bushes. The aphids, which vary in colour from green to reddish-brown, are distinguished from all other rose-infesting species by the long, black siphunculi.

FIG 258. Beech aphids (*Phyllaphis fagi*) are coated with white, flocculent wax.

This is particularly well demonstrated in the beech aphid (*Phyllaphis fagi*), colonies of which develop from spring onwards on the underside of leaves of beech (Fig. 258). In this case, infestations on the young leaves can lead to dieback and extensive distortion of shoots.

Among tree aphids, species of *Periphyllus* on sycamore and on maples exhibit an unusual phenomenon in that normal breeding can be interrupted in summer by the production of first-instar nymphs of two very different body forms: these are known as dimorphs. Following egg hatch in the spring, normal nymphs develop into adult viviparous females (Fig. 259). At the height of summer, however, colonies of some species die out and the insects survive as tiny first-instar nymphs (dimorphs) that undergo an extended period of aestivation. These dimorphs either have very long, fine, wavy body hairs on parts of the head, abdomen and appendages, or such hairs modified into flattened, leaf-like structures.[3] In the former case, the

FIG 259. Leaves of maple trees are often infested by *Periphyllus* spp., including the generally common *P. testudinaceus*.

dimorphs typically aestivate in tightly compacted groups on the underside of leaves, as in *Periphyllus acericola*; in the latter, as typified by *P. testudinaceus* and the introduced Californian maple aphid (*P. californiensis*), the dimorphs aestivate as scattered individuals. On cessation of the period of aestivation the dimorphs continue their development and eventually become adults.

Minute, superficially aphid-like insects are sometimes found on the underside of leaves of young deciduous oak trees. These creatures – oak leaf phylloxerans (*Phylloxera glabra*) – cause disease-like spotting on expanded leaves. Damage becomes more and more extensive as the season progresses, the spots coalescing and affected leaf tissue eventually turning brown. Heavy infestations can lead to premature leaf fall. The life history of oak leaf phylloxera is different from that of aphids in that all female individuals are oviparous, each depositing eggs on the leaves in distinctive groups. Such eggs are often arranged side by side in a partial circle, reminiscent of the markings around a clock face, with the maternal female at the centre. After several generations of asexual forms, even smaller-bodied, winged sexual forms are produced, before winter eggs are finally laid in crevices on the bark of host plants. Phylloxerans are sometimes reported on young holm oak trees imported into Britain from southern Europe (e.g. from Italy), but these are a different species – probably most frequently *P. ilicis*.

Young conifer trees host a range of aphids, including lachnids (especially *Cinara* spp.) (family Aphididae, subfamily Lachninae) and gall-inducing aphid-like adelgids (family Adelgidae). Adelgids are discussed later (p. 284). Lachnids (large or very large aphids, usually with short, hairy, cone-like siphunculi) include essentially needle-infesting species such as the grey pine-needle aphid (*Schizolachnus pineti*) and many, such as brown spruce aphid (*Cinara pilicornis*), cypress aphids (*C. cupressi* and *C. cupressivora*), juniper aphid (*C. juniperi*)

FIG 260. Juniper aphid (*Cinara juniperi*) is a common and widely distributed pest.

(Fig. 260) and large pine aphid (*C. pinea*), that develop on the shoots, branches and stems of their respective hosts. Cypress aphids are responsible for widespread and severe damage to Leyland cypress trees and hedges. Lachnids excrete vast quantities of honeydew and their colonies are commonly ant-attended. The mutually beneficial relationship between aphid and ant is such that colonies are frequently enclosed within protective earthen canopies constructed by their honeydew-seeking guardians. As pests, lachnids cause discoloration and premature loss of needles; they also have an adverse effect on plant vigour, and infestations can result in the death of branches. In addition, infested plants are frequently blackened by sooty moulds, an unwelcome sight on both nursery stock and established ornamentals. A few lachnids, including the large willow aphid (*Tuberolachnus salignus*) and the rose root aphid (*Maculolachnus submacula*), attack broadleaved trees and shrubs. Colonies of the latter occur in summer on

FIG 261. Rose root aphid (*Maculolachnus submacula*) colonies are protected by earthen shelters constructed by ants.

the roots and stem bases of rose bushes and, as in the case of their conifer-based cousins, are often protected by earthen, ant-constructed shelters (Fig. 261). Infestations of green spruce aphid (*Elatobium abietinum*) (family Aphididae, subfamily Aphidinae) can be a significant problem on spruce trees, resulting in bronzing of needles and extensive defoliation. This abundant and important conifer pest often damages young Christmas trees (Chapter 11).

Scale insects

Scale insects are important crop pests, and they are of particular significance in subtropical and tropical parts of the world. Several species flourish in cooler countries such as Britain, and some of these can reach pest status on hardy ornamentals (Table 13). Today, the British fauna includes many species that have their origins in southern Europe or have settled here from further afield. However, some foreign pests such as cymbidium scale (*Lepidosaphes machili*),

TABLE 13. Examples of scale insects associated with hardy ornamentals.

Species	*Remarks*
Family Diaspididae (armoured scales)	
Euonymus scale (*Unaspis euonymi*)	Mainly on Japanese spindle, especially in southern England
Juniper scale (*Carulaspis juniperi*)	Mainly on cypresses, junipers and other Pinaceae
Mussel scale (*Lepidosaphes ulmi*)	Polyphagous on broadleaved hosts
Rose scale (*Aulacaspis rosae*)	Mainly on rose and *Rubus*
Willow scale (*Chionaspis salicis*)	Polyphagous on broadleaved hosts
Family Coccidae (soft scales)	
Brown scale (*Parthenolecanium corni*)	Polyphagous on broadleaved trees and shrubs
Brown soft scale (*Coccus hesperidum*)	Polyphagous; occurs outdoors but mainly in greenhouses
Horse chestnut scale (*Pulvinaria regalis*)	Polyphagous on broadleaved trees
Lichtensia viburni	Mainly on ivy and *Viburnum tinus*
Nut scale (*Eulecanium tiliae*)	Polyphagous on broadleaved trees and shrubs
Peach scale (*Parthenolecanium persicae*)	Polyphagous; occurs outdoors but mainly in greenhouses
Yew scale (*Parthenolecanium pomeranicum*)	Monophagous on yew
Family Eriococcidae	
Ash scale (*Pseudochermes fraxini*)	Mainly on ash; especially on older trees
Beech scale (*Cryptococcus fagisuga*)	Monophagous on beech; mainly on older trees
Elm scale (*Eriococcus spuria*)	Monophagous on elm; mainly on older trees

hemispherical scale (*Saissetia coffeae*) and orchid scale (*Diaspis boisduvalii*) survive only under artificial conditions. As with many sap feeders, scale insects often excrete vast quantities of sticky honeydew and this (along with sooty moulds) often contaminates host plants. Soiled plants in nurseries can be unmarketable, even if growth is unaffected.

Scale insects exhibit many unique features. Adult females are typically sedentary, with relatively large, piercing mouthparts but no clear subdivision between head and body; also, legs (usually) and wings are wanting, and eyes are typically represented merely by patches of pigmented tissue. In armoured scales (family Diaspididae), the flattened, pear-shaped body is protected by a distinctive (often oyster- or mussel-shaped) covering called a test, formed from wax and cast nymphal skins. By contrast, female soft scales or wax scales (family Coccidae) are typified by their more or less tortoise-shaped body that comes to form a hardened, smooth or wax-coated scale-like cover, protecting the underlying batch of eggs. As in *Pulvinaria* spp., the egg mass may be contained within a prominent white ovisac constructed of flocculent wax. Sometimes, the ovisac also encloses the female body, as in *Lichtensia viburni* which occurs on hosts such as holly, ivy and *Viburnum tinus*. In other instances, e.g. nut scale (*Eulecanium tiliae*) and *Parthenolecanium* spp., no such ovisac is formed. Male scale insects, when present in the lifecycle, are unique in that they lack mouthparts, and either are wingless or possess just a single pair of wings. Such insects are minute (frequently less than a millimetre long) and usually escape attention, although the pupal scales from which the adults emerge are often very noticeable on infested plants. This is spectacularly so in species such as euonymus scale (*Unaspis euonymi*) (Fig. 262), where the male scales greatly outnumber, and are far more obvious than, those of females. Many species breed both sexually and

FIG 262. Euonymus scale (*Unaspis euonymi*) is a devastating pest of ornamental spindle plants.

FIG 263. Ornamental juniper bushes are sometimes heavily infested by juniper scale (*Carulaspis juniperi*).

parthenogenetically, i.e. with or without males; in others, males are quite unknown. Brown scale (*Parthenolecanium corni*) and, as already mentioned in Chapter 8, mussel scale (*Lepidosaphes ulmi*) are primarily parthenogenetic, although races with a sexual phase are reported on some hosts.

Willow scale (*Chionaspis salicis*) is a single-brooded species that infests a range of outdoor ornamental trees and shrubs. In spring, following the hatching of overwintered eggs, first-instar nymphs (called crawlers) swarm on the bark of host plants. At this time, being deep red in colour, they are sometimes mistaken for bryobia mites or spider mites. The crawlers soon disperse, and then settle down to feed and develop. The adult stage is reached in the summer, both females and males being produced. Exceptionally for a scale insect, the males are either winged or wingless, the latter state predominating. Not all scale insects overwinter as eggs. Juniper scale (*Carulaspis juniperi*) (Fig. 263), for instance, pass the winter as mated females, eggs being laid in the spring. Conversely, species such as brown scale overwinter as nymphs. Both the first- and second-instar nymphs are mobile, and they initially feed on the young growth of host plants. In autumn, they move to the twigs and branches, where they settle down for the winter. Here, they gradually change in colour from green to brown. In the following spring the nymphs finally become sedentary and go on to complete their development. A similar developmental pattern is shared by other species, such as elm scale (*Eriococcus spuria*).[4] In the case of horse chestnut scale (*Pulvinaria regalis*), however, mobility extends into adulthood, the young females migrating from the young twigs to the stem or trunk and main branches of host plants before eventually becoming sedentary and laying eggs. Dense colonies of egg-laying females of horse chestnut scale often accumulate on the bark of older hosts, and these have become a common sight on amenity trees in many of our towns and cities. This Asiatic species was unknown in Britain up until the 1960s; since then it has become firmly established both here and in mainland Europe.

Miscellaneous

In addition to scale insects, several other sap-feeding pests occur on hardy ornamentals. Such pests, even when present only on the underside of leaves, frequently attract attention owing to the extensive discoloration caused to the foliage. Examples include phillyrea whitefly (*Siphoninus latifolia*), rhododendron whitefly (*Dialeurodes chittendeni*), rhododendron lace bug (*Stephanitis rhododendri*), privet thrips (*Dendrothrips ornatus*) and rose thrips (*Thrips fuscipennis*), and a wide range of polyphagous or host-specific leafhoppers. The last-mentioned include the stunningly beautiful rhododendron hopper (*Graphocephala fennahi*) (Fig. 264) which was introduced into Britain from North America in the 1930s. Nefarious pests such as common green capsid (*Lygocoris pubulinus*), potato capsid (*Closterotomus norvegicus*)[5] and European tarnished plant bug (*Lygus rugulipennis*) also invade nursery stock. They often cause noticeable leaf tattering, discoloration and shoot distortion on young trees, shrubs and herbaceous plants. However, the bugs themselves are often overlooked as they immediately scurry away when disturbed; also, by the time that damage is noticed, the pests may already have dispersed. Non-insect sucking pests include alder leaf rust mite (*Acaricalus paralobus*), ash rust mite (*Aculus epiphyllus*), azalea bud & rust mite (*Aculus atlantazaleae*) and, of course, spider mites. The ubiquitous two-spotted spider mite (*Tetranychus urticae*), for example, is a constant threat on a wide range of broadleaved hosts. Also, conifer spinning mite (*Oligonychus ununguis*) is often of significance on young spruce trees; this pest has a marked impact on its hosts, and can cause the death of seedlings and transplants.

FIG 264. Rhododendron hopper (*Graphocephala fennahi*), introduced from North America in the 1930s, is a particularly attractive leafhopper.

DEFOLIATORS

A roll call of defoliating pests on ornamental trees, shrubs and flowers would be very extensive and, presented here, rather meaningless. On rose bushes alone, at least 40 pest species (mostly moths and sawflies) may occur at one time or another. Birches, ornamental crab-apples, hawthorns, poplars, oaks and willows are also saddled with a particularly wide range of such pests. These include larvae of winter moth (*Operophtera brumata*) (potentially a major pest), March moth (*Alsophila aescularia*) and mottled umber moth (*Erannis defoliaria*), all of which have flightless adult females (see Chapter 7). Winter moth adults occur in greatest numbers in November and December. Eggs are then laid singly on the bark of host plants. They hatch from late March or early April onwards. The larvae then attack the developing buds, flowers and foliage of a wide range of host plants before eventually pupating in the soil, usually in late May or early June. The life history of mottled umber moth is similar. March moths, however, occur from mid-February onwards, eggs being deposited by the totally wingless females in distinctive batches. These form compact bands around the twigs of host plants. The eggs hatch in April.

Other geometrids to inhabit nurseries include brimstone moth (*Opisthograptis luteolata*) (Fig. 265), which is by no means uncommon on rosaceous nursery stock, and peppered moth (*Biston betularia*). Larvae of both species occur in two colour forms: brown or green. Peppered moth larvae feed on various trees and shrubs, including young conifers, but they cause most concern when on plants such as chrysanthemum and pot marigold. At up to 50 mm or so in length, they are amongst the largest of British geometrids. However, their impact as pests is far exceeded by many much smaller species.

FIG 265. Brimstone moth (*Opisthograptis luteolata*) larvae are minor pests of various broadleaved trees and shrubs. Unlike most geometrids they possess four pairs of functional abdominal prolegs.

Very large moth larvae (some approaching, if not exceeding 80 mm in length) sometimes summon attention on nursery stock, especially in the later stages of their development when they rapidly strip the foliage from shoots and branches. Examples include larvae of eyed hawk moth (*Smerinthus ocellata*) on ornamental crab-apple and willow, lime hawk moth (*Mimas tiliae*) on lime, privet hawk moth (*Sphinx ligustri*) on shrubs such as lilac, privet and snowberry, and puss moth (*Cerura vinula*) on willow trees. Elephant hawk moth (*Deilephila elpenor*) larvae similarly browse on busy lizzie and fuchsia plants, both outdoors and under protection. Such larvae most often occur in just ones or twos, and are usually discovered when almost fully grown. They are ephemeral pests, rather than harbingers of future on-site devastation. Little or nothing is to be gained, therefore, from killing them and, in the interests of conservation, growers are usually encouraged to offer a reprieve, allowing the larvae to complete their development *in situ* or on suitable wild hosts nearby.

Larvae of many noctuid moths attack ornamental plants, ranging from highly polyphagous woodland species to more specialist feeders such as delphinium moth (*Polychrysia moneta*) (outside applied circles usually known as the golden plusia moth) and mullein moth (*Cucullia verbasci*). The colourful larvae of the latter often destroy the flower spikes and leaves of cultivated mullein plants (Fig. 266); they also occur on buddleia and cape figwort. As polyphagous pests, angle-shades moth (*Phlogophora meticulosa*), cabbage moth (*Mamestra brassicae*) and tomato moth (*Lacanobia oleracea*) frequently breed on outdoor herbaceous ornamentals. However, these pests are of greater significance when present on protected crops (Chapter 10). The same is true of gothic moth (*Naenia typica*), whose young larvae, prior to hibernation, feed gregariously on a range of herbaceous ornamentals. Among

FIG **266.** Mullein moth (*Cucullia verbasci*) larvae are gregarious and voracious feeders. They cause extensive damage and quickly ruin host plants.

FIG 267. Dark dagger moth (*Acronicta tridens*) larvae feed mainly on the foliage of rosaceous trees and shrubs.

the defoliating noctuids associated with trees and shrubs, no individual species stands out from the pack as especially damaging. However, larvae of some are more likely to attract attention than others: notably, the brightly coloured larvae of dark dagger moth (*Acronicta tridens*) (Fig. 267) and grey dagger moth (*A. psi*) (Fig. 268), which often bask in sunshine on the leaves of their food plants. Rarities such as alder moth (*A. alni*) (Fig. 269) might also be discovered.

FIG 268. Grey dagger moth (*Acronicta psi*) larvae sometimes attract attention in nurseries, but are not important pests.

FIG 269. Alder moth (*Acronicta alni*) larvae are instantly recognised by their unique coloration and spatula-like body hairs.

FIG 270. Vapourer moth (*Orgyia antiqua*) is a generally common pest of trees and shrubs. The highly active, day-flying males (above middle) and highly mobile larvae (above) are far more often noticed than the sedentary, totally wingless females.

Densely hairy larvae of ermine moths and tiger moths often occur in outdoor nurseries, especially in weedy sites. Garden tiger moth (*Arctia caja*) and white ermine moth (*Spilosoma lubricipeda*) are examples. Such larvae (those of the former commonly known as woolly bears) feed on various low-growing herbaceous plants, but are usually insufficiently numerous to be regarded as important pests.

Pests such as vapourer moth (*Orgyia antiqua*) (Fig. 270) and yellow-tail moth (*Euproctis similis*) (Fig. 271) are also frequent denizens of nurseries, and both possess hairy, colourful, sun-loving larvae. Vapourer moth larvae feed from spring to early summer, each eventually pupating in an expansive silken cocoon spun on the food plant or on a nearby post, fence or building. Adults appear from July onwards and often remain alive well into October. The female is a bloated, sedentary and virtually wingless creature which, on emerging from the pupa, remains on

FIG 271. (Above left) Yellow-tail moth (*Euproctis similis*) is one of a wide range of species whose larvae (above right) occur on broadleaved ornamental trees and shrubs in commercial nurseries.

her cocoon, awaiting the arrival of a mate. By contrast, the fully winged males are very active. They often attract attention during sunny weather, when careering wildly through the air in search of potential brides. After mating, each female lays a large batch of eggs and then dies. The eggs hatch in the following spring. Yellow-tail moth is also single brooded, adults occurring in July and August. Eggs are laid in batches on the foliage of host plants and then coated in hairs from the female's anal tuft. The eggs hatch a week or so later. At first, the larvae feed gregariously. However, they soon disperse and each then spins a tiny cocoon under a flake of bark or in some other sheltered situation within which to overwinter. Activity is resumed in the spring, and larvae usually complete their development in June. Moth pests with truly gregarious larvae are commonly encountered on hardy ornamental nursery stock (see under web formers, below). These include buff-tip moth (*Phalera bucephala*), whose unmistakeable fluffy, black and golden-yellow larvae feed in large compact masses on various broadleaved trees and shrubs. Towards the end of their development, however, they tend to become more or less solitary feeders. Buff-tip moth larvae do not inhabit silken webs.

Few butterflies qualify as pests of ornamental plants. There is the potential for damage to geranium and pelargonium plants from the invasive geranium bronze butterfly (*Cacyreus marshalli*) – if this African pest continues its northward advance through Europe (see Chapter 12). However, currently, our key butterfly antagonists are large white butterflies (*Pieris brassicae*) and small white butterflies (*P. rapae*), which sometimes lay their eggs on ornamentals such as mignonette, nasturtium and stock. As on vegetable brassicas (Chapter 6), larvae of both species cause extensive and rapid defoliation of such hosts. However, infestations on these ornamentals do not materialise every year. Populations of cabbage white butterflies are frequently boosted by immigrants from abroad. Other migratory pests of ornamentals include diamond-back moth (*Plutella xylostella*) and silver Y

FIG 272. Bordered straw moth (*Heliothis peltigera*) is an uncommon summer visitor, whose larvae feed on pot marigold.

moth (*Autographa gamma*) as regular immigrants, and bordered straw moth (*Heliothis peltigera*) (Fig. 272) as an infrequent visitor from the subtropics. Diamond-back moth larvae occur on various brassicaceous plants, including rock cress and wallflower, and those of silver Y moth are polyphagous on a range of mainly herbaceous hosts, including geraniums, pot marigolds and snapdragons. Pot marigold also serves as a food source for bordered straw moth larvae.

FIG 273. Damage to the foliage of geranium plants by geranium sawfly (*Protemphytus carpini*) larvae is often extensive. Larvae feed on the underside of leaves and usually escape attention.

Sawfly larvae are often voracious foliage feeders, and various species can be of concern on herbaceous ornamentals. The widely distributed geranium sawfly (*Protemphytus carpini*), for example, causes noticeable defoliation on geraniums (Fig. 273). The dull-coloured larvae feed gregariously on the underside of the

FIG 274. Solomon's seal sawfly (*Phymatocera aterrima*) larvae are highly gregarious and voracious feeders. (I. Howells)

leaves but often go undetected until damage is well advanced. The related viola sawfly (*P. pallipes*) is a pest of cultivated violets. Other defoliating species that affect the vigour and quality of cultivated herbaceous plants include columbine sawfly (*Pristiphora aquilegia*)[6] and Solomon's seal sawfly (*Phymatocera aterrima*); the latter, a gregarious species (Fig. 274), is often very numerous and will then cause complete destruction of host plants. Both pests are common in private gardens and commercial nurseries. Iris sawfly (*Rhadinoceraea micans*) also warrants a

FIG 275. Geum sawfly (*Monophadnoides geniculatus*) larvae attack ornamentals such as meadowsweet and wood avens.

mention, the larvae being especially harmful to butterfly iris and to *Iris laevigata*. Larvae of geum sawfly (*Monophadnoides geniculatus*) (Fig. 275), pests of *Filipendula* and *Rubus* as well as *Geum*, invite additional comment as their bodies are armed with an array of branched spines. Similarly endowed sawfly larvae occur on other hosts, notably *Periclista lineolata* on the leaves of oak trees.

Of the many sawflies associated with trees and shrubs, those with gregarious larvae are of particular concern in nurseries. Species such as hazel sawfly (*Croesus septentrionalis*), for example, can be very significant pests, the larvae totally stripping the foliage from the shoots and branches of young trees. Alder, birch, hazel, poplar, rowan and willow are frequently damaged, their denuded branches remaining as mere skeletons; fortunately, however, the unopened buds are unaffected and plants do recover. The black and reddish-brown adults of hazel sawfly occur in the spring. Eggs are then laid in the leaf veins of host plants and hatch about two weeks later. Larvae rest fully exposed on the leaves, each grasping the leaf edge with its thoracic legs and with the body arched upwards over the head. If disturbed, the larvae thrash their bodies violently in the air in a concerted attempt to discourage a potential enemy. Such behaviour is also demonstrated by larvae of other sawflies, including the often abundant lesser willow sawfly (*Nematus pavidus*) on alder, poplar and willow. Fully grown hazel sawfly larvae eventually drop to the ground and pupate in the soil, each in a dark brown cocoon. A second generation of adults appears in the summer, producing a brood of larvae in late summer and autumn. The gregarious larvae of poplar sawfly (*Trichiocampus viminalis*), a pest of poplar and willow, are superficially similar in appearance to those of hazel sawfly but noticeably hairy. Also, unlike those of hazel sawfly, they shelter in groups on the underside of host leaves, which they devour from below.

FIG **276.** Oak slug sawfly (*Caliroa annulipes*) larvae feed on the leaves of lime, oak and, less frequently, beech, birch and sallow.

FIG 277. Large rose sawfly (*Arge ochropus*) larvae are very similar in appearance to those of variable rose sawfly (*A. pagana*). The former, shown here, is less widely distributed.

The slug-like larvae of so-called 'slug sawflies' also often feed gregariously on the leaves of trees and shrubs. Usually, the underside of an infested leaf is pared away, the upper surface staying more or less intact. The remnants of damaged leaves often turn brown, so that heavily infested branches appear scorched as if damaged by fire. Common examples of such pests include oak slug sawfly (*Caliroa annulipes*) (Fig. 276) on lime and oak (occasionally also on other hosts, including birch) and rose slug sawfly (*Endelomyia aethiops*) on rose. In addition, pear slug sawfly (*C. cerasi*), the well-known fruit pest (Chapter 7), occurs on a wide range of rosaceous woody ornamentals; unlike their near relatives, pear slug sawfly larvae are solitary and feed fully exposed (albeit covered in slime) on the upper surface of leaves. They frequently cause extensive damage on young nursery trees, especially rowan.

Various other sawflies have a propensity to attack nursery stock. These include banded rose sawfly (*Allantus cinctus*), large rose sawfly (*Arge ochropus*) (Fig. 277), variable rose sawfly (*Arge pagana*) (Fig. 278) and some others on rose bushes, fox-coloured sawfly (*Neodiprion sertifer*) and pine sawfly (*Diprion pini*) on young pine trees, and a veritable cocktail of species on hosts such as birch, oak, poplar and willow. At the other extreme, some trees and shrubs have but one sawfly pest: false acacia, the host of false acacia sawfly (*Nematus tibialis*) (Fig. 279), and goat's beard, home of aruncus sawfly (*Nematus spiraeae*), are examples. False

FIG 278. Variable rose sawfly (*Arge pagana*) is often present on rose bushes in gardens and nurseries.

acacia sawfly does not rate as particularly important, but aruncus sawfly causes significant defoliation. Lilac and privet bushes being raised in nurseries are sometimes attacked by *Macrophya punctumalbum*, a distinctive black-bodied sawfly with bright red hind femora and prominent white markings on the thorax and legs. This sawfly is essentially parthenogenetic, males being very rare. Eggs are laid in fully expanded leaves from June onwards, and the slowly developing

FIG 279. (Above left) False acacia sawfly (*Nematus tibialis*) is a North American species and has been firmly established in Britain for many years. (Above right) Larvae feed only on false acacia, and pose no threat to other plants.

larvae feed throughout the summer. Holing of infested foliage can be extensive and is very noticeable; ash is also an acceptable host.

The largest sawfly larvae to be found on nursery stock (individuals up to 50 mm long) are those of the large birch sawfly (*Cimbex femoratus*). The solitary, unmistakable creatures rest during the daytime tightly curled, pouffe-like, on the underside of birch leaves. They feed at night and eventually pupate on the food plant in large, reddish-brown, barrel-shaped cocoons. The stout-bodied, fast-flying adults are characterised by their strongly clubbed antennae. They occur from May to July, but are rarely noticed. The somewhat smaller species *C. luteus* breeds on poplar and smooth-leaved willows; its larvae are sometimes found curled up on the leaves of trees in nurseries or stool beds.

Although of greatest significance as a root-feeding larval pest, adult vine weevils (*Otiorhynchus sulcatus*) cause extensive notching of the leaves of containerised and open-bedded nursery stock. Hosts range from herbaceous plants (including alpines) to coniferous and broadleaved trees and shrubs, and the extent of leaf-edge notching on plants such as cherry laurel, lily-of-the-valley and rhododendron is often spectacular. Notching of leaf edges is also practiced by many other species, including clay-coloured weevil (*O. singularis*) and various leaf weevils (genera *Phyllobius* and *Polydrusus*). Feeding by adult weevils is not necessarily restricted to the foliage. Adult clay-coloured weevils, for example,

FIG 280. The robust-bodied weevil *Barynotus obscurus* is a pest of rose and certain other ornamentals.

FIG 281. Figwort weevil (*Cionus scrophulariae*) is a generally common pest of cape figwort and related plants.

often browse on the buds, leaf stalks and bark of plants; they may also ring-bark and kill young seedlings. On young trees and shrubs, loss of buds frequently results in misshapen plants, sporting forked shoots and a proliferation of unsolicited side shoots. Species such as strawberry weevil (*O. ovatus*) are a particular problem on young conifers, and nut leaf weevil (*Strophosoma melanogrammum*)[7] has a propensity to ring-bark larch seedlings. The rather stout-bodied weevil *Barynotus obscurus* (Fig. 280), a species sometimes mistaken for a vine weevil, is particularly partial to flowers of ornamentals such as primulas, roses and violets.

Some weevils cause major foliage damage as both adults and larvae. These include mullein weevil (*Cionus hortulanus*) on dark mullein, and figwort weevil (*C. scrophulariae*) (Fig. 281) on *Buddleja globosa*, cape figwort and mullein. The slime-coated, superficially slug-like larvae (Fig. 282) feed openly on the leaves,

FIG 282. Figwort weevil larvae are very destructive pests.

FIG 283. Lily beetle (*Lilioceris lilii*) has become an important pest, especially in southern England. Adults (above left) and the excrement-coated larvae (above right) defoliate host plants.

removing the surface tissue. Windowing of infested leaves is often extensive. Fully fed larvae pupate in rounded, parchment-like cocoons, each attached to a leaf or other surface, and adults emerge two to three weeks later. There are usually two generations annually. Adults of the second eventually overwinter.

Leaf beetles are also important in nurseries. The adults and, notably, their gregarious larvae, browse on the foliage and sometimes inflict extensive damage. Examples include lily beetle (*Lilioceris lilii*) (Figs 283) (a non-indigenous species, first found breeding in Britain in 1940),[8] viburnum leaf beetle (*Pyrrhalta viburni*) on ornamental viburnums (including guelder-rose), plus a wide range of defoliating species on poplars and willows (see Chapter 11). Water-lily beetle (*Galerucella nymphaeae*) can similarly prove troublesome in nurseries where aquatic plants are being raised.

Not all defoliating pests are insects. Slugs and snails, for example, can cause significant damage to the leaves, young shoots and flowers of herbaceous plants. These nocturnal creatures also attack succulent woody plants, including laburnum saplings.

Web formers

Among web-forming pests, small ermine moths (*Yponomeuta* spp.) are probably the best known. Several species occur on hardy ornamentals, in particular allied small ermine moth (*Y. cagnagella*) on spindle (both European and Japanese cultivars) and common small ermine moth (*Y. padella*) on blackthorn and hawthorn. Both of these species share similar lifecycles, the adults occurring in July and August. Eggs, arranged in overlapping rows (similar to the tiles on a

FIG 284. Allied small ermine moth (*Yponomeuta cagnagella*) larvae (above left) pupate in dense, white cocoons (above right).

roof), are laid on the bark of host plants to form scale-like batches. They are then coated with a protective secretion that hardens when in contact with the air. Most eggs hatch a few weeks later. However, the larvae do not emerge. Instead, they remain beneath the scale, protected against the elements, until the following spring. In May, larvae venture forth to attack the bursting buds and unfurling leaves, and eventually form expansive webs on the shoots and branches. Pupation takes place in June, each larva spinning a silken cocoon within the communal web. These pupal cocoons vary from species to species. Those of common small ermine moth, for example, are flimsy, transparent and pendulous, whereas those of allied small ermine moth are white, dense and virtually opaque (Fig. 284).

Hawthorn webber moth (*Scythropia crataegella*) and social pear sawfly (*Neurotoma saltuum*) have already been cited as gregarious web-forming pests in orchards (Chapter 7). Both also occur from time to time in nurseries on cotoneaster, hawthorn and certain other Rosaceae. Porphyry knot-horn moth (*Trachycera suavella*)[9] is another cotoneaster-feeding species. This can infest nursery stock but is associated mainly with wild blackthorn. The larvae feed during the spring, in the shelter of webs formed along the shoots of host plants. These habitations sometimes attract attention, especially as dead leaf fragments and quantities of frass accumulate in the webbing. The adult moths are active during the summer. As another example, juniper webber moth (*Dichomeris marginella*) is sometimes responsible for the destruction and death of juniper foliage. Attacks on young container-grown plants are most important, the brown-bodied larvae (known as juniper webworms) feeding gregariously on the foliage in May and June amongst a loose network of silken threads.

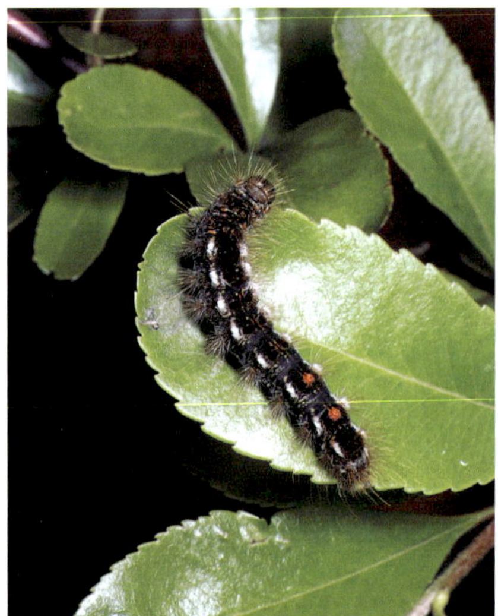

FIG 285. Brown-tail moth (*Euproctis chrysorrhoea*) larvae are clothed in urticating hairs that cause skin irritation and dermatitis in man.

Brown-tail moth (*Euproctis chrysorrhoea*) and lackey moth (*Malacosoma neustria*), two well-known and prolific web formers, also occur in nurseries. The former (although locally distributed) is of particular concern and currently appears to be on the increase. Brown-tail moth larvae (Fig. 285) have been a societal problem for many years, not only inflicting widespread damage to rosaceous trees and shrubs but also (owing to their urticating hairs) causing skin irritation and dermatitis in man. Well over 200 years ago, the botanist William Curtis famously described plague-like invasions of brown-tail moth larvae in London,[10] and local outbreaks (mainly in south-eastern English coastal or estuarine districts) have been commonplace since that

FIG 286. Overwintering webs of brown-tail moth (*Euproctis chrysorrhoea*) occur locally on cotoneaster, hawthorn and various other rosaceous hosts.

time. When hedgerows and other amenity areas become infested, local authorities are often minded to take remedial action. In Canvey Island, for example, following the Second World War, prisoners of war (POWs) were specifically tasked with destroying the overwintering communal larval tents (Fig. 286). Today's nurserymen usually eradicate the pest from their holdings by cutting out and burning the larval tents or by applying selective insecticides against the young larvae.

Leaf tiers

Although not communal web formers, larvae of tortrix moths often construct individual shelters by tying leaves together with silk. Such habitations, which often incorporate blossoms or might simply be a single rolled or folded leaf, are sometimes sufficiently characteristic to enable the causal agent to be identified without further investigation. Tied or rolled leaves, however, cannot necessarily be taken as the work of tortricids, since members of several other lepidopteran groups (e.g. families Gelechiidae, Oecophoridae, Pyralidae and Yponomeutidae) often share this habit.

Tortrix moths are important pests of hardy ornamental nursery stock, especially broadleaved trees and shrubs. Some, such as carnation tortrix moth (*Cacoecimorpha pronubana*), straw-coloured tortrix moth (*Clepsis spectrana*) and various species of *Cnephasia*, are also of significance on herbaceous plants. Barred fruit tree tortrix moth (*Pandemis cerasana*), fruit tree tortrix moth (*Archips podana*) and Leche's twist moth (*Ptycholoma lecheana*) feature amongst the most common species, especially in the vicinity of woodlands. *Acleris rhombana*, *Ditula angustiorana* and autumn apple tortrix moth (*Syndemis musculana*) also warrant a mention, although there are many other equally deserving candidates; this is especially so on rose bushes, where members of several genera (including *Acleris*, *Archips*, *Croesia*, *Epiblema* and *Hedya*) are frequently encountered. However, reaching a consensus on the relative significance of the various species which attack ornamental plants is difficult, if not impossible, owing to local differences and, of course, the range of plants under cultivation at any particular site. Two highly polyphagous species, both of which first became breeding species in Britain during the twentieth century, justify further attention: light brown apple moth (*Epiphyas postvittana*) (Fig. 287) and carnation tortrix moth. Light brown apple moth, an Australasian species, was first seen breeding in Britain on Japanese spindle in Cornwall. Subsequently, it became well established on various hosts in both Cornwall and Devon.[11] Today, the larvae (Fig. 288) occur in abundance on a vast range of hardy and greenhouse-grown ornamentals in southwest England nurseries, and its geographical range now extends eastwards into East Anglia and northwards to many other parts of Britain. Unlike the situation in its native Australia, however, this insect is not a pest in apple

FIG 287. Light brown apple moth (*Epiphyas postvittana*), an Australasian species, is most abundant in southwest England, but has greatly extended its range in recent years. Males (above left) are distinguished from females (above right) by the dark distal half of each forewing.

orchards, although it is now reported causing damage in English cherry orchards and vineyards. As for carnation tortrix moth, this is one of our most frequently reported tortricids on hardy herbaceous ornamentals in southern England, but it is especially damaging in greenhouses; the larvae also feed on many woody hosts, coincidentally including Japanese spindle upon which it is often abundant.[12] This pest (whose presence is often betrayed by the appearance in spring, summer or autumn of the bright-orange, diurnal, sun-loving adult males) is indigenous to the Mediterranean region, and was first found breeding in Britain in 1906. Outdoors, it is at the northern edge of its range in England as it is unable to survive low temperatures. The January 2°C isotherm is thought to represent the limit to its natural range.[13] The young females of carnation tortrix moth, their bloated bodies distended and weighed down with eggs, rarely fly.

FIG 288. Light brown apple moth (*Epiphyas postvittana*) larvae feed on a wide range of ornamental trees and shrubs.

In addition to attacking broadleaved plants, some tortricids are known to attack young or seedling conifers. Common examples include autumn apple tortrix moth on spruce and larch, *Ditula angistiorana* on juniper, larch and yew, and straw-coloured tortrix moth on pine seedlings.

LEAF MINERS

Many leaf-mining insects are associated with hardy ornamental trees and shrubs, and several are by no means uncommon invaders of nursery stock. Growth of lightly infested hosts is often unaffected by such pests (apart, perhaps, from slight distortion and disfigurement of individual leaves). However, heavy infestations can be debilitating and of direct significance, especially on young plants. Leaf miners also attack outdoor herbaceous plants. Mines are formed mainly by dipterous or lepidopterous larvae, most of which construct distinctive blotches or linear galleries. Several sawflies and a few beetles also have leaf-mining larvae. Blotch mines are essentially simple habitations which can be very restricted in size or may be more extensive. Those inhabited by larvae of *Phytomyza aquilegiae* in the leaves and stipules of columbine, for example, are often rather large and prominent (Fig. 289). At the extreme (albeit on a needle-

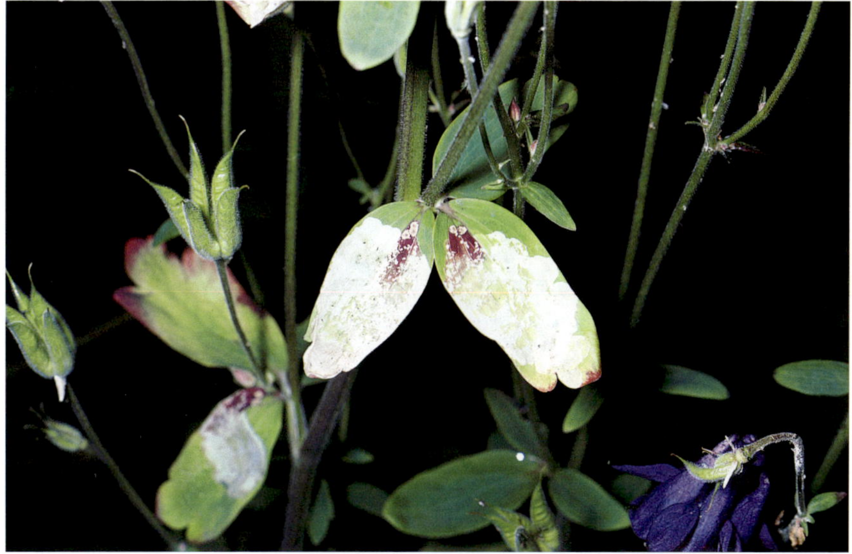

FIG 289. Blotch mines formed on columbine by larvae of *Phytomyza aquilegiae* are very obvious.

FIG 290. The pattern of frass deposited in blotch mines formed on laburnum by larvae of *Leucoptera laburnella* is very characteristic.

leaved host), larvae of the larch casebearer moth (*Coleophora laricella*) frequently destroy the entire contents of invaded larch needles, reducing them to pallid, empty shells. Linear mines, typical of a wide range of pests, commence as narrow channels that meander through the leaf and gradually widen in proportion to the size of the developing larva. In some instances, larval mines are at first linear but subsequently develop into distinct blotches – as in the case of the beech leaf-mining weevil (*Orchestes fagi*)[14] on beech and the moth *Acrocercops brongniardella* on oak.

The overall appearance of a leaf mine (whether a blotch, a linear gallery or otherwise) is frequently sufficiently diagnostic to allow the species responsible for its creation to be identified. It might also be possible to produce meaningful keys to species, as in the lepidopteran families Gracillariidae and Nepticulidae.[15] A mine's position on the leaf can be a useful guide – for example, whether visible from above or from below; whether towards the centre or at the margin. Frass deposits in mines are also often characteristic. The swirling, wave-like arrangement of frass grains in blotch mines formed on laburnum leaves by larvae of the moth *Leucoptera laburnella* (Fig. 290) is an outstanding example. In general, a leaf-mining moth larva deposits frass in a single, more or less continuous trail. Dipterous leaf-mining larvae, however, typically produce two parallel lines of frass. In the case of sawfly larvae, frass is usually scattered at random throughout the mine. However, it is sometimes deposited in a plug-like clump or even expelled at intervals through a slit in the leaf surface.

Structurally, leaf-mining larvae often differ markedly from their non-mining, perhaps leaf-browsing, relatives.[16] In some leaf-mining moth larvae, for example, thoracic legs and abdominal prolegs are absent, or virtually so; also, in several leaf-mining sawfly larvae the body is often noticeably flattened and abdominal prolegs poorly developed, reduced in number or entirely absent.

Most leaf miners are solitary feeders, although there may well be more than one mine on an infested leaf or leaflet. The multitude of blotch mines of the invasive horse chestnut leaf miner moth (*Cameraria ohridella*) on heavily infested leaves of horse chestnut trees and the extensive linear mines of *Lyonetia clerkella*, which sometimes occur in numbers on the leaves of ornamental cherry trees and other hosts, are examples. In some instances, as in the case of the geum leaf-mining sawfly (*Metallus gei*), multiple mines in one and the same leaf coalesce; the individual larvae then come to feed and develop gregariously. A few leaf miners, however, are gregarious from the outset, as in the case of the dipteran *Cerodontha iridis* whose larvae are known as gregarious iris leaf miners.

Although many insects are leaf miners throughout their development, some are ephemeral miners and the larvae later come to feed externally. The larvae of the moth *Caloptilia syringella* (known as lilac leaf miners), for example, which feed gregariously, initially mine the leaves of lilac, privet and various other members of the Oleaceae. Later, they inhabit large, frass-filled leaf rolls or tent-like shelters. These habitations are very disfiguring, and often a common sight on young bushes in June and again in late summer.

Phytomyza ilicis, an agromyzid pest of holly, is unusual amongst leaf miners in that the egg is laid in the midrib where, following egg hatch (usually in late May or June), the larva begins to feed. Development is slow and, at the end of the summer, the still small larva finally enters the leaf blade. Here, feeding continues throughout the winter as the cold-tolerant larva gradually increases the size of its mine. Eventually, an irregular, sub-linear blotch is formed, and this is clearly visible from above. Pupation takes place in the spring, the adult emerging from the mine through a tiny hole in the leaf surface. Damaged leaves remain on infested plants long after the mines have been vacated, and are a common sight on nursery stock as well as on established holly bushes and hedges.

FIG 291. Leaf mines formed by larvae of *Phyllocnistis unipunctella* are inconspicuous, and resemble slug slime trails.

Although of no consequence, the long, linear larval mines of the moth *Phyllocnistis unipunctella* (Fig. 291) (a leaf miner on both black poplar and Lombardy poplar) deserve a passing mention. These appear as inconspicuous, silvery traceries, more reminiscent of slug slime trails than leaf mines, and are often present on the leaves of nursery stock. Such mines are formed as a result of the unique feeding habits of the larvae, which are sap feeders (rather than tissue feeders) throughout their development.[17] Members of the family Gracillariidae (e.g. *Caloptilia* spp. and *Phyllonorycter* spp.) share a sap-feeding habit, but in their first instar only. On a world scale, another species of *Phyllocnistis*, the citrus leaf miner moth (*P. citrella*), is an important pest in citrus orchards. This species has spread westwards from southeast Asia and is now common in many parts of southern Europe. The mines, which are much more obvious than those of *Phyllocnistis unipunctella*, are sometimes present on containerised citrus trees imported into Britain as ornamentals. However, findings are typically restricted to plants bearing old, unoccupied mines, located on the underside of leaves. In the genus *Phyllonorycter*, several species are associated with hardy ornamental trees and shrubs, their mines ranging from small, inconsequential blotches between the major veins to elongated ones that, as in the case of the firethorn leaf miner moth (*P. leucographella*), can cause noticeable distortion of affected leaves. Brown blotch mines of *P. messaniella* are a common sight on holm oak, and can be very disfiguring when on young trees. The leaves of holm oak trees are also damaged by larvae of *Stigmella suberivora*, which form conspicuous linear mines.

GALL INHABITANTS

True bugs

Adelgids are aphid-like creatures that frequently include a distinctive gall-inhabiting phase in their intricate lifecycle. They are commonly known as conifer woolly aphids (because of the flocculent masses of white wax secreted by the non-galling stages) and are important forestry pests.[18] Adelgids are often of significance in Christmas tree plantations (see Chapter 11); conifers being raised or planted as ornamentals are also attacked. Larch adelges (*Adelges laricis*) (Fig. 292) and the two spruce-infesting pineapple-gall adelges *A. abietis* and *A. viridis* are among the more common examples to be found in nurseries. Larch adelges does not form galls on larch (the secondary host of all three species). However, on spruce trees it inhabits small, typically creamy and waxy, pineapple-like galls on the shoots. Such galls are readily distinguished from the larger, greenish ones induced by *A. abietis* and the rather elongated structures characteristic of *A. viridis*.

Among true aphids, several species are responsible for the development of leaf curling (often described as galls or pseudogalls) and other symptoms on broadleaved trees and shrubs. Also, various members of the subfamily Eriosomatinae induce the development of distinctive galls (Table 14, p. 286).

FIG 292. When on spruces, larch adelges (*Adelges laricis*) induces the development of creamy, pineapple-like galls.

In most instances, such aphids overwinter in the egg stage on deciduous woody hosts, galling being initiated in the spring. In the case of holocyclic species, winged aphids produced in the galls then migrate in summer to secondary herbaceous plants, with a return migration to winter hosts taking place in the autumn.

Jumping plant lice (commonly described as psyllids or suckers) not infrequently occur in hardy ornamental nurseries, and a few species are responsible for galling leaves. Ash leaf gall sucker (*Psyllopsis fraxini*), for example, overwinters in the egg stage on the shoots of ash trees. The eggs hatch at about bud burst, and the first-instar nymphs then invade the unfurling leaves. The edges of attacked leaves curl downwards to enclose the nymphs, the leaf tissue eventually becoming tinged with red or purple. The nymphs feed gregariously within their galls, exuding drops of honeydew and also producing large quantities of flocculent wax. The adult stage is reached from June or July onwards, there being just one generation annually. Although they have little or no impact on plant growth, galls on young ash trees are unsightly. Box sucker (*Psylla buxi*), which inhabits cabbage-like galls on the terminal growth of box plants, is another single-brooded, gall-inhabiting species. These galls, and also sooty moulds that develop on excreted honeydew, disfigure hosts and check the growth of heavily infested plants.

TABLE 14. Examples of aphids inducing galls or gall-like symptoms on hardy ornamentals.

Species	*Primary host*	*Symptom(s)*	*Secondary host(s)*
Subfamily Aphidinae			
Black bean aphid (*Aphis fabae*)	Mainly spindle	Leaf curling and distortion	Various herbaceous plants
Cherry blackflies (*Myzus cerasi*/ *M. pruniavium*)	*Prunus*	Distortion of the terminal growth	Various herbaceous plants
Cryptomyzus korschelti	*Ribes*	Reddish leaf blistering and distortion	Woundworts
Hawthorn/carrot aphid (*Dysaphis crataegi*)	Hawthorn	Reddish-tinged leaf swellings	Carrot and other Apiaceae
Leaf-curling plum aphid (*Brachycaudus helichrysi*)	*Prunus*	Leaf curling and distortion	Asteraceae
Privet aphid (*Myzus ligustri*)	Privet	Longitudinal leaf rolling	None
Subfamily Eriosomatinae			
Currant root aphid (*Eriosoma ulmi*)	Elm	Marginal leaf rolling	*Ribes* (roots)
Elm leaf gall aphid (*Tetraneura ulmi*)	Elm	Bean-like outgrowth from upper surface of leaves	Poaceae (roots)
Lettuce root aphid (*Pemphigus bursarius*)	Lombardy poplar	Reddish, purse-like gall on petiole	Lettuce, sow-thistles etc.
Poplar spiral-gall aphid (*Pemphigus spyrothecae*)	Mainly Lombardy poplar	Swollen and twisted petiole	None

Bay sucker (*Trioza alacris*) is an introduced species that first appeared in Britain in the 1920s.[19] It is often common on bay laurel, both on young and mature plants, the wax-coated nymphs developing within tightly rolled and swollen leaf galls (Fig. 293). Infestations are disfiguring and of particular concern on nursery plants, the shoots of which may be killed. Plants are also contaminated by sticky honeydew and sooty moulds. Bay sucker is usually single brooded, but in favourable conditions there can be a second generation.

Pittosporum sucker (*Trioza vitreoradiata*) is a relatively recent arrival in Britain, and has rapidly become well established on pittosporum in Cornwall and the Isles of Scilly, including nursery stock.[20] Infested plants are disfigured by

FIG 293. Bay sucker (*Trioza alacris*) galls are very disfiguring to the foliage of bay laurel plants.

pit-like leaf galls within which the nymphs develop, and this has a particular impact on plants raised for indoor decorative displays. Although not forming galls, the eucalyptus sucker (*Ctenarytaina eucalypti*) is yet another Australasian psyllid that has found a home in Britain. It infests the youngest growth, and attacks often occur on young eucalyptus trees, especially in southern England and the Channel Islands; the pest also occurs in Ireland.

Gall midges

Gall midge larvae frequently cause damage to plants in nurseries. Violet leaf midge (*Dasineura affinis*), for example, is a potentially serious, multi-brooded pest of violets being raised as bedding plants. It is also a notorious garden pest. Adults appear from May onwards, and eggs are deposited mainly in the furled margins of the youngest leaves. The eggs hatch a few days later. The margins of infested leaves become greatly swollen and tightly rolled upwards (Fig. 294), enclosing the developing whitish to whitish-orange larvae. During the summer, larvae are fully fed in about six weeks. They then pupate *in situ* and the next generation of adults emerges some ten days later.[21] Arabis midge (*D. alpestris*) is another multi-brooded pest, occurring in both gardens and nurseries. The reddish larvae feed gregariously in galls formed at the leaf bases of rock cress and related plants. As a result, the central growth of infested plants is often destroyed. During the growing season, the terminal shoots are also attacked. Far less damaging, but nevertheless particularly obvious, rose leaf midge (*D. rosarum*) causes the leaflets of rose bushes to develop into pod-like galls, each enclosing several (up to 50), relatively large, pinkish larvae. Unlike the previous two species, this pest completes just one generation annually.

FIG 294. Violet leaf midge (*Dasineura affinis*) is an often persistent pest of violets, both outdoors and under glass. Each leaf-edge gall encloses several larvae.

The hemerocallis gall midge (*Contarinia quinquenotata*), a damaging pest of early- and mid-season-flowering day-lilies, is also single brooded. This pest (in Britain, first discovered in a London garden in the late 1980s)[22] is steadily increasing its range, and damage has been reported in various parts of southern England, especially in and around London. Adults are active in the spring, eggs then being laid in the flower buds. Larvae develop gregariously during the late spring and early summer, infested buds swelling but failing to open. Later-flowering cultivars produce buds after the egg-laying period and are unaffected.

Gall midges often become established on trees and shrubs but they are rarely of significance. Nevertheless, a few species are known to have a deleterious impact on hardy ornamentals being raised in nurseries. The hawthorn button-top midge (*Dasineura crataegi*) and the oak terminal-shoot gall midge (*Arnoldiola quercus*) are examples. Both affect the young vegetative growth of their respective hosts. Hawthorn button-top midge is often abundant, depositing eggs in the developing shoot tips. The whitish larvae feed gregariously, and infested shoot tips develop into compact, rosette-like galls that eventually turn black. Fully fed individuals finally drop to the ground and pupate in the soil. There are several generations annually. Attacked hawthorn plants are not only disfigured, especially as the vacated galls often remain *in situ* for many years, but are also misshapen, and this affects the quality of stock plants. Oak terminal-shoot gall midge attacks the terminal shoots of oak trees, preventing the development of shoots and eventually causing dieback and death. Attacks in nurseries affect the vigour and overall structure of young trees, and are especially important on two- and three-year-old plants. The midge has two generations annually, the periods of egg-laying coinciding neatly with the main periods of growth of oaks in spring and summer.

FIG 295. Honey-locust gall midge (*Dasineura gleditchiae*) hails from North America and is now firmly established in southern England. When tinged with red or purple the galls are attractive, and sometimes mistaken for flowers. Blue tits feed avidly on the gall-inhabiting larvae.

Since its first appearance on honey-locust in England in the early 1980s, honey-locust gall midge (*Dasineura gleditchiae*) has become increasingly common. Adults are active from late May onwards, and eggs are then deposited on the young leaflets. Infested leaflets develop into swollen, yellowish-green to purplish-red, pod-like galls (Fig. 295) within which the gregarious, whitish to whitish-orange larvae develop. Pupation takes place in the galls and the next generation of midges emerges shortly afterwards. There are either two or three generations in the year, larvae of the final generation overwintering in the soil. The cascades of swollen galls are colourful and rather attractive, but their blackened, dead remains (before they eventually drop from infested trees) are unsightly. Insectivorous birds, especially blue tits, frequently visit infested trees and feed avidly on the larvae and pupae.

Yew gall midge (*Taxomyia taxi*) also deserves special mention. This midge attacks cowtail pine as well as yew. Adults are active in late May and June, eggs being laid singly in the buds of host plants. The eggs hatch one to three weeks later. First-instar larvae take either two or (more commonly) fourteen months to develop, thereby determining the duration of the lifecycle.[23] In the case of one-year galls, these become no more than swollen buds; two-year galls, however, develop into large, artichoke-like rosettes up to 40 mm or so in diameter. Larvae embarking upon a one-year course of development remain within the galls throughout the summer, autumn and winter, eventually pupating in the spring about six weeks before the emergence of the adults. Most larvae, however, remain in the galls for two summers, autumns and winters. Vacated galls eventually die and their brown remains often linger on infested hosts for up to two or more years. Heavy infestations cause stunting of plants and are of particular significance on nursery stock. Two chalcid parasitoids are

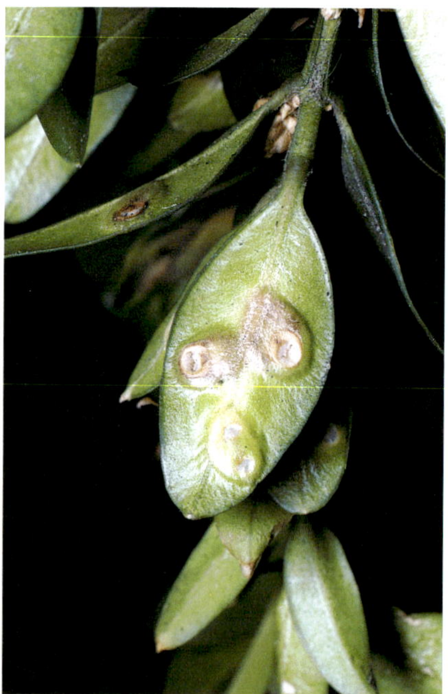

FIG 296. Box leaf mining midge (*Monarthropalpus buxi*) larvae feed inside swollen, gall-like mines on the underside of leaves.

commonly associated with yew gall midge: *Mesopolobus diffinis* (a multi-brooded species) and *Torymus nigritarsus* (which is single brooded). The former is of particular significance in regulating larval populations in one-year galls, whereas the latter restricts its attacks to hosts in two-year galls.[24] Although studied in the field, the occurrence and impact of these natural enemies do not appear to have been assessed in nurseries.

As a gall midge, the box leaf mining midge (*Monarthropalpus buxi*) is of interest in that the larvae essentially mine within the rather fleshy leaves of box. Each mine develops into a blister-like swelling with a partly sunken centre (Fig. 296). These 'galls' are clearly visible from below and also cause discoloration of the upper leaf surface. There are often several 'galls' on each infested leaf. Barnes[25] alluded to box leaf mining midge as 'one of the earliest known midges in historic times' – the insect having been first described by the French entomologist Étienne Louis Geoffroy in 1764. Development of this species is slow, larvae taking up to ten months to reach maturity. They survive in the 'galls' throughout the winter and eventually pupate in the spring, shortly before the emergence of adults.

The gall midge *Resseliella oculiperda* is sometimes of importance on sites where fruit trees or rose bushes are grafted, the pest depositing eggs in slits or other wounds on newly budded root stock. Following egg hatch, the larvae (known as red bud borers) develop gregariously within the cambium between scion and stock. Larvae are fully grown in about three weeks. They then drop to the ground to pupate in the soil, each in a silken cocoon. There are typically three generations annually, larvae of the final brood overwintering in their subterranean cocoons and pupating in the spring. Damaged grafts fail to take; they eventually wither and die.

Gall wasps

Cynipid gall wasps breed on various trees and shrubs, especially oak – over 75 species (including *Andricus*: 54 species; *Biorhiza*: one species; *Cynips*: seven species; *Neuroterus*: ten species) are associated with oak in Europe.[26] Members of all the above-cited genera occur on oak trees in Britain, including scrub oaks, although few are of any significance on nursery stock. Galls formed by cynipids occur on various parts of host plants, including roots, leaves, inflorescences and fruits, and are often very spectacular. The oak leaf cherry-gall cynipid (*C. quercusfolii*), for example, forms colourful cherry-like galls on the underside of leaves (Fig. 297), especially on English oak and sessile oak. The less striking galls formed by the marble gall wasp (*A. kollari*), however, are more frequently encountered. As previously mentioned in the New Naturalist series,[27] marble galls were historically harvested and then used as a source of dye or tannin (the latter to make ink, among other things); also, the causal insect (a non-native British species) may well have been accidentally introduced to Britain in the first half of the nineteenth century, following the importation of galls for use in the cloth industry. Marble galls are sometimes incorrectly described as 'oak apples'. However, the latter description is more correctly applied to the large, spongy, apple-sized galls formed by the oak-apple gall wasp (*B. pallida*).

FIG 297. Oak leaf cherry-gall cynipid (*Cynips quercusfolii*) is one of many gall-inducing cynipid wasps associated with young oak trees.

Lifecycles of cynipid gall wasps are highly complex, and often include asexual and bisexual generations that might involve an alternation of host species. This is well illustrated by the acorn cup gall cynipid (*A. quercuscalicis*), a continental species that was first confirmed breeding in Britain (in Devon) in 1956 and is now widely distributed. Adult females are active in the early spring and lay their eggs on the developing flowers of Turkey oak. Larvae of a bisexual generation then feed in galls formed on the catkins. Following the production of adult males and females, eggs are eventually deposited in the fruit (acorn) primordia of English oak trees. As the infested acorns develop, large, irregular and sticky mounds of greenish tissue develop, each enclosing a single whitish larva. These so-called knopper galls later harden and turn brown. In autumn, they drop to the ground. Larvae within them then pupate and adult females of the next asexual generation appear in the following year. Knopper galls are sometimes noticed on fruiting nursery stock but are of no importance.

Members of the genus *Neuroterus* are tiny wasps, no more than a few millimetres long. They also exhibit complex lifecycles, involving both bisexual and asexual generations. Oak leaf spangle-gall cynipid (*N. quercusbaccarum*), for example, is a widespread and generally abundant species. Females of the asexual generation lay eggs in the male catkins of oak trees. Larvae then develop in currant-like galls that finally become dark red. Pupation takes place in June. Adults of a bisexual generation then emerge, and mated females eventually lay eggs in the underside of the expanded leaves. Following egg hatch, disc-like spangle galls (up to 100 or more on each infested leaf) (Fig. 298) develop, each containing a single larva. In October, the galls drop to the ground. Larvae overwinter in their galls. They then pupate, shortly before the emergence of the next generation of adult (asexual) females. The related oak leaf blister-gall cynipid (*N. numismalis*) also induces the development of spangle galls, and there

FIG 298. Galls of the oak leaf spangle-gall cynipid (*Neuroterus quercusbaccarum*) are very numerous and may exceed 100 or more per infested leaf.

can be 1,000 or more on a single leaf. Such galls, however, are smaller than those of the previous species, and they have a silky, golden-brown appearance and a distinct central pit. Spangle galls have little or no adverse effect on plant growth, although infested foliage looks unhealthy as if diseased.

Gall wasps (*Diplolepis* spp.) are also associated with rose bushes, especially the rose smooth pea-gall cynipid (*D. eglanteriae*) and the rose spiked pea-gall cynipid (*D. nervosa*). Both species form conspicuous, pea-like galls on the underside of the young leaflets, those of rose spiked pea-gall cynipid bearing several spiky outgrowths. Such galls are single chambered (unilocular), and each encloses a single larva. Although sometimes found on nursery stock, the galls are more frequent on wild, rather than cultivated, bushes. The same is true of the bedeguar gall wasp (*D. rosae*), whose large, multi-chambered, moss-like galls often attract attention in the countryside.

Sawflies

Gall-inhabiting sawflies (genus *Pontania*) are sometimes associated with willows being raised in nurseries, albeit as minor pests. Willow bean-gall sawfly (*P. proxima*), a pest of crack willow and white willow, is an example. Bean-gall sawflies are considered in more detail in Chapter 11. Several other sawfly larvae, formerly included in the genus *Pontania* but now treated separately, inhabit rolled or folded leaf edges. *Phyllocolpa leucaspis* and *P. leucosticta* on common sallow, pussy willow and other broadleaved willows are examples. However, these habitations are not classified as galls.

Gall mites

Gall mites infest a wide range of outdoor ornamental trees and shrubs (Table 15, overleaf). Symptoms following attacks by the mites include an upward or downward (often tight) rolling of the leaf margins, and the development of colourful bead-, nail-, pimple- or pouch-like galls. The spectacular displays of tiny bead-like galls on the leaves of maple and sycamore – induced by maple bead-gall mite (*Artacris cephaloneus*) and sycamore gall mite (*Aculops acericola*), respectively – frequently attract attention on both cultivated and wild hosts. Larger, pouch-like galls, such as those inhabited by maple leaf gall mite (*Eriophyes macrochelus*), also occur. These leaf galls sometimes distort foliage but they rarely if ever affect the growth of host plants. The elongate, finger-like nail galls induced by lime nail-gall mite (*E. tiliae*), which may be as long as 15 mm, are particularly eye-catching. Again, however, even when very numerous, they appear to have little or no adverse effect on the growth of host plants. Nevertheless, infestations are considered unsightly and therefore have a detrimental effect on

TABLE 15. Examples of gall-inducing eriophyid mites (family Eriophyidae) associated with hardy ornamental nursery stock.

Host Plant	*Mite Species*	*Type of Gall*[*]
Alder	Alder erineum mite (*Acalitus brevitarsus*)	Erinea on underside of leaves
Alder	*Eriophyes inangulis*	Pouch-like galls in angles of the major veins
Alder	Alder bead-gall mite (*Eriophyes laevis*)	Large, pouch-like galls
Ash	Ash inflorescence gall mite (*Eriophyes fraxinivorus*)	Distorted inflorescences
Beech	*Aceria stenaspis stenaspis*	Marginal leaf rolls
Beech	Beech leaf-vein gall mite (*Eriophyes nervisequus*)	Narrow erinea on the upper surface of leaves, along the major veins
Beech	Beech erineum gall mite (*Eriophyes nervisequus fagineus*)	Erinea on underside of leaves
Birch	Birch witches' broom mite (*Acalitus rudis*)	Swollen buds ('big-buds')
Birch	Birch bead-gall mite (*Aceria leionotus*)	Small, pimple-like galls
Birch	*Aceria longisetosus*	Erinea on underside of leaves
Broom	Broom gall mite (*Eriophyes genistae*)	Distorted and enlarged (fleshy and hairy) buds
Elder	Elder leaf mite (*Epitrimerus trilobus*)	Distorted leaves
Elm	Elm leaf blister mite (*Eriophyes filiformis*)	Pouch-like galls
Elm	Elm bead-gall mite (*Aculus ulmicola*)	Bead-like galls
False acacia	*Vasates robiniae*	Marginal leaf rolls
Greenweed	Broom gall mite (*Eriophyes genistae*)	Distorted and enlarged (fleshy and hairy) buds
Hawthorn	*Eriophyes pyri crataegi*	Small, blister-like galls
Hawthorn	Hawthorn leaf gall mite (*Phyllocoptes goniothorax*)	Marginal leaf rolls
Hazel	Filbert bud mite (*Phytoptus avellanae*)†	Swollen buds ('big-buds')
Hornbeam	Hornbeam leaf gall mite (*Eriophyes macrotrichus*)	Interveinal furrowing on leaves
Lime	*Aceria exilis*	Hairy, pimple-like galls in angles of the major veins
Lime	Lime leaf erineum mite (*Eriophyes leiosoma*)	Erinea on underside of leaves
Lime	*Phytoptus tetratrichus*†	Marginal leaf rolls
Lime, common	Lime nail-gall mite (*Eriophyes tiliae*)	Long, nail-like galls
Lime, small-leaved	*Eriophyes tiliae lateannulatus*	Stumpy, nail-like galls
Maple	*Eriophyes eriobius*	Erinea on underside of leaves

Maple	Maple bead-gall mite (*Artacris cephaloneus*)	Small, bead-like galls
Poplar	Poplar erineum mite (*Phyllocoptes populi*)	Erinea on underside of leaf
Rowan	*Eriophyes pyri sorbi*	Small, blister-like galls
Spindle	Spindle leaf-roll gall mite (*Eriophyes convolvens*)	Marginal leaf rolls
Sycamore	Sycamore leaf gall mite (*Artacris macrorhynchus*)	Short, finger-like galls
Sycamore	*Eriophyes eriobius pseudoplatani*	Erinea on underside of leaves, mainly alongside or at junctions of the major veins
Sycamore	*Eriophyes psilomerus*	Small erinea on underside of leaves
Walnut	Walnut leaf erineum mite (*Aceria erinea*)	Large erinea on underside of leaves
Whitebeam	*Eriophyes pyri arianus*	Small, blister-like galls
Willow	Willow leaf gall mite (*Aculops tetanothrix*)	Hairy, pouch-like galls
Willow	*Aculus truncatus*	Marginal leaf rolls
Yew	Yew gall mite (*Cecidophyopsis psilaspis*)	Swollen buds

* On upper surface of leaves unless stated otherwise.
† Family Phytoptidae.

the perceived quality of nursery stock. The same is true, for example, of the small, blister-like leaf galls on young rowan trees attacked by *E. pyri sorbi*. Gall mites also often induce the development of large erinea on the underside of leaves. Viewed from above such galls appear as swellings between the major veins. Below, they are lined with dense felt-like or velvet-like mats of short hairs amongst which the causal mites feed and breed. The hairs clothing the erinea often appear translucent, whitish or light brown, but they are sometimes more colourful. Red-tinged erinea formed on the leaves of beech trees by *E. nervisequus fagineus* (Fig. 299) are an example.

Apart from marginal leaf-roll galls, eriophyid leaf galls are usually distributed more or less randomly over infested leaf blades. However, this is not always so. Erinea formed on the underside of sycamore leaves by *Eriophyes eriobus pseudoplatani*, for example, are typically located at the junctions of the major veins, and the same is true of the pouch-like galls induced on alder by *E. inangulis*. Similarly, the beech leaf-vein gall mite (*E. nervisequus*) induces narrow, furrow-like erinea that run along the major veins on the upper side of leaves.

FIG 299. The colourful erinea inhabited by *Eriophyes nervisequus fagineus* are sometimes found on the leaves of ornamental beech trees.

Some gall mites invade the buds and inflorescences of plants. *Aceria stenaspis*, for example, causes distortion of the new growth and often kills the opening buds of beech trees. Others, including the birch witches' broom mite (*Acalitus rudis*) on birch and the filbert bud mite (*Phytoptus avellanae*) on hazel, cause the invaded buds to swell and sometimes to develop into grotesque, hairy outgrowths, as is also the case with broom gall mite (*E. genistae*) (Fig. 300) on both broom and greenweed. Yew gall mite (*Cecidophyopsis psilaspis*) induces the development of big-buds on yew, and also causes distortion and death of young shoots; this mite is often a pest in nurseries, and the galls are sometimes mistaken for those initiated by yew gall midge (see p. 289). Azalea bud & rust mite, a North American species now established on azaleas in southern England, causes not only distortion of the new growth but also extensive russeting of tissue. Various other eriophyids also cause russeting; examples to be found in

FIG 300. Buds of broom and greenweed invaded by broom gall mite (*Eriophyes genistae*) become swollen, fleshy and characteristically downy.

nurseries include *Aculus aucuparia* on rowan, apple rust mite (*A. schlechtendali*) on crab-apple, ash rust mite on ash, plum rust mite (*A. fockeui*) on various kinds of ornamental cherry, and false acacia rust mite (*Vasates allotrichus*) on false acacia. Of these, ash rust mite is particularly damaging, and heavy infestations result in the death of young shoots.

SHOOT AND STEM BORERS

Larvae of leopard moth (*Zeuzera pyrina*) and rosy rustic moth (*Hydraecia micacea*) occasionally cause damage in nurseries. Those of the former bore in the wood of young trees and those of the latter feed within the stems of plants such as chrysanthemum, dahlia, hollyhock and iris. Larvae of the frosted orange moth (*Gortyna flavago*), a close relative of the rosy rustic moth, are sometimes also charged with attacking the root stocks of herbaceous hardy ornamentals, although they rarely occur in nurseries.

Ash bud moth (*Prays fraxinella*) is sometimes an important shoot-boring pest of young ash trees. From June or July onwards, eggs are laid on the twigs but they do not hatch until the autumn. Larvae commence life as miners in leaves and other tissue, before eventually hibernating. In spring, the larvae feed within the young shoots, which then wilt and die. Loss of terminal shoots affects the structure of young trees, paired side shoots (laterals) becoming dominant so that subsequent growth is forked. The poplar cloaked bell moth (*Gypsonoma aceriana*) similarly causes forked growth on poplars, and is often of importance in stool beds (sites where plants are regularly coppiced at ground level) and nurseries.[28] The shoot-boring larvae develop during May and June. Characteristically, frass is expelled as a tell-tale, tube-like protrusion near the base of each infested terminal shoot.

Rose shoot sawfly (*Ardis brunniventris*) is a potentially important pest of rose, and can inflict considerable damage on young bushes. Adults, which have a very protracted period of activity, occur from May onwards. Eggs are then deposited singly in the terminal buds and hatch a few days later. Initially, the larvae feed on the developing leaf tissue but then each bores into a shoot and begins to tunnel downwards within the pith (Fig. 301). Wet, black frass is expelled through the larval entry hole, and this often betrays the presence of the pest. When fully fed the larva escapes from the base of the damaged shoot, leaving behind a distinctive exit hole. The invaded shoot eventually wilts and dies. This species has just one generation annually, larvae overwintering in the soil, each in an earthen cell, and pupating in the spring. Longitudinally rolled, drooping leaves

FIG 301. Rose shoot sawfly (*Ardis brunniventris*) larvae are destructive pests of rose. Larvae feed internally, each burrowing downwards within a young shoot.

on the terminal shoots of rose bushes are often thought to be due to shoot-boring pests such as rose shoot sawfly. In reality, however, they are caused by the leaf-rolling rose sawfly (*Blennocampa pusilla*). These characteristic leaf rolls are initiated by the egg-laying female who, usually after depositing some eggs, uses her ovipositor to probe the tissue on either side of the midrib. This causes the leaf to roll downwards. A tight, tube-like shelter is formed, within which the sawfly larvae subsequently develop. Infestations in nurseries can be extensive and affect the vigour of young bushes; infested plants are also unsightly.

Young conifer trees are damaged by various shoot-boring larvae. Juniper shoot moth (*Argyresthia dilectella*) larvae, for example, cause death of young juniper shoots and are sometimes of concern in nurseries. *A. trifasciata*, an invasive southern European species, also infests junipers and, in the Netherlands, has caused particularly severe damage to the juniper known as pencil cedar (cv. Sky Rocket).[29] Having successfully crossed the English Channel (probably in association with infested plants), this insect has become widely established in England and has also been found in Wales.[30] The cypress tip moth (*A. cupressella*), a North American species that mines within the shoots of cypresses and junipers, is yet another new arrival in Britain.[31] To date, however, neither of these newcomers has become a commercial problem here.

Pine shoot moth (*Rhyacionia buoliana*) is frequently reported causing damage to young pine trees, and significant outbreaks sometimes occur in nurseries. The pretty, orange-red, silver-marked adults occur mainly in late June and throughout July, eggs being laid close to the terminal buds. Following egg hatch, each larva mines within the base of a needle before entering a lateral bud and then overwintering. In early spring, the larva again becomes active and invades a terminal bud or shoot to continue its development. Pupation takes place in the larval habitation in June, adults emerging two to three weeks later. Both before and following hibernation, characteristic silken tents incorporating exuded resin are formed around the larval feeding sites, and these become particularly obvious in bright, sunny weather. Attacks on the leading shoots of pine trees result in one of three damage symptoms.[32] Sometimes, all buds and shoots are killed and this culminates in subsequent forking of growth as shoots from below are stimulated to develop. More commonly, however, although the terminal shoot or bud is killed, some or all of the side shoots survive; the extent of future distortion then depends upon the number and vigour of the side shoots that eventually arise. Repeated attacks cause stunting of trees and result in the appearance of stag-headed (multi-forked) leaders. The third, least common, symptom (yet that most frequently cited in descriptions of the pest) is the resulting looped, so-called 'post-horn', deformation of the main stem. This characteristic feature develops if a young infested leader keels over at its base but then recovers and again becomes dominant.

CHAPTER 10

Pests of Plants in Protected Cultivation

CROPS HAVE LONG BEEN grown under protection, culminating in the cultivation of plants in purpose-built structures formerly known as glasshouses but more commonly nowadays called greenhouses. Greenhouses are either fixed or mobile and often heated structures, permanently glazed in glass or plastic and tall enough to walk through. They protect plants from the worst of the elements (e.g. extremes of heat and cold), optimise exposure to light and extend growing seasons. They also allow tender plants (such as cucumbers, peppers and tomatoes) to be produced in regions where their cultivation might otherwise be very limited if not impossible. Increasingly, nowadays, high walk-in tunnels (polytunnels) – temporary plastic-covered structures that provide an intermediate level of environmental protection between heated greenhouses and open-field conditions – are appearing in the landscape. However, these typically unheated structures (including French tunnels and Spanish tunnels: temporary single- and multi-bay structures, respectively) do not qualify as greenhouses and are not discussed further: nor are temporary low-level shelters, such as cloches, cold frames and plastic sheeting.

The greenhouse microclimate (light, heat and humidity) is often strictly controlled, and this not only affects plant growth but also impacts on pests and other organisms. Temperatures in heated greenhouses, for example, are often kept at about 20–30°C during the daytime, optimising crop development and production but also providing ideal breeding conditions for pests such as whiteflies and spider mites. The epithet 'protected' is typically applied to crops raised in greenhouses. Mushrooms too are considered protected crops, and pests associated with these two quite distinct and highly specialised areas of horticulture (i.e. greenhouse plants and mushrooms) are discussed separately, below.

LIFE IN GREENHOUSES

Aphids

Aphids are persistent greenhouse pests, and are of importance both as direct feeders and as potential virus vectors. Peach/potato aphid (*Myzus persicae*), for example, readily transmits carnation latent virus (CLV), chrysanthemum virus B (CVB), cucumber mosaic virus (CMV) and more besides. Potato aphid (*Macrosiphum euphorbiae*) is also a virus vector. Aphids in heated greenhouses typically breed parthenogenetically throughout the year and, as in the case of rose aphid (*Macrosiphum rosae*), they do so even if outdoor populations undergo a sexual phase and survive the winter in the egg stage. Some greenhouse plants are particularly suitable hosts for aphids. Chrysanthemums, for example, attract the attention of several species. These include chrysanthemum aphid (*Macrosiphoniella sanborni*), melon & cotton aphid (*Aphis gossypii*), mottled arum aphid (*Aulacorthum circumflexum*) (Fig. 302), peach/potato aphid, small chrysanthemum aphid (*Coloradoa rufomaculata*), *Dactynotus tanaceti* and *Macrosiphoniella oblonga*. As for protected vegetable crops, lettuces host at least six species (Table 16). Contamination of host plants by honeydew and cast nymphal skins is often a consequence of an aphid infestation. This is notably so in the case of violet aphid (*Myzus ornatus*), an entirely parthenogenetic species that is rarely found out of doors. This aphid is a persistent pest of African violets and many other greenhouse-grown plants. In common with peach/potato aphid, it is also a well-known virus vector. Violet aphid persists on hosts as scattered individuals, albeit often with many present on each infested leaf, bud or flower. At the other extreme, as illustrated by chrysanthemum aphid, dense colonies

FIG 302. Mottled arum aphid (*Aulacorthum circumflexum*) infests many greenhouse plants.

TABLE **16.** Examples of aphids associated with greenhouse vegetable crops.

Species	*Host(s)*
Currant/lettuce aphid (*Nasonovia ribisnigri*)	Lettuce
Glasshouse & potato aphid (*Aulacorthum solani*)	Aubergine, lettuce, sweet pepper, tomato
Melon & cotton aphid (*Aphis gossypii*)	Aubergine, celery, courgette, cucumber, lettuce, marrow, melon, sweet pepper
Mottled arum aphid (*Aulacorthum circumflexum*)	Lettuce
Peach/potato aphid (*Myzus persicae*)	Aubergine, celery, Chinese cabbage, courgette, cucumber, lettuce, marrow, sweet pepper, spinach, tomato
Potato aphid (*Macrosiphum euphorbiae*)	Aubergine, lettuce, tomato

often develop on host plants (in this case in late summer and early autumn), buds and flowers then becoming noticeably distorted.

Aphid colonies in greenhouses support a range of parasitoids, predators and pathogens. These either arrive fortuitously as natural invaders or gain a foothold following their release during biological control or integrated pest management (IPM) programmes. In respect of IPM, four species of aphid are especially targeted by growers:

- **glasshouse & potato aphid and potato aphid** – using the parasitoid wasps *Aphelinus abdominalis* and *Aphidius ervi*;
- **melon & cotton aphid and peach/potato aphid** – using the parasitoid wasp *Aphidius colemani*, the predatory midge *Aphidoletes aphidimyza* and the entomopathogenic fungus *Lecanicillium longisporum*.

Whiteflies

Whiteflies commonly become established in greenhouses, attacking a wide range of vegetable crops and ornamentals. The glasshouse whitefly (*Trialeurodes vaporariorum*) (Fig. 303) is most often encountered, and this important pest has a detrimental effect on the growth of host plants. Whiteflies excrete large quantities of honeydew, upon which sooty moulds soon develop. Such contamination often means that harvested fruits, such as cucumbers, peppers and tomatoes, must be washed before sale or otherwise rejected. Whiteflies, their bodies more or less coated in white, mealy wax, often rest in considerable numbers on the leaves of host plants, but they readily take flight if disturbed. Eggs are laid in distinctive circular groups on the underside of leaves and hatch just over a week later. At first, the mobile first-instar nymphs wander over the leaves but eventually they settle

FIG 303. Glasshouse whitefly (*Trialeurodes vaporariorum*) is a major pest of greenhouse crops such as tomato.

permanently to become flattened, sedentary, scale-like nymphs. Such individuals pass through several nymphal stages before becoming non-feeding pseudo-pupae – equivalent to the true pupae of higher (holometabolous) insects. These pseudo-pupae, which in common with sedentary nymphs are white in appearance, and bear several long marginal and dorsal waxen processes, eventually erupt as the new adult whiteflies emerge. Development from egg to adult takes just under a month at normal greenhouse temperatures. Although essentially a pest of protected crops, during the summer months glasshouse whiteflies also breed on a wide range of outdoor plants growing in the vicinity of infested greenhouses.

Over the past 20 years or so, commercial greenhouses in Britain have sometimes become infested by tobacco whitefly (*Bemisia tabaci*), a tropical and subtropical pest that most often slips into the country on imported poinsettia plants or cuttings. Unlike glasshouse whitefly, tobacco whiteflies tend to occur as scattered individuals on infested leaves. The eggs, too, are deposited singly rather than in groups. Development of this pest is somewhat slower than that of glasshouse whitefly for any given temperature, but its life history and habits are otherwise similar. In British greenhouses, the pest has been found mainly on ornamentals, and on edible crops such as sweet pepper and tomato. Tobacco whitefly is an important virus vector, being capable of transmitting over 100 different kinds. Plant Health authorities rightly demand elimination of infestations of this potentially very harmful and highly polyphagous pest. To date, constant vigilance (and the adoption of appropriate statutory control measures when infestations have been found) has prevented the pest from becoming established here (see Chapter 12).

Glasshouse whiteflies are frequently parasitised by the wasp *Encarsia formosa*, a tiny parasitoid whose potential as a biocontrol agent has been known for many

FIG 304. Glasshouse whitefly nymphs parasitised by the wasp *Encarsia formosa* are characteristically black – a good indication that biological control is under way.

years.[1] The wasps lay their eggs singly in the older nymphal scales of the host, and the parasitoid larvae subsequently feed internally before eventually pupating. New adult wasps emerge from parasitised scales about two weeks after eggs were laid, and there is a succession of generations throughout the growing season. Parasitised whitefly scales are readily distinguished from healthy (unparasitised) ones, as they soon turn black (Fig. 304). This allows growers adopting biocontrol measures to confirm that released parasitoids have become established. Although it is an important enemy of glasshouse whitefly, *E. formosa* has little impact on tobacco whitefly. The entomopathogenic fungus *Lecanicillium muscarium*,[2] however, is active against both species.

Leafhoppers

Protected crops, including vegetable plants and a range of ornamentals, are often attacked by leafhoppers, of which the glasshouse leafhopper (*Hauptidia maroccana*) (Fig. 305) is a common example. This species is particularly troublesome on tomato, the foliage of infested plants becoming pallid and speckled with white, where the cell contents have been withdrawn. The tiny eggs are laid in the veins on the underside of host leaves, each inserted through a small slit made in the epidermis. They hatch about a week later at normal greenhouse temperatures. The pale-coloured nymphs then feed on the

FIG 305. Glasshouse leafhopper (*Hauptidia maroccana*) is often present in heated greenhouses.

underside of the leaves for about a month before eventually moulting into adults. Cast nymphal skins are a common sight on the underside of infested leaves, remaining as a clear indication of the causal organism even in the absence of adults and nymphs. The chrysanthemum leafhopper (*Eupteryx melissae*) is also a frequent greenhouse inhabitant, but attacks occur mainly on cultivated herbs such as lemon balm, mint and sage.

The leafhopper *Empoasca decipiens*, a generally common species on various outdoor plants, including potato, is also known to breed on protected crops and has recently become a particular problem on sweet peppers. High temperatures (35°C and 30°C, respectively) favour egg and nymphal development,[3] so it is well suited to heated greenhouse conditions.

Infestations of glasshouse leafhopper are often arrested following the release of *Anagrus atomus*, a minute mymarid wasp currently available as a biocontrol agent. It is also commonplace in nature. Owing to their minute size and delicate appearance, mymarid wasps are often known as fairy-flies. At only about a millimetre long, they are amongst the smallest of all British insects. Eggs of *A. atomus* are deposited in those of leafhoppers, each host egg subsequently turning from green to red as a parasitoid develops within. The parasitoid eggs hatch a couple of days or so after oviposition, and each parasitoid larva then passes through two instars before eventually pupating.[4] *E. decipiens* is also victimised by *A. atomus*, but chrysanthemum leafhopper is not.

Mirids (capsids) and other plant bugs

Phytophagous mirid (capsid) bugs frequently cause damage to greenhouse plants, especially in weedy sites. The European tarnished plant bug (*Lygus rugulipennis*), for example, often invades greenhouses during the summer, notably following

FIG 306. Common nettle capsid (*Liocoris tripustulatus*) sometimes invades greenhouses, and has recently been recognised as a pest.

the mass appearance of young adults in July. The bugs then feed on a range of hosts, including chrysanthemum and cucumber. In recent years the common nettle capsid (*Liocoris tripustulatus*), a distinctive and rather stout-bodied species (Fig. 306), has also been recognised as a pest in greenhouses. This insect is often abundant in nettle beds, where it feeds on the buds and fruits, and sometimes invades nearby greenhouses to feed on plants such as cucumber, sweet pepper and tomato. Such detrimental behaviour has been noted in both Britain and the Netherlands.[5] As mentioned earlier (Chapter 5), this leafhopper also occurs on potato crops.

As particularly highlighted in the case of orchards and soft-fruit plantations, mirids (capsids) and related bugs are natural predators of pests on various outdoor crops. Few species, however, are currently reared commercially for release in biocontrol programmes. Of those that are, the southern European species *Macrolophus melanotoma*[6] (a narrow, green-bodied insect with reddish eyes) is recommended for use against whiteflies on greenhouse-grown tomato crops. *M. melanotoma* also feeds on aphids, spider mites, moth eggs and so forth. However, when prey is in short supply the bugs become phytophagous sap feeders. They then cause damage to a range of plants, including aubergine, cherry tomato (upon which it causes fruit drop) and gerbera. *Orius laevigatus* and *O. majusculus*, known as minute pirate bugs, are similarly released into greenhouses to control thrips. In the absence of thrips they feed on pollen, and also attack aphids, mites and various other small invertebrates. As close relatives of anthocorid bugs (*Anthocoris* spp.), pirate bugs are voracious feeders and, once established, they become highly effective predators. Both species occur naturally in the British Isles.

Scale insects

Scale insects are often persistent greenhouse pests, especially on perennial ornamentals (including ferns and orchids). Many species occur under protection,[7] of which brown soft scale (*Coccus hesperidum*) (Fig. 307) is a particularly abundant example. Brown soft scale breeds continuously on a wide range of hosts, completing several overlapping generations annually. Infested plants are often weakened. They also become sticky with honeydew and further disfigured by sooty moulds. As mentioned elsewhere (e.g. in Chapter 9), scale insects typically develop to adulthood through an egg and several nymphal stages. However, brown soft scale is ovoviviparous, the mature females giving birth to nymphs rather than depositing eggs; the eggs (which possess a definite shell) hatch whilst still within the body of the parent.[8] Scale insects in greenhouses sometimes attract the attention of tiny parasitoid wasps, some of which may have been deliberately introduced as biocontrol agents. Populations of brown soft scale, for example, are targeted by *Metaphycus helvolus*, an exotic encyrtid wasp of African origin, whose larvae feed on the developing nymphal scales. Host feeding by the adult female parasitoids (see Chapter 4, p. 92) also occurs, resulting in the death of a large number of nymphal scales. *M. helvolus* is ineffective against armoured scales (family Diaspididae).

FIG 307. Brown soft scale (*Coccus hesperidum*) is a persistent pest, and a frequent problem on protected ornamental plants.

Mealybugs

Although rarely found outdoors in Britain,[9] mealybugs often infest ornamentals being raised in greenhouses. Frequented hosts include cacti, ferns, lilies, orchids and vines. The glasshouse mealybug (*Pseudococcus viburni*)[10] also attacks tomato plants. Mealybugs are close relative of scale insects, but they remain mobile

FIG 308. Long-tailed mealybug (*Pseudococcus longispinus*) is one of several species of mealybug found in heated greenhouses.

throughout their nymphal and adult stages. Typically of subtropical and tropical origin, most greenhouse-inhabiting species are favoured by hot, humid conditions. They then breed continuously and complete several generations annually. Mealybugs are typically powdered or coated with wax. Their bodies are also fringed by wax-coated spines, including backwardly directed caudal processes. In some species, as in the case of the long-tailed mealybug (*P. longispinus*) (Fig. 308), the latter are greatly elongated. By contrast, the caudal processes of the citrus mealybug (*Planococcus citri*) are rather short and stout. Mealybugs tend to occur in groups (colonies). Honeydew can be excreted in considerable quantities and this sometimes accumulates amongst the insects as large viscous droplets.

Wax-coated colonies of root mealybugs (*Rhizoecus* spp.) sometimes develop around the root balls of containerised greenhouse-grown ornamentals. Attacked plants tend to develop dull-coloured foliage and to wilt, as if suffering from drought. The insects produce honeydew and this commonly attracts ants. These then become their guardians, as they often do in the case of root- and leaf-inhabiting aphids.

For many years, adults and larvae of *Cryptolaemus montrouzieri* (a small, greenish-black to orange ladybird from Australia) have been used in greenhouses to combat foliage-feeding mealybugs. They are efficient predators, well capable of regulating or eliminating infestations so long as temperatures do not drop below about 20°C. When mealybugs are scarce, aphids and soft scales become alternative prey; the ladybird larvae also resort to cannibalism. Larvae of *C. montrouzieri* are unusual in that their bodies are coated in white, flocculent wax. They appear, therefore, somewhat mealybug-like. The adult beetles are highly active creatures and sometimes escape into the wild. However, unlike the exotic harlequin ladybird (*Harmonia axyridis*) (see Chapter 12), *C. montrouzieri* does not pose a threat to our native fauna.

The encyrtid parasitoid *Leptomastix dactylopii* is also released into protected environments as a biocontrol agent, specifically to combat citrus mealybug infestations. This wasp deposits its eggs singly in third-instar mealybug nymphs. The larvae subsequently feed as endoparasitoids and eventually pupate within the mummified remains of their hosts. *L. dactylopii* is credited with particularly effective host-seeking ability and is well able to deal with dispersed populations. Its close relative *L. epona* is a host-specific parasitoid of the glasshouse mealybug.

Thrips

Thrips frequently attack greenhouse-grown ornamentals and also vegetable crops such as aubergines, cucumbers and lettuces. Tomato plants, however, are rarely damaged directly by thrips. Nowadays, onion thrips (*Thrips tabaci*) and western flower thrips (*Frankliniella occidentalis*) are usually the commonest of our greenhouse-inhabiting species. Both infest a wide range of plants and breed throughout the year in heated greenhouses, completing up to ten or more generations annually. Western flower thrips (a North American species unknown in Britain until outbreaks were reported in greenhouses from the mid-1980s onwards – see Chapter 12) is now a firmly established and widely distributed pest of protected crops. In suitable locations it also breeds outdoors, at least during the summer months. Although it infests a wide range of hosts, damage is of greatest significance on greenhouse-grown chrysanthemums and cucumber plants (Fig. 309). On chrysanthemum, silvering of foliage is commonplace; also, the flowers become blanched and distorted, and appear desiccated. On cucumber, extensive leaf flecking occurs and attacks on young developing fruits can result in considerable malformation. Other susceptible hosts include African violet, cyclamen (Fig. 310), primula, sweet pepper and various bedding plants.

Western flower thrips has received considerable attention from applied entomologists, owing to its direct impact on crops, but especially because of its role in transmitting plant viruses and its proven ability to develop resistance to pesticides. It is a highly efficient virus vector, especially the males,[11]

FIG 309. Western flower thrips (*Frankliniella occidentalis*) is now firmly established in Britain, where it attacks a wide range of greenhouse-grown crops. Flowers of cucumber and various other plants are often affected.

FIG 310. Onion thrips (*Thrips tabaci*) is a common greenhouse inhabitant. Damage occurs on various vegetable crops and also on ornamentals such as cyclamen.

transmitting important viruses such as impatiens necrotic spot virus (INSV) and tomato spotted wilt virus (TSWV). Interestingly, this insect was the first thrips in which males were shown to produce an aggregation pheromone – one to which young virgin females are attracted.[12] Also, anal droplets produced by second-instar nymphs include chemicals that function as an alarm pheromone, eliciting a response in both nymphs and adults.[13] Western flower thrips reproduces sexually and parthenogenetically. Eggs are laid in plant tissue (leaves, floral parts and fruits) and hatch within a week at normal greenhouse temperatures. Individuals then pass through two nymphal feeding stages before dropping to the ground, where the transformation to adulthood (through a propupal and a pupal stage – see Appendix I, p. 414) takes place. Development from egg to adult occupies up to three weeks at temperatures of 20–30°C.[14] The propupal and pupal stages of western flower thrips also occur on host plants – in chrysanthemum and cucumber flowers for example. Development of onion thrips follows a similar pattern. However, unlike western flower thrips, onion thrips is almost entirely parthenogenetic, and pupation always occurs on the ground.

In addition to the above-mentioned species, glasshouse thrips (*Heliothrips haemorrhoidalis*), a native of Brazil, is a frequent inhabitant of greenhouses in Britain and other parts of northern Europe. Plants with smooth, leathery leaves are favoured as hosts.[15] Examples include azaleas, calla lilies and seedling rhododendrons. The pest, which breeds continuously in heated greenhouses, is intolerant of cold conditions. Nevertheless, it has been found breeding outdoors in southern England and the Isles of Scilly.[16] Typical of thrips damage, infested leaves develop silvery or whitish flecks. As on calla lilies, flower petals also become marked and discoloured. Dracaena thrips (*Parthenothrips dracaenae*), which has distinctively broadened and banded wings, is another tropical or subtropical species that has become established in northern Europe on protected ornamentals. It is often abundant, for example, on dracaena plants, palms and ornamental rubber-trees. Breeding by this species is mainly parthenogenetic. The adults and nymphs feed on the underside of leaves, causing significant discoloration. In addition, the upper surface of affected foliage becomes peppered with silvery markings. Infestations often develop on specimen plants in conservatories and other suitably protected environments. Other thrips known to occur under glass in Britain include carnation thrips (*Thrips atratus*), chrysanthemum thrips (*T. nigropilosus*), gladiolus thrips (*T. simplex*), lily thrips (*Liothrips vaneeckei*) and rose thrips (*T. fuscipennis*).[17]

Beetles

Large blue flea beetles (*Altica lythri*) are frequently attracted to fuchsia plants growing outdoors or in greenhouses and polythene tunnels, especially in sites where their natural hosts, such as great willowherb, marsh willowherb and rose-bay, are allowed to flourish. The adult beetles, which overwinter in a variety of sheltered situations, become active from May onwards. They then congregate in numbers on suitable host plants. Eventually, batches of distinctive, whitish-orange eggs are laid on the underside of leaves. The eggs hatch two to three weeks later. Larvae then feed on the leaves before eventually pupating in the soil. New adults make their appearance in late August or September, but soon disperse to take up their winter quarters, there being just one generation annually. Infested leaves become notched and holed, and are also contaminated by pellets of black excrement. In Wales, albeit in outdoor plots, the pest has also been reported causing damage to the leaves of large-flowered evening primrose.[18]

FIG 311. Vine weevil (*Otiorhynchus sulcatus*) is a major pest of horticultural crops, both outdoors and in greenhouses.

Greenhouse-grown fuchsias also attract adult vine weevils (*Otiorhynchus sulcatus*) (Fig. 311), one of our most destructive pests. The weevils, which are wingless, are active mainly at night. They then often feed on the foliage of host plants, biting out distinctive notches in the leaf margins. Other pot plants, particularly begonias, cyclamens and primulas, are similarly targeted. The soil-inhabiting larvae (Fig. 312) attack the plant roots and are capable of causing extensive damage. Adults and larvae of the lesser strawberry weevil (*O. rugosostriatus*), another flightless species, similarly damage greenhouse-grown pot plants.

FIG 312. Vine weevil larvae feed on the roots of host plants, and are often abundant in greenhouses.

As specialist feeders, lily beetles (*Lilioceris lilii*) are also unwelcome visitors to greenhouses, where they are well able to survive. If unchecked, they cause extensive damage to their hosts. The slug-like larvae, coated in black excrement, have become a familiar sight on cultivated lilies, both outdoors and under glass, as have the crimson and black adults.

Moths

Greenhouses are commonly inhabited by lepidopterous pests, many of which are no doubt attracted into such structures by night-time illumination. Most tend to be polyphagous species, of which generally common noctuids such as angle-shades moth (*Phlogophora meticulosa*) (Fig. 313), cabbage moth (*Mamestra brassicae*) and tomato moth (*Lacanobia oleracea*) (Fig. 314) are examples. The rather plump larvae of angle-shades moth (sometimes described as leech-like, owing to the

FIG 313. Angle-shades moth (*Phlogophora meticulosa*) is often present in greenhouses.

FIG 314. Tomato moth (*Lacanobia oleracea*) frequently breeds in greenhouses.

habit of extending the anterior parts of the body) occur in two colour forms: brown and green. These feed mainly on the foliage of their hosts, and are especially renowned for the damage they cause to greenhouse-grown ornamentals such as chrysanthemums and geraniums; they also attack lettuces. Adults may be encountered at any time of year, but they are most numerous in late summer and autumn. Larvae resulting from autumn-laid eggs feed throughout the winter and produce adults in the spring. These are followed by larvae that develop during the summer months. Larvae of cabbage moth frequently occur on greenhouse ornamentals such as carnations, chrysanthemums, Peruvian lilies and pinks. They damage the foliage, but are rarely of great significance. Tomato moth, however, is a particularly harmful greenhouse pest. Eggs are laid in large, untidy batches which often more or less cover the entire underside of a leaf. They hatch about a week later. The larvae then invade various hosts, their attention in greenhouses being directed to cucumber, lettuce, sweet pepper and tomato plants and also to ornamentals (including carnations, cyclamens and pinks). The larvae feed on the leaves; as on tomato, they also bore into developing and ripe fruits. Two generations can develop annually under greenhouse conditions, but the time of year when larvae pupate appears to govern the duration of the pupal stage.[19] The polymorphic larvae are essentially pale green, yellowish brown or brown, in each case with distinctive longitudinal stripes and the body finely speckled with white. Other noctuids to find sanctuary in greenhouses include gothic moth (*Naenia typica*) (Fig. 315) and large yellow underwing moth (*Noctua pronuba*) (Fig. 316). Gothic moth larvae attack plants such as chrysanthemums, fuchsias and geraniums, and are initially gregarious feeders (Fig. 317). Those of large yellow underwing moth (Fig. 318) (as climbing cutworms – see Chapter 6, p. 154) attack a range of

FIG 315. Gothic moth (*Naenia typica*) sometimes occurs in greenhouses.

FIG 316. Large yellow underwing moth (*Noctua pronuba*) is a common pest of greenhouse-grown and outdoor plants.

FIG 317. Gothic moth (*Naenia typica*) larvae feed on various plants, including greenhouse-grown fuchsia.

FIG 318. Large yellow underwing moth larvae have a wide host range. They often attack ornamental plants in greenhouses.

FIG 319. (Above left) Pearly underwing moth (*Peridroma saucia*) is a regular but generally uncommon migrant to Britain. (Above right) The larvae feed on various greenhouse crops, and are sometimes found on imported produce, including lettuce.

greenhouse ornamentals, including carnations, chrysanthemums, pinks and primulas. The tropical and subtropical Mediterranean brocade moth (*Spodoptera littoralis*), whose larvae are also designated climbing cutworms – in this case Mediterranean climbing cutworms – has also been found on occasions in British greenhouses. So too have other alien Lepidoptera, typically introduced in association with plants imported from abroad (see Chapter 12). Plump-bodied larvae of the pearly underwing moth (*Peridroma saucia*) (Fig. 319) – specifically designated 'variegated cutworms' – sometimes occur in greenhouses, especially on chrysanthemum, pelargonium, cucumber and tomato plants. The larvae also feed on lettuce. Although the moth is a natural migrant to Britain, its presence here most often follows the importation of infested plants from abroad.

Greenhouse-grown brassica plants are sometimes attacked by diamond-back moth (*Plutella xylostella*), especially in years when this migratory pest is abundant. Similarly, silver Y moths (*Autographa gamma*) not infrequently enter greenhouses. Their eggs are then deposited on various plants, ranging from ornamentals such as carnations, chrysanthemums, geraniums and pelargoniums to vegetable crops such as lettuces. On ornamentals, the larvae are particularly destructive to buds and flowers.

In spite of their frequency on outdoor plants, larvae of geometrid moths (i.e. looper caterpillars) rarely occur on protected crops. Nevertheless, the slender, essentially green-bodied larvae of the common carpet moth (*Chloroclysta truncata*) sometimes attract attention on ornamentals such as geraniums. Individuals typically rest with the anterior part of the body curled beneath the abdomen, and the head positioned upside down close to the sixth abdominal segment.

Particularly in Cornwall and Devon, larvae of the light brown apple moth (*Epiphyas postvittana*) feed on a wide range of outdoor and protected ornamentals, including azalea, bay laurel, cape figwort, Californian lilac, camellia, Chilean fire bush, daisy-bush, firethorn, honeysuckle, New Zealand tea tree, pittosporum, skimmia, Japanese spindle and witch alder. The pest, which hails from Australia, is essentially double-brooded, but with overlapping generations. Adults occur from May to October and the leaf-tying larvae feed in June and July, and again from September to April. Damage to pot plants, including young containerised shrubs, can be considerable. In common with many related species, pupation typically takes place in the larval habitation. Under glass, adults sometimes emerge during mid-winter. Other leaf-tying species in greenhouses include flax tortrix moth (*Cnephasia asseclana*), a single brooded pest of various herbaceous ornamentals and lettuces, and *C. stephensiana* which commonly damages the leaves of pot plants such as geraniums. The straw-coloured tortrix moth (*Clepsis spectrana*) attacks a range of plants, especially cyclamens (hence the alternative common name cyclamen tortrix moth) and roses. As well as attacking leaves and young shoots, straw-coloured moth larvae also destroy buds and flowers, often boring into rose buds before the flowers have had a chance to unfurl. On cyclamens, the larvae also destroy the fruits and seeds. Outdoors, straw-coloured strawberry tortrix moth is double brooded, larvae of the second generation undergoing a period of obligatory winter diapause. In some greenhouses, however, continuously breeding, non-diapausing, populations have developed, and these can complete several generations annually.[20] The highly polyphagous carnation tortrix moth (*Cacoecimorpha pronubana*) (Fig. 320) is similarly double brooded outdoors. However, breeding is continuous under suitable greenhouse conditions, with several indistinct generations being completed annually. Eggs of carnation tortrix moth are deposited in greenish batches (egg rafts) on the leaves of host plants, the individual eggs overlapping one another like roof tiles. The

FIG 320. Carnation tortrix moth (*Cacoecimorpha pronubana*). (Above left) Males are very active, but females are mainly sedentary. (Above right) Egg rafts occur on the leaves of host plants, and on other surfaces.

FIG 321. Carnation tortrix moth (*Cacoecimorpha pronubana*) larvae are highly polyphagous, and feed on a wide range of plants.

egg rafts also occur on wooden stakes, greenhouse frames and panes of glass. Sexual dimorphism is pronounced, the smaller, darker-coloured, day-flying males (individuals up to 18 mm wingspan) contrasting with the larger, paler and mainly sedentary females (individuals up to 24 mm wingspan). Larvae vary considerably in general appearance, depending on the food plant,[21] but are usually some shade of green (Fig. 321).

True flies

In late summer or autumn, greenhouses and polytunnels are often invaded by common crane flies (*Tipula paludosa*). These may then lay eggs and thereby initiate larval infestations in beds and containers, including seedling trays. As in the case of outdoor crops, the larvae (leatherjackets) attack the roots and other underground parts of host plants. They also emerge at night to feed on leaves in contact with the compost or ground. Where eggs are laid in heated greenhouses, pest development is often accelerated compared with that of outdoor populations, and new adults may well appear as early as the following March or April.

Sciarid flies, also known as fungus gnats, often occur in greenhouses in association with bedding plants, pot plants, cuttings and seedlings. The adults are tiny, long-legged and delicate-looking, and they breed continuously in heated greenhouses so long as conditions remain favourable. Although extremely active, sciarid flies tend to skip over the surface of beds rather than fly. They are especially at home where the soil or compost is damp and has a high organic content. Eggs are usually laid in the growing media, close to host plants. Following egg hatch, the larvae feed on root hairs for three to four weeks, checking growth and sometimes causing plants to wilt, collapse and die. Sciarid larvae (which are translucent-white, narrow-bodied maggots with a distinct, shiny black head) also burrow into corms, roots and stems, usually where plant tissue has been invaded by moulds and other micro-organisms. Fully grown individuals usually pupate in the soil, each in a flimsy silken cocoon, and new adults emerge a week or two later. Sciarid flies are well-known carriers of fungal pathogens such as *Phytophthora* spp. and *Pythium* spp., and they readily spread spores from one place or plant to another. *Bradysia difformis*[22] is the most common sciarid in British greenhouses, although *B. ocellaris*,[23] known as the moss fly, is often associated with orchids. There is also the cucumber sciarid fly (*Pnyxia scabiei*), an unusual species in that the females are wingless and the males either fully or partially winged.[24] Sciarid flies are also associated with mushroom crops (see below).

Glasshouse wing-spot flies (the ephydrids *Scatella stagnalis* and *S. tenuicosta*) are often mistaken for sciarid flies. However, their larvae are not damaging to plants as they merely feed on algae growing in nutrient-film troughs, on propagation benches and elsewhere. Nevertheless, the adults can be a nuisance and might then be classified as pests, especially if they occur as contaminants in harvested lettuces. Hymenopterous parasitoids introduced into greenhouses to control pests have also sometimes become contaminants in plastic-wrapped lettuces, and suffered the same indignity. Other tiny flies causing minor problems in greenhouses include *Bryophaenocladius furcatus*. This is a parthenogenetic non-biting midge whose yellowish-green larvae feed on mosses and lichens. They sometimes damage the roots of ornamental plants.

Various midges inhabit greenhouses, including *Aphidoletes aphidimyza* whose reddish-orange larvae feed within aphid colonies. This predator is frequently released into greenhouses to augment biocontrol by aphidophagous parasitoids. However, there are limits to its use, as it does not readily become established on rockwool-grown crops owing to the poor survival of the midge pupae on artificial flooring. Another predatory midge, *Feltiella acarisuga*,[25] is often introduced to combat spider mites. Midges that are pests include violet leaf midge (*Dasineura affinis*), which can be troublesome under glass as well as outdoors (Chapter 9). It completes at least five generations annually and, if conditions allow, breeding continues throughout the year.

Greenhouse-grown ornamentals, including chrysanthemum and many other Asteraceae, are attacked by chrysanthemum leaf miner (*Chromatomyia syngenesiae*).[26]

FIG 322. Chrysanthemum leaf miner (*Chromatomyia syngenesiae*) has a wide host range and is a generally common pest in greenhouses.

Adult females of this ubiquitous pest form conspicuous more or less oval feeding punctures in the leaves (each up to 1 mm across), the female using her ovipositor to break through the surface and then imbibing sap issuing from the wound. Later, eggs are deposited singly in the underside of leaves. They hatch a few days later. Larvae then mine within the leaves, individuals forming extensive brownish-white galleries just below the upper surface (Fig. 322). Larvae are fully fed in one to two weeks. Pupation then takes place in a brownish puparium, formed at the end of the larval mine. The new adult emerges a week or so later.[27] There are several overlapping generations during the summer, and breeding can continue throughout the year in greenhouses where AYR (all year round) chrysanthemums are produced. Infestations on ornamentals are disfiguring, and also weaken and kill hosts. Although mainly a pest of ornamentals, especially Asteraceae, chrysanthemum leaf miner frequently attacks greenhouse-grown lettuces. Populations in greenhouses are sometimes supplemented during the summer by adults reared on outdoor plants. Wild hosts include groundsel and sow-thistles, upon which there are typically two generations annually.

Tomato leaf miner (*Liriomyza bryoniae*) is another economically important greenhouse pest, found mainly in southern England and the Channel Islands. The lifecycle is similar to that of the previous species, although eggs are deposited in the upper surface of leaves and pupation takes place in the soil rather than in the larval mine. Other dipterous leaf miners to inhabit glassshouses include celery fly (*Euleia heraclei*) and carnation fly (*Delia cardui*). Larvae of the former produce distinctive blotch mines in the leaves of celery plants, whereas those of the latter feed within the leaves of carnations, pinks and sweet williams. Alien leaf miners such as the American serpentine leaf miner (*Liriomyza trifolii*) and the South American leaf miner (*L. huidobrensis*) also sometimes appear in British greenhouses. These are both notifiable pests under Plant Health regulations and are discussed further in Chapter 12.

TABLE 17. Some commercially available biocontrol agents for use in greenhouses.

Biocontrol agent	*Kind of organism*	*Target pests*
Amblyseius cucumeris	Predatory mite – Mesostigmata: Phytoseiidae	Thrips
Anagrus atomus	Parasitoid wasp – Hymenoptera: Mymaridae	Leafhoppers
Aphelinus abdominalis	Parasitoid wasp – Hymenoptera: Aphelinidae	Aphids
Aphidius colemani	Parasitoid wasp – Hymenoptera: Aphidiidae	Aphids
Aphidius ervi	Parasitoid wasp – Hymenoptera: Aphidiidae	Aphids
Aphidoletes aphidimyza	Predatory midge – Diptera: Cecidomyiidae	Aphids
Cryptolaemus montrouzieri	Predatory ladybird – Coleoptera: Coccinellidae	Mealybugs
Dacnusa sibirica	Parasitoid wasp – Hymenoptera: Braconidae	Leaf miners
Diglyphus isaea	Parasitoid wasp – Hymenoptera: Eulophidae	Leaf miners
Encarsia formosa	Parasitoid wasp – Hymenoptera: Aphelinidae	Whiteflies
Feltiella acarisuga	Predatory midge – Diptera: Cecidomyiidae	Spider mites
Hypoaspis miles	Predatory mite – Mesostigmata: Laelapidae	Sciarid flies, thrips
*Lecanicillium longisporum**	Entomopathogenic fungus – anamorphic Hypocreales	Aphids
*Lecanicillium muscarium**	Entomopathogenic fungus – anamorphic Hypocreales	Whiteflies (thrips – incidental)
Leptomastix dactylopii	Parasitoid wasp – Hymenoptera: Encyrtidae	Mealybugs
Leptomastix epona	Parasitoid wasp – Hymenoptera: Encyrtidae	Mealybugs
*Macrolophus caliginosus***	Predatory mirid – Hemiptera: Miridae	Whiteflies, spider mites
Metaphycus helvolus	Parasitoid wasp – Hymenoptera: Encyrtidae	Soft scales
Orius laevigatus	Predatory bug – Hemiptera: Anthocoridae	Thrips
Orius majusculus	Predatory bug – Hemiptera: Anthocoridae	Thrips
Phytoseiulus persimilis	Predatory mite – Mesostigmata: Phytoseiidae	Spider mites
Steinernema carpocapsae	Entomopathogenic nematode – Rhabditida: Steinernematidae	Vine weevils
Steinernema feltiae	Entomopathogenic nematode – Rhabditida: Steinernematidae	Sciarid flies

* Formerly regarded as an isolate of *Lecanicillium lecanii*.

** Now synonymised with *Macrolophus melanotoma*.

Following man's intervention, infestations of chrysanthemum leaf miner and tomato leaf miner in greenhouses are often targeted by the hymenopterous parasitoids *Dacnusa sibirica* and *Diglyphus isaea*, both of which are available from commercial biocontrol suppliers (Table 17). Given the chance, these parasitoids would also attack American serpentine leaf miner and South American leaf miner. However, this is not an option where (as in the case of these two alien pests) rapid eradication of an infestation is required. There are many fundamental differences between the two parasitoids, both of which occur naturally in Britain. For example, *D. sibirica* (a tiny, dark-brown to black wasp with long antennae) is an endoparasitoid which deposits its eggs singly inside first- or second-instar host (leaf miner) larvae. Following egg hatch the young parasitoid larva does not develop further until after the host has pupated. It then passes through two further growth stages before finally pupating, still within the remains of its host. As an ectoparasitoid, *D. isaea* (a tiny, metallic-green wasp with short antennae) attacks second- and third-instar host larvae, paralysing them by using the ovipositor. An egg is then placed within the mine, alongside the comatose host. Following cgg hatch, the parasitoid larva commences to feed, passing through three instars before finally pupating in the host's mine. In *Diglyphus*, but not in *Dacnusa*, host feeding (see Chapter 4, p. 92) by adult females is a prerequisite for egg development.

Mites

In addition to its role as an important pest of outdoor crops, two-spotted spider mite (*Tetranychus urticae*) is notorious for the damage it causes in greenhouses. In such situations – where it is frequently known as the glasshouse red spider mite – breeding occurs throughout the spring and summer on a wide range of vegetable crops, including cucumber, dwarf French bean, sweet pepper and tomato. Ornamentals such as AYR chrysanthemums, roses and many kinds of pot plant are also attacked. At the height of summer, mites often disperse in numbers to outdoor crops, escaping through roof ventilators and other openings, and each then being wafted away by the wind on a fine thread of silk. Breeding in greenhouses continues into September, but declines noticeably once day-length drops below about 14 hours and growth of host plants becomes less vigorous. Eventually, only adult females remain alive, and these wander away from host plants to seek suitable overwintering sites. The winter females, which are characteristically brick-red in colour, are often found in clusters amongst leaf litter or in sheltered situations in or on the greenhouse structure. In particular, the metal supporting brackets of heating pipes are places where such mites congregate.[28] Summer females, by contrast, are typically greenish in appearance, with a pair of dark patches visible through the body wall. A second species, the carmine spider mite (*Tetranychus cinnabarinus*), also occurs in greenhouses, especially on ornamentals such as arum lily, carnation, pink and various cacti (Fig. 323). Vegetable crops such as aubergine and tomato are also susceptible to attack. These mites do not have an obligatory diapausing phase, and they breed continuously so long as conditions remain favourable. Non-diapausing strains of two-spotted spider mite also occur in greenhouses.

FIG 323. Infestations of carmine spider mite (*Tetranychus cinnabarinus*) are sometimes found in greenhouses, especially on carnations, pinks and, as here, on cacti such as rat-tail cactus.

Carmine spider mites are distinctly red in appearance and remain so throughout the year. In addition to direct feeding damage – where affected leaves often appear pallid, specked and blanched – heavy infestations of spider mites result in plants becoming clothed in silk webbing. So-called false spider mites, characterised by their inability to produce webbing, also infest greenhouse ornamentals. *Brevipalpus obovatus*, a typically parthenogenetic and exotic species that has become established in Europe following numerous accidental introductions, is most often encountered.

Microscopic eriophyid mites occasionally infest greenhouse plants. Such pests include chrysanthemum leaf rust mite (*Epitrimerus alinae*) and tomato russet mite (*Aculops lycopersici*), both of which cause leaf bronzing and distortion on their respective hosts. In addition, the tomato erineum mite (*Aceria lycopersici*) inhabits white erinea on the stems and petioles of tomato plants.

Various tarsonemid mites inhabit greenhouses. These include the little-known fern mite (*Hemitarsonemus tepidariorum*), and more familiar species such as the cyclamen mite (*Phytonemus pallidus*). Fern mite was first described in 1903 and long thought to be restricted to England. However, it is now known to occur in Central and North America. Although associated mainly with mother spleenwort, upon which it can be very damaging (causing a condition described as fern mite disease),[29] it has been found on other ferns, including *Polystichum* and *Pteris*. Cyclamen mite is damaging to a wide range of greenhouse ornamentals, especially African violet, begonia, cyclamen and ivy. Heavy infestations result in considerable distortion and stunting, if not death, of hosts. The mites breed continuously under suitable greenhouse conditions and several overlapping generations are completed annually. The subspecies *Phytonemus pallidus fragariae* has already been cited as an important pest of strawberry crops (Chapter 8); the subspecies *P. pallidus asteris* attacks Michaelmas daisies,[30] especially *Aster novi-belgii*. A third tarsonemid species, the broad mite (*Polyphagotarsonemus latus*), ranks as another secretive, light-shy and often overlooked pest of greenhouse plants, with potential to cause considerable harm to a wide range of crops. Significant injury to the fruits of greenhouse-grown aubergines, cucumbers, sweet peppers and tomatoes has been reported,[31] the fruit surfaces becoming extensively crazed by a network of russeted, calloused tissue (Fig. 324). Damage to pot plants (gloxinias, grape ivy, ivy, kangaroo vine and zebra plant are examples) can also be severe. Attacks result in considerable malformation, stunting and discoloration, and can be very persistent. It is not unknown for growers (unaware of the presence of the pest) to believe that resultant distortion and bronzing are features of the particular cultivar or cultivars being raised. Broad mites, in common with other tarsonemids, produce rather large, oval eggs – at about 0.11 mm in length, reaching if not exceeding about half the body length of the egg-laying female.[32] Broad mite eggs are adorned by mushroom-like tubercles. Nowadays, broad mite appears less common than formerly, probably as a result of the activities of predatory mites such as *Amblyseius cucumeris*[33] introduced into greenhouses to combat thrips. Whether the same is true of cyclamen mite is less certain.

FIG 324. Tomatoes infested with broad mite (*Polyphagotarsonemus latus*) are severely damaged and quite unmarketable.

Other mites known to be damaging in greenhouses include cucumber mite (*Tyrophagus neiswanderi*) and grainstack mite (*T. longior*), the latter historically known to growers as French 'fly'. Both are bulbous, translucent-whitish, soft-bodied mites with long bristles, and are close relatives of bulb mites (*Rhizoglyphus* spp.) (Chapter 9). Species of *Tyrophagus* are potentially damaging to cucumber plants grown on straw bales or in traditional manure-based beds. Cucumber mites, in particular, are especially numerous in straw and in horse manure that has yet to decompose. Another compost-loving species, the mould mite (*T. putrescentiae*), is known to cause damage in mushroom houses (see below).

Nowadays, biocontrol of mites in greenhouses is often routine, and the predatory mite *Phytoseiulus persimilis* is frequently employed to keep spider mites in check. Predatory mites are also used against various other greenhouse pests, including sciarid flies and thrips (Table 17). Unlike phytoseiids, such as *Amblyseius cucumeris* and *P. persimilis* (which are plant-inhabiting mites), the predatory mite *Hypoaspis miles* is a soil-dwelling species; both adults and juveniles prey on the larvae of sciarid flies and other invertebrates, including thrips that as fully developed nymphs drop to the ground in order to pupate.

FIG 325. Celery plants suffering from boron deficiency are sometimes attacked by common earwigs (*Forficula auricularia*). Affected tissue is soon contaminated by masses of black frass.

Miscellaneous pests

Earwigs (*Forficula auricularia*) frequently occur in greenhouses, where they cause damage to the foliage and flowers of various plants. Chrysanthemums, Michaelmas daisies, dahlias and the like are often attacked, especially when outdoor-raised plants have been brought into greenhouses in the autumn. Earwigs also graze on the cracked stems of celery plants suffering from boron deficiency, extending the initial sites of tissue injury and contaminating plants with pellets of black frass (Fig. 325).

Chrysanthemum, cucumber and lettuce leaves in contact with the ground are sometimes damaged by garden springtails (*Bourletiella hortensis*), lucerne-fleas (*Sminthurus viridis*) and white blind springtails such as *Onychiurus armatus*. Such attacks most often occur on plants growing in unsterilised soils. Springtails, including *O. armatus* and other species of *Onychiurus*, are also known to target tomato seedlings.[34]

Although of very minor significance, cockroaches such as the American cockroach (*Periplaneta americana*), the common cockroach (*Blatta orientalis*) and the German cockroach (*Blatella germanica*) are sometimes found in heated greenhouses, especially where hygiene is poor. The adults and nymphs emerge at night and then attack seeds and seedlings.

Greenhouses sometimes offer suitable accommodation to invertebrate pests other than insects and mites: millepedes, molluscs, nematodes, symphylids and woodlice are examples.[35] The glasshouse millepede (*Oxidus gracilis*), a pest of tropical origin, is often found in heated structures. It is renowned for causing damage to cucumber plants, the adults and juveniles browsing on the surface of roots and the base of stems. Eggs of this millepede are laid in small batches in the soil. They hatch about ten days later into first-stage juveniles. These possess just three pairs of legs and few body segments. Glasshouse millepedes develop through several juvenile stages, additional legs and body segments being added at each moult until adulthood is reached. This species breeds throughout the year and completes two generations annually. Spotted snake millepede (*Blaniulus guttulatus*) also attacks greenhouse plants, including carnations and chrysanthemums, biting into the stems just below soil level. Attacks also occur on bulbs, corms and other plant material previously damaged by other factors. As for woodlice, the blunt snout pillbug (*Armadillidium nasatum*) (Fig. 326) is often a common but minor pest in heated greenhouses.

FIG 326. Blunt snout pillbugs (*Armadillidium nasatum*) are often numerous in greenhouses, and sometimes cause damage to young plants.

FIG 327. Snails, such as garden snail (*Cornu aspersum*), often enter greenhouses, and are sometimes troublesome pests. They often roost and overwinter in empty pots and other containers.

Slugs and snails often enter greenhouses through gaps in the base or frames. They are also accidentally carried into such structures on or in pots, trays and boxes that have been left standing on the ground outside. The garden slug (*Arion hortensis*) and the keeled slug (*Tandonia budapestensis*) are typically subterranean species, and they mostly damage roots, corms and bulbs. Field slugs (*Deroceras reticulatum*), however, graze on the aerial parts of plants, as do snails such as the garden snail (*Cornu aspersum*)[36] (Fig. 327). Slugs and snails are active mainly at night, and surface-feeding species can then be very destructive to seedlings and young plants; they also destroy the leaves, buds and flowers of older plants.

Among nematode pests, chrysanthemum nematode (*Aphelenchoides ritzemabosi*) feeds and breeds as both an ectoparasite and an endoparasite, attacking the buds and leaves of a range of greenhouse plants. Several thousand nematodes can occur in a single leaf, individuals gaining access to the innermost tissue via the stomata. Affected leaves turn brown and eventually die. Damage tends to commence on the lowermost leaves and gradually progresses upwards as the infestation spreads. Development from egg to adult takes up to two weeks and includes a series of motile juvenile stages. Stem nematode (*Ditylenchus dipsaci*), a polyphagous endoparasitic pest of various outdoor crops, also attacks a range of greenhouse-grown plants. Root-infesting nematodes in greenhouses include cactus cyst nematode (*Heterodera cacti*) on cacti, clover cyst nematode (*Heterodera trifolii*) on carnation, and potato cyst nematodes (*Globodera* spp.) on aubergine and tomato. On occasions, polyphagous pests such as dagger nematodes (*Xiphinema* spp.), root-knot nematodes (*Meloidogyne* spp.) and root-lesion nematodes (*Pratylenchus* spp.) also occur.

Natural biocontrol agents in greenhouses

As outlined throughout this chapter, biocontrol agents (many of which are of non-British origin)[37] are often deliberately released into greenhouses to combat pests. When used correctly, these are capable of stemming the tide of pest outbreaks, reducing if not eliminating the need for standard chemical treatments. Naturally occurring parasitoids, predators and pathogens also enter greenhouses, where they usually play only a minor role in reducing pest numbers. Commonly encountered insects include hymenopterous parasitoids, lacewings, ladybirds and predatory bugs and midges, all of which also attack pests in other cropping situations. Not all find the greenhouse environment congenial or settle there. However, some undoubtedly do so, perhaps then augmenting commercially supplied biocontrol agents.

Insects aside, jumping spiders such as the well-known zebra spider (*Salticus scenicus*) certainly find the warmth of greenhouses to their liking. They are highly agile and competent daytime hunters, stalking and seizing various invertebrates, including leafhoppers and adult tortrix moths. The generally common and relatively large, blackish-brown, orb-web spider *Araneus umbraticus* is also a frequent although often overlooked greenhouse inhabitant. This species has an unusually flattened body, allowing it to squeeze into crevices in the greenhouse structure. The spiders tend to hide during the daytime but emerge at night. They can then be seen as motionless sentinels on their webs, awaiting the arrival of suitable prey.

PESTS OF MUSHROOM CROPS

British and Irish mushroom production is based almost exclusively on the white button mushroom, a close relative of the well-known field mushroom. However, particularly in mainland Europe (as in the famous limestone caves near Saumur in northwest France), various other species are also cultivated. Also abroad, wild edible fungi are often collected commercially, including highly prized and very expensive truffles (especially Piedmont truffles).[38] In recent years, truffle production in Europe has been initiated on specially seeded sites known as truffières or truffle orchards. Typically, young hazel or oak trees are inoculated with truffle spores or mycelium and then planted out in the hope that marketable sporophores (the edible fruiting bodies) will eventually be produced. Speculatively, in 1999, one such site was initiated in Hertfordshire.[39]

Various invertebrates are associated with wild and cultivated mushrooms. However, apart from certain flies, especially phorid flies (whose larvae tunnel within the sporophores), such antagonists are rarely observed by field naturalists. Pests of cultivated mushrooms range from species that cause direct damage (attacking either the fungal mycelium or the developing sporophores) to those that are primarily or merely of nuisance value. The latter may swarm over the spawn and production beds, and are usually (as in the case of bacterium-feeding organisms) an indication of poor compost quality. Mushroom pests known to cause direct damage include various insects, mites and nematodes.[40]

Springtails

Tiny (up to 1.5 mm in long), often bluish-black springtails, collectively known as gunpowder-mites (see Fig. A.1, p. 410), sometimes occur in great swarms in mushroom beds. Here, they feed on the fungal mycelium and also attack the developing sporophores, on which they form characteristically dry pits from which minute channels meander through the stalks and caps. Gunpowder-mites are often cited generically as *Hypogastrura* spp., but records are clouded by misidentifications. In recent years, collembolan (springtail) systematics has also undergone considerable revision.[41] Most records of springtails from British and Irish mushroom beds probably refer to *Ceratophysella denticulata* (often misidentified as *Hypogastrura armata*), *Hypogastrura manubrialis*, *Proisotoma minuta* and *Xenylla welchi*. In the past, the last mentioned has been erroneously described as *X. mucronata*, for which there are no confirmed British or Irish records. As well as being generally abundant in soils and leaf litter, springtails of one species or another also inhabit caves and greenhouses (where mushrooms may also be grown).

True flies

Members of four dipteran families – Cecidomyiidae (cecid midges or gall midges), Phoridae (phorid flies or scuttle flies), Sciaridae (sciarid flies or fungus gnats) and Sphaeroceridae (lesser dung flies) – are frequently associated with cultivated mushrooms. These insects display a range of habits and life histories bordering on the bizarre. Cecid midges demonstrate the extreme, often bypassing an adult stage in their lifecycle and reproducing as larvae – a process known as paedogenesis. Mushroom cecids are minute (about 1 mm long), flimsy-bodied insects, and five mushroom-infesting species are known in Britain: two in the subfamily Porricondylinae (*Henria psalliotae* and *Heteropeza pygmaea*) and three in the subfamily Lestremiinae (*Lestremia cinerea*, *Mycophila barnesi* and *M. speyeri*). Apart from *L. cinerea*, all are paedogenetic. Owing to their minute size, the adults are rarely seen, even though those of some species sometimes occur in mushroom houses in their thousands. Larvae of cecids are characterised by the presence of two dark spots (eye-spots) just behind the minute head. They feed mainly on mycelium in the compost, and their numbers can become astronomical. In the case of *M. speyeri*, larval densities approaching a quarter of a million per square metre of compost are reproductively limiting, leading to population decline and a change from paedogenetic to sexual reproduction. The latter culminates in the production of adults via so-called 'imago larvae' (adult-destined larvae) and pupae.[42] Details of paedogenetic development, which is completed in less than a week, vary from species to species. In *H. pygmaea* the first-instar larva becomes a mother larva, within which several embryos (destined to become daughter larvae) develop. The mother larva then moults into a hemipupa, from which the daughter larvae eventually emerge; this kind of development is termed pupal paedogenesis. In *M. barnesi* and *M. speyeri*, where true larval paedogenesis occurs, a hemipupa is not formed, the daughter larvae emerging directly from the maternal larva. Regarding the evolution of paedogenesis within mushroom-infesting cecids, at the most primitive level *H. psalliotae* passes through three larval instars in both sexual and paedogenetic lifecycles; this compares with just one larval instar in *H. pygmaea*, where the greatest degree of evolutionary degeneration is to be found. *Mycophila* spp., albeit on a different evolutionary line, usually develop through two larval instars (whether breeding paedogenetically or not).[43] In terms of pest status, *H. pygmaea* and *M. speyeri* are the most important and most frequently encountered species, followed by *M. barnesi*. Although it is very common in nature, *L. cinerea* is rarely found in mushroom houses, probably because it is diurnal and requires light in order to lay eggs. *H. psalliotae* was found once, breeding in compost from a mushroom crop in Cornwall, and is our rarest species.[44] This species undergoes pupal paedogenesis and one individual can give rise to as many as 96 offspring.[45]

Phorid flies are dark, somewhat hump-backed insects with (unlike cecid midges and sciarid flies) short, inconspicuous antennae. One species, *Megaselia halterata*, is a potentially important mushroom pest which first came to prominence in 1953. In that year, significant outbreaks occurred on mushroom farms in several parts of England, including Kent, Lancashire and Norfolk, but especially in and around Worthing in West Sussex. Consequently, the pest became known as the Worthing phorid. In the following year, severe damage also occurred on mushroom farms in Surrey and East Sussex, areas that had been unaffected in 1953.[46] Females of this species deposit their eggs in the compost, and the maggot-like larvae subsequently feed on the developing fungal mycelium. Modern production techniques, however, have largely (although not entirely) eliminated the pest, which has now greatly declined in status. Larvae of this phorid do not attack the sporophores, but those of a second species,

FIG 328. Larvae of phorid flies, such as *Megaselia nigra*, occur in both wild and cultivated mushrooms.

M. nigra, typically do so. Adults of *M. nigra* are active from June to December but, as their eggs are deposited only in the light, cultivated crops growing in the dark usually escape attack.[47] In late summer and autumn wild mushrooms are frequently infested, the larvae (Fig. 328) riddling the caps and stalks with tunnels (Fig. 329) which then become invaded by bacterial pathogens. Although nowadays usually regarded as minor pests, phorid flies in mushroom houses can be a nuisance to pickers. They have been implicated as a cause of bronchial asthma[48] and rhinoconjunctivitis.[49]

Sciarid flies (see p. 318) are active in mushroom houses for much of the year, as they often are in greenhouses. Eggs are laid singly or in small batches in the casing material or close to the developing sporophores and hatch a few days later. The translucent-white, black-headed larvae (Fig. 330) (as previously described) then feed within the compost and casing material, and also burrow

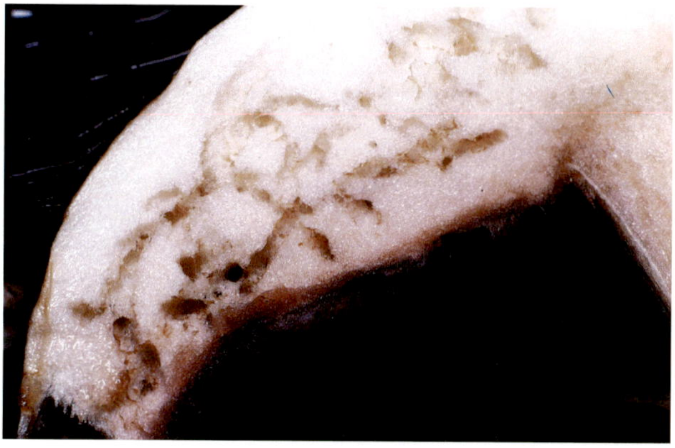

FIG 329. Damage caused to mushroom fruiting bodies by larvae of phorid flies is often extensive.

FIG 330. Larvae of sciarid flies thrive in damp composts, and are often present in greenhouses and mushroom houses.

within the young, developing mushrooms (pinheads); less frequently, they enter the tissue of mature mushrooms, directly affecting the marketability of the crop. Sciarid larvae can also have an adverse effect on yields and the overall size of mushrooms.[50] As in greenhouses, larvae feed for up to a month before finally pupating, each in a silken cocoon. Adults emerge a week or two later. Sciarid flies readily act as vectors of mites and nematodes. They also spread the spores of pathogens such as *Verticillium fungicola*, the cause of a disease known as dry bubble – currently the most important fungal pathogen in mushroom houses. Spores of *V. fungicola* can also be transported by phorid flies. For many years, *Lycoriella castanescens*[51] was the most frequently recorded sciarid on British mushroom farms.[52] Recently, however, the American species *L. ingenua*[53] has also come to the fore. Species of *Bradysia* associated with mushroom growing include *B. brunnipes* and also the newcomer *B. lutaria*.[54]

Lesser dung flies have long been known to be associated with cultivated mushroom crops.[55] The larvae feed in compost, grass cuttings and other rotting vegetable matter (including the dung of herbivorous animals), but are rarely mentioned as pests. In recent years, however, *Pullimosina heteroneura* has become a frequent inhabitant of mushroom houses, and sometimes acts as a vector of pathogenic fungi and mites.[56] With their hump-backed appearance and short antennae, the adults may easily be mistaken for phorids. However, the wing venation is characteristic (see Fig. A.5, p. 417);[57] also, unlike those of phorids, the compound eyes are red.

Mites

Various mites are to be found in mushroom beds. These include the mushroom mite (*Tarsonemus myceliophagus*), a formerly important pest, first recorded in Kent in 1956.[58] Mushroom mites feed primarily on fungal hyphae; they also sever the tissue attaching sporophores to the mycelium, resulting in discoloration at the base of the stalks. When heavy infestations develop, the sporophores themselves become covered in mites and eggs, and they are then more extensively damaged.

Microscopic red pepper mites (*Pygmephorus* spp., especially *P. mesembrinae*),[59] although not considered pests, also attract attention in mushroom beds when they appear in large, pale reddish-brown swarms on the surface of the compost and developing mushrooms. Such mites feed on weed moulds such as *Trichoderma* spp., and their presence is primarily an indication of poor hygiene during compost preparation.

Hairy, soft-bodied, tyroglyphid mites – *Caloglyphus* spp., *Histiostoma* spp. and *Tyrophagus* spp. – frequently occur in mushroom cultures, where they feed on the fungal mycelium and also form small depressions in the developing sporophores. These pits, unlike those excavated by springtails (see above), are typically moist, because the damaged tissue becomes broken down by bacteria. Like grainstack mite (already cited as a pest of greenhouse-grown cucumbers) the mites develop to adulthood through egg, protonymphal and tritonymphal stages. In some tyroglyphids, however, a highly specialised hypopal stage (equivalent to a deutonymph) also arises, typically when feeding conditions are unfavourable or when colonies become overcrowded. The tiny hypopus is specifically adapted as a phoretic (hitchhiking) dispersal stage, being distinctly flattened and short-legged, with a hard body shell and a ventral plate (the sucker plate) which bears several pairs of suckers. By adhering to passing insects, such as sciarid flies, the hypopi are readily transferred from one place to another. Once in a suitable location they dismount and eventually develop (via a tritonymphal stage) into adults. Hypopi are often produced by *Caloglyphus* spp. and *Histiostoma* spp., but rarely if ever in *Tyrophagus* spp.

Mushroom beds are also suitable habitats for predatory mites, including long-legged mushroom mites (*Linopodes* spp.). These fast-moving predators often run over the casing material and developing sporophores, where they feed avidly on other mites (including mushroom mites) and nematodes. Predatory mites in the genus *Parasitus* (e.g. *P. fimetorum*) also abound in mushroom compost. They feed on nematodes and various other invertebrates, including cecid and sciarid larvae.[60] Other named predators in mushroom houses include *Arctoseius cetratus* and *Digamasellus fallax*. Both are phoretic on sciarid flies, the former as adult females and the latter as deutonymphs.[61]

Nematodes

Growing media used in mushroom houses are often ideal substrates for the development of bacteria which aid decomposition. Nematodes that feed on such bacteria can become extremely numerous, forming dense writhing masses which project upwards from the surface of the casing material. Although not directly harmful to the crop, the presence of such nematodes is an indication that growing conditions may be poor. As for pests, two species (*Aphelenchoides composticola* and *Ditylenchus myceliophagus*), known as mushroom spawn nematodes, feed on fungal mycelia. When present in mushroom beds they can have an adverse effect on cropping.[62] Development follows that of their outdoor counterparts, individuals passing to adulthood through egg and several juvenile stages. The lifecycle of *A. composticola* is completed in just over a week at 23°C and in ten days at 13°C,[63] allowing particularly rapid increase in populations in mushroom beds. *D. myceliophagus*, however, develops much more slowly, the complete lifecycle at these temperatures taking 18 and 42 days, respectively.[64] When populations in mushroom houses explode, the nematodes clump together on the beds or elsewhere, and in spite of the small size of individuals (*A. composticola*, c. 0.5 mm long; *D. myceliophagus*, c. 1 mm long) they are then readily visible. On occasions, nematode-trapping fungi (*Arthrobusta* spp.)[65] form grey patches on the surface of mushroom beds in the immediate vicinity of nematode-infested mushroom mycelium.

CHAPTER 11

Pests of Miscellaneous Crops

A REVIEW OF THE NATURAL history of plant pests would be incomplete without considering those associated with specialist crops that have so far escaped attention. Novel or so-called 'alternative' arable crops also deserve to be mentioned. Together, such crops range from long-established ones, some of which have in today's market conditions largely if not entirely ceased to be produced in Britain, to new introductions yet to be exploited commercially on a field scale.

ARABLE CROPS

Flax and linseed

Flax and linseed crops have been cultivated for many years,[1] the former for fibre (notably in Ireland) and the latter as a source of oil and protein. In 1996, winter as opposed to spring linseed was introduced to British farms, increasing the potential of linseed as a drought-resistant arable break crop. Flax and linseed crops are often invaded by polyphagous plant bugs, including common green capsid (*Lygocoris pabulinus*), European tarnished plant bug (*Lygus rugulipennis*) and potato capsid (*Closterotomus norvegicus*)[2], and these are most numerous around the field margins, especially in the vicinity of hedges.[3] The flowering crops are also very attractive to thrips, with at least 18 species known to occur on flax alone.[4] Field thrips (*Thrips angusticeps*) and banded or banded-wing thrips (*Aeolothrips intermedius*[5] and *A. tenuicornis*) are the most frequently encountered species, and they are particularly numerous on linseed crops growing on light, stony soil. Field thrips can be very damaging, but species of *Aeolothrips* probably act mainly as predators (see Chapter 6).

Flea beetles have long been known as pests of flax crops, and since the early 1990s both the flax flea beetle (*Longitarsus parvulus*) and the large flax flea beetle (*Aphthona euphorbiae*) have also become of considerable significance on linseed. In Ireland, flax flea beetle holds sway, and is said to prefer cultivated flax to any other food plant.[6] Adults overwinter in woody and other sheltered areas, and emerge in the spring. In warm weather they migrate in numbers to spring-sown crops, arriving at about the time of germination and seedling emergence. The beetles then feed on the developing leaves, cotyledons and hypocotyls, damage sometimes resulting in the death of plants or even complete crop failure. As long ago as 1838 Robert Patterson of Belfast[7] announced that:

> *As linen is the staple manufacture of this part of the country, and gives employment in various departments to many thousand persons, the flax crop is naturally regarded as one of very high importance; yet here a diminutive insect had the hardihood to interfere, and, despite of all the efforts of man, nearly destroyed in many parts of the county Down, in the summer of 1827, the entire crop of flax. The minute assailant was a little jumping beetle (*Haltica parvula*), resembling that called the turnip-fly, but much smaller.*

Eggs of flax flea beetles are laid in the soil and hatch two or more weeks later. Larvae then feed on the roots, becoming fully grown and pupating about a month later. New adults appear after a further two weeks or so, usually in August, the beetles feeding briefly on a range of plants before eventually entering hibernation. In the 1990s, flax flea beetle was considered a 'nationally scarce' British insect.[8] However, it no longer deserves such status, the recent boost in populations no doubt being a direct result of the increased area of linseed grown in England and Wales over the past two decades.

A few minor pests are also associated with flax and linseed crops. These include leaf miners such as *Phytomyza horticola* and the polyphagous larvae of flax tortrix moth (*Cnephasia asseclana*) and *C. longana*. One or two opportunist feeders, more frequently associated with weeds, are also recorded on linseed. The lime-speck pug moth (*Eupithecia centaureata*), whose larvae feed on the flowers of plants such as knapweed, ragwort and scabious, is an example.[9]

Novel crops

Relatively little is known about the pests of novel industrial oil and fibre crops growing under British conditions, and comments about them are often largely speculative. In springtime, brassicaceous oilseed crops such as Abyssinian mustard[10] and Ethiopian mustard certainly attract pollen beetles (*Meligethes aeneus*).

FIG 331. Essig's lupin aphid (*Macrosiphum albifrons*) is a damaging pest of lupins. It is also a virus vector.

However, compared with oilseed rape, such crops are not necessarily ideal hosts. Abyssinian mustard, for example, is less favoured for egg-laying.[11] Tolerance or resistance to turnip flea beetles (e.g. *Phyllotreta cruciferae*) is also known to occur, as has been demonstrated in the case of Ethiopian mustard and gold-of-pleasure.[12, 13]

Non-brassicaceous oilseed crops such as borage, evening primrose, lupin, safflower and sunflower appear largely pest free, although they may well invite the attention of aphids and thrips. Borage plants, for example, host black bean aphid (*Aphis fabae*) plus a few other species, and safflower is a known host of peach/potato aphid (*Myzus persicae*) and potato aphid (*Macrosiphum euphorbiae*).[14] Furthermore, field-grown lupins can support Essig's lupin aphid (*Macrosiphum albifrons*) (Fig. 331) – a pest

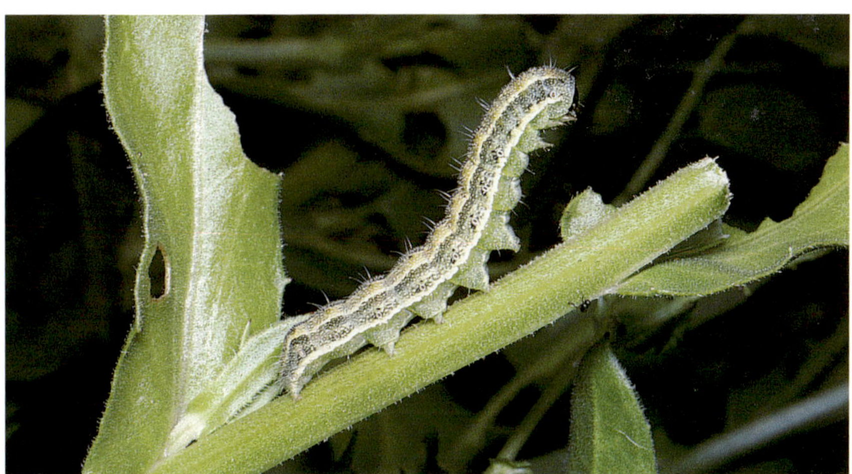

FIG 332. Bordered straw moth (*Heliothis peltigera*), an uncommon migrant to Britain, breeds on pot marigold.

that not only causes direct damage but also carries and transmits bean yellow mosaic virus (BYMV). Pot marigold (potentially, yet another oilseed crop) is attacked by several pests. Black bean aphid, potato aphid, bordered straw moth (*Heliothis peltigera*) (Fig. 332), large yellow underwing moth (*Noctua pronuba*), turnip moth (*Agrotis segetum*) and the polyphagous chrysanthemum leaf miner (*Chromatomyia syngenesiae*)[15] are examples, all of which damage pot marigold plants growing as ornamentals;[16] given the opportunity at least some of them may find field crops to their liking.

Pest infestations on some host plants (novel or otherwise) are largely if not entirely restricted to the establishment phase – i.e. to the initial stages of growth from seed to seedling. Large striped flea beetle (*Phyllotreta nemorum*), for example, damages the seedlings of otherwise pest-free crops such as hemp. This novel crop is currently being grown on a small scale in Britain as a source of fibre.[17] Stinging nettles also have potential to be grown as fibre crops, and they have been trialled as such in experimental plots. In the wild, nettles are attacked by many phytophagous insects,[18] including nettle aphid (*Microlophium carnosum*), leafhoppers and various other plant bugs. Certain butterflies and moths are also associated with nettles: mother of pearl moth (*Pleuroptya ruralis*),[19] peacock butterfly (*Inachis io*), small magpie moth (*Eurrhypara hortulata*) and small tortoiseshell butterfly (*Aglais urticae*) are examples. However, foliage-infesting insects such as these are most unlikely to become genuinely harmful to cultivated nettles. On the contrary, particularly in the case of butterflies, such insects are welcome elements of the British fauna, both in town and country. Many other insects are also associated with wild nettles.[20]

Finally, black bean aphid is known to attack quinoa (a grain crop of Andean origin), as are the European tarnished plant bug and larvae of tortrix moths (e.g. *Cnephasia* spp.). In Denmark, the cloudy tortoise beetle (*Cassida nebulosa*) and the moth *Scrobipalpa atriplicella* have also been recorded on quinoa.[21] Neither of these insects is of pest status in Britain, although the former has sometimes been found on sugar beet plants.

BASKET WILLOWS

Today, basket-willow production is a highly localised and minor industry, former beds in various wetland areas of Britain (including Lancashire, the Severn valley, the Thames valley and parts of East Anglia) having long since been lost. Basket-willow beds are still to be found in the Somerset levels, although today little more than 100 ha remain. Almond willow and osier are the dominant species in

FIG 333. Large willow aphid (*Tuberolachnus salignus*) is one of the world's largest aphids. Note the cone-like siphunculi, typical of the subfamily Lachninae, and the large tubercle arising from the fourth abdominal segment.

cultivation, dominated by the almond willow cultivar Black Maul. In the past, purple willow was also grown, primarily on sandy soils in the Ribble valley, Lancashire. On a small scale, willows are raised in various parts of the country for garden and landscape uses (including erosion control); they are also widely planted as an on-farm biomass crop.

Traditional wetland willow beds form a unique wildlife habitat, and the willows themselves are an important, and often essential, food source for a broad range of creatures. Some of these feed on the foliage, and others invade the canes and stools. Aphids, for example, are frequent inhabitants of willow beds, colonies of one species or another regularly inhabiting the young shoots, leaves and canes (Table 18). The aphid assemblage includes the large willow aphid (*Tuberolachnus salignus*)[22] (Fig. 333). At over 5 mm in length, this is amongst the world's largest aphids, but it falls well short of species such as the giant fir aphid (*Cinara confinis*) and the giant oak aphid (*Stomaphis quercus*). Although aphids are not considered of major significance in basket-willow beds, large willow aphid and, to a lesser extent, black willow aphid (*Pterocomma salicis*) are potentially of some importance as they are known to have a detrimental qualitative and quantitative effect on the yield of host plants.[23]

TABLE **18.** Examples of aphids associated with basket willows.

Species	*Remarks*
Subfamily APHIDINAE	
Black willow aphid (*Pterocomma salicis*)	On young shoots, especially of osier
Small willow aphid (*Aphis farinosa*)	On young shoots
Willow/carrot aphid (*Cavariella aegopodii*)	On young shoots, especially of almond willow
Subfamily CHAITOPHORINAE	
Osier leaf aphid (*Chaitophorus beuthami*)	On foliage
Subfamily LACHNINAE	
Large willow aphid (*Tuberolachnus salignus*)	On bark of shoots and stems

Colonies of spider mites (usually *Schizotetranychus schizopus*) are sometimes found on narrow-leaved willows. Infested foliage, when viewed from above, appears extensively mottled with yellow. The mites inhabit the underside of the leaves, close to the midrib, and sometimes produce an amazing abundance of webbing. In extreme cases, webs extend way beyond the foliage to engulf the adjacent shoots and developing canes. On willow trees, the silk sometimes cloaks entire trunks and branches.[24]

Various leaf-browsing moth larvae frequent basket-willow beds. Examples include those of cream-bordered green pea moth (*Earias clorana*) (Fig. 334), puss moth (*Cerura vinula*) (Fig. 335) and the communal web-inhabiting species *Yponomeuta rorrella*. None, however, can be considered of real significance. The

FIG **334.** Cream-bordered green pea moth (*Earias clorana*) larvae sometimes feed on the foliage of basket willows.

FIG 335. Puss moth (*Cerura vinula*) larvae are amongst the largest insects to be found in willow beds, but are of little or no importance as pests.

same is true of defoliating sawfly larvae, such as those of the lesser willow sawfly (*Nematus pavidus*) (Fig. 336). Leaf beetles are of greater importance and they often occur in abundance on willows (see under biomass crops, below). Heavy infestations lead to extensive defoliation; buds and young shoots are also damaged.

Leaf-mining insects, such the moths *Phyllonorycter salicicolella* and *P. viminiella* and the sawfly *Heterarthrus microcephalus*, the larvae of which form blotch mines,

FIG 336. Lesser willow sawfly (*Nematus pavidus*) larvae feed gregariously and cause extensive defoliation.

FIG 337. Willow weevil (*Cryptorhynchus lapathi*) is one of the most damaging pests in basket willow beds.

may also be encountered in basket-willow beds. However, they are not important antagonists. Nor is the purely sap-imbibing leaf miner *Phyllocnistis saligna*, which forms inconspicuous, serpentine, silvery galleries; this species breeds mainly on purple willow rather than almond willow or osier. Old records exist of basket willows being invaded by the agromyzid fly *Phytobia cambii*. The very long and thin, nematode-like larvae mine within the stems, causing noticeable flecking of affected tissue. Signs of this pest are most likely to be found at harvest time, and damaged wands are rendered unsuitable for basket-making.[25]

The willow weevil (*Cryptorhynchus lapathi*) (Fig. 337) is a significant pest of basket-willows. It is also associated with alder and poplar. In northern Europe, including Britain, the lifecycle of this weevil extends over two years. Adults occur in the late spring, from mid-May onwards, emerging after a period of hibernation. They hide by day at the base of plants and are rarely seen. At night, however, they crawl up the canes to feed on the new shoots, the tips of which often keel over and eventually turn black. The robust-bodied, somewhat bulky weevils are sluggish, and do not appear to fly, even though they have fully developed wings.[26] Eggs are laid in the rods (canes) and stools (coppiced stumps) from late May or early June to early autumn and hatch about three weeks later. The larvae (known as willow and poplar borers) feed slowly and eventually hibernate, typically whilst still in their first instar. They resume feeding in the following spring, forming long tunnels in the canes and stools. Damaged rods are rendered useless for basket-making. Larvae are usually fully grown in July. They then pupate, each having excavated a bulbous pupal cell at the end of its feeding gallery. The adult stage is reached after about two weeks. However, the weevils do not emerge but remain *in situ* until the following year. In the Netherlands[27] the two-year lifecycle is synchronised such that adults tend to

FIG 338. Red-tipped clearwing moth (*Synanthedon formicaeformis*) often breeds in basket willow beds.

occur only in even years and larvae in odd years. Such synchrony, however, has not been observed in Britain.[28]

Wood-boring larvae of the red-tipped clearwing moth (*Synanthedon formicaeformis*) also feed within willow stools, particularly osier, but they tunnel more superficially than willow weevil larvae and are far less damaging. The diurnal, wasp-like adults (Fig. 338) occur mainly in June and July, and are sometimes to be seen in basket-willow beds, especially when foraging for nectar on flowering weeds or basking in sunshine. They are a welcome sight for naturalists rather than true pests.

Colourful leaf-edge galls caused by the osier leaf-folding midge (*Rabdophaga marginemtorquens*)[29] (Fig. 339) often attract attention on narrow-leaved willows, including osier. These galls, arranged as a continuous series along a leaf margin, develop into yellowish-green, reddish-tinged swellings, each enclosing a small,

FIG 339. Narrow-leaved willows are sometimes infested by osier leaf-folding midge (*Rabdophaga marginemtorquens*). Typically, each leaf-edge swelling (gall) encloses a tiny orange-coloured larva.

FIG 340. Galls initiated by the mite *Aculus truncatus* are reminiscent of those inhabited by osier leaf-folding midge larvae, but occur on the leaves of purple willow.

orange-coloured larva – similar-looking galls are formed by the gall mite *Aculus truncatus*, but these occur only on purple willow (Fig. 340). Fully fed midge larvae overwinter in the soil and pupate in the spring, there being just one generation annually. Although seemingly innocuous, heavy infestations on young plants are considered damaging.[30] Various other gall midges breed on willows, including the willow button-top midge (*Rabdophaga heterobia*)[31] whose larvae feed gregariously in galled terminal and lateral buds, preventing shoot development (Fig. 341). There are two generations annually and pupation occurs within the galls, the dead remains of which persist on host plants long after leaf fall. This pest occurs mainly on almond willow.

Gall-inhabiting larvae of sawflies (*Pontania* spp.) often occur in abundance on the leaves of willows. The two species most often encountered in basket-willow beds are *P. triandrae* (Fig. 342) on almond willow and willow pea-gall sawfly (*P. viminalis*) on purple willow. The latter insect also attacks osiers. Adults of *P. triandrae* appear in May and deposit

FIG 341. Willow button-top midge (*Rabdophaga heterobia*) prevents the development of terminal shoots, resulting in the production of unwanted laterals.

FIG 342. The sawfly *Pontania triandrae* infests almond willow, and is often common in basket willow beds.

eggs in the leaf buds of host plants. Subsequently, pale, reddish-tinged, hollow, bean-like galls develop on the expanded leaves, each protruding from the upper and lower surfaces of the leaf blade and enclosing a single larva. When fully grown the larvae vacate their galls. They then pupate in cocoons spun in the ground or in sheltered situations elsewhere. A second generation of adults emerges in July. If galls are massed on the uppermost leaves of tall canes, their combined weight can cause plants to become bent, reducing the quality and, hence, value of the harvested rods. Galls of willow pea-gall sawfly are rounded, pinkish to orange-red in appearance, and usually present in only small numbers. This is a far less damaging species.

BIOMASS CROPS

Miscanthus

Miscanthus is a non-indigenous, bamboo-like grass, which has been grown in the UK since the 1990s, either as *Miscanthus sinensis* or as the hybrid *M.* × *giganteus*. The crop is perennial and woody, and often attains a height of three to four metres – hence the alternative common name elephant grass. Although it is largely pest-free in Britain, larvae of common rustic moth (*Mesapamea secalis*) have been found feeding in the young shoots of recent plantings.[32] Also, cereal leaf aphid (*Rhopalosiphum maidis*) can invade the crop during the summer months. The latter species has been cited as a potential vector of barley yellow dwarf virus (BYDV) on miscanthus.[33] However, miscanthus is not considered a suitable host for bird-cherry/oat aphid (*R. padi*), the most important vector of BYDV in the UK.[34]

Poplars and willows

In recent years, short-rotation coppice (SRC) poplars and willows have been grown increasingly as perennial biomass crops, and this has served greatly to increase on-farm biodiversity, not only of invertebrates but also of other wildlife such as birds.[35] It would be superfluous here to delve into details, as so many creatures utilise such plants and habitats. However, mention should be made of a few SRC inhabitants that are classified as pests. Infestations of leaf beetles, for example, can result in significant yield losses,[36] and on clones of some willow cultivars they can cause extensive damage.[37] Several species are involved, of which the blue osier leaf beetle (*Phratora vulgatissima*)[38] and to a lesser extent the brassy willow leaf beetle (*P. vitellinae*)[39] and the brown willow leaf beetle (*Galerucella lineola*) (Fig. 343) are most important. Damage is caused not only by the adult beetles but also by their gregarious, leaf-feeding larvae that have voracious, seemingly insatiable, appetites. Blue osier leaf beetles and brown willow leaf beetles are especially numerous on willows low in phenol glucosides,[40] whereas the reverse is true in the case of brassy willow leaf beetles.[41] Some willow genotypes seem to be less susceptible to beetle attack than others,[42] indicating that plant breeding has a role in combating such pests. The use of high-yielding cultivars to overcome losses from defoliating pests such as leaf beetles has also

FIG 343. Brown willow leaf beetle (*Galerucella lineola*) is one of many species to attack willows.

FIG 344. Poplar sawfly (*Trichiocampus viminalis*) larvae typically feed gregariously.

been advocated.[43] Foliage damage on poplars and willows is also caused by poplar flea beetles (*Crepidodera aurea*) and willow flea beetles (*C. aurata*).[44]

As for defoliating caterpillars, poplars and/or willows are ideal food plants for species such as gregarious poplar sawfly (*Nematus melanaspis*), lesser willow sawfly, poplar sawfly (*Trichiocampus viminalis*) (Fig. 344) and willow sawfly (*N. salicis*). These pests all have gregarious larvae and can be damaging. Other insects, not necessarily of particular significance but likely to attract attention on account of their large size or colourful appearance, include the larvae of buff-tip moth (*Phalera bucephala*), poplar hawk moth (*Laothoe populi*), puss moth and white satin moth (*Leucoma salicis*).

Finally, aphids (notably the large willow aphid and, to a lesser extent, the black willow aphid) deserve a passing mention as pests of SRC willows since, particularly under dry conditions, infestations can lead to the death of stools.

CHRISTMAS TREES

On-farm production of Christmas trees centres around Norway spruce, silver firs (especially Caucasian fir) and to a lesser extent pine trees. All of these are attractive food sources for a wide range of pests, including many conifer-inhabiting specialists, of which aphids (including lachnids), adelgids, sawflies and mites are of greatest importance.[45] Polyphagous soil inhabitants, notably chafer grubs and vine weevil (*Otiorhynchus sulcatus*) larvae, also cause problems (the latter primarily attacking seedlings in seedbeds), as might other generalist antagonists such as clay-coloured weevil (*O. singularis*), large pine weevil (*Hylobius abietis*) (Fig. 345) and leatherjackets.

FIG **345.** Large pine weevil (*Hylobius abietis*) is a minor pest in Christmas tree plantations.

Young spruce trees are commonly invaded by green spruce aphid (*Elatobium abietinum*). This important pest can cause extensive discoloration (Fig. 346) and eventual loss of needles (notably from autumn through to late spring), and is feared by many a Christmas tree grower. Severe attacks in the year of sale have resulted in entire crops being rendered useless. Symptoms of attack are similar to those induced by conifer spinning mite (*Oligonychus ununguis*). However, mite-damaged shoots (even in the subsequent absence of the mites) can be

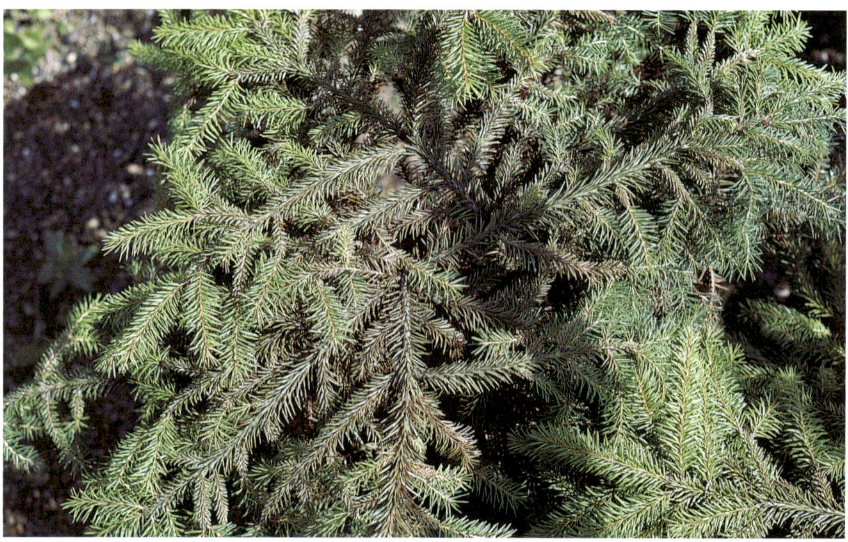

FIG **346.** Green spruce aphid (*Elatobium abietinum*) is capable of causing extensive damage to Christmas trees.

distinguished by the presence of silken webbing and empty mite egg shells. Conifer spinning mite is a serious problem on Norway spruce trees, especially in southern and eastern England. Infestations are also, occasionally, found on pine trees.

Spruces in Christmas tree plantations are frequently infested by brown spruce aphids (*Cinara pilicornis*).[46] These insects inhabit the shoots and excrete vast quantities of honeydew upon which black sooty moulds eventually develop. Related species of *Cinara* infest various other conifers, including those cultivated as ornamentals (Chapter 9). Such aphids are often attended by ants which milk them for honeydew (effectively treating them as aphid 'cows'); where aphids are clustered on the bark, ants frequently protect them by constructing earthen shelters over the colonies. Dense colonies of the related grey pine-needle aphid (*Schizolachnnus pineti*) often occur on the needles of pine trees. These aphids also excrete vast quantities of sticky honeydew, amongst which debris (such as wind-borne seeds of thistles and other weeds) often accumulates. Heavy infestations of this pest render pine Christmas trees unmarketable.[47]

Norway spruce trees are often damaged by the spruce pineapple-gall adelges (*Adelges abietis*),[48] a species that breeds within distinctive pineapple-like swellings on the shoots. Other adelgids associated with Christmas trees include the silver fir migratory adelges (*A. nordmanniana*)[49] and the Scots pine adelges (*Pineus pini*).[50] The former causes considerable distortion of needles and dieback of shoots. Adelgids, which differ from true aphids by the total absence of siphunculi and by their characteristically very short antennae, have complex life histories involving a range of distinctive morphs and reproductive strategies.[51] In common with true aphids, some adelgids are anholocyclic (breeding entirely parthenogenetically throughout the growing season) and others are holocyclic (interrupting their parthenogenetic lifestyle with a sexual phase involving both males and females). Adelgids may also be autoecious or heteroecious. Autoecious species are restricted to just one kind of host, as in the case of the spruce pineapple-gall adelges on silver fir trees; heteroecious species exhibit an annual alternation between a primary and a secondary host, as in the case of the silver fir migratory adegles which alternates between silver fir trees and oriental spruce.

Christmas trees are also hosts of various root-infesting aphids, in particular spruce root aphids (*Pachypappa tremulae* and *P. vesicalis*); the colonies (accompanied by flocculent masses of white wax) are most often seen when young plants are lifted or when the root balls of container-grown nursery plants are examined.

Young pine trees, including those being raised as Christmas trees, are sometimes attacked by pine shoot moth (*Rhyacionia buoliana*), the larvae of which cause characteristic damage on the developing shoots (see Chapter 9, p. 299).

FIG 347. Fox-coloured sawfly (*Neodiprion sertifer*) is one of several sawflies whose larvae feed on young pine trees, including those in Christmas tree plantations.

Defoliating sawfly larvae are also of importance. These include those of the fox-coloured sawfly (*Neodiprion sertifer*) (Fig. 347), a single-brooded species, and the pine sawfly (*Diprion pini*), a mainly, but not entirely, double-brooded species. Larvae of both species feed from May to July; second-brood larvae of the latter species are active from August to the beginning of October. The colourful larva of *D. similis*, an introduced species from North America, may also be found on young pine trees, at least in southern England. The widely distributed gregarious spruce sawfly (*Pristiphora abietina*) also damages Christmas trees, especially those being raised in the vicinity of established spruce plantations. The same is true of spruce bell moth (*Epinotia tedella*), whose larvae initially mine and later feed openly upon the needles of spruce trees. Damage caused by large pine weevils is also most prevalent in plantations sited close to coniferous woodlands, especially if the latter include stands of recently felled trees. The adult weevils typically feed on the bark just above the root collar and are especially damaging to small transplants.

HERBS

Lavender, rosemary and many other herbs are frequently decorated with blobs of spittle (cuckoo-spit), within which nymphs of the common froghopper (*Philaenus spumarius*) develop (Fig. 348). Each protective envelope is formed when the nymph injects air into a watery liquid expelled from the anus, the air being forced by abdominal contractions along a canal-like groove on the underside of the body. From June onwards, after five sedentary nymphal instars, the highly active adult stage is reached. Eggs, however, are not deposited until September. These overwinter and hatch in the spring.

FIG 348. Common froghopper (*Philaenus spumarius*) nymphs develop within a protective mass of spittle. They occur on a wide range of plants, and are often abundant on herbaceous plants, including lavender, rosemary and other herbs.

Other sap-feeding inhabitants of cultivated herbs include the chrysanthemum leafhopper (*Eupteryx melissae*) (Fig. 349), also widely known as the sage leafhopper. This pest is often abundant on herbs such as lemon balm, mint, sage and thyme. Adults and nymphs quickly disfigure the foliage of their hosts, the leaves becoming pale-speckled and otherwise discoloured (Fig. 350). Cast nymphal skins also contaminate the underside of leaves – often a tell-tale sign of

FIG 349. Chrysanthemum leafhopper (*Eupteryx melissae*) is an important pest of herbs and various other plants.

FIG 350. Damage to sage and other herbs invaded by chrysanthemum leafhopper (*Eupteryx melissae*) is often severe.

leafhopper infestations. Damaged plants are unsightly and lack vigour; they are also unmarketable. Mint plants sometimes also host colonies of mint aphid (*Ovatus crataegarius*), a small heteroecious species that usually overwinters in the egg stage on hawthorn. The aphid is of little significance commercially, except perhaps on protected plants, but can be a nuisance in kitchen gardens. Other aphids likely to be found on herbs include hawthorn/parsley aphid (*Dysaphis apiifolia* ssp. *petroselini*) and willow/carrot aphid (*Cavariella aegopodii*) on parsley (both particularly damaging pests of protected parsley crops), and peach/potato aphid on basil. Glasshouse & potato aphid (*Aulacorthum solani*) and melon & cotton aphid (*Aphis gossypii*) sometimes attack protected herbs, the former especially sage and the latter mainly basil, coriander, lemon-scented verbena and parsley.

Mint moth (*Pyrausta aurata*) is a minor pest of cultivated mint, out of doors and under protection. The attractive, purple and yellow-marked adults (Fig. 351) are active in sunshine during May and June, with members of a second generation appearing in the summer. First-brood larvae feed amongst spun leaves in June and July, producing an abundance of black frass, and eventually pupate in silken cocoons formed on the food plant. Second-brood larvae are present during the autumn, fully fed individuals overwintering in silken cocoons and pupating in the spring. The larvae (Fig. 352), which are very active if disturbed, also feed on marjoram, sage and thyme.

FIG 351. Mint moth (*Pyrausta aurata*) is a common pest of mint. Both outdoor and protected crops are attacked.

FIG 352. Mint moth larvae feed amongst spun leaves, and are very active when disturbed.

Herbs are also invaded by leaf beetles. Mint leaf beetle (*Chrysolina menthastri*), for example, although most often associated with wild water mint, is sometimes found on cultivated plants. The metallic, golden-green adults (Fig. 353) and blackish-bodied larvae cause noticeable defoliation. However, attacks are usually insignificant unless the pest is abundant. In recent years, rosemary plants in southern England have been attacked by an exotic, southern European species, the rosemary beetle (*C. americana*)[52] (Fig. 354). This insect, first found breeding here in 1994,[53] has been causing considerable concern amongst gardeners. The pest also breeds on other Lamiaceae, including lavender, sage and thyme. Although it is now well established in Britain,[54] fears that lavender crops in Norfolk or elsewhere in England may be at risk are probably unfounded. Certainly, the pest does not appear to be a significant problem on cultivated rosemary or lavender crops in southern Europe or elsewhere in its natural range.[55]

FIG 353. Mint leaf beetle (*Chrysolina menthastri*) is a minor pest of cultivated mint.

FIG 354. Rosemary beetle (*Chrysolina americana*) has quickly established itself in Britain, following its discovery here as a breeding species in the 1990s.

HOPS

Hop production in Britain was formerly of considerable significance, at its height in the nineteenth century exceeding 29,000 ha,[56] concentrated mainly in Hereford and Worcester, and extending from Hampshire, through Sussex into Kent. By the end of the twentieth century, however, the area in production had shrunk to well below 3,000 ha. Today, hop gardens are still to be found in southeast England (mainly in Kent) and the West Midlands, with a few isolated pockets persisting elsewhere, as in Alton, Hampshire. Production systems are also changing, with a move away from traditional, labour-intensive high poles and wire-work (reaching up to 6 m) in favour of dwarf or hedgerow cultivars that are grown as continuous hedgerows, supported to half this height by strings or netting. Mechanical harvesting has also replaced the gangs of hop pickers that would arrive annually from the poorer parts of nearby cities. There have also been various changes in the status of hop pests; some considered of significance 50 or so years ago are now rarely, if ever, encountered.

As in the past, damson/hop aphid (*Phorodon humuli*) features as the most important pest of hops, and is widely regarded as a major limiting factor to crop production. The aphid is also a vector of viruses, including hop mosaic virus (HoMV). Damson/hop aphid, which overwinters in the egg stage on blackthorn and various other wild and cultivated species of *Prunus*, arrives on hops from late May or early June onwards. The immigration from primary (winter) hosts is long-lasting, and in some years persists into early August or even later. Colonies on hop plants soon develop on the tips of the bines, and also appear on the lateral growth, eventually spreading onto the developing cones. Considerable damage can result; growth is disrupted, vigour is reduced and plants are contaminated by sticky honeydew and sooty moulds. Damson/hop aphid has gained notoriety for its ability to develop resistance to pesticides, and the resulting unreliability of chemical treatments has been a thorn in the side of many a hop grower. Also, owing to the dense summer growth of traditional (tall) hop plants, spraying against the pest after mid-July can be difficult. Treatment of dwarf hops, however, poses less of a problem. Predators such as earwigs, anthocorid bugs and ladybirds often play a part in reducing damson/hop aphid numbers.[57] Accordingly, the activities of such predators (preceded by the application of a translocatable aphicide to the stem bases in advance of aphid immigration) can be an effective pest management strategy. However, natural enemies alone or in combination with a stem-base treatment cannot be guaranteed to provide adequate control. This is especially so in hot, dry summer weather that encourages aphid build-up and limits uptake of soil-applied pesticides. Usefully, following on from experimental studies,[58] a new aphid-resistant dwarf cultivar (cv. Boadicea) – hailed as a world first – is now available to twenty-first-century hop growers.

Various other sap-feeding insect pests occur in hop gardens. These include thrips, froghoppers, leafhoppers and mirids (capsids). Well-known species include hop capsid (*Closterotomus fulvomaculatus*), red and black froghopper (*Cercopis vulnerata*), hop leafhopper (*Evacanthus interruptus*), loganberry leafhopper (*Ribautiana tenerrima*) and rose leafhopper (*Edwardsiana rosae*). Compared with aphids, however, these are merely bit players.

Hop bines are invaded by a wide range of lepidopterous pests, including defoliators such as angle-shades moth (*Phlogophora meticulosa*), cabbage moth (*Mamestra brassicae*), clouded drab moth (*Orthosia incerta*), knotgrass moth

FIG 355. In hop gardens, pale tussock moth (*Calliteara pudibunda*) larvae are known as hop-dogs.

(*Acronicta rumicis*), pale tussock moth (*Calliteara pudibunda*), peppered moth (*Biston betularia*), powdered quaker moth (*O. gracilis*), vapourer moth (*Orgyia antiqua*) and silver Y moth (*Autographa gamma*). There are also defoliating leaf-rollers such as fruit tree tortrix moth (*Archips podana*), rose tortrix moth (*A. rosana*), *Cnephasia longana*, straw-coloured tortrix moth (*Clepsis spectrana*) and summer fruit tortrix moth (*Adoxophyes orana*). However, none of these can be considered a major pest. Nevertheless, the hairy larvae of pale tussock moth (Fig. 355) and the pencil-like larvae of peppered moth (Fig. 356) are known locally in hop-growing circles as hop-dogs and hop-cats, respectively, suggesting a long-standing association with the crop.[59] In the past, larvae of the comma butterfly (*Polygonia c-album*), in the nineteenth century a common inhabitant of English hop gardens,[60] were also described as hop-cats. Comma butterflies, however, no longer warrant pest status in hop gardens. This insect nowadays breeds mainly on nettles and is a welcome

FIG 356. In hop gardens, peppered moth (*Biston betularia*) larvae are known as hop-cats.

FIG 357. (Above left) Currant pug moth (*Eupithecia assimilata*) adults and (above right) larvae are frequent inhabitants of hop gardens.

sight in the countryside and elsewhere. Among present-day foliage-browsing species on cultivated hops, larvae of the currant pug moth (*Eupithecia assimilata*) (Fig. 357) are probably most frequently reported, this small geometrid having become more numerous in hop gardens in recent years.

Only two species of British Lepidoptera are restricted to hop: the leaf miner *Cosmopterix zieglerella*[61] and the buttoned snout moth (*Hypena rostralis*). Although cited as minor pests of cultivated hop in mainland Europe,[62] neither has pest status in Britain, although the buttoned snout moth was formerly reported breeding in commercial hop gardens as well as on wild hop. Although still widespread in southern England, buttoned snout moth has markedly declined since the 1950s[63] and is now found only in association with wild hosts. Both species are currently classified as nationally scarce under the UK Biodiversity Action Plan.

Larvae of *Ostrinia nubilalis* were found recently on dwarf hops in Kent, the larvae boring upwards within the stems and causing dieback of cone-bearing shoots.[64] *O. nubilalis* was formerly a rare migrant moth in Britain, but is now well established on waste land adjacent to the Thames estuary and in various other parts of southern England.[65] Abroad, the larvae (known as European corn borers) (Fig. 358) are important pests of maize and sweet corn. In Britain, however, they are associated mainly with mugwort.[66]

Rosy rustic moth (*Hydraecia micacea*) is another stem-boring pest, and the larvae commonly attack hop plants, especially in weedy sites.[67] The insect overwinters in the egg stage. In spring, following egg hatch, the larvae burrow within the pith of the bines; unlike European corn borers they typically tunnel downwards. Later, they invade the roots and crowns. Weedy sites also encourage a

FIG 358. Although of greater significance as pests of maize or sweet corn, European corn borer (*Ostrinia nubilalis*) larvae (albeit of a different biological race) are known to attack hop bines.

range of polyphagous soil pests, including chafers, leatherjackets, garden swift moth (*Hepialus lupulinus*), ghost swift moth (*H. humuli*), wingless weevils (*Otiorhynchus* spp.) and wireworms.

Hop root weevil (*Mitoplinthus caliginosus*)[68] (Fig. 359) has been known as a pest of English hops since the 1930s. This secretive and rather immobile, dull-coloured, often mud-encrusted insect usually escapes attention, and hides away during the daytime at the base of the bines or in the upper reaches of the

FIG 359. Hop root weevil (*Mitoplinthus caliginosus*) is a secretive and nowadays rarely encountered pest.

soil. This behaviour is reminiscent of that of clay-coloured weevils, which also sometimes inhabit hop gardens. Hop root weevil lays its eggs singly, mainly from late summer to early winter, either in the underground parts of the bines or in the rootstock. Following egg hatch the larvae mine within the cortex before entering the pith, development lasting anything from nine to eighteen months.[69] Nowadays, the pest appears to be of little or no significance in our remaining hop gardens. The same is true of hop strig midge (*Contarinia humuli*), which was formerly an injurious pest in various English hop-growing districts,[70] and is now perhaps merely a museum piece.

Two-spotted spider mite (*Tetranychus urticae*) (already discussed in earlier chapters in relation to several other crops) is an important pest in hop gardens, and second only to damson/hop aphid as a target for pesticide treatments.[71] This important pest can have a major impact on hop yields and quality, and is often of particular significance on dwarf hops. Adult females overwinter in various sheltered situations, especially in cracks in wooden hop poles, but also amongst dry leaf litter, under stones and in the soil. In the spring, the mites become active and invade the young hop bines to begin breeding. As the season advances, the mites constantly move upwards onto the young shoots; they also spread to the developing cones. Breeding eventually ceases, and in September newly reared winter females finally depart from the bines and enter hibernation.

NUT CROPS

Nowadays, nut-growing in the British Isles is a minor activity, largely restricted to the production of hazelnuts (as cobnuts or filberts) and, to a lesser extent, walnuts. Sweet chestnut trees are planted mainly for amenity purposes or as a coppice crop (e.g. for trellis work or timber poles); the fruits ripen here (at least they do so in southern England), but there is no commercial production. Most of our edible chestnuts are imported from Italy. Cobnuts and filberts (raised in sites known as plats) are concentrated in Kent, the traditional heartland of the British nut industry. However, even here, the area dedicated to nut-growing has declined dramatically over the years. That having been said, confidence in nuts (albeit as a minor crop) is increasing, and there have been several recent plantings. As in the case of traditional fruit orchards (Chapter 7), long-term nut plats are important wildlife habitats.[72] Their presence in the landscape, therefore, has considerable environmental benefits. Traditional English walnut orchards, with their large, imposing trees, are now a rare sight, although a few are still to be found, as in Worcestershire and on the Essex/Suffolk border.

Cobnuts and filberts

As a generally common component of many a hedgerow, copse or woodland habitat, hazel acts as a food source or refuge for an abundance of wildlife. Many phytophagous species associated with this generally abundant wild shrub (along with their entourage of parasitoids and predators) also occur in cultivated nut plats. Frequently encountered pests include aphids, leafhoppers, leaf miners and an array of leaf-browsing herbivores. Hazel aphids (*Myzocallis coryli*), for example, although present mainly on the underside of expanded leaves (Fig. 360), sometimes attract attention. However, even when numerous, the aphids are not particularly damaging, although infested foliage and branches are often contaminated by aphid-excreted honeydew and blackened by sooty moulds. The large hazel aphid (*Corylobium avellanae*) infests young shoots, but is a less common species. Leafhoppers, such as *Edwardsiana avellanae*, and the nut leaf blister moth (*Phyllonorycter coryli*), although often abundant, are also of little or no consequence in nut plats. As for leaf-browsers, gregarious larvae such as those of buff-tip moth are capable of causing noticeable (but localised) defoliation, as are those of hazel sawfly (*Croesus septentrionalis*). If numerous, solitary-feeding larvae of winter moth (*Operophtera brumata*), March moth (*Alsophila aescularia*), mottled umber moth (*Erannis defoliaria*) and various other species also inflict appreciable leaf damage, especially in sites close to deciduous woodlands. Adult leaf weevils (e.g. *Phyllobius* spp. and *Polydrusus* spp.) are often abundant in springtime, albeit as ephemeral visitors. These include nut leaf weevil (*Strophosoma melanogrammum*)[73] (a relatively bulbous species with characteristically protruding compound eyes) which has a strong affinity with hazel.

FIG 360. Hazel aphids (*Myzocallis coryli*) colonise the underside of leaves. They do not cause distortion but infested foliage, shoots and branches are contaminated by honeydew and sooty moulds.

FIG 361. Hazel nut weevil (*Balaninus nucum*) is an important pest of cobnut and filbert.

Among weevils, hazel nut weevil (*Balaninus nucum*)[74] (Fig. 361) is probably the most significant insect pest of cobnut and filbert, damage being caused by both adults and larvae. Eggs are laid in June, each placed singly in a developing nutlet through a tiny hole drilled through the wall by the female weevil. The larva feeds on the developing nut during the summer, before escaping through the hardening shell by enlarging the original oviposition hole. It then works its way into the soil, to form an earthen cell in which to overwinter. Hazel nut weevil larvae remain in a state of diapause for one or more winters before eventually pupating. Crop yields can be greatly depleted following the activities of this pest. A further toll on nut crops around harvest time results from raids launched by grey squirrels, particularly in the vicinity of woodlands.

Some invertebrate pests specifically target the buds of hazel plants. These include the larvae of nut bud tortrix moth (*Epinotia tenerana*) and the generally common and widely distributed filbert bud mite (*Phytoptus avellanae*). In addition, larvae of the tortrix moth *Gypsonoma dealbana* (which, as young larvae, bite into buds after overwintering)[75] distort the growth of young shoots, each larva later bunching the leaves of a terminal shoot together with silk to form a distorted, fist-like habitation. Filbert bud mite, which is a potentially significant pest, spends the winter months within swollen, galled buds. The mites also overwinter in the developing female flowers and male catkins. In spring, adult female mites emerge and deposit eggs on the underside of expanding or expanded leaves. These eggs give rise to microscopic protonymphs that wander about and feed before eventually moulting into summer deutonymphs, which soon settle down alongside the major leaf veins. These nymphs are more or less sedentary, dorsoventrally flattened individuals, with few but noticeably broad 'tergites'. Eventually, the summer deutonymphs moult into adults of more normal appearance (individuals about 0.3 mm long and sausage-shaped, and finely cross-striated by numerous, very narrow 'tergites' and 'sternites' – see Appendix I, p. 424). These mites then invade the developing terminal buds. Here, breeding recommences, and continues throughout the autumn and winter months. As in summer, development includes egg, protonymphal and deutonymphal stages, the deutonymphs (here called winter deutonymphs) being essentially similar in appearance to adults but smaller. Rather than bursting open, the invaded buds are induced to swell, and from September onwards they become very obvious, and reminiscent of big-buds inhabited by gall mites on blackcurrant bushes (Chapter 8). Particularly in winter, the swollen buds (packed with literally thousands of mites) are a familiar sight on wild hazel bushes, and it is no surprise that cultivated plants in nut plats are also attacked. When free-living (i.e. when not in their galls), microscopic creatures such as gall mites are readily spread by wind and rain, on insects and, accidentally, by man.[76]

Walnuts

Walnut trees (in Britain primarily common walnut) are attacked by various pests. These range from wood-boring goat moth (*Cossus cossus*) and leopard moth (*Zeuzera pyrina*) larvae to leaf-inhabiting pests such as aphids, defoliating insects and gall mites. Infestations by goat moth, whose enormous pink, naked-looking larvae (individuals up to 100 mm long) form deep tunnels in the base of older trees, often persist in the same tree for many years. Leopard moth larvae, if present, feed mainly in the stems of young trees or in the younger branches of older ones. Among foliage pests, the large walnut aphid (*Panaphis juglandis*)[77] and the small walnut aphid (*Chromaphis juglandicola*) are monophagous, being specific to walnut. Both are yellowish in colour, with short, stumpy siphunculi. They overwinter in the egg stage. In summer, large walnut aphids typically inhabit the

FIG 362. Large walnut aphid (*Panaphis juglandis*) colonies develop along the midrib on the upper surface of leaves.

upper surface of the leaves, forming a double row of developing nymphs along the midrib (Fig. 362). Colonies of small walnut aphid, however, occur as scattered individuals on the underside of the leaves. Of the two species, the latter is less often encountered. Defoliating pests are usually of minor importance on walnut, even when numerous. These include leaf-browsing weevils (*Phyllobius* spp., for example), and a few leaf-tying and defoliating lepidopterans, including light brown apple moth (*Epiphyas postvittana*). None, however, is of real significance. Leaves galled by mites are commonplace on walnut trees. The walnut leaf gall mite (*Aceria tristriatus*), for example, forms tiny, maroon, pimple-like galls (Fig. 363) and the walnut leaf erineum mite (*A. erinea*) inhabits large blister-like erinea, each up to 15 mm or more in length (Fig. 364). Heavy infestations of the latter cause distortion and senescence of leaves, and the presence of erinea on the leaves of seedlings and mature trees is by no means unusual. Both species are deuterogenous (see Chapter 7, p. 192).

FIG 363. The tiny pimple-like galls initiated by walnut leaf gall mites (*Aceria tristriatus*) are often very numerous.

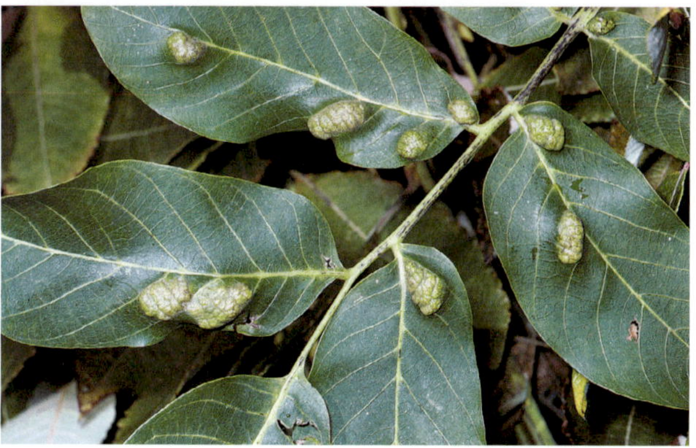

FIG 364. The large, felt-like galls inhabited by walnut leaf erineum mites (*Aceria erinea*) are a common sight on walnut trees.

Developing walnut fruits are attacked by codling moth (*Cydia pomonella*), the notorious pest of apples (Chapter 7). They are also utilised as breeding sites by the related acorn moth (*C. splendana*). The latter is superficially similar in appearance to codling moth, and has a similar life history, but is most frequently associated with oak and sweet chestnut trees. At or close to maturity, walnuts are also plundered by rooks and grey squirrels.

OUTDOOR FLOWER BULB CROPS

Bulb growing in Britain is largely confined to Lincolnshire, Cornwall and the Isles of Scilly, and currently extends to around 4,000 ha dedicated mainly to the production of daffodils (including narcissi). Other bulbs, corms, rhizomes and tubers (e.g. anemones, crocuses, gladioli, hyacinths, irises, lilies, snowdrops and tulips) are also grown but are of far less significance. Relatively few pests are associated with outdoor bulb and corm crops. However, their ranks do include a few specialists such as large narcissus fly (*Merodon equestris*) and bulb scale mite (*Steneotarsonemus laticeps*)[78] (see below).

Insects

Aphids are rarely found on field-grown bulb and corm crops, although species such as black bean aphid, glasshouse & potato aphid, peach/potato aphid, potato aphid and shallot aphid (*Myzus ascalonicus*) do occur on occasions. They are then of particular significance as potential virus vectors (Table 19). By contrast, dry bulbs and corms in store are commonly attacked by aphids. Mangold aphid (*Rhopalosiphoninus staphyleae*), mottled arum aphid (*Aulacorthum circumflexum*), shallot aphid and tulip bulb aphid (*Dysaphis tulipae*) are examples. If infested bulbs or corms are planted out, colonies of aphids can subsequently develop on the young shoots and in some cases may even spread onto the flowerheads.

In springtime, large narcissus flies are often to be seen foraging or resting in bulb fields and their surroundings. These hairy, bumblebee-like hover flies (Fig. 365) are well-known pests of daffodils, and a major threat to bulb-growing in southwest England. In recent years, they have also caused concern in the bulb fields of Lincolnshire. Although associated mainly with daffodils, large narcissus fly sometimes attacks other bulbous plants, such as hyacinths, irises and snowdrops. However, the bulb-infesting larvae are unable to complete their development in tulip bulbs as these rot too rapidly if invaded. The warmth-loving adults are active in the field from spring to early summer at

TABLE 19. Examples of pest-transmitted viruses on bulb and corm crops.

Virus	*Host(s)*	*Vectors*
Arabis mosaic virus (ArMV)	Daffodil	Dagger nematodes
Bean yellow mosaic virus (BYMV)	Freesia, gladiolus	Aphids
Cucumber mosaic virus (CMV)	Daffodil, gladiolus, lily, tulip	Aphids
Freesia mosaic virus (FMV)	Freesia	Aphids
Lily symptomless virus (LSV)	Lily	Aphids
Narcissus degeneration virus (NDV)	Daffodil	Aphids
Narcissus late season yellows virus (NLSYV)	Daffodil	Aphids
Narcissus latent virus (NLV)	Daffodil	Aphids
Narcissus yellow stripe virus (NYSV)	Daffodil	Aphids
Raspberry ringspot virus (RpRSV)	Daffodil	Needle nematodes
Strawberry latent ringspot virus (SLRV)	Daffodil	Dagger nematodes
Tobacco rattle virus (TRV)	Daffodil, gladiolus	Stubby-root nematodes
Tobacco ringspot virus (TRSV)	Gladiolus	Dagger nematodes
Tomato black ring virus (TBRV)	Daffodil	Needle nematodes
Tomato ringspot virus (ToRSV)	Gladiolus	Dagger nematodes
Tulip breaking virus (TBV)	Lily, tulip	Aphids

temperatures above *c.* 20°C and are often to be seen sunning themselves on or in the close vicinity of host plants. They feed on the flowers of various plants, including dandelions and other Asteraceae, and are often particularly attracted to the daisy-like flowers of mesembs (mesembryanthemums).[79, 80] These South African succulents have become naturalised in various places frequented by large narcissus flies, especially in the Isles of Scilly and in Cornwall.[81]

FIG 365. Large narcissus flies (*Merodon equestris*) occur in several colour forms. Both brown (above left) and black, red-tipped (above right) forms are common bumblebee mimics.

FIG **366.** Large narcissus fly (*Merodon equestris*) larvae feed singly inside bulbs, which are soon destroyed.

Eggs of large narcissus flies are laid singly in cracks in the soil during June and early July, usually close to the base of daffodil bulbs. The eggs hatch about a fortnight later. Each larva then migrates to the base plate of a suitable bulb and burrows inside to commence feeding. A few weeks later the central tissue of the bulb is invaded (Fig. 366). Here, a large cavern filled with masses of black frass and rotting tissue is eventually formed. Although the pest usually completes its development in one and the same bulb, if bulbs are small then several may have to be utilised to enable the larva to complete its development. Most larvae are fully fed by the onset of winter. They then overwinter before eventually pupating in the soil or in the neck region of infested bulbs. Adults emerge from early May onwards. In forcing sheds, however, the flies appear very much earlier.

Maggot-like larvae are sometimes found feeding gregariously inside lifted daffodil bulbs (Fig. 367), and these are sometimes thought to represent a

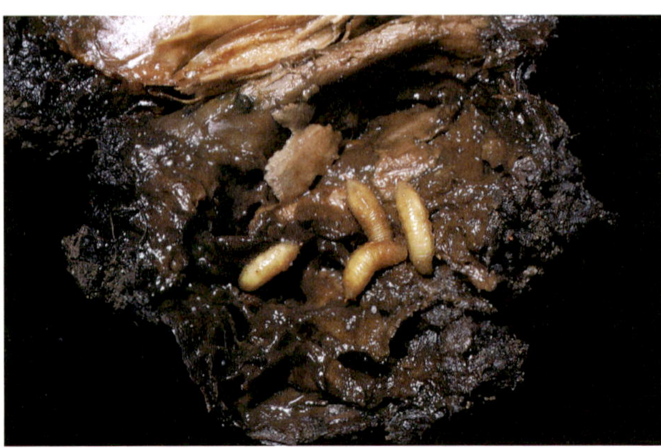

FIG **367.** Small narcissus fly (*Eumerus* spp.) larvae are gregarious feeders.

particularly heavy infestation of large narcissus fly. However, the culprits invariably prove to be larvae of small narcissus flies, usually *Eumerus tuberculatus*.[82] Small narcissus flies are secondary pests that most often restrict their attacks to diseased or mechanically damaged bulbs. Daffodil bulbs infected with basal rot (*Fusarium oxysporum* f. sp. *narcissi*), for example, are frequently targeted. Adults of *E. tuberculatus* appear in the early spring. Eggs are then laid in association with unhealthy bulbs, typically in groups of five or six but sometimes more. Larvae appear a few days later, and these invade the bulbs in order to feed. Fully fed larvae pupate in the neck region of the infested bulb, and adults emerge about two weeks later. Larvae of a second brood feed during the summer, and these complete their development in the autumn. They then vacate the remnants of the infested bulbs, to overwinter in the soil. Pupation takes place in the spring. A second species of small narcissus fly, *E. strigatus*, has a similar life history but a much wider host range, including not only various kinds of bulbs but also carrots, onions, parsnips and potatoes.

Leaf-browsing insects on bulbs and corms are few and far between, although larvae of polyphagous pests such as angle-shades moth and cabbage moth are sometimes encountered, particularly on the foliage of anemones and gladioli. Specialist feeders such as the adults and larvae of lily beetle (*Lilioceris lilii*) and the gregarious larvae of iris sawfly (*Rhadinoceraea micans*) may also be found on lilies and irises, respectively. The leaves of irises also host dipterous leaf miners: either *Cerodontha ireos* (on yellow flag) or *C. iridis* (on stinking iris and certain other cultivated species).

Mites

Bulb scale mite is of particular significance on forced daffodils.[83] Heavy infestations affect flower quality and also lead to reductions in crop yields. The pest is favoured by high temperatures, the lifecycle from egg to adult being completed in about a month at 20°C and twice as rapidly at bulb-forcing temperatures. The mites inhabit the gaps between the bulb scales and if infested bulbs are sliced open horizontally evidence of their presence can be seen as brownish markings at the angles of the scales. These symptoms are similar to those caused by stem nematodes (*Ditylenchus dipsaci*). However, in the case of nematode attack discoloration is more extensive, appearing as brownish streaks amongst the scales. In the field, the development of bulb scale mite is greatly protracted, especially immediately following planting out in the autumn and during the winter. Activity and breeding escalate in spring and early summer in response to increased temperatures. The mites then occur within the bulbs and on the aerial parts of plants. However, by the time of lifting in mid-summer

FIG 368. Bulb mites (*Rhizoglyphus* spp.) often breed in rotting bulbs.

most mites have retreated back into the bulbs. Attacks in the field are indicated by the emergence of dwarfed, distorted flowers, and by the presence of sickle-shaped leaves with saw-toothed edges; also, young leaves lack their typical greyish bloom and so appear bright green.

Bulb mites (*Rhizoglyphus* spp.) (Fig. 368) are glistening, bulbous-bodied, largely colourless creatures, with reddish-brown appendages and long body hairs. They occur in abundance in soils, especially in association with damp or diseased organic matter, and often breed on rotting bulbs, corms and tubers (and less often on sound ones), both in the field and under protection. Breeding is continuous, so long as conditions remain favourable, and attacks can lead to the complete breakdown of tissue. Two species are involved: the long-haired *Rhizoglyphus callae* and somewhat shorter-haired *R. echinops*. Attacks are usually launched on previously damaged or diseased material, so the mites are essentially secondary pests. Unlike the former species, *R. echinops* is said to favour sound as opposed to rotting bulbs, and the two species do not breed together.[84] Phoretic hypopi (see Chapter 10, p. 333) sometimes appear in their lifecycle as a microscopic dispersal stage,[85] individuals attaching themselves temporarily to passing insects such as small narcissus flies and thereby hitching a lift from one breeding site to another.

Nematodes

Foliage emerging from daffodil bulbs infested by stem nematodes typically bear small, raised, elongated lesions, called spickels. Similarly, flower stems of tulips arising from heavily infested bulbs are bent; they also develop lesions that eventually split open. In addition, nematode-infested bulbs frequently rot, making them liable to be invaded by bulb mites or small narcissus flies. Like aphids, nematodes are also important vectors of virus disease (Table 19).

TEASELS

Since Roman times, the seed heads of cultivated teasel (known as Fuller's teasel) have been used to raise the nap or pile of high-quality cloth. However, commercial teasel-growing, traditionally centred in Somerset, is now virtually non-existent. At the last count there was just one UK-based merchant (in Huddersfield, Yorkshire). The seed heads of cultivated teasels are essentially similar to those of wild teasel plants, but noticeably longer. Also, the tips of the awns (slender, bristle-like appendages) in cultivated seed heads are bent (crooked) rather than straight, thereby making them suitable for carding. Teasel is a biennial crop, with seed planted in April of the first year, and plants maturing and producing seed heads in year two.

Over the years, the main pest of cultivated teasel plants has been stem nematode, a highly polyphagous species of considerable economic importance in both agriculture and horticulture. Stem nematode was first described, and named, in 1857 by the famous German plant pathologist Julius Kühn,[86] following the collection of material from the seed heads of teasel plants; teasel, therefore, is classified as the type host. Stem nematode has a major impact on the growth of teasel plants, causing considerable stunting and distortion. In addition, the midrib and base of infested leaves become swollen, a symptom described as cabbagy. Also, seed heads often fail to develop or, when they do, they become soft and malformed, and are then unfit for carding purposes.

Few insect pests are associated with teasel. Of these, maggots of the agromyzid leaf miner *Phytomyza ramosa*[87] (Fig. 369) infest the leaves, each forming a linear mine along the midrib, with lateral branches extending into the lamina. *P. ramosa* (a pest known to growers as teasel fly) has two or more generations

FIG **369.** Teasel fly (*Phytomyza ramosa*) larvae tunnel within the midrib of leaves, and are a particular problem on first-year plants.

annually, and young larvae overwinter within the rosette leaves of first-year plants. *Agromyza dipsaci*, a single-brooded leaf miner, also occurs on teasel plants, each larva forming a brown, funnel-shaped blotch along the margin of an expanded leaf. To what extent agromyzid leaf miners are (or perhaps, more correctly, have been) of significance on cultivated teasel plants is unclear. However, teasel growers have long viewed teasel fly as a pest, and in the 1960s the insecticides DDT and malathion were commonly applied at fortnightly intervals during the summer to combat infestations.[88] When they referred to teasel fly, growers may not always have meant the leaf miner. On occasions, they might have been referring to teasel marble moth (*Endothenia gentianaeana*), whose larvae develop within the seed heads of teasel plants. These larvae feed on the pith during the autumn, and the resulting cavity becomes filled with masses of blackish frass intermixed with strands of silken webbing (Fig. 370). After harvest, the damaged teasel heads collapse or disintegrate. Larvae of another small British moth, the rosy conch moth (*Cochylis roseana*), feed on teasel seeds, at least in the wild, but these do not enter the central pith of the seed heads.[89]

Nowadays, interest in European teasel pests (not all of which occur in the UK) arises largely from workers in North America. They seek to use such organisms as possible biological control agents to combat teasel plants that have become established in the US as invasive, non-indigenous weeds.[90]

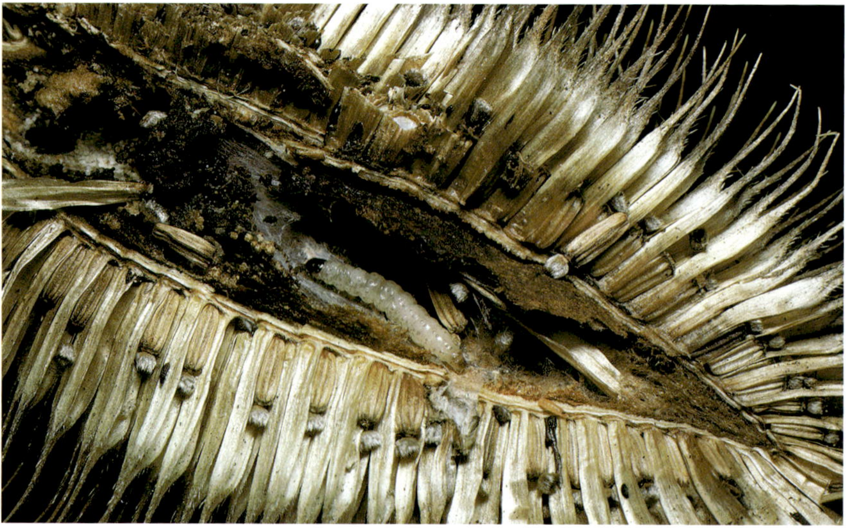

FIG 370. Teasel marble moth (*Endothenia gentianaeana*) larvae feed within the seed heads of teasel plants, which then disintegrate.

WATERCRESS

The commercial production of watercress is located mainly in chalk or limestone areas of southern England (especially Dorset, Hampshire and Wiltshire), where fresh, uncontaminated, alkaline water emanates from springs or boreholes at a steady temperature of 10°C or 11°C.[91] Although formerly of considerable importance, the crop has declined considerably over the years, and production currently stands at about 2,000 tonnes annually, obtained from around 60 ha. Watercress grown commercially today is derived from dark-green stock that originated in the US, the hybrid brown watercress of former years (favoured owing to its frost tolerance) having long since been superseded.

Pests in watercress beds

Freshwater amphipods[92] (*Gammarus* spp.) and freshwater snails (e.g. *Lymnaea* spp.) are natural inhabitants of watercress beds. By ridding beds of decaying plant material, they help to maintain healthy growing conditions and are generally considered beneficial. Occasionally, however, if populations become excessive, such scavengers can have an adverse effect on plant growth. They then qualify as pests. When numerous, snails, if not amphipods, may also be included as contaminants in harvested crops, as can aquatic chironomid midge larvae (especially those of *Metriocnemus hirticollis*). Watercress beds are also attractive to birdlife, and this can be something of a problem. Woodpigeons, for example, sometimes graze on plants around the periphery of beds, and house sparrows, linnets and other small birds can be troublesome in seedbeds. Mallards, moorhens and swans, and various other species (nowadays even including little egrets), cause incidental mechanical damage by wading through the crop, especially in frosty conditions; plants may also be uprooted by birds searching the shallows for invertebrate prey.

Insect pests include aphids, which often invade watercress beds during the summer months. Buckthorn/potato aphid (*Aphis nasturtii*) – a bright yellow to yellowish-green species that overwinters in the egg stage on common buckthorn – is probably most frequently encountered. However, the ubiquitous peach/potato aphid also occurs, as does cabbage aphid (*Brevicoryne brassicae*). All three species are vectors of turnip mosaic virus (TuMV). Summer infestations of red currant/arrow-grass aphid (*Aphis triglochinis*) – a brownish-green species that overwinters as eggs on red currant – are found on occasions; they cause mottling and distortion of leaves, symptoms easily mistaken for those of virus infection.

The watercress beetle (*Phaedon cochleariae*) is occasionally a problem in

FIG 371. Watercress beetle (*Phaedon cochleariae*) larvae are gregarious feeders.

watercress beds. The adult beetles emerge from hibernation in the spring and eventually deposit eggs in small cavities bitten into the surface of the leaves. Following egg hatch the larvae feed gregariously (Fig. 371), each grazing away the upper leaf tissue and often causing extensive damage. Larvae feed for about three weeks before pupating. Adults of a second generation appear shortly afterwards, usually in June and July. Second-brood larvae occur during the summer, and these eventually give rise to adults in August or September. These either hibernate or, in particularly favourable seasons, may produce a third brood of larvae. Watercress beetle is often common on wild watercress plants, and was formerly of some significance on brassica seed crops, especially white mustard. Mustard beetle (*P. armoraciae*), a slightly larger species, has a similar life history, and also attacks watercress.

Watercress plants are also subject to attack by adult flea beetles, especially the small striped flea beetle (*Phyllotreta undulata*). Shot-holing of the foliage, caused by the adults, often attracts attention but is rarely significant.

Following their dispersal in the summer from oilseed rape and other brassicaceous plants upon which they were reared, young adult cabbage seed weevils (*Ceutorhynchus assimilis*)[93] and cabbage stem weevils (*C. pallidactylus*)[94] are often attracted to watercress beds prior to seeking overwintering sites. They graze on the foliage and also bite into the leafstalks, causing noticeable wounds that can downgrade crops. Such infestations appear to be far more frequent nowadays than they used to be, probably reflecting the greater preponderance of oilseed rape crops in the farming landscape. Adult pollen beetles (essentially *Meligethes aeneus*) produced on oilseed rape crops are also ephemeral visitors to watercress beds, but they are not harmful. The young adults arrive on the crop in the early summer, invading the flowers in search of pollen, and soon disperse. Their main claim to fame is fooling some observers into believing an outbreak of watercress beetle has arisen!

The watercress stem miner (*Hydrellia nasturtii*) is known to attack cultivated watercress plants, although there appear to be no recent records. The larvae of this fly mine superficially within the stems, seemingly without affecting plant growth. Although usually overlooked, the mines are often invaded by the bright red larvae of chironomid midges (commonly known as bloodworms); the mines are then readily discernable in harvested produce.[95]

Limnephilus lunatus, a caddis fly, is a common inhabitant of commercial watercress beds. The long-lived adults are on the wing from early summer onwards, but breeding is delayed until the autumn. Eggs are then laid in batches on the leaves and stems of watercress plants, just above the surface of the water. Each batch (perhaps containing several hundred eggs) is enclosed in a rounded gelatinous mass that swells on absorption of water and finally reaches 10 mm or so in diameter.[96] Unless low temperatures intervene, the eggs hatch about three weeks later. The aquatic, case-inhabiting larvae then feed throughout the winter and spring on submerged parts of plants. At each growth stage the larvae occupy distinctive tube-like cases – those of first-instar larvae constructed from sand grains; those of second and third instars from pieces of the food plant; and those of fourth- and fifth-instar individuals once again from sand grains. Pupation takes place inside the final larval case, usually in May or early June, and adults emerge shortly afterwards. Feeding by caddis fly larvae results in direct damage to leaves, stems and roots. In addition, particularly in winter, pieces of severed tissue often float away and are then lost.

Although most frequently reported on land-based crops such as oilseed rape and stubble turnips (see Chapter 4), turnip sawfly (*Athalia rosae*) has recently appeared during the autumn in watercress beds in Hampshire. The larvae skeletonise leaves but are of greatest significance as contaminants in the harvested crop.

CHAPTER 12

Alien Pests

OVER THE YEARS, THE SPECTRUM of crop pests in this country has been extended by the addition of various newcomers from abroad. Such pests sometimes arrive by natural means, perhaps following an expansion of their ranges in Europe. However, the introduction of many others is artificial and usually but not always accidental. Many such organisms, having become permanently established, are now accepted as residents (welcome or otherwise) and have long since shed their 'alien' label. Crop pests that regularly arrive in Britain as natural migrants, and augment existing British populations, also do not deserve to be classified as aliens. Common examples include angle-shades moth (*Phlogophora meticulosa*), diamond-back moth (*Plutella xylostella*) and large white butterfly (*Pieris brassicae*), all of which have been discussed in earlier chapters. Silver Y moth (*Autographa gamma*) and other migrants to Britain that usually do not survive a British winter require a similar dispensation. There are also a few migratory species that arrive on occasions and might then become established, remaining as residents only so long as conditions remain suitable. Turnip sawfly (*Athalia rosae*) (as discussed in Chapter 4) is a particularly good example.

Climate change, particularly the impact of global warming, could lead to natural invasion of Britain by pests that until now have remained well away from our shores. It might also allow new pests to flourish, or introduced ones and also native species to colonise areas previously unsuitable for them. The converse, however, may be true for species disadvantaged by increasing temperatures. Natural spread of many insects is currently taking place in Europe and, as a direct or indirect result, several have arrived in Britain. Oak processionary moth (*Thaumetopoea processionea*) is a very recent example and one that has made the media headlines. Spread of invasive species (whether pests, pathogens or weeds)

FIG 372. The spread of firethorn leaf miner moth (*Phyllonorycter leucographella*) has been studied in some detail since the pest's first arrival in Britain in the late 1980s.

is inevitably often aided by man. However, as in the case of the invasive firethorn leaf miner moth (*Phyllonorycter leucographella*) (Fig. 372) from southern Europe, although perhaps initially producing distribution outliers, this does not necessarily impact significantly on the natural rate or pattern of spread.[1]

International trade in plants or plant products is considered the major pathway for introductions from abroad. Over 100 years ago, albeit specifically related to scale insects, Newstead observed that:

> *The occurrence of certain species of Coccids in countries so widely separated and so completely isolated has undoubtedly been brought about by the importation of plants, which is now so rapidly carried on in all parts of the world. The fixed, inert character of the Coccids, the minute size of their larvae, render them the easiest of all insects to be carried long distances; and what is equally important, on their arrival in a new country they may easily escape the eyes of the untrained horticulturist, who ... would be unable to detect the almost microscopic young which might be lurking in a hundred places.*[2]

Such comments are equally valid for many other alien pests. Almost 90 per cent of human-mediated introductions to the UK during the period 1970 to 2003, for example, resulted from the importation of ornamental plants.[3]

The European Community seeks to minimise the risks faced by Member States from the introduction of alien pests. Plant Health Directive 2000/29/EC, for example, identifies protective measures to oppose the introduction of organisms deemed harmful to plants or plant products, and to prevent their spread.[4] These restrictions cover a large number of organisms, many of which are named specifically. Plant Health (quarantine) authorities maintain constant vigilance. However, as history has proven, it is unrealistic to expect that every unwelcome new arrival can be intercepted and prevented from breeding or becoming established in a new country. Also, when outbreaks of new pests are discovered it might not always be possible to eradicate them. Containment, where eradication is impractical or has failed, can also prove a lost cause. The situation in Britain and Ireland, as elsewhere in the world, is one of constant pressure on Plant Health authorities, pressure that is increased by open borders and by ever-increasing international trade in plants and plant products. There are notable exceptions, but most non-native pests established in Britain over the past 200 or so years have come from continental Europe and, to a lesser extent, Australasia, East Asia and North America.[5]

TRUE BUGS

Several long-established aphid pests of British crops are of North American ancestry. These include the potato aphid (*Macrosiphum euphorbiae*), first recorded in Britain in 1917, and woolly aphid (*Eriosoma lanigerum*), the notorious apple pest that first arrived here in the 1700s. Further additions to the British list have been made over the years, including Essig's lupin aphid (*M. albifrons*) which arrived from North America in 1981,[6] and the peach leaf-roll aphid (*Myzus varians*) (Fig. 373) which was first discovered here in 1970. The last-mentioned species is associated with clematis and peach trees (the former acting as the secondary, summer, host and the latter as the primary host upon which overwintering eggs are laid) and is possibly of Japanese origin. It probably found its way to Britain via mainland Europe. Well established aphids of non-British origin also persist on a range of other plants. These include the North American species *Illinoia*

FIG 373. (Above left) Peach leaf-roll aphid (*Myzus varians*) inhabits tight leaf-edge rolls on peach trees (above right). It is seen occasionally in Britain, where it was first found in 1970.

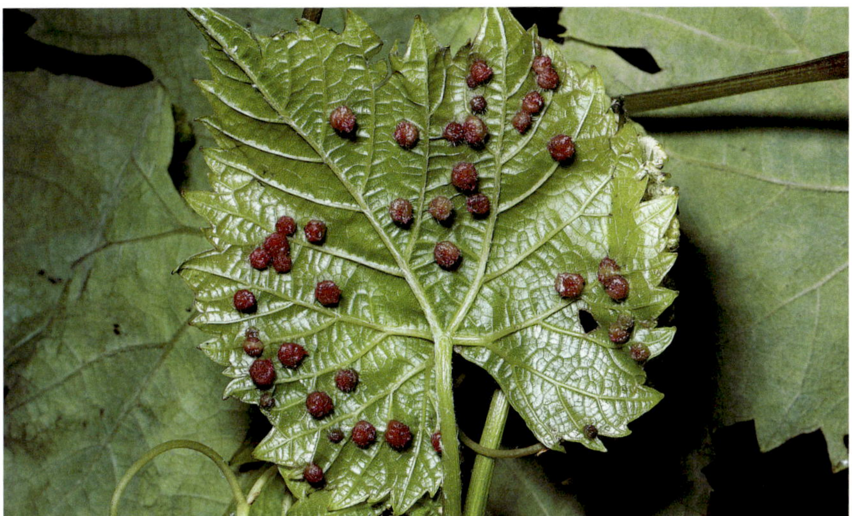

FIG 374. Grape phylloxera (*Viteus vitifoliae*) leaf galls are found occasionally in British vineyards.

azaleae and *I. lambersi* on azaleas, and the Asiatic species *Paracolopha morrisoni*, *Takecallis arundicolens*, *T. arundinariae* and *T. taiwanus* on bamboos. Various conifer-infesting aphids (e.g. several *Cinara* spp.) are also of non-British origin, as are several adelgids (family Adelgidae).[7] However, these are of greater significance as forestry pests.

Grape phylloxera (*Viteus vitifoliae*),[8] a minute aphid-like creature, hails from North America and following its accidental introduction to Europe in 1863 it infamously devastated the French wine industry. Over two million hectares of vines were destroyed, a catastrophe that became known as the great wine blight. Today, this much feared pest is of worldwide significance. However, it is largely kept under control by grafting grapevines onto American rather than European rootstocks, the former being either tolerant or resistant to attack. The earlier history of grape phylloxera in the UK (as documented from 1863 to 1990) was one of infrequent outbreaks and eradication.[9] Today, the pest is considered as established in Britain, but infestations here are thought to be contained. Grape phylloxera has a highly complex and fascinating life history, involving both root-inhabiting and leaf-inhabiting forms, known as radicolae and gallicolae, respectively. The lifecycle can also include both sexual and asexual phases, but the former is very rare under European conditions. Typically in Europe (including Britain) the pest breeds parthenogenetically on the roots of grapevines, where radicolae induce the formation of elongated galls. On

FIG 375. Wisteria scale (*Eulecanium excrescens*) is one of the world's largest scale insects. Established infestations of this Asian pest were first found in London in 2001.

occasions, gallicolae appear and these invade the aerial parts of host plants. Here they inhabit warty, greenish to red or purplish-red galls, which develop on the leaves (Fig. 374). Breeding within these galls is again parthenogenetic, with several generations being completed during the year.

Scale insects are primarily subtropical and tropical insects, and foreign imports have plagued these shores for years. Many introduced species are associated with protected environments, including greenhouses and hothouses. Others, however, are well capable of surviving outdoors. The invasive horse chestnut scale (*Pulvinaria regalis*) from Asia, which now 'adorns' street and parkland trees in many of our towns and cities, is an all too common example. Amongst other recent arrivals, special mention should be made of wisteria scale (*Eulecanium excrescens*) (Fig. 375), an exceptionally large species (the helmet-like adult females measuring up to 13 mm in length), which has become established in London on wisteria and certain other ornamental shrubs.[10] In its native China, wisteria scale is a recognised pest of fruit trees. Outdoor plants in London also now play host to cottony cushion scale (*Icerya purchasi*),[11] an insect of Australian origin.[12] Today, this important polyphagous crop pest (Fig. 376) is well established in southern Europe, and is often common in citrus orchards and on many other trees and shrubs, including acacia and pittosporum (both of which, in the distant past, have hosted greenhouse infestations in Britain).[13] In northern Europe, however, it is more typically restricted to protected environments. In common with those of most scale insects, the nymphs of cottony cushion scale remain active whilst in their first instar. Thereafter they become sedentary on the twigs and branches prior to moulting into adults. Cottony cushion scale is hermaphroditic, the adult females producing sperm and fertilising their own eggs.

FIG 376. Cottony cushion scale (*Icerya purchasi*).

Following its accidental introduction on nursery stock exported from China in 1870, the subtropical San José scale (*Diaspidiotus perniciosus*)[14] quickly became a highly destructive pest of fruit trees in the US. Since then it has also spread to many other parts of the globe, including southern Europe. In 1898, in the wake of earlier scares surrounding Colorado beetles (see below), fears were raised that the importation of scale-infested pears from California might result in the pest becoming established in Britain. However, expert opinion at the time considered such fears to be groundless.[15] The introduction of modern insecticides has greatly reduced the significance of San José scale as a fruit pest. Today, however, there is some evidence of a resurgence in the pest's fortunes.[16]

Over the past half century or so the alien tobacco whitefly (*Bemisia tabaci*)[17] has posed a major threat to European crops. The pest was first seen in Britain in 1987, on imported poinsettia cuttings, but the outbreak was quickly contained and the pest successfully eliminated. Since then, there has been a veritable flood of interceptions on poinsettia and other plants. Tobacco whitefly is a notifiable pest[18] and, as before, implementation of appropriate control measures has kept the pest at bay. Parts of mainland Europe, however, have succumbed, and tobacco whitefly is now established on outdoor and protected crops throughout the Mediterranean region; it is also found in greenhouses further north. In Britain, greenhouse crops such as aubergine, cucumber, sweet pepper, tomato and various ornamentals are at greatest risk, and constant vigilance is considered vital to maintain Britain's *Bemisia*-free status. On a world scale, tobacco whitefly is rated amongst the 100 most important alien invasive organisms.[19] As well as being highly polyphagous, tobacco whitefly is also a notorious vector of plant viruses, including cucurbit yellow stunting disorder virus (CYSDV) and tomato yellow leaf curl virus (TYLCV). In common with glasshouse whitefly (*Trialeurodes vaporariorum*)[20] (Chapter 10), with which it can coexist, tobacco whitefly also causes direct damage to host plants and excretes considerable quantities of honeydew upon which sooty moulds soon develop. Tobacco whitefly is generally regarded as a species complex, comprising several distinct biotypes, of which at least four are known to occur in Europe. Biotypes B and Q (the former sometimes known as the poinsettia strain) are most important and most widely distributed.

Again on a world scale, spiralling whitefly (*Aleurodicus dispersus*) is considered an important invasive species. Originally discovered in South America, this interesting species is a potentially major pest of tropical and subtropical crops. It is highly polyphagous, and attacks plants of many different families, including ornamentals and vegetable crops.[21] Spiralling whiteflies occur mainly on the underside of leaves. However, on crops such as aubergine, banana, citrus and tomato, they also invade the fruits. Infested leaves are characterised by the presence of sinuous, waxen trails, which are formed by the adult females and into which eggs are deposited. These white traceries often traverse widely over the leaf surface (Fig. 377) and, viewed casually, they may be mistaken for the work of leaf miners. The pest excretes considerable quantities of honeydew, and host plants often become tainted with sooty moulds. Over the past 30 years or so,

FIG 377. Spiralling whitefly (*Aleurodicus dispersus*) deposits eggs amongst a convoluted tracery of wax.

FIG 378. Elaeagnus sucker (*Cacopsylla fulguralis*) is a recent arrival in Britain, and causes extensive discoloration of the foliage of its food plant.

spiralling whitefly has spread rapidly across the Pacific region. It has also now reached Africa and off-shore European locations such as the Canary Islands and Madeira. Although unlikely to survive outdoors in Europe, other than in the warmest of regions, infestations could conceivably develop more widely on greenhouse-grown or hothouse ornamentals, and on protected vegetable crops such as aubergine and tomato. The pest poses little or no threat to Britain, but with the ever-increasing movement of plants and plant products as a result of international trade, and the seemingly insatiable demand for exotic plants, its eventual appearance (if not survival) here cannot be totally ruled out. Alien whiteflies, albeit mainly tobacco whiteflies, are frequently intercepted on plant material imported into Britain. Recent examples include the anthurium whitefly (*Crenidorsum aroidephagus*), the banded-winged whitefly (*Trialeurodes abutiloneus*) (Table 20) and the castor whitefly (*T. ricini*).[22]

Mention has already been made in Chapter 9 of several alien plant bugs that became established in Britain during the twentieth century. These include three psyllids (superfamily Psylloidea): bay sucker (*Trioza alacris*), eucalyptus sucker (*Ctenarytaina eucalypti*) and pittosporum sucker (*T. vitreoradiata*). Elaeagnus sucker (*Cacopsylla fulguralis*) (Fig. 378) is yet another but more recent psyllid invader (Table 20). This Asiatic bug first appeared in the Channel Islands in 2002. Soon afterwards it spread to mainland Britain, where it is now widely distributed. Infested elaeagnus bushes can be damaged severely,[23] but the pest does not pose a threat to other cultivated plants.

In 2006, the platanus lace bug (*Corythucha ciliata*)[24] (Fig. 379), a native of North America, was discovered in a Bedfordshire nursery on London plane and oriental plane trees. The pest was believed to have arrived via France and Italy, from where the infested trees had been imported some years previously (Table 20).[25]

TABLE 20. Examples of alien phytophagous insects discovered or intercepted in Britain, and for which (from 2001 to 2009) Plant Health Notices were issued on behalf of Defra[26] by the Central Science Laboratory.[27]

Pest	*Order: Family*	*Remarks*
Allium leaf miner (*Phytomyza gymnostoma*)	Diptera: Agromyzidae	Found on garden-grown leeks in Wolverhampton in 2003 and now locally established – Notice No. 35 (July 2004).
Anthurium whitefly (*Crenidorsum aroidephagus*)	Hemiptera: Aleyrodidae	Found by the Plant Health & Seeds Inspectorate (PHSI) in 2006 on *Anthurium* leaves imported from Mauritius – Notice No. 45 (August 2006).
Asian miscanthus aphid (*Melanaphis sorini*)	Hemiptera: Aphididae	Found in 2006 at a nursery in Hampshire on *Miscanthus* plants imported from Israel – Notice No. 44 (September 2006).
Banded-winged whitefly (*Trialeurodes abutiloneus*)	Hemiptera; Aleyrodidae	Intercepted in 2005 by PHSI at Gatwick airport on hibiscus plants imported from the US (also found in a commercial nursery) – Notice No. 39 (April 2005).
Chilli thrips (*Scirtothrips dorsalis*)	Thysanoptera: Thripidae	A regularly intercepted pest – Notice No. 40 (May 2006).
Cycad aulacaspis scale (*Aulacaspis yasumatsui*)	Hemiptera: Diaspididae	Found in a garden centre in England in 2006 on cycad plants imported from Vietnam via the Netherlands – Notice No. 42 (May 2006).
Elaeagnus sucker (*Cacopsylla fulguralis*)	Hemiptera: Psyllidae	First found in Guernsey in March 2002 on elaeagnus, and subsequently found in various parts of England – Notice No. 32 (June 2002).
Japanese wax scale (*Ceroplastes ceriferus*)	Hemiptera: Coccidae	Intercepted on rubber-trees and yellow-woods imported from the Netherlands in 1999 and 2000. Previously found on smooth Japanese

		maple imported from Japan in 1921 and on yellow-woods imported from the US in 1995 and 1999 – Notice No. 34 (October 2002).
Onion aphid (*Neotoxoptera formosana*)	Hemiptera: Aphididae	First found in the UK in September 1999, on Welsh onions in Surrey – Notice No. 29 (February 2001).
Palm borer moth (*Paysandisia archon*)	Lepidoptera: Castniidae	First found in Sussex in 2002. Subsequently, in Kent in 2007, several adults emerged from large palm trees – *Phoenix canariensis* – imported from Spain in 2005 – Notice No. 49 (May 2007).
Platanus lace bug (*Corythucha ciliata*)	Hemiptera: Tingidae	Found by PHSI in 2006 on two nurseries in Bedfordshire on plane trees imported from France and Italy – Notice No. 46 (October 2006).
South American tomato moth (*Tuta absoluta*)	Lepidoptera: Gelechiidae	Following its discovery in southern Europe, in 2006, infested tomato fruits imported from Spain have subsequently been found in the UK – Notice No. 56 (April 2009)
Western corn rootworm (*Diabrotica virgifera virgifera*)	Coleoptera: Chrysomelidae	Found close to Heathrow airport and near Gatwick airport in 2003, and subsequently eradicated – Notices No. 36 (March 2004) and No. 37 (July 2005).
White peach scale (*Pseudaulacaspis pentagona*)	Hemiptera: Diaspididae	Found in England in 2006/7 on Indian bean-tree and peach. Also intercepted on occasions on imported kiwi fruit, lilac and peach – Notice No. 52 (September 2007).
Wisteria scale (*Eulecanium excrescens*)	Hemiptera: Coccidae	Established in London since 2001, mainly on wisteria – Notice No. 33 (July 2002).

FIG 379. Platanus lace bug (*Corythucha ciliata*) is not indigenous to Britain, but infested trees were found in a Bedfordshire nursery in 2006.

FIG 380. Green vegetable bug (*Nezara viridula*) is now established in Britain. The nymph, illustrated here, is far more colourful than the mainly dull green adult.

The greatest threat posed by this bug lies in its ability, in conjunction with the fungal pathogens *Apiognomonia veneta*[28] and *Ceratocystis fimbriata* f. sp. *platani*, to cause the decline and death of host trees. Other aliens to have entered Britain include the lace bug *Stephanitis takeyai*, from Japan, on lily of the valley bush,[29] and the highly polyphagous green vegetable bug (*Nezara viridula*) (Fig. 380) – the latter probably of East African or Mediterranean origin. Green vegetable bug is well established in southern Europe, and in 2003 it was found breeding in the London area.[30] Interestingly, in February 2005, 132 live adults were discovered on a Devon nursery amongst a consignment of terracotta pots imported from Italy.[31] Solitary interceptions of green vegetable bugs have also been made in Britain.

Not all alien bugs associated with plants are pests. The non-British predatory mirid *Deraeocoris flavilinea* (see Chapter 7) is an example.

THRIPS

Western flower thrips (*Frankliniella occidentalis*) (WFT) is one of the most infamous invasive insect pests to have reached Britain in recent years. Following a major expansion of its natural range in North America during the early 1980s, the thrips also began to spread internationally. It reached mainland Europe in about 1983, and in 1986 an outbreak was found for the first time in Britain – on chrysanthemums in a commercial greenhouse in Cambridge. The pest's reputation as both a polyphagous feeder and an important virus vector had preceded it, and confirmation of its arrival in Britain caused considerable alarm within the horticultural industry. Concern was heightened by its discovery shortly afterwards on a nursery that both propagated and distributed chrysanthemum cuttings. Subsequent surveys confirmed that over 500 customers of the nursery had unwittingly received infested plants. This triggered widespread publicity and promulgation of advice on how to tackle the problem. However, owing in part to its small size, rapid rate of breeding and ability to develop resistance to insecticides, the pest proved very difficult to control. By the end of 1988 WFT was still located on over 300 sites in the UK, having thwarted attempts to eradicate or contain it. A case was cited where, on a large commercial nursery, around a million ornamental pot plants and hanging-basket plants had become infested. Here, an added difficulty in advising on control measures was the unknown risk of phytotoxicity from chemical treatments.[32] Today, WFT is accepted as an indelibly established pest of protected crops in Britain (Chapter 10), joining the ranks of other long-established non-native residents such as glasshouse thrips (*Heliothrips haemorrhoidalis*) and onion thrips (*Thrips tabaci*) – the former a tropical species and the latter probably of eastern Mediterranean origin.

In the wake of WFT, the melon thrips (*Thrips palmi*) from southeast Asia is also causing concern in Britain. This polyphagous and invasive species first arrived in Europe in the 1970s. Although not a permanent European resident, outbreaks have occurred from time to time, and the pest is currently viewed as presenting a potential risk to various crops. Greenhouse ornamentals and protected food crops such as aubergine, cucumber, lettuce, melon, sweet pepper and tomato are particularly vulnerable. In the year 2000, infestations of melon thrips were discovered on all-year-round (AYR) chrysanthemums in greenhouses in Sussex. However, although by then well established (indicative of what might happen if vigilance were to be relaxed), the pest was eventually eradicated.[33] Other non-European thrips attracting the attention of Plant Health authorities include chilli thrips (*Scirtothrips dorsalis*)[34] and poinsettia thrips (*Echinothrips americanus*).[35] These aliens constitute a potential threat to greenhouse crops in Britain, and both have been intercepted in recent years.

BEETLES

Colorado beetle (*Leptinotarsa decemlineata*)[36] is a major worldwide pest of potato crops, capable of causing widespread and complete defoliation.[37] It is also, arguably, one of our most notorious crop pests, even though it does not reside in these islands and few UK farmers or members of the public will have ever seen one, alive or dead. The pest is greatly feared, and posters displaying the distinctive, yellow and black adults (Fig. 381) were long on display in police stations and government offices, calling for help in keeping these islands free of this unwelcome interloper.

Colorado beetle was once restricted to the semi-desert regions of Colorado, in the US, where it bred on wild solanaceous plants, especially buffalobur nightshade.[38] In the nineteenth century, following man's pioneering encroachment into the west (and the introduction of potato plants, which quickly proved ideal hosts), the beetle spread rapidly eastwards across the

FIG 381. Colorado beetle (*Leptinotarsa decemlineata*) is one of the world's most feared crop pests. Fortunately, it is not established in Britain.

FIG 382. Colorado beetle eggs are laid in batches on the leaves of potato plants.

country. By 1874 it had reached the Atlantic seaboard of both the US and southeast Canada. It had also by then developed into a devastating potato pest. Colorado beetles soon arrived in mainland Europe, and reference has already been made (in Chapter 5) to the introduction of statutory measures (the Destructive Insects Act of 1877) to protect British crops from such pests. In the same year, importation of potato haulm (the stalks or stems of potato plants) from the US was also banned. The first British outbreak of Colorado beetle on a potato crop occurred in 1901, near Tilbury docks in Essex. Although the pest managed to overwinter, it was then eradicated. Breeding colonies of Colorado beetle also appeared in Britain in later years, especially during the 1940s and early 1950s when there were over 150 outbreaks. These were also eliminated, as were colonies found in Kent in 1976 and Sussex in 1977.[39] The pest did, however, become temporarily established in the Channel Islands during the 1940s, before eventually being ousted. Invasions resulted from sea-borne adults that drifted ashore, having first taken flight in France. The beetles are known to survive for up to ten days in sea water and, if conditions are suitable, they are then still capable of taking flight.[40] Britain and Ireland continue to be successful in keeping the Colorado beetle at bay. However, this is not the case in mainland Europe. There, the pest became established in western France, near Bordeaux, around 1920. Since then it has spread inexorably northwards, southwards and eastwards. Colorado beetle is now resident in many parts of central, eastern and southern Europe, including the near continent (Belgium, France and the Netherlands).[41] Owing to its close proximity to France, Jersey is under constant threat of direct invasion, especially during the migratory flight period of the adult beetles each spring. The importance of potatoes to the island's economy highlights the need to limit the risk of invasion. Plant Health (Jersey) laws

FIG 383. Since its appearance in mainland Europe in 1992, western corn rootworm (*Diabrotica virgifera virgifera*) has spread very rapidly. The pest was found in Britain, near Heathrow airport, in 2003.

require regular beach inspections to 'ensure no live Colorado beetles survive on Island beaches thus preventing flight and establishment of a breeding colony', and field inspections of early potato crops, for adults, eggs (Fig. 382) and larvae to 'ensure no colonies of Colorado beetle are established within the crop'. As for mainland Britain, adults are intercepted in most (if not all) years. However, these arrive not as migrants but as contaminants in consignments of imported plants or plant products. Lettuces and other leafy vegetables, in which adults may be hiding, constitute the greatest risk.[42] Climatically, much of southern England is currently suitable for the establishment of Colorado beetle. However, global warming over the next half century or so may allow colonisation to occur far more widely, and to extend across Ireland.[43]

Western corn rootworm (*Diabrotica virgifera virgifera*) (Fig. 383) is a major North American pest of maize (including sweet corn). Following its discovery near Belgrade international airport in 1992, the pest has also become firmly established in mainland Europe. Its range now extends well beyond Serbia into Austria, the Czech Republic, Italy, Poland and the Ukraine. It has also appeared elsewhere, as in Belgium, England, France, Germany, the Netherlands and Switzerland. In England, western corn rootworm was first detected in 2003, when 92 adults were caught in pheromone traps placed in forage maize crops near Heathrow and Gatwick airports.[44] Detections in the vicinity of airports have also been made in many other countries, including – in addition to the original discovery in the former Yugoslavia – Belgium (Zaventem, Brussels), France (Le Bourget, Orly and Roissy, Paris), Italy (e.g. Venezia) and the Netherlands (Schiphol). Adult western corn rootworms feed on the aerial parts of plants, but most harm is done by the soil-inhabiting larvae which attack the roots. Also, greatest damage is caused in the absence of crop rotation, where maize is grown continuously. Corn rootworms are major pests in the US.[45] They cause significant crop losses which, along with the cost of treatments, famously amount to around US$ 1 billion annually. Accordingly, the pests are widely known as billion dollar bugs. Infestations of western corn rootworm have already resulted in economic damage on maize crops in Serbia and surrounding countries, including Bulgaria, Croatia, Hungary and Romania. To date, however, this is not the case elsewhere in Europe. Steps were taken to prevent the spread of western corn rootworm within the European Community, and in several instances the pest was successfully eliminated. However, infestations have persisted in several member states, albeit often (as in England) on a very local scale. In September 2008, in recognition of air transport as a major invasion pathway, the Plant Health (England) (Amendment) Order 2008[46] was issued. This Amendment, which came into force on 1 October 2008, states that:

> *Where there is a high risk of the introduction of* Diabrotica virgifera *Le Conte from any aircraft landing at an airport in England, the Secretary of State may designate a zone around the airport ('a designated zone').*

Restrictions apply within a designated zone, including a stipulation that maize can be grown just once in any two consecutive years. It remains to be seen whether such measures, along with others already in force,[47] will prove effective and whether western corn rootworm can be permanently eradicated from these islands. Currently, western corn rootworm is thought to be at the northern edge of its range in Britain. However, it has been suggested that by 2050, in the wake of climate change, much of England could become climatically suitable for the pest. Also, if the area of maize-growing were also to increase, western corn rootworm may well become an economic problem here.[48] Fears have been expressed that western corn rootworm might attack cereal crops other than maize or sweet corn. However, although the pest can breed on barley, wheat and certain grass weeds, fecundity of adults is then compromised as are larval survival rates.[49]

For many years the exotic Australian ladybird *Cryptolaemus montrouzieri* has been used in greenhouses and hothouses to control mealybugs, especially the citrus mealybug (*Planococcus citri*). Occasionally, adults have escaped into the wild. However, as tropical insects with a lack of cold tolerance, such insects are very unlikely to survive a British winter, except in the mildest of areas.[50] Also, owing to their greatly restricted host range, any survivors or their progeny are unlikely to have any adverse impact on the British fauna and would probably eventually die from lack of suitable food. This is in marked contrast to the situation created

FIG 384. Harlequin ladybird (*Harmonia axyridis*) has spread rapidly in Britain, following its first discovery in 2004. It is now firmly established.

by the harlequin ladybird (*Harmonia axyridis*),[51] a recent addition to the British fauna. Harlequin ladybirds (Fig. 384) are natives of Asia, and they have also been marketed for many years as biocontrol agents (BCAs), for use against aphids and scale insects, although never in Britain. In recent years, following its arrival in southeastern England in 2004, this highly invasive species has become firmly established. Unlike *C. montrouzieri*, harlequin ladybirds are serious competitors of other ladybirds, out-competing them and leading to serious declines in populations of indigenous species.[52] Nevertheless, coexistence with native species, such as the seven-spot ladybird (*Coccinella septempunctata*), is reported.[53] In spite of its attractive appearance, in both the adult and larval stages, and its ability to reduce aphid numbers on many crops, it is generally considered an unwelcome addition to our fauna. Harlequin ladybirds are also minor pests of crops. In dry conditions, for example, they not only imbibe juices from overripe fruits such as pears but, during their search for moisture, also damage grapes, raspberries and other soft-skinned fruits. Furthermore, following reflex bleeding, whereby haemolymph is exuded from the body, an obnoxious odour is produced. This contaminates fruits, and has become a particular problem for winegrowers in both America and mainland Europe. If the ladybirds are present at harvest time and are then crushed with the grapes, they can eventually affect the aroma and flavour of the wine.[54] This is especially so with traditional high-pressure grape pressing, but less so in the case of modern lower-pressure production systems.

Wingless weevils (*Otiorhynchus* spp.) have long been recognised as important crop pests in Britain, and in recent years their ranks have been swelled by newcomers from abroad. The privet weevil (*O. crataegi*)[55] (Fig. 385), for example, appeared in Berkshire in the 1980s. This is a relatively small, southern European

FIG 385. Privet weevil (*Otiorhynchus crataegi*) has been established in southern England since the 1980s.

FIG 386. Several alien species of *Otiorhynchus*, including *O. salicicola*, have been found recently on ornamental plants in England.

species (adults about 5 mm long), the adults of which cause damage to the leaves of privet hedges and ornamental shrubs such as lilac. Other non-British species to have become established here include *O. armadillo* and *O. salicicola* (Fig. 386), both of which were found recently in southwest London.[56]

TRUE FLIES

Over the past two decades the agromyzid fly *Phytomyza gymnostoma*[57] has emerged from obscurity to become a pest of leek and onion crops, especially in central Europe. The insect has also greatly extended its range, and is now present in many parts of Europe, including Britain. The first UK outbreak occurred in 2003, in a private garden in the West Midlands. Subsequent observations confirmed that the

FIG 387. American serpentine leaf miner (*Liriomyza trifolii*) is most often imported on chrysanthemum cuttings. This important North American pest was first found in Britain in 1977.

pest was also present in other non-commercial sites (e.g. allotments) in the same area.[58] There are two generations annually; adults occur in spring and early autumn, and larvae – known as allium leaf miners – feed in May and in the late autumn. Attacked plants are often invaded by white rot (*Sclerotium cepivorum*) and other pathogens. At least abroad, the pest aestivates during the summer as pupae formed (in puparia) at the end of the larval feeding galleries. The winter is also passed in the pupal stage. Although it is yet to be found on commercial crops in the UK, the pest's appearance in this country is viewed with concern. The reasons for its sudden emergence as a pest are unknown.

Dipterous leaf miners are also important greenhouse pests (Chapter 10), and these sometimes include non-native species accidentally introduced with plants imported from abroad. Two New World species in particular have grabbed the headlines: the American serpentine leaf miner (*Liriomyza trifolii*) (Fig. 387) and, more recently, the South American leaf miner (*L. huidobrensis*). American serpentine leaf miner was first found in Britain in 1977, followed in 1989 by the first recorded outbreak of the South American leaf miner. Since then, there have been many incursions, although nowadays the former species occurs far less frequently than in the past. Both species have also been found in greenhouses in Ireland.[59] American serpentine leaf miner, which has now become established in parts of Europe and elsewhere in the Old World, is most often introduced on chrysanthemum cuttings from places such as the Canary Islands, Denmark, Kenya, Malta, the Netherlands and the US.[60] South American leaf miner also gains entry on infested plant material, notably cut flowers and pot plants, and is especially damaging on gerbera and verbena; edible crops such as cucumber, lettuce and tomato are also at particular risk.[61] Apart from leaf mines, which tend to vary in appearance from one species to another,[62] the first sign of these alien pests is often the presence of adult feeding punctures in the leaves (Fig. 388). These appear as tiny speckles, but are indistinguishable

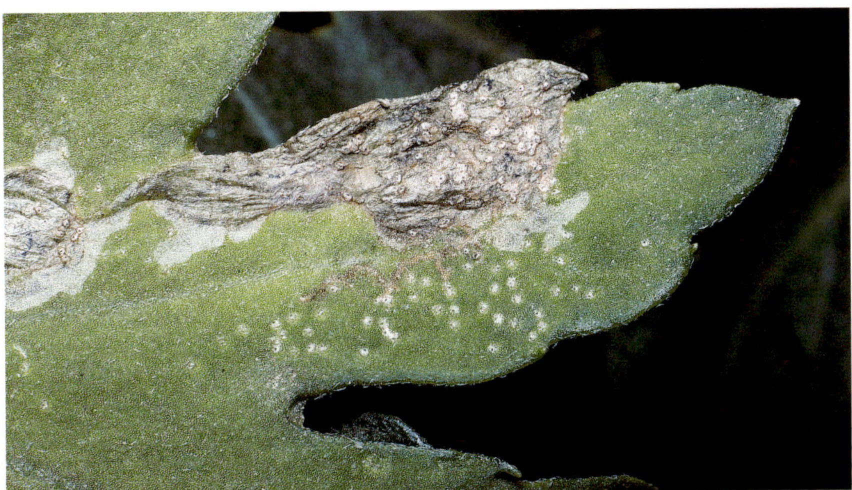

FIG 388. Adult feeding punctures are often the first indication of an outbreak of American serpentine leaf miner (*Liriomyza trifolii*) and other such pests.

from those produced by non-exotic species of *Liriomyza*. At *c.* 0.2 mm in diameter, however, they are distinctly smaller than those produced by our native chrysanthemum leaf miner (*Chromatomyia syngenesiae*) (Chapter 10). Afforded the opportunity, alien leaf miners may also spread to outdoor plants.[63] However, they are not thought capable of surviving British winters in unprotected situations.

Larvae of non-British tephritid flies (large fruit flies) are found occasionally inside fresh fruits imported from abroad. These include European cherry fruit fly (*Rhagoletis cerasi*) (Fig. 389) and Mediterranean fruit fly (*Ceratitis capitata*)[64]

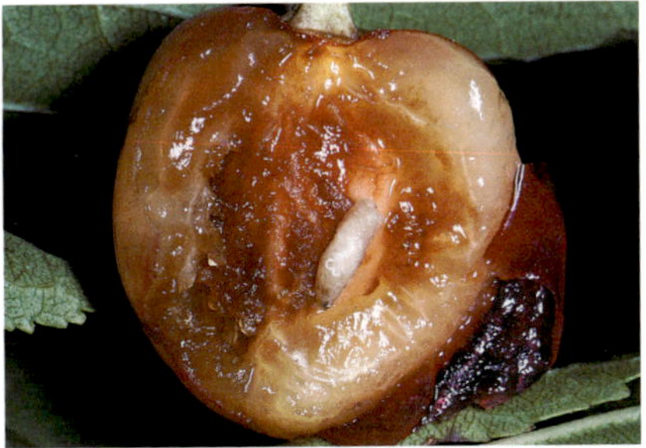

FIG 389. (Above left) European cherry fruit fly (*Rhagoletis cerasi*) is a common pest of cherries in mainland Europe, but does not occur in Britain. (Above right) Larvae occur occasionally in imported cherries, and drowned ones are sometimes found in jars of preserved sour cherries.

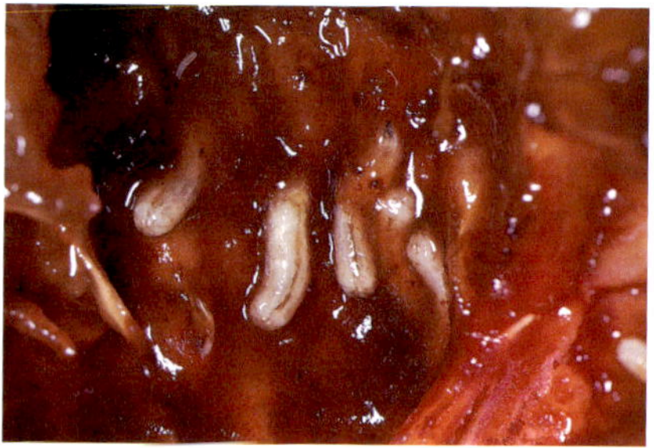

FIG 390. (Above left) Mediterranean fruit fly (*Ceratitis capitata*) is a major tropical and subtropical pest of fruit crops. (Above right) Larvae feed gregariously, and are occasionally intercepted in citrus and other fruits imported from warmer parts of the world.

(Fig. 390). Larvae of the former occur singly in sweet and sour cherries, whereas those of the latter feed gregariously in oranges, nectarines, peaches and many other fruits. Casual imports such as these are unlikely to survive, even if adults were to be produced, and they are not currently seen as presenting a risk to the British fruit-growing industry.

MOTHS AND BUTTERFLIES

Over the years, several alien moths have become established in Britain.[65] These include pests such as the carnation tortrix moth (*Cacoecimorpha pronubana*) from southern Europe, and the light brown apple moth (*Epiphyas postvittana*) and the summer fruit tortrix moth (*Adoxophyes orana*) from Australasia (see earlier

FIG 391. Platanus leaf miner moth (*Phyllonorycter platani*) is a recent arrival in mainland Europe, and the relatively large leaf mines are now found on plane trees in Britain.

FIG 392. Since its first discovery in Macedonia in the late 1970s or early 1980s, horse chestnut leaf miner moth (*Cameraria ohridella*) has spread rapidly across Europe. Nowadays, the characteristic leaf mines are abundant on horse chestnut trees in England.

chapters). The straw-coloured apple moth (*Blastobasis decolorella*), a species originating in Madeira, has also become a pest since its arrival in Britain (Chapter 7). The British moth fauna has been boosted further by several alien leaf-mining species. These too are regarded as pests if the larvae damage cultivated plants in amenity areas, garden centres, nurseries or private gardens. Examples of European origin include the firethorn leaf miner moth and the platanus leaf miner moth (*Phyllonorycter platani*) (Fig. 391). Visible proof of the destruction capable of being meted out by such pests is dramatically demonstrated by yet another species, the horse chestnut leaf miner moth (*Cameraria ohridella*) (Fig. 392). In this case, mines can be exceedingly numerous and often come to occupy the complete leaf area available to them, heavily infested foliage turning brown and falling prematurely.[66] Although horse chestnut trees are severely affected, red horse chestnut (a red-flowering hybrid between horse chestnut and red buck-eye) is resistant to attack. Horse chestnut leaf miner moth, a tiny (wings *c.* 4 mm long) and highly invasive species, was unknown to science until its discovery in Macedonia in the late 1970s or early 1980s. It has since spread rapidly across Europe, and is now firmly established in Britain.

Leaf miners that have successfully entered mainland Europe from other parts of the globe include the citrus leaf miner moth (*Phyllocnistis citrella*) (Fig. 393) and *Phyllonorycter issikii* (both from Asia – the former on citrus (family Rutaceae); the latter on lime (family Tiliaceae)), and North American pests such as *Parectopa robiniella* and *Phyllonorycter robiniella* (both on false acacia).[67] As previously mentioned (Chapter 9), mines of the citrus leaf miner moth are sometimes present on the leaves of ornamental citrus plants imported into Britain. However, to date, signs of *Phyllonorycter issikii* and the two leaf-mining species associated with false acacia have not been found here. In 1995, another North

FIG 393. Mines formed by citrus leaf miner moth (*Phyllocnistis citrella*) larvae are sometimes found on ornamental citrus plants imported into Britain.

FIG 394. American grapevine leaf miner moth (*Phyllocnistis vitegenella*) is a recent arrival in Europe, but is not thought likely to pose a threat to British vineyards.

American pest, the American grapevine leaf miner moth (*Phyllocnistis vitegenella*) (Fig. 394), was discovered in northeast Italy.[68] This species has since spread to Slovenia. British vineyards, however, are not under threat.

Britain maintains vigilance for a range of other exotics. These include tropical or subtropical pests which sometimes arrive in association with imported plants. By way of example, larvae of banana moth (*Opogona sacchari*) (known as sugar cane borers) are found occasionally. They feed within the woody or fleshy stems of imported ornamentals (e.g. genera *Dracaena*, *Ficus* and *Hibiscus*), and betray their presence by expelling large quantities of dry frass. The larvae are versatile feeders, and also attack the leaves and leaf stalks of herbaceous plants such as begonias and African violets. Abroad, the larvae are of particular concern as pests of banana plants and sugar cane; they are also known to feed on stored potato tubers.[69] Apart from larvae occasionally imported with bananas, the first infestation in Britain occurred in a greenhouse in East Sussex in 1971, when *c.* 3,000 of 11,000 rubber-plant cuttings were affected.[70] Although well capable of persisting in heated greenhouses and other protected environments, banana moth (a tropical or subtropical pest of African origin) is unable to survive outdoors in Britain. The same probably holds true for another stem-boring alien, the palm borer moth (*Paysandisia archon*). Following its accidental introduction, this South American pest is now established in southern Europe (France, Italy and Spain), and has since been reared from palm trees imported into Britain from mainland Europe (Table 20). Palm borer moth is large (adults have a wingspan of *c.* 100 mm) and colourful, with olive-brown forewings and red, black and white hindwings. Depending on conditions, the pest completes its lifecycle in one to three years. Palm trees of various genera are attacked, including Europe's only native species *Chamaerops humilis*.[71]

Following its colonisation of southern Europe, the geranium bronze butterfly (*Cacyreus marshalli*) from South Africa has become a focus of attention as a pest of cultivated geranium and pelargonium plants. The larvae mine the leaves, and bore into the flower buds and terminal shoots. They also feed openly on the expanded leaves. Various cultivars are attacked, although those with scented leaves tend to be avoided.[72] The first European interception of this small but attractive butterfly was made in 1978, when the pest was found on greenhouse-grown geraniums in the UK. This infestation was quickly eradicated. Later, in the wake of its accidental introduction to the Balearic Islands in the mid- to late 1980s,[73] the pest eventually spread (as predicted)[74] to mainland Europe. It now breeds in various places, including southern France, Italy, Portugal and Spain. Its second appearance in the UK was in 1997, in East Sussex, the pest probably having been introduced on nursery plants imported from Iberia.[75]

FIG 395. Mediterranean brocade moth (*Spodoptera littoralis*) is reared occasionally from larvae imported into Britain on chrysanthemum cuttings and other greenhouse plants.

Mediterranean brocade moth (*Spodoptera littoralis*) (Fig. 395) is a notorious, polyphagous pest of tropical and subtropical agriculture. Exceptionally, back in September 1963, the pest was found on AYR chrysanthemums at over 20 sites in Britain – ranging from southern England to Scotland. These infestations, linked to chrysanthemum cuttings imported from the Canary Islands, were all subsequently eliminated. The pest has also appeared in more recent years, following the importation of carnation, chrysanthemum, hibiscus and various other ornamentals. Eggs of Mediterranean brocade moth are laid in large, compact batches, often containing several hundred eggs. These are usually placed on the underside of leaves, and are then covered in hair-like scales from the female's abdomen. These egg batches are easily overlooked, and typically form the stage at which the pest is introduced to importing countries.[76] Following egg hatch, the larvae feed in small groups. From the fourth instar onwards, however,

FIG 396. Mediterranean brocade moth (*Spodoptera littoralis*) larvae are commonly known as Mediterranean climbing cutworms.

FIG 397. In tropical countries, scarce bordered straw moth (*Helicovera armigera*) is a major pest of cotton and other tropical crops. Larvae, known as Old World bollworms, cause extensive damage, and are found occasionally in Britain on imported plants and plant products.

they become solitary. Older larvae typically hide in the soil during the daytime, emerging at night and ascending plants to feed. Such larvae (known as Mediterranean climbing cutworms) (Fig. 396) cause extensive defoliation. They are also damaging to buds, flowers and stems.

Imported chrysanthemum cuttings (as well as other plants) have also been a pathway for the introduction of other aliens into British greenhouses. Examples of notifiable pests include the African carnation tortrix moth (*Epichoristodes acerbella*) and the scarce bordered straw moth (*Helicovera armigera*).[77] Larvae of the latter (Fig. 397) are known as Old World bollworms, and can be very destructive. However, significant outbreaks have not been observed in Britain. Other non-natives introduced from time to time include the golden twin-spot moth (*Chrysodeixis chalcites*) and the slender burnished brass moth (*Diachrysia orichalcea*). Both of these species are closely related to the well-known silver Y moth, and their larvae are semi-loopers (possessing just three pairs of abdominal prolegs).

Protected horticultural crops in northern Europe are also under threat from various other alien Lepidoptera. These include the marshland pyralid moth (*Duponchelia fovealis*). This polyphagous species is a resident of the Canary Islands and the Mediterranean area, where the larvae feed on a range of marshland plants. In recent years, however, the same insect has appeared on a wide range of

FIG 398. (Above left) Gypsy moth (*Lymantria dispar*), here a male, is a potentially devastating pest. (Above right) The larvae feed on a wide range of broadleaved trees and shrubs.

protected crops in northern Europe. These include ornamentals, as well as vegetables such as celery and lettuce. Cultivated aquatic plants are also attacked. The larvae, which favour damp conditions, attack the crowns and base of stems, causing plants to wilt, collapse and die. The first outbreak in the UK occurred on heuchera plants in a West Midlands nursery in 1999.[78] Although also recorded more recently in Britain, the pest is not established here. Another alien, the box-tree pyralid (*Diaphania perspectalis*),[79] is amongst our most recent arrivals, adults having been captured in light traps in southern England in 2008. This highly invasive pest, a native of eastern Asia (China, Japan and Korea), causes extensive defoliation of box plants and is a threat to nursery stock as well as to bushes in parks and gardens. In Europe, it was first recorded in Germany in 2007, having been introduced from China via a nursery in the Netherlands.[80]

Other aliens to have appeared in Britain in recent years include gypsy moth (*Lymantria dispar*) (Fig. 398), an outbreak of which was discovered in the Epping

FIG 399. This gelechiid moth, believed to be a species new to science, was reared from gregarious larvae boring inside cyclamen corms imported into Britain from Asia in the 1990s.

FIG 400. Oriental fruit moth (*Cydia molesta*) does not occur in Britain, but larvae are sometimes intercepted in peaches and other fruits imported from southern Europe.

area in 1995.[81] This formerly native species (then not considered a pest) became extinct in Britain just over 100 years ago. Of far lesser significance was a gelechiid moth (family Gelechiidae) whose larvae were found infesting imported cyclamen corms, also in the 1990s. Although larvae were reared through to adulthood, the identity of this Asiatic species (believed to be new to science) (Fig. 399) was never established.

As in the case of tephritid flies (see above), larvae of non-British moths are sometimes found feeding inside imported fruits. These include those of the oriental fruit moth (*Cydia molesta*) (Fig. 400), a pest of apricots, nectarines, peaches and other rosaceous fruits. Oriental fruit moth is well entrenched in southern Europe, but (global warming aside) the British climate is not thought suitable for its establishment.[82]

SAWFLIES AND GALL WASPS

Except as forestry pests, alien sawflies are rarely a cause for concern in these islands. Nevertheless, some long-established foreign species occur here on ornamental plants, including aruncus sawfly (*Nematus spiraeae*), false acacia sawfly (*N. tibialis*) and Solomon's seal sawfly (*Phymatocera aterrima*) (Chapter 9).[83] Recent newcomers to Britain on ornamentals are few and far between, but the barberry sawfly (*Arge berberidis*), a notorious pest in central and southern Europe, can now be counted as a resident.[84] This sawfly has quickly become established in southern England, probably having been first introduced on infested nursery stock in the late 1990s. The rather plump, unmistakable larvae (Fig. 401) feed on the foliage of barberry, and are capable of causing extensive, and sometimes complete, defoliation of bushes. Mahonia, a close relative of barberry, is also attacked.

FIG 401. Barberry sawfly (*Arge berberidis*) has recently become established in Britain. The plump-bodied larvae cause extensive defoliation of barberry and related plants.

Various alien gall wasps have become established in Britain, especially on oak trees. These include long-established species such as the marble gall wasp (*Andricus kollari*) and the acorn cup gall cynipid (*A. quercuscalicis*), as well as more recent arrivals such as *A. grossulariae* and *A. lucidus*. Such gall wasps are associated mainly with wild hosts, and it would be pushing boundaries to regard these as crop pests (except when they occur on nursery stock in commercial holdings). Additional newcomers to Britain include a gall wasp on eucalyptus, thought to be the eucalyptus gall wasp (*Ophelimus maskelli*). This Australian pest, which is currently causing problems in New Zealand and many non-antipodean countries, recently appeared in the London area (in 2005), and seems poised to become more widely distributed in Britain.

MITES

Owing to their small size, it is not surprising that phytophagous mites sometimes arrive undetected on imported plant material. However, symptoms of attack (such as webbing, discoloration or blotching of leaves in the case of spider mites; galling or bronzing of tissue in the case of gall mites and rust mites) often help to betray their presence, either on initial inspection of plants or subsequently. In recent years, bamboo mite (*Stigmaeopsis celarius*)[85] has been found on nursery-grown bamboo plants in several counties in southern England, having previously escaped detection. This century has also seen interceptions of other alien spider mites, including citrus brown mite (*Eutetranychus orientalis*)[86] and citrus spider mite (*Panonychus citri*). Most new arrivals, however, have been gall mites or rust mites (Table 21). Of these, greatest concern surrounds mites on bay laurel and fuchsia: bay big-bud mite (*Cecidophyopsis malpighianus*) and bay rust mite (*Calepitrimerus russoi*) on the former; fuchsia gall mite (*Aculops fuchsiae*) on the latter. Bay big-bud mite is a Mediterranean species and, along with bay rust mite (a central and eastern European species), has become well established on nursery-grown bay laurel in northern Europe, notably in Belgium. The appearance of these mites in Britain, therefore, is not unexpected, since Belgium is a major exporter of bay laurel plants. Buds infested by bay big-bud mite become extremely enlarged, discoloured and distorted, affecting the appearance and growth of plants. Conversely, bay rust mite causes severe bronzing, necrosis and desiccation of leaves, resulting in premature leaf fall. The fuchsia gall mite is currently causing considerable alarm, not least amongst members of the British Fuchsia Society and local fuchsia clubs in Britain. This South American species, unknown prior to its discovery in Brazil in 1972, causes extensive stunting, distortion and discoloration of infested plants, and has quickly established itself as a highly significant pest. In 1981, the mite was accidentally introduced to North America, where it then spread rapidly. In the early 2000s, outbreaks occurred in mainland Europe, notably in Brittany, France. More recently, the pest has been found in Guernsey, Jersey and in several locations in mainland Britain, including Hampshire, Kent and Middlesex.

MISCELLANEOUS PESTS

Several vertebrate pests of UK crops are of foreign origin. These include grey squirrels, rabbits and ring-necked parakeets, all of which have been mentioned in earlier chapters. Potato cyst nematodes, which (along with potato plants) have their origins in South America, have also been discussed elsewhere (Chapter 5). As for other exotics, attention here will be restricted to alien terrestrial flatworms.

Over the years, Britain has been invaded by various species of alien terrestrial flatworm.[87] However, until the arrival of the much publicised New Zealand flatworm (*Arthurdendyus triangulatus*)[88] (Fig. 402), these non-native species raised little or no concern. The New Zealand flatworm was first recorded outside its native country in 1963, when it was found in a garden in Northern Ireland. This was followed, in 1965, by its discovery in Scotland.[89] Since then the flatworm,

TABLE 21. Alien phytophagous mites discovered or intercepted in Britain, and for which (from 2005 to 2008) Plant Health Notices were issued on behalf of Defra[90] by the Central Science Laboratory.[91]

Species	*Family*	*Remarks*
Bay big-bud mite (*Cecidophyopsis malpighianus*)	Eriophyidae	Found on bay laurel in London in 2005 and 2006 – Notice No. 43 (June 2006)
Bay rust mite (*Calepitrimerus russoi*)	Eriophyidae	Found in northeast Yorkshire in May 2007 on young greenhouse-grown bay laurel saplings imported from Belgium – Notice No. 53 (November 2007)
Fuchsia gall mite (*Aculops fuchsiae*)	Eriophyidae	First found on fuschia plants in the Channel Islands in 2006 and in southern England in September 2007 – Notice No. 38 (June 2005*); Notice No. 51 (September 2007); Notice No. 54 (August 2008)
Goji gall mite (*Aceria kuko*)	Eriophyidae	Found in England in 2008, on Goji berry plants imported from China via the Netherlands and Guernsey – Notice No. 55 (October 2008)
Onion mite (*Aceria tulipae*)	Eriophyidae	Found on onion sets imported from the Netherlands in 2006 – Notice No. 41 (May 2006)
Swamp cypress rust mite (*Epitrimerus taxodii*)	Eriophyidae	Found in Herefordshire in October 2006 on swamp cypress trees imported from France – Notice No. 47 (November 2006).

* Notice issued in advance of the pest's discovery in Britain.

which feeds on earthworms, has spread considerably, albeit accidentally aided by man, and it is now also established in England, the Republic of Ireland and the Isle of Man. The distribution and spread of New Zealand flatworm have been studied by various workers, often with the aid of the general public, and its progress as an invasive species is well documented.[92] In spite of having greatly extended its range, the pest is still most abundant in Northern Ireland and

FIG 402. New Zealand flatworm (*Arthurdendyus triangulatus*) has become a much-publicised invader, and is especially common in Northern Ireland and Scotland. It feeds on earthworms, and is an unwelcome import.

Scotland, where conditions for its survival appear especially favourable. In 1980 another alien planarian predator of earthworms, the Australian flatworm (*Australoplana sanguinea* var. *alba*)[93] (Fig. 403), was found in the Isles of Scilly.[94] This species has since become widely distributed in southern and western Britain, although it has not attained the same status as its antipodean cousin. In recent years, other species have also been discovered in Britain. These include *Arthurdendyus albidus*, a then undescribed alien flatworm found in Scotland in association with camellia plants previously imported from New Zealand,[95] and two Australian flatworms: *Kontikia ventrolineata*[96] and *Fletchamia sugdeni*, the latter introduced into Britain along with tree ferns.[97]

An earthworm predator such as the New Zealand flatworm is not, of course, a plant pest. However, such organisms can have a direct impact on international horticultural trade (see below). In Britain, and elsewhere in Europe, the flatworm

FIG 403. Australian flatworm (*Australoplana sanguinea* var. *alba*), an invader from Australasia, was found in the Isles of Scilly in 1980. It has since extended its range in Britain and is now well established, especially in the southwest.

therefore attracted the attention of Plant Health authorities. Alien terrestrial flatworms are also regarded as undesirables, because they can have both a direct and an indirect impact on ecosystems. Although this is not always the case,[98] numbers of earthworms can be reduced 'to the point of elimination'.[99] Loss of earthworms as a result of the activities of New Zealand flatworms could affect soil aeration and structure, leading to waterlogging,[100] and in lowland pastures this might result in rushes and other undesirable plants subsequently gaining ground. Evidence to support such expectations, however, remains largely anecdotal. Earthworms, whose value to agriculture is well documented,[101] are also a key component in animal food chains. Not surprisingly, therefore, concerns have been expressed that their reduction or loss in the wake of flatworm predation might have an adverse effect on blackbirds, badgers, moles and other creatures that regularly feed upon them.[102] As a consequence, since 1992, the New Zealand flatworm has been scheduled under the British Countryside and Wildlife Act 1991 as a species 'which may not be released or allowed to escape into the wild'. Alien species 'which threaten ecosystems, habitats or species', are also covered by Article 8h of the Convention on Biological Diversity (CBD),[103] which seeks to prevent their introduction or to control or eradicate them. Over the years, New Zealand flatworms have also been blitzed by the popular press. Sensational newspaper headlines from Northern Ireland, for example, include: 'Alien flatworms turn the native stock into soup', 'Kill the Kiwi', 'Killer worms threaten Ulster farms' and 'MP unearths horror of All Black worm'![104] Reference to soup arises from the flatworm's feeding habits. On locating an earthworm, the flatworm secretes enzymes that break down the body of its prey. The flatworm then imbibes the resulting mush.

FIG 404. New Zealand flatworms (*Arthurdendyus triangulatus*) and their pea-like egg capsules are readily transported from site to site in pots and other plant containers.

Although often present in the wild (as in grassland sites in Northern Ireland and Scotland), New Zealand flatworms are especially numerous in botanic gardens, home gardens and plant nurseries. Here, they hide during daylight hours under plastic sheets, plant containers, rocks, stones and so on, curled up on beds of mucus. New Zealand flatworms are hermaphroditic creatures, and they reproduce by producing egg capsules (Fig. 404). These are deposited in the soil, and are often also hidden amongst compost inside plant pots and other containers. Movement of containerised plants from one site to another, therefore, generates a risk of spreading the pest. In the 1990s, Plant Health authorities in Europe became aware of the possibility and consequences of countries becoming infested through international plant trade. Accordingly, strict quarantine measures were introduced to prevent the importation of New Zealand flatworms, whether alone or in association with plants or other items.[105] This raised the profile of the pest. It also placed an additional burden on growers wishing to export containerised plants, especially those operating in areas known to be infested.

APPENDIX I

Main Features of Invertebrate Pests and Their Natural Enemies

INSECTS

Insects (class Insecta) are included in the phylum Arthropoda, invertebrate animals characterised by their usually hardened exoskeleton (body shell), segmented bodies and jointed limbs.[1] Unlike other arthropods, the body of an adult insect is divided into three distinct parts: the head (which bears a single pair of antennae, and usually eyes and mouthparts); the thorax (which usually bears three pairs of legs and two pairs of wings); and the abdomen (which lacks legs but in some groups bears cerci or filaments at the hind end).

The following groups of insects include plant pests, parasitoids or predators in Britain and Ireland:

Subclass **Apterygota** (primitive, wingless insects)
Order **Collembola** (springtails)[2]

Subclass **Pterygota** (winged insects)
Order **Saltatoria** (crickets, grasshoppers etc.)[*]
Order **Dermaptera** (earwigs)
Order **Dictyoptera** (cockroaches)[*]
Order **Hemiptera** (true bugs)
Order **Thysanoptera** (thrips)
Order **Neuroptera** (lacewings etc.)[†]
Order **Coleoptera** (beetles)
Order **Diptera** (true flies)
Order **Lepidoptera** (butterflies and moths)

Order **Trichoptera** (caddis flies)*
Order **Hymenoptera** (ants, bees, sawflies, wasps etc.)

* Of very limited significance as plant pests.
† Includes parasitic or predacious species only.

The subclass Pterygota is often subdivided into the Exopterygota and the Endopterygota. The Exopterygota includes orders in which metamorphosis (i.e. the change from one body form to another) is gradual. Development from egg to adult then typically involves a series of more or less adult-like juvenile stages, each known as a nymph. Wings typically develop externally as flattened, sac-like pads (wing pads), which become larger each time the nymph moults from one growth stage (instar) to the next. The final-instar nymph eventually transforms into a fully winged adult. This process is regarded as incomplete metamorphosis (hemimetabolous development). By contrast, members of the Endopterygota undergo complete metamorphosis (holometabolous development), in which wings develop internally. Here, the juvenile stages between egg and adult are known as larvae. These are very different in appearance from the adult, and the change from larval to adult form takes place abruptly during a non-feeding stage known as the pupa. Unlike nymphs, larvae lack compound (multifaceted) eyes, although they may possess one or more pairs of simple (single-lensed) eyes called stemmae.[3] Also, larvae do not possess external wing pads.[4]

Accounts of the features of insects down to family level, if not beyond, are available in many texts[5] and such details need not be repeated fully here. However, for general guidance, brief comments on the key features and status of the various groups containing (or of relevance to) pests of cultivated plants are presented below. Modern reviews of specific groups of importance on crops are also readily available.[6]

Order Collembola (springtails)

Springtails are small, primitive, wingless creatures, with mainly biting mouthparts. A sucker-like tube (the collophore) is present on the underside of the first abdominal segment and a forked, tail-like springing organ (the furcula) is usually present on the fourth; the furcula enables individuals to spring into the air when disturbed. Metamorphosis is slight, and the immature stages are similar in appearance to adults. Springtails often abound in soil, leaf litter and other habitats, and they play an important role in the breakdown of organic matter. Various species of *Hypogastrura* (the so-called gunpowder-mites) (family Hypogastruridae) (Fig. A.1) occur in mushroom houses. Soil-inhabiting white blind springtails (*Onychiurus* spp.) (family Onychiuridae) feed mainly on the roots

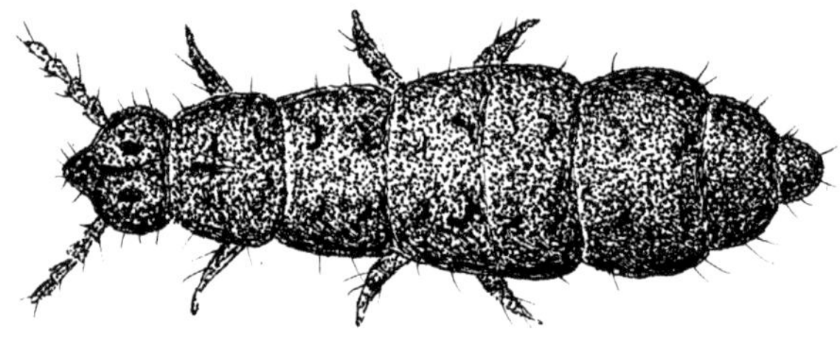

FIG A.1 A gunpowder-mite (Collembola: Hypogastruridae).

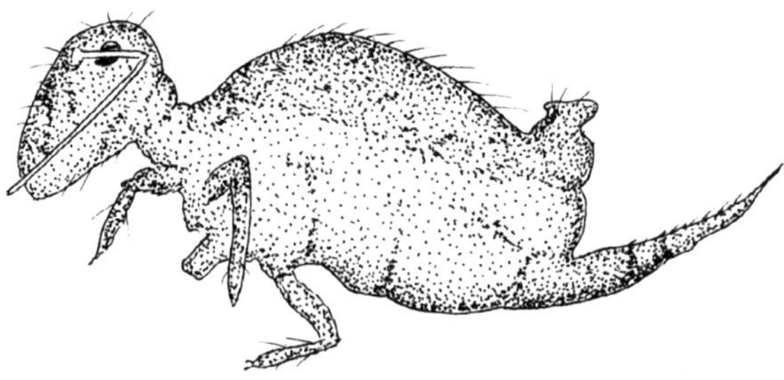

FIG A.2 A lucerne-flea (*Sminthurus viridis*) (Collembola: Sminthuridae).

of plants, including seedlings of field and greenhouse crops, and a few species are predators of soil-inhabiting nematodes. The family Sminthuridae also includes plant pests, of which the garden springtail (*Bourletiella hortensis*) and the lucerne-flea (*Sminthurus viridis*) (Fig. A.2) are the best-known examples.

Cited genera (i.e. those cited in the text) are included in the following families:

ONYCHIURIDAE – *Onychiurus*;
HYPOGASTRURIDAE – *Ceratophysella, Hypogastrura, Xenylla*;
ISOTOMIDAE – *Proisotoma*;
SMINTHURIDAE – *Bourletiella, Sminthurus*.

Order Saltatoria (crickets, grasshoppers etc.)

Saltatorians (formerly included, along with cockroaches, in the order Orthoptera) are medium-sized to large, stout-bodied, usually saltatorial (jumping) insects, with chewing mouthparts, large compound eyes and usually two pairs of wings. The forewings, or tegmina, are leathery and the hindwings membranous; however, either one or both pairs of wings may be reduced or absent. Development includes egg and nymphal stages and is hemimetabolous. Although mole crickets (family Gryllotalpidae) and bush-crickets (family Tettigoniidae) are known to damage plants, no saltatorians are of economic importance as crop pests in Britain. Indeed, the mole cricket (*Gryllotalpa gryllotalpa*) is a very rare, endangered species in these islands and is protected under Schedule 5 of the Wildlife & Countryside Act 1981. The largest saltatorian family (the Acrididae) includes locusts and short-horned grasshoppers; however, no such species are pests in northern Europe.

Cited genera are included in the following families:

TETTIGONIIDAE – *Leptophyes, Phaneroptera;*
ACRIDIDAE – *Locusta.*

Order Dermaptera (earwigs)

Earwigs are elongate, omnivorous insects, with mouthparts adapted for biting and chewing. The forewings (elytra) are short and horny, and the hindwings are membranous, semicircular and fan-like. Both sexes possess prominent anal cerci (a pair of forceps-like appendages) that arise from the hind-most abdominal segment. Development is hemimetabolous, with individuals passing through an egg and several nymphal stages. Earwigs (family Forficulidae), essentially the common earwig (*Forficula auricularia*), are of significance on cultivated plants as both pests and predators.

Order Dictyoptera (cockroaches and mantises)

This order includes cockroaches (suborder Blattodea) and mantises (suborder Mantodea). Cockroaches are small to large, stout-bodied and somewhat flattened insects with a large, shield-like prothorax, two pairs of wings, long, thread-like antennae and prominent anal cerci. The forewings (tegmina) are leathery and the hindwings membranous, folding away longitudinally when not in use. The mouthparts are adapted for chewing. Development is hemimetabolous, and includes an egg and numerous nymphal stages. Eggs are laid *en masse* in purse-like capsules known as oothecae. Cockroaches are of little or no importance as plant pests, but they occasionally cause damage to plants in heated greenhouses and hothouses. Mantises are carnivorous, mainly tropical insects; they do not occur in Britain or Ireland.

Cited genera of cockroaches are included in the following family:

BLATTIDAE – *Blatta, Blatella, Periplaneta.*

Order Hemiptera (true bugs)

True bugs range from minute to large insects, characterised by their piercing, needle-like, suctorial mouthparts and, usually, two pairs of wings. Development is hemimetabolous. Parthenogenesis (asexual reproduction, with or without an egg stage) is commonplace, and lifecycles are frequently highly complex. Although the Hemiptera was formerly regarded as comprising just two suborders (the Heteroptera and the Homoptera), molecular studies[7] support replacement of the Homoptera by the Auchenorrhyncha and the Sternorrhyncha, both of which then become suborders.

In the suborder Heteroptera, the mouthparts arise from the front of the head and the point of attachment is flexible. Characteristically, the forewings (known as hemelytra) have a horny basal area and a membranous tip, but the hindwings are entirely membranous. Also, when at rest, the wings overlap and are held flat over the more or less dorsoventrally flattened body. Many heteropterans are phytophagous (plant feeders), and plant pests occur in several families. These include various ground bugs (Lygaeidae), lace bugs (Tingidae), leaf bugs (Piesmatidae), mirids or capsids (Miridae) and shield bugs (Pentatomidae). Some shield bugs and most mirids (capsids) are predacious, as are damsel bugs (Nabidae), flower bugs (Anthocoridae) and members of the Microphysidae.

Cited genera within the suborder Heteroptera are included in the following families:

ACANTHOSOMATIDAE – *Acanthosoma*;
PENTATOMIDAE – *Dolycoris, Nezara, Palomena, Pentatoma*;
PIESMATIDAE – *Piesma*;
TINGIDAE – *Corythucha, Stephanitis*;
NABIDAE – *Aptus*;
ANTHOCORIDAE – *Anthocoris, Orius*;
MIRIDAE – *Atractotomus, Blepharidopterus, Camplylomma, Closterotomus, Deraeocoris, Dicyphus, Heterotoma, Liocoris, Lygocoris, Lygus, Macrolophus, Malacocoris, Orthotylus, Phytocoris, Pilophorus, Plagiognathus, Psallus, Stenodema.*

Members of the former Homoptera range from minute to large insects. The mouthparts arise from the back of the head and the point of attachment is rigid; also, when at rest, the wings (when present) are typically held over the body in a sloping, roof-like posture. Unlike heteropterans, the forewings are uniform throughout, either being horny (then termed elytra) (as in the suborder Auchenorrhyncha) or entirely membranous (as in the suborder Sternorrhyncha). All species are phytophagous and many are important virus vectors. Plant pests are of significance in several families. These include, in the Auchenorrhyncha: froghoppers (Cercopidae), leafhoppers (Cicadellidae) and planthoppers (e.g. delphacid leafhoppers – Delphacidae) (Fig. A.3); and in the Sternorrhyncha:

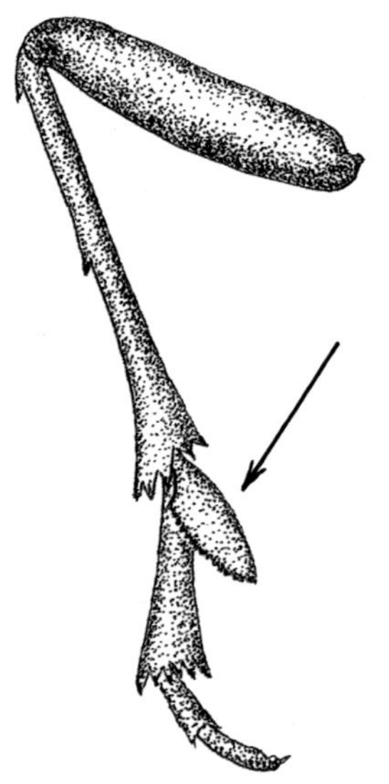

FIG A.3 Hind leg of a delphacid leafhopper (Hemiptera: Delphacidae), showing apical spur (arrowed).

adelgids (Adelgidae), aphids (Aphididae),[8] armoured scales (Diaspididae), mealybugs (Pseudococcidae), phylloxerans (Phylloxeridae), psyllids (Psyllidae), soft scales (Coccidae) and whiteflies (Aleyrodidae).

Cited genera within the suborder Auchenorrhyncha are included in the following families:

CERCOPIDAE – *Cercopis, Philaenus*;
FLATIDAE – *Metcalfa*;
MEMBRACIDAE – *Stictocephala*;
CICADELLIDAE – *Aguriahana, Alnetoidia, Aphrodes, Cicadella, Circulifer, Edwardsiana, Empoasca, Eupterycyba, Eupteryx, Euscelis, Evacanthus, Fieberiella, Graphocephala, Hauptidia, Macrosteles, Ribautiana, Typhlocyba, Zygina*;
DELPHACIDAE – *Javesella*.

Cited genera within the suborder Sternorrhyncha are included in the following families:

PSYLLIDAE – *Cacopsylla, Psylla, Psyllopsis*;
TRIOZIDAE – *Trioza*;
SPONDYLIASPIDAE – *Ctenarytaina*;
ALEYRODIDAE – *Aleurodicus, Aleyrodes, Bemisia, Crenidorsum, Dialeurodes, Siphoninus, Trialeurodes*;
APHIDIDAE – *Acyrthosiphon, Amphorophora, Anuraphis, Aphis, Aploneura, Aulacorthum, Brachycaudus, Brevicoryne, Cavariella, Chaetosiphon, Chaitophorus, Chromaphis, Cinara, Coloradoa, Corylobium, Cryptomyzus, Dactynotus, Dysaphis, Elatobium, Eriosoma, Hyadaphis, Hyalopteroides, Hyalopterus, Hyperomyzus, Illinoia, Macrolophium, Macrosiphoniella, Macrosiphum, Maculolachnus, Megoura, Melanaphis, Metopolophium, Microlophium, Myzocallis, Myzus, Nasonovia, Neotoxoptera, Ovatus, Pachypappa, Panaphis, Paracolopha, Pemphigus, Periphyllus, Phorodon, Phyllaphis, Pterochloroides, Pterocomma, Rhopalosiphoninus, Rhopalosiphum, Schizolachnus, Sitobion, Stomaphis, Takecallis, Tetraneura, Tuberolachnus*;

ANOECIIDAE – *Anoecia*;
ADELGIDAE – *Adelges, Pineus*;
PHYLLOXERIDAE – *Aphanostigma, Phylloxera, Viteus*;
DIASPIDIDAE – *Aulacaspis, Carulaspis, Chionaspis, Diaspidiotus, Epidiaspis, Lepidosaphes, Pseudaulacaspis, Quadraspidiotus, Unaspis*;
COCCIDAE – *Ceroplastes, Coccus, Eulecanium, Lichtensia, Parthenolecanium, Pulvinaria, Saissetia, Sphaerolecanium*;
ERIOCOCCIDAE – *Cryptococcus, Eriococcus, Pseudochermes*;
PSEUDOCOCCIDAE – *Balanococcus, Planococcus, Pseudococcus, Rhizoecus*;
MARGARODIDAE – *Icerya*.

Order Thysanoptera (thrips)

Thrips (often known as thunderflies) are minute, elongate insects, with asymmetrical mouthparts adapted for piercing, lacerating and sucking. Wings, when present, are strap-like, with marginal hair-like fringes and few or no veins. Development of a thrips is intermediate between that of hemimetabolous and holometabolous insects, and includes an egg, two nymphal and two or three inactive, non-feeding stages termed propupae and pupae; nymphs are similar in appearance to adults, but wingless and paler in colour. Thrips are essentially phytophagous, although predacious (or partly predacious) species also occur. Some thrips are important vectors of plant-pathogenic viruses.

Cited genera are included in the following families:

AEOLOTHRIPIDAE – *Aeolothrips*;
THRIPIDAE – *Anaphothrips, Aptinothrips, Chirothrips, Dendrothrips, Echinothrips, Frankliniella, Heliothrips, Kakothrips, Limothrips, Parthenothrips, Scirtothrips, Taeniothrips, Thrips*;
PHLAEOTHRIPIDAE – *Liothrips*.

Order Neuroptera (ant-lions, lacewings etc.)

The order Neuroptera includes various small to large, soft-bodied, mainly predacious insects, with biting mouthparts. Wing venation is complex; the veins form a net-like pattern and often fork near the wing margin. Development is holometabolous, and includes egg, larval and pupal stages. The most important predators (suborder Planipennia) are brown lacewings (family Hemerobiidae), green lacewings (family Chrysopidae) and powdery lacewings (family Coniopterygidae). Adults of some species are pollen feeders, but others are predacious. Lacewing larvae are entirely predacious.

Cited genera are included in the following families:

CHRYSOPIDAE – *Chrysopa, Chrysoperla, Cunctochrysa, Nineta*;
HEMEROBIIDAE – *Hemerobius*;
CONIOPTERYGIDAE – *Conwentzia, Coniopteryx, Semidalis.*

Order Coleoptera (beetles)

Beetles are minute to large insects, with biting mouthparts. Characteristically, the forewings (elytra) are horny, and meet in a straight line along the midline of the back; the hindwings are membranous but can be reduced or entirely absent. Development is holometabolous, and includes egg, larval and pupal stages. Beetle larvae usually have a distinct head, biting mouthparts and three pairs of thoracic legs, although legs are lacking in some groups (as in weevils).

Plant pests occur in several families, and the following are of particular significance: apionid weevils (Apionidae), chafers (Scarabaeidae), click beetles (Elateridae), fruitworm beetles (Byturidae), flea beetles (Chrysomelidae, subfamily Halticinae), leaf beetles (Chrysomelidae), leaf-roll weevils (Rhynchitidae), pollen beetles (Nitidulidae), pulse beetles (Bruchidae) and true weevils (Curculionidae).

Predators of pests are also well represented. These include: ground beetles (Carabidae), ladybirds (Coccinellidae), rove beetles (Staphylinidae) and solider beetles (Cantharidae). In addition, larvae of a small number of beetles (e.g. *Aleochara bilineata* and *A. bipustulata* – Staphylinidae, subfamily Aleocharinae) are parasitoids.

Cited genera are included in the following families:

CARABIDAE – *Amara, Anchomenus, Bembidion, Clivina, Demetrias, Dromius, Harpalus, Nebria, Poecilus, Pterostichus, Trechus, Zabrus*;
HYDROPHILIDAE – *Helophorus*;
SILPHIDAE – *Aclypea*;
STAPHYLINIDAE – *Aleochara, Oligota, Staphylinus, Tachyporus*;
SCARABAEIDAE – *Amphimallon, Gnorimus, Hoplia, Melolontha, Phyllopertha, Serica*;
BUPRESTIDAE – *Agrilus*;
ELATERIDAE – *Agriotes, Athous, Ctenicera*;
CANTHARIDAE – *Cantharis, Rhagonycha*;
BOSTRYCHIDAE – *Sinoxylon*;
NITIDULIDAE – *Meligethes*;
CRYPTOPHAGIDAE – *Atomaria*;
BYTURIDAE – *Byturus*;
COCCINELLIDAE – *Adalia, Chilocorus, Coccinella, Cryptolaemus, Exochomus, Harmonia, Propylea, Stethorus*;

CERAMBYCIDAE – *Tetrops*;
BRUCHIDAE – *Bruchus*;
CHRYSOMELIDAE – *Agelastica, Cassida, Chrysolina, Diabrotica, Galerucella, Gastrophysa, Leptinotarsa, Lilioceris, Oulema, Phaedon, Phratora, Pyrrhalta*;
CHRYSOMELIDAE (subfamily Halticinae) – *Altica, Aphthona, Batophila, Chaetocnema, Crepidodera, Longitarsus, Neocrepidodera, Phyllotreta, Psylliodes*;
RHYNCHITIDAE – *Involvulus, Neocoenorrhinus*;
ATTELABIDAE – *Byctiscus, Deporaus*;
APIONIDAE – *Eutrichapion, Protapion*;
CURCULIONIDAE – *Anthonomus, Balaninus, Barynotus, Barypeithes, Ceutorhynchus, Cionus, Cryptorhynchus, Furcipes, Hylobius, Hypera, Magdalis, Mecinus, Mitoplinthus, Orchestes, Otiorhynchus, Peritelus, Philopedon, Phyllobius, Polydrusus, Scolytus, Sitona, Strophosoma, Xyleborinus, Xyleborus.*

Order Diptera (true flies)

True flies are minute to large insects, characterised by the presence of just one pair of wings, the hind pair being reduced to small balancing organs called halteres. The mouthparts of adults are usually suctorial, but are sometimes adapted for piercing, as in biting midges, mosquitoes and horse flies. Development is holometabolous, and usually includes egg, larval and pupal stages. Fly larvae (often known as maggots) are apodous (legless), the head is usually small and inconspicuous, and the mouthparts are usually simple. In the suborder Nematocera, however, larvae usually have a distinct head, although this is often retracted into the thorax. In the suborder Cyclorrhapha the larval mouthparts are typically modified into hook-like structures (sometimes described as 'mouth-hooks'); these form part of the cephalopharyngeal skeleton[9] (Fig. A.4) and are used to rasp or tear at tissue which can then be imbibed in a semi-digested, partly liquid form. In the suborder Cyclorrhapha the pupa is formed within the cast skin of the final-instar larva, which comes to form a protective barrel-like structure called a puparium.

FIG A.4 Mouthparts of a fly larva (suborder Cyclorrhapha). Note mouth-hook on extreme left.

(a)

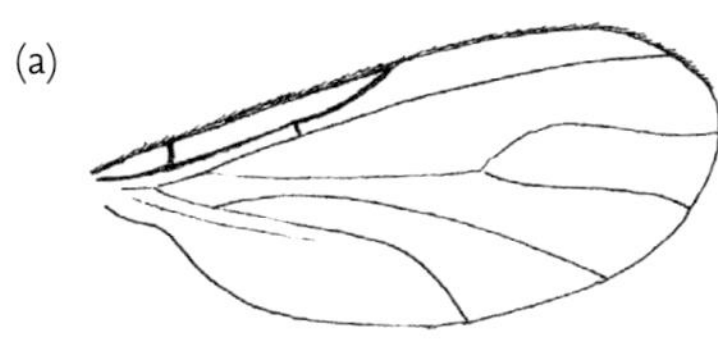

(b)

(c)

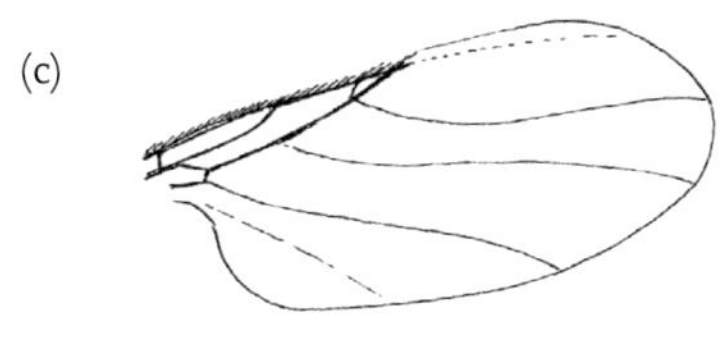

FIG A.5 Forewing venation:
(a) a sciarid fly (Sciaridae);
(b) a lesser dung fly (Sphaeroceridae); and
(c) a phorid fly (Phoridae).

Plant pests are present in many families. In the suborder Nematocera these include bibionid flies (Bibionidae), crane flies (Tipulidae) and sciarid flies (Sciaridae) (Fig. A.5a), and in the suborder Cyclorrhapha: anthomyiid flies (Anthomyiidae), cereal flies (Opomyzidae), gall midges (Cecidomyiidae), large fruit flies (Tephritidae), leaf-miner flies (Agromyzidae), lesser dung flies (Sphaeroceridae) (Fig. A.5b), small fruit flies (Drosophilidae), scuttle flies (Phoridae) (Fig. A.5c), shore flies (Ephydridae) and timothy flies (Scathophagidae).

Predators (as adults or as larvae) occur in several families. In the suborder Nematocera these include gall midges (Cecidomyiidae); in the suborder Brachycera long-legged flies (Dolichopodidae), empidid dance flies (Empididae), hybotid dance flies (Hybotidae) and stiletto flies (Therevidae); in the suborder Cyclorrhapha hover flies (Syrphidae).

In addition, members of the family Tachinidae (suborder Cyclorrhapha) are of considerable importance as parasitoids.

Cited genera within the suborder Nematocera are included in the following families:

TIPULIDAE – *Nephrotoma, Tipula;*
CHIRONOMIDAE – *Bryophaenocladius, Metriocnemus;*
BIBIONIDAE – *Bibio, Dilophus;*
SCIARIDAE – *Bradysia, Lycoriella, Pnyxia.*

Cited genera within the suborder Brachycera are included in the following families:

EMPIDIDAE – *Empis;*
HYBOTIDAE – *Platypalpus.*

Cited genera within the suborder Cyclorrhapha are included in the following families:

CECIDOMYIIDAE – *Aphidoletes, Arnoldiola, Cerodontha, Clinodiplosis, Contarinia, Dasineura, Feltiella, Haplodiplosis, Henria, Heteropeza, Janetiella, Lasioptera, Lestodiplosis, Lestremia, Mayetiola, Monarthropalpus, Mycophila, Oblodiplosis, Phytomyza, Putoniella, Rabdophaga, Resseliella, Sitodiplosis, Taxomyia*;
PHORIDAE – *Megaselia*;
SYRPHIDAE – *Episyrphus, Eumerus, Melangyna, Merodon, Pipiza, Syrphus*;
TEPHRITIDAE – *Bactrocera, Ceratitis, Euleia, Pliorecepta, Rhagoletis*;
PSILIDAE – *Psila*;
SPHAEROCERIDAE – *Pullimosina*;
OPOMYZIDAE – *Geomyza, Opomyza*;
EPHYDRIDAE – *Hydrellia, Scatella*;
DROSOPHILIDAE – *Scaptomyza*;
AGROMYZIDAE – *Agromyza, Cerodontha, Chromatomyia, Hexomyza, Liriomyza, Napomyza, Phytobia, Phytomyza, Pseudonapomyza*;
CHLOROPIDAE – *Cetema, Chlorops, Meromyza, Oscinella*;
TACHINIDAE – *Compsilura, Cyzenis, Elodia, Nemorilla, Pales, Pelatachina, Phryxe*;
SCATHOPHAGIDAE – *Nanna, Scathophaga*;
ANTHOMYIIDAE – *Delia, Pegomya, Phorbia*;
MUSCIDAE – *Mesembrina*.

Order Lepidoptera (butterflies and moths)

Butterflies and moths are familiar, minute to large insects, characterised by their often colourful, scale-coated wings and suctorial mouthparts which often form a long, coiled proboscis (tongue). Development is holometabolous and includes egg, larval and pupal stages. Larvae (frequently designated caterpillars) have a distinct head and biting mouthparts, three pairs of thoracic legs and, usually, single pairs of prolegs (false legs) on the third to sixth and the tenth abdominal segments; those on the tenth (last) abdominal segment are often termed anal claspers. Prolegs are sometimes absent from the third to fifth abdominal segments, as in most members of the family Geometridae; such larvae move with a looping gait and are often termed loopers. Semi-loopers (with prolegs present on just the fifth, sixth and tenth abdominal segments) also occur, as in the family Noctuidae (subfamily Plusiinae). Prolegs are unjointed and in lepidopterans (cf. sawfly larvae, below) usually armed with chitinous hooks known as crotchets, the number and arrangement of which are often characteristic. Lepidopterous larvae are essentially phytophagous, and usually armed with biting mouthparts; there are, however, some sap-imbibing species. A few species are cannibalistic or partly predacious, as in the dunbar moth (*Cosmia trapezina*) (family Noctuidae). Many groups include plant pests, of which members of the families Gelechiidae, Geometridae, Gracillariidae, Hepialidae, Lymantriidae, Noctuidae, Pieridae, Pyralidae, Tortricidae and Yponomeutidae are most important.

Cited genera are included in the following families:

HEPIALIDAE – *Hepialus*;
NEPTICULIDAE – *Stigmella*;
TISCHERIIDAE – *Tischeria*;
INCURVARIIDAE – *Lampronia*;
COSSIDAE – *Cossus, Zeuzera*;
CASTNIIDAE – *Paysandisia*;
ZYGAENIDAE – *Agalopa*;
LYONETIIDAE – *Bucculatrix, Leucoptera, Lyonetia*;
HIEROXESTIDAE – *Opogona*;
GRACILLARIIDAE – *Acrocercops, Callisto, Caloptilia, Cameraria, Parectopa, Parornix, Phyllonorycter*;
PHYLLOCNISTIDAE – *Phyllocnistis*;
SESIIDAE – *Synanthedon*;
GLYPHIPTERIGIDAE – *Glyphipterix*;
CHOREUTIDAE – *Choreutis*;
YPONOMEUTIDAE – *Acrolepiopsis, Argyresthia, Evergestis, Plutella, Prays, Scythropia, Swammerdamia, Yponomeuta, Ypsolopha*;
EPERMENIIDAE – *Epermenia*;
COLEOPHORIDAE – *Coleophora*;
ELACHISTIDAE – *Elachista*;
OECOPHORIDAE – *Batia, Carcina, Depressaria, Diurnea*;
GELECHIIDAE – *Anarsia, Dichomeris, Gelechia, Recurvaria, Scrobipalpa, Tuta*;
BLASTOBASIDAE – *Blastobasis*;
MOMPHIDAE – *Cosmopterix, Spuleria*;
COCHYLIDAE – *Cochylis*;
TORTRICIDAE – *Acleris, Adoxophyes, Ancylis, Archips, Argyrotaenia, Cacoecimorpha, Celypha, Choristoneura, Clepsis, Cnephasia, Croesia, Cydia, Ditula, Enarmonia, Endothenia, Epiblema, Epichoristodes, Epinotia, Epiphyas, Exapate, Gypsonoma, Hedya, Neosphaleroptera, Pammene, Pandemis, Ptycholoma, Rhopobota, Rhyacionia, Spilonota, Syndemis*;
PYRALIDAE – *Agriphila, Chrysoteuchia, Cryptoblabes, Diaphania, Duponchelia, Eurrhypara, Evergestis, Ostrinia, Pleuroptya, Pyrausta, Trachycera, Udea*;

PAPILIONIDAE – *Iphiclides*;
PIERIDAE – *Aporia, Pieris*;
LYCAENIDAE – *Cacyreus, Satyrium, Thecla*;
NYMPHALIDAE – *Aglais, Cynthia, Inachis, Nymphalis, Polygonia*;
LASIOCAMPIDAE – *Eriogaster, Euthrix, Gastropacha, Malacosoma, Odonestis, Poecilocampa*;
GEOMETRIDAE – *Abraxas, Agriopis, Alcis, Alsophila, Biston, Campaea, Chloroclysta, Colotois, Crocalis, Ectropis, Epirrita, Erannis, Eupithecia, Lycia, Operophtera, Opisthograptis, Ourapteryx, Pasiphila, Peribatodes, Phigalia, Selenia, Theria*;
SPHINGIDAE – *Acherontia, Deilephila, Laothoe, Mimas, Smerinthus, Sphinx*;
NOTODONTIDAE – *Cerura, Phalera*;
DILOBIDAE – *Diloba*;
THAUMETOPOEIDAE – *Thaumetopoea*;
LYMANTRIIDAE – *Calliteara, Euproctis, Leucoma, Lymantria, Orgyia*;
ARCTIIDAE – *Arctia, Hyphantria, Spilosoma*;
NOLIDAE – *Nola*;
NOCTUIDAE – *Acronicta, Agrotis, Allophyes, Amphipyra, Apamea, Cerapteryx, Conistra, Cosmia, Cucullia, Earias, Eupsilia, Euxoa, Gortyna, Graphiphora, Helicoverpa, Heliothis, Hydraecia, Hypena, Lacanobia, Lithophane, Luperina, Mamestra, Melanchra, Mesapamea, Mesoligia, Naenia, Noctua, Oligia, Oria, Orthosia, Peridroma, Phlogophora, Spodoptera*;
NOCTUIDAE (subfamily Plusiinae) – *Autographa, Chrysodeixis, Diachrysia, Polychrysia*.

Order Trichoptera (caddis flies)

Caddis flies are small to large insects, with often vestigial mouthparts. The wings are coated with minute hairs and are typically held in a sloping, roof-like posture when at rest. Development is holometabolous, and includes egg, larval and pupal stages. Caddis fly larvae are aquatic, and they inhabit protective cases made from plant debris, sand grains etc. The family Limnephilidae includes a few pests of watercress and aquatic ornamental plants, including water-lilies. *Halesus radiatus* and *Limnephilus marmoratus* are examples.

Order Hymenoptera (ants, bees, sawflies, wasps etc.)

Hymenopterans are minute to large insects, with usually two pairs of more or less transparent, membranous wings, the hindwings being the smaller pair. The mouthparts are adapted for biting but also, sometimes, for lapping and sucking. In the suborder Apocrita (ants, bees and wasps) the body has a waist-like constriction between the first and second abdominal segments, but there is no such constriction in the suborder Symphyta (sawflies and wood-wasps). Development in Hymenoptera is holometabolous, and includes egg, larval and pupal stages; in some sawflies, there is also an active but non-feeding prepupal stage. Some parasitic forms aside, larvae have an often well-developed head and biting mouthparts. Legs are often absent, as in the suborder Apocrita and in stem-boring sawflies (family Cephidae). However, larvae of most sawflies (families Argidae, Cimbicidae, Diprionidae and Tenthredinidae) are caterpillar-like, and possess three pairs of thoracic legs and seven or eight pairs of abdominal prolegs which, unlike those of butterfly and moth larvae, lack crotchets; abdominal prolegs are absent in the family Pamphiliidae. Sawfly larvae are entirely phytophagous, and many are important pests. The suborder Apocrita includes many parasitoids that are important natural enemies of such pests. These range from minute insects (some less than 0.25 mm long) to rather large species with an overall body length of several centimetres.

Cited genera within the suborder Symphyta are included in the following families:

PAMPHILIIDAE – *Neurotoma*;
CEPHIDAE – *Cephus*, *Janus*;
ARGIDAE – *Arge*;
CIMBICIDAE – *Cimbex*;
DIPRIONIDAE – *Diprion*, *Neodiprion*;
TENTHREDINIDAE – *Allantus*, *Ametastegia*, *Ardis*, *Athalia*, *Blennocampa*, *Caliroa*, *Cladius*, *Croesus*, *Dolerus*, *Empria*, *Endelomyia*, *Heterarthrus*, *Hoplocampa*, *Macrophya*, *Metallus*, *Micronematus*, *Monophadnoides*, *Nematus*, *Pachynematus*, *Periclista*, *Phyllocolpa*, *Phymatocera*, *Pontania*, *Priophorus*, *Pristiphora*, *Protemphytus*, *Rhadinoceraea*, *Trichiocampus*.

Cited genera within the suborder Apocrita are included in the following families:

ICHNEUMONIDAE – *Amblysteles*, *Aptesis*, *Campoplex*, *Collyria*, *Glypta*, *Hemiteles*, *Itoplectis*, *Lathrolestes*, *Phradis*, *Phygadeuon*, *Phytodietus*, *Pristomerus*, *Phradis*, *Scambus*, *Tersilochus*;
BRACONIDAE – *Ascogaster*, *Bracon*, *Cotesia*, *Dacnusa*, *Macrocentrus*, *Microgaster*;
APHIDIIDAE – *Aphidius*, *Diaeretiella*, *Praon*;
CYNIPIDAE – *Andricus*, *Biorhiza*, *Cynips*, *Diastrophus*, *Diplolepis*, *Neuroterus*, *Trybliographa*;
TORYMIDAE – *Torymus*;

PTEROMALIDAE – *Macroglenes, Mesopolobus, Pteromalus, Stenomalus, Trichomalus;*
ENCYRTIDAE – *Copidosoma, Leptomastix, Litomastix, Metaphycus;*
APHELINIDAE – *Aphelinus, Aphytis, Encarsia;*
EULOPHIDAE – *Cirrospilus, Diglyphus, Chrysocharis, Omphale, Ophelimus, Tetrastichus;*
TRICHOGRAMMATIDAE – *Trichogramma;*
MYMARIDAE – *Anagrus;*
PLATYGASTRIDAE – *Leptacis, Platygaster;*
FORMICIDAE – *Lasius;*
VESPIDAE – *Vespa, Vespula;*
APIDAE – *Apis.*

MITES

Mites, along with creatures such as harvestmen and spiders (see below), are included in the class Arachnida. Unlike insects, mites and other arachnids lack wings and antennae, and most possess four pairs of legs. Excluding ticks engorged with blood,[10] mites are typically minute to small creatures, no more than a few millimetres in length at best. The body is subdivided into the gnathosoma (which bears the mouthparts and a pair of sensory, leg-like, pedipalps) and the idiosoma, which is usually inconspicuously delineated into the anterior propodosoma (which bears the first two pairs of legs) and the posterior hysterosoma (which bears the third and fourth pairs). The mouthparts include a pair of fang-like chelicerae, and these are often modified into needle-like probes that are used to penetrate the plant or animal hosts prior to imbibing the sap or body contents.

The following groups of mites include plant pests:

Subclass **Acari** (mites)[11]
  Order **Mesostigmata**[*†]
  Order **Prostigmata**[†]
  Order **Astigmata**[*]
  Order **Cryptostigmata**[*]

[*] Of very limited significance as plant pests.
[†] Includes predacious as well as pest species.

Mites usually develop through an egg, a six-legged so-called 'larva' and up to three eight-legged nymphal stages known, respectively, as protonymphs, deutonymphs and tritonymphs. Within the order Prostigmata, however, members of the superfamily Eriophyoidea (see below) lack a 'larval' stage; also, in tarsonemid mites (superfamily Tarsonemoidea), active nymphs are wanting, the 'larva' passing to adulthood after a quiescent, non-feeding pupa-like stage enclosed within the bloated and cast 'larval' skin. Terminology is somewhat ambiguous, and this last-mentioned stage is variously described as a nymph or a pupa.[12]

Order Mesostigmata

Mesostigmatid mites include mainly debris- or soil-inhabiting species; adults range from 0.2 to 2.0 mm in length. Members of the family Phytoseiidae are oval to elongate-oval, with an undivided and weakly sclerotized dorsal shield covering most of the body[13]. Several species are important predators of gall mites, rust mites, spider mites and other small invertebrates. Members of the family Parasitidae are typically oval-bodied, strongly sclerotized, mainly brown-bodied mites with a divided or undivided dorsal shield, and there are both predacious and detritus-feeding species. Such mites abound in leaf litter, and are often numerous in cultivated mushroom beds.

Cited genera are included in the following families:

PHYTOSEIIDAE – *Amblyseius, Euseius, Phytoseiulus, Phytoseius, Typhlodromus*;
LAELAPIDAE – *Hypoaspis*;
PARASITIDAE – *Parasitus*;
ASCIDAE – *Arctoseius*;
DIGAMASELLIDAE – *Digamasellus*.

Order Prostigmata

This is the main order of phytophagous mites. Most members are weakly sclerotized and 0.1–1.0 mm long. The order includes gall mites and rust mites (superfamily Eriophyoidea), several of which are important pests. Such mites are microscopic, and often pear-shaped or spindle-shaped. Unlike other mites, they are characterised by the presence of just two pairs of legs, and by the more or less elongated hysterosoma – the upper and lower parts of which are annulated by so-called 'tergites' and 'sternites', respectively (Fig. A.6). Spider mites (family Tetranychidae) (superfamily Tetranychoidea) and tarsonemid mites (family Tarsonemidae) (superfamily Tarsonemoidea) are also plant pests, as are various members of the families Eupodidae (superfamily Eupodoidea), Pygmephoridae and Siteroptidae (superfamily Tarsonemoidea). Predacious mites occur in the families Anystidae, Stigmaeidae and Trombidiidae.

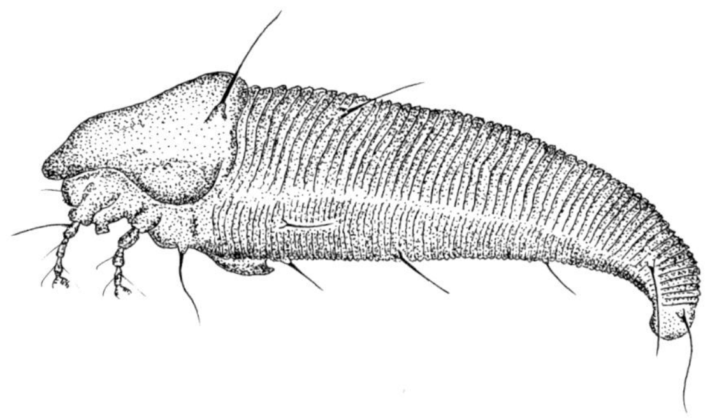

FIG A.6 A typical eriophyid mite.

Cited genera are included in the following families:

PHYTOPTIDAE – *Phytoptus*;
ERIOPHYIDAE – *Abacarus, Acalitus, Aceria, Aculops, Aculus, Artacris, Calepitrimerus, Cecidophyopsis, Colomerus, Diptacus, Epitrimerus, Eriophyes, Phyllocoptes, Vasates*;
TARSONEMIDAE – *Hemitarsonemus, Phytonemus, Polyphagotarsonemus, Steneotarsonemus, Tarsonemus*;
PYGMEPHORIDAE – *Pygmephorus*;
SITEROPTIDAE – *Siteroptes*;
EUPODIDAE – *Linopodes*;
PENTHALEIDAE – *Halotydeus, Penthaleus*;
STIGMAEIDAE – *Zetzellia*;
TETRANYCHIDAE – *Amphitetranychus, Bryobia, Eotetranychus, Eutetranychus, Oligonychus, Panonychus, Schizotetranychus, Stigmaeopsis, Tetranychus*;
TENUIPALPIDAE – *Brevipalpus, Cenopalpus*;
ANYSTIDAE – *Anystis*;
TROMBIDIIDAE – *Allothrombium*.

Order Astigmata

Astigmatids are oval, weakly sclerotized, phytophagous, parasitic or predacious mites, 0.2–1.5 mm long; several are skin parasites of birds and mammals. Members of the family Acaridae are bulbous and translucent or pearly white in appearance, with long hairs on the body, and they often abound in damp, mouldy situations. Members of a few genera (e.g. *Rhizoglyphus* and *Tyrophagus*) have a deleterious impact on plants and are considered pests.

Cited genera are included in the following families:

ACARIDAE – *Acarus, Caloglyphus, Rhizoglyphus, Tyrophagus, Tyrolichus*;
GLYCYPHAGIDAE – *Lepidoglyphus*;
HISTIOSTOMATIDAE – *Histiostoma.*

Order Cryptostigmata

Cryptostigmatids (often known as beetle mites) are heavily sclerotized and 0.2–1.5 mm long, with a characteristically shield-like idiosoma that bears a pair of wing-like expansions. Most species are vegetarian and inhabitants of leaf litter. One species, the cherry beetle mite (*Humerobates rostrolamellatus*) (family Mycobatidae), can be a very minor pest on fruit trees.

OTHER INVERTEBRATE GROUPS

Harvestmen and spiders

Harvestmen (order Opiliones) and spiders (order Araneae) are entirely predacious on small invertebrates, and are often important natural enemies of plant pests. Particularly useful groups include comb-footed spiders (family Theridiidae), crab spiders (family Thomisidae), jumping spiders (family Salticidae), money spiders (family Linyphiidae), orb-web spiders (e.g. family Argiopidae) and wolf spiders (family Lycosidae). Unlike mites (see above), spiders have the body clearly divided into two main sectors: the cephalothorax and the opisthosoma. In harvestmen, these two regions are broadly united.

Cited genera of spiders are included in the following families:

THERIDIIDAE – *Theridion*;
TETRAGNATHIDAE – *Tetragnatha*;
ARGIOPIDAE – *Araneus*;
THOMISIDAE – *Misumena*;
SALTICIDAE – *Salticus.*

Nematodes

Although they are unlikely to attract the attention of most field naturalists, mention must be made of plant-parasitic nematodes (formerly known as eelworms), whose detrimental activities can be of considerable economic importance in both agriculture and horticulture. In farming circles, the devastation caused by cyst nematodes on potato and sugar beet crops, for example, is legendary (see Chapter 5). Nematodes (phylum Nematoda)[14] are non-segmented, thread-like creatures, and many species are parasites of plants or animals including man. Those of medical or veterinary significance are commonly known as roundworms. There are also a vast number of soil-inhabiting species that feed on bacteria. Plant-parasitic nematodes are microscopic (adults usually no more than 0.1–1.0 mm long), and are characterised by their specialised suctorial mouthparts which are armed with a needle-like stylet (mouth-spear), used to penetrate the cell walls of their hosts. A moisture-film thickness of 2–5 μm is considered ideal for nematode movement.[15]

Nematodes typically develop to adulthood via an egg and several juvenile stages. Many plant-parasitic species are free-living. These attack plant roots in order to feed but otherwise exist independently within the soil. Others invade host plants as second-stage juveniles, and then feed, develop and breed internally. Several species of plant-parasitic nematodes introduce and spread virus diseases. Members of the following two classes (sometimes regarded as orders) include pests of agricultural or horticultural crops:

Class/Order **Tylenchida**
Family TYLENCHIDAE (e.g. *Ditylenchus*)
Family HETERODERIDAE (e.g. *Globodera, Heterodera, Meloidogyne*)
Family HOPLOLAIMIDAE (e.g. *Aphelenchoides, Pratylenchus*)

Class/Order **Dorylaimida**
Family DORYLAIMIDAE (e.g. *Longidorus, Xiphinema*)
Family TRICHODORIDAE (e.g. *Paratrichodorus, Trichodorus*)

In addition, some nematodes, known as entomopathogenic nematodes (EPNs), are parasitic on insects and are useful natural enemies of plant pests. Members of the class Rhabditida (e.g. *Heterorhabditis*: family Heterorhabditidae; *Steinernema*: family Steinernematidae) and the class Mermithida (e.g. *Mermis*: family Mermithidae) are well-known examples. In addition, the rhabditid nematode *Phasmarhabditis hermaphrodita* is a parasite of slugs and snails.

Various other micro-organisms also attack plant pests. These include entomopathogenic bacteria, fungi and viruses.[16]

Slugs and snails

Slugs and snails (phylum Mollusca: class Gastropoda) require no description, other than to comment that they do not possess jaws but feed by rasping at plant tissue with a tongue-like structure (the radula) which is armed with thousands of minute hook-like teeth. Slugs in particular are frequently troublesome pests, of which the following are amongst the most important: the field slug (*Deroceras reticulatum*) (family Agriolimacidae), the garden slug (*Arion hortensis*) (family Arionidae) and the keeled slug (*Tandonia budapestensis*)[17] (family Milacidae). Terrestrial snails (family Helicidae) are sometimes also of significance, especially *Cepaea* spp., the garden snail (*Cornu aspersum*)[18] and the strawberry snail (*Trochulus striolatus*);[19] in addition, freshwater snails (e.g. *Lymnaea* spp.) (family Lymnaeidae) are sometimes a nuisance in watercress beds. The impact of slugs and snails on man, however, extends well beyond that of simplistic crop damage or contamination of harvested produce,[20] and their role in ecosystems and biological food chains should not be ignored.

Centipedes and millepedes

Centipedes and millepedes (phylum Arthropoda: class Myriapoda) often occur in association with damp soil and leaf litter, and the latter are occasionally damaging to cultivated plants. Centipedes (order Chilopoda) (which are essentially carnivorous) differ from millepedes (order Diplopoda) in having distinctly flattened bodies and one pair of legs, rather than two, on each ambulatory segment. Pest species of millepede include the black millepede (*Cylindroiulus londinensis*) (family Iulidae), the flat millepede (*Polydesmus angustus*) (family Polydesmidae), the glasshouse millepede (*Oxidus gracilis*) (family Paradoxomatidae) and the spotted snake millepede (*Blaniulus guttulatus*) (family Blaniulidae).

Symphylids

Symphylids (phylum Arthropoda: class and order Symphyla) are tiny, white-bodied creatures up to 8 mm long, with (as adults) 14 body segments, 12 pairs of legs, a pair of long antennae and a pair of anal cerci arising from the hind-most body segment. Symphylids are generally abundant in damp soils, where they feed on decaying animal and plant matter; the rootlets and root hairs of healthy plants are also attacked. Two groups are known to damage crops: glasshouse symphylids (*Scutigerella immaculata*) (family Scutigerellidae) and open-ground symphylids (*Symphyella* spp.) (family Symphylidae).

Woodlice

Woodlice (phylum Arthropoda: class Crustacea: order Isopoda) are small, distinctly segmented often grey-bodied creatures, with seven pairs of legs and two pairs of antennae (one pair being very small and inconspicuous). Although feeding mainly on decaying vegetable matter, woodlice sometimes graze on the roots and stems of healthy plants, including seedlings in greenhouses and cold frames. Members of the families Armadillidiidae (*Armadillidium* spp.), Oniscidae (*Oniscus asellius*) and Porcellionidae (*Porcellio* spp.) cause damage to plants.

Amphipods

Amphipods (phylum Arthropoda: class Crustacea: order Amphipoda) are laterally compressed, shrimp-like creatures with numerous thoracic and abdominal appendages. Although mainly marine scavengers or detritus feeders, a few species (including *Gammarus* spp.) occur in freshwater and may be troublesome in watercress beds.

Terrestrial flatworms

Terrestrial flatworms (phylum Platyhelminthes: class Turbellaria: order Tricladida), also known as land planarians, are not strictly plant pests. Some alien species, however, have become of significance environmentally as unwelcome predators, especially when preying upon earthworms. On environmental grounds, this has resulted in the implementation of Plant Health measures (notably in relation to the exportation and importation of containerised plants) to prevent their spread from one country to another.

Cited genera are included in the following family:

GEOPLANIDAE – *Arthurdendyus, Australoplana, Fletchamia, Kontikia.*

APPENDIX II

Plant-Pathogenic Viruses

Virus	Acronym	Family	Genus	Vectors
Agropyron mosaic virus	AgMV	Potyviridae	*Rymovirus*	Mites
Arabis mosaic virus	ArMV	Comoviridae	*Nepovirus*	Nematodes
Barley yellow dwarf virus	BYDV	Luteoviridae	*Luteovirus*	Aphids
Bean yellow mosaic virus	BYMV	Potyviridae	*Potyvirus*	Aphids
Beet chlorosis virus	BChV	Luteoviridae	*Polerovirus*	Aphids
Beet curly top virus	BCTV	Geminiviridae	*Curtovirus*	Leafhoppers
Beet leaf curl virus	BLCV	Rhabdoviridae	*Nucleorhabdovirus*	Leaf bugs
Beet mild yellowing virus	BMYV	Luteoviridae	*Luteovirus*	Aphids
Beet mosaic virus	BMV	Potyviridae	*Potyvirus*	Aphids
Beet western yellows virus	BWYV	Luteoviridae	*Polerovirus*	Aphids
Beet yellows virus	BYV	Closteroviridae	*Closterovirus*	Aphids
Black raspberry necrosis virus	BRNV	–	*Sadwavirus* (?)	Aphids
Blackcurrant reversion virus	BRV	Comoviridae	*Nepovirus*	Mites
Broad bean stain virus	BBSV	Comoviridae	*Comovirus*	Weevils
Broad bean true mosaic virus	BBTMV	Comoviridae	*Comovirus*	Weevils
Carnation latent virus	CLV	Flexiviridae	*Carlavirus*	Aphids
Carrot motley dwarf virus, a complex of:	CMDV			
carrot mottle virus	CMoV	–	*Umbravirus*	Aphids
carrot red leaf virus	CtRLV	Luteoviridae	–	Aphids
Cauliflower mosaic virus	CaMV	Caulimoviridae	*Caulimovirus*	Aphids
Chrysanthemum virus B	CVB	Bromoviridae	*Cucumovirus*	Aphids
Cocksfoot mild mosaic virus	CMMV	–	*Sobemovirus*	Leaf beetles
Cocksfoot mottle virus	CoMV	–	*Sobemovirus*	Leaf beetles
Cucumber mosaic virus	CMV	Bromoviridae	*Cucumovirus*	Aphids
Cucurbit yellow stunting disorder virus	CYSDV	Closteroviridae	*Crinivirus*	Whiteflies
Freesia mosaic virus	FMV	Potyviridae	*Potyvirus*	Aphids
Gooseberry vein-banding virus	GVBV	Caulimoviridae	*Badnavirus*	Aphids
Hop mosaic virus	HoMV	Flexiviridae	*Carlavirus*	Aphids

Virus	Acronym	Family	Genus	Vectors
Impatiens necrotic spot virus	INSV	Bunyaviridae	*Tospovirus*	Thrips
Lily symptomless virus	LSV	Flexiviridae	*Carlavirus*	Aphids
Narcissus degeneration virus	NDV	Potyviridae	*Potyvirus*	Aphids
Narcissus late season yellows virus	NLSYV	Potyviridae	*Potyvirus*	Aphids
Narcissus latent virus	NLV	Potyviridae	*Macluravirus*	Aphids
Narcissus yellow stripe virus	NYSV	Potyviridae	*Potyvirus*	Aphids
Parsnip yellow fleck virus	PYFV	Sequiviridae	*Sequivirus*	Aphids
Pea early browning virus	PEBV	–	*Tobravirus*	Nematodes
Plum pox virus	PPV	Potyviridae	*Potyvirus*	Aphids
Potato leaf roll virus	PLRV	Luteoviridae	*Polerovirus*	Aphids
Potato mop top virus	PMTV	–	*Pomovirus*	Fungi
Potato virus Y	PVY	Potyviridae	*Potyvirus*	Aphids
Raspberry leaf mottle virus	RLMV	–	–	Aphids
Raspberry leaf spot virus	RLSV	–	–	Aphids
Raspberry ringspot virus	RpRSV	Comoviridae	*Nepovirus*	Nematodes
Raspberry vein chlorosis virus	RVCV	Rhabdoviridae	–	Aphids
Rubus yellow net virus	RYNV	Caulimoviridae	*Badnavirus*	Aphids
Ryegrass mosaic virus	RgMV	Potyviridae	*Rymovirus*	Mites
Strawberry crinkle virus	SCV	Rhabdoviridae	*Cytorhabdovirus*	Aphids
Strawberry latent ringspot virus	SLRV	–	*Sadwavirus*	Nematodes
Strawberry mottle virus	SMoV	–	*Sadwavirus*	Aphids
Tobacco rattle virus	TRV	–	*Tobravirus*	Nematodes
Tobacco ringspot virus	TRSV	Comoviridae	*Nepovirus*	Nematodes
Tomato black ring virus	TBRV	Comoviridae	*Nepovirus*	Nematodes
Tomato ringspot virus	ToRSV	Comoviridae	*Nepovirus*	Nematodes
Tomato spotted wilt virus	TSWV	Bunyaviridae	*Tospovirus*	Thrips
Tomato yellow leaf curl virus	TYLCV	Geminiviridae	*Begomovirus*	Whiteflies
Tulip breaking virus	TBV	Potyviridae	*Potyvirus*	Aphids
Turnip mosaic virus	TuMV	Potyviridae	*Potyvirus*	Aphids

Endnotes

Chapter 1: Plant Pests and Their Natural Enemies

1 Imms, 1947.
2 Where names of two alternate host plants form the basis of the common name of an aphid – cited as the primary (winter) host followed by that of the secondary (summer) host – these are separated by a solidus rather than the more commonly used en-rule or hyphen: thus, 'blackberry/cereal aphid' rather than 'blackberry–cereal aphid' or 'blackberry-cereal aphid'. This allows a hyphen to be used without ambiguity or confusion (as in the case of the bird-cherry/oat aphid) and is compatible with the use of hyphens in the common names of pests such as 'diamond-back moth', 'angle-shades moth' etc.
3 Finch & Collier, 2000.
4 Lindley, 1831.
5 See, for example, Wiseman (1990).
6 van Gelder, 1991.
7 Armer, 2004.
8 Frohne & Pfänder, 2005.
9 Aplin *et al.*, 1975.
10 Mattiacci *et al.*, 1994.
11 Peumans & van Damme, 1995.
12 For example, Gatehouse *et al.*, 1997, 1999.
13 Lehrman *et al.*, 2008.
14 Stork, 1980.
15 Redfern *et al.*, 2002.
16 Emmet *et al.*, 1985.
17 Silk produced by insects and other arthropods, including spider mites and spiders, is secreted as a liquid that is forced through the narrow opening of a spinneret. This gives the silk strength by lining up the molecules, to form a solid but flexible, semicrystalline thread. In insect larvae, as in Lepidoptera and Hymenoptera, the silk emanates from a pair of spinnerets in the head, which open near the base of the lower lip (labium). In spider mites, a silk-producing spinneret is located on each pedipalp. Spiders produce their silk from spinnerets located on the abdomen.
18 Pest species of aphid in the aerial plankton have been monitored for many years as part of the Rothamsted Insect Survey, using specially designed suction traps (e.g. Macaulay *et al.*, 1988).
19 Vandermeer, 1989.
20 Andow, 1991.
21 Nilsson, 2003.
22 Alford, 1979.
23 Pauer, 1975; Luff, 1987.
24 Cook *et al.*, 2007.
25 Hokkanen, 1991.
26 See Walters *et al.*, 2003.
27 Pistorius *et al.*, 2009.
28 For example, Frampton & Wratten, 2000.
29 For example, Haque & Ebing, 1983.
30 Vänninen & Hokkanen, 1988.
31 For example, Frank, 1996.
32 Nilsson, 2003.
33 Symondson *et al.*, 2002.
34 Altieri, 1999.
35 Greaves & Marshall, 1987; Thomas, 1996.
36 Crop margins are often described as headlands. However, the term 'headland' more correctly refers to the turning area for farm machinery within the crop, and is typically restricted to just two ends of a field.
37 Thomas *et al.*, 1991, 1992; MacLeod *et al.*, 2004.

Chapter 2: An Overview of Cereal Pests

1 Cox, 2000.
2 Graham & Alford, 1981.
3 Savage, 1977.
4 Port & French, 1984.
5 Fidler, 1936a.
6 For example, Maskell, 1959.
7 Coll & Blackshaw, 1996.
8 See Chapter 3, Endnote 19.
9 Gair, 1964.
10 Bassett, 1978.
11 Balachowsky, 1962.
12 Petherbridge & Thomas, 1936a.
13 Nye, 1959.
14 For example, Gough, 1947, 1949, 1957.
15 Long, 1960; Dobson, 1961.
16 Gough, 1946.
17 Ryan, 1975.
18 Synonym: *Scatophaga stercorarium.*
19 Jones, 1975.
20 Lawton, 1956.
21 Vickerman, 1982.
22 Thomas, 1933.
23 Thomas, 1934.
24 Frew, 1924.
25 Synonym: *Stenomalina micans.*
26 Kearns, 1931.
27 Synonym: *Crepidodera ferruginea.*
28 Petherbridge & Thomas, 1936b.
29 For example, Rézbányai-Reser, 1985.
30 Balachowsky, 1972.
31 Haggett, 1957.
32 Phillips & Parsons, 2005.
33 Salt, 1931.
34 For example, Goosey *et al.*, 2005.
35 Vickerman & Wratten, 1979.
36 Walters *et al.*, 1983.
37 Carter *et al.* 1980.
38 Stone, 1977.
39 Siphunculi (also known as cornicles) are the pair of often tube-like structures arising from the abdomen of an aphid, and from which alarm pheromones and other defensive secretions are emitted. Features of the siphunculi vary from species to species, and in some groups they are cone-like, pore-like or absent.
40 Also known as the corn leaf aphid.
41 *Metapolophium* is a misspelling.
42 Leather *et al.*, 1984.
43 For example, Miller & Rasochová, 1997.
44 Acronyms for the various isolates are derived in part from the scientific names of their respective vectors: RP, for example, standing for *__R__hopalosiphum __p__adi*; MA for *__M__acrosiphum* (= *Sitobion*) *__a__venae*; PA for *Rhopalosiphum __p__adi* and *Sitobion __a__venae.*
45 A'Brook & Dewar, 1980.
46 Shirota *et al.*, 1983.
47 Carter *et al.*, 1980.
48 Dransfield, 1979.
49 For example, Sunderland, 1975; Vickerman & Sunderland, 1975; Edwards *et al.*, 1979.
50 Holland *et al.*, 1994.
51 For example, Kromp, 1999.
52 Synonyms: *Agonum dorsale, Platynus dorsalis.*
53 Sotherton, 1984, 1985.
54 Thomas *et al.*, 1991, 1992; MacLeod *et al.*, 2004.
55 Frank & Reichhart, 2004.
56 van Huizen, 1977.
57 For example, Sharga, 1933; Lewis, 1959.
58 Oakley, 1980.
59 Nielsen & Nielsen, 2002.
60 Basedow, 1977.
61 Miller & Halton, 1961.
62 Oakley *et al.*, 1998.
63 Synonym: *Pirene penetrans.*
64 For example, Doane *et al.*, 1989.
65 Barnes, 1956.
66 McMahon, 1962.
67 Empson & Gair, 1982.
68 As cited in Pauly, 2002.
69 Enock, 1909.
70 Golightly & Woodville, 1974.
71 Hodson, 1929.
72 Synonym: *Oulema lichenis.*
73 Balachowsky, 1963.
74 Synonym: phleum mottle virus.
75 A'Brook & Benigno, 1972.
76 Mason, 1958.
77 Roebuck, 1923.
78 For example, Vickerman & O'Bryan, 1979.
79 Sotherton, 1990.
80 For example, Feare, 1978.
81 Deans, 1979; Wright & Isaacson 1978.
82 Gough, 1955a.
83 Spencer, 1973.
84 Duthoit, 1968.
85 Synonym: *Tyroglyphus casei.*
86 Synonym: *Glycyphagus destructor.*
87 Griffiths *et al.*, 1976.
88 For example, Cherewick & Robinson, 1958.
89 Suski, 1974.
90 Cooper, 1940.
91 Empson & Gair, 1982.
92 Gair *et al.*, 1969.
93 Kerry & Crump, 1977.
94 Franklin, 1965.

Chapter 3: Grasslands

1 Glen *et al.*, 1991.
2 Edwards & Evans, 1950.
3 Miles *et al.*, 1941.
4 Roberts, 1919, 1921, 1922.
5 Gough & Evans, 1942.

6 Gray *et al.*, 1947.
7 Milne, 1956.
8 Synonym: *Crepidodera ferruginea.*
9 Bevan, 1962.
10 Murray & Clements, 1995.
11 Jackson, 1920, 1922.
12 Synonym: *Apion* spp.
13 Blackshaw, 1991.
14 White & French, 1968.
15 Blackshaw & D'Arcy-Burt, 1997.
16 Morris, 1921, 1922.
17 Synonym: *Philudoria potatoria.*
18 Gair, 1959.
19 Confusingly, the name *Crambus culmella* (or *Crambus culmellus*) was formerly applied to *Agriphila straminella*; *Chrysoteuchia culmella* was then cited as either *Crambus hortuella* (or *Crambus hortuellus*).
20 Thompson, 1942.
21 Nye, 1958.
22 Thomas, 1934.
23 Thomas, 1938.
24 Stokes, 1957.
25 Jones, 1940a; Barnes, 1946.
26 Miller, 1918.
27 Barnes, 1930.
28 Jones, 1940b.
29 Metcalfe, 1933.
30 Milne, 1960.
31 Harris, 1966.
32 Barnes, 1935; King *et al.*, 1935.
33 Empson, 1956.
34 Spencer, 1973.
35 Mühle, 1971.
36 *Metapolophium* is a misspelling.
37 For example, Kendall *et al.*, 1996.
38 Morris, 1971.
39 Frazier & Posnette, 1956.
40 Also known as the American grass thrips.
41 Gibson, 1976.
42 Mulligan, 1960.
43 Catherall & Chamberlain, 1975.
44 For example, Skoracka & Kuczynski, 2006.
45 Gould & Winfield, 1962.
46 Chada, 1956.
47 Hardison, 1959.

Chapter 4: The World of Oilseed Rape Pests

1 Alford, 2003.
2 Erucic acid in rapeseed oil causes heart problems, and also has other detrimental effects; glucosinolates affect the thyroid gland, leading to hormonal imbalance.
3 For example, Williams, 1989.
4 Rawlinson & Williams, 1991.
5 Glen *et al.*, 1989.
6 Also known as Trowse mustard.
7 Also known as clevers.
8 Jay & Smith, 1995.
9 Walsh & Tomlinson, 1985.
10 George, 1957.
11 Büchs, 2003.
12 Synonym: *Calocoris norvegicus.*
13 Hoßfeld, 1963.
14 Bonnemaison & Jourdheiul, 1954; Alford, 1979.
15 Williams & Carden, 1961.
16 For example, Marshall, 1783; Yarrell, 1837; Curtis, 1860.
17 Yarrell, 1837.
18 Benson, 1952.
19 Marshall, 1783.
20 Yarrell, 1837.
21 For example, Müller & Brakefield, 2003.
22 In a splendid colour plate, Yarrell (1837) illustrates the puparium of a tachinid parasitoid partially enclosed within the remains of a turnip sawfly larva.
23 Cameron, 1882.
24 Marshall, 1783.
25 Winfield, 1992.
26 Gabry *et al.*, 1998.
27 Blackman, 1965, 1967.
28 George, 1957.
29 Furk *et al.*, 1990.
30 Gratwick, 1992.
31 'Green bud' is the growth stage when clusters of buds are clearly visible but petals are still hidden. This is followed by 'yellow bud', when petals become visible but are yet to emerge.
32 Ekbom & Borg, 1996.
33 Williams & Free, 1978.
34 Fritzsche, 1957.
35 Alford & Gould, 1975; Free & Williams, 1978.
36 See Endnote 31 above.
37 Richardson, 2008.
38 Osborne, 1960; Winfield, 1963.
39 Nilsson & Andreasson, 1987.
40 Nilsson & Ahmed, 2006.
41 Friedrichs, 1920.
42 Synonym: *Pterostichus cupreus.*
43 Büchs & Nuss, 2000.
44 Büchs, 2003.
45 Hokkanen *et al.*, 2003.
46 Synonym: *Metarhizium anisopliae.*
47 Butt *et al.*, 1998.
48 Kirk *et al.*, 1995.
49 Synonym: *Ceutorhynchus obstrictus.* In the 1990s, following the examination of type material (the original specimens upon which descriptions and names of species are based), the virtually unused name *obstrictus* was resurrected for the cabbage seed weevil. Regrettably, the name *assimilis* (that had been used for cabbage seed weevil for over 200

years) was then transferred to the species universally known as *Ceutorhynchus pleurostigma* – i.e. the turnip gall weevil. This has since caused utter confusion in applied entomology, a problem which should have been predicted and could easily have been avoided from the outset. In line with the rules of zoological nomenclature the changes have been adopted in recent checklists (e.g. Morris, 2003; Duff, 2008), although they are not given precedence here.

50 Ferguson & Williams, 1993.
51 Williams, 2003a.
52 Alford *et al.*, 1996.
53 Murchie *et al.*, 1997b.
54 Dmoch, 1998.
55 Murchie & Williams, 1998.
56 Synonym: *Ceutorhynchus quadridens.*
57 Graham & Gould, 1980.
58 Winfield, 1961.
59 Broschewitz & Daebeler, 1987.
60 Alford *et al.*, 2003.
61 Dechert & Ulber, 2004.
62 Synonym: *Ceutorhynchus floralis.*
63 Buhl, 1960.
64 Williams *et al.*, 1987a, 1987b.
65 When pods shatter prematurely some or all seeds drop to the ground and are lost. Yield reductions following severe pod midge infestations can be considerable.
66 Williams, 2003b.
67 Williams & Walton, 1990.
68 Murchie *et al.*, 1999a.
69 Murchie *et al.*, 1997a.
70 Bartlet, 1996.
71 Bernays & Chapman, 1994.
72 Brunel *et al.*, 1989.
73 Prescher & Büchs, 1998.

Chapter 5: Pests of Beet, Mangold and Potato Crops

1 Also known as mangel or mangelwurzel.
2 Tomato, of course, is also of South American origin.
3 Shaw, 1970a, b.
4 Broadbent & Heathcote, 1954; Shaw, 1954.
5 Fisken, 1959a, b.
6 Jones & Dunning, 1972.
7 For example, Bell, 1983.
8 Smith, 1972.
9 Kershaw, 1964.
10 Synonym: *Calocoris norvegicus.*
11 Walton & Staniland, 1929.
12 Dunning, 1957.
13 Stewart, 1968.
14 Schewket Bay, 1930.
15 Voigt *et al.*, 2007.
16 Dewar *et al.*, 2000.
17 French & White, 1960.
18 Synonym: *Philopedon plagiatus.*
19 Jones *et al.*, 1947.
20 Parker & Howard, 2001.
21 For example, Edwards & Dennis, 1960.
22 Gratwick, 1989.
23 Petherbridge & Stapley, 1937.
24 Jones & Dunning, 1972.
25 Whitehead & Hooper, 1970.
26 Cooper, 1971.
27 Anon., 2006.
28 Taylor, 1978.
29 Winslow, 1954.
30 Winslow, 1955.
31 Southey *et al.*, 1982.
32 Petherbridge & Jones, 1944.
33 Trudgill, 1986.
34 Stone, 1973.
35 Jones & Dunning, 1972.
36 Gratwick, 1989.
37 Corbett, 1973.
38 Based on Gratwick, 1989.
39 Anderson, 2005.
40 Kennedy, 1996.
41 Jones & Dunning, 1972.

Chapter 6: Pests of Field Vegetables

1 Field beans (an agricultural break crop in cereal rotations) and broad beans (a vegetable crop) are forms of the same species (vars *minor* and *major*, respectively). They are attacked by a similar range of pests.
2 Dunn, 1959a.
3 Dunn, 1959b.
4 Philips *et al.*, 1999.
5 Buczacki & Harris, 2005.
6 Dunn & Wright, 1955b.
7 McVean *et al.*, 1999.
8 Dunn & Wright, 1955a.
9 Kunert *et al.*, 2005.
10 Kunert *et al.*, 2008.
11 Geigy *et al.*, 2005.
12 Libbrecht *et al.*, 2007.
13 Formerly described under *Lecanicillium lecanii.*
14 Synonym: *Erynia neoaphidis.*
15 Synonym: *Metarhizium anisopliae.*
16 Chandler, 1997.
17 Gough, 1955b.
18 Williams, 1914.
19 Synonym: *Aeolothrips fasciatus.*
20 Synonym: *Calocoris norvegicus.*
21 Hering, 1951.
22 Bretherton *et al.*, 1979.
23 Arkle, 1891.
24 Shaw, 1959; French & White, 1960.
25 Synonym: *Apanteles glomeratus.*
26 For example, Mattiacci *et al.*, 1995.

27 Baker, 1970.
28 van Alphen, 1980.
29 Jackson, 1920.
30 Synonym: *Apion vorax.*
31 Cockbain *et al.*, 1975; 1982.
32 Synonym: *Ceutorhynchus quadridens.*
33 Leroi, 1973.
34 Synonym: *Platyparea poeciloptera.*
35 Smith, 1989.
36 Synonym: *Ophiomyia simplex.*
37 Barnes, 1937.
38 Gilbertson *et al.*, 1985.
39 Spencer, 1973.
40 Coaker, 1973.
41 Simmonds, 1974.
42 Jary & Edelsten, 1944.
43 Coppock, 1974.
44 Petherbridge *et al.*, 1942.
45 Petherbridge & Wright, 1943.
46 Baker *et al.*, 1942.
47 Wright & Ashby, 1946.
48 Gratwick, 1992.
49 Wright *et al.*, 1947.
50 Burn, 1982.
51 Jones, 1975.
52 Lewis *et al.*, 1975.
53 Wright & Geering, 1948.
54 Wright *et al.*, 1961.
55 Balachowsky, 1966.
56 Cameron, 1938; Wright & Geering, 1948.
57 Miles, 1958.
58 Ellis & Scatcherd, 2007.
59 Finch & Collier, 1983; Finch *et al.*, 1986.
60 Synonym: *Ceutorhynchus assimils*, but see comments in Chapter 4 Endnote 49.
61 Protozoans are regarded as non-filamentous members of the kingdom Protista. However, although retained as terms of convenience, neither is used in modern taxonomy.
62 Synonym: *Harpalus aeneus.*
63 For example, Coaker & Williams, 1963; Mitchell, 1963.
64 Finch, 1989.
65 Misidentification: *Cothonaspis rapae.* Synonym: *Idiomorpha rapae.*
66 Wishart & Monteith, 1954.
67 Wishart *et al.*, 1957.
68 Synonym: *Empusa muscae.*
69 Coaker & Finch, 1971.
70 Bowden *et al.*, 1983.
71 Esbjerg *et al.*, 1986; Esbjerg, 1988.
72 Vallotton, 1969.
73 Theobald, 1907; Warburton, 1926; Bevan & Uncles, 1958.
74 Synonym: *Pirene graminea.*
75 Kutter, 1934.
76 Barnes, 1946.
77 Thomas, 1946.
78 Bardner *et al.*, 1971.
79 Bardner *et al.*, 1984.
80 Franklin, 1978.
81 Hooper & Southey, 1978.
82 Yuksel, 1960.
83 Gratwick, 1992.
84 Goodey, 1941.

Chapter 7: Life in Orchards

1 Co. Armagh is often known as the apple county or Ireland's orchard county.
2 Based on Alford, 2007.
3 Based on Alford, 2007.
4 Traditional orchards are considered priority habitats for wildlife.
5 Bradley *et al.*, 1973, 1979.
6 Theobald, 1928.
7 Synonym: *Apocheima pilosaria.*
8 Heddergott, 1962.
9 Ormerod, 1898; Theobald, 1909.
10 Synonym: *Chloroclystis rectangulata.*
11 Alford, 1978a.
12 Synonym: *Argyresthia arcella.*
13 Synonym: *Rhynchites caeruleus.*
14 Haggett, 1950.
15 Winfield, 1964.
16 Also known as the red-belted clearwing moth.
17 Miles, 1930.
18 Synonym: *Xyleborus saxeseni.*
19 Also known as the apple ermine moth.
20 Also known as the orchard ermine moth.
21 Leather, 1986.
22 Theobald, 1909.
23 Emmet, 1989.
24 Emmet *et al.*, 1996.
25 On apple, the stage of development in spring when flower/fruit buds are fully exposed and surrounded by a cluster of opening leaves but petals have yet to appear.
26 Light, 1980.
27 Schmidt, 1970.
28 Stroyan, 1963.
29 Bell, 1983.
30 Synonym: *Plesiocoris rugicollis.*
31 For example, Fryer, 1914; Smith, 1920.
32 Butler, 1923.
33 Carpenter, 1920.
34 Petherbridge & Thorpe, 1928.
35 Petherbridge & Husain, 1918; Austin, 1929, 1931.
36 Taksdal, 1983.
37 Synonym: *Psylla mali.*
38 Synonym: *Psylla pyricola.*
39 Winfield *et al.*, 1985.
40 Synonyms: *Aspidiotus perniciosus; Comstockaspis pernicosa; Quadraspidiotus perniciosus.*

41 Kozár *et al.*, 1996.
42 Wyss, 1995.
43 Schliesske, 1995, 2004.
44 Easterbrook, 1979.
45 Easterbrook, 1978.
46 For example, Easterbrook & Fuller, 1986.
47 Solomon & Locke, 2000.
48 Cranham, 1973.
49 Cranham, 1972.
50 Various acaricides formerly used in orchards to control fruit tree red spider mite have long since ceased to be effective.
51 Alford, 1978b.
52 Taylor, 1949.
53 Vernon, 1971b.
54 Theobald, 1909.
55 de Jong & Beeke, 1956.
56 Vogel *et al.*, 1956.
57 Bradley *et al.*, 1979.
58 Petherbridge, 1928.
59 Stapley, 1934.
60 Synonym: *Rhynchites aequatus.*
61 Massee, 1954.
62 Alford, 1973.
63 Rings, 1970.
64 Groves, 1951.
65 Glen, 1982.
66 For example, van Frankenhuyzen *et al.*, 2002.
67 Alford, 1980.
68 Easterbrook, 1985.
69 For example, Collyer, 1952; Solomon, 1982.
70 Collyer, 1964; Solomon, 1975.
71 For example, Collyer, 1953a, 1953b, 1953c.
72 Glen, 1975, 1977.
73 Speyer, 1933.
74 Myers, 1927.
75 See Wheeler, 2001.
76 Nau & Brooke, 2003.
77 Sigsgaard, 2004.
78 Scutareanu *et al.*, 1999.
79 Solomon & Locke, 2000.
80 Glen & Milsom, 1978.
81 Putnam, 1955.
82 McEwan *et al.*, 2001.
83 Killington, 1936.
84 Herting, 1974.
85 Lyon & Göldlin de Tiefenau, 1974.
86 Cross & Jay, 2001.
87 Zijp & Blommers, 2002a.
88 Babendreier, 2000.
89 Imms, 1918.
90 Zijp & Blommers, 2002b.
91 d'Aguilar *et al.*, 1974.
92 Morley & Rait-Smith, 1933.
93 Wajnberg & Hassan, 1994.
94 Massee, 1954.
95 Solomon *et al.*, 2000; Fitzgerald & Solomon, 2002.
96 Glen, 1975, 1977.
97 Synonym: *Amblyseius finlandicus.*
98 Cuthbertson *et al.*, 2003.
99 Cuthbertson, 2004.
100 MacRae & Croft, 1996.
101 Zhang, 1998.
102 Solomon *et al.*, 1976; Solomon & Glen, 1979.
103 Newton, 1964, 1972.

Chapter 8: Life in Soft-Fruit Plantations

1 Hurst, 1969.
2 For example, Whitehead & Wood, 1946.
3 Wood, 1950.
4 Dicker, 1952.
5 Jones, 1986.
6 Newstead, 1903.
7 Wardlow & Ludlam, 1975.
8 Petherbridge & Thorpe, 1928.
9 Dicker, 1939b; Hill, 1952a.
10 Taksdal & Sørum, 1971; Easterbrook, 1996, 2000.
11 Easterbrook, 1997.
12 Easterbrook, 1991.
13 Strawberry mite was first described as distinct from the cyclamen mite (*Phytonemus pallidus*) by Zimmermann (1905), who applied the name *fragariae* to specimens associated with strawberry plants in Europe. Over the years, however, its status as a distinct species has been questioned. Ewing & Smith (1934) and Smith & Goldsmith (1936), for example, concluded that the American cyclamen mite and the European strawberry mite were identical. Van Eyndhoven & Groenewold (1959) and Karl (1965a), however, reported minor structural differences between the two mites; host-plant differences have also been demonstrated (Wiesmann, 1941; Karl, 1965a). Separate specific status does not appear justified. However, strawberry mite is arguably most usefully regarded as a subspecies of *P. pallidus*, at least in applied circles.
14 Alford, 1972.
15 Storkan & Lembright, 1955.
16 Stenseth & Nordby, 1976.
17 van Eyndhoven, 1955.
18 Vernon, 1971a.
19 Sheldon, 1925; Turner, 1968.
20 For example, Heddergott, 1955; Alford & Docherty, 1974.
21 Petherbridge, 1920.
22 Synonym: *Olethreutes lacunana.*
23 Alford, 1975.
24 Madge, 1964.
25 Dicker, 1972.
26 Dicker, 1939a.
27 Gordon *et al.*, 1988.

28 Lawson *et al.*, 1988.
29 Benson, 1953.
30 Miles, 1932.
31 Miles, 1936.
32 Gordon & Woodford, 1994.
33 See Heath (1983) for further details.
34 Synonym: *Rhynchites germanicus.*
35 Jary, 1931, 1932.
36 Dicker, 1947.
37 Synonym: *Rhynchites caeruleus.*
38 Taylor, 1971.
39 Kearns & Walton, 1933.
40 Steer, 1932.
41 Massee, 1954; Luff, 1974.
42 Briggs, 1957.
43 Vernon, 1971a; Alford, 2007.
44 Greenslade, 1963.
45 Brown, 1961.
46 French *et al.*, 1968.
47 Brock *et al.*, 1964.
48 Sykes, 1969.
49 Shaw, 1956.
50 Hellqvist *et al.*, 2006.
51 Hill, 1952b.
52 Carpenter, 1909.
53 Bierne, 1943.
54 Shaw, 1957.
55 Barnes, 1926.
56 Gordon & Hargreaves, 1973; Woodford & Gordon, 1978.
57 Gunn & Foster, 1978.
58 For example, Pitcher & Webb, 1952.
59 Massee, 1928; Jary *et al.*, 1938.
60 Smith, 1960.
61 Healthy flower buds are more or less coated in grey hairs and have a downy appearance. On reverted bushes, however, the flower buds are virtually hairless, so they appear distinctly reddish. There are also characteristic differences in the appearance of leaves (see Lees, 1922).
62 Fenton *et al.*, 1993; Roberts *et al.*, 1993.
63 Fenton *et al.*, 1995.
64 Gordon & Taylor, 1976.
65 Macintyre & Foster, 1977.
66 For example, Savage, 1978.
67 For example, Vernon & Dennis, 1965.
68 Synonym: *Plinthus caliginosus.*
69 Fidler, 1936b.
70 For example, Fox-Wilson, 1925; Fidler, 1936b.
71 Ibbotson & Edwards, 1954.
72 For example, Theobald, 1909.
73 For example, Moorhouse *et al.*, 1992.
74 The UK black currant industry, for instance, was particularly concerned about vine weevil in the 1980s. This followed the decline in the use of persistent organochlorine insecticides and a noticeable resurgence of the pest.
75 Pickett *et al.*, 1996.
76 Stenseth & Vik, 1979; Buxton, 1996.
77 Alford, 1996.
78 Synonym: *Amblyseius finlandicus.*
79 Synonym: *Neoseiulus californicus.*
80 Synonym: *Neoseiulus cucumeris.*
81 Simmonds, 1970.
82 Smith, 1990.
83 Dicker, 1944.
84 Hanni & Luik, 2006.
85 Barnes, 1948a.
86 Cameron, 1885.
87 Turner, 1968.
88 Alford, 1984.
89 Alford, 1976.
90 Turner, 1968.
91 Vernon, 1971a.
92 Alford, 1976.
93 Hawkins *et al.*, 1993.
94 Dicker, 1939a.
95 Synonym: *Apanteles.*
96 Lipa, 1977.
97 Brock *et al.*, 1964.
98 Dicker, 1939a.
99 Synonym: *Neoaplectana bibionis.*
100 Miller & Bedding, 1981, 1982.
101 Synonym: *Entomophora planchoniana.*
102 Synonym: *Metarhizium anisopliae.*

Chapter 9: Hardy Ornamentals

1 Pape, 1964; Becker, 1974; Alford, 1991.
2 Fly honeysuckle is attacked by the fly-honeysuckle aphid (*Hyadaphis foeniculi*), but not the honeysuckle aphid.
3 See Stroyan, 1977.
4 Synonym: *Gossyparia spuria.*
5 Synonym: *Calocoris norvegicus.*
6 Synonym: *Pristiphora alnivora.*
7 Synonym: *Strophosomus melanogrammus.*
8 Fox-Wilson, 1942, 1943.
9 Synonym: *Numonia suavella.*
10 Curtis, 1782.
11 Baker, 1968.
12 Bradley *et al.*, 1973.
13 Herfs, 1963.
14 Synonym: *Rhynchaenus fagi.*
15 Emmet *et al.*, 1985; Emmet, 1976.
16 Hering, 1951.
17 Emmet, 1985.
18 Carter, 1971.
19 Miles, 1928.
20 Martin & Malumphy, 1995.
21 Barnes, 1948b.
22 Halstead & Harris, 1990.
23 Redfern, 1975.
24 Redfern & Cameron, 1995; Redfern & Hunter, 2005.
25 Barnes, 1948.

26 Schwenke, 1982.
27 Imms, 1947.
28 Strouts & Winter, 1994.
29 Stigter & van Frankenhuysen, 1992.
30 White, 2003.
31 Agassiz & Tuck, 1999.
32 Scott, 1972.

Chapter 10: Pests of Plants in Protected Cultivation

1 Speyer, 1927.
2 Formerly described under *Lecanicillium lecanii.*
3 Raupach *et al.*, 2002.
4 MacGill, 1934.
5 For example, Ulenberg *et al.*, 1986.
6 Synonym: *Macrolophus caliginosus.*
7 Becker, 1974.
8 Annecke, 1966.
9 The citrophilous mealybug (*Pseudococcus calceolariae*) and the New Zealand flax mealybug (*Balanococcus diminutus*) are exceptions. Both occur outdoors in southwest England, the latter as a relatively recent arrival in Britain (Bartlett, 1981).
10 Synonyms: *Pseudococcus affinis* and *P. obscurus.*
11 van de Wetering *et al.*, 1999.
12 Kirk & Hamilton, 2004; Hamilton *et al.*, 2005.
13 Teerling *et al.*, 1993.
14 Gaum *et al.*, 1994.
15 Scott Brown & Simmonds, 2006.
16 Robinson & Collins, 2005.
17 Morison, 1957; Hussey *et al.*, 1969.
18 Port & Guile, 1986.
19 Lloyd, 1920.
20 van de Vrie, 1991.
21 Fisher, 1924.
22 Synonym: *Bradysia paupera.*
23 Synonym: *Bradysia tritici.*
24 Speyer, 1922.
25 Synonym: *Therodiplosis persicae.*
26 Synonym: *Phytomyza syngenesiae.*
27 Cohen, 1936.
28 Speyer, 1928.
29 Cameron, 1925.
30 Karl, 1965a.
31 For example, Cross & Bassett, 1982.
32 Karl, 1965b.
33 Synonym: *Neoseiulus cucumeris.*
34 Brown, 1954.
35 Hussey *et al.*, 1969.
36 Synonym: *Helix aspersa.*
37 Copping, 2009.
38 Also known as white truffle or Italian white truffle, but not to be confused with the unrelated pig truffle that is also sometimes called white truffle (see de Rougemont, 1989).
39 Spooner & Roberts, 2005.
40 Hussey *et al.*, 1969; Fletcher & Gaze, 2007.
41 For example, Deharveng, 2004.
42 Wyatt, 1964.
43 Wyatt, 1967.
44 Wyatt, 1959.
45 Wyatt, 1960.
46 Moreton & John, 1955.
47 Hussey, 1959.
48 For example, Truitt, 1951.
49 Cimarra *et al.*, 1999.
50 White, 1986.
51 Synonym: *Lycoriella auripila.*
52 Hussey & Gurney, 1968.
53 Synonyms: *Lycoriella mali* and *L. solani.*
54 White & Smith, 2000; White *et al.*, 2000.
55 Austin, 1937.
56 Fletcher & Gaze, 2007.
57 Pitkin, 1989.
58 Moreton, 1958.
59 Synonyms: *Bakerdania mesembrinae, Pediculaster mesembrinae* and *Siteroptes mesembrinae.*
60 For example, Al-Amidi & Downes, 1990; Al-Amidi *et al.*, 1991.
61 Binns, 1972, 1973.
62 Arrold & Blake, 1968.
63 Caryol, 1967.
64 Caryol, 1964.
65 Spooner & Roberts (2005) briefly review the mechanisms employed by fungi to trap their nematode prey.

Chapter 11: Pests of Miscellaneous Crops

1 Flax is one of the world's oldest cultivated plants (de Rougemont, 1989).
2 Synonym: *Calocoris norvegicus.*
3 For example, Ferguson *et al.*, 1997.
4 Morison, 1943.
5 Synonym: *Aeolothrips fasciatus.*
6 Rhynehart, 1922.
7 Patterson, 1838.
8 Hyman & Parsons, 1992.
9 Ferguson *et al.*, 1997.
10 A white-flowering crop with deeply penetrating taproots, especially favoured owing to its drought tolerance; also known as crambe.
11 Ekbom & Borg, 1996.
12 Also known as false flax.
13 For example, Pachagounder *et al.*, 1998; Elliott & Rakow, 1999.
14 Blackman & Eastop, 2006.
15 Synonym: *Phytomyza syngenesiae.*
16 Alford, 1991.
17 Hemp crops have sometimes attracted the unwelcome attention of drug users, who mistakenly believe the plants contain viable amounts of cannabis. In reality, however, the

amounts of hallucinogenic drug (cannabis) that can be extracted from such plants are at best minimal.
18 Perrin, 1975.
19 Synonym: *Sylepta ruralis.*
20 Davis, 1983.
21 Sigsgaard *et al.*, 2008.
22 Also known as the giant willow aphid.
23 Collins *et al.*, 2001.
24 Duncan & Lindquist, 1989.
25 Barnes, 1933.
26 Doom, 1966.
27 ter Pelkwijk, 1946; Doom, 1966.
28 Smith & Stott, 1964.
29 Synonym: *Rhabdophaga marginemtorquens.*
30 Strong *et al.*, 1993.
31 Synonym: *Rhabdophaga heterobia.*
32 Nixon, 1997.
33 Huggett, 1996.
34 Huggett *et al.*, 1999.
35 For example, Sage *et al.*, 2006.
36 Sage & Tucker, 1997.
37 Kendall *et al.*, 1996.
38 Synonym: *Phyllodecta vulgatissima.*
39 Synonym: *Phyllodecta vitellinae.*
40 Kendall *et al.*, 1996.
41 Pasteels & Rowell-Rahier, 1992.
42 Wiltshire *et al.*, 1997; Peacock *et al.*, 2001, 2002.
43 Bell *et al.*, 2006.
44 Synonyms: *Chalcoides aurea* and *C. aurata*, respectively.
45 Carter & Winter, 1998.
46 Also known as spruce shoot aphids.
47 Carter & Winter, 1998.
48 Also known as the pineapple gall woolly aphid.
49 Also known as the silver fir woolly aphid.
50 Also known as the European pine woolly aphid.
51 Varty, 1956; Carter, 1971.
52 Also known as the rosemary leaf beetle.
53 Halstead, 1996.
54 For example, Mabbott & Salisbury, 2006.
55 Balachowsky, 1963.
56 Burgess, 1964.
57 For example, Campbell, 1978; Aveling, 1981.
58 Darby & Campbell, 1996.
59 A hop-dog is also a long-handled, iron-toothed tool traditionally used by hop growers to lever hop poles out of the ground; along with other farming implements, one is portrayed as part of the village sign for Otham in Kent.
60 Pratt, 1986–7.
61 Synonym: *Cosmopteryx eximia.*
62 Balachowsky, 1966.
63 Bretherton *et al.*, 1983.
64 Campbell & Tregidga, 2004.
65 Goater, 1986.
66 There are two genetically distinct races of *Ostrinia nubilalis*, the E race (associated with hop and mugwort) and the Z race (associated with maize and sweet corn). The latter is a major pest in southern Europe and is currently expanding its natural range northwards, as in Germany (e.g. Schmitz *et al.*, 2002). To date, the Z race has not been found in Britain. European corn borer is also an important pest in North America.
67 French *et al.*, 1973.
68 Synonym: *Plinthus caliginosus.*
69 Collingwood, 1954.
70 Massee, 1942.
71 For example, Garthwaite & Thomas 2004.
72 Game, 1995.
73 Synonym: *Strophosomus melanogrammus.*
74 Synonym: *Curculio nucum.*
75 Bradley *et al.*, 1979.
76 Schliesske, 2004.
77 Synonym: *Callaphis juglandis.*
78 *Stenotarsonemus* is a misspelling.
79 Also known as dewplants.
80 Hodson, 1932.
81 Preston & Sell, 1988.
82 Hodson, 1927.
83 Hodson, 1934.
84 Hughes, 1961.
85 Hodson, 1928.
86 In January 2008, the Federal Biological Research Centre for Agriculture and Forestry in Germany became the Julius Kühn Institute (JKI).
87 Synonym: *Chromatomyia ramosa.*
88 Topham, 1968.
89 Cheesman, 1996.
90 Rector *et al.*, 2006.
91 Stevens, 1983.
92 Amphipods are often incorrectly described as freshwater shrimps.
93 Synonym: *Ceutorhynchus obstrictus*; see Chapter 4 Endnote 49.
94 Synonym: *Ceutorhynchus quadridens.*
95 Taylor, 1928.
96 Gower, 1967.

Chapter 12: Alien Pests

1 Nash *et al.*, 1995.
2 Newstead, 1901.
3 Smith *et al.*, 2007.
4 In this Directive, a harmful organism is defined as 'any species, strain or biotype of plant, animal or pathogenic agent harmful to plants or plant products'.
5 Smith *et al.*, 2005.
6 Carter *et al.*, 1984.

7 Carter, 1971; Carter & Maslen, 1983.
8 Synonyms: *Daktulosphaira vitifoliae*; *Phylloxera vitifolia*.
9 Bartlett, 1984; Bartlett & Savage, 1993.
10 Malumphy, 2005.
11 Also known as the fluted scale.
12 Watson & Malumphy, 2004.
13 Green, 1926, 1931.
14 Synonyms: *Aspidiotus perniciosus*; *Quadraspidiotus perniciosus*.
15 Discussions with the Board of Agriculture on the risks to British crops posed by San José scale are summarised by Newstead (1901).
16 For example, www.purdue.edu/fff/FFF08/FFF08-02.pdf
17 Also known as the sweet potato whitefly.
18 Suspected outbreaks of notifiable, non-native pests must be reported immediately to Plant Health authorities.
19 Lowe *et al.*, 2000.
20 Glasshouse whitefly is also a non-European species, but is now endemic throughout western Europe – in Britain primarily as a greenhouse pest (see Chapter 10).
21 For example, Lambkin, 1999.
22 www.defra.gov.uk/planth/interc/intercold.htm
23 Malumphy & Halstead, 2003.
24 '*Corythuca*' also appears in the literature, but is a misspelling. In North America, where plane trees (*Platanus* spp.) are called sycamores, the pest is known as the sycamore lace bug. However, this is inappropriate in Europe, where the name sycamore is ascribed specifically to *Acer pseudoplatanus*, a tree that is not attacked by platanus lace bug. N.B. In Scotland, adding further confusion, sycamore trees are commonly known as plane trees!
25 Malumphy *et al.*, 2007.
26 Department for the Environment, Food & Rural Affairs – formerly the Ministry of Agriculture, Fisheries & Food (MAFF).
27 On 1 April 2009, the Central Science Laboratory became part of The Food and Environment Research Agency (Fera).
28 Synonym: *Gnomonia veneta*.
29 Halstead & Malumphy, 2003.
30 Barclay, 2004.
31 Reid, 2006.
32 Baker *et al.*, 1993.
33 Cannon *et al.*, 2007.
34 Also known as the yellow tea thrips.
35 Also known as the impatiens thrips.
36 In America, known as the Colorado potato beetle or the potato bug.
37 Hare, 1990.
38 There are many alternative common names, including: buffalobur, Colorado bur, horned nightshade, Kansas thistle, Mexican thistle and Texas thistle.
39 Bartlett, 1980.
40 Dunn, 1949.
41 Balachowsky, 1963.
42 For example, Bartlett, 1980, 1983, 1990.
43 Baker *et al.*, 1998.
44 Ostojá-Starzewski, 2005.
45 There are several species or subspecies of corn rootworm in the USA, not only the western corn rootworm but also the northern corn rootworm (*Diabrotica barberi*) and the southern corn rootworm (*D. undecimpunctata howardi*).
46 www.opsi.gov.uk/si/si2008/uksi_20082411_en_1
47 Cannon *et al.*, 2005.
48 Baker *et al.*, 2000, 2003; MacLeod *et al.*, 2007.
49 For example, Branson & Ortman, 1967, 1970; Breitenbach *et al.*, 2005.
50 Majerus, 1994.
51 Also known as the multicoloured Asian ladybird and the Halloween ladybird.
52 Koch, 2003.
53 Hironori & Katsuhiro, 1997.
54 In North America, known as 'ladybug taint'.
55 Formerly known as the Mediterranean hawthorn weevil.
56 Barclay, 2003.
57 Synonym: *Napomyza gymnostoma*.
58 Collins & Lole, 2005.
59 Dunne & O'Connor, 1989; Hume *et al.*, 1990.
60 Bartlett & Powell, 1981.
61 For example, Cheek & Cannon, 2003.
62 www.csl.gov.uk/specialInterest/liriomyza.pdf
63 For example, Powell, 1981.
64 Also known as the Med fly.
65 Agassiz, 1996.
66 For example, Gilbert & Grégoire, 2003.
67 The highly invasive false acacia gall midge (*Obolodiplosis robiniae*), although having spread very rapidly and widely in central, southeastern and western Europe following its discovery in northeastern Italy in 2003 (Glavendekic & Roques, 2009), has also yet to be found in Britain.
68 Posenato *et al.*, 1997.
69 Oldham, 1928.
70 Moreton, 1974.
71 Drescher & Dufay, 2002.
72 Lupi & Jucker, 2005.
73 Eitschberger & Stamer, 1990.
74 Sarto i Monteys, 1992.
75 Holloway, 1998.
76 Powell, 1979.

77 Synonym: *Heliothis armigera.*
78 Defra Plant Pest Notice No. 27, September 1999.
79 Synonym: *Glyphodes perspectalis.*
80 Krüger, 2008.
81 Cannon *et al.* 2004.
82 Bradley *et al.*, 1979.
83 Benson, 1935.
84 Halstead, 2004.
85 Synonym: *Schizotetranychus celarius.*
86 Also known as the oriental red mite.
87 Yeates (1998) provides a wealth of information.
88 Synonym: *Artioposthia triangulata.*
89 Willis & Edwards, 1977.
90 See Endnote 26, above.
91 See Endnote 27, above.
92 For example, Boag *et al.*, 1994; Alford *et al.*, 1996; Jones & Boag, 1996; Moore *et al.*, 1998; Murchie *et al.*, 2004.
93 Synonym: *Geoplana sanguinea* var. *alba.*
94 Jones, 1981.
95 Jones & Gerard, 1999.
96 Synonym: *Parakontikia ventrolineata.*
97 Specifically, soft tree ferns; Cannon & Baker, 2007.
98 For example, Boag, 2000.
99 For example, Blackshaw, 1990.
100 Haria *et al.*, 1998.
101 For example, Davis *et al.*, 1992; Bailey *et al.*, 1999.
102 For example, Alford, 1998; Cannon *et al.*, 1999; Boag, 2000.
103 An international treaty 'to sustain the diversity of life on Earth'.
104 Moore *et al.*, 1998.
105 Unger, 1998.

Appendix I: Main Features of Invertebrate Pests and Their Natural Enemies

1 Arthropods, which greatly outnumber all other known animal species in the world, are subdivided into various classes: e.g. the Arachnida (harvestmen, mites, pseudoscorpions, scorpions and spiders), the Crustacea (amphipods, crabs, crayfish, lobsters, shrimps and woodlice), the Insecta (insects) and the Myriapoda (centipedes and millepedes).
2 Some authorities (e.g. Gullan & Cranston, 1994) exclude Collembola from the Insecta, and regard them, along with proturans and diplurans – orders Protura and Diplura, respectively – as non-insect hexapods (six-legged creatures). Insects are then treated as a subclass within the class Hexapoda and the terms Apterygota (wingless insects) and Pterygota (winged insects) abandoned.
3 Simple eyes in adult insects are called ocelli.
4 The terms nymph and larva are sometimes defined or applied differently: cf., for example, in the *New Naturalist* series Imms (1947) and Corbet & Brooks (2008).
5 For example, Imms, 1947; Chinery, 1993; Hill, 1994; Alford, 1999.
6 For example, Blackman & Eastop, 1984; Carter, 1984; Lewis, 1997; Wheeler, 2001; van Emden & Harrington, 2007.
7 von Dohlen & Moran, 1995.
8 The family Aphididae includes several subfamilies (e.g. Callaphidinae, Chaitophorinae, Eriosomatinae and Lachninae) which, in older schemes, were usually granted full family status.
9 The mouthparts of several pest species are illustrated by Smith (1989).
10 Ticks are included in the suborder Metastigmata (= Ixodida).
11 Classification schemes for mites also exist in which the Mesostigmata, Prostigmata etc. are regarded either as suborders or super orders.
12 Evans *et al.*, 1961; Baker & Wharton, 1964; Jeppson *et al.*, 1975.
13 Sclerotization, as in insects and mites, is the process whereby the outer layer of the body (the cuticle) is hardened and tanned (darkened) by formation of the protein sclerotin.
14 Wallace, 1963; Southey, 1978; Bridge & Starr, 2007.
15 Wallace, 1958, 1963.
16 Helyer *et al.*, 2003.
17 Synonym: *Milax budapestensis.*
18 Synonym: *Helix aspersa.*
19 Synonym: *Hygromia striolata.*
20 Dussart, 2003.

References

A'Brook, J. & Benigno, D. A. (1972). The transmission of cocksfoot mottle and phleum mottle viruses by *Oulema melanopa* and *O. lichenis*. *Annals of Applied Biology* **72**, 169–76.

A'Brook, J. & Dewar, A. M. (1980). Barley yellow dwarf virus infectivity of alate aphid vectors in west Wales. *Annals of Applied Biology* **96**, 51–8.

Agassiz, D. J. L. (1996). *Invasions of Lepidoptera into the British Isles*. In: *The Moths and Butterflies of Great Britain and Ireland. Vol. 3* (ed. Emmet, A. M.), pp. 9–36. Harley Books, Colchester.

Agassiz, D. J. L. & Tuck, K. R. (1999). The cypress tip moth *Argyresthia cupressella* Walsingham, 1890 (Lepidoptera: Yponomeutidae) new to Britain. *Entomologist's Gazette* **50**, 11–16.

Aguilar, J. d', Celli, D. & Chambon, J. P. (1974). *Parasites des mineuse*. In: *Les organismes auxillaires en verger de pommiers* (eds Milaire, H. G., Baggioloni, M., Gruys, P. & Steiner, H.). OILB/srop (IOBC/wprs) Brochure No. 3, pp. 71–9.

Al-Amidi, A. H. K. & Downes, M. J. (1990). *Parasitus bituberosus* (Acari: Parasitidae), a possible agent for biological control of *Heteropeza pygmaea* (Diptera: Cecidomyiidae) in mushroom compost. *Experimental and Applied Acarology* **8**, 13–25.

Al-Amidi, A. H. K., Dunne, R. & Downes, M. J. (1991). *Parasitus bituberosus* (Acari: Parasitidae): an agent for control of *Lycoriella solani* (Diptera: Sciaridae) in mushroom crops. *Experimental and Applied Acarology* **11**, 159–66.

Alford, D. V. (1972). The effect of *Tarsonemus fragariae* Zimmermann (Acarina: Tarsonemidae) on strawberry yields. *Annals of Applied Biology* **70**, 13–18.

Alford, D. V. (1973). The clouded drab moth, *Orthosia incerta* (Hfn.) (Lep., Noctuidae), a pest of orchard fruit. *Bulletin of Entomological Research* **62**, 383–90.

Alford, D. V. (1975). Specific feeding preferences of tortricid larvae on flowering strawberry plants. *Plant Pathology* **24**, 54–8.

Alford, D. V. (1976). Observations on *Litomastix aretas*, an encyrtid parasite of the strawberry tortrix moth. *Annals of Applied Biology* **84**, 1–5.

Alford, D. V. (1978a). The true identity of the cherry fruit moth in Britain. *Plant Pathology* **27**, 35–7.

Alford, D. V. (1978b). Observations on the specificity of pheromone-baited traps for *Cydia funebrana* (Treitschke) (Lepidoptera: Tortricidae). *Bulletin of Entomological Research* **68**, 97–103.

Alford, D. V. (1979). Observations on the cabbage stem flea beetle, *Psylliodes chrysocephala*, on winter oil-seed rape in Cambridgeshire. *Annals of Applied Biology* **93**, 117–23.

Alford, D. V. (1980). *Blastobasis decolorella* (Wollaston) (Lepidoptera: Blastobasidae), a potentially serious apple pest. *Plant Pathology* **29**, 145–6.

Alford, D. V. (1984). *A Colour Atlas of Fruit Pests*. Wolfe, London.

Alford, D. V. (1991). *A Colour Atlas of Pests of Ornamental Trees, Shrubs and Flowers*. Wolfe, London.

Alford, D. V. (1996). Adult vine weevil activity in black currant plantations in South West England. *Mitteilungen aus der Biologischen Bundesanstalt für Land- und Forstwirtschaft Berlin-Dahlem* **316**, 31–5.

Alford, D. V. (1998). Potential problems posed by non-indigenous terrestrial flatworms in the United Kingdom. *Pedobiologia* **42**, 574–8.

Alford, D. V. (1999). *A Textbook of Agricultural Entomology*. Blackwell Science, Oxford.

Alford, D. V. (ed.) (2003). *Biocontrol of Oilseed Rape Pests*. Blackwell Science, Oxford.

Alford, D. V. (2007). *Pests of Fruit Crops*. Manson, London.

Alford, D. V. & Docherty, A. (1974). The distribution of eggs of *Acleris comariana* (Lepidoptera: Tortricidae) on strawberry plants. *Plant Pathology* **23**, 156–9.

Alford, D. V. & Gould, H. J. (1975). Surveys of pest incidence on oil-seed rape in the UK. *Proceedings of the 8th British Insecticide and Fungicide Conference* **2**, 489–95.

Alford, D. V., Lole, M. J. & Emmett, B. J. (1996a). Alien terrestrial planarians in England & Wales, and implications for horticultural trade. *Proceedings of the Brighton Crop Protection Conference: Pests & Diseases* **3**, 1083–8.

Alford, D. V., Nilsson, C. & Ulber, B. (2003). *Insect Pests of Oilseed Rape Crops*. In: *Biocontrol of Oilseed Rape Pests* (ed. Alford, D. V.), pp. 9–41. Blackwell Science, Oxford.

Alford, D. V., Walter, K. F. A., Williams, I. H. & Murchie, A. K. (1996b). A commercially low-cost strategy for the management of seed weevil populations on winter oilseed rape in the UK. *Proceedings of the Brighton Crop Protection Conference – Pests & Diseases* **2**, 609–14.

Alphen, J. J. M. van (1980). Aspects of the foraging behaviour of *Tetrastichus asparagi* Crawford and *Tetrastichus* spec. (Eulophidae), gregarious egg parasitoids of the asparagus beetles *Crioceris asparagi* L. and *C. duodecimpunctata* L. (Chrysomelidae). I. Host-species selection, host-stage selection and host discrimination. *Netherlands Journal of Zoology* **30**, 307–25.

Altieri, M. A. (1999). The ecological role of biodiversity in agroecosystems. *Agriculture, Ecosystems & Environment* **74**, 19–31.

Anderson, R. (2005). An annotated list of the non-marine Mollusca of Britain and Ireland. *Journal of Conchology* **38**, 607–38.

Andow, D. A. (1991). Vegetational diversity and arthropod population response. *Annual Review of Entomology* **36**, 561–86.

Annecke, D. P. (1966). Biological studies on the immature stages of soft brown scale, *Coccus hesperidum* Linnaeus (Hemiptera: Coccoidea). *South African Journal of Agricultural Science* **9**, 205–28.

Anonymous (2006). *Pocket Guide to Varieties of Potatoes – 2006*. NIAB, Cambridge.

Aplin, R. T., d'Arcy Ward, R. & Rothschild, M. (1975). Examination of the large white and small white butterflies (*Pieris* spp.) for the presence of mustard oil glycosides. *Journal of Entomology Series A* **50**, 73–8.

Arkle, J. (1891). The diamond-back moth (*Plutella cruciferarum*). *The Entomologist* **24**, 256–60.

Armer, C. A. (2004). Colorado potato beetle toxins revisited: evidence the beetle does not sequester host plant glycoalkaloids. *Journal of Chemical Ecology* **30**, 883–8.

Arrold, N. P. & Blake, C. D. (1968). Some effects of the nematodes *Ditylenchus myceliophagus* and *Aphelenchoides composticola* on the yield of the cultivated mushroom. *Annals of Applied Biology* **61**, 161–6.

Austin, M. D. (1929). Observations on the eggs of the apple capsid (*Plesiocoris rugicollis* Fall.) and the common green capsid (*Lygus pabulinus* Linn.). *Journal of the South-Eastern Agricultural College, Wye, Kent* **26**, 136–44.

Austin, M. D. (1931). A contribution to the biology of the apple capsid (*Plesiocoris rugicollis* Fall.) and the common green capsid (*Lygus pabulinus* Linn.). *Journal of the South-Eastern Agricultural College, Wye, Kent* **28**, 153–68.

Austin, M. D. (1937). Notes on the status of flies of the family Sphaeroceridae (Borboridae) in the economy of cultivated mushrooms. *Proceedings of the Royal Entomological Society of London, Series A* **12**, 15–16.

Aveling, C. (1981). The role of *Anthocoris* species (Hemiptera: Anthocoridae) in the integrated control of the damson-hop aphid (*Phorodon humuli*). *Annals of Applied Biology* **97**, 143–53.

Babendreier, D. (2000). Life history of *Aptesis nigrocincta* (Hymenoptera: Ichneumonidae) a cocoon parasitoid of the apple sawfly, *Hoplocampa testudinea* (Hymenoptera: Tenthredinidae). *Bulletin of Entomological Research* **90**, 291–7.

Bailey, A. P., Rehman, T., Park, J., Keatinge, J. D. H. & Tranter, R. B. (1999). Towards a method for the economic evaluation of environmental indicators for UK integrated farming systems. *Agriculture, Ecosystems and Environment* **72**, 145–58.

Baker, C. R. B. (1968). Notes on *Epiphyas* (= *Austrotortrix*) *postvittana* (Walker), (Lep., Tortricidae). *Entomologist's Gazette* **19**, 167–72.

Baker, C. R. B., Barker, I., Bartlett, P. W. & Wright, D. W. (1993). *Western flower thrips, its introduction and spread in Europe and role as a vector of tomato spotted wilt virus*. In: *Plant Health and the Single European Market* (ed. Ebbles, D.). BCPC Monograph No. 54, pp. 355–60.

Baker, E. W. & Wharton, G. W. (1964). *An Introduction to Acarology*. Macmillan, New York.

Baker, F. T., Ketteringham, I.E., Bray, S. P. V. & White, J. H. (1942). Observations on the biology of the carrot fly (*Psila rosae* Fab.): assembling and oviposition. *Annals of Applied Biology* **29**, 115–25.

Baker, R. H. A., Cannon, R. J. C. & MacLeod, A. (2003). Predicting the potential distribution of alien pests in the UK under global climate change: *Diabrotica virgifera virgifera*. *Proceedings of the BCPC International Congress, Crop Science & Technology* **2**, 1201–8.

Baker, R. H. A., MacLeod, A., Cannon, R J. C., Jarvis, C. H., Walters, K. F. A., Barrow, E. M. & Hulme, M. (1998). Predicting the impacts of a non-indigenous pest on the UK potato crop under global climate change: reviewing the evidence for the Colorado beetle, *Leptinotarsa decimlineata*. *Proceedings of the Brighton Conference – Pests & Diseases* **3**, 979–84.

Baker, R. H. A., Sansford, C. E., Jarvis, C. H., Cannon. R. J. C., MacLeod, A. & Walters, K. F. A. (2000). The role of climatic mapping in predicting the potential geographic distribution of non-indigenous pests under current and future climates. *Agriculture, Ecosystems & Environment* **82**, 57–71.

Baker, R. R. (1970). Bird predation as a selective pressure on the immature stages of the cabbage butterflies, *Pieris rapae* and *P. brassicae*. *Journal of Zoology, London* **162**, 43–59.

Balachowsky, A. S. (ed.) (1962). *Entomologie Appliquée a l'Agriculture. Tome I. Coléoptères. Premier volume.* Masson, Paris.

Balachowsky, A. S. (ed.) (1963). *Entomologie Appliquée a l'Agriculture. Tome I Coléoptères, Second Volume.* Mason, Paris.

Balachowsky, A. S. (ed.) (1966). *Entomologie Appliquée a l'Agriculture. Tome II. Lépidoptères. Premier Volume.* Masson, Paris.

Balachowsky, A. S. (ed.) (1972). *Entomologie Appliquée a l'Agriculture. Tome II. Lépidoptères. Deuxiéme volume.* Masson, Paris.

Barclay, M. V. L. (2003). *Otiorhynchus* (*s. str.*) *armadillo* (Rossi, 1792) and *Otiorhynchus* (*s. str.*) *salicicola* Heyden, 1908 (Curculionidae: Entominae: Otiorhynchini) – two European vine weevils established in Britain. *The Coleopterist* **12**, 41–56.

Barclay, M. V. L. (2004). The green vegetable bug *Nezara viridula* (L., 1758) (Hem.: Pentatomidae) new to Britain. *Entomologist's Record and Journal of Variation* **116**, 55–8.

Bardner, H. M., Edwards, C. A., Arnold, M. K. & Rogerson, J. P. (1971). The symptoms of attack by swede midge (*Contarinia nasturtii*) and effects on the yield of swedes. *Entomologia Experimentalis et Applicata* **14**, 223–33.

Bardner, R., Fletcher, K. M. & Hamon, N. (1984). *Resseliella* sp. (Diptera: Cecidomyiidae) attacking field beans (*Vicia faba* L.). *Crop Protection* **3**, 53–7.

Barnes, H. F. (1926). The gall midges of blackberries and raspberries. *Journal of Pomology and Horticultural Science* **5**, 137–40.

Barnes, H. F. (1930). On the biology of the gall midges (Cecidomyidae) attacking meadow foxtail grass (*Alopecurus pratensis*), including the description of one new species. *Annals of Applied Biology* **17**, 339–66.

Barnes, H. F. (1933). A cambium miner of basket willows (Agromyzidae) and its inquiline gall midge (Cecidomyidae). *Annals of Applied Biology* **20**, 498–519.

Barnes, H. F. (1935). Notes on the timothy grass flies (*Amaurosoma* spp.). *Annals of Applied Biology* **22**, 259–66.

Barnes, H. F. (1937). The asparagus miner (*Melanagromyza simplex* H. Loew) (Agromyzidae: Diptera). *Annals of Applied Biology* **24**, 574–8.

Barnes, H. F. (1946a). *Gall Midges of Economic Importance. Vol. I: Gall Midges of Root and Vegetable Crops.* Crosby Lockwood & Son, London.

Barnes, H. F. (1946b). *Gall Midges of Economic Importance. Vol. II: Gall Midges of Fodder Crops.* Crosby Lockwood & Son, London.

Barnes, H. F. (1948a). *Gall Midges of Economic Importance. Vol. III: Gall Midges of Fruit.* Crosby Lockwood & Son, London.

Barnes, H. F. (1948b). *Gall Midges of Economic Importance. Vol. IV: Gall Midges of Ornamental Plants and Shrubs.* Crosby Lockwood & Son, London.

Barnes, H. F. (1956). *Gall Midges of Economic Importance. Vol. VII: Gall Midges of Cereal Crops.* Crosby Lockwood & Son, London.

Bartlet, E. (1996). Chemical cues to host-plant selection by insect pests of oilseed rape. *Agricultural Zoology Reviews* **7**, 89–116.

Bartlett, P. W. (1980). Interception and eradication of Colorado beetle in England and Wales, 1958–1977. *Bulletin OEPP/EPPO Bulletin* **10**, 481–9.

Bartlett, P. W. (1981). *Trionymus diminutus* (Leonardi) (Homoptera: Pseudococcidae) infesting New Zealand flax in England. *Plant Pathology* **30**, 56–8.

Bartlett, P. W. (1983). Interception of Colorado beetle in England and Wales, 1978–1982. *Bulletin OEPP/EPPO Bulletin* **13**, 559–62.

Bartlett, P. W. (1984). Grape phylloxera: is it in Britain? *The Garden* **109**, 207–9.

Bartlett, P. W. & Powell, D. F. (1981). Introduction of American serpentine leaf miner, *Liriomyza trifolii*, into England and Wales and its eradication from commercial nurseries, 1977–81. *Plant Pathology* **30**, 185–93.

Bartlett, P. W. & Savage, D. (1993). Grape phylloxera (*Daktulosphaira vitifoliae*): quarantine status in the United Kingdom. In: *Plant Health and the Single European Market* (ed. Ebbles, D.). BCPC Monograph No. 54, pp. 367–70.

Basedow, T. (1977). Über den Flug der Weizengallmucken *Contarinia tritici* (Kirby) und *Sitodipsosis mosellana* (Gehin) (Diptera, Cecidomyidae) in Beziehung zur Windrichtung und zu Weizenfeldern. *Zeitschrift für Angewandte Entomologie* **83**, 173–83.

Bassett, P. (1978). Damage to winter cereals by *Zabrus tenebrioides* (Goeze) (Coleoptera: Carabidae). *Plant Pathology* **27**, 48.

Becker, P. (1974). *Pests of Ornamental Plants.* MAFF Bulletin 97. HMSO, London.

Bell, A. C. (1983). The life-history of the leaf-curling plum aphid *Brachycaudus helichrysi* in Northern Ireland and its ability to transmit potato virus YC(AB). *Annals of Applied Biology* **102**, 1–6.

Bell, A. C., Clawson, S. & Watson, S. (2006). The long-term effect of partial defoliation on the yield of short-rotation willow. *Annals of Applied Biology* **148**, 97–103.

Bennett, S. H. (1955). The biology, life history and methods of control of the leaf curling plum aphid, *Brachycaudus helichrysi*, (Kltb.). *Journal of Horticultural Science* **30**, 252–9.

Benson, R. B. (1935). The alien element in the British sawfly fauna. *Annals of Applied Biology* **22**, 754–68.

Benson, R. B. (1952). Hymenoptera (Symphyta). *Handbooks for the Identification of British Insects* **VI (2b)**, 1–137.

Benson, R. B. (1953). A new British *Nematus* (Hym., Tenthredinidae) attacking black-currant. *Entomologist's Monthly Magazine* **89**, 60–3.

Bernays, E. A. & Chapman, R. F. (1994). *Host-plant Selection by Phytophagous Insects.* Chapman & Hall, New York.

Bevan, W. J. (1962). Observations on damage to grassland in East Yorkshire by larvae of the common leaf weevil, *Phyllobius pyri* L. and notes on its biology. *Journal of the British Grassland Society* **17**, 194–7.

Bevan, W. J. & Uncles, J. J. (1958). Studies on soil population of *Contarinia pisi* Winn. in 1957 in Yorkshire and Lancashire. *Annals of Applied Biology* **46**, 529–35.

Bierne, B. P. (1943). Some observations on the biology and control of the raspberry moth (*Incurvaria rubiella* Bjerk.) in Ireland. *Economic Proceedings of the Royal Dublin Society* **3**, 221–6.

Binns, E. S. (1972). *Arctoseius cetratus* (Sellnick) (Acarina: Ascidae) phoretic on mushroom sciarid flies. *Acarologia* **14**, 351–6.

Binns, E. S. (1973). *Digamasellus fallax* Leitner (Mesostigmata : Digmasellidae) phoretic on mushroom sciarid flies. *Acarologia* **15**, 10–17.

Blackman, R. L. (1965). Studies on specificity in Coccinellidae. *Annals of Applied Biology* **56**, 336–8.

Blackman, R. L. (1967). The effects of different aphid foods on *Adalia bipunctata* L. and *Coccinella 7-punctata* L. *Annals of Applied Biology* **59**, 207–19.

Blackman, R. L. & Eastop, V. F. (2000). *Aphids on the World's Crops. An Identification and Information Guide.* Third edition. John Wiley & Sons, Chichester.

Blackman, R. L. & Eastop, V. F. (2006). *Aphids on the World's Herbaceous Plants and Shrubs. Volume 1. Host Lists and Keys.* John Wiley, Chichester.

Blackshaw, R. P. (1990). Studies on *Artioposthia triangulata* Dendy (Tricladida: Terricola), a predator of earthworms. *Annals of Applied Biology* **116**, 169–76.

Blackshaw, R. P. (1991). Leatherjackets in grassland. *Proceedings of the British Grassland Society Conference. Strategies for Weed, Disease and Pest Control in Grassland* 6.1–6.12.

Blackshaw, R. P. & D'Arcy-Burt, S. (1997). Spatial distribution of bibonid larvae in agricultural grassland. *Entomologia Experimentalis et Applicata* **84**, 17–25.

Boag, B. (2000). The impact of the New Zealand flatworm on earthworms and moles in agricultural land in western Scotland. *Aspects of Applied Biology* **62**, 79–84.

Boag, B., Palmer, L. F., Neilson, R. & Chambers, S. J. (1994). Distribution and prevalence of the predatory planarian *Artioposthia triangulata* (Dendy) (Tricladida: Terricola) in Scotland. *Annals of Applied Biology* **124**, 165–71.

Bonnemaison, L. & Jourdheuil, P. (1954). L'altise d'hiver du colza (*Psylliodes chrysocephala* L.). *Annales des Épiphyties* **5**, 345–524.

Bowden, J., Cochrane, J., Emmett, B. J., Minall, T.E. & Sherlock, P. L. (1983). A survey of cutworm attacks in England and Wales, and a descriptive population model for *Agrotis segetum* (Lepidoptera: Noctuidae). *Annals of Applied Biology* **102**, 29–47.

Bradley, J. D., Tremewan, W. G. & Smith, A. (1973). *British Tortricoid Moths. Cochylidae and Tortricidae: Tortricinae.* Ray Society, London.

Bradley, J. D., Tremewan, W. G. & Smith, A. (1979). *British Tortricoid Moths. Tortricidae: Olethreutinae.* Ray Society, London.

Breitenbach, S., Heimbach, U., Gloyna, K. & Thieme, T. (2005). Possible host plants for larvae of western corn rootworm (*Diabrotica virgifera virgifera*). *Plant Protection and Plant Health in Europe: Introduction and Spread of Invasive Species, BCPC Symposium Proceedings No. 81*, pp. 217–18.

Bretherton, R. F., Goater, B. & Lorimer, R. I. (1979). *Noctuidae.* In: *The Moths and Butterflies of Great Britain and Ireland. Volume* 9 (eds Heath, J. & Emmet, A. M.), pp. 120–278. Curwen Books, London.

Bretherton, R. F., Goater, B. & Lorimer, R. I. (1983). *Noctuidae (Part II) and Agaristidae.* In: *The Moths and Butterflies of Great Britain and Ireland. Volume 10.* (eds Heath, J. & A. M. Emmet, A. M.), pp. 36–413. Harley Books, Colchester.

Bridge, J. & Starr, J. L. (2007). *Plant Nematodes of Agricultural Importance.* Manson, London.

Briggs, J. B. (1965). Biology of some ground beetles (Col., Carabidae) injurious to strawberries. *Bulletin of Entomological Research* **56**, 79–93.

Broadbent, L. & Heathcote, G. D. (1954). Sources of overwintering *Myzus persicae* (Sulzer) in England. *Plant Pathology* **4**, 135–7.

Brock, A. M., Collingwood, C. A. & White, J. H. (1964). The currant clearwing moth (*Aegeria tipuliformis* (Clerck)) as a pest of black currants. *Annals of Applied Biology* **53**, 243–9.

Broschewitz, B. & Daebeler, F. (1987). Beitrag zür Biologie und Schadwirkung des Gefleckten Kohltriebrusslers (*Ceutorhynchus quadridens* Panz.) an Winterraps. *Nachrichtenblatt für den Pflanzenschutz in der DDR* **41**, 34–7.

Brown, E. B. (1954). Springtail damage to tomatoes. *Plant Pathology* **3**, 87–8.

Brown, E. B. (1961). Linnet damage to strawberry fruit. *Plant Pathology* **10**, 41–2.

Brunel, E., Grootaert, P. & Medquida, J. (1989). Entomofaune associée à la floraison du colza (*Brassica napus* L.): note preliminaire sur les Dolichopoididae et les Empididae (Insectes: Diptera). *Mededelingen van de Faculteit Landbouwwetenchappen Rijksuniversiteit Gent* **54**, 727–37.

Büchs, W. (2003). *Predators as Biocontrol Agents of Oilseed Rape Pests.* In: *Biocontrol of Oilseed Rape Pests* (ed. Alford, D. V.), pp. 279–98. Blackwell Science, Oxford.

Büchs, W. & Nuss, H. (2000). First steps to assess the importance of epigaeic active polyphagous predators on oilseed rape insect pests with soil pupating larvae. *IOBC/wprs Bulletin* **23**, 151–63.

Buczacki, S. & Harris, K. M. (2005). *Pests, Diseases & Disorders of Garden Plants.* Third edition. Collins, London.

Buhl, C. (1960). Beobachtungen über vermehrtes Schadauftreten der Kohlschotenmücke (*Dasyneura brassicae* Winn.) an Raps und Rübsen in Schleswig-Holstein. *Nachrichtenblatt des Deutschen Pflanzenschutzdienst (Braunschweig)* **12**, 1–6.

Burgess, A. H. (1964). *Hops: Botany, Cultivation and Utilization.* Leonard Hill, London.

Burn, A. J. (1982). The role of predator searching efficiency in carrot fly egg loss. *Annals of Applied Biology* **101**, 154–9.

Butler, E. A. (1923). *A Biology of the British Hemiptera-Heteroptera.* Witherby, London.

Butt, T. M., Carreck, N. L., Ibrahim, L. & Williams, I. H. (1998). Honey-bee-mediated infection of pollen beetle (*Meligethes aeneus* Fab.) by the insect-pathogenic fungus, *Metarhizium anisopliae. Biocontrol Science and Technology* **8**, 533–8.

Buxton, J. H. (1996). Current status of vine weevil as a pest in the UK. *Mitteilungen aus der Biologischen Bundesanstalt für Land- und Forstwirtschaft Berlin-Dahlem* **316**, 1–11.

Cameron, P. (1882). *A Monograph of the British Phytophagous Hymenoptera. Vol. 1.* Ray Society, London.

Cameron, P. (1885). *A Monograph of the British Phytophagoius Hymenoptera. Vol. II.* Ray Society, London.

Cameron, R. (1938). A study of the natural control of the pea moth, *Cydia nigricana*, Steph. *Bulletin of Entomological Research* **29**, 277–313.

Cameron, W. P. L. (1925). The fern mite. (*Tarsonemus tepidariorum*, Warburton). *Annals of Applied Biology* **12**, 93–112.

Campbell, C. A. M. (1978). Regulation of the damson-hop aphid (*Phorodon humuli* (Schrank)) on hops (*Humulus lupulus* L.) by predators. *Journal of Horticultural Science* **53**, 235–42.

Campbell, C. A. M. & Tregidga, E. (2004). European corn borer *Ostrinia nubilalis* (Hb.) (Lep.: Pyralidae) on hops in Kent. *Entomologist's Record and Journal of Variation* **116**, 219–20.

Cannon, R. J. C. & Baker, R. H. A. (2007). Invasive, non-native plant pests. *Outlooks on Pest Management* **18**, 130–4.

Cannon, R. J. C., Baker, R. H. A., Taylor, M. C. & Moore, J. P. (1999). A review of the status of the New Zealand flatworm in the UK. *Annals of Applied Biology* **135**, 597–614.

Cannon, R. J. C., Koerper, D., Ashby, S., Baker, R. [H. A.], Bartlett, P. W., Brookes, G., Burgess, R., Cheek, S., Evans. H. F., Hammon, R. [P.], Head, J., Nettleton, G., Robinson, J., Slawson, D. [D.], Taylor, M. C., Tilbury, C. A. & Ward, M. (2004). Gypsy moth, *Lymantria dispar*, outbreak in northeast London, 1995–2003. *International Journal of Pest Management* **50**, 259–73.

Cannon, R. J. C., Matthews, L., Cheek, S., Baker, R. H. A., MacLeod, A. & Bartlett, P. W. (2005). Surveying and monitoring western corn rootworm (*Diabrotica virgifera virgifera*) in England & Wales. *Plant Protection and Plant Health in Europe: Introduction and Spread of Invasive Species, BCPC Symposium Proceedings No. 81*, pp. 155–60.

Cannon, R. J. C., Matthews, L., Collins, D. W., Agallou, E., Bartlett, P. W., Walters, K. F. A., Macleod, A., Slawson, D. D. & Gaunt, A. (2007). Eradication of an invasive alien pest, *Thrips palmi. Crop Protection* **26**, 1303–14.

Carpenter, G. H. (1909). Injurious insects and other animals observed in Ireland during the year 1908. *Economic Proceedings of the Royal Dublin Society* **1**, 589–611.

Carpenter, G. H. (1920). Injurious insects and other animals observed in Ireland during the years 1916, 1917, and 1918. *Economic Proceedings of the Royal Dublin Society* **2**, 259–72.

Carter, C. I. (1971). *Conifer woolly aphids (Adelgidae) in Britain.* Forestry Commission Bulletin 42. HMSO, London.

Carter, C. I., Fourt, D. F. & Bartlett, P. W. (1984). The lupin aphid's arrival and consequences. *Antenna* **8**, 129–32.

Carter, C. I. & Maslen, N. R. (1982). *Conifer Lachnids.* Forestry Commission Bulletin 58. HMSO, London.

Carter, C. [I.] & Winter, T. [G.] (1998). *Christmas Tree Pests.* Forestry Commission Field Book 17. The Stationery Office, London.

Carter, D. J. (1984). *Pest Lepidoptera of Europe with special reference to the British Isles.* Dr W. Junk, Dordrecht.

Carter, N., McLean, I. F. G., Watt, A. D. & Dixon, A. F. G. (1980). Cereal aphids: a case study and review. *Applied Biology* **5**, 271–348.

Caryol, J.[-]C. (1967). Etude du cycle evolutif d'*Aphelenchoides composticola. Nematologica* **13**, 23–32.

Caryol, J.-C. (1964). Etudes preliminaires sur le cycle evolutif de *Ditylenchus myceliophagus* Goodey. *Nematologica* **10**, 361–8.

Catherall, P. L. & Chamberlain, J. A. (1975). Occurrence of agropyron mosiac virus in Britain. *Plant Pathology* **24**, 155–7.

Chada. H. L. (1956). Biology of the winter grain mite and its control in small grains. *Journal of Economic Entomology* **49**, 515–20.

Chandler, D. (1997). Selection of an isolate of the insect pathogenic fungus *Metarhizium anisopliae* virulent to the lettuce root aphid, *Pemphigus bursarius. Biocontrol Science and Technology* **7**, 95–104.

Cheek, S. & Cannon, R. J. C. (2003). Alien pests: management of plant quarantine species in UK glasshouses. *Pesticide Outlook* **14**, 273–5.

Cheesman, O. D. (1996). Life histories of *Cochylis roseana* and *Endothenia gentianaeana* (Lepidoptera: Tortricidae) on wild teasel. *The Entomologist* **115**, 65–80.

Cherewick, W. J. & Robinson, A. G. (1958). A rot of smutted inflorescences of cereals by *Fusarium poae* in association with the mite *Siteroptes graminum. Phytopathology* **48**, 232–4.

Chinery, M. (1993). *Field Guide to the Insects of Britain & Northern Europe.* Third edition. HarperCollins, London.

Cimarra, M., Martínez-Cócerea, C., Chamorro, M., Cabrera, M., Robledo, T., Alonso, A., Castellano, A., Bartololme, J. M. & Lombardero, M. (1999). Occupational asthma caused by champignon flies. *Allergy* **54**, 521–5.

Coaker, T. H. (1973). Insecticidal control of the cabbage leaf miner, *Phytomyza rufipes* Meig., attacking calabrese. *Plant Pathology* **22**, 51–7.

Coaker, T. H. & Finch, S. (1971). Cabbage root fly, *Erioischia brassicae* (Bouché). *Report of the National Vegetable Research Station for 1970*, pp. 23–42.

Coaker, T. H. & Williams, D. A. (1963). The importance of some Carabidae and Staphylinidae as predators of the cabbage root fly, Erioischia brassicae (Bouché). *Entomologia Experimentalis et Applicata* **6**, 156–64.

Cockbain, A. J., Bowen, R. & Bartlett, P. W. (1982). Observations on the biology and ecology of *Apion vorax* (Coleoptera: Apionidae), a vector of broad bean stain and broad bean true mosaic viruses. *Annals of Applied Biology* **101**, 449–57.

Cockbain, A. J., Cook, S. M. & Bowen, R. (1975). Transmission of broad bean stain virus and Echtes Ackerbohnenmosaik- Virus to field beans (*Vicia faba*) by weevils. *Annals of Applied Biology* **81**, 331–9.

Cohen, M. (1936). The biology of the chrysanthemum leaf-miner, *Phytomyza atricornis* Mg. (Diptera: Agromyzidae). *Annals of Applied Biology* **23**, 612–32.

Collingwood, C. A. (1954). The hop root weevil. *Plant Pathology* **3**, 63–5.

Collins, C. M., Rosado, R. G. & Leather, S. M. (2001). The impact of the aphids *Tuberolachnus salignus* and *Pterocomma salicis* on willow trees. *Annals of Applied Biology* **138**, 133–40.

Collins, D. W. & Lole, M. (2005). *Phytomyza gymnostoma* Loew (Diptera: Agromyzidae), a leaf mining pest of leek and onion new to Britain. *Entomologist's Monthly Magazine* **141**, 131–7.

Collyer, E. (1952). Biology of some predatory insects and mites associated with the fruit tree red spider mite (*Metatetranychus ulmi* (Koch)) in southeastern England. I. The biology of *Blepharidopterus angulatus* (Fall.) (Hemiptera-Heteroptera, Miridae). *Journal of Horticultural Science* **27**, 117–29.

Collyer, E. (1953a). Biology of some predatory insects and mites associated with the fruit tree red spider mite (*Metatetranychus ulmi* (Koch)) in south-eastern England. II. Some important predators of the mite. *Journal of Horticultural Science* **28**, 85–97.

Collyer, E. (1953b). Biology of some predatory insects and mites associated with the fruit tree red spider mite (*Metatetranychus ulmi* (Koch)) in south-eastern England. III. Further predators of the mite. *Journal of Horticultural Science* **28**, 98–113.

Collyer, E. (1953c). Biology of some predatory insects and mites associated with the fruit tree red spider mite (*Metatetranychus ulmi* (Koch)) in south-eastern England. IV. The predator-mite relationship. *Journal of Horticultural Science* **28**, 246–59.

Collyer, E. (1964). The effect of an alternative food supply on the relationship beween two *Typhlodromus* species and *Panonychus ulmi* (Koch) (Acarina). *Entomologia Experimentalis et Applicata* **7**, 120–4.

Cook, S. M., Zhan, Z. R. & Pickett, J. A. (2007). The use of push-pull strategies in Integrated Pest Management. *Annual Review of Entomology* **52**, 375–400.

Cooper, J. I. (1971). The distribution in Scotland of tobacco rattle virus and its nematode vectors in relation to soil type. *Plant Pathology* **20**, 51–8.

Cooper, K. W. (1940). Relations of *Pediculopsis graminum* and *Fusarium poae* to central bud rot of carnations. *Phytopathology* **30**, 853–9.

Copping, L. G. (2009). *The Manual of Biocontrol Agents.* Fourth edition. BCPC, Alton.

Coppock, L. J. (1974). Notes on the biology of carrot fly in eastern England. *Plant Pathology* **23**, 93–100.

Corbet, P. S. & Brooks, S. J. (2008). *Dragonflies.* Collins, London.

Corbett, D. C. M. (1973). *Pratylenchus penetrans. Commonwealth Institute of Helminthology Descriptions of Plant-parasitic Nematodes Set 2, No. 25*, 4.

Cox, M. L. (2000). The current status of *Psylliodes luteola* (Müller, O. F., 1776) (Chrysomelidae) in the U.K. *The Coleopterist* **9**, 55–63.

Cranham, J. E. (1972). Influence of temperature on hatching of winter eggs of fruit-tree red spider mite, *Panonychus ulmi* (Koch). *Annals of Applied Biology* **70**, 119–37.

Cranham, J. E. (1973). Variation in the intensity of diapause in winter eggs of fruit tree red spider mite, *Panonychus ulmi. Annals of Applied Biology* **75**, 173–82.

Cross, J. V. & Bassett, P. (1982). Damage to tomato and aubergine by broad mite, *Polyphagotarsonemus latus* (Banks). *Plant Pathology* **31**, 391–3.

Cross, J. V. & Jay, C. N. (2001). Exploiting the parasitoids *Lathrolestes ensator* and *Platygaster demades* for control of apple sawfly and apple leaf midge in IPM in apple orchards. *IOBC/wprs Bulletin* **24**, 161–5.

Curtis, J. (1860). *Farm Insects: Being the Natural History and Economy of the Insects Injurious to the Field Crops of Great Britain and Ireland, and also those which infest barns and granaries.* Blackie & Sons, Glasgow.

Curtis, W. (1782). *A Short History of the Brown Tail Moth.* White, Sewell, Johnson, Strahan & Faulder, London.

Cuthbertson, A. G. S. (2004). Unnecessary pesticide applications in Northern Ireland apple orchards due to mis-identification of a beneficial mite species. *Research Journal of Chemistry and Environment* **8**, 77–8.

Cuthbertson, A. G. S., Fleming, C. C. & Murchie, A. K. (2003). Detection of *Rhopalosiphum insertum* (apple-grass aphid) predation by the predatory mite *Anystis baccarum* using molecular gut analysis. *Agricultural & Forest Entomology* **5**, 219–25.

Darby, P. & Campbell, C. A. M. (1996). Aphid-resistant hops – the key to integrated pest management in hops. *Proceedings of the Brighton Crop Protection Conference – Pests & Disease* **3**, 893–8.

Davis, B. N. K. (1983). *Naturalists' Handbook No. 1. Insects on Nettles.* Richmond Publishing Co., Slough.

Deans, I. R. (1979). Feeding of brent geese on cereal fields in Essex and observations on the subsequent loss of yield. *Agro-Ecosystems* **5**, 283–8.

Dechert, G. & Ulber, B. (2004). Interactions between the stem-mining weevils *Ceutorhynchus napi* Gyll. and *Ceutorhynchus pallidactylus* (Marsh.) (Coleoptera: Curculionidae) in oilseed rape. *Agricultural & Forest Entomology* **6**, 193–8.

Deharveng, L. (2004). Recent advances in Collembola systematics. *Pedobiologia* **48**, 415–33.

Dewar, A. M., Haylock, L. A., Bean, K. M., Garner, B. H. & Boyce, R. (2000). The ecology and control of the two-spotted spider mite, *Tetranychus urticae*, in sugar beet. *Proceedings of the BCPC Conference – Pests & Diseases* **3**, 913–8.

Dicker, G. H. L. (1939a). The morphology and biology of the bramble-shoot webber, *Notocelia uddmanniana* L. (Tortricidae). *Annals of Applied Biology* **26**, 710–38.

Dicker, G. H. L. (1939b). Insects associated with cultivated forms of *Rubus. Transactions of the Society for British Entomology* **6**, 115–36.

Dicker, G. H. L. (1944). *Tachyporus* (Col., Staphylinidae) larvae preying on Aphides. *Entomologist's Monthly Magazine* **80**, 71.

Dicker, G. H. L. (1947). Control of the strawberry rhynchites (*Rhynchites germanicus* Herbst) with notes on its biology. *Journal of Pomology and Horticultural Science* **23**, 63–70.

Dicker, G. H. L. (1952). The biology of the strawberry aphid, *Pentatrichopus fragaefolii* (Cock.), with special reference to the winged form. *Journal of Horticultural Science* **27**, 151–78.

Dicker, G. H. L. (1972). An effect of cultural practice on populations of *Clepsis spectrana* (Treits.) (Lep., Tortricidae) on black currant. *Plant Pathology* **21**, 67–8.

Dmoch, J. (1998). Kairomones and searching behavior of *Trichomalus perfectus* Walker. *IOBC/wprs Bulletin* **21**, 171–6.

Doane, J. F., DeClerck-Floate, R., Arthur, A. P. & Affolter, F. (1989). Description of the life stages of *Macroglenes penetrans* (Kirby) (Hymenoptera: Chalcidoidea,, Pteromalidae), a parasitoid of the wheat midge, *Sitodiplosis mosellana* (Géhin) (Diptera: Cecidomyiidae). *Canadian Entomologist* **121**, 1041–8.

Dobson, R. M. (1961). Observations on natural mortality, parasites and predators of wheat bulb fly, *Leptohylemyia coarctata* (Fall.). *Bulletin of Entomological Research* **52**, 281–91.

Dohlen, C. D. von & Moran, N. A. (1995). Molecular phylogeny of the homoptera: a paraphyletic taxon. *Journal of Molecular Evolution* **41**, 211–23.

Doom, D. E. (1966). The biology, damage and control of the poplar and willow borer, *Cryptorrhynchus lapathi. Netherlands Journal of Plant Pathology* **72**, 233–40.

Dransfield, R. D. (1979). Aspects of host–parasitoid interactions of two aphid parasitoids, *Aphidius urticae* (Haliday) and *Aphidius uzbekistanicus* (Luzhetski) (Hymenoptera: Aphidiidae). *Ecological Entomology* **4**, 307–16.

Drescher, J. & Dufay, A. (2002). Importation of mature palms: a threat to native and exotic palms in Mediterranean areas? *Palms* **46**, 179–84.

Duff, A. G. (ed.) (2008). *Checklist of beetles of the British Isles.* 2008 edition. A. G. Duff, Wells.

Duncan, R. & Lindquist, E. E. (1989). An unusually copious production of webbing by a willow-inhabiting spider mite, *Schizotetranychus schizopus* (Zacher). *Canadian Entomologist* **121**, 1037–9.

Dunn, E. (1949). Colorado beetle in the Channel Islands, 1947 and 1948. *Annals of Applied Biology* **36**, 525–34.

Dunn, J. A. (1959a). Biology of the lettuce root aphid. *Annals of Applied Biology* **47**, 475–91.

Dunn, J. A. (1959b). The survival in soil of apterae of the lettuce root aphid, *Pemphigus bursarius* (L.). *Annals of Applied Biology* **47**, 766–71.

Dunn, J. A. & Wright, D. W. (1955a). Population studies of the pea aphid in East Anglia. *Bulletin of Entomological Research* **46**, 369–87.

Dunn, J. A. & Wright, D. W. (1955b). Overwintering egg populations of the pea aphid in East Anglia. *Bulletin of Entomological Research* **46**, 389–92.

Dunne, R. & O'Connor, J. P. (1989). Some insects (Thysanoptera: Diptera) of economic importance, new to Ireland. *Irish Naturalists' Journal* **23**, 63–4.

Dunning, R. A. (1957). Mirid damage to seedling beet. *Plant Pathology* **6**, 19–20.

Duso, C. & Skuhravá, M. (2004). First record of *Obolodiplosis robiniae* (Haldeman) (Diptera: Cecidomyiidae) galling leaves of *Robinia pseudoacacia* L. (Fabaceae) in Italy and Europe. *Frustula Entomologica* **25**, 117–22.

Dussart, G. B. J. (ed.) (2003). Slugs & Snails: Agricultural, Veterinary & Environmental Perspectives. *BCPC Symposium Proceedings No. 80*, 324.

Duthoit, C. M. G. (1968). Cereal leaf miner in the South-east Region. *Plant Pathology* **17**, 61–3.

Easterbrook, M. A. (1978). The life-history and bionomics of *Epitrimerus piri* (Acarina: Eriophyidae) on pear. *Annals of Applied Biology* **88**, 13–22.

Easterbrook, M. A. (1979). The life-history of the eriophyid mite *Aculus schlechtendali* on apple in South-east England. *Annals of Applied Biology* **91**, 287–96.

Easterbrook, M. A. (1985). The biology of *Blastobasis decolorella* (Wollaston) (Lepidoptera: Blastobasidae), a potentially serious pest of apple. *Entomologist's Gazette* **36**, 167–72.

Easterbrook, M. A. (1991). Species of thrips associated with flowers of late-flowering strawberries. *The Entomologist* **110**, 5–10.

Easterbrook, M. A. (1996). Damage to strawberry fruits by the European tarnished plant bug, *Lygus rugulipennis*. *Brighton Crop Protection Conference. Pests & Diseases* **3**, 867–72.

Easterbrook, M. A. (1997). The phenology of *Lygus rugulipennis*, the European tarnished plant bug, on late-season strawberries, and control with insecticides. *Annals of Applied Biology* **131**, 1–10.

Easterbrook, M. A. (2000). Relationship between the occurrence of misshapen fruit on late-season strawberry on the United Kingdom and infestation by insects, particularly the European tarnished plant bug, *Lygus rugulipennis*. *Entomologia Experimentalis et Applicata* **96**, 59–67.

Easterbrook, M. A. & Fuller, M. M. (1986). Russeting of apples caused by apple rust mite *Aculus schlechtendali* (Acarina: Eriophyidae). *Annals of Applied Biology* **109**, 1–9.

Edwards, C. A. & Dennis, E. B. (1960). Observations on the biology and control of the garden swift moth. *Plant Pathology* **9**, 95–9.

Edwards, C. A., Sunderland, K. D. & George, K. S. (1979). Studies on polyphagous predators of cereal aphids. *Journal of Applied Ecology* **16**, 811–23.

Edwards, E. E. & Evans, J. R. (1950). Observations on the biology of *Corymbites cupreus* F. (Coleoptera, Elateridae). *Annals of Applied Biology* **37**, 249–59.

Eitschberger, U. & Stamer, P. (1990). *Cacyreus marshalli* Butler, 1898, eine neue Tagfalterart für die europaïsche Fauna? (Lepidoptera, Lycaenidae). *Atalanta* **21**, 101–8.

Ekbom, B. & Borg, A. (1996). Pollen beetle (*Meligethes aeneus*) oviposition and feeding preference on different host plant species. *Entomologia Experimentalis et Applicata* **78**, 291–9.

Elliott, R. H. & Rakow, G. F. W. (1999). Resistance of *Brassica* and *Sinapis* species to flea beetles, *Phyllotreta cruciferae*. *Proceedings of the 10th International Rapeseed Congress, Canberra, Australia*. [CD]

Ellis, S. A. & Scatcherd, J. E. (2007). Bean seed fly (*Delia platura*, *Delia florilega*) and onion fly (*Delia antiqua*) incidence in England and an evaluation of chemical and biological control options. *Annals of Applied Biology* **151**, 259–67.

Emden, H. F. van & Harrington, R. (eds) (2007). *Aphids as Crop Pests*. CAB International, Wallingford.

Emmet, A. M. (1976). Nepticulidae. In: *The Moths and Butterflies of Great Britain and Ireland. Volume 1* (ed. Heath, J.), pp. 171–267. Blackwell Scientific Publications: Oxford.

Emmet, A. M. (1985). Phyllocnistidae. In: *The Moths and Butterflies of Great Britain and Ireland. Volume 2* (eds Heath, J. & Emmet, A. M.), pp. 363–8. Harley Books: Colchester.

Emmet, A. M. (1989). *Phyllonorycter leucographella* (Zeller, 1850) (Lep. Gracillariidae) in Essex: a species new to Britain. *Entomologist's Record & Journal of Variation* **101**, 189–94.

Emmet, A. M., Langmaid, J. R., Bland, K. P., Corley, M. F. V. & Razowski, J. (1996). *Coleophoridae*. In: *The Moths and Butterflies of Great Britain and Ireland. Vol. 3. Yponomeutidae – Elachistidae* (ed. Emmet, A. M.), pp. 126–338. Harley Books, Colchester.

Emmet, A. M., Watkinson, I. A. & Wilson, M. R. (1985). Gracillariidae. In: *The Moths and Butterflies of Great Britain and Ireland. Volume 2* (eds Heath, J. & Emmet, A. M.), pp. 244–363. Harley Books, Colchester.

Empson, D. W. (1956). Cocksfoot moth investigations. *Plant Pathology* **5**, 12–18.

Empson, D. W. & Gair, R. (1982). *Cereal Pests*. Second edition. MAFF Bulletin 186. HMSO: London.

Enock, F. (1909). *Clinodoplosis equestris* (Wagner); an insect new to Great Britain. *The Entomologist* **42**, 217–19.

Esbjerg, P. (1988). Behaviour of 1st- and 2nd-instar cutworms (*Agrotis segetum* Schiff.) (Lep., Noctuidae): the influence of soil moisture. *Journal of Applied Entomology* **105**, 295–302.

Esbjerg, P., Nielsen, J. K., Philipsen, H., Zethner, O. & Øgård, L. (1986). Soil moisture as mortality factor for cutworms, Agrotis segetum Schiff. (Lep., Noctuidae). *Journal of Applied Entomology* **102**, 277–85.

Evans, A. C. & Gough, H. C. (1942). Observations on some factors influencing growth in wireworms of the genus *Agriotes* Esch. *Annals of Applied Biology* **29**, 168–75.

Evans, G. O., Sheals, J. G. & Macfarlane, D. (1961). *The Terrestrial Acari of the British Isles. Vol. 1. Introduction and biology*. Trustees of the British Museum Natural History, London.

Ewing, H. E. & Smith, F. F. (1934). The European tarsonemid strawberry mite identical with the American cyclamen mite. *Proceedings of the Entomological Society of Washington* **36**, 267–8.

Eyndhoven, G. L. van (1955). *Bryobia* from *Hedera*, apple and pear (Acar., Tetran.). *Entomologische Berichten (Amsterdam)* **15**, 340–47.

Eyndhoven, G. L. van & Groenewold, H. (1959). On the morphology of *Steneotarsonemus pallidus* and *S. fragariae* (Acar., Tars.). *Entomologische Berichten (Amsterdam)* **19**, 123–4.

Feare, C. J. (1978). The ecology of damage by rooks (*Corvus frugilegus*). *Annals of Applied Biology* **88**, 329–34.

Fenton, B., Malloch, G., Brennan, R. M., Jones, A. T., Gordon, S. C., McGavin, W. J. & Birch, A. N. E. (1993). Taxonomic evaluation of three reputed species of *Cecidophyopsis* mite on *Ribes*. *Acta Horticulturae* **352**, 535–8.

Fenton, B., Malloch, G., Jones., A. T., Amrine, J. W. Jr, Gordon, S. C., A'Hara, S., McGavin, W. J. & Birch, A. N. (1995). Species identification of *Cecidophyopsis* mites (Acari: Eriophyidae) from different *Ribes* species and countries using molecular genetics. *Molecular Ecology* **4**, 383–7.

Ferguson, A. W., Fitt, B. D. L. & Williams, I. H. (1997). Insect injury to linseed in south-east England. *Crop Protection* **16**, 643–52.

Ferguson, A. W. & Williams, I. H. (1993). Studies of the oviposition deterring pheromone of the cabbage seed weevil (*Ceutorhynchus assimilis* Payk.): behavioural bioassays and oviposition by weevils wintered in the laboratory. *IOBC/wprs Bulletin* **16**, 193–201.

Fidler, J. H. (1936a). Some notes on the biology and economics of some British chafers. *Annals of Applied Biology* **23**, 409–27.

Fidler, J. H. (1936b). On the first instar larvae of some species of *Otiorrhynchus* found on strawberries, with notes on their biology. *Bulletin of Entomological Research* **27**, 369–76.

Finch, S. (1989). Ecological considerations in the management of *Delia* pest species in vegetable crops. *Annual Review of Entomology* **34**, 117–37.

Finch, S. & Collier, R. H. (2000). Host-plant selection by insects – a theory based on 'appropriate/inappropriate' landings by pest insects of cruciferous plants. *Entomologia Experimentalis et Applicata* **96**, 91–102.

Finch, S. & Collier, R. H. (1983). Emergence of flies from overwintering populations of cabbage root fly pupae. *Ecological Entomology* **8**, 29–36.

Finch, S., Collier, R. H. & Skinner, G. (1986). Local population differences in emergence of cabbage root flies from south-west Lancashire: implications for pest forecasting and population divergence. *Ecological Entomology* **11**, 139–45.

Fisher, R. C. (1924). The life-history and habits of *Tortrix pronubana* Hb., with special reference to the larval and pupal stages. *Annals of Applied Biology* **11**, 395–447.

Fisken, A. G. (1959a). Factors affecting the spread of aphid-borne viruses in potato in eastern Scotland. I. Overwintering of potato aphids, particularly *Myzus persicae* (Sulzer). *Annals of Applied Biology* **47**, 264–73.

Fisken, A. G. (1959b). Factors affecting the spread of aphid-borne viruses in potato in eastern Scotland. II. Infestation of the potato crop by potato aphids, particularly *Myzus persicae* (Sulzer). *Annals of Applied Biology* **47**, 274–86.

Fitzgerald, J. D. & Solomon, M. G. (2002). Distribution of predatory phytoseiid mites in commercial cider apple orchards and unsprayed apple trees in the UK: implications for biocontrol of phytophagous mites. *International Journal of Acarology* **28**, 181–6.

Fletcher, J. T. & Gaze, R. H. (2007). *Mushroom Pest and Disease Control*. Manson, London.

Fox-Wilson, G. (1925). The mining habits of *O. rugifrons* larva. *Entomologist's Monthly Magazine* **61**, 273–6.

Fox-Wilson, G. (1942). The lily beetle, *Crioceris lilii* Scop. *Journal of the Royal Horticultural Society* **67**, 165–8.

Fox-Wilson, G. (1943). The lily beetle, Crioceris lilii Scopoli: its distribution in Britain (Coleoptera). Proceedings of the Royal Entomological Society of London. Series A 18, 85–6.

Frampton, G. F. & Wratten, S. D. (2000). Effects of benzimadazole and triazole fungicide use on epigeic species of Collembola in wheat. *Ecotoxicology and Environmental Safety* **46**, 64–72, 363.

Frank, T. (1996). Species diversity and activity densities of epigeic and flower visiting arthropods in sown weed strips and adjacent fields. *IOBC/wprs Bulletin* **19**, 101–5.

Frank, T. & Reichhart, B. (2004). Staphylinidae and Carabidae overwintering in wheat and sown wildflower areas of different age. *Bulletin of Entomological Research* **94**, 209–17.

Frankenhuizen, A. van, Stigter, H. & Dickler, E. (2002). *Schädliche und nützliche Insekten und Milben an Kern- und Steinobst in Mitteleuropa*. Ulmer, Stuttgart.

Franklin, M. T. (1965). A root-knot, *Meloidogyne naasi* n. sp., on field crops in England and Wales. *Nematologica* **11**, 79–86.

Franklin, M. T. (1978). Meloidogyne. In: *Plant Nematology*. Third edition (ed. Southey, J. F.), pp. 98–124. HMSO, London.

Frazier, N. W. & Posnette, A. F. (1956). Leafhopper transmission of a clover virus causing green petal disease in strawberry. *Nature* **177**, 1040–41.

Free, J. B. & Williams, I. H. (1978). A survey of the damage caused to crops of oil-seed rape (*Brassica napus* L.) by insect pests in south-central England and their effect on seed yield. *Journal of Agricultural Science, Cambridge* **90**, 417–24.

French, N., John, M. E. & Moreton, B. D. (1968). The control of strawberry-seed beetle (*Harpalus rufipes* Deg.); with observations on the damage it causes and that by linnets (*Carduelis cannabina cannabina* (L.)). *Annals of Applied Biology* **62**, 241–8.

French, N., Ludlam, F. A. B. & Wardlow, L. R. (1973). Biology, damage and control of rosy rustic moth, *Hydraecia micacea* (Esp.), on hops. *Plant Pathology* **22**, 58–64.

French, R. A. & White, J. H. (1960). The diamond-back moth outbreak of 1958. *Plant Pathology* **9**, 77–84.

Frew, J. G. H. (1924). *Chlorops taeniopus* Meig. (the gout fly of barley). *Annals of Applied Biology* **11**, 175–219.

Friedrichs, K. (1920). Untersuchungen über den Rapsglanzkäfer in Mechlenburg. *Zeitschrifrt für Angewandte Entomologie* **7**, 1–36.

Fritzsche, R. (1957). Zur Biologie und Ökologie der Rapsschädlinge aus der Gattung *Meligethes*. *Zeitschrift für Angewandte Entomologie* **40**, 222–80.

Frohne, D. & Pfänder, H. J. (2005). *Poisonous Plants.* Second Edition. Manson Publishing, London.

Fryer, J. C. F. (1914). Preliminary notes on damage to apples by capsid bugs. *Annals of Applied Biology* **1**, 107–12.

Furk, C., Hines, C. M., Smith, S. D. J. & Devonshire, A. L. (1990). Seasonal variation of susceptible and resistant variants of *Myzus persicae*. *Proceedings of the Brighton Crop Protection Conference – Pests & Diseases* **3**, 1207–12.

Gabry, B., Henryk, G., Sobota, G. & Halarewicz-Pacan, A. (1998). Reduction of the cabbage aphid, *Brevicoryne brassicae* (L.), population by *Diaeretiella rapae* (McIntosh) on oilseed rape, white mustard, and *Brassica* vegetables. *IOBC/wprs Bulletin* **21**, 197–203.

Gair, R. (1959). A tortricid caterpillar affecting timothy seed crops. *Plant Pathology* **8**, 95–6.

Gair, R. (1964). Crambid moth caterpillar attacks on cereals. *Plant Pathology* **13**, 159–60.

Gair, R., Mathias, P. L. & Harvey, P. N. (1969). Studies of cereal nematode populations and cereal yields under continuous or intensive culture. *Annals of Applied Biology* **63**, 503–12.

Game, M. (1995). Cobnuts and conservation. *British Wildlife* **6**, 380–3.

Garthwaite, D. G. & Thomas, M. R. (2004). *Pesticide Usage Survey Report 204: Hops in Great Britain 2004.* Defra, London.

Gatehouse, A. M. R., Davison, G. M., Newell, C. A., Merryweather, A., Hamilton, W. D. O., Burgess, E. P. J., Gilbert, R. J. C. & Gatehouse, J. A. (1997). Transgenic potato plants with enhanced resistance to the tomato moth, *Lacanobia oleracea*: growth room trials. *Molecular Breeding* **3**, 49–63.

Gatehouse, A. M. R., Davison, G. M., Stewart, J. N., Gatehouse, L. N., Kumar, A., Geoghegan, I. E., Birch, A. N. E. & Gatehouse, J. A. (1999). Concanavalin A inhibits development of tomato moth (*Lacanobia oleracea*) and peach-potato aphid (*Myzus persicae*) when expressed in transgenic potato plants. *Molecular Breeding* **5**, 153–65.

Gaum, W. G., Giliomee, J. H. & Pringle, K. L. (1994). Life history and life tables of western flower thrips, *Frankliniella occidentalis* (Thysanoptera: Thripidae), on English cucumbers. *Bulletin of Entomological Research* **84**, 219–24.

Geiger, F., Bianchi, F. J. J. A. & Wäckers, F. L. (2005). Winter ecology of the cabbage aphid *Brevicoryne brassicae* (L.) (Homo., Aphididae) and its parasitoid *Diaeretiella rapae* McIntosh (Hym., Braconidae: Aphidiidae). *Journal of Applied Entomology* **129**, 563–6.

Gelder, W. M. J. van (1991). *Chemistry, Toxicology, and Occurrence of Steroidal Glycoalkaloids: Potential Contaminants of the Potato (*Solanum tuberosum *L.).* In: *Poisonous Plant Contamination of Edible Plants* (ed. Rizk, A.-F. M.), pp. 117–56. CRC Press, Boca Raton.

George, K. S. (1957). Preliminary investigations on the biology and ecology of the parasites and predators of *Brevicoryne brassicae* (L.). *Bulletin of Entomological Research* **48**, 619–29.

George, K. S. (1974). Damage assessment aspects of cereal aphid attack in autumn- and spring-sown cereals. *Annals of Applied Biology* **77**, 67–74.

Gibson, R. W. (1976). Effects of cutting height on the abundance of the eriophyid mite *Abacarus hystrix* (Nalepa) and the incidence of ryegrass mosaic virus in ryegrass. *Plant Pathology* **25**, 52–6.

Gilbert, M. & Grégoire, J.-C. (2003). Visual, semi-quantitative assessments allow accurate estimates of leafminer population densities: an example comparing image processing and visual evaluation of damage by the horse chestnut leafminer *Cameraria ohridella* (Lep., Gracillariidae). *Journal of Applied Entomology* **127**, 354–9.

Gilbertson, R. L., Manning, W. J. & Ferro, D. N. (1985). Association of the asparagus miner with stem rot caused in asparagus by *Fusarium* species. *Phytopathology* **75**, 1188–91.

Glavendekic, M. & Roques, A. (2009). Invasive species following new crops. In: *Crop Plant Resistance to Biotic and Abiotic Factors: Current Potential and Future Demands* (eds Feldmann, F., Alford, D. V. & Furk, C.), pp. 328–37. DPG, Braunschweig.

Glen, D. M. (1975). The effects of predators on the eggs of codling moth *Cydia pomonella*, in a cider-apple orchard in south-west England. *Annals of Applied Biology* **80**, 115–19.

Glen, D. M. (1977). Predation of codling moth eggs *Cydia pomonella*, the predators responsible and their alternative prey. *Journal of Applied Ecology* **14**, 445–56.

Glen, D. M. (1982). *Syndemis musculana* (Hübner) (Lepidoptera: Tortricidae), a new leaf roller attacking apples in the United Kingdom. *Plant Pathology* **31**, 269–71.

Glen, D. M., Cuerden, R. & Butler, R. C. (1991). Impact of the field slug *Deroceras reticulatum* on establishment of ryegrass and white clover in mixed swards. *Annals of Applied Biology* **119**, 155–62.

Glen, D. M., Jones, H. & Fieldsend, J. K. (1990). Damage to oilseed rape seedlings by the field slug *Deroceras reticulatum* in relation to glucosinolate concentration. *Annals of Applied Biology* **117**, 197–207.

Glen, D. M. & Milsom, N. F. (1978). Survival of mature larvae of codling moth (*Cydia pomonella*) on apple trees and ground. *Annals of Applied Biology* **90**, 133–46.

Goater, B. (1986). *British Pyralid Moths: a guide to their identification.* Harley, Colchester.

Golightly, W. H. & Woodville, H. C. (1974). Studies of recent outbreaks of saddle gall midge. *Annals of Applied Biology* **77**, 97–101.

Goodey. T. (1941). Observations on a giant race of stem eelworm, *Anguillulina dipsaci*, attacking broad beans, *Vicia faba* L. *Journal of Helminthology* **19**, 114–22.

Goosey, H. B., Hatfield, P. G., Lenssen, A. W., Blodgett, S. L., Kott, R. W. & Spezzano, T. M. (2005). The potential role of sheep in dryland grain production systems. *Agriculture, Ecosystems and Environment* **111**, 349–53.

Gordon, S. C. & Hargreaves, A. J. (1973). Raspberry cane midge. *Report of the Scottish Horticultural Research Institute for 1972*, p. 80.

Gordon, S. C., McKinlay, R. G., Riley, R. G. & Osborne, P. (1988). Observations on the biology and distribution of the double dart moth (*Graphiphora augur* (Fabricius)) in Scotland, and on damaged caused by larvae to red raspberry. *Crop Research* **28**, 157–67.

Gordon, S. C. & Taylor, C. E. (1976). Some aspects of the biology of the raspberry leaf and bud mite (*Phyllocoptes* (*Eriophyes*) *gracilis* Nal.) Eriophyidae in Scotland. *Journal of Horticultural Science* **51**, 501–8.

Gordon, S. C. & Woodford, J. A. T. (1994). Cantharid beetle feeding damage to *Rubus* plants in eastern Scotland. *Journal of Horticultural Science* **69**, 727–30.

Gough, H. C. (1946). Studies on wheat bulb fly, *Leptohylemyia coarctata*, Fall. I. Biology. *Bulletin of Entomological Research* **37**, 251–71.

Gough, H. C. (1947). Studies on wheat bulb fly, *Leptohylemyia coarctata*, Fall. II. Numbers in relation to crop damage. *Bulletin of Entomological Research* **37**, 439–54.

Gough, H. C. (1949). Studies on wheat bulb fly, *Leptohylemyia coarctata*, Fall. III. A survey of infestation in Yorkshire. *Bulletin of Entomological Research* **40**, 267–77.

Gough, H. C. (1955a). Grazing of winter corn by the rabbit (*Oryctolagus cuniculus* (L.)). *Annals of Applied Biology* **43**, 720–34.

Gough, H. C. (1955b). *Thrips angusticeps* Uzel attacking peas. *Plant Pathology* **4**, 53.

Gough, H. C. (1957). Studies on wheat bulb fly (*Leptohylemyia coarctata* (Fall.)). IV. – The distribution of damage in England and Wales in 1953. *Bulletin of Entomological Research* **48**, 447–57.

Gould, H. J. & Winfield, A. L. (1962). Red-legged earth mite. *Plant Pathology* **11**, 157–9.

Gower, A. M. (1967). A study of *Limnephilus lunatus* Curtis (Trichoptera; Limnephilidae) with reference to its life cycle in watercress beds. *Transactions of the Royal Entomological Society of London* **119**, 283–302.

Graham, C. W. & Alford, D. V. (1981). The distribution and importance of cabbage stem flea beetle (*Psylliodes chrysocephala* (L.)) on winter oilseed rape in England. *Plant Pathology* **30**, 141–5.

Graham, C. W. & Gould, H. J. (1980). Cabbage stem weevil (*Ceutorhynchus quadridens*) on spring oilseed rape in southern England and its control. *Annals of Applied Biology* **95**, 1–10.

Gratwick, M. (ed.) (1989). *Potato Pests.* MAFF Reference Book 187. HMSO, London.

Gratwick, M. (ed.) (1992). *Crop Pests in the UK. Collected edition of MAFF leaflets.* Chapman & Hall, London.

Gray, R. A. H., Peet, W. V. & Rogerson, J. P. (1947). Observations on the chafer grub problem in the Lake District. *Bulletin of Entomological Research* **37**, 455–68.

Greaves, M. P. & Marshall, E. J. P. (1987). *Field margins: definitions and statistics.* In: *Field Margins* (eds May, J. M. & Greig-Smith, P. W.), BCPC Monograph No 35, 85–94.

Green, E. E. (1926). Observations on British Coccidae. X. *Entomologist's Monthly Magazine* **62**, 172–83.

Green, E. E. (1931). Observations on British Coccidae. XIII. *Entomologist's Monthly Magazine* **67**, 99–106.

Greenslade, P. J. M. (1963). Daily rhythms of locomotor activity in some Carabidae (Coleoptera). *Entomologia Experimentalis et Applicata* **6**, 171–80.

Griffiths, D. A, Wilkin, D. R., Southgate, B. J. & Lynch, S. M. (1976). A survey of mites in bulk grain stored on farms in England and Wales. *Annals of Applied Biology* **82**, 180–85.

Groves, J. R. (1951). *Adoxophyes orana* F. R. (Lep., Tortricidae), a moth new to Britain. *Entomologist's Monthly Magazine* **87**, 259.

Gullan, P. J. & Cranston, P. S. (1994). *The Insects: An Outline of Entomology.* Chapman & Hall, London.

Gunn, L. C. & Foster, G. N. (1978). Observations on the phenology of raspberry cane midge (*Resseliella theobaldi* (Barnes), Diptera, Cecidomyiidae) in the west of Scotland. *Horticultural Research* **17**, 99–105.

Haggett, G. (1950). The life history and habits of *Zeuzera pyrina* Linn. (*aesculi* Linn.) in Britain. *The Entomologist* **83**, 73–81.

Haggett, G. (1957). Larvae of the British Lepidoptera not figured in Buckler. *Proceedings of the South London Entomological and Natural History Society* **1955**, 152–63.

Halstead, A. J. (1996). Possible breeding by the rosemary beetle, *Chrysolina americana* L. in Britain. *British Journal of Entomology and Natural History* **9**, 107–8.

Halstead, A. J. (2004). Berberis sawfly, *Arge berberidis* Schrank (Hymenoptera: Argidae), a pest new to Britain. *British Journal of Entomology and Natural History* **17**, 131–5.

Halstead, A. J. & Harris, K. M. (1990). First British record of a gall midge pest of day lily (*Hemerocallis fulva* L.). *British Journal of Entomology and Natural History* **3**, 1–2.

Halstead, A. J. & Malumphy, C. P. (2003). Outbreak in Britain of *Stephanitis takeyai* Drake & Mao (Hemiptera, Tingidae), a pest of *Pieris japonica*. *British Journal of Entomology and Natural History* **16**, 3–6.

Hamilton, J. G. C., Hall, D. R. & Kirk, W. D. J. (2005). Identification of a male-produced aggregation pheromone in the western flower thrips *Frankliniella occidentalis*. *Journal of Chemical Ecology* **31**, 1369–79.

Hanni, L. & Luik, A. (2006). Parasitism of raspberry beetle (*Byturus tomentosus* F.) larvae in different cropping techniques of red raspberry. *Agronomy Research* **4** (special issue), 187–90.

Haque, A. & Ebing, W. (1983). Toxicity determination of pesticides to earthworms in the soil substrate. *Zeitschrift für Pflanzenkrankheiten und Pflanzenschutz* **90**, 395–408.

Hardison, J. R. (1959). Evidence against *Fusarium poae* and *Siteroptes graminum* as causal agents of silver top of grasses. *Mycologia* **51**, 712–28.

Hare, J. D. (1990). Ecology and management of the Colorado potato beetle. *Annual Review of Entomology* **35**, 81–100.

Haria, A. H., McGrfath, S. P., Moore, J. P., Bell, J. P. & Blackshaw, R. P. (1998). Impact of the New Zealand flatworm (*Artioposthia triangulata*) on soil structure and hydrology in the UK. *The Science of the Total Environment* **215**, 259–65.

Harris, K. M. (1966). Gall midge genera of economic importance (Diptera: Cecidomyiidae) Part 1: Introduction and subfamily Cecidomyiinae; supertribe Cecidomyiidi. *Transactions of the Royal Entomological Society of London* **118**, 313–58.

Hawkins, B. A., Thomas, M. B. & Hochberg, M. E. (1993). Refuge theory and biological control. *Science* **262**, 1429–32.

Heath, J. (ed.) (1983). *The Moths and Butterflies of Great Britain and Ireland. Volume 1.* Harley Books, Colchester.

Heddergott, H. (1955). Zur Biologie und Bekämpfung des Erdbeerwicklers *Acleris* (*Acalla*) *comariana* Zell. *Zeitschrift für Pflanzenkrankheiten und Pflanzenschutz* **62**, 220–35.

Heddergott, H. (1962). Zur Biologie von *Thecla betulae* L. (Lep., Lycaenidae). *Anzeiger für Schädlingskunde* **35**, 152–4.

Hellqvist, S., Jurie, E. & Löfstedt, C. (2006). Oviposition and flight period of the currant shoot borer *Lampronia capitella*. *Journal of Applied Entomology* **130**, 491–4.

Helyer, N., Brown, K. & Cattlin, N. D. (2003). *A Colour Handbook of Biological Control in Plant Protection.* Manson, London.

Herfs, W. (1963). Freilanduntersuchungen zur Klimaresistenz des Nelkenwicklers (*Tortrix pronubana* Hb.) und der Möglichkeit seiner Einbürgerung in Deutschland. II. Versuche zur Klimaresistenz und Beurteilung der Einbürgerungsmöglichkeit. *Zeitschrift für Angewandte Entomologie* **52**, 1–38.

Hering, E. M. (1951). *Biology of the Leaf Miners.* W. Junk, 's-Gravenhage.

Herting, B. (1974). *Les tachinaires.* In: *Les organismes auxillaires en verger de pommiers* (eds Milaire, H. G., Baggioloni, M., Gruys, P. & Steiner, H.). OILB/srop (IOBC/wprs) Brochure No. 3, pp. 171–85.

Hill, A. R. (1952a). Observations on *Lygus pabulinus* (L.), a pest of raspberries in Scotland. *Annual Report of the East Malling Research Station for 1951*, pp. 181–2.

Hill, A. R. (1952b). The bionomics of *Lampronia rubiella* (Bjerkander), the raspberry moth, in Scotland. *Journal of Horticultural Science* **27**, 1–13.

Hill, D. S. (1994). *Agricultural Entomology.* Timber Press, Oregon.

Hironori, Y. & Katsuhiro, S. (1997). Cannibalism and interspecific predation in two predatory ladybirds in relation to prey abundance in the field. *Entomophaga* **42**, 153–63.

Hodson, W. E. H. (1927). The bionomics of the lesser bulb flies, *Eumerus strigatus*, Flyn., and *Eumerus tuberculatus*, Rond., in south-west England. *Bulletin of Entomological Research* **17**, 373–84.

Hodson, W. E. H. (1928). The bionomics of the bulb mite, *Rhizoglyphus echinops*, Fumouze & Robin. *Bulletin of Entomological Research* **19**, 187–200.

Hodson, W. E. H. (1929). The bionomics of *Lema melanopa*, L. (Criocerinae), in Great Britain. *Bulletin of Entomological Research* **20**, 5–14.

Hodson, W. E. H. (1932). The large narcissus fly, *Merodon equestris*, Fab. (Syrphidae). *Bulletin of Entomological Research* **23**, 429–48.

Hodson, W. E. H. (1934). The bionomics of the bulb-scale mite, *Tarsonemus approximatus*, Banks, var. *narcissi*, Ewing. *Bulletin of Entomological Research* **25**, 177–85.

Hokkanen, H. M. T. (1991). Trap cropping in pest management. *Annual Review of Entomology* **36**, 119–38.

Hokkanen, H. M. T., Menzler-Hokkanen, I. & Butt, T. M. (2003). *Pathogens of Oilseed Rape Pests.* In: *Biocontrol of Oilseed Rape Pests* (ed. Alford, D. V.), pp. 299–322. Blackwell Science, Oxford.

Holland, J. M., Thomas, S. R. & Courts, S. (1994). Phacelia tanacetifolia *flower strips as a component of integrated farming.* In: *Field Margins: Integrated Agriculture and Conservation* (ed. Boatman, N.), BCPC Monograph No. 58, pp. 215–20.

Holloway, J. (1998). Geranium bronze *Cacyreus marshalli* Butl. *Atropos* **4**, 3–6.

Hooper, D. J. & Southey, J. F. (1978). Ditylenchus, Anguina *and related genera.* In: *Plant Nematology* Third edition (ed. Southey, J. F.), pp. 78–97. HMSO, London.

Hoßfeld, R. (1963). Synökologischer Vergleich der Fauna von Winter- und Sommerrapsfeldern. *Zeitschrift für Angewandte Entomologie* **52**, 209–54.

Huggett, D. A. J. (1996). Potential aphid pests of the biomass crop *Miscanthus. Proceedings of the 1996 Brighton Crop Protection Conference – Pests & Diseases* **1**, 427–8.

Huggett, D. A. J., Leather, S. R. & Walters, K. F. A. (1999). Suitability of the biomass crop *Miscanthus sinensis* as a host for the aphids *Rhopalosipum padi* (L.) and *Rhopalosiphum maidis* (F.), and its susceptibility to the plant luteovirus Barley Yellow Dwarf Virus. *Agricultural & Forest Entomology* **1**, 143–9.

Hughes, A. M. (1961). *The mites of stored food.* MAFF Technical Bulletin No. 9. HMSO, London.

Huizen, T. H. P. van (1977). The significance of flight activity in the life cycle of *Amara plebeja* Gyll. (Coleoptera, Carabidae). *Oecologia* **29**, 27–41.

Hume, H., Dunne, R. & O'Connor, J. P. (1990). *Liriomyza huidobrensis* (Blanchard) (Diptera: Agromyzidae), an imported pest new to Ireland. *Irish Naturalists' Journal* **23**, 325–6.

Hurst, G. W. (1969). Shallot aphid in south-east England. *Plant Pathology* **18**, 62–6.

Hussey, N. W. (1959). Biology of mushroom phorids. *Mushroom Science* **4**, 260–70.

Hussey, N. W. & Gurney, B. (1968). Biology and control of the sciarid *Lycoriella auripila* Winn. (Diptera: Lycoriidae) in mushroom culture. *Annals of Applied Biology* **62**, 395–403.

Hussey, N. W., Read, W. H. & Hesling, J. J. (1969). *The Pests of Protected Cultivation. The Biology and Control of Glasshouse and Mushroom Pests.* Edward Arnold, London.

Hyman, P. S. & Parsons, M. S. (1992). *A review of the scarce and threatened Coleoptera of Great Britain. Part 1. UK Nature Conservation: 3.* Joint Nature Conservation Committee, Peterborough.

Ibbotson, A. & Edwards, C. A. T. (1954). The biology and control of *Otiorrhynchius clavipes* Bonsd. (Rhyn. Coleop.), a pest of strawberries. *Annals of Applied Biology* **41**, 520–35.

Imms, A. D. (1918). Observations on *Pimpla pomorum* Ratz., a parasite of the apple blossom weevil (including a description of the male by Claude Morley, F.Z.S.). *Annals of Applied Biology* **4**, 211–27.

Imms, A. D. (1947). *Insect Natural History.* Collins, London.

Jackson, D. J. (1920). Bionomics of weevils of the genus *Sitones* injurious to leguminous crops in Britain. Part I. *Annals of Applied Biology* **7**, 269–98.

Jackson, D. J. (1922). Bionomics of weevils of the genus *Sitona* injurious to leguminous crops in Britain. Part II. *Sitona hispidula* F., *S. sulcifrons* Thun and *S. crinita* Herbst. *Annals of Applied Biology* **9**, 93–115.

Jary, S. G. (1931). A note on the strawberry and raspberry bud weevil, *Anthonomus rubi* (Herbst). *Journal of the South-Eastern Agricultural College, Wye, Kent* **28**, 147–52.

Jary, S. G. (1932). The strawberry blossom weevil *Anthonomus rubi* (Herbst). *Journal of the South-Eastern Agricultural College, Wye, Kent* **30**, 171–82.

Jary, S. G., Austin, M. D. & Pitcher, R. S. (1938). The control of big bud mite, *Eriophyes ribis* (Westw.) Nal. by lime sulphur. *Journal of the South-Eastern Agricultural College, Wye, Kent* **42**, 82–92.

Jary, S. G. & Edelsten, H. M. (1944). *Acrolepia assectella* Zell. (Lep. Plutellidae) in England. *Entomologist's Monthly Magazine* **80**, 14–15.

Jay, C. N. & Smith, H. G. (1995). The effect of beet western yellows virus on the growth and yield of oilseed rape. *Proceedings 9th International Rapeseed Congress, Cambridge, UK*, pp. 664–6.

Jeppson, L. R., Keifer, H. H.& Baker, E. W. (1975). *Mites Injurious to Economic Plants.* University of California Press, Berkeley.

Jones, A. T. (1986). Advances in the study, detection and control of viruses and virus diseases of *Rubus*, with particular reference to the United Kingdom. Crop Research **26**, 127–71.

Jones, D. P. (1940a). Gall midges (Cecidomyidae) affecting grass-seed production in mid-Wales and West Shropshire, together with descriptions of two new species. *Annals of Applied Biology* **27**, 533–44.

Jones, D. P. (1940b). Oviposition in gall midges (Cecidomyidae) affecting seed production in grasses. *Journal of Animal Ecology* **9**, 328–35.

Jones, D. P., Petherbridge, F. R. & Jenkins, A. C. (1947). Beet carrion beetle in England and Wales. *Agriculture, London* **54**, 375–7.

Jones, F. G. W. & Dunning, R. A. (1972). *Sugar Beet Pests.* MAFF Bulletin 162. HMSO, London.

Jones, H. D. (1981). A specimen of the Australian land planarian *Geoplana sanguinea* (Moseley) var. *alba* (Dendy) from the Isles of Scilly. *Journal of Natural History, London* **15**, 837–43.

Jones, H. D. & Boag, B. (1996). The distribution of New Zealand and Australian terrestrial flatworms (Platyhelminthes: Turbellaria: Tricladida: Terricola) in the British Isles – the Scottish survey and MEGALAB WORMS. *Journal of Natural History, London* **30**, 955–75.

Jones, H. D. & Gerard, B. M. (1999). A new genus and species of terrestrial planarian (Platyhelminthes; Tricladida; Terricola) from Scotland, and an emendation of the genus *Artioposthia*. *Journal of Natural History, London* **33**, 387–94.

Jones, M. G. (1975). The predators of wheat-bulb fly. *Annals of Applied Biology* **80**, 128–30.

Jones, O. T. (1975). Damage to carrots by larvae of *Napomyza carotae* Spencer (Diptera: Agromyzidae). *Plant Pathology* **24**, 62.

Jong, D. J. de & Beeke, H. (1956). Vroege wormstekigheid bij appel veroorzaakt door *Pammene argyrana* Hb. (Tortricidae, Lepid). *Mededelingen van de Directie Tuinbouw* **19**, 100–4.

Karl, E. (1965a). Untersuchungen zur Morphologie und kologie von Tarsonemiden gärtnerischer Kulturpflanzen. I. *Tarsonemus pallidus* Banks. *Biologisches Zentralblatt* **84**, 47–80.

Karl, E. (1965b). Untersuchungen zur Morphologie und Ökologie von Tarsonemiden gärtnerischer Kulturpflanzen. II. *Hemitarsonemus latus* (Banks), *Tarsonemus confusus* Ewing, *T. talpae* Schaarschmidt, *T. setifer* Ewing, *T. smithi* Ewing und *Tarsonemoides belemnitoides* Weis-Fogh. *Biologisches Zentralblatt* **84**, 331–57.

Kearns, H. G. H. (1931). The larval and pupal anatomy of *Stenomalus micans* Ol. (Pteromalidae), a chalcid endoparasite of the gout-fly (*Chlorops taeniopus* Meig.), with some details of the life history of the summer generation. *Parasitology* **23**, 380–95.

Kearns, H. G. H. & Walton, C. L. (1933). The adult raspberry beetle as a cause of serious blossom injury. *Journal of Pomology and Horticultural Science* **11**, 53–5.

Kendall, D. A., George, S. & Smith, B. D. (1996). Occurrence of barley yellow dwarf viruses in some common grasses (Gramineae) in south west England. *Plant Pathology* **45**, 29–37.

Kendall, D. A., Hunter, T., Arnold, G. M., Liggitt, J., Morris, T. & Wiltshire, C. W. (1996). Susceptibility of willow clones (*Salix* spp.) to herbivory by *Phyllodecta vulgatissima* (L.) and *Galerucella lineola* (Fabr.) (Coleoptera, Chrysomelidae). *Annals of Applied Biology* **129**, 379–90.

Kennedy, T. F. (1996). The control of slug damage to seedling beet, in Ireland, with special reference to band placement of slug pellets. *Slug & Snail Pests In Agriculture, BCPC Symposium Proceedings No. 66*, pp. 377–82.

Kerry, B. R. & Crump, D. H. (1977). Observations on fungal parasites of females and eggs of the cereal cyst-nematode, *Heterodera avenae*, and other cyst nematodes. *Nematologica* **23**, 193–201.

Kershaw, W. J. S. (1964). *Piesma quadratum* (Fieb.) in East Anglia. *Journal of Agricultural Science, Cambridge* **63**, 393–5.

Killington, F. J. (1936). *A Monograph of the British Neuroptera. Volume I.* Ray Society, London.

King, L. A. L., Meikle, A. A. & Broadfoot, A. (1935). Observations on the timothy grass fly (*Amaurosoma armillatum* Zett.). *Annals of Applied Biology* **22**, 267–78.

Kirk, W. D. J., Ali, M. & Breadmore, K. N. (1995). The effects of pollen beetles on the foraging behaviour of honey bees. *Journal of Apicultural Research* **34**, 15–22.

Kirk, W. D. J. & Hamilton, J. G. C. (2004). Evidence for a male-produced sex pheromone in the western flower thrips *Frankliniella occidentalis*. *Journal of Chemical Ecology* **30**, 167–74.

Koch, R. L. (2003). The multicolored Asian lady beetle, *Harmonia axyridis*: a review of its biology, uses in biological control, and non-target impacts. *Journal of Insect Science* **3:32**, 16 pp. Available online: [insectscience.org/3.32]

Kozár, F., Hippe, C. & Mani, E. (1996). Morphometric analyses of the males of *Quadraspidiotus* species (Hom., Diaspididae) found in European orchards or their vicinity. *Journal of Applied Entomology* **120**, 433–7.

Kromp, B. (1999). Carabid beetles in sustainable agriculture: a review on pest control efficay, cultivation impacts and enhancement. *Agriculture, Ecosystems and Environment* **74**, 187–228.

Krüger, E. O. (2008). *Glyphodes perspectalis* (Walker, 1858) – neu für die Fauna Europas (Lepidoptera: Crambidae). *Entomologische Zeitschrift* **118**, 81–3.

Kunert, G., Otto, S., Röse, U. S. R., Gershenzon, J. & Weisser, W. W. (2005). Alarm pheromone mediates production of winged dispersal morphs in aphids. *Ecology Letters* **8**, 596–603.

Kunert, G., Schmoock-Ortlepp, K., Reismann, U., Creutzburg, S. & Weisser, W. W. (2008). The influence of natural enemies on wing induction in *Aphis fabae* and *Megoura viciae* (Hemiptera: Aphididae). *Bulletin of Entomological Research* **98**, 57–62.

Kutter, H. (1934). Weitere Untersuchungen über *Kakothrips robustus* Uzel und *Contarinia pisi* Winn., sowie deren Parasiten, insbesondere *Pirene graminea* Hal. *Mitteilungen der Schweizerischen Entomologischen Gesellschaft* **16**, 1–82.

Lambkin, T. A. (1999). A host list for *Aleurodicus dispersus* Russell (Hemiptera: Aleyrodidae) in Australia. *Australian Journal of Entomology* **38**, 373–6.

Lane, A. (1984). *Bulb Pests.* MAFF Reference Book 51. HMSO, London.

Lawson, H. M., Wiseman, J. S. & Wright, G. McN. (1988). Effects of injury of the double dart moth on fruit and vegetative cane production in red raspberry cv. Glen Moy. *Crop Research* **28**, 169–75.

Lawton, R. (1956). Observations on the wheat stem fly with special reference to oviposition. *Plant Pathology* **5**, 123–7.

Leather, S. R. (1986). Insects on bird cherry. 1. The bird cherry ermine moth, *Yponomeuta evonymellus* (L.) (Lepidoptera: Yponomeutidae). *Entomologist's Gazette* **37**, 209–13.

Leather, S. R., Carter, N., Walters, K. F. A., Chroston, J. R., Thornback, N., Gardner, S. M. & Watson, S. J. (1984). Epidemiology of cereal aphids on winter wheat in Norfolk, 1979–1981. *Journal of Applied Ecology* **21**, 103–14.

Lees, A. H. (1922). Leaf character in reverted black currants. *Annals of Applied Biology* **9**, 49–68.

Lehrman, A., Åhman, I. & Ekbom, B. (2008). Effect of pea lectin expressed transgenically in oilseed rape on pollen beetle life-history parameters. *Entomologia Experimentalis et Applicata* **127**, 184–90.

Leroi, B. (1973). A study of natural populations of the celery leaf-miner, *Philophylla heraclei* L. (Diptera, Tephritidae). II. Importance of changes of mines for larval populations. *Researches on Population Ecology* **15**, 163–82.

Lewis, T. (1959). The annual cycle of *Limothrips cerealium* Haliday (Thysanoptera) and its distribution in a wheat field. *Entomologia Experimentalis et Applicata* **2**, 187–203.

Lewis, T. (ed.) (1997). *Thrips as Crop Pests.* CAB International, Wallingford.

Lewis, T., Wall, C., Macaulay, E. D. M. & Greenway, A. R. (1975). The behavioural basis of a pheromone monitoring system for pea moth, *Cydia nigricana*. *Annals of Applied Biology* **80**, 257–74.

Libbrecht, R., Gwynn, D. M. & Fellowes, M. D. E. (2007). *Aphidius ervi* preferentially attacks the green morph of the pea aphid, *Acyrthosiphon pisum*. *Journal of Insect Behavior* **20**, 25–32.

Light, W. I. St. G. (1980). Surveys of apple-grass aphid on apple in southern England, 1965–76. *Plant Pathology* **29**, 136–9.

Lindley, G. (1831). *A Guide to the Orchard and Kitchen Garden.* Longman, Rees, Orme, Brown & Green, London.

Lipa, J. J. (1977). Infection of *Notocelia uddmanniana* L. (Lepidoptera Tortricidae) by the microsporidian *Nosema carpocapsae* Paillot. *Acta Protozoologica* **16**, 201–5.

Lloyd, Ll. (1920). The habits of the glasshouse tomato moth, *Hadena* (*Polia*) *oleracea*, and its control. *Annals of Applied Biology* **7**, 66–102.

Long, D. B. (1960). The wheat bulb fly, *Leptohylemyia coarctata* Fall. A review of current knowledge of its biology. *Rothamsted Experimental Station Report for 1959*, pp. 216–29.

Lowe, S., Browne, M., Boudjelas, S. & De Poorter, M. (2000). *100 of the World's Worst Invasive Alien Species. A selection from the Global Invasive Species Database.* Published by The Invasive Species Specialist Group (ISSG) a specialist group of the Species Survival Commission (SSC) of the World Conservation Union (IUCN), 12 pp.

Luff, M. L. (1974). Aspects of damage by strawberry ground beetle (*Pterostichus madidus* (F.)). *Plant Pathology* **23**, 101–4.

Luff, M. L. (1987). Biology of polyphagous ground beetles in agriculture. *Agricultural Zoology Reviews* **2**, 237–78.

Lupi, D. & Jucker, C. (2005). The butterfly *Cacyreus marshalli* in northern Italy, and susceptibility of commercial cultivars of *Pelargonium*. *Plant Protection and Plant Health in Europe: Introduction and Spread of Invasive Species, BCPC Symposium Proceedings No. 81*, pp. 249–50.

Lyon, J. P., Göldlin de Tiefenau, P. (1974). *Les syrphes predateurs des pucerons.* In: *Les organismes auxillaires en verger de pommiers* (eds Milaire, H. G., Baggioloni, M., Gruys, P. & Steiner, H.). OILB/srop (IOBC/wprs) Brochure No. 3, pp. 163–70.

Mabbott, P. & Salisbury, A. (2006). The establishment of the rosemary beetle Chrysolina americana (L.) in London, 1998-2005. The London Naturalist **85**, 163–6.

Macaulay, E. D. M., Tatchell, G. M. & Taylor, L. R. (1988). The Rothamsted Insect Survey '12-metre' suction trap. *Bulletin of Entomological Research* **78**, 121–9.

MacGill, E. I. (1934). On the biology of *Anagrus atomus* Hal.: an egg parasite of the leaf-hopper *Erythroneura pallidifrons* Edwards. *Parasitology* **26**, 57–63.

Macintyre, I. D. & Foster, G. N. (1977). Autumn mortality in the raspberry leaf and bud mite (*Phyllocoptes gracilis* (Nalepa), Eriophyidae). *Horticultural Research* **17**, 47–50.

MacLeod, A., Baker, R. H. A., Cheek, S., Eyre, D. & Cannon, R. J. C. (2007). Pest risk analysis for *Diabrotica virgifera virgifera*. [www.defra.gov.uk/planth/pra/diab.pdf]

MacLeod, A., Wratten, S. D., Sotherton, N. W. & Thomas, M. B. (2004). 'Beetle banks' as refuges for beneficial arthropods in farmland: long-term changes in predator communities and habitat. *Agricultural & Forest Entomology* **6**, 147–54.

MacRae, I. V. & Croft, B. A. (1996). Differential impact of egg predation by *Zetzellia mali* (Acari: Stigmaeidae) on *Metaseiulus occidentalis* and *Typhlodromus pyri* (Acari: Phytoseiidae). *Experimental & Applied Acarology* **20**, 143–54.

Madge, D. S. (1964). The light reactions and feeding activity of larvae of the cutworm *Tryphaena pronuba* L. (Lepidoptera: Noctuidae). Part II. Field investigations. *Entomologica Experimentalis & Applicata* **7**, 105–14.

Majerus, M. E. N. (1994). *Ladybirds.* HarperCollins, London.

Malumphy, C. P. (2005). *Eulecanium excrescens* (Ferris) (Hemiptera: Coccidae), an Asian pest of woody ornamentals and fruit trees, new to Britain. *British Journal of Entomology and Natural History* **18**, 45–9.

Malumphy, C. P., & Halstead, A. J. (2003). *Cacopsylla fulguralis* (Kuwayama), an Asian jumping plant louse (Hemiptera: Psyllidae), causing damage to *Elaeagnus* in Britain. *British Journal of Entomology and Natural History* **16**, 89–91.

Malumphy, C. P., Reid, S. & Eyre, D. (2007). The platanus lace bug, *Corythucha ciliata* (Say) (Hemiptera: Tingidae), a nearctic pest of plane trees, new to Britain. *British Journal of Entomology & Natural History* **20**, 233–40.

Marshall, D. (1783). Account of the black canker caterpillar, which destroys the turnips in Norfolk. *Philosophical Transactions of the Royal Society of London* **73**, 217–22.

Martin, J. H. & Malumphy, C. P. (1995). *Trioza vitreoradiata*, a New Zealand jumping plant louse (Homoptera, Psylloidea), causing damage to *Pittosporum* spp. in Britain. *Bulletin of Entomological Research* **85**, 253–8.

Maskell, F. E. (1959). Wireworm distribution in East Anglia. *Plant Pathology* **8**, 1–7.

Mason, E. C. (1958). Notes on the life-history and host range of the tortrix *Cnephasia longana* (Haworth) (Lep., Tortricidae). *Entomologist's Monthly Magazine* **94**, 79–80.

Massee, A. M. (1928). The life-history of the black currant gall mite, *Eriophyes ribis* (Westw.) Nal. *Bulletin of Entomological Research* **18**, 297–309.

Massee, A. M. (1942). Some important pests of the hop. *Annals of Applied Biology* **29**, 324–6.

Massee, A. M. (1954). *The Pests of Fruit and Hops.* Third edition. Crosby Lockwood & Son, London.

Mattiacci, L., Dicke, M. & Posthumus, M. A. (1994). Induction of parasitoid attracting synomone in Brussels sprouts plants by feeding of *Pieris brassicae* larvae: role of mechanical damage and herbivore elicitor. *Journal of Chemical Ecology* **20**, 2229–47.

Mattiacci, L., Marcel, D. & Posthumus, M. A. (1995). β-glucosidase: an elicitor of herbivore-induced plant odor that attracts host-searching parasitic wasps. *Proceedings of the National Academy of Science of the United States of America* **92**, 2036–40.

McEwan, P., New, T. R. & Whittington, A. E. (eds) (2001). *Lacewings in the Crop Environment.* Cambridge University Press, Cambridge.

McMahon, E. (1962). Wheat blossom midge investigations. *The Scientific Proceedings of the Royal Dublin Society Series B* **1**, 47–57.

McVean, R. I. K., Dixon, A. F. G. & Harrington, R. (1999). Causes of regional and yearly variation in pea aphid numbers in eastern England. *Journal of Applied Entomology* **123**, 495–502.

Metcalfe, M. E. (1933). *Dasyneura leguminicola* (Lint.), the clover-seed midge. *Annals of Applied Biology* **20**, 185–204.

Miles, H. W. (1928). The bay-psyllid, *Trioza alacris* Flor. *North West Naturalist* **3**, 8–14.

Miles, H. W. (1932). Biological studies of sawflies infesting *Ribes. Bulletin of Entomological Research* **23**, 1–15.

Miles, H. W. (1936). On the biology of *Emphytus cinctus*, L., and *Blennocampa waldheimi*, Gimm. (Hym, Symphyta). *Bulletin of Entomological Research* **27**, 467–73.

Miles, H. W., Petherbridge, F. R. & Jary, S. G. (1941). Wireworms and agriculture. *Journal of the Royal Agricultural Society of England* **102**, 171–88.

Miles, M. (1930). On the life-history of *Blastodacna atra* Haw., the pith moth of the apple. *Annals of Applied Biology* **17**, 775–95.

Miles, M. (1958). Studies of British anthomyiid flies. IX.–Biology of the onion fly, *Delia antiqua* (Mg.). *Bulletin of Entomological Research* **49**, 405–14.

Miller, B. S. & Halton, P. (1961). The damage to wheat kernels caused by the wheat blossom midge (*Sitodiplosis mosellana*). *Journal of the Science of Food and Agriculture* **12**, 391–8.

Miller, D. (1918). Limitation of injurious insects by beneficial species. *New Zealand Journal of Agriculture* **17**, 12–18.

Miller, L. A. & Bedding, R. A. (1981). Disinfecting blackcurrant cuttings of *Synanthedon tipuliformis*, using the insect parasitic nematode, *Neoaplectana bibionis. Environmental Entomology* **10**, 449–53.

Miller, L. A. & Bedding, R. A. (1982). Field testing of the insect parasitic nematode, *Neoaplectana bibionis* (Nematoda: Steinernematidae) against currant borer moth, *Synanthedon tipuliformis* (Lep.: Sesiidae) in blackcurrants. *BioControl* **27**, 109–14.

Miller, W. A. & Rasochová, L. (1997). Barley yellow dwarf viruses. *Annual Review of Phytopathology* **35**, 167–90.

Milne, A. (1956). Biology and ecology of the garden chafer, *Phyllopertha horticola* (L.). II.–The cycle from egg to adult in the field. *Bulletin of Entomological Research* **47**, 23–42.

Milne, D. L. (1960). The gall midges (Diptera : Cecidomyidae) of clover flower-heads. *Transactions of the Royal Entomological Society of London* **112**, 73–108.

Mitchell, B. (1963). Ecology of two carabid beetles, *Bembidion lampros* (Herbst) and *Trechus quadristriatus* (Schrank). I. Life cycles and feeding behaviour. *Journal of Animal Ecology* **32**, 289–99.

Moore, J. P., Dynes, C. & Murchie, A. K. (1998). Status and public perception of the 'New Zealand flatworm', *Artioposthia triangulata. Pedobiologia* **42**, 563–71.

Moorhouse, E. R., Charnley, A. K. & Gillespie, A. T. (1992). A review of the biology and control of the vine weevil, *Otiorhynchus sulcatus* (Coleoptera: Curculionidae). *Annals of Applied Biology* **121**, 431–54.

Moreton, B. D. (1974). *Opogona sacchari*, an imported pest of *Ficus elastica decora. Plant Pathology* **23**, 163–4.

Moreton, B. D. & John, M. E. (1955). The mushroom phorid fly epidemic of 1953. *Plant Pathology* **4**, 9–11.

Morison, G. D. (1943). Notes on Thysanoptera found on flax (*Linum usitatissimum* L.) in the British Isles. *Annals of Applied Biology* **30**, 251–9.

Morison, G. D. (1957). A review of the British glasshouse Thysanoptera. *Transactions of the Royal Entomological Society of London* **109**, 467–534.

Morley, C. & Rait-Smith, W. (1933). The hymenopterous parasites of the British Lepidoptera. *Transactions of the Royal Entomological Society of London* **81**, 133–83.

Morris, H. M. (1921). The larval and pupal stages of the Bibionidae. *Bulletin of Entomological Research* **12**, 221–32.

Morris, H. M. (1922). The larval and pupal stages of the Bibionidae.–Part II. *Bulletin of Entomological Research* **13**, 189–95.

Morris, M. G. (1971). Differences between the invertebrate faunas of grazed and ungrazed chalk grasslands. IV. Abundance and diversity of Homoptera-Auchenorhyncha. *Journal of Applied Ecology* **8**, 37–52.

Morris, M. G. (2003). An annotated check list of British Curculionoidea (Col.). *Entomologist's Monthly Magazine* **139**, 193–225.

Mühle, E. (1971). *Krankheiten und Schädlinge der Futtergräser.* Hirzel, Leipzig.

Müller, C. & Brakefield, P. M. (2003). Analysis of a chemical defense in sawfly larvae: easy bleeding targets predator wasps in late summer. *Journal of Chemical Ecology*, 2683–94.

Mulligan, T. E. (1960). The transmission by mites, host-range and properties of ryegrass mosaic virus. *Annals of Applied Biology* **48**, 575–9.

Murchie, A. K., Moore, J. P., Walters, K. F. A. & Blackshaw, R. P. (2004). Invasion of agricultural land by the earthworm predator, *Arthurdendyus triangulatus* (Dendy). *Pedobiologia* **47**, 920–3.

Murchie, A. K., Polaszek, A. & Williams, I. H. (1999). *Platygaster subuliformis* (Kieffer) (Hym., Platygastridae) new to Britain, an egg-larval parasitoid of the brassica pod midge *Dasineura brassicae* Winnertz (Dipt., Cecidomyiidae). *Entomologist's Monthly Magazine* **135**, 217–22.

Murchie, A. K., Smart, L. E. & Williams, I. H. (1997a). Responses of *Dasineura brassicae* and its parasitoids *Platygaster subuliformis* and *Omphale clypealis* to field traps baited with organic isothiocyanates. *Journal of Chemical Ecology* **23**, 917–26.

Murchie, A. K. & Williams, I. H. (1998). A bibliography of the parasitoids of the cabbage seed weevil (*Ceutorhynchus assimilis* Payk.). *IOBC/wprs Bulletin* **21**, 163–9.

Murchie, A. W., Williams, I. H. & Alford, D. V. (1997b). Effects of commercial insecticide treatments to winter oilseed rape on parasitism of *Ceutorhynchus assimilis* Paykull (Coleoptera: Curculionidae) by *Trichomalus perfectus* (Hymenoptera: Pteromalidae). *Crop Protection* **16**, 199–202.

Murchie, A. K., Williams, I. H. & Perry, J. N. (1999b). Edge distributions of *Ceutorhynchus assimilis* and its parasitoid *Trichomalus perfectus* in a crop of winter oilseed rape (*Brassica napus*). *BioControl* **44**, 379–90.

Murray, P. J. & Clements, R. O. (1995). Distribution and abundance of three species of *Sitona* (Coleoptera, Curculionidae) in grassland in England. *Annals of Applied Biology* **127**, 229–37.

Myers, J. G. (1927). Natural enemies of the pear leaf-curling midge, *Perrisia pyri*, Bouché (Dipt., Cecidom.). *Bulletin of Entomological Research* **18**, 129–38.

Nash, D. R., Agassiz, D. J. L., Godfray, H. C. J. & Lawton, J. H. (1995). The pattern of spread of invading species: two leaf-mining moths colonizing Great Britain. *Journal of Animal Ecology* **64**, 225–33.

Nau, B. S. & Brooke, S. E. (2003). The contrasting range expansion of two species of *Deraeocoris* (Hemiptera–Heteroptera) in south-east England. *British Journal of Entomology and Natural History* **16**, 44–5.

Newstead, R. (1901). *Monograph of the Coccidae of the British Isles. Volume I.* Ray Society, London.

Newstead, R. (1903). *A Monograph of the British Coccidae. Vol. II.* Ray Society, London.

Newton, I. (1964). Bud-eating by bullfinches in relation to the natural food-supply. *Journal of Applied Ecology* **1**, 265–79.

Newton, I. (1972). *Finches.* Collins, London.

Nielsen, L. B. & Nielsen, B. O. (2002). Density and phenology of soil gallmidges (Diptera: Cecidomyiidae) in arable land. *Pedobiologia* **46**, 1–14.

Nijveldt, W. (1969). *Gall Midges of Economic Importance. Vol. VIII. Miscellaneous.* Crosby Lockwood & Sons, London.

Nilsson, C. (2003). *Parasitoids of Pollen Beetles.* In: *Biocontrol of Oilseed Rape Pests* (ed. Alford, D. V.), pp. 73–85. Blackwell Science, Oxford.

Nilsson, C. & Ahmed, B. (2006). Parasitoids of pollen beetles in Sweden – part of a strategy against pyrethroid resistance. *Proceedings of the International Symposium on Integrated Pest Management in Oilseed Rape, 3rd – 5th April 2006, Göttingen, Germany.* [CD]

Nilsson, C. & Andreasson, B. (1987). Parasitoids and predators attacking pollen beetles (*Meligethese aeneus* F.) in spring and winter rape in southern Sweden. *IOBC/wprs Bulletin* **10**, 64–73.

Nixon, P. M. I. (1997). Does the common rustic moth *Mesapamea secalis* (L.) represent an economic threat to Miscanthus? *Aspects of Applied Biology* **49**, 137–42.

Nye, I. W. B. (1958). The external morphology of some of the dipterous larvae living in the Gramineae of Britain. *Transactions of the Royal Entomological Society of London* **110**, 411–87.

Nye, I. W. B. (1959). The distribution of shoot-fly larvae (Diptera, Acalypterae) within pasture grasses and cereals in England. *Bulletin of Entomological Research* **50**, 53–62.

Oakley, J. N. (1980). Damage to barley germ by *Limothrips* spp. (Thysanoptera: Thripidae). *Plant Pathology* **29**, 99.

Oakley, J. N., Cumbleton, P. C., Corbett, S. J., Saunders, P., Green, D. I., Young, J. E. B. & Rogers, R. (1998). Prediction of wheat blossom midge activity and risk of damage. *Crop Protection* **17**, 145–9.

Oldham, J. N. (1928). *Hieroxestis subcervinella*, Wlk., an enemy of the banana in the Canary Islands. *Bulletin of Entomological Research* **19**, 147–66.

Ormerod, E. A. (1898). *Handbook of Insects Injurious to Orchard and Bush Fruits, with Means of Prevention and Remedy*. Simkin, Marshall, Hamilton, Kent & Co., London.

Osborne, P. (1960). Observations on the natural enemies of *Meligethes aeneus* (F.) and *M. viridescens* (F.) [Coleoptera: Nitidulidae]. *Parasitology* **50**, 91–110.

Ostojá-Starzewski, J. C. (2005). The western corn rootworm *Diabrotica virgifera virgifera* Le Conte (Col., Chrysomelidae) in Britain: distribution, description and biology. *Entomologist's Monthly Magazine* **141**, 175–82.

Pachagounder, P., Lamb, R. J. & Bodnaryk, R. P. (1998). Resistance to the flea beetle *Phyllotreta cruciferae* (Coleoptera: Chrysomelidae) in false flax, *Camelina sativa* (Brassicaceae). *Canadian Entomologist* **130**, 235–40.

Pape, H. (1964). *Krankheiten und Schädlinge der Zierpflanzen und ihre Bekämpfung*. Paul Parey, Berlin.

Pasteels, J. M. & Rowell-Rahier, M. (1992). The chemical ecology of herbivory on willows. *Proceedings of the Royal Society of Edinburgh* **98B**, 63–73.

Patterson, R. (1838). *Letters on the Natural History of the Insects Mentioned in Shakespeare's Plays. With Incidental Notices of the Entomology of Ireland*. Orr, London.

Pauer, R. (1975). Zur Ausbreitung der Carabiden in der Agrarlandschaft, unter besonderer Berücksichtigung der Grenzbereiche verschiedener Feldkulturen. *Zeitschrift für Angewandte Zoologie* **62**, 457–89.

Pauly, P. J. (2002). Fighting the hessian fly. American and British responses to insect invasion, 1776-1789. *Environmental History* **7**, 485–507.

Peacock, L., Herrick, S. & Harris, J. (2002). Interactions between the willow beetle *Phratora vulgatissima* and different genotypes of *Salix viminalis*. *Agricultural & Forest Entomology* **4**, 71–9.

Peacock, L., Lewis, M. & Powers, S. (2001). Volatile compounds from *Salix* spp. varieties differing in susceptibility to three willow beetle species. *Journal of Chemical Ecology* **27**, 1943–51.

Pelkwijk, A. J. ter (1946). Onderzoek naar de biologie van de elzensnuitkever, *Cryptorrhynchus lapathi* L. *Tijdschrift over Plantenziekten* **52**, 22–5.

Perrin, R. M. (1975). The role of perennial stinging nettle, *Urtica dioica*, as a reservoir of beneficial natural enemies. *Annals of Applied Biology* **81**, 289–97.

Petherbridge, F. R. (1920). The life history of the strawberry tortrix moth, *Oxygrapha comariana* (Zeller). *Annals of Applied Biology* **7**, 6–10.

Petherbridge, F. R. (1928). How the ribbon-like scars on apples are made by the apple sawfly (*Hoplocampa testudinea* Klug). *Journal of Pomology and Horticultural Science* **7**, 60–2.

Petherbridge, F. R. & Husain, M. A. (1918). A study of the capsid bugs found on apple trees. *Annals of Applied Biology* **4**, 179–205.

Petherbridge, F. R. & Jones, F. G. W. (1944). Beet eelworm (*Heterodera schachtii* Schm.) in East Anglia, 1934–1943. *Annals of Applied Biology* **31**, 320–32.

Petherbridge, F. R. & Stapley, J. H. (1937). Cutworms as sugar-beet pests, and their control. *Journal of the Ministry of Agriculture and Fisheries* **44**, 43–9.

Petherbridge, F. R. & Thomas, I. (1936a). Damage to wheat by *Helophorus nubilus* F. *Annals of Applied Biology* **23**, 640–48.

Petherbridge, F. R. & Thomas, I. (1936b). The common rustic moth, *Apamea* (*Hadena*) *secalis* L., attacking winter cereals. *Annals of Applied Biology* **23**, 649–52.

Petherbridge, F. R. & Thorpe, W. H. (1928). The common green capsid bug (*Lygus pabulinus*). *Annals of Applied Biology* **15**, 446–72.

Petherbridge, F. R. & Wright, D. W. (1943). Further observations on the biology and control of the carrot fly (*Psila rosae* F.). *Annals of Applied Biology* **30**, 348–58.

Petherbridge, F. R., Wright, D. W. & Davies, P. G. (1942). Investigations on the biology and control of the carrot fly (*Psila rosae* F.). *Annals of Applied Biology* **29**, 380–92.

Peumans, W. J. & Damme, E. J. M. van (1995). The role of lectins in plant defence. *Histochemical Journal* **27**, 253–71.

Philips, S. W., Bale, J. S. & Tatchell, G. M. (1999). Escaping an ecological dead-end: asexual overwintering and morph determination in the lettuce root aphid *Pemphigus bursarius* L. *Ecological Entomology* **24**, 336–44.

Phillips, J. W. & Parsons, M. S. (2005). The history, ecology and current status of the Brighton Wainscot *Oria musculosa* (Hübner) (Lepidoptera: Noctuidae): is this species on the verge of extinction in the United Kingdom. *British Journal of Entomology and Natural History* **18**, 81–100.

Pickett, J. A., Bartlett, E., Buxton, J. H., Wadhams, L. J. & Woodcock, C. M. (1996). Chemical ecology of adult vine weevil. *Mitteilungen aus der Biologischen Bundesanstalt für Land- und Forstwirtschaft Berlin-Dahlem* **316**, 41–5.

Pistorius, J., Bischoff, G. & Heimbach, U. (2009). Bienenvergiftung durch Wirkstoffabrieb von Saatgutbehandlungsmitteln während der Maisaussaat im Frühjahr 2008. *Journal für Kulturpflanzen* **61**, 9–14.

Pitcher, R. S. & Webb, P. C. R. (1952). Observations on the raspberry cane midge (*Thomasiniana theobaldi* Barnes). II. "Midge Blight", a fungal invasion of the raspberry cane following injury by *T. theobaldi*. *Journal of Horticultural Science* **27**, 95–100.

Pitkin, B. R. (1989). Lesser dung flies. Diptera: Sphaeroceridae. *Handbooks for the Identification of British Insects* **10 (5e)**, 1–175.

Port, C. M. & French, N. (1984). Damage to spring barley by larvae of *Dilophus febrilis* (L.) (Bibionidae: Diptera). *Plant Pathology* **33**, 133–4.

Port, C. M. & Guile, C. T. (1986). Outbreaks of flea beetles, *Altica* spp., on heather and other flowering plants. *Plant Pathology* **35**, 575–7.

Posenato, G., Girolami, V. & Zangheri, S. (1997). La minatrice americana un nuovo fillominatore della vite. *Informatore Agrario* **15**, 75–7.

Powell, D. F. (1979). Combining methyl bromide fumigation with cold storage to eradicate *Spodoptera littoralis* on chrysanthemum cuttings. *Plant Pathology* **28**, 178–80.

Powell, D. F. (1981). The eradication campaign against American serpentine leaf miner, *Liriomyza trifolii*, at Efford Experimental Station. *Plant Pathology* **30**, 195–204.

Pratt, C. R. (1986–7). A history and investigation into the fluctuations of *Polygonia c-album* L.: the comma butterfly. *Entomologist's Record and Journal of Variation* **98**, 197–203, 244–50; **99**, 21–7, 69–80.

Prescher, S. & Büchs, W. (1998). Der Einflu abgestufter Extensivierungsma nahmen im Raps- und Erbsenanbau auf nützliche Fliegen (Diptera, Brachycera). *Gesunde Pflanzen* **50**, 213–8.

Preston, C. D. & Sell, P. D. (1988). The Aizoaceae naturalized in the British Isles. *Watsonia* **17**, 217–44.

Putnam, W. L. (1955). Bionomics of *Stethorus punctillum* Weise (Coleoptera: Coccinellidae) in Ontario. *Canadian Entomologist* **87**, 9–33.

Raupach, K., Borgemeister, C., Hommes, M., Poehling, H.-M. & Sétamou, M. (2002). Effect of temperature and host plants on the bionomics of *Empoasca decipiens* (Homoptera: Cicadellidae). *Crop Protection* **21**, 113–19.

Rawlinson, C. J. & Williams, I. H. (1991). Pests, diseases and effects of crop protection on single- and double-low winter rape. *Bulletin SROP/wprs – Proceedings of the OILB Meeting, Rothamsted, UK, March 1990*, pp. 74–88.

Rector, B. G., Harizanova, V., Sforza, R., Widmer, T. & Wiedenmann, R. N. (2006). Prospects for biological control of teasels, *Dipsacus* spp., a new target in the United States. *Biological Control* **36**, 1–14.

Redfern, M. (1975). The life history and morphology of the early stages of the yew gall midge *Taxomyia taxi* (Inchbald) (Diptera: Cecidomyiidae). *Journal of Natural History* **9**, 513–33.

Redfern, M. & Cameron, R. A. D. (1995). Population dynamics of the yew gall midge *Taxomyia taxi* and its chalcid parasitoids: a 24-year study. *Ecological Entomology* **18**, 365–78.

Redfern, M. & Hunter, M. D. (2005). Time tells: long-term patterns in the population dynamics of the yew gall midge, *Taxomyia taxi* (Diptera: Cecidomyiidae), over 35 years. *Ecological Entomology* **30**, 86–95.

Redfern, M., Shirley, P. R., & Bloxham, M. (2002). British Plant Galls. Identification of Galls on Plants and Fungi. *Field Studies* **10**, 207–531.

Reid, S. (2006). A significant interception of the green vegetable bug, *Nezara viridula* (Linnaeus) (Hemiptera: Pentatomidae) in the UK. *Entomologist's Record and Journal of Variation* **118**, 123–5.

Rézbányai-Reser, L. (1985). *Mesapamea* - Studien II. *Mesapamea remmi* sp. n. aus der Schweiz, sowie Beiträge zur Kenntnis der westpaläarktischen Arten der Gattung *Mesapamea* Heinicke, 1959. *Entomologische Berichte Luzern* **14**, 127–48.

Rhynehart, J. G. (1922). On the life-history and bionomics of the flax flea-beetle (*Longitarsus parvulus*, Payk.), with descriptions of the hitherto unknown larval and pupal stages. *Scientific Proceedings of the Royal Dublin Society* **16**, 497–541.

Richardson, D. M. (2008). *Pollen beetle in the UK; the start of a resistance problem? EPPO/OEPP Bulletin* **38**, 73–4.

Rings, R. W. (1970). Contributions to the bionomics of the green fruitworms: the life history of *Orthosia hibisci*. *Journal of Economic Entomology* **63**, 1562–8.

Roberts, A. W. R. (1919). On the life history of 'wireworms' of the genus *Agriotes*, Esch., with some notes on that of *Athous haemorrhoidalis*, F. Part I. *Annals of Applied Biology* **6**, 116–35.

Roberts, A. W. R. (1921). On the life history of 'wireworms' of the genus *Agriotes*, Esch., with some notes on that of *Athous haemorrhoidalis*, F. Part II. *Annals of Applied Biology* **8**, 193–215.

Roberts, A. W. R. (1922). On the life history of 'wireworms' of the genus *Agriotes*, Esch., with some notes on that of *Athous haemorrhoidalis*, F. Part III. *Annals of Applied Biology* **9**, 306–24.

Roberts, I. M., Duncan, G. II, Amrine, J. W. Jr & Jones, A. T. (1993). Morphological and ultrastructural studies on three species of *Cecidophyopsis* mites (Acari: Eriophyidae) on *Ribes*. *Acta Horticulturae* **352**, 591–5.

Robinson, J. & Collins, D. W. (2005). Two records of *Heliothrips haemorrhoidalis* (Bouché) (Thysanoptera, Thripidae) breeding outdoors at Kew Gardens and in the Isles of Scilly. *Entomologist's Monthly Magazine* **141**, 67–8.

Roebuck, A. (1923). On the occurrence of leaf-eating sawflies on cereals in Britain. *Bulletin of Entomological Research* **13**, 267–9.

Rougemont, G. M. de (1989). *A Field Guide to the Crops of Britain and Europe*. Collins, London.

Ryan, M. F. (1975). The natural mortality of wheat bulb fly pupae, *Leptohylemyia coarctata* (Fall.) (Dipt., Anthomyiidae). *Plant Pathology* **24**, 27–30.

Sage, R. [B.], Cunningham, M. & Boatman, N. (2006). Birds in willow short-rotation coppice compared to other arable crops in central England and a review of bird census data from energy crops in the UK. *Ibis* **148**, 184–97.

Sage, R. B. & Tucker, K. (1997). Invertebrates in the canopy of willow and poplar short rotation coppices. *Aspects of Applied Biology* **49**, 105–11.

Salt, G. (1931). Parasites of the wheat-stem sawfly, *Cephus pygmaeus*, Linnaeus, in England. *Bulletin of Entomological Research* **22**, 479–545.

Sarto i Monteys, V. (1992). Spread of the Southern African Lycaenid butterfly, *Cacyreus marshalli* Butler, 1898, (Lep: Lycaenidae) in the Balearic Archipelago (Spain) and considerations on its likely introduction to continental Europe. *Journal of Research on the Lepidoptera* **31**, 24–34.

Savage, M. J. (1977). Damage to cereals by larvae of *Bibio johannis* (L.) and *Bibio hortulanus* (L.) (Bibionidae, Diptera). *Plant Pathology* **26**, 199.

Savage, M. J. (1978). Damage to vines by *Colomerus vitis* (Pgst.) (Prostigmata: Eriophyidae). *Plant Pathology* **27**, 147–8.

Schewket Bay, N. (1930). Zur Biologie der phytophagen Wanze *Dicyphus errans* Wolff (Capsidae). *Zeitschrift für Wissenschaftliche Insektenbiologie* **25**, 179–83.

Schliesske, J. (1995). Gallmilben an Obstgewächsen. Morphologie und Symptomatologie. *Schriftenreiher der Deutschen Phytomedizinischen Gesellschaft* **5**, 1–288.

Schliesske, J. (2004). Zur Biologie arboricoler Gallmilben (Acari, Eriophyoidea). *Entomologie Heute* **16**, 51–69.

Schmidt, G. (1970). Die deutschen Namen wichtiger Arthropoden. *Mitteilungen aus der Biologischen Bundesanstalt für Land- und Forstwirtschaft Berlin-Dahlem* **137**, 1–222.

Schmitz, G., Rothmeier, I., Greib, G., Ro -Nickoll, M. & Bartsch, D. (2002). Zum Ausbreitungsprozess und *Ostrinia nubilalis* Hbn.) in Nordwestdeutschland. *Zeitschrift für Pflanzenkrankheiten und Pflanzenschutz* **109**, 624–9.

Schwenke, W. (ed.) (1982). *Die Forstschädlinge Europas. Vierter Band.* Paul Parey, Hamburg.

Scott, T. M. (1972). *The Pine Shoot Moth and Related Species.* Forestry Commission Forest Record 83. HMSO, London.

Scott Brown, A. S. & Simmonds, M. S. J. (2006). Leaf morphology of hosts and nonhosts of the thrips *Heliothrips haemorrhoidalis* (Bouché). *Botanical Journal of the Linnean Society* **152**, 109–30.

Scutareanu, P., Lingeman, R., Drukker, B. & Sabelis, M. W. (1999). Cross-correlation analysis of fluctuations in local populations of pear psyllids and anthocorid bugs. *Ecological Entomology* **24**, 354–62.

Seymour, P. R. (1989). *Invertebrates of Economic Importance in Britain. Common and Scientific Names.* HMSO, London.

Sharga, U. S. (1933). Biology and life history of *Limothrips cerealium* Haliday and *Aptinothrips rufus* Gmelin feeding on Gramineae. *Annals of Applied Biology* **20**, 308–26.

Shaw, M. J. P. (1954). Overwintering of *Myzus persicae* (Sulzer) in north-east Scotland. *Plant Pathology* **4**, 137–8.

Shaw, M. J. P. (1970a). Effects of population density on alienicolae of *Aphis fabae* Scop. II. The effect of crowding on the production of alatae in the laboratory. *Annals of Applied Biology* **65**, 191–6.

Shaw, M. J. P. (1970b). Effects of population density on alienicolae of *Aphis fabae* Scop. II. The effects of crowding on the expression of migratory urge among alatae in the laboratory. *Annals of Applied Biology* **65**, 197–203.

Shaw, M. W. (1956). *Lampronia capitella* in Scotland. *Plant Pathology* **5**, 75.

Shaw, M. W. (1957). Damage by rosy rustic moth larvae in Scotland, 1956. *Plant Pathology* **6**, 135–6.

Shaw, M. W. (1959). The diamond-back moth *Plutella maculipennis* (Curtis). A historical review with special reference to its occurrence in Scotland in 1958. *Transactions of the Royal Highland and Agricultural Society of Scotland*, pp. 1–24.

Sheldon, W. G. (1925). *Peronea comariana*, Zeller, and its variation. *The Entomologist* **58**, 281–5.

Shirota, Y., Carter, N., Rabbinge, R. & Ankersmit, G. W. (1983). Biology of *Aphidius rhopalosiphi*, a parasitoid of cereal aphids. *Entomologia Experimentalis et Applicata* **34**, 27–34.

Sigsgaard, L. (2004). Oviposition preference of *Anthocoris nemorum* and *A. nemoralis* for apple and pear. *Entomologia Experimentalis et Applicata* **111**, 215–23.

Sigsgaard, L., Jacobsen, S. E. & Christiansen, J. L. (2008). Quinoa, *Chenopodium quinoa*, provides a new host for native herbivores in northern Europe: Case studies of the moth, *Scrobipalpa atriplicella*, and the tortoise beetle, *Cassida nebulosa*. *Journal of Insect Science* **8:49**, 4 pp. [Available online: insectscience.org/8.49]

Simmonds, S. P. (1970). The possible control of *Steneotarsonemus pallidus* on strawberries by *Phytoseiulus persimilis*. *Plant Pathology* **19**, 106–7.

Simmonds, S. P. (1974). Onions attacked by *Acrolepia assectella* (Zell.). *Plant Pathology* **23**, 49.

Skoracka, A. & Kuczynski, L. (2006). Is the cereal rust mite, *Abacarus hystrix* really a generalist? – Testing colonization performance on novel hosts. *Experimental and Applied Acarology* **38**, 1–13.

Smith, B. D. (1960). The behaviour of the black currant gall mite (*Phytoptus ribis* Nal.) during the free living phase of its life cycle. *Long Ashton Agricultural and Horticultural Research Station Annual Report for 1959*, pp. 130–36.

Smith, B. D. & Stott, K. G. (1964). The life history and behaviour of the willow weevil *Cryptorrhynchus lapathi* L. *Annals of Applied Biology* **54**, 141–51.

Smith, K. G. V. (1989). An introduction to the immature stages of British flies. Diptera larvae, with notes on eggs, puparia and pupae. *Handbook for the Identification of British Insects* **10 (14)**, 1–280.

Smith, K. G. V. (1990). Hemiptera (Anthocoridae and Miridae) biting man. *Entomologist's Monthly Magazine* **26**, 96.

Smith, K. M. (1920). Investigation of the nature and cause of the damage to plant tissue resulting from the feeding of capsid bugs. *Annals of Applied Biology* **7**, 40–55.

Smith, K. M. (1972). *A Textbook of Plant Virus Diseases.* Third edition. Longman, London.

Smith, L. M. & Goldsmith, E. V. (1936). The cyclamen mite, *Tarsonemus pallidus*, and its control in field strawberries. *Hilgardia* **10**, 53–94.

Smith, R. M., Baker, R. H. A., Malumphy, C. P., Hockland, S., Hammon, R P., Ostojá-Starzewski, J. C. & Collins, D. W. (2005). Non-native invertebrate plant pests established in Great Britain an assessment of patterns and trends. *BCPC Symposium Proceedings No. 81*, pp. 119–24.

Smith, R. M., Baker, R. H. A., Malumphy, C. P., Hockland, S., Hammon, R P., Ostojá-Starzewski, J. C. & Collins, D. W. (2007). Recent non-native invertebrate plant pest establishments in Great Britain: origins, pathways, and trends. *Agricultural & Forest Entomology* **9**, 307–26.

Solomon, M. G. (1975). The colonization of an apple orchard by predators of the fruit tree red spider mite. *Annals of Applied Biology* **80**, 119–22.

Solomon, M. G. (1982). Phytophagous mites and their predators in apple orchards. *Annals of Applied Biology* **101**, 201–3.

Solomon, M. G., Cross, J. V., Fitzgerald, J. D., Campbell, C. A. M., Jolly, R. L., Olszak, R. W., Niemczyk, E. & Vogt, H. (2000). Biocontrol of pests of apples and pears in northern and central Europe – 3. Predators. *Biocontrol Science & Technology* **10**, 101–38.

Solomon, M. E. & Glen, D. M. (1979). Prey density and rates of predation by tits (*Parus* spp.) on larvae of codling moth (*Cydia pomonella*) under bark. *Journal of Applied Ecology* **16**, 49–59.

Solomon, M. E., Glen, D. M., Kendall, D. A. & Milsom, N. F. (1976). Predation of overwintering larvae of codling moth (*Cydia pomonella* (L.)) by birds. *Journal of Applied Ecology* **13**, 341–52.

Solomon, M. G. & Locke, T. (2000). *Pests and Diseases of Fruit and Hops.* In: *Pest and Disease Management Handbook* (ed. Alford, D. V.), pp. 258–316. Blackwell Science, Oxford.

Sotherton, N. W. (1984). The distribution and abundance of predatory arthropods overwintering on farmland. *Annals of Applied Biology* **105**, 423–9.

Sotherton, N. W. (1985). The distribution and abundance of predatory Coleoptera overwintering in field boundaries. *Annals of Applied Biology* **106**, 17–21.

Sotherton, N. W. (1990). The effects of six insecticides used in UK cereal fields on sawfly larvae (Hymenoptera: Tenthredinidae). *Proceedings of the Brighton Crop Protection Conference – Pests & Diseases* **3**, 999–1004.

Southey, J. F. (ed.) (1978). *Plant Nematology.* Third edition. HMSO, London.

Southey, J. F., Alphey, T. J. W., Cooke, D. A., Whiteway, J. A. & Mathias, P. L. (1982). Surveys of beet cyst nematode in England 1977–80. *Plant Pathology* **31**, 163–9.

Spencer, K. A. (1973). *Agromyzidae (Diptera) of Economic Importance.* Dr W. Junk, The Hague.

Speyer, E. R. (1922). Mycetophilid flies as pests of the cucumber plant in glass-houses. *Bulletin of Entomological Research* **13**, 255–9.

Speyer, E. R. (1927). An important parasite of the greenhouse white-fly (*Trialeurodes vaporariorum*, Westwood). *Bulletin of Entomological Research* **17**, 301–8.

Speyer, E. [R.] (1928). The red spider mite (*Tetranychus telarius* L.). *Journal of Pomology* **6**, 161–71.

Speyer, W. (1933). Wanzen (Heteroptera) an Obstbäumen. *Zeitschrift für Pflanzenkrankheiten und Pflanzenschutz* **43**, 113–38.

Spooner, B. & Roberts, P. (2005). *Fungi.* Collins, London.

Stapley, J. H. (1934). The apple fruit miner (*Argyresthia conjugella* Zell.). *Journal of the South-Eastern Agricultural College, Wye, Kent* **34**, 87–92.

Steer, W. (1932). Further observations on the habits of the raspberry beetle (*Byturus tomentosus* Fabr.) with special reference to the control of the pest by means of derris. *Journal of Pomology and Horticultural Science* **10**, 1–16.

Stenseth, C. & Nordby, A. (1979). Damage, and control of the strawberry mite *Steneotarsonemus pallidus* (Acarina: Tarsonemidae), on strawberries. *Journal of Horticultural Science* **51**, 49–54.

Stenseth, C. & Vik, J. (1979). The effect of black polyethylene mulch on the development of *Otiorhynchus sulcatus* on strawberry plants. *Gartneryrket* **69**, 912–4.

Stevens, C. P. (1983). *Watercress – production of the cultivated crop.* ADAS/MAFF Reference Book 136. Grower Books, London.

Stewart, R. K. (1968). The biology of *Lygus rugulipennis* Poppius (Hemiptera : Miridae) in Scotland. *Transactions of the Royal Entomological Society of London* **120**, 437–57.

Stigter, H. & Frankenhuysen, A. van (1992). *Argyresthia trifasciata*, een nieuwe beschadiger van coniferen in Nederland (Lepidoptera: Yponomeutidae, Agryresthiinae). *Entomologische Berichten (Amsterdam)* **52**, 33–7.

Stokes, B. M. (1957). *Mayetiola dactylis* Kieffer in cocksfoot grass. *Plant Pathology* **6**, 127–30.

Stone, A. R. (1973). *Heterodera pallida* n.sp. (Nematoda: Heteroderidae), a second species of potato cyst nematode. *Nematologica* **18**, 591–606.

Stone, L. E. W. (1977). The incidence and economic significance of pests in cereals in England and Wales. *Proceedings of the British Crop Protection Conference – Pests and Diseases* **3**, 713–20.

Stork, N. E. (1980). Role of waxblooms in preventing attachment to brassicas by the mustard beetle, *Phaedon cochleariae. Entomologica Experimentalis et Applicata* **28**, 100–7.

Storkan, R. C. & Lembright, H. W. (1955). Tarpaulin fumigation of strawberry plants with methyl bromide for mite control and plant response. *Down to Earth* **11**, 12–14.

Strong, D. R., Larsson, S. & Gullberg, U. (1993). Heritability of host plant resistance to herbivory changes with gallmidge density during an outbreak on willow. *Evolution* **47**, 291–300.

Strouts, R. G. & Winter, T. G. (1994). *Diagnosis of ill-health in trees.* Research for Amenity Trees No. 2. HMSO, London.

Stroyan, H. L. G. (1963). *The British Species of* Dysaphis *Börner (*Sappaphis *auctt.* nec *Mats). Part II. The Subgenus* Dysaphis sensu stricto. HMSO, London.

Stroyan, H. L. G. (1977). Homoptera Aphidoidea. *Handbooks for the Identification of British insects* **2 (4a)**, 1–130.

Sunderland, K. D. (1975). The diet of some predatory arthropods in cereal crops. *Journal of Applied Ecology* **12**, 507–15.

Sunderland, K. D., Fraser, A. M. & Dixon, A. F. G. (1986). Distribution of linyphiid spiders in relation to capture of prey in cereal fields. *Pedobiologia* **29**, 367–75.

Suski, Z. W. (1974). A revision of *Siteroptes cerealium* (Kirchner) complex (Acarina, Heterostigmata, Pyemotidae). *Annales Zoologici* **30**, 509–35.

Sykes, G. B. (1969). Experiments on the control of currant clearwing moth (*Synanthedon tipuliformis* (Clerck)) on gooseberries. *Plant Pathology* **18**, 119–21.

Symondson, W. O. C., Sunderland, K. D. & Greenstone, M. H. (2002). Can generalist predators be effective biocontrol agents? *Annual Review of Entomology* **47**, 561–94.

Taksdal, G. (1983). *Orthotylus marginalis* Reuter and *Psallus ambiguus* Fallén (Heteroptera, Miridae) causing stony pits in pears. *Acta Agriculturae Scandinavica* **33**, 205–8.

Taksdal, G. & Sørum, O. (1971). Capsids (Heteroptera, Miridae) in strawberries, and their influence on fruit malformation. *Journal of Horticultural Science* **46**, 43–50.

Taylor, C. E. (1971). The raspberry beetle (*Byturus tomentosus*) and its control with alternative chemicals to DDT. *Horticultural Research* **11**, 107–12.

Taylor, C. E. (1978). *Plant-parasitic Dorylaimida: Biology and Virus Transmission.* In: *Plant Nematology*, Third edition (ed. Southey, J. F.), pp. 232–43. HMSO, London.

Taylor, H. V. (1949). *The Plums of England.* Crosby Lockwood & Sons, London.

Taylor, T. H. (1928). The watercress stem-miner. *Entomologist's Monthly Magazine* **64**, 126–8.

Teerling, C. R., Pierce, H. D., Borden, J. H. & Gillespie, D. R. (1993). Identification and bioactivity of alarm pheromone in the western flower thrips, *Frankliniella occidentalis. Journal of Chemical Ecology* **19**, 681–97.

Theobald, F. V. (1907). Report on economic zoology for the year ending April 1st, 1907. *Journal of the South-Eastern Agricultural College, Wye, Kent* **16**, 29–180.

Theobald, F. V. (1909). *The Insect and Other Allied Pests of Orchard, Bush and Hothouse Fruits and Their Prevention and Treatment.* Theobald, Wye.

Theobald, F. V. (1928). The apple leaf skeletoniser (*Hemerophila pariana*, Clerck). *Journal of the South-Eastern Agricultural College, Wye, Kent* **7**, 1–10.

Thomas, C. F. G. (1996). Field margin terminology and definitions: towards a unified semantic perspective. *Field Margins Newsletter* **6/7**, 35–7.

Thomas, D. C. (1946). A study of the distribution of the swede midge (*Contarinia nasturtii* Kieffer) in Devon and symptoms of its attack on various plants. *Annals of Applied Biology* **33**, 77–81.

Thomas, I. (1933). On the bionomics and structure of some dipterous larvae infesting cereals and grasses. I. *Opomyza florum* Fabr. *Annals of Applied Biology* **20**, 707–21.

Thomas, I. (1934). On the bionomics and structure of some dipterous larvae infesting cereals and grasses. II. *Opomyza germinationis* L. *Annals of Applied Biology* **21**, 519–29.

Thomas, I. (1938). On the bionomics and structure of some dipterous larvae infesting cereals and grasses. III. *Geomyza (Balioptera) tripunctata* Fall. *Annals of Applied Biology* **25**, 181–96.

Thomas, M. B., Wratten, S. D. & Sotherton, N. W. (1991). Creation of 'island' habitats in farmland to manipulate populations of beneficial arthropods: predator densities and emigration. *Journal of Applied Ecology* **28**, 906–17.

Thomas, M. B., Wratten, S. D. & Sotherton, N. W. (1992). Creation of 'island' habitats in farmland to manipulate populations of beneficial arthropods: predator densities and species composition. *Journal of Applied Ecology* **29**, 524–31.

Thompson, H. W. (1942). *Crambus hortuellus* Hb. as a grassland pest. *Annals of Applied Biology* **29**, 393–8.

Topham, P. N. (1968). The fuller's teasel. *Proceedings of the Botanical Society of the British Isles* **7**, 377–81.

Trudgill, D. L. (1986). Yield losses caused by potato cyst nematodes: a review of the current position in Britain and prospects for improvements. *Annals of Applied Biology* **108**, 181–98.

Truitt, G. W. (1951). The mushroom fly as a cause of bronchial asthma. *Annals of Allergy* **9**, 513–6.

Turner, J. R. G. (1968). The ecological genetics of *Acleris comariana* (Zeller) (Lepidoptera: Tortricidae), a pest of strawberry. *Journal of Animal Ecology* **37**, 489–520.

Ulenberg, S. A., Goffau, L. J. W. de, Frankenhuyzen, A. van & Burger, H. C. (1986). Bijzondere aantastingen door insecten in 1985. *Entomologische Berichten (Amsterdam)* **46**, 163–71.

Unger, J.-G. (1998). The impact of quarantine regulations for terrestrial flatworms on international trade. *Pedobiologia* **42**, 579–84.

Vallotton, R. (1969). Contribution à la biologie de la Cécidomyie du pois *Contarinia pisi* Winn. (Diptera, Cecidomyiidae) avec étude particulière du phénomène de la diapause. *Mitteilungen der Schweizerischen Entomologischen Gesellschaft* **42**, 241–93.

Vandermeer, J. (1989). *The Ecology of Intercropping.* Cambridge University Press, Cambridge.

Vänninen, I. & Hokkanen, H. [M. T.] (1988). Effect of pesticides on four species of entomopathogenic fungi *in vitro*. *Annales Agriculturae Fenniae* **27**, 345–53.

Varty, I. W. (1956). *Adelges insects of silver firs.* Forestry Commission Bulletin No. 26. HMSO, Edinburgh.

Vernon, J. D. R. & Dennis, E. B. (1965). A survey of pest and disease control methods on strawberries in the Cheddar and Draycott areas of Somerset: 1963-64. *Plant Pathology* **14**, 169–73.

Vernon, J. D. R. (1971a). Observations on the biology and control of tortricid larvae on strawberries. *Plant Pathology* **20**, 73–80.

Vernon, J. D. R. (1971b). Observations on the biology and control of the plum fruit moth. *Plant Pathology* **20**, 106–10.

Vickerman, G. P. (1982). Distribution and abundance of *Opomyza florum* (Diptera: Opomyzidae) in cereal crops and grassland *Annals of Applied Biology* **101**, 441–7.

Vickerman, G. P. & O'Bryan, M. (1979). Partridges and insects. *Annual Review of the Game Conservancy* **9**, 35–43.

Vickerman, G. P. & Sunderland, K. D. (1975). Arthropods in cereal crops: nocturnal activity, vertical distribution and aphid predation. *Journal of Applied Ecology* **12**, 755–66.

Vickerman, G. P. & Wratten, S. D. (1979). The biology and pest status of cereal aphids (Hemiptera: Aphididae) in Europe: a review. *Bulletin of Entomological Research* **69**, 1–32.

Vogel, W., Klinger, J. & Wildbolz, Th. (1956). *Pam[m]ene rhediella* Clerck, der Bodenseewickler, ein bisher übersehener Obstschädling. *Mitteilungen der Schweizerischen Entomolgischen Gesellschaft* **29**, 283–302.

Voigt, D., Gorb, E. & Gorb, S. (2007). Plant surface-bug interactions: *Dicyphus errans* stalking along trichomes. *Arthropod-Plant Interactions* **1**, 221–43.

Vrie, M. van de (1991). *Tortricids in Ornamental Crops in Greenhouses.* In: *World Crop Pests, Volume 5, Tortricid Pests, Their Biology, Natural Enemies and Control* (eds Geest, L. P. S. van der & Evenhuis, H. H.), pp. 515–39. Elsevier, Amsterdam.

Wajnberg, E. & Hassan, S. A. (1994). *Biological Control with Egg Parasitoids.* CAB International, Wallingford.

Wallace, H. R. (1958). Movement of eelworms. I. The influence of pore size and moisture content of the soil on the migration of larvae of the beet eelworm, *Heterodera schachtii* Schmidt. *Annals of Applied Biology* **46:** 74–85.

Wallace, H. R. (1963). *The Biology of Plant Parasitic Nematodes.* Edward Arnold, London.

Walsh, J. A. & Tomlinson, J. A. (1985). Viruses affecting winter oilseed rape (*Brassica napus* ssp. *oleifera*). *Annals of Applied Biology* **107**, 485–95.

Walters, K. F. A., Watson, S. J. & Dixon, A. F. G. (1983). Forecasting outbreaks of the grain aphid *Sitobion avenae* in East Anglia. *Proceedings of the 10th International Congress of Plant Protection* **1**, 168.

Walters, K. F. A., Young, J. E. B., Kromp, B. & Cox, P. D. (2003). *Management of Oilseed Rape Pests.* In: *Biocontrol of Oilseed Rape Pests* (ed. Alford, D. V.), pp. 43–71. Blackwell Science, Oxford.

Walton, C. L. & Staniland, L. N. (1929). The common green capsid bug (*Lygus pabulinus*) as a pest of sugar beet. *Long Ashton Agricultural and Horticultural Research Station Report for 1929*, pp. 99–100.

Warburton, C. (1926). Annual report for 1926 of the zoologist. *Journal of the Royal Agricultural Society* **87**, 352–6.

Wardlow, L. R. & Ludlam, F. A. B. (1975). Biological studies and chemical control of brown scale (*Parthenolecanium corni* (Bouché)) on red currant. *Plant Pathology* **24**, 213–16.

Watson, G. W. & Malumphy, C. P. (2004). *Icerya purchasi* Maskell, cottony cushion scale (Hemiptera: Margarodidae), causing damage to ornamental plants growing outdoors in London. *British Journal of Entomology and Natural History* **17**, 105–9.

Weihrauch, F. (2005). Evaluation of a damage threshold for two-spotted spider mites, *Tetranychus urticae* Koch (Acari: Tetranychidae), in hop culture. *Annals of Applied Biology* **146**, 501–9.

Wetering, F. van de, Hoek, M. van de, Goldbach, R. & Peters, D. (1999). Differences in tomato spotted wilt virus vector competency between males and females of *Frankliniella occidentalis*. *Entomologia Experimentalis et Applicata* **93**, 105–12.

Wheeler, A. G. Jr (2001). *Biology of the Plant Bugs (Hemiptera: Miridae).* Cornell University Press, Ithaca.

White, J. H. & French, N. (1968). Leatherjacket damage to grassland. *Journal of the British Grassland Society* **23**, 326–9.

White, M. J. (2003). *Argyresthia trifasciata* Staudinger (Lep.: Yponomeutidae) – new for Wales. *Entomologist's Record & Journal of Variation* **115**, 225–6.

White, P. F. (1986). The effect of sciarid larvae (*Lycoriella auripila*) on cropping of the cultivated mushroom (*Agaricus bisporus*). *Annals of Applied Biology* **109**, 11–17.

White, P. F. & Smith, J. E. (2000). *Bradysia lutaria* (Winn.) (Dipt., Sciaridae) – a recent addition to the British fauna and a pest of the cultivated mushroom (*Agaricus bisporus*). *Entomologist's Monthly Magazine* **136**, 165–7.

White, P. F., Smith, J. E. & Menzel, F. (2000). Distribution of Sciaridae (Dipt.) species infesting commercial mushroom farms in Britain. *Entomologist's Monthly Magazine* **136**, 207–10.

Whitehead, A. G. & Hooper, D. J. (1970). Needle nematodes (*Longidorus* spp.) and stubby-root nematodes (*Trichodorus* spp.) harmful to sugar beet and other field crops in England. *Annals of Applied Biology* **65**, 339–50.

Whitehead, T, & Wood, C. A. (1946). Virus diseases of the strawberry. 1. The field problem in North Wales. *Journal of Pomology and Horticultural Science* **22**, 119–33.

Wiesmann, R. (1941). Untersuchungen über die Biologie und Bekämpfung der Erdbeermilbe *Tarsonemus pallidus* (*fragariae* Z.) Banks. *Landwirtschaftliches Jahrbuch der Schweiz* **55**, 259–329.

Williams, C. B. (1914). The pea thrips (*Kakothrips robustus*). *Annals of Applied Biology* **1**, 222–46.

Williams, I. H. (1989). Pest incidence on single low and double low oilseed rape cultivars. *Aspects of Applied Biology* **23**, 277–86.

Williams, I. H. (2003a). *Parasitoids of Cabbage Seed Weevil*. In: *Biocontrol of Oilseed Rape Pests* (ed. Alford, D. V.), pp. 97–112. Blackwell Science, Oxford.

Williams, I. H. (2003b). *Parasitoids of Brassica Pod Midge*. In: *Biocontrol of Oilseed Rape Pests* (ed. Alford, D. V.), pp. 113–23. Blackwell Science, Oxford.

Williams, I. H. & Free, J. B. (1978). The feeding and mating behaviour of pollen beetles (*Meligethes aeneus* Fab.) and seed weevils (*Ceutorhyhchus assimilis* Payk.) on oilseed rape (*Brassica napus* L.). *Journal of Agricultural Science, Cambridge* **91**, 453–9.

Williams, I. H., Martin, A. P. & Kelm, M. (1987a). The phenology of the emergence of brassica pod midge (*Dasineura brassicae* Winn.) and its infestation of winter oil-seed rape (*Brassica napus* L.). *Journal of Agricultural Science, Cambridge* **108**, 579–89.

Williams, I. H., Martin, A. P. & Kelm, M. (1987b). The phenology of the emergence of brassica pod midge (*Dasineura brassicae* Winn.) and its infestation of spring oil-seed rape (*Brassica napus* L.). *Journal of Agricultural Science, Cambridge* **109**, 309–14.

Williams, I. H. & Walton, M. (1990). A bibliography of the parasitoids of the brassica pod midge (*Dasineura brassicae* Winn.). *IOBC/wprs Bulletin* **13**, 46–52.

Williams, J. J. W. & Carden, P. W. (1961). Cabbage stem flea beetle in East Anglia. *Plant Pathology* **10**, 85–95.

Willis, R. J. & Edwards, A. R. (1977). The occurrence of the land planarian *Artioposthia triangulata* (Dendy) in Northern Ireland. *Irish Naturalists' Journal* **19**, 113–16.

Wiltshire, C. W., Kendall, D. A., Hunter, T. & Arnold G. M. (1997). Host-plant preferences of two willow-feeding leaf beetles (Coleoptera, Chrysomelidae). *Aspects of Applied Biology* **49**, 113–20.

Winfield, A. L. (1961). Observations on the biology and control of the cabbage stem weevil, *Ceutorhynchus quadridens* (Panz.), on Trowse mustard (*Brassica juncea*). *Bulletin of Entomological Research* **52**, 589–600.

Winfield, A. L. (1963). A study on the effects of insecticides on parasites of larvae of blossom beetles (*Meligethes aeneus* F., Coleoptera: Nitidulidae). *Entomologia Experimentalis et Applicata* **6**, 309–18.

Winfield, A. L. (1964). The biology and control of the cherrybark tortrix moth. *Plant Pathology* **13**, 115–20.

Winfield, A. L. (1992). Management of oilseed rape pests in Europe. *Agricultural Zoology Reviews* **5**, 51–95.

Winfield, A. L., Hancock, M., Jackson, A. W. & Hammon, R. P. (1985). Pear sucker (*Psylla pyricola*) in south-east England. *IOBC/wprs Bulletin* **7**, 45–54.

Winslow, R. D. (1954). Provisional lists of host plants of some root eelworms (*Heterodera* spp.). *Annals of Applied Biology* **41**, 591–605.

Winslow, R. D. (1955). The hatching responses of some root eelworms of the genus *Heterodera*. *Annals of Applied Biology* **43**, 19–36.

Wiseman, B. R. (1990). Plant resistance to insects in the southeastern United States: an overview. *The Florida Entomologist* **73**, 351–8.

Wishart, G. (1957). Surveys of parasites of *Hylemya* spp. (Diptera: Anthomyiidae) that attack cruciferous crops in Europe. *Canadian Entomologist* **89**, 510–17.

Wishart, G. & Monteith, E. (1954). *Trybliographa rapae* (Westw.) (Hymenoptera: Cynipidae), a parasite of *Hylemya* spp. (Diptera: Anthomyiidae). *Canadian Entomologist* **86**, 145–54.

Wood, C. A. (1950). The strawberry aphid, *Pentatrichopus fragaefolii* (Theob.), in North Wales, with special reference to the maintenance of healthy strawberry stocks in non-fruit-growing areas. *Journal of Horticultural Science* **26**, 22–34.

Woodford, J. A. T. & Gordon, S. C. (1978). The history and distribution of raspberry cane midge (*Resseliella theobaldi* (Barnes)) = *Thomasiniana theobaldi* Barnes), a new pest in Scotland. *Horticultural Research* **17**, 87–97.

Wright, D. W. & Ashby, D. G. (1946). Bionomics of the carrot fly (*Psila rosae* F.). I. The infestation and sampling of carrot crops. *Annals of Applied Biology* **33**, 69–77.

Wright, D. W. & Geering, Q. A. (1948). The biology and control of the pea moth, *Laspeyresia nigricana*, Steph. *Bulletin of Entomological Research* **39**, 57–84.

Wright, D. W., Geering, Q. A. & Ashby, D. G. (1947). The insect parasites of the carrot fly, *Psila rosae*, Fab. *Bulletin of Entomological Research* **37**, 507–29.

Wright, D. W., Geering, Q. A. & Dunn, J. A. (1961). Varietal differences in the susceptibility of peas to attack by the pea moth, *Laspeyresia nigricana* (Steph). *Bulletin of Entomological Research* **41**, 663–77.

Wright, E. N. & Isaacson, A. J. (1978). Goose damage to agricultural crops in England. *Annals of Applied Biology* **88**, 334–8.

Wyatt, I. J. (1959). A new genus and species of Cecidomyiidae (Diptera) infesting mushrooms. *Proceedings of the Royal Entomological Society of London, Series B* **28**, 175–9.

Wyatt, I. J. (1960). Cecidomyiidae as pests of cultivated mushrooms. *Annals of Applied Biology* **48**, 430–32.

Wyatt, I. J. (1964). Immature stages of Lestremiinae (Diptera : Cecidomyiidae) infesting cultivated mushrooms. *Transactions of the Royal Entomological Society of London* **116**, 15–27.

Wyatt, I. J. (1967). Pupal paedogenesis in the Cecidomyiidae (Diptera) 3 – A reclassification of the Heteropezini. *Transactions of the Royal Entomological Society of London* **119**, 71–98.

Wyss, E. (1995). The effects of weed strips on aphids and aphidophagous predators in an apple orchard. *Entomologia Experimentalis et Applicata* **75**, 43–9.

Yarrell, W. (1837). Some observations on the economy of an insect destructive to turnips. *Transactions of the Zoological Society of London* **2**, 67–70.

Yeates, G. W. (ed.) (1998). OECD Workshop on Terrestrial Flatworms, New Zealand 1998. *Pedobiologia* **42**, 385–584.

Yuksel, H. S. (1960). Observations on the life cycle of *Ditylenchus dipsaci* on onion seedlings. *Nematologica* **5**, 289–96.

Zhang, Z.-Q. (1998). Biology and ecology of trombidiid mites (Acari: Trombidioidea). *Experimental and Applied Acarology* **22**, 139–5.

Zijp, J.-P. & Blommers, L. H. M. (2002a). Apple sawfly *Hoplocampa testudinea* (Hym., Tenthredinidae) and its parasitoid *Lathrolestes ensator* in Dutch apple orchards (Hym., Ichneumonidae, Ctenopelmatinae). *Journal of Applied Entomology* **126**, 265–74.

Zijp, J.-P. & Blommers, L. H. M. (2002b). Surival mode between the yearly reproduction periods, and reproductive biology of *Scambus pomorum* (Hymenoptera: Ichneumonidae: Pimplinae), a parasitoid of the apple blossom weevil *Anthonomus pomorum* (Coleoptera: Curculionidae). *Entomologia Generalis* **26**, 29–46.

Zimmermann, H. (1905). Eine neue Tarsonemusart auf Gartenerdbeeren. *Zeitschrift des Mährischen Landesmuseums, Brünn* **5**, 91–102.

Indexes

PLANT INDEX

Plant names include references to their respective products (e.g. fruits)

GENERAL INDEX

* = *see also* individual groups and/or species

The New Naturalist Library

1. *Butterflies* — E. B. Ford
2. *British Game* — B. Vesey-Fitzgerald
3. *London's Natural History* — R. S. R. Fitter
4. *Britain's Structure and Scenery* — L. Dudley Stamp
5. *Wild Flowers* — J. Gilmour & M. Walters
6. *The Highlands & Islands* — F. Fraser Darling & J. M. Boyd
7. *Mushrooms & Toadstools* — J. Ramsbottom
8. *Insect Natural History* — A. D. Imms
9. *A Country Parish* — A. W. Boyd
10. *British Plant Life* — W. B. Turrill
11. *Mountains & Moorlands* — W. H. Pearsall
12. *The Sea Shore* — C. M. Yonge
13. *Snowdonia* — F. J. North, B. Campbell & R.Scott
14. *The Art of Botanical Illustration* — W. Blunt
15. *Life in Lakes & Rivers* — T. T. Macan & E. B. Worthington
16. *Wild Flowers of Chalk & Limestone* — J. E. Lousley
17. *Birds & Men* — E. M. Nicholson
18. *A Natural History of Man in Britain* — H. J. Fleure & M. Davies
19. *Wild Orchids of Britain* — V. S. Summerhayes
20. *The British Amphibians & Reptiles* — M. Smith
21. *British Mammals* — L. Harrison Matthews
22. *Climate and the British Scene* — G. Manley
23. *An Angler's Entomology* — J. R. Harris
24. *Flowers of the Coast* — I. Hepburn
25. *The Sea Coast* — J. A. Steers
26. *The Weald* — S. W. Wooldridge & F. Goldring
27. *Dartmoor* — L. A. Harvey & D. St. Leger Gordon
28. *Sea Birds* — J. Fisher & R. M. Lockley
29. *The World of the Honeybee* — C. G. Butler
30. *Moths* — E. B. Ford
31. *Man and the Land* — L. Dudley Stamp
32. *Trees, Woods and Man* — H. L. Edlin
33. *Mountain Flowers* — J. Raven & M. Walters
34. *The Open Sea: I. The World of Plankton* — A. Hardy
35. *The World of the Soil* — E. J. Russell
36. *Insect Migration* — C. B. Williams
37. *The Open Sea: II. Fish & Fisheries* — A. Hardy
38. *The World of Spiders* — W. S. Bristowe
39. *The Folklore of Birds* — E. A. Armstrong
40. *Bumblebees* — J. B. Free & C. G. Butler
41. *Dragonflies* — P. S. Corbet, C. Longfield & N. W. Moore
42. *Fossils* — H. H. Swinnerton
43. *Weeds & Aliens* — E. Salisbury
44. *The Peak District* — K. C. Edwards
45. *The Common Lands of England & Wales* — L. Dudley Stamp & W. G. Hoskins
46. *The Broads* — E. A. Ellis
47. *The Snowdonia National Park* — W. M. Condry
48. *Grass and Grasslands* — I. Moore
49. *Nature Conservation in Britain* — L. Dudley Stamp
50. *Pesticides and Pollution* — K. Mellanby
51. *Man & Birds* — R. K. Murton
52. *Woodland Birds* — E. Simms
53. *The Lake District* — W. H. Pearsall & W. Pennington
54. *The Pollination of Flowers* — M. Proctor & P. Yeo
55. *Finches* — I. Newton
56. *Pedigree: Words from Nature* — S. Potter & L. Sargent
57. *British Seals* — H. R. Hewer
58. *Hedges* — E. Pollard, M. D. Hooper & N. W. Moore
59. *Ants* — M. V. Brian
60. *British Birds of Prey* — L. Brown
61. *Inheritance and Natural History* — R. J. Berry
62. *British Tits* — C. Perrins
63. *British Thrushes* — E. Simms
64. *The Natural History of Shetland* — R. J. Berry & J. L. Johnston

65. *Waders* — W. G. Hale
66. *The Natural History of Wales* — W. M. Condry
67. *Farming and Wildlife* — K. Mellanby
68. *Mammals in the British Isles* — L. Harrison Matthews
69. *Reptiles and Amphibians in Britain* — D. Frazer
70. *The Natural History of Orkney* — R. J. Berry
71. *British Warblers* — E. Simms
72. *Heathlands* — N. R. Webb
73. *The New Forest* — C. R. Tubbs
74. *Ferns* — C. N. Page
75. *Freshwater Fish* — P. S. Maitland & R. N. Campbell
76. *The Hebrides* — J. M. Boyd & I. L. Boyd
77. *The Soil* — B. Davis, N. Walker, D. Ball & A. Fitter
78. *British Larks, Pipits & Wagtails* — E. Simms
79. *Caves & Cave Life* — P. Chapman
80. *Wild & Garden Plants* — M. Walters
81. *Ladybirds* — M. E. N. Majerus
82. *The New Naturalists* — P. Marren
83. *The Natural History of Pollination* — M. Proctor, P. Yeo & A. Lack
84. *Ireland: A Natural History* — D. Cabot
85. *Plant Disease* — D. Ingram & N. Robertson
86. *Lichens* — Oliver Gilbert
87. *Amphibians and Reptiles* — T. Beebee & R. Griffiths
88. *Loch Lomondside* — J. Mitchell
89. *The Broads* — B. Moss
90. *Moths* — M. Majerus
91. *Nature Conservation* — P. Marren
92. *Lakeland* — D. Ratcliffe
93. *British Bats* — John Altringham
94. *Seashore* — Peter Hayward
95. *Northumberland* — Angus Lunn
96. *Fungi* — Brian Spooner & Peter Roberts
97. *Mosses & Liverworts* — Nick Hodgetts & Ron Porley
98. *Bumblebees* — Ted Benton
99. *Gower* — Jonathan Mullard
100. *Woodlands* — Oliver Rackham
101. *Galloway and the Borders* — Derek Ratcliffe
102. *Garden Natural History* — Stefan Buczacki
103. *The Isles of Scilly* — Rosemary Parslow
104. *A History of Ornithology* — Peter Bircham
105. *Wye Valley* — George Peterken
106. *Dragonflies* — Philip Corbet & Stephen Brooks
107. *Grouse* — Adam Watson & Robert Moss
108. *Southern England* — Peter Friend
109. *Islands* — R. J. Berry
110. *Wildfowl* — David Cabot
111. *Dartmoor* — Ian Mercer
112. *Books and Naturalists* — David E. Allen
113. *Bird Migration* — Ian Newton
114. *Badger* — Timothy J. Roper
115. *Climate and Weather* — John Kington